*A Coat of
Many Colors*

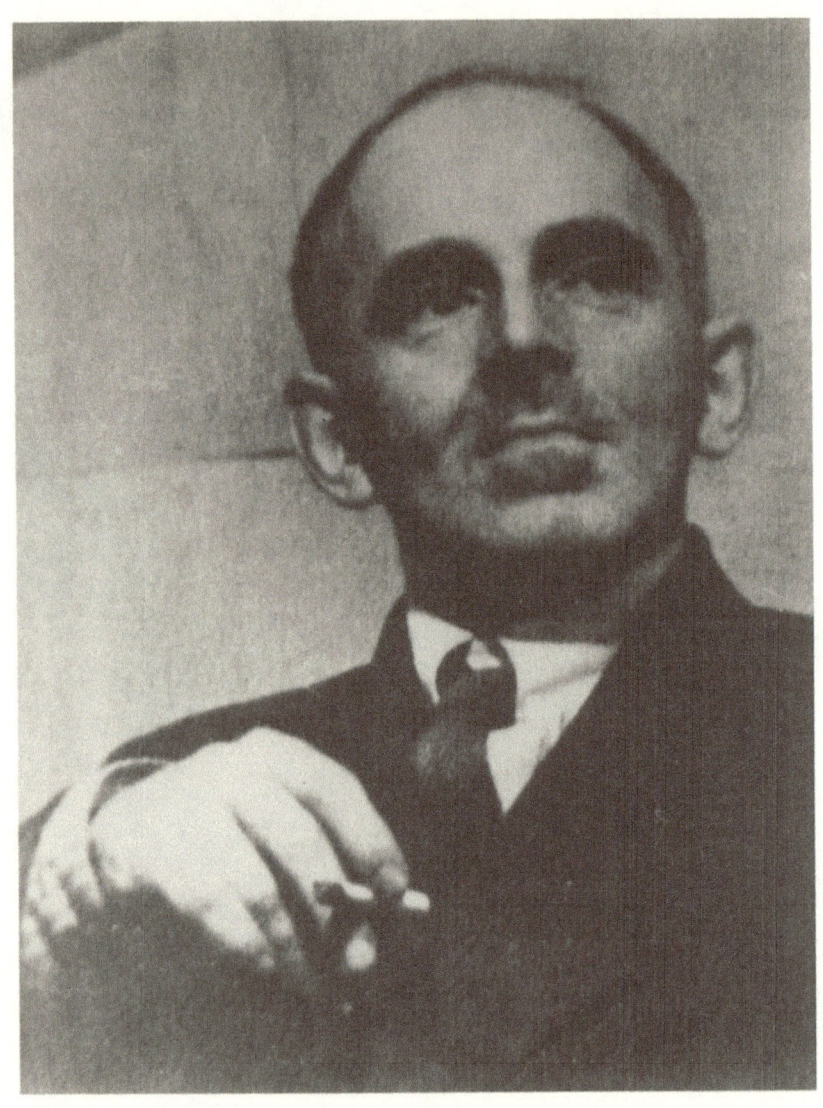

Osip Mandelstam (early 1930s).

A Coat of Many Colors

OSIP MANDELSTAM AND HIS MYTHOLOGIES OF SELF-PRESENTATION

GREGORY FREIDIN

University of California Press
Berkeley / Los Angeles / London

University of California Press
Berkeley and Los Angeles, California
University of California Press, Ltd.
London, England
© 1987 by
The Regents of the University of California

Printed in the United States of America
1 2 3 4 5 6 7 8 9

Library of Congress Cataloging-in-Publication Data

Freidin, Gregory.
  A coat of many colors.

  Bibliography: p.
  Includes index.
  1. Mandel'shtam, Osip, 1891–1938—Criticism and
interpretation. I. Title.
PG3476.M355Z64 1986   891.71'3   85-16440
ISBN 0-520-05438-5 (alk. paper)
ISBN: 978-0-520-26916-3

*For my parents
and in memory of
Ivy Litvinov*

CONTENTS

	PREFACE	ix
	ACKNOWLEDGMENTS	xv
I	*The Charisma of Poetry and the Poetry of Charisma*	1
	Nomen Est Omen; Siamese Twins; The Holy as Paradigm; In Place of a Biography	
II	*Mysteries of Breathing: 1909–1912*	34
	On a Lone Winter Evening; Conjugal Conjugations; A Most Ineligible Bachelor; Between Law and Grace	
III	*Le Nouvel Hippolyte and Phaedra-Russia: 1915–1916*	56
	The Theater of the Lyric; Le Nouvel Hippolyte; Phaedra-Russia and the Night Sun; Mandelstam Between *Stone* and *Tristia*	
IV	*Setting the Stage: Prolepsis in* Tristia, *1915–1917*	84
	Three Books; An Ending and a Beginning; Exchanging Gifts: Tsvetaeva and Mandelstam	

Contents

V   *The Question of Return: Themes and Variations, 1918–1920*   124

Flight from Ilium; The Addressee as Reader; Two More Readers Reading; Extended Family; Variations

VI   *Revolutions and the Poetics of a Dying Age*   154

History's Wheels; The Inner Form of Fin de Siècle; Poetics, Scholarship, Ideology; The Word's Suffering and Magic

VII   *Dying as Metaphor and the Ironic Mode: 1920–1930*   187

Mandelstam's and the Commune's Trains; An Offering of Dead Bees; Oedipus, Antigone, and the Forgotten Word; The Irony and the Prose of the NEP; What Happened to the Coat

VIII   *History and Myth: 1930–1938*   222

Between the Wolfhound and the Wolf; Hippolytus and Hephaestus; Hoofprints in the Black Earth; The Story of the "Ode"; Two Josephs; Image and Likeness

APPENDICES   273

I. *The Mandelstam–Gornfel'd Affair*

II. *A Note on Pasternak*

NOTES   277

BIBLIOGRAPHY   385

INDEX   411

PREFACE

At this moment the fate of the Russian writer has become the most intriguing, the most fruitful literary topic in the whole world: he is either being imprisoned, pilloried, internally exiled, or simply kicked out. ANDREI SINIAVSKII, "Literary Process in Russia"

I wish to present the poet Osip Mandelstam as the focal point of a complex cultural phenomenon—perhaps a cult—in which art extends effortlessly into biography, history, politics, and above all the sphere of communal values held sacred by the poet's readers. There are few authors in this century whose works are so thoroughly identified with their days, and both together with the expectations and catastrophes of modernity. Even among the great poets of his generation (Akhmatova, Maiakovskii, Tsvetaeva, Pasternak), Mandelstam has come to define the fullest complement of features making up Russia's symbolic authorial figure: a poet of genius, a witness, a man who began at the culture's periphery and soon moved into its center, a dervish indifferent to worldly success, a fearless fighter for the dignity of man, and finally, a persecuted outcast, an exile, a prisoner, a victim, and in the end a martyr to Stalinist terror.

This reputation notwithstanding, most students of Mandelstam are aware that the poet's *life* was not endowed with this sort of unity. What unusual coherence it had came from his poetry and prose (both written in the person of the "lyric I") and from a common temptation to attribute to exceptional figures some of the culture's most prized human qualities on an extraordinary scale. *A Coat of Many Colors* offers a perspective that helps to ground Mandelstam's poetry and prose in the patterns of his culture and the events of his time, to account for the remarkable narrative integrity of his writings, and, most important, to examine his career in light of modern Russian authorship, an institution with strong charismatic propensities.

Like other poets of his own and preceding generations (foremost among them Aleksandr Blok, as the Formalist critics were first to point out), Mandelstam was the author of his own "myth," or, rather, "myths of the poet." He worked consistently at designing a figure that could serve as a unifying epic or dramatic center for a variety of lyric gestures. He was thus able to satisfy a major condition for being a lyric poet in contemporary Russia, namely, to compose poetry capable of projecting a powerful, integrative self. Such a self had to be grounded not only in the particular circumstances and consciousness of the poet as an individual but also in the consciousness of the audience; in short, in the culture of the body social to which the poet appealed. Furthermore, the self had to be flexible, able to respond to the rapidly changing world, yet stable enough to remain recognizable, allowing the poet to maintain narrative continuity in self-presentation. Such a figure had to create the possibility for "naturalizing" the new, for integrating or joining it with the familiar. Contemporary poets, beneficiaries of the nineteenth-century comparative mythology, understood that this was to be accomplished in large measure by having the protagonist project narrative patterns intentionally designed both to emulate ancient myth *and* to absorb modern historical matter. How Mandelstam, with his particular circumstances and background, went about satisfying these desiderata of modern Russian poetry constitutes the subject of this study.

Although I do not limit myself to any one aspect of the Mandelstam phenomenon, I focus precisely on these partially overlapping and often homologous patterns of self-presentation. Of crucial importance for the understanding of Mandelstam's poetic project as a historical phenomenon, these patterns have functioned as a source from which readers have spun the threads of Mandelstam myths and his *mythologies,* that is, the rationalizations of the poet's stance. Hence the title of this book, with its echoes of Roland Barthes's study *Mythologies,* which first alerted me to the interaction between verbal imagination, ideology, and social practice. Modern Russian poetry, with its incredible power over readers—many of whom would admit to their profound puzzlement over its sense—offers a tantalizing case study for anyone interested in this interaction.

Trying to understand the nature of the extraordinary symbolic power of modern Russian poets, I have conceptualized Russian literary authorship as a "charismatic institution," drawing on the work of Max Weber, Emile Durkheim, and Edward Shils. I aim to provide a systematic account of the imperatives—social and psychological as well as literary—that the institution of Russian literary authorship has imposed on the poet and the way it has tended to shape the expectations of the reading public. To offer an illustration, Mandelstam's use of "verbal magic," that is, his reliance on folkloric formulas, received a significant reinforcement from his university training as a philologist, was thematized in his verse in the figure of a shamanlike poet, and was amplified and made more effective by his incantatory, ecstatic style of recitation. At the same time, as a metaphor for poetry, "verbal magic" and related terms became an accepted part of the reader's own vocabulary, signaling an implicit acknowledgment of the poet's supernatural or merely extraordinary—and therefore charismatic—attributes. In turn, these claims were themselves imposed on the poet by the institution of Russian authorship into which he had been born and whose charismatic propensity intensified in the intoxicating, vertiginous atmosphere of the prerevolutionary decade.

It is a unique feature of Russian (and European) modernism that the view of poetry as a charismatic calling—a gift that obligates—was inseparable from a great scholarly and popular interest in comparative mythology and religion. In this respect, the theoretical framework of *Essay on the Gift*, produced by Mandelstam's contemporary, anthropologist Marcel Mauss, offers an important supplement to literary-rhetorical analysis proper. Its application makes possible an integral view of literary exchange—as genre, theme, device, and ritual. The approach is particularly suited to the study of Acmeist poetry, and especially Mandelstam, for it parallels uncannily both the doctrine and the practice of Acmeism, which based its poetics on the principles of simultaneity of successive stages in poetic tradition and obligatory creative exchange.

In sum, this book offers a multifaceted view of the phenomenon of Mandelstam: the poet's writings, the social and cultural context of his career, his created biography and posthumous reception. But above all, I intend it as an essay in the anatomy of the cult of a modern Russian poet, a scholarly tribute from one who grew up, like many of his compatriots, spellbound by the aura emanating from the names of Blok and Tsvetaeva, Pasternak and Akhmatova, Maiakovskii and Mandelstam.

With the exception of the introductory chapter, which includes a discussion of my approach and a grudging biographical sketch of Mandelstam, the book is organized in roughly chronological order. However, the periodization I have chosen follows the landmarks in the development of Mandelstam's mythologies of self-presentation rather than the major events of his life. Chapters 2 and 3 deal with Mandelstam's search for suitable narrative vehicles for his poetry among the mythological and ideological repertoires available to the young members of Russia's educated elite between the two revolutions. Chapters 4 and 5 offer a hypothetical account of how these narrative vehicles functioned as controlling patterns in both the composition and the reception of Mandelstam's post-1915 poetry (primarily *Tristia*). The 1920s form the subject of chapters 6 and 7, in which I examine both the shift in Mandelstam's mythologies and the contemporary ideology and scholarship that may have determined particular interpretations of his art. A mutual determination of the collective and personal history, of the accidental and symbolic in the last decade of Mandelstam's life, is the main theme of the concluding chapter.

Although I have tried to cover Mandelstam's entire career, some major works, notably "The Slate Ode," "1 January 1924," and the cycle "Verses on the Unknown Soldier," have not been dealt with in depth. This was due in part to the nature of my study, which does not depend on any single work, in part to the lengthy explications that these difficult works would have demanded, and, most important, to the comprehensive and profound treatment these poems have already received in the works of Omry Ronen (regrettably, his most recent and monumental contribution, *An Approach to Mandelstam* [Jerusalem, 1983], reached me after the final draft of this study had been completed).

With a few exceptions, Mandelstam's writings are cited according to what has been the standard edition of his works: Osip Mandel'štam, *Sobranie sochinenii* (Collected Works), 3 vols. [vol. 4 (supplementary)], edited by G. Struve and B. Filippov, vol. 1, 2d ed. (n.p., Inter-Language Literary Associates, 1967), vol. 2, 2d ed. (n.p., Inter-Language Literary Associates, 1971), vol. 3 (n.p., Inter Language Literary Associates, 1969), and vol. 4, edited by G. Struve, N. Struve, and B. Filippov (Paris: YMCA Press, 1981). Poems in this edition, including versions, are numbered consecutively, but for the reader's convenience I refer to them in the text by title or by first line and date, the latter either supplied by Mandelstam or established by his editors: for example, "Ia ne uvizhu znamenitoi Fedry" (I shall not see the famous Phèdre, 1914). In the case of notes and occasional short references in the text, poems are referred to by volume as well as by number. For example, *SS* 1:123 designates poem number 123 in volume 1 (this should not be confused with page references, e.g., *SS* 1, p. 123).

I have also relied on the two more or less comprehensive Soviet collections of Mandelstam's poetry: the 1928 *Stikhotvoreniia* and the more recent volume of the same title edited by N. Khardzhiev and

Preface

published in 1973. I refer to them as *Stikhotvoreniia* (1928) and (1973), respectively. Another frequently cited source is the two-volume memoirs of the poet's wife, the late Nadezhda Mandelstam. Although both volumes exist in a good English translation, for the sake of precision and consistency I have cited the original Russian editions. These are abbreviated as NM 1 (*Vospominaniia* [New York: Chekhov Publishing Corporation, 1970]) and NM 2 (*Vtoraia kniga* [Paris: YMCA Press, 1972]). A list of other abbreviations precedes the notes.

Regarding transliteration, I have relied on the Library of Congress system throughout the study (hence Boris Eikhenbaum, Iurii Tynianov), bowing to the traditional spelling only in the case of a few well-known names such as Tolstoy, Gogol, Mandelstam. However, in the case of bibliographical references involving sources in Russian, I have adhered to the Library of Congress system uniformly, with Tolstoy becoming Tolstoi; Herzen, Gertsen; and Mandelstam, Mandel'shtam.

Because translating from one language to another is an interpretive enterprise, I have tried to offer my own translation of both poetry and prose. The few exceptions to this rule are fully acknowledged.

ACKNOWLEDGMENTS

Throughout all the years of my work on Mandelstam, my greatest debt has been to Robert P. Hughes. The project originated in his seminar on Mandelstam in 1973 at the University of California at Berkeley, and since then I have relied on his knowledge, advice, and support, which he offered with rare tact and generosity. I also wish to express my appreciation to my Stanford colleague William Mills Todd III for his invaluable intellectual stimulation and encouragement, from early discussions of my dissertation to comments on the finished manuscript. He has helped me to keep this study on a steady course. I am very grateful to Clarence Brown, who has always been forthcoming with valuable information, advice, and criticism. He kindly introduced me to the Mandelstam Archive at the Firestone Library at Princeton University in 1978 and provided the intellectual companionship that helped me to rethink my Mandelstam project. I benefited enormously from the advice and criticism of Boris Gasparov, a most generous interlocutor, who read my manuscript chapter by chapter as I prepared the final draft. Whatever illusions I may have had about my doctoral dissertation were dispelled by the witty and provocative commentary of Edward J. Brown. Six years later, he kindly agreed to subject the final manuscript to a like treatment, and I can regret only that I was unable to answer all his questions adequately. I am also greatly indebted to Lazar Fleishman for his careful, sometimes sobering, but always tolerant and thoughtful reading of the manuscript. Simon Karlinsky offered many helpful suggestions regarding the work, especially the chapter dealing with the poetic exchange between Tsvetaeva and Mandelstam.

Among my colleagues in the field of Russian literature, I owe a particular debt to Robert A. Maguire who followed my work and, in

Acknowledgments

informal conversations, helped me to identify the main themes my study subsequently developed. For many years, the late Gleb Petrovich Struve shared with me some of his unpublished Mandelstam materials as well as criticism and advice with great kindness.

I wish to express my appreciation to Reginald Zelnik for his stimulating and broad-minded support of this study. Throughout the years he has provided a thoughtful commentary, and his perspective as a social historian, as well as his understanding of the political and cultural outlook of the Russian intelligentsia, helped me to see the Mandelstam phenomenon in a new light. His advice on the manuscript has been invaluable.

Many important comments and suggestions have come from my colleagues and friends who closely followed my work on the project or read portions of the manuscript: Burton Benedict, Marion Benedict, Joseph Brodsky, Monika Dudli Frenkel, Leopold Haimson, Herbert Lindenberger, John Malmstad, Irina Paperno, and David Wellbery. Darra Goldstein helped me to obtain copies of rare printed materials from the Soviet Union. Katia Hawkanson assisted me in organizing the Russian portions of the manuscript.

Many of the specific, historical issues that I address in this book were often discussed and formulated as general propositions at the Mellon Faculty Seminar on Interpretation, Stanford University, in which I have participated since 1978. I wish to thank all my seminar colleagues for their intellectual stimulation, companionship, and support.

I would also like to take this opportunity to thank my instructors and advisers, formal and informal, who gave liberally of their time and knowledge during my years as a graduate student at the University of California at Berkeley. I am especially grateful to Hugh McLean, Martin Malia, Czeslaw Milosz, and Francis J. Whitfield, whose singular styles of thought, in speaking and writing, have influenced my own.

I owe an inestimable debt of gratitude to my wife, Victoria E. Bonnell. Albeit imperceptibly, this book bears a profound imprint of her intellectual rigor, knowledge, and intuition, as well as of her insight as a historian and sociologist. Always forthcoming with sharp and provocative advice, she was equally generous with moral support and assistance, from which I benefited at every stage of my research and preparation of the manuscript. This study is truly a joint effort.

My project would not have been possible without the extensive institutional support provided me since its inception. In 1976 a fellowship from the International Research and Exchanges Board (IREX) supported me during the initial stages of the dissertation research at

Acknowledgments

the University Library in Helsinki, Finland. A grant from the American Philosophical Society and another from the Center for Research in International Studies, Stanford University, enabled me to begin research in the Mandelstam Archive at the Firestone Library, Princeton University, the New York Public Library, and the Butler Library, Columbia University, in the summer of 1979. An American Council of Learned Societies Fellowship for Recent Recipients of a Ph.D. and a sabbatical leave from Stanford University in 1980–1981 enabled me to proceed with my research at the Dow Library, University of California at Berkeley, the Green Library, Stanford University, and the Hoover Library and Archive. A Summer Grant from the National Endowment for the Humanities in 1982 allowed me to start writing. A Pew Foundation Grant and a Howard Foundation Fellowship supported me during my leave of absence from Stanford University in 1982–1983, making it possible for me to finish a draft of the manuscript. During my work on the project I have benefited from the generous advice and assistance of Edward Kasinec (New York Public Library), Hilja Kukk (Hoover Institution Library), and Wojciech Zalewski (Stanford University Libraries).

Finally, I wish to thank Sheila Levine and Barbara Ras, my editors at the University of California Press, for their efforts on behalf of my manuscript.

I

The Charisma of Poetry and the Poetry of Charisma

NOMEN EST OMEN

And they said unto him, We have dreamed a dream, and there is no interpreter of it. And Joseph said unto them, Do not interpretations belong to God? tell me them, I pray you.   GENESIS 40:8

A man's name is one of the main constituents of his person and perhaps a part of his psyche.   SIGMUND FREUD, Totem and Taboo

But how can I tear myself away from you, my dear Egypt of things?
   MANDELSTAM, The Egyptian Stamp

Now, it is a matter of coincidence that Mandelstam, whose first name happened to be Osip, was a namesake of the biblical interpreter and dreamer. But once his parents decided to name their firstborn Joseph, the Egyptian career of Israel's most beloved son became an easily available exemplar for Mandelstam—one of the measures of his life's progress. To use Joseph in this way became especially tempting to Mandelstam after he had decided to pursue the vocation of lyric poet—in a way, a born dreamer and interpreter of dreams. This vocation was valued highly in the Egypt of his time but had still to be properly conferred on a man of Jewish origin.[1] To spin this much meaning out of something so random and insignificant as a poet's first name may seem a trifle archaic. Still, a vague hope that a famous namesake can influence one's life is deeply embedded in Western culture, the majority of whose members bear *Christian* names, that is, live under the guidance and protection, however attenuated by modernity, of a particular holy woman or man.[2] In Russian culture (and Mandelstam's mother was at home in it)[3] this tradition remained relatively strong. Russians of Mandelstam's time were more likely to celebrate the day of the namesake saint (*imianiny*) than their own date of birth, and the Russian Orthodox custom of naming a child after the saint on whose day that child was born remained common.[4] Moreover, in the age of Nietzsche, Frazer, and Freud, a revival of the archaic possessed the imprimatur of ultimate modernity, and it was cultivated assiduously in Mandelstam's own milieu. We need not look further than *Anno Domini,* a collection of poetry by *Anna* Akhmatova, to be convinced that a contemporary poet did not treat his or her Christian name as an anachronism whose purpose would have been better served by a unique license plate number à la Zamiatin's *We.*[5] By the same token, the name Joseph was simply too suggestive for Mandelstam to be ignored completely. There will be more than one occasion to consider what Mandelstam himself made of it. But the fact that sometime in January 1891 Emile and Flora Mandelstam decided to call their first child Joseph—a decision neither magical nor prophetic and yet bearing the traces of a belief in both magic and prophecy—prompts an appeal to the Old Testament legend to elucidate the conceit on which this study is based.

According to the Book of Genesis, when Pharaoh's butler and baker offended their master, they were thrown into jail to await the disposition of their fate. There they met another prisoner, Joseph, a Hebrew slave of Captain Potiphar who had been condemned for trying to rape his master's wife. Of course he was innocent, and although it was true that he had fled her chambers leaving his garment in her hands, he did so not as a bungling rapist but as a loyal employee who preferred to suffer the wrath of a scorned woman than yield to the amorous embraces of his master's wife. Be that as it may, one day Joseph noticed that his two cellmates looked especially vexed. They were troubled, Joseph learned, by the dreams they had had the previous night. Neither knew how to make sense of the complex symbolism of his dream, and, unable to engage a reputable interpreter, they could not take advantage of the precious knowledge that the nocturnal signs both promised and concealed. Here Joseph could help. But first he had to persuade the dreamers to divulge those enigmatic symbols that God, or perhaps demons, had conveyed to them in the privacy of their sleep. Like other unusual signs, dreams had to be treated with the utmost seriousness, as something directly relevant to the fate of an individual, family, country, or tribe. A record left by a higher power, they were a means of gaining insight into the workings of individual or collective fate;

and as such, they could benefit the dreamer just as much as the dreamer's enemy. It was therefore more prudent to remain ignorant about the meaning of the dream rather than to rely on a chance interpreter who might use one's omens to his own advantage. Why else would the two prisoners be so reluctant to tell Joseph their dreams? Then, as today, dream interpretation called for a trusted and reputable private specialist whose practice depended on loyalty and discretion, qualities that in turn were supported by the diviner's social ties and, indirectly, by the amount of his fee. In no respect did Joseph fit this description.

He managed, however, to convince his cellmates that they had no need for a professional when they had the good luck of sharing a jail with him. For he was a born dreamer and interpreter of dreams, one whose know-how came from God and therefore did not depend on the three conditions of professionalism: training, experience, and payment. "Interpretations belong to God," he insisted, implying that he himself had been ordained to play the role of God's hermetic messenger.[6] Had they still been enjoying the perquisites of courtiers, the butler and the baker would probably have shrugged off the arrogant claim of this humble and unlicensed soothsayer, but the sudden loss of station, indeed of all social and psychological support, must have made them too vulnerable to decline any solution, no matter how improbable. Besides, was there not something special about this Hebrew who had inexplicably escaped execution despite the gravity of the accusation against him and, equally inexplicably, had been placed by the warden in charge of the entire jail (Gen. 39:21–23)? Still, the baker remained reticent and would tell Joseph his dream only after he had heard the favorable interpretation of the butler's nocturnal omens. His change of heart would suggest that he attributed to Joseph's talent a power to shape as well as disclose one's fate—a modicum of extraordinary, demonic power. What made Joseph appear an even stranger character was that his plea for a reward followed rather than preceded the service and took the form of a request for a favor unconstrained by a contractual bond. The ensuing events proved Joseph's interpretations correct, as later on they would corroborate his understanding of Pharaoh's dream. And Pharaoh was so impressed by Joseph's gift ("the spirit of God") that he made him his highest viceroy. This is one way of retelling part of the Joseph legend, the story of a miserable slave who became, after Pharaoh, the most powerful man in Egypt.

A more analytical retelling might be based on Max Weber's conceptions of charismatic authority.[7] Unlike traditional authority and that of the rational-legal type, which exist in a relatively stable social milieu, charismatic authority depends on the beliefs of groups seized by "enthusiasm, despair or hope."[8] Often this authority becomes vested in an individual who believes himself, and is believed to be, endowed with "supernatural, superhuman or at least specifically exceptional powers or qualities."[9] Ultimately, these extraordinary "gifts" signify the charismatic individual's intimate contact with what he and society perceive as "sacred"[10] or "central" to their universe; in turn, proximity to fate endows such a leader with an exceptional ability to order or disorder the core of forces that "make sense" of the world, whether in the area of politics, high art, religion, popular culture, or science.[11] In this respect, what distinguishes a charismatic figure, group, or institution from its ordinary counterpart in society is not a matter of a particular program—the program merely conducts the current of authority—but the difference in intensity of expression between the feebly electrified "periphery" of a culture and the always steaming, awesome powerhouse of its "center."[12]

For a charismatic figure to emerge, the claim to possession of the gift must be recognized by others.[13] In fact, what distinguishes the sociological notion of charismatic authority from the notion of charisma, including its biblical, Pauline usage,[14] is the indispensable symbiosis between the leader and his following that transforms charisma into a relational, mediating entity, not simply a divine gift held by a specific figure. Given the extraordinary nature of charisma, recognition of a charismatic person by a group occurs outside the daily round of life,[15] and in this respect the proof that a charismatic figure offers must be perceived not only as effective but also as magical, irrational, unpredictable—in short, extraordinary. "Originally," Weber wrote, it was "always a miracle."[16] Perhaps the central paradox of charismatic authority involves the disparity between the holder's total dependence on the group's recognition (hence the instability of charismatic authority)[17] and the absolute obedience the power of this individual commands as long as possession of the gift is acknowledged.[18] Thus proof and obedience, although interdependent, are dissociated in the followers' minds. On the one hand, a disciple submits to the leader out of a sense of "inner compulsion," not in exchange for miracles or mundane rewards, and considers failure in devotion to be a "dereliction of duty." To understand this paradox, recall how adamantly Christ refused to make faith conditional on miracles even as he was performing miracles for the sake of his disciples' faith. On the other hand, the leader's failure to pass the test of repeated proof can transform all the vertical bonds within his following into last year's snow.

Confronted with a situation of disorientation and acute distress, Joseph claimed a special grace that, in the words of the Bible, "gave him favor in the eyes" of Potiphar and his wife, the butler, the baker, and even Pharaoh and that allowed him, in those same eyes, to transform uncertainty into order. And even though the people in distress were inclined to "recognize" the signs of God's favor in Joseph, they did so only after he had furnished them with the sine qua non of charisma—the twofold "proof" of his divine hermeneutic skill. First, the events predicted by him did indeed come to pass, which prompted his promotion by Pharaoh and gave Joseph the opportunity to preside over the prevention of disorder. This was unusual, but it was not enough to distinguish a charismatic divine from a wise man undertaking these tasks as a way of earning a living. Only in combination with Joseph's strangeness and the disinterested nature of his performance does his work begin to radiate the aura of a truly extraordinary gift.

This second, less evident aspect of proof involved both the absence of remuneration and Joseph's unusual freedom from the customary bonds of family and tribe. His seeming indifference to personal gain and virtual independence from ordinary human obligations made Joseph's aptitude for dream interpretation appear brilliant and unalloyed. This is not to say that Joseph expected no rewards for his insights; he did. Rather, the rewards had to be as extraordinary as his gift—very different from the fee a professional charges. Nor did he undertake his interpretations in the hope of enriching his family, though it eventually benefited from his generosity. Even more important, prior to his elevation by Pharaoh, Joseph had no regular standing in Egyptian society, and his spectacular performances, if anything, must have made him even more of a stranger to it.[19] This lack of social face—this empty space in place of a fixed identity—made Joseph an excellent screen on which to project the anxieties and desires of his not always hospitable hosts. The nearly tragic incident with the wife of Captain Potiphar gives us some idea of how good a screen one could make of Joseph's many-colored coat. Among its many different patches, a butler, a baker, a pharaoh, his captain and his captain's wife, and, finally, Joseph's own brothers had little trouble finding colors that matched the glow of their own nightmares and dreams.

THE SIAMESE TWINS

For us, who are not initiated into the simple mystery of the exorcist's soul—into his power over the word which transforms word into deed—this may be laughable only because we have forgotten the soul of the people and, perhaps, the true soul in general.
        ALEKSANDR BLOK, "The Poetry of Spells and Incantations"

The Charisma of Poetry

> *Sometimes I think*
> *I am a Dutch cock*
> *or I am*
> *the king of Pskov.*
> *And sometimes*
> *I like best of all*
> *my own name*
> *Vladimir Maiakovskii.*
>
> VLADIMIR MAIAKOVSKII, Vladimir Maiakovskii: A Tragedy

Mandelstam's career was, of course, different from that of his ancient namesake, and yet the story of Joseph provides more than one illuminating analogy to the phenomenon of Mandelstam—the totality of his art and his life in the imagination of his readers. Mandelstam was and still is a charismatic poet, just as Joseph was a charismatic diviner and not merely an anonymous vehicle for interpreting dreams. Mandelstam's "gift" went beyond his verbal art to permeate the whole of what his readers and, I assume, he himself perceived as his personality. Consonant with the early Formalist dictum that an artist's life must be judged as a work of art, Mandelstam's poetry, like that of his more illustrious contemporaries, is difficult to separate from the legendary biographical aura that has surrounded it; indeed, even difficult to separate from the way he looked to his audience as he recited his verse:

> Mandelstam's face was not striking at first glance. Thin, with slight, irregular features, he reminded one in his whole aspect of the people in Chagall's paintings. But then he began to read, in a singsong way and slightly rocking to the rhythm of the verse. Blok and I were sitting side by side. Suddenly he touched my sleeve softly and with his eyes pointed toward the face of Osip Emil'evich. I have never seen a human face so transformed by inspiration and self-abandonment. Mandelstam's homely, unassuming face had become the face of a visionary and prophet. Aleksandr Aleksandrovich [Blok] was also astonished by this.[20]

He was indeed. Himself a foremost visionary of his time, Blok made the following professionally astute note in his diary after attending Mandelstam's recital: "Clearly an *artiste*. His poetry emerges out of dreams—of a very special kind that abide wholly within the realm of art."[21] For Blok the "realm of art" was the chief among the variety of realms of religious experience.[22]

To cut such an awe-inspiring figure at moments of poetic "possession" was to be seen as someone so close to the culture's "center" as to be on intimate terms with the inner workings of fate, a privilege granted only to visionaries and prophets.[23] At least since Nikolai

Gogol's masterful performances at the Aksakovs',[24] public recitals in Russia have constituted an important moment in the author's interaction with his reader. In this century, poets have benefited from this institution enormously, as witnessed by the mesmerizing artistry of Blok, the provocative antics of the Futurists, especially Maiakovskii's spellbinding recitals,[25] and the "shamanistic" séances of Osip Mandelstam.[26] To the extent that the word of such a poet was perceived as having transcendent attributes (and Mandelstam, for one, did not flinch at referring to the poetic word as Logos),[27] the poet's capacity to make himself transparent to the word contributed greatly to the affirmation of his charismatic aura. People who attended these performances could feel the presence of the spirit possessing the poet; they could hear the poet's oracle and feel close to the sacred, which in ordinary life remained concealed.[28] At moments of particularly profound despair or enthusiasm, a poet's reading might even be experienced as a sort of *tremendum mysteriosum*, a sensation on a continuum with the biblical "fear of God." Consider, for instance, the impression that Mandelstam's reading made on his friend Nikolai Khardzhiev, a literary scholar and art historian who attended the poet's recital in November 1932. Khardzhiev's testimony is especially significant as it comes from a private letter to Boris Eikhenbaum, a colleague and a scholar of great sophistication (italics are mine):

> Mandelstam is the only consolation. He is a poet of genius, of valor, a heroic man. A gray-bearded patriarch, Mandelstam presided as shaman for *two and a half hours*. He recited every poem that he had written (in the past two years) in chronological order!
>
> They were such terrifying exorcisms that many people took fright.
>
> Even Pasternak was afraid—he lisped: "I envy your freedom. For me you are a new Khlebnikov. And just as alien to me as he is. I need a non-freedom."

And, Khardzhiev continued, when some of those who did not "take fright" challenged the poet publicly, Mandelstam "answered them with the haughtiness of a captive emperor—or a captive poet."[29]

Both the correspondent and the addressee had known and admired Mandelstam for many years,[30] and nothing could have been further from Khardzhiev's mind than advertising Mandelstam's success in a friendly missive. All the more striking, then, the description of Mandelstam's attributes: a genius (possessed by a spirit), a heroic man (superhuman), a patriarch (in line with Abraham, Isaac, Jacob, Joseph), a shaman (a sorcerer and master of metapsychosis), an exorcist, a terror- and fear-inspiring figure (*tremendum mysteriosum*), a captive emperor (of Rome among the Huns?), and only lastly—to sum up all of these extraordinary powers—a poet.[31] Equally revealing was Pasternak's proclaiming Mandelstam the second Velemir Khlebnikov (1885–1922),[32] that mysterious genius of Russian modernism who enjoyed the reputation of a "fool in Christ,"[33] a holy man, indeed, a Christ figure, even among the allegedly cold-blooded and no-nonsense Formalists. Viktor Shklovskii, for one, a writer not famous for his Christian piety, could compare Khlebnikov's death to the Crucifixion and his readers to the Sanhedrin and the Roman Guard, while Jakobson could take this comparison as a starting point for his seminal essay "On a Generation That Squandered Its Poets" (1931).

> Forgive us for yourself and for others whom we will kill. The state is not responsible for the destruction of people. When Christ lived and spoke it did not understand His Aramaic, and it has never understood simple human speech. The Roman Soldiers who pierced Christ's hands are no more to blame than the nails. Nevertheless, it is very painful for those whom they crucify.[34]

It is well known that Khlebnikov was not persecuted by the state, but died of a gangrenelike disease while being cared for by his friend, the artist Pavel Miturich.[35]

Mandelstam's exalted standing, his famous hauteur,[36] has coexisted with, indeed has drawn sustenance from, his reputation as a bungler and a pariah, a reputation that his own writings often seconded. He could count himself among the stars of the most luminous constellation of Russian poetry, next to Derzhavin and Lermontov, as he did in the 1923 "Slate Ode," and at the same time complain of profound inadequacy in a bitterly ironic "Pindaric fragment," "He Who Found a Horseshoe," where he likened himself to the lucky charm "fragment" of a once magnificent racing steed. To follow Mandelstam's characterization of his fictional alter ego Parnok in *The Egyptian Stamp* (1928), his lot was that of a "mosquito prince," "a prince of bad luck, a Collegial Assessor from the city of Thebes"[37]—the rank of the humiliated proud misfits from the Petersburg Thebes of Gogol and Dostoevsky.

There is a famous line of Marina Tsvetaeva, a paraphrase of Pangloss's optimistic motto, which helps us to grasp Mandelstam's ambiguous self-image—this fusion of princely hubris with the humility of an insignificant and annoying insect: "In this most Christian of worlds, poets are Yids!"[38] When Tsvetaeva fired this shot at the philistines in 1924, many poets, including Mandelstam, could have testified that she was speaking for their generation. Her pungent ethnic metaphor implied, first, that in contemporary society one could do better than be a Jew; second, that those who shared her calling were treated as and had the fate of the culture's proverbial outcasts; and third, since the name was applied to a poet, a figure of recognized symbolic power, that the true center of modern Russian culture was not with those "most Christian" but with their opposites—the antipodal "Yids." As chance would have it, Mandelstam fit Tsvetaeva's bill doubly: figuratively, as a poet, and literally, as a Jew; indeed, he was known to some of his contemporaries as *zinaidin zhidenok* ("Zinaida's [Gippius] little Yid").[39] But then, seen from the stage on which the poet's drama was unfolding, what ranked low on the philistine scale of values took the pride of place in the sacred realm. The poet's audience was assigned a less enviable function. Confronted with Tsvetaeva's heavy-handed irony, a sympathetic reader was in effect forced to recognize (or to pretend to recognize) in the poet an innocent and sacred victim and to cast himself in the role of a lowbrow Jew-hating philistine, thereby acknowledging twice and at his own expense the extraordinary moral and sacred power of poets. Mandelstam's lines from a 1924 poem—a distant echo of Byron's "I was born for opposition"—carried a similar ring:

> Нет, никогда ничей я не был современник,
> Мне не с руки почет такой.
> О как противен мне какой-то соименник,
> То был не я, то был другой.
>
> No, never have I ever been anybody's contemporary,
> Such honor doesn't suit me well.
> Oh how disgusted I am with that namesake,
> It was not I, it was another.

And yet it was he himself who

> Я с веком поднимал болезненные веки —
> Два сонных яблока больших,
>
> Together with the century I raised my painful eyelids—
> Two large sleepy orbs.

And it was to him that

> И мне гремучие рассказывали реки
> Ход воспаленных тяжб людских.
>
> The rumbling rivers related to me . . .
> The course of the fevered disputes of men.[40]

Further, Tsvetaeva's words point to one of the most important contemporary assumptions concerning poetry. Russian society extended to the poets a measure of *serious* consideration, with all the profound ambiguity that such consideration implied. In this regard, Mandelstam's reply to his wife about the death by firing squad in 1921 of his friend Nikokai Gumilev has become proverbial: "Fool, it is a good thing that we live in a country where people are shot for their verse."[41] For it is degradation and persecution, whether real or imagined, on the one hand and reverence and veneration on the other that conjoin to form the "fate of the poet"—a term with obvious supernatural implications used by the pre- and postrevolutionary Russian critics writing on the inside or the outside.[42] There is little that is surprising in this dualism, for few things seal one's bond with the sacred better than a little spilled blood or its mimetic counterparts.[43] As a medium of sacralization, this blood might have taken the form of cranberry juice, as it did in Aleksandr Blok's self-mocking *Puppet Theater,* or some less apparently ironic imitation such as ink, as in Maiakovskii's poem addressed to the suicide Esenin,[44] or the real stuff that flowed abundantly during the "literalist" years of World War I, the revolution, civil war, and the construction of the new Soviet state. Even when wars, revolutions, or the secret police failed to oblige, one could put a bullet through one's heart, as Maiakovskii did in 1930, timing his suicide to coincide with Easter week.[45] Analyzing Maiakovskii's testament, Roman Jakobson summed up the function of a created biography-fate in the poet's oeuvre:

> The letter with its several literary motifs and with Maiakovskii's own death in it is so closely interrelated with his poetry that it can be understood only in the context of his poetry.[46]

That an artist aestheticizes everything, including the sacred, is a matter of common sense, especially in post-Nietzschean modernism. What is particular about a charismatic poet is that he imbues a fact of life, one as serious as death, with the aura of the sacred as soon as it becomes a "literary fact."[47] When, in the words of Mandelstam's 1922 poem, "The Age,"

> Кровь-строительница хлещет
> Горлом из земных вещей,
>
> Blood the builder is gushing out of the throat
> Of earthly things,

the poet's own blood could be used to "glue together" the broken "vertebrae of the two centuries."[48]

For a poet, then, this assumption of seriousness "in this most Christian of the worlds" amounted to the necessity of cultivating the double identity of a pariah-king. "My poor Joseph," Nadezhda Mandelstam wrote, echoing Mandelstam's own poetry, "he remembered that in his veins there coursed the blood of shepherds, patriarchs, and kings."[49] Unique and mysterious people, these, who can, it seems, illuminate the sacred core of their culture in such a way as to appear fused with it—culture's Siamese twins.

THE HOLY AS PARADIGM

If a man experiences this feeling, becomes infected with the state of the soul which the author has experienced, and feels his unity with other people, then the object causing this state is art; where this infection does not take place . . . there is no art.   LEO TOLSTOY, "What Is Art"

The sight of a mathematician who produces without effort the square of some ten-digit number fills us with a certain wonderment. But too often do we fail to see that a poet raises a phenomenon to the tenth power, and the modest appearance of a work of art frequently deceives us with respect to the monstrously condensed reality which it possesses.
   OSIP MANDELSTAM, "The Morning of Acmeism" (1913)

In his classic study *Elementary Forms of the Religious Life*, Emile Durkheim concluded that the sacred in one important sense represented a projection of the collective interest of society onto the superhuman sphere.[50] From there, after gaining the higher sanction and becoming a *sacred* principle, this will of the collective body for survival (or its will for self-representation, according to Geertz)[51] could command universal assent, even though an individual's interest and instinct may run counter to it. "The worshipper," Durkheim wrote, "believes himself to be held to certain manners of acting which are imposed upon him by the nature of the sacred principle with which he feels he is in communion."[52] What Durkheim called the "sacred principle" represented a sort of archetypal paradigm—a formulaic, concentrated model of social being that differed from other forms of group consciousness or activity by the higher degree of symbolic intensity (the presence of "mana," or the like) that members of a given community ascribed to it.[53]

Elaborating on Weber's sociology of charismatic authority, Edward Shils also put a special emphasis on intensity as a fundamental attribute of the "charismatic center," and it is not surprising that a charismatic poet, Osip Mandelstam, a junior contemporary of Durkheim and Weber, began one of his earliest essays on the nature of poetry by stressing the "monstrously condensed reality" of the poetic word—this pure paradigm encompassing the infinity of its variants.[54] That another contemporary, Sigmund Freud, made intensity a fundamental notion of his essentially paradigmatic economy of the human psyche and society (the Oedipus complex) suggests that we are dealing here with a case of historical congeniality.[55] Apparently, in turn-of-the-century Europe, intensity in association with the paradigmatic (or, as in Mandelstam, the "condensed reality" of a mathematical formula)[56] denoted a phenomenon commanding the sort of reverence and respect afforded hidden springs of a tremendous power. What the students of society and of the individual psyche were attempting to analyze was what the poet Mandelstam, together with other artists, tried to appropriate and display in ample measure. But this shared fascination with the intensely paradigmatic provides only one reason why the "demystifiers" and the "mystagogues" seem so well suited to each other. Not only the object of their concern, the power of the extraordinary over the routine of life, but also the very choice of the object was in harmony with the growing interest that an increasingly "rationalized" European society took in the demons of unreason slipping through the "positive" scientific net.[57]

In order to make this "sociology" relevant to the matter at hand, we must approach the phenomenon of modern Russian literature as something that is sacredly paradigmatic in relation to the society's round of life: its symbolic microcosm, with the major authors its stellar bodies.[58] In this respect, literature as a whole would represent a specific product (symbolic and intense) of a common social interest, defined not by separate individuals or social groups[59] but by what amounts to a sine qua non of a social body, a never-ending performance in which society represents itself to itself.[60] Literature, then, as a potential locus of the sacred, should have been treated *seriously,* even with reverence, by the Russians, and indeed it has been. Khardzhiev's letter to Eikhenbaum, quoted earlier, is a telling example of this phenomenon, enough so for us to pause here to consider it briefly against the background of another example of the literary-social paradigm, Aleksandr Blok.

It is a truth universally acknowledged that the famous poets of modern Russia, Mandelstam among them, have a personal following that borders on a cult. No doubt a complex phenomenon, it involves a strong tendency toward identification with the poet on the part of the reader, both individually and en masse. Such identification is implied in the very idea of intensity, which denotes a relation of quantity be-

The Holy as Paradigm

tween qualitatively similar entities, and without this underlying similitude the notion of intensity will not make any sense. The interdependence between poet and reader is most evident in the following excerpt about Aleksandr Blok, which comes from a highly specialized scholarly study of his manner of recitation by S. N. Bernshtein, a pioneer of Saussurian structuralism in Russia (italics are mine):[61]

> Generations shall cherish the emotional memory of the poet now gone. But we, his contemporaries "born in mute years," we are linked to him with an especially intimate link. And for us, who *recognize* in his poetic legacy the features of our own aesthetically metamorphosed sense of the world, the untimely passing away of the poet appears profoundly *symbolic:* together with him, under the pressure of the catastrophic events of recent years, there passes away *our spiritual universe,* and we, survivors of our own age, we are condemned to becoming our own historians. . . .
>
> By fixing the image of Aleksandr Blok, we, historians of our own time, an already passing epoch, epigones of the prerevolutionary attitudes, strive to *mirror* for the ages to come *our own image* and to pass on over the heads of the living to the distant descendants our ardor no longer comprehensible to the contemporaries who have managed to submit their psychological makeup to the demands of the current moment.[62]

In this introduction, Bernshtein considers it self-evident that while the reader and the poet share their experience of the age, only the poet, a privileged child of the age, can serve as a symbolic medium of communion with the epoch. Thus, in order to transfix his age for posterity, indeed to assure his own cultural survival, Bernshtein, a reader peripheral to the Blok cult, turned to the center of it, to the acknowledged *profound symbol* of his generation, its "paradigm," Blok the poet.

A similar pattern of identification informs Nikolai Khardzhiev's letter. In the enthusiastic and terrifying Stalinist 1932, the third year of total mobilization, most intellectuals (no matter how loyal) must have experienced a sense of constraint, running the gamut from minor discomforts to the sense or state of captivity.[63] As readers, Khardzhiev and Eikhenbaum no doubt shared these sentiments with Mandelstam, but it was his experience that was recognized as ultimately intense: he, the symbolic, central figure of the culture, implicitly likened to the cultivated Rome seized by the barbarians, behaved as a "captive emperor, or poet," while they, by implication, paid him court, being peripheral to him but still in his orbit. For the duration of the recital at least, he was the center of their universe, and as a result every *intense* sensation, even fear (of which every soul had plenty in those days), appeared as something generated by the poet himself. No doubt, some of the poems were politically risqué, and the very sight of this alleged relic of the past commanding an actual stage in the present must have appeared extraordinary. Other factors contributed to this impression: Mandelstam's rather unusual appearance (a "patriarch" to Khardzhiev, he looked like a "dervish" to Lidiia Ginzburg),[64] his frequent reliance on verbal formulas akin, and kin, to spells and exorcisms as well as his "shamanistic"[65] way of reciting poetry. All of this, in combination or separately, would have sufficed for tuning the mind of the audience—stressed as it was by the uncertainties of the Stalin revolution—to the awe-inspiring wavelength. These people expected to experience fear as well as awe, admiration, elation, and other strong sensations in the presence of a poet of Mandelstam's reputation. And he expected to serve as an emotional catalyst for their catharsis. Such is the paradox of charisma, particularly the so-called charisma of reversal characteristic of millenarian movements and sects.[66] The example of Maiakovskii's last and failed recital—a devastating fiasco precisely because he tried so hard—shows that an audience with a different set of expectations cannot be moved even by one who had the reputation as Russia's foremost Orpheus.[67] By contrast, those who came to hear Mandelstam were prepared to be captivated by him for "two and a half hours." And since both poets were more than amply endowed with talent, the question of the relative merit of their poetry should not be raised. It is a vexing vicissitude of the charismatic mission that one can prove one's possession of the gift only to those who are thoroughly inclined to believe in it.

Apparently, Mandelstam and his audience shared not only a culture but a specific set of expectations that the poet was able to personify; and one can be fairly certain that Mandelstam appeared to those who gathered to hear him (and, no doubt, to himself) as a symbol of the community of his admirers, while they perceived themselves as attenuated variants of the poet-paradigm. Each harbored a smoldering spark from the poet's charismatic fire. And as long as they could see the fire in the poet, they affirmed the presence of the spark in their own selves—the periphery and the center exchanging signals of *mutual recognition*. As to the fire, its source lay elsewhere, in some other exemplars, ingrained in the collective memory of the culture, whose identities the poet willingly assumed. Properly speaking, these deeply etched images—the archetypal poet-healer,[68] poet-magician, poet-shaman, in short, the omnipotent poet—had been conjured up in a dream long before Mandelstam could put them to use.

The Holy as Paradigm

> Быть может, прежде губ уже родился шепот,
> И в бездревесности кружилися листы,
> И те, кому мы посвящаем опыт,
> До опыта приобрели черты.
>
> 1933

> Perhaps, the whisper was born before the lips,
> And leaves once swirled in a woodlessness,
> And those to whom we dedicate our work
> Have, before our work, acquired their features.[69]

With this in mind, we might imagine the poet's audience and his sympathetic readers as people who are dreaming the poet's interpretation of their own old and powerful dreams. For it was only through a combined effort of both parties (conscious *and* unreflective) that a community of literary worship could begin to arise.

Mandelstam was by no means unaware of the mechanism of this reciprocal arrangement, nor of the culture's need for repeated reenactment of its own sacred "dreams," foremost among them the dream about death and resurrection. In the later poetry this awareness is expressed with virtually analytic precision. Consider a few lines, including an evangelical closure, from his 1934 poem on the death of Andrei Belyi, focused on the moving atmosphere of a Russian literary funeral:

> Дышали шуб меха. Плечо к плечу теснилось,
> Кипела киноварь здоровья — кровь и пот —
> Сон в оболочке сна, внутри которой снилось
> На полшага продвинуться вперед.
> . . . .
> Как будто я повис на собственных ресницах
> И, созревающий и тянущийся весь,
> Покуда не сорвусь, разыгрываю в лицах
> Единственное, что мы знаем днесь.
>
> Январь 1934

> Fur coats heaved. And shoulders rubbed.
> Blood, sweat—vermillion of health was seething.
> A dream wrapped in a dream; inside it, you were dreaming
> Of moving forward, if for half an inch.
> . . . .
> I feel as if suspended from my own eyelashes—
> And so ripening, and so all-stretching—
> Till I fall off, I reenact
> That one and only thing we know unto this day.[70]

As Mandelstam himself put it in his essay on Blok, in order to sustain itself culture required a cult,[71] and the cult he had in mind was one practiced by the community of authors and readers—in Russia a significant "community of worship" among the educated people and one that knew how to make itself heard.

Far from being esoteric, this point of view has been common currency for nearly a century and a half, beginning with the exaltation of Pushkin by Gogol in 1834, when Russia's future archetypal poet was still a robust thirty-five. What follows is a small portion of this extraordinary document, which later would serve as a model for the adulation not only of Pushkin but of Nikolai Gogol himself (italics are mine):[72]

> Pushkin constitutes an extraordinary and, perhaps, unique manifestation of the Russian spirit: this is a Russian man in his [mature] development, which he will perhaps achieve in two hundred years. In him the Russian nature, the Russian soul, Russian language, Russian character found a reflection of such purity, such *unalloyed purity* as only a landscape can achieve when reflected on the convex surface of a magnifying glass.[73]

In the latter half of the nineteenth century, the authority of authorship became so great that it was not uncommon for an educated Russian to seek moral and spiritual advice from a writer even in a personal encounter, as one would from a Russian Orthodox "holy man," or more precisely, "holy old man" (*starets*).[74] Reflected in this phenomenon is what one historian defined as a tendency of Eastern Christianity toward the "dispersal of the holy" outside the confines of the established church,[75] a tendency very much encouraged and magnified by the tremendous pressures experienced by Russian society in the decades following the emancipation of the enserfed peasants.

In fact, in some instances the institution of secular authorship and *starchestvo* existed in a kind of symbiotic relationship, with writers—themselves venerated as spiritual leaders and healers—going on pilgrimages to the retreats famous for their holy sages. Konstantin Leont'ev ended his life as a monk at the Optina Hermitage, and Dostoevsky, fascinated by the institution, visited Optina often and presented a vivid description of it at the beginning of *The Brothers Karamazov*.[76] Nikolai Leskov responded to the society's interest in the ascetic "holy men" by producing a cycle of exemplary novellas about secular "righteous men" (*pravedniki*) and later retold with his characteristic pungency the lives of the early saints, those distant cousins of the Russian *startsy*.[77] Tolstoy, too, is known to have visited the Optina Hermitage, where he extolled the merits of his adaptation of the New Testament, referring to it—some say immodestly—as "my own gospel."[78] The radical left promoted a *starets* from its own ranks: Nikolai Chernyshevskii, a vastly influential figure. Although temperamentally unsuited for the role of personal guru in the manner of Dostoevsky or Tolstoy, he was nevertheless considered a veritable prophet, as a contemporary put it, the greatest man born since Paul and Jesus Christ.[79] In exile for most of his productive life, this Symeon Stylites of Russian socialism helped to shape the personalities of many educated young men and women, among them Lenin, for generations.[80] The focus of this momentous accomplishment was *What Is to Be Done*, a novel of exemplary personalities whose extraordinary appeal among contemporary youth was apparently unrelated to the novel's flaws in craftsmanship, as compared with the "classical" Russian novel. Obviously, on the readers' scale of values, the questions of artistic merit could not outweigh the *holy* attributes of the symbolic Chernyshevskii: a suffering author mirrored in his protagonists and in the gospel of social justice and individual fulfillment that they preached. What appears to one generation as aesthetic ineptitude might appear to another as a lofty spareness of form or freedom from self-indulgent embellishment, as the antiaesthetic aesthetics of the post-1881 Tolstoy demonstrate most amply. The type of proof offered by a charismatic literary figure might change, but the change itself need not affect the intensity of the literary charisma.

The reasons why literature in Russia has come to occupy what Shils would call a central position in the elite culture require a separate study, but some of the more important aspects of this process need to be sketched here to give historical depth to the career of the poet Mandelstam. The process received its perhaps most decisive impetus from a historical coincidence: the famous parting of the ways, the alienation of the elite from the state in the wake of the Decembrist Rebellion (1825),[81] which was taking place against the background of a great creative outburst in imaginative literature dominated at the time by the European Romanticism that tended to privilege alienation in sentiment and, in the realm of spirit, the aesthetic sphere. This constellation of circumstances had unanticipated consequences, among them, the transformation of Russian literature into a sole *social* institution that the "society" could claim in its entirety, for it did not owe it to anyone but itself.[82] In the Durkheimian sense especially, the leading spokesmen of the educated society seized on literature as an "encyclopedia of Russian life," to use the phrase with which Vissarion Belinskii defined *Eugene Onegin*.

However, apart from being a convenient ethnosocial compendium, literature for the generations after Pushkin served less as the *Encyclopédie* and more as a revered secular *Summa* of exemplary paradigms of its place and epoch.[83] Exacerbated by the backwardness of the largely peasant country and the inflexibility of the ancien régime, the rift between educated society and the state grew ever wider. With time it became a three-way split, alienating one from the other: the educated upper and middle classes, the "people," meaning the lower strata of rural and urban life, and the increasingly decrepit but still powerful autocracy. Under these conditions the lone "voluntary" and open institution of Russia continued to soak up and imitate some of those functions that other Western countries entrusted to the church, political parties, schools, universities, and, of course, the press. Represented by Dostoevsky, Tolstoy, Turgenev, Chernyshevskii, and Chekhov, to name the more famous, Russian literature appeared capable of holding the totality of Russian experience in its embrace. And it is as a matter of course that Russian literature, a "paradigm" of Russian culture, had developed along the way its own pantheon of "holy men," consisting of authors and their protagonists and not unrelated to the traditional veneration of saints. Viewed against this background, Tolstoy's decision to abandon "literature" in favor of propagating a new form of ethical spirituality by means of "unembellished" verbal structures would have had to be invented had it not taken place in 1881. In a way, Tolstoy's last three decades constituted an apotheosis of the seriousness of Russian literature and at the same time served as its last global and unqualified success.

The expansion of the professions and of industry in the latter half of the nineteenth century and the dramatic easing of censorship, the legalization of political parties and other voluntary associations, and the high standards of public education for the middle and upper classes after the Revolution of 1905 all contributed to the rapidly growing differentiation of educated Russian society.[84] An educated man or woman residing in either of the two capitals could enjoy the best of what cosmopolitan prewar Europe had to offer, even if living on a modest income or, like Mandelstam, on no income at all. When in 1910 Tolstoy escaped from his estate and shortly afterward, like his Anna, died at a railroad station (for him a symbol of unwelcome modernity), his readers were aware that they might have lost the last Russian author with a "total" grasp.[85] The age of differentiation had commenced and with it the nagging questions about the special, all-embracing position of Russian letters.[86] "We used to be 'prophets,'" Blok wrote, commenting wistfully on bygone days in his "On the Present State of Russian Symbolism" (1910), and he contrasted that higher calling with the current, trivial "request to be 'poets.'"[87] It might appear that charismatic energy was flowing out of Russian poetry. In fact nothing was further from the truth. There cannot be a better environment for the dispersal of charisma than the time when old convictions, even if undermined, continue to exist side by side with new uncertainties.

Virtually in the same breath Blok insisted that the "motherland" and society, or, as he put it, "the people," found in poetry their highly focused paradigm. The "soul" of the Russian people and the "soul" of Russia were projected onto the microcosm of the poet's soul,[88] and in this sense, a poet could be seen as a holy man, his *intense* holiness derived from the dispersed holiness of the native land and the people. Needless to say, not every one agreed. But when in late 1910 Dmitrii Merezhkovskii ventured to express his doubts concerning Blok's claims on this privilege, Blok was ready with an unequivocal response that forced Merezhkovskii to withdraw his objections and offer an apology. "Motherland is akin to her son—man," Blok wrote in what he intended as an open letter to Merezhkovskii:

> When she is healthy and at rest, her entire body becomes as sensitive as a healthy human body; not a single point is anesthetized; everything breathes, sees; she answers every blow by raising her head in anger; to every caress she responds tenderly and passionately. Her organs of feelings are multifarious and their range is very great. Who, then, plays the role of the organs of this being, so like us and so dear?
>   The role of these organs is played and must be played by all people. As to us, writers, who are free from all but human obligations, we must play the role of the subtlest and most important organs of her feelings. We are not her blind instincts—we are her heartaches, her thoughts, ideas, the impulses of her will.[89]

IN PLACE OF A BIOGRAPHY

Do not forget me, torment me, but do
Give me a name, do give me a name:
It will be easier for me, do understand me,
In this pregnant and profound blue.
OSIP MANDELSTAM (1923)

It was against this ambiguous background of exalted expectations for poetry and poets and the fear that the time of great literature was passing away[90] that Mandelstam's first selection of poems appeared in a major journal—the August 1910 issue of the Petersburg *Apollon*. Half a century later, typescripts and amateur collections of his poetry, much of it heroically preserved by his widow, were furtively passed from hand to hand in Moscow and Leningrad, while in the United States

The Charisma of Poetry

Boris Filippov and Gleb Struve were launching a multivolume edition of his writings. The major landmarks of these fifty-odd years included two great wars and an assortment of smaller ones; two major revolutions from below (February and October 1917); one (the Stalin revolution) from above, with its total mobilization, colossal construction, famine, and the catastrophic proliferation of the Gulag; and eventually, after Stalin's death, the still incomplete de-Stalinization. The full brunt of these events fell on the shoulders of Mandelstam's generation, men and women born during the last decade of what, through the haze of nostalgia, appears an innocent and civil age. Most of them were crushed by the enormous weight of the new, "not calendar but real twentieth century," in Akhmatova's chilling phrase, and have disappeared into the anonymity of its mass graves.

But there were others, admittedly few, who, however glorious or inglorious their lives and deaths, managed to preserve their names or, better, managed to have their names closely associated with the image of their epoch.

> Одни
> > на монетах изображают льва,
>
> Другие —
> > голову;
>
> Разнообразные медные, золотые и бронзовые лепешки
> С одинаковой почестью лежат в земле.
> Век, пробуя их перегрызть, оттиснул на них свои зубы.
> Время срезает меня, как монету,
> И мне уже не хватает меня самого, —
> Не хватает, не достает — и я ищу сравнения...
>
> Москва, 1923

> Some
> > stamp a lion on their coins,
>
> Others—
> > a head;
>
> Different copper, gold and bronze pancakes
> Lie in the earth with equal honor.
> The age, trying to crack them, has imprinted them with its teeth.
> Time is filing me down like a coin,
> And I am no longer sufficient unto myself,
> Not sufficient, not enough—and I am looking for a comparison...

Mandelstam wrote these lines late in 1923, around the time he began work on his autobiography, having sat through only the first act or two of the drama that was his epoch. The part he had seen impressed

In Place of a Biography

him enough to turn it into a vehicle for the poetic narrative of his own personal drama. Hence the title of his recollections: not a "story of my life" but *The Noise of Time,* sparely and emphatically. What remained for Mandelstam to hear and see before his death in 1938 in a concentration camp somewhere in the Far East loomed larger still and was making, as it continued to move, a louder and crasser sound. "We live," says one of his ambiguous descriptions of the epoch in 1922, "in the shadow of an unfinished temple dedicated to a deity yet unknown."[91] Indeed, we have to strain our eyes to keep the poet's personal biography in view, so thoroughly has it blended with the pall cast by the blessedly unfinished house of worship. Like the fact of his first name, the facts of his life were accidental—in themselves ordinary. And only retouched by the narrative of his readers' historical memory and the narrative patterns of his own art did they amount to what we casually call a biography while having in mind something far more purposeful—a poet's "fate." That story, specifically the childhood years, is well told by Mandelstam himself in his autobiographical *The Noise of Time* (1925) and admirably amplified and contextualized in the critical biography by Clarence Brown.[92] What I offer here is not so much an outline of Mandelstam's childhood and youth (with a small addendum on his life in the late 1920s) as a discussion of the typology used to compose a by now well-known story. Events pertaining to the rest of Mandelstam's life will be invoked in subsequent chapters as we move from poem to poem.

Mandelstam was Jewish, went to the Tenishev School, and grew up in St. Petersburg. Now, to be born a Jew, as Mandelstam was, might not have meant much if he and his age had not decided to dwell on it, however gingerly the one and obsessively the other. Boris Pasternak, also a Jew and a poet of the same generation, did not make much of his ethnic origins, and in his case, too, the age seems to have chosen to let sleeping dogs lie.[93] Nor was there anything extraordinary or unique about Mandelstam's family. Middle class, moderately well-off, and settled in St. Petersburg, his parents succeeded in giving their three boys (Osip was the oldest) a good education. All three graduated from one of St. Petersburg's more "progressive" schools, where children of different social, ethnic, and religious backgrounds were more or less harmoniously mixed in pursuit of physical health, knowledge, and civic virtue. The liberal aristocratic parents of another famous Russian author and Tenishev graduate, Vladimir Nabokov, would not have settled for less. Nor would a Karaiti Jew, B. N. Sinani. This physician, who sat in council with the members of the terrorist section of the

Socialist-Revolutionary (S-R) party, sent his son Boris to the Tenishev School, where he and Osip Mandelstam were to strike up an important and memorable friendship.

In Mandelstam's later reconstruction of his childhood, composed in the early 1920s, his family (more precisely, his parents, for about his siblings there was not a word) appeared as something fragile and insubstantial, a pair of interlopers pretending to belong to the St. Petersburg of the Russian Orthodox feast days and military parades. For what from the outside might have seemed a solid leather merchant's household—music lessons, French governesses, the dacha, instruction in the Talmud, private school for the boys—turned out to be a slapdash affair tossed about on Russia's uncertain seas overwhelmed by the "noise of time" whistling and clapping in the rigging. Whether true to life or imagined, this family portrait matched nicely with Mandelstam's metaphor of the deceptively decorous Imperial capital: a magnificent covering of pomp and circumstance thrown over the twitching body of the snorting, expiring Imperial "beast."[94] That the family was Jewish and lived in a country where the majority of their coreligionists were banished from central Russia by law[95] might or might not have been relevant as a feature of the family's life experience. In either case, the state's anti-Semitism made *narrative* sense, for it possessed all the satisfying attributes of "poetic justice" one might find in ethically balanced plot lines. For, no matter how grotesquely and paradoxically, the family did mirror the state: as they tried to assimilate, unevenly and with hesitation, into the larger Russian life, the Mandelstams unwittingly recapitulated the ambiguous career of the "Petersburg Russia" as she attempted to "assimilate" into the community of Europe's better pedigreed states. Not unlike this "assimilated" European country, the assimilated Mandelstams were neither quite Jewish nor quite Russian—two slates waiting to be erased and reinscribed.

To the extent that the Tenishev School reflected the interests and concerns of the capital city (public gatherings were often held in its capacious assembly hall),[96] Mandelstam found himself in a milieu where literature and politics formed the main preoccupations and were often hard to separate. There must have been other more romantic concerns, but about them he chose to say nothing. Russia—she was the elected bride, at least by retrospective intention. And in order to appeal to her, boys like Mandelstam read the *The Erfurt Program,* tempered their character and intellect according to the still risqué Herzen, and composed mystico-symbolic verse. "Metal shavings from the Obukhov Plant and the latest issue of *The Balance,*" both sitting under his desk, were the two items that defined the compass of his interests before

In Place of a Biography

graduation.⁹⁷ The first was emblematic of the boy's politics (in substance Marxist and in temperament heroically Socialist-Revolutionary)⁹⁸ and invoked one of St. Petersburg's more radical factories. There on March 2, 1907, the sixteen-year-old Mandelstam made a propaganda speech on the occasion of plaster falling from the ceiling of the State Duma—an innocent event, as it later turned out, which only resembled a possible plot of the sinister autocratic state.⁹⁹ The other, "the most civilized journal" in Russia, in the words of one historian,¹⁰⁰ had served since 1904 as the central organ for the expression of the Russian Symbolists' refined sensibility and profound sense.

It goes without saying that for those like Mandelstam who marched into impressionable adolescence in step with the decomposition of the old state and were propelled into their youth by the explosion of the 1905 revolution, a combination of these two interests may indeed have been a matter of course. Literature, the Russian tradition taught one to expect, would prophesy the cause that, according to the ideology of Russian populism, would be acted upon by the heroic martyrs.¹⁰¹ Thus Boris Savinkov, the mastermind of a series of political assassinations, was also a rather fashionable author of modernist novels, published under the pen name Ropshin. And Ivan Kaliaev, known to the Socialist-Revolutionary underground as "the Poet," executed two of Savinkov's assassination plots, one leading to the death of Minister of the Interior Pleve and the other, in which Kaliaev threw the bomb, killing the Grand Duke Sergei Aleksandrovich in 1905. Kaliaev, too, had cultivated a taste for modern literature. According to Savinkov, he particularly admired Blok, Briusov, and Bal'mont, who seem to have been integral to his political activity:

> For those who knew him [Kaliaev] intimately, his love for art and love for the revolution were illuminated by the same flame—unconscious, timid but profound and powerful religious feeling. He came to terrorism following his own, original route, seeing in it not only the best form of political struggle but also a moral, perhaps religious, sacrifice.¹⁰²

In those heady days, one could travel in the opposite direction, too, as did Mandelstam's future mentor, the major Symbolist guru Viacheslav Ivanov, who proudly declared his membership in a group called the Mystical Anarchists.¹⁰³ How well Mandelstam understood this tradition and how it affected him! In *The Noise of Time,* in the chapter entitled "The Bookcase," he comes across the portrait of the poet Semen Nadson (1862–1887), the rage of his parents' generation, which provides him with a pretext for developing, albeit in the ironic mode, the singularly important charismatic theme. This passage, with its complex elaboration of the metaphor of burning, is worth citing here at length.

> The 1880's in Vilno as mother recalled them. It was everywhere the same: sixteen-year-old girls tried to read John Stuart Mill and at the public recitals one could see luminous personalities who—with a certain dense admixture of pedal, a fainting away on the *piano* passage, and blank features—played the latest thing of the leonine Anton. But what actually happened is that the intelligentsia with Buckle and Rubinstein and led by the luminous personalities—who in their beatific idiocy completely lost the way—resolutely turned to the practice of self-immolation. Like high tar-coated torches the adherents of the People's Will Party burned for all the people to see, with Sofia Perovskaia and Zheliabov, and all of them, all of provincial Russia and all of the students smouldered in sympathy: not one single green leaf was to be left. . . . Semen Afanasievich Vengerov, a relative of mine on my mother's side (the family in Vilno and school memories), understood nothing of Russian literature and studied Pushkin as a professional task, but "one thing" he understood. His "one thing" was: the heroic character of Russian literature. He was a fine one with his heroic character when he would drag slowly along Zagorodnyi Prospekt from his apartment to the card catalogue, hanging on the elbow of his aging wife and smirking into his dense ant beard.[104]

All this was written by the man who admired Skriabin's "The Poem of Fire," tracing its sensibility to the self-immolation of the Russian Old Believers martyring themselves for Christ.[105]

Upon their graduation from the Tenishev School in the summer of 1907, Boris Sinani and Osip Mandelstam, both age sixteen, traveled to the village of Raivola, Finland, where, at a conspiratorial retreat, they applied for membership in the Fighting (that is, terrorist) Organization of the Socialist-Revolutionary party. For whatever reason (most likely their age), the boys' petition to join the ranks of those who "burned up" was rejected.[106] Soon afterward Boris Sinani died, and Mandelstam set out on his first tour of Europe. He spent his time largely in Paris, enjoying cafe life, composing, making friends among compatriots, attending the Sorbonne, and translating French poetry.[107] In Paris, he attended a memorial meeting for one of the founders of the S-R party and a leader of the Fighting Organization, Gersh Gershuni, who "burned up" from lung cancer in a Zurich hospital on March 17, 1908. Mikhail Karpovich, who befriended Mandelstam in Paris, recalled this occasion:

Gershuni died in Paris [sic] in the spring of 1908 and the S.-R.'s arranged a gathering in his memory. Mandelstam expressed the strongest desire to go there with me, but I don't think politics had anything to do with it. It was of course the personality and the fate of Gershuni that attracted him. The principal speaker was B. V. Savinkov. The moment he began to speak, Mandelstam sat bolt upright, got up from his seat, and listened to the whole speech standing in the aisle. He listened to it in a kind of trance, his mouth half open and his eyes half closed and his whole body leaning over so far backwards that I was even afraid he might fall. I must confess that he made a rather comic sight.[108]

The posture described by Karpovich strongly recalls Mandelstam's "trances" during his recitals.[109]

In the summer of 1908, having postponed his decision to enroll at Heidelberg, he returned to St. Petersburg to remain there until the summer of the following year. These months, when the young man gave himself up to the intellectual and artistic life of the capital, were decisive for Mandelstam's subsequent career as a poet. Perhaps most important, he was introduced to Viacheslav Ivanov and began visiting his "Tower," *the* literary salon in St. Petersburg and, in more ways than one, a true academy for the *pléiade* of Mandelstam's generation.[110]

Among poets of Ivanov's stature not one could rival him in erudition, authority, and energy—qualities that this man, who had studied with Mommsen (Roman history) and Saussure (Sanskrit),[111] combined to produce the most comprehensive "charismatic" program for poets and poetry in modern Russia.[112] Bringing together a post-Nietzschean mysterial Christianity and the achievements of contemporary scholarship in philology, anthropology, and comparative mythology,[113] Ivanov integrated them into the populist ideology of the Russian intelligentsia (the sanctifying seriousness of the popular and archaic imagination)[114] and into the religious sensibility of his contemporaries.[115] He was able to produce such a satisfying aesthetic, religious, and political synthesis that a young man like Mandelstam could not help being stunned and seduced. Not only could most of the contradictions of contemporary Russian life find their resolution in Ivanov's all-embracing catholicity, but, most important, they could accommodate splendidly, all too splendidly, the wildest ambition of a young poet—to assume the role of a condensed representation of all the society considered to be serious and sacred.

A letter Mandelstam wrote from Paris to V. V. Gippius (pen name Bestuzhev), a Symbolist poet and his Tenishev teacher of Russian literature, contains an intellectual self-portrait of Mandelstam a year before he came to know personally the author of *Guiding Stars* and, later, *Cor ardens*. The portion of this letter that I cite here conveys succinctly what it meant for a young man to drift in the cross-currents of different, often conflicting, ideological trends competing in the relative freedom of post-1905 Russia. This is a sixteen-year-old Mandelstam, overexposed to the grand solutions to the grand riddle of life and completely unsure about the type into which to cast his own self at the moment. The letter was dated April 19, 1908.

> I have always seen in you a representative of some dear and at the same time hostile principle, and, I have to add, it is precisely the ambiguity of this principle that constituted its charm.
>
> Now I understand that this principle is nothing other than religious culture—whether Christian or not I do not know—but religious in any case.
>
> Brought up in a nonreligious milieu (the family and school), I have long yearned for religion hopelessly and platonically—but with an ever-increasing self-awareness. My first religious experience goes back to my juvenile infatuation with the Marxist dogma and is inseparable from this infatuation.
>
> But the bond linking religion and social issues was broken for me already in my childhood.
>
> At the age of fifteen, I went through the purifying flame of Ibsen and, although I did not adhere to the religion of the will [Nietzsche?], I have taken the position of religious individualism [Lev Shestov] and against collectivism. . . .
>
> Tolstoy and Hauptmann, the two greatest apostles of love of mankind, have been assimilated ardently but abstractly, as was the "philosophy of norm" [neo-Kantianism: Cohen, Windelbandt].
>
> My religious consciousness has never transcended Knut Hamsun and the worship of "Pan," that is, an intuitive [*nesoznannyi*] God, and to this day it constitutes my religion (Oh, do not worry, this is not "maeonism," and in general I have nothing in common with Minskii). . . .
>
> I have no definite feelings toward society, God and man—but because of this I love life, faith and love all the more.[116]

Whoever could put that kind of house in order could not fail to gain a number of very interesting disciples among the young people who would continue to absorb and systematize what society's common sense could not assimilate or hold in abeyance. A little over a year later (June 1909), after he had met Ivanov and been taken into the fold, Mandelstam appended the following declaration to a very brief note to the "very respected and dear Viacheslav Ivanovich":

In Place of a Biography

> Your seeds have fallen deep into my soul, and I take fright as I look at their enormous shoots.
> I cherish the hope of meeting you somewhere this summer.
> Almost spoiled by you,
> but straightened out,
>
> Osip Mandelstam[117]

The relief provided by Ivanov from contradictions may not have been complete,[118] but the friendship between the young man and his mentor lasted for years.[119] What is more significant, the conceptual vocabulary that Ivanov imparted to Mandelstam was never entirely abandoned.[120]

A young poet torn between Nietzschean individualism and the deep populist yearning for a "catholic" or "symphonic" union (*sobornoe edinenie*) with the people could breathe a sigh of relief after finding a comfortable footing in Ivanov's elaborate construct. So, too, could the poet who now found himself perplexed by the limitations of action and the questionable effectiveness of boundless thought, limitations of ethics as a form of religion, and limitations of the available "institutional" religions as means of satisfying a deep spiritual need. For Ivanov, a lone poet if he were a true "hermitage" poet (*keleinyi poet*), served as "the organ of popular [*narodnyi*] consciousness,"[121] and his poetry was efficacious, active, a true deed, like "a prayer of Brahmin."[122] One who felt dissatisfied with institutionalized religion but found atheism or agnosticism equally wanting (as did Mandelstam) could also find relief in Ivanov's views. For the contemporary religious experience of Christianity was, according to Ivanov, historically incomplete, waiting to be reunited with its suppressed but original other half—the religion of Dionysus.[123] And it was the task of the "hermitage" poet to assume the heavy burden of reawakening this dormant truth in the mind of the people by invoking in his art the magic of symbol and myth.[124]

What a "hermitage" poet was to the throng, symbol was to myth, and myth was to the sacred collective consciousness of the people [*narod, der Volk*].[125] Each link in this chain differed from its preceding link by a higher degree of intensity, and all contributed to the charismatic mana possessed by a poet—the *theurgos*, author, creator—who has focused on himself all their intensity. Further, the theories of Viacheslav the Magnificent (as his admirers referred to him on occasion) provided a powerful antidote to the creeping toxins of "differentiation" that threatened to deprive Russian Literature and Poetry of their capital L and P. The acknowledged crisis of the sacred permeating modern Russian society, including the realm of letters, needed only a minute grafting of Hegelian dialectics to be convincingly transformed into the prelude to an imminent and total sacralization. This operation Ivanov performed with consummate skill.

Finally, Ivanov's teaching, however esoteric his work may seem to us, did not wander far from the humanistic curriculum of a contemporary European university, which made the course work of a student like Mandelstam a relevant and rich source of material for poetry as well as a current and satisfying view of the world.[126] In lifestyle, too, university learning and modernism found a happy alliance in Viacheslav Ivanov, for a student privileged enough to attend the famous nighttime vigils at the "Tower" stood a good chance of running into one of his instructors at the University of St. Petersburg.[127]

It would, of course, be misleading to limit Mandelstam's intellectual background to Ivanov's influence alone. In the presence of Aleksandr Blok, Mikhail Kuzmin, Andrei Belyi, Innokentii Annenskii, Valerii Briusov, Zinaida Gippius, and, of course, the proto-Futurist movement, the literary life of the two capitals was too rich for one to be loyal to a single guru. Moreover, Ivanov's authority in the 1910s began to ebb. To what extent Ivanov shaped or, as scholars used to say, influenced Mandelstam may be an open question, but one could hardly argue that there was another body of literature associated with a single figure that was more heterogeneous and more inclusive of the contemporary ideological vocabulary than Ivanov's writings. For a while, within the limited space of Petersburg's cultural elite, Ivanov represented a modernist "encyclopedia of Russian life." And what better mentor could one find to learn the craft from and later (or even simultaneously) to individuate from and to attack.

For Mandelstam's generation, a period of apprenticeship was followed by a period of individuation that coincided with what has become known in the history of Russian literature as the crisis of Symbolism. This series of critical debates concerning the nature of the Russian Symbolist movement culminated in the famous four-part exchange, with Ivanov, Blok, and Belyi insisting on a sacred theurgist mission for the movement and Briusov, in a recent about-face, denying that anything but aesthetics would ever matter for a true Symbolist.[128] The specifics of the agenda aside, the debate represented a clash not so much of scenarios for the future or the past of Symbolism as of discourses, and in this respect there can be little doubt that the vocabulary of Viacheslav Ivanov had triumphed. Blok, the foremost poet at the time, acknowledged this in his talk "On the Contemporary State of Russian Symbolism," delivered on April 8, 1910, a week after Ivanov's statements. It was not a polite exaggeration when Blok referred to his own, and for him crucially important, address as a Baedeker to the world that Viacheslav Ivanov had just mapped out in his "Testaments of Symbolism." The relations between the two poets soon soured, but for years to come Blok continued to indicate that his April address was one of the two most significant essays he had ever written.[129] He reprinted it without any changes as a separate brochure eleven years later.

An incident involving Valerii Briusov and Nikolai Gumilev, who at the time considered himself to be in Briusov's orbit, is even more instructive. Believing that he had the younger generation on his side,[130] Briusov must have been quite surprised to receive an endorsement of Blok's speech from his disciple Nikolai Gumilev. The future theoretician and founder of Acmeism, who was busy preparing a revolt against the *diktat* of Ivanov,[131] saw in Blok's variations on the theme from the "Testament" of Viacheslev the Magnificent a form in which he could accept Ivanov's central notion of art as theurgy—if not through symbol, then through myth.[132] And even if the style that the Acmeists, particularly Gumilev and Mandelstam, would later advocate was relatively sober and better "balanced" between this and the other mysterious world, the two were never prepared to give up the global claims for poetry that bore a recognizable imprint of Ivanov's old program. In fact, not only Acmeists but the Futurists, too, defined themselves in opposition to "theurgist" Symbolism, while keeping the substantial portion of the lofty vocabulary intact.[133] This type of indirect acknowledgment speaks volumes about the importance of Ivanov's writings for the contemporary discourse on poetry. The "ideas came from Viacheslev Ivanov himself," Mandelstam was prepared to acknowledge in the early 1920s, defining the Acmeist and indirectly the Futurist achievement as the introduction into Russian poetry of a new "taste."[134]

Mandelstam was not present at the debates concerning the crisis of Symbolism, although he followed them with great interest. During the fall and winter of 1909–10 he was studying Romance languages and philosophy at Heidelberg. One more year would pass before he established himself as a student at the University of St. Petersburg. The activities and landmarks during this intervening year included his first entry into print in the *Apollon,* involvement in the literary politics surrounding this journal,[135] attendance at the "Academy of Verse," the Poets' Guild,[136] meetings at the St. Petersburg Religious-Philosophical Society,[137] and further (albeit unsuccessful) attempts to publish his poetry in *Russkaia mysl'*.[138] And baptism. Whatever else Mandelstam's baptism might have meant, it assured him of matriculating at the University of St. Petersburg.[139] Enigmatically, he was baptized not as a Russian Orthodox, which perhaps might have carried the stigma of capitulation before the religious intolerance of the state, nor as a Roman Catholic, however much he felt fascinated by the glory of the Roman Church, but as a Finnish Methodist.[140] Given the position of the Methodists in the religiously intolerant Russian Empire, they were an unlikely choice for someone in search of a fictitious baptismal certificate, which suggests that Mandelstam's baptism was more of a conversion than a pro forma ceremony for a Russian Jew seeking to enroll at the University of St. Petersburg. Be that as it may, Methodism never surfaced in his art, unless one wishes to locate it in the poet's abundant enthusiasm,[141] whereas both Roman Catholicism and Russian Orthodoxy played a significant role in the "narrative" of his life.

With the publication of his poetry in *Apollon*, the "mute" years of Mandelstam's life come to an end, and whatever we know about his life henceforth becomes inseparable from his prose and poetry.

> Issue no. 9 of *Apollon,* which I received today, contains five poems by a young lyric poet Joseph [*sic*] Emilievich Mandelstam whose acquaintance I made in Hankö [Finland] in July of the current year. . . . Mandelstam is very young: he is 20 or 21. He graduated from the Tenishev School and subsequently went to Heidelberg University (as a Jew, he could not enter the University of St. Petersburg), where for half a year he studied Romance languages. At the Tenishev, he was either an S-R or an S-D, and even made an inflammatory speech before the workers of his district. . . . Now he is ashamed of his previous revolutionary activity and considers it his calling to pursue the career of a lyric poet.[142]

So wrote an older friend of Mandelstam, Sergei Pavlovich Kablukov, making an entry in his diary on August 18, 1910, which might as well be considered, to paraphrase Clarence Brown, the birthday of Mandelstam the poet. At least for the purposes of this study, there was no other Mandelstam. Thus, in order to provide an understanding of his place in modern Russian culture, I shall focus on his identity as a "Russian poet," more specifically, on the narrative of self-presentation—the way he shaped his self in his gesture and art.

Such an approach is justified even when it involves the second half of the 1920s, when Mandelstam's muse fell silent, or to put it simply, when he ceased to compose poetry. For these were not altogether "mute" years. Both his autobiographical prose, *The Noise of Time* (1925), and his novella *The Egyptian Stamp* (1928) were events in modern Russian literature, even if they were marked by self-mockery on the part of the once loftily charismatic poet. For Mandelstam, as for other poets of his generation, this period between 1924 and 1929 was a time of changing landmarks. The perplexing Russian society of the New Economic Policy (NEP), with its conflicting value systems, the difficulty of earning a living by literary free-lancing, and, finally, the appearance of a new generation of readers and writers with different expectations and tastes greatly attenuated the "centrality" of poetry. To add insult to injury, Mandelstam, whose earnings from writing had never amounted to a reliable income, had to undertake money-making literary projects (editing and translating) in order to earn a living, it would seem, for the first time in his life. Charismatic poetry as it had taken shape over the preceding century was, needless to say, inimical to enterprising activity of this kind. According to the memoirs of the poet's widow, to whom we owe the canonical view of Mandelstam, these were not the most glorious years of her husband's career,[143] for this was the period when the narrative consistency of life in art was most difficult to maintain.

It was only in the 1930s, with the institution of strict controls over literature, that the state began to provide an economic cushion for the officially recognized but nevertheless still free-lance authors. By contrast, under the NEP the relative autonomy of literature from the state went hand in hand with economic insecurity for writers and poets. Together with the shift of poetry from the center to the periphery of the culture, these not entirely personal reasons could not but affect the choice of style and form, and in *The Egyptian Stamp* in particular, Mandelstam switched from the high gear of an almost mystical identification with the age to the low gear of historicizing, ironic prose narrative. One could no longer write, as Mikhail Zoshchenko once put it, as though nothing had happened.[144] This was true for lyric poetry as much as prose fiction.[145]

The poet had two choices—to disappear from the scene or to start looking for new paths.[146] In *The Egyptian Stamp*, Mandelstam went so far as to jettison those parts of his former self—the instinctive humanity of the intelligentsia and the no less instinctive attachment to the "culture" of ballets and operas at the Mariinskii, as well as the touchingly exasperated gestures of a bungler and "weakling"—that might brand him as a "has-been" or, in the parlance of the day, a "carryover" from the antediluvian tsarist period (*perezhitok*).[147] It was one such "carryover," the Populist litterateur A. G. Gornfel'd, who in 1928 accused Mandelstam of literary piracy. Apparently through no fault of Mandelstam, Gornfel'd's pre-1917 translation of Coster appeared under the name of Mandelstam, who had only served as editor (see chapters 7 and 8 as well as Appendix I). As Nadezhda Mandelstam suggested decades later, this ultimately wrongful accusation and Mandelstam's travails to clear his name helped him to regain his "sense of his inner certitude," without which he could not function as a poet.[148] Or we might say, the painful experience allowed him once again to counterpose himself to, and hence to identify with, the entire world—the fundamental source of strength for a charismatic poet. The rapidly growing polarization of society further amplified Mandelstam's estrangement from the community of writers, raising a personal misfortune to the level of an objective correlative.

Upon his return to Moscow from an extended tour of Armenia in 1930, things slowly began to fall into place. Before long, Mandelstam was able to reestablish in his life a bohemian equilibrium and to resume the lifestyle of a charismatic poet, something that he found difficult to sustain under the materialist NEP. His continuing estrangement from the writers' establishment formed one part of the equilibrium, and it was counterbalanced by the privileged status he was able to enjoy thanks to his friends in high places. His chief patron, Nilokai Bukharin, who admired Mandelstam's art and was still a powerful figure in the party hierarchy, was able to arrange for the poet a special state pension which, although meager monetarily, entitled him to such pleasantries as free public transportation and, no minor matter in a famine-stricken country, food privileges reserved for the very important servants of the state.[149] In addition to this already extraordinary gift, the Mandelstams moved into their own apartment, a true luxury in those very difficult years.[150] Whatever label one might wish to put on that literary *skandal* that the Mandelstams ironically christened the "Dreyfus Affair,"[151] it prepared him well for the decade to come. The resumption of total mobilization in the Stalin revolution and the accompanying cult of the supreme leader brought to an end the complex and, many thought, complacent pluralism of the NEP years.[152] What followed was a long period of inclement weather, poorly suited for habitation but one in which a poet of cultivated singularity and charismatic tradition could go on producing lyric poetry of high seriousness or perish tragically in a concentration camp—or, as happened to Mandelstam, do both.

There is a 1913 poem by Mandelstam that he originally intended to call "The Palace Square," referring to the square before the Winter Palace in St. Petersburg. Knowing what we know now about Mandelstam's life and death, it reads almost like an outline of his future. But if we look at it from the vantage point of 1913, it appears as a thematic variation on the charismatic tradition of Russian poetry and poets. Shaped in the form of a poetic prayer, it consists of only two stanzas. In the first Mandelstam sets up the historical props that in the second will begin to look like the shadows cast by the praying poet.

> Заснула чернь. Зияет площадь аркой.
> Луной облита бронзовая дверь.
> Здесь арлекин вздыхал о славе яркой,
> И Александра здесь замучил зверь.
>
> Курантов бой, и тени государей...
> Россия, ты на камне и крови,
> Участвовать в своей последней каре
> Хоть тяжестью меня благослови!
> 1913

The rabble is asleep! The arch of the square is yawning.
The moonlight has spilled over the bronze door.
Here dreamed the Harlequin about his brilliant glory,
And Alexander here was gored and stomped on by the beast.

The chimes of time and the shadows of the Tsars...
You, Russia, who rest on stone and blood,
To partake of your iron punishment
Even in heaviness, do give me your blessing![153]

There is magic in such "answered prayers," the kind of magic that tradition associates with the poetic word—it heals, it casts a spell, it prophesies. And just as it is not necessary to believe in Santa Claus in order to covet a present at Christmas, it is not necessary to believe in the magic of the word in order to continue expecting from poets the coveted assurance that they indeed possess the extraordinary gift and would share it with us, if only on rare and special occasions. How was it possible for Mandelstam or, for that matter, any poet of his stature to attract to himself so much mana? This question requires different and complementary answers, each focusing on a certain aspect of the culture in which the gift and the proofs of its extraordinary nature are displayed and recognized. The answer offered in this study involves an examination of Mandelstam's mythologies[154] of self-presentation in relation to the larger narrative patterns of Russian culture that provided the lexicon and the grammar as well as the outer frame for the poet's work.

II

Mysteries of Breathing: 1909–1912

> И ты с беспечного детства
> Ищи сочетания слов.
> VALERII BRIUSOV (1908)

ON A LONE WINTER EVENING

> *If you can puzzle that out, you shall be your own master, and I'll give you the whole world and a new pair of skates.*
> HANS CHRISTIAN ANDERSEN, The Snow Queen

> Мы были праздничные дети,
> Моя сестра и я.
> Плела нам радужные сети
> Коварная змея.
> FEDOR SOLOGUB (1906)

> Стекла стынут от холода,
> Но сердце знает,
> Что лед растает—
> Весенне будет и молодо.
> MIKHAIL KUZMIN (1908)

> "Did you know that great Plotinus is said to have made the remark that he was ashamed to have a body?" asked Settembrini.
> THOMAS MANN, Magic Mountain

The first readers of the first *Stone* (1913) must have been surprised when they opened the book to discover on page one a poem with a pointedly ephemeral title, "Breathing" (1909). It read:

34

On a Lone Winter Evening

Дано мне тело — что мне делать с ним,
Таким единым и таким моим?

За радость тихую дышать и жить,
Кого, скажите, мне благодарить?

Я и садовник, я же и цветок,
В темнице мира я не одинок.

На стекла вечности уже легло
Мое дыхание, мое тепло.

Запечатлеется на нем узор,
Неузнаваемый с недавних пор.

Пускай мгновения стекает муть —
Узора милого не зачеркнуть.

1909

A body is given me—what shall I do with it,
So whole and so mine?

For the quiet joy of breathing and living,
Whom, tell me, should I thank?

I am both a gardener and a flower I am, too;
In the prison of the world, I am not alone.

On the window panes of eternity, settled
My breathing, my warmth.

A design shall be imprinted on them,
Unrecognizable since not long ago.

Let the dregs of the moment drip down—
The sweet design cannot be crossed out.[1]

To begin with, the metrical arrangement was somewhat unusual. For in the Russian tradition, one does not often encounter a poem consisting of six couplets of iambic pentameter, each having a contiguous masculine rhyme (a a, b b, c c, etc.). The syntax, especially in line five, was also bound to raise eyebrows. It lay somewhere between the correct literary language and a slightly precious colloquial, unconstrained speech, a feature that made it very difficult to put one's finger on the intention of the poem.[2] Was Mandelstam completely serious or only half-serious? Was he parodying? And if he was, then whom—himself? Fedor Sologub?[3] Mikhail Kuzmin?[4] Konstantin Bal'mont?[5] Some obscure poet? Or was it, perhaps, the result of a premature entry into the world of letters by an incautious Jew who did not feel quite at home with all the intricacies of the Russian language?[6] Maybe one should avert one's eyes to spare the poor soul further embarrassment.

Mysteries of Breathing: 1909–1912

And yet the poem, published in 1910 in the fashionable *Apollon*, possessed enough charm, enough touching innocence to have earned the poet a modicum of enviable notoriety. He would not have placed it at the beginning of his first *and* second book (1913, 1916) had it been otherwise. In a way, "Breathing," with all of its engaging, unthreatening incongruities and childish innocence, projected a character that could easily become emblematic of the "young poet" Mandelstam[7]—a man whom his friend Georgii Ivanov remembered as taking offense at the smallest, often imaginary slights while inviting his companions to join in the laughter over his own eccentricities or clumsiness.[8] Thus it is possible to treat "Breathing" as a sort of a snapshot (the more artless, the more telling) of the poet in his late teens and very early twenties—a collector's item with which the reader begins the work of tracing the outlines of the poet's public face.

I am not sure what these six couplets, especially in a translation, convey to a non-Russian reader, but one who grew up in Petersburg-Leningrad or even Moscow might imagine a city apartment in winter, frozen window panes with intricate patterns of hoarfrost, and, seeping through, the sickly and eerie winter light. One might imagine a child sitting by the window, trying to melt with his breath a circle in the ice through which to peek outside. I say a child not merely because of the third couplet, but because of the whole infantile tone of the poem—its spareness and naiveté, its almost primitive rhyming pattern, its wobbly syntax ("I am both a gardener and a flower I am, too"), and its unselfconscious bragging in the conclusion.[9] What we have here, then, is a mental picture of a child daydreaming by a frozen window in the middle of winter, say, around Christmas time. He is daydreaming because of inactivity enforced by the weather, because of the utopian season, and because, very likely, he has just read Hans Christian Andersen's "The Snow Queen,"[10] which may help explain why this seemingly "soft" poem opened *Stone*, a collection with such a hard and laconic name.

Andersen's boy Kay, who would later follow the Snow Queen to the North Pole, caught his first glimpse of her in a similar setting—through a peephole thawed out in the frozen pane of glass. A year later, she kindled in him a desire to compose the word ETERNITY out of crystals of ice. Had Kay's heart not been melted by Gerda's kiss, he would have finished the assignment successfully and, as promised, would have inherited the world. But he was saved by Gerda. The moral: give up ambitions and dreams and instead of chasing after snow queens who promise the world, stick with Grandma and the trusty, if a bit simple, Gerda. However sensible, this was no way to be a poet. The poet—more precisely, the poet of Mandelstam's generation—must do both: breathe a naively warm, ice-melting breath while composing ETERNITY out of the delicate cold crystals. For Mandelstam, who, incidentally, suffered from asthma,[11] breathing often stood for poetry, and it makes sense—if we wish to understand what it meant for him to be a poet—to take a closer look at what it meant in those days for a poet to "breathe."

CONJUGAL CONJUGATIONS

Vowels are women, consonants are men.
KONSTANTIN BAL'MONT,
Poetry as Magic (1916)

In 1909, commenting on one of the more risqué poems by Briusov, Innokentii Annenskii made an enigmatic statement concerning the significance of the theme of eros in poetry.[12] Characteristic of the contemporary regard for positive science, his remark began with an invocation of physiology, yet it brings to mind not the work of, say, Sechenov but rather the post-Freudian writings of a Lacan, a Barthes, or a Derrida.[13] According to Annenskii, the uses of eroticism in Briusov's poetry, "thanks to the poet's intuition, endow with a new and profound meaning" what, for a physiologist, "constitutes an established fact," namely, that there exists "a kinship between the centers of speech and sexual feeling." Omitting Annenskii's detour into the Greek conception of the ineffable (an appeal to the authority of antiquity no less characteristic of the times),[14] we find "profound meaning" in the suggestion that the eroticism of Briusov's poetry "illuminates not so much sexual love as the process of [artistic] creativity, that is, the *sacred play with words.*"[15] For Annenskii believed that the erotic thematism of verbal art went beyond any specific thematic pattern—a love poem is about a poet in love—but, more important, constituted a discourse on, and an imitation of, the very essence of poetry.[16]

Mandelstam echoed Annenskii's suggestion in one of his earliest poems, "The heart is clothed as though in a cloud" (1909–10?).[17] And although the poem was never published, for it apparently did not satisfy the standard that the poet set for himself, its message, delivered with all the artlessness of a novice, discloses with uncharacteristic directness some of Mandelstam's early but lasting thoughts on the subject of a poet's calling and the nature of verbal art. Equally significant, it demonstrates, as perhaps no other poem composed before 1915, that the Acmeist[18] pathos of his first two collections—their classical decorum and architectural precision—served as a facade or, better, as a dialectical opposite concealing great emotional intensity and the ardent mind of a "Southerner." This dialectic did not escape some of the astute readers of Mandelstam's first two *Stones*. Early in 1914, Nikolai Gumilev took note of it when he welcomed Mandelstam's first *Kamen'* (1913),[19] as did Vladislav Khodasevich two years later in a review of recent poetry. Khodasevich wrote:

> O. Mandelstam apparently favors a cold and measured minting of lines. The movement of his verse is slow and calm. However, from time to time in his poetry, there bursts through the emphatic reserve a pathos which one would like to trust as genuine just because the poet has tried (or knew how to pretend that he has tried) to conceal it.[20]

In Khodasevich's sense, the poem I will discuss here conceals nothing. On the contrary, it is precisely the unabashed display of central Symbolist notions concerning poetry, some echoing Lermontov's "Molitva," some literally transposed from Briusov's "Poetu,"[21] that recommends it to our consideration. The following is a literal translation.

> Как облаком сердце одето
> И камнем прикинулась плоть,
> Пока назначенье поэта
> Ему не откроет Господь.
>
> Какая-то страсть налетела,
> Какая-то тяжесть жива;
> И призраки требуют тела,
> И плоти причастны слова.
>
> Как женщины, жаждут предметы,
> Как ласки, заветных имен,
> Но тайные ловит приметы
> Поэт, в темноту погружен.
>
> Он ждет сокровенного знака,
> На песнь, как на подвиг, готов:
> И дышит таинственность брака
> В простом сочетании слов.
>
>   [1909–10?]

> The heart is clothed, as though in a cloud,
> And the flesh pretends to be stone
> Until the vocation of a poet
> Is revealed to him by the Lord.
>
> Some kind of passion has seized [him],
> Some kind of heaviness is alive;

> And specters demand a body,
> And words are in communion with flesh.
>
> Like women yearning for a caress, objects
> Yearn for cherished names,
> But grasping the long-cherished omens,
> The poet is in darkness submerged.
>
> He is awaiting the secret sign,
> Ready for the song as for an ordeal:
> And the conjugal mystery is breathing
> In a plain conjugation of words.[22]

Lest it escape the reader, the last two lines of the poem constitute a pun on the rather elevated Russian term for marriage, *brakosochetanie*. Hence Mandelstam's *tainstvo* BRAKA and SOCHETANIE *slov* (literally, "the mystery of marriage" and "conjugation of words"), which I tried to render into English on the basis of a similar etymological wordplay (conjugal conjugations).

Whatever the merits of "The Heart" (as I shall refer to the poem), and it rather fails the test of present-day, if not contemporary, tastes, one cannot help being astonished at how programmatic this tongue-tied declaration turned out to be for Mandelstam's subsequent development. An apparent example of poetic anticipation, it need not be taken as a proof of the poet's clairvoyance or extraordinary grip on fate. Rather, "The Heart" testifies to the essential fidelity of the more mature Mandelstam to a set of ideas that he had selected from the available "ideology" of poetry and made his own at the very outset of his career. This is what makes it methodologically permissible to use the language of this poem as a descriptive and analytical tool to discuss the evolution and the repertoire of Mandelstam's "mythologies" of self-presentation. The petrified flesh of the poem's speaker ("And the flesh is masquerading as stone") is an obvious starting point for a discussion of Mandelstam's poetry, in which the word "stone" was to play such a prominent role.

Mandelstam's choice of *Stone* for the title of his three major collections (1913, 1916, 1923) contrasts sharply with the negative, and quite common, connotation that this word carried in "The Heart." After all, for the flesh to pretend to be stone constitutes an affliction, one that Mandelstam obviously considered bad enough to merit divine intervention. Three years after the composition of the poem, after he had become the author of *Stone,* the terms were to be, quite literally, reversed. A switch as emphatic as this one could not help having a programmatic significance. For the earlier Mandelstam, the word "flesh" with its capacity for erotic connotation was obviously preferable to "stone," coming closer to the ultimate value and essence of poetry; for the Mandelstam of the Acmeist period, the opposite was obviously the case. To recall Dante, Mandelstam's poetry during the period of the Acmeist tour de force might be seen as a latter-day "Rime petrose," in which the old Symbolist workhorse "music" was retired in favor of the *Acmeist*[23] "architecture" as poetry's controlling metaphor.[24]

Yet one need not be carried away with this dualism, whatever its merit as a category of classification. Even if we accept Gumilev's by now traditional periodization, according to which in the year of nineteen hundred and twelve the Symbolist Mandelstam died to be reborn as an Acmeist,[25] his pointed inclusion of his "Symbolist" verse into the three *Stones* should indicate that the matter was not that simple. Even the 1912 sonnet "Casino," exemplary of the new movement according to Gumilev, began with a barely concealed jibe against a somewhat embarrassing Acmeist insistence on joie de vivre: "I am not an admirer of preconceived joy."[26] Granted, the Symbolists, too, were mocked ("The soul is hanging over the damned abyss"), but their long and illustrious history of bitter romantic irony (Blok's *Puppet Theater*) could assimilate such irreverence as a matter of course. While hesitant and uncertain about the direction his poetry was to take in 1912, Mandelstam was a solid presence on the literary scene in 1916 and much more so in 1923 when his collections, in fact, included a larger pool of his "soft" pre-Acmeist poems. What other reasons might he have had in mind for representing both the "soft" and the "hard" poems in all of his three *Stones*?

I suggest that, at least in part, Mandelstam's persistent desire to start *ab ovo*[27] may be traced to the epic framing of the lyric made so effective by the "trilogy" of Aleksandr Blok. This new generic convention placed a great value on the notion of "origins"[28]—as an instance prefiguring the poet's eventual fate—and demanded that earlier poetry be included in later collections where it would play the role of an epic reference point, at the same time providing a vocabulary and a grammar for the entire lyric narrative.[29] Mandelstam was fully conscious of this principle as well as of its association with Aleksandr Blok. In 1922, marking the first anniversary of the poet's death, he declared with authority (italics are mine):

> To establish a poet's literary genealogy, his literary sources, his *kinship group* and origins means to find right away a firm ground under our feet. It is not necessary for a critic to reply to the question

"what did the poet want to say?" but it is his duty to answer the question "where did he come from?"[30]

For Mandelstam circa 1913—who only at the last moment decided to switch the title of his first collection from the receptive "seashell" to the active and aggressive "stone"[31]—it must have been important for the poet to create a sharply ambivalent connotation for one of the central symbols of his poetry. With that accomplished, "stone" could become a major item in his lexicon, an emblem of the poet's identity, and establish a relation of antithetical tension, explicit or implied, among the images—one of the most important rules in Mandelstam's poetic grammar. Thus, when it appeared in his later poetry, "stone" was capable of generating a specifically Mandelstamian ambivalence[32] on its own, conveying the connotations of the ordinary usage as well as those of its opposite, "flesh"—something that had hitherto required the presence of both words in close proximity to each other. The reader of *Stone* (1913) would be led by the title to expect something less than ephemeral, but encountering "Breathing," he was confronted with a double oxymoron even before he had the time to turn to the second page of the collection. Nor was this oxymoronic tension relieved in the concluding poem of the book ("Notre Dame," 1912), where the "firmament Notre Dame" was presented as an extended simile of Adam's body both "visually" and by means of the obvious paronomastic wordplay (Dame—A-dam). In short, "stone," whatever its other connotations, became a compact, one-word invocation of the poet's "grammar"—a set of rules, characterized by the meeting of extremes, according to which Mandelstam's poetry was to make sense.[33] I can think of no better formulation of this principle than the lines from the 1923 "Ode on Slate":

> Кто я? Не каменщик прямой,
> Не кровельщик, не корабельщик:
> Двурушник я, с двойной душой.
> Я ночи друг, я дня застрельщик.

> Who am I? Not an upright stone mason,
> Not one who raises roof beams, not a mariner:
> A double dealer am I, with a double soul.
> I am night's friend, I am day's vanguard soldier.[34]

In order to read this equivocally unequivocal declaration with profit, the reader should keep in mind that it was issued by the author of three *Stone*s, a poet who had "raised the roof beams" in his version of Sappho's epithalamia,[35] and one who had navigated a series of poetic ships, including the ship of the new state in "The Twilight of Freedom" (1918) and one that creaked and swayed in the "Pindaric Fragment" ("He Who Found a Horseshoe," 1923), composed shortly before the "Slate Ode."

But to return now to the discussion of "The Heart," this pattern of tension, although still in embryonic form, is already discernible in the first two lines of the second stanza. After the poet has received from God the sign of his vocation, the "body" ("flesh") begins to exchange its attributes with "heaviness" ("stone"), its antithetical counterpart.[36] The world has become sexually polarized, charged with erotic tension, and, to follow Annenskii, with the tension of verbal creativity as well: "objects" are "yearning for" special names in the same way as "women yearn for caresses," ready to receive the imprint of the poet's personal myth-making vocabulary.[37]

To follow Mandelstam's reasoning here, limiting oneself to satisfying their desire (indulging in erotic or love poetry) would be both too easy and too incautious—it would mean forfeiting a much dearer reward awaiting the poet who has been able to pass through and beyond this ordeal by temptation. The "long-cherished omens" that he is trying to grasp in the "dark" of solitude (unmoved as he is by the things "yearning" without) are signs of the reward accorded to those who are "ready for a song as for an ordeal." For these poets, their vocation is inseparable from a calling to prophecy or martyrdom. At the very least, it signifies an acceptance of an ascetic vow in the service of some supreme mystery, say, Beauty or Truth.[38] When the "secret sign" the poet has been awaiting finally arrives, he will experience an epiphany and fuse with the ultimate, or whoever represents that category in the latest Symbolist charts ("the mystery of marriage breathing in a plain conjunction of words"). Perhaps it was Viacheslav Ivanov's interpretation of Pushkin's "The Poet and the Crowd" that Mandelstam had in mind as he was composing "The Heart." Adding to Pushkin's Romantic dialogue a pinch of religious syncretism, a dash of mysticism, a sprinkling of Hegelian dialectics, and a good dose of the venerable Russian populism, Ivanov was able to transform Pushkin's eternal rift between the autonomous poet and the slavish "crowd" thirsting for instruction into a stage preceding the eventual fusion of the two parties in a transcendent absolute. One relevant passage, taken from a collection of essays, *Across the Stars* (1909), runs as follows:

> Tragic is a genius who has not understood himself [his destiny?], who has nothing to offer the Crowd, because for the sake of new revelations (and he is to say only the new), his spirit draws him, first,

to a solitary communion with his god. In the calm of the wilderness, in the secret change of visions and sounds, for the Crowd redundant and incomprehensible, he must await "the wafting of the subtle cool" [breeze] and the "epiphany" of the god.... The poet departs—for the sake of the "sweet sounds and prayers." The Schism [between the poet and the people] has taken place.... Hence an artist's withdrawal as the fundamental phenomenon of the modern history of spirit....

His focusing on himself constituted a passive self-affirmation of the active element in response to the active self-affirmation, on the part of the Crowd, of the rigid and passive element. This pride of the poet shall be redeemed by [his] suffering of solitude; but his loyalty to the spirit will manifest itself in the fortifying ordeal [*podvig*] of his secret, "thoughtful" action.[39]

A scenario of this sort was itself a product of a marriage of two prominent offspring of romantic idealism—aesthetic mysticism and nationalism, or populism—a marriage that a Russian intellectual of the period did not need to be asked to celebrate.

To continue with the poem, one may have prudishly expected that when the final stage preceding the supreme prize is reached—"the borderline of conception," as Blok called it[40]—it would be quite unlike the siren call of "things" that Mandelstam so admirably left behind. Alas, this ultimate stage, too, is presented with the aid of erotic vocabulary.[41] What has changed, however, is that the analogous images of the coda evince an aura of the sacred,[42] encapsulating in an aphoristic closure, first, Annenskii's remark discussed above (Mandelstam's "breathing"); second, Ivanov's poetics of Dionysian afflatus and self-sacrifice ("the song as an ordeal");[43] and third, Blok's thematics of a redemptive mystical marriage of the poet and his mystical bride[44] (the latter two in opposition to Briusov's "aestheticism").

> Он ждет сокровенного знака,
> На песнь, как на подвиг, готов:
> И дышит таинственность брака
> В простом сочетании слов.
>
> He is awaiting the secret sign,
> Ready for the song as for an ordeal:
> And the conjugal mystery is breathing
> In a plain conjunction of words.

The word "plain" in this concluding stanza—here an unexpected attribute of the mystical revelation of poetry—also carries an additional meaning, one similar to what Blok had in mind when he spoke with reverence about the magical power of popular imagination in his "Poetry of Spells and Incantations" and "The Elemental Force and Culture."[45] In fact, juxtaposing one of the incantations cited by Blok with Mandelstam's description of a poet's state before the "call" (the "heart clothed in a cloud" and the "flesh pretending to be stone") allows one to read the poem as a clash of two opposing forces—the "black magic" of uninspired everyday life and the "white," extraordinary "magic" of a poet's calling:

> "I shall clothe myself in a cloud, stud myself with many stars," says the exorcist; and behold, he is already a magus, sailing inside a cloud, girded with the Milky Way.[46]

Expressed with a naive openness in "The Heart," these categories of the contemporary ontological grammar of poetry—the identification of verbal art with eros, ecstatic states, ascesis, magic, and the sacred—may not catch the eye of today's reader, but both a closer reading and their apparent reemergence in his later poetry strongly suggest that they continued to maintain their hold on the poet's thinking even in the period of the Acmeist Sturm und Drang.[47] In retrospect, judging by the development of Mandelstam's thematics, it appears that attempts to suppress their presence in *Stone* I and II were dictated not so much by the "anxiety of influence"—they were, after all, identified with Mandelstam's Symbolist mentors—as by the lack of an appropriately defined "identity," a persona that the ideological climate of the time made necessary even in a lyric unfolding of this ontological formula. To put it less abstractly, during the years when one could buy a postcard with Blok's portrait (beginning in 1909, at least),[48] the contemporary scenario for success called for the presence of a distinct protagonist in one's lyric poetry. In 1909–1910, when "The Heart" was most likely composed, that protagonist still remained to be shaped. But as Mandelstam's output in the prewar years testifies, he kept busy at the task, accomplishing it in an original manner and in a very short time.

One indication that Mandelstam was casting about for ways to adapt to the contemporary conventions for poetry may be found in his essay on François Villon (1910), where the French poet, apparently an ideal type for Mandelstam, is presented as an androgyne, his feminine hypostasis identical in gender with the "real woman," France:

> France, captured by foreigners, has shown herself to be a real woman. Like a woman in captivity, she paid attention mostly to the toiletry trifles of her daily life and culture, while keeping a curious eye on the victors. . . .

> The feminine passivity of the epoch left an indelible imprint on Villon's fate and his character. . . .
> A lyric poet is, by his very nature, a bisexual creature capable of countless divisions for the sake of the inner dialogue. . . . There is no one [besides Villon] in whom this "lyric hermaphroditism" has manifested itself with such sharpness. What an assortment of charming duos: a distressed man and a comforter, a mother and a child, a judge and an accused, a proprietor and a pauper.[49]

Whether it is immediately obvious or not, this description of Villon is compatible with, and serves as a counterpart to, the "mystical marriage" with which Mandelstam concluded his poem. Although the "relationship" between Villon and the France of his time does not fit snugly enough into the Blokian mystical pattern, the choice of erotic metaphor together with emphasis on the identity between the poet on the one hand and his country and the age on the other indicates a certain kinship with Blok's myth or Ivanov's "Eros of the whole and the universal."[50] From here it was only a short step to some version of the charismatic invocation "O my Russia, o my wife," an appeal from Blok's famous 1908 cycle.[51] Mandelstam, in his own way, would take this step later, but not before he had the time to "fashion" his self,[52] that is, become ready for the "ordeal" of a Russian poet's charismatic mission.

A MOST INELIGIBLE BACHELOR

> *A Yid is being married to a frog.*   ALEKSANDR PUSHKIN (1833)
>
> *Why do we need a second-class Rubanovich when we have a first-class Rubanovich (Osip Mandelstam)?*
>   ALEKSANDR BLOK, Letter to Andrei Belyi (1911)

Mandelstam's meditative poetry, interspersed throughout the first two collections (*Stone* I and II), speaks of the poet's sense of loneliness and rejection that are relieved only when he turns to larger cultural systems: Byzantium, Rome, the Catholic Middle Ages, Gothic and other epochal architectural monuments, the tradition of European literature, and, of course, ancient Greece. I shall refrain from speculating why this should have been so, turning instead to what the poems looked like then as well as to Mandelstam's intrinsic rationalizations of his preference for this Acmeist "anchorite" diet. In the eyes of contemporaries, these themes, although related to the "other" Mandelstam, as Khodasevich had suggested,[53] became the hallmark of the Acmeist poet. A typical example of such a reading may be found in a 1917 survey of modern poetry written by an important and far-sighted critic, D. Vygotskii, who could appreciate Mandelstam's poetry despite his Futurist sympathies:

> From the aesthetic point of view, a book of poetry, *Kamen'*, by O. Mandelstam, the most talented poet among the "Hyperboreans," [Acmeists] is the most significant. Even more static and cold than Gumilev, marching solemnly in a luxuriant mantle of words, he nevertheless is capable of making his solemnity more attractive. Never abandoning his pathos, never even trying to speak in everyday simple words, he remains wholesome in his stiffness. A skillful painter, he at the same time invests some of his poems with a philosophical element, and his attempts to create the philosophy of music, the philosophy of architecture, and even the philosophy of sport cannot be considered uninteresting. And still, how cold and dispassionate all of this is, how far it is from life, how ineradicable in all of this is the smell of an ancient book with pages grown yellow from use. How characteristic it is for Mandelstam (and the entire school that he represents) that he knows nothing, not only about nature, but about love. Even for love he is too good, I would say, too lazy.[54]

One may assume that many shared Vygotskii's reservations, since Viktor Zhirmunskii, a critic close to the Acmeists, especially Akhmatova and the author of *Kamen'*, used virtually the same terms and insisted on the lack of the personal element in the lyric poetry Mandelstam composed between 1912 and 1915. Drawing a sharp line between the earlier Symbolist poet and his later Acmeist reincarnation, Zhirmunskii wrote in 1916:

> In Mandelstam's mature verse, we no longer find his soul, his personal human moods; in general, the element of an emotional, lyric content, in its immediate poetic expression [*pesennoe vyrazhenie*], moves into the background, as in the work of the other "Acmeists." But Mandelstam is unaware not only of the lyric of love or the lyric of nature (common themes of emotional, personal poetry), but, generally, he never speaks about himself, his soul, about his immediate perception of life, either external or inner.[55]

Criticism of this sort should not be taken at face value, for the poet that Vygotskii and Zhirmunskii had in mind was the same man who wrote in 1912, "I tremble from the cold—I want to die," "There—I could not love, / Here—I fear to love," and, in 1913, "Joseph sold into Egypt could not have grieved more."[56]

Taking a close look at the passage from Zhirmunskii, one begins to discern what might have obscured the critic's view and, more important, what had prevented Mandelstam from indulging the taste of some of his most respected readers. Zhirmunskii's insistence on the "immediacy" of expression, the "immediacy" of perception, on the "human" and "personal" thematics as the sui generis attributes of the lyric, which in his opinion were lacking in Mandelstam, indicates that he took one set of conventions—no doubt characteristic of the still dominant Symbolism and very much alive in a Futurist like Maiakovskii—as a given of lyric poetry, as something that was not conventional at all. Even more surprising, since it came from a scholar, Zhirmunskii's statement implied the possibility, indeed the existence, of lyric poetry that eschewed mediation in favor of immediacy—a contradiction in terms when one deals with representation of re-presentation, that is, with verbal art. In fact, these aspects of the lyric that Zhirmunskii took for granted constituted a specific "confessional" mode, a matter of tradition and choice, which put a high premium on a poet's "sincerity" of expression[57]—a mode that Blok practiced with consummate skill.[58]

In a different ideological climate, say, in Pushkin's time, with a better awareness of the conventional nature of art and, more important, without the emphatically charismatic view of poetry, one could fake sincerity and do this as often as the need arose, assuming it with as much difficulty or ease as any other mask.[59] Not so in Mandelstam's time, when poets cultivated both in their work and in the minds of their readers the notion of poetry as a source of ultimate truth, which, needless to say, made the requirement for sincerity central to contemporary poetic practice.[60] "I know that deception is unthinkable in [a poet's] vision."[61] These words, affirming a common Symbolist belief in the truthfulness of a poet's inner experience, were spoken by Mandelstam in 1911, the year of his poetic debut in *Apollon,* and they may indicate that he took this ideological desideratum to heart. Or, since he never published the poem in question, that he knew better. In either case (and the two interpretations are not incompatible), the convention could not be ignored.

But it was not simple for Mandelstam to disclose in his poetry important elements of his "vision" with the "immediacy" demanded by the poetic convention he had apparently internalized. He was, after all, a Jew, and although he could find a sympathetic ear for a disclosure of his predicament, his milieu, on the whole, was either hostile or indifferent to "confessions" of this sort, incapable, in any case, of recognizing in them any charismatic value. Consequently, the thematics of the "mystical marriage" that he attempted to develop early on and that an ethnic Russian could exploit naturally would have looked rather ridiculous coming from the pen of one Osip Mandelstam, a young poet whom some of the Petersburg literati used to call "Zinaida's [Gippius] little Yid" (*Zinaidin zhidenok*).[62] The remark made by Aleksandr Blok, the chief authority on mystical marriages with Russia, had a similar, if more charitable, ring to it.[63] In short, the "mystical marriage," while desired, appeared unthinkable, and the rich thematics that might have been developed on the basis of this frustration could not be "confessed."

BETWEEN LAW AND GRACE

Let us try to develop Philosophical Letters *like a photographic negative. Perhaps those areas that become bright will turn out to be about Russia, after all.* OSIP MANDELSTAM, "Petr Chaadaev" (1914)

Two strategies, traceable in Mandelstam's early poetry, seem to be defined by this antithesis between the contemporary assumptions concerning poetry and poets and the personal problems that Mandelstam had to face as a Russian Jew growing up and living in St. Petersburg in the final decades of the old regime. One strategy belonged to the "Symbolist" period and found expression in an involved development of the confessional theme, so involved, in fact, that it took modern readers a while to figure out what this "confession" was about.[64] The other strategy, which has established Mandelstam's public persona as a decorous, philosophical, and formidably cultivated poet, bore the imprint of Acmeist thematics and style and took the form of large-scale cultural and historiosophic edifices in which the poet, in part an outcast, could find well-defined and honorable points of self-reference. In this section I shall concentrate on the first of these strategies.

Composed in 1910, neither of the two "encoded" poems below happened to be included in *Stone* I, II, or III, although they appeared as part of a selection of Mandelstam's poems in *Apollon* in 1911. I shall cite them here in my own, emphatically literal translation.

Из омута злого и вязкого
Я вырос, тростинкой шурша,
И страстно, и томно, и ласково
Запретною жизнью дыша.

И никну, никем не замеченный,
В холодный и топкий приют,
Приветственным шелестом встреченный
Коротких осенних минут.

Я счастлив жестокой обидою
И в жизни, похожей на сон,

Between Law and Grace

Я каждому тайно завидую
И в каждого тайно влюблен.

Ни сладости в пытке не ведаю,
Ни смысла я в ней не ищу;
Но близкой, последней победою,
Быть может, за всё отомщу.

1910

Out of an evil and miry pool,
I have grown—a rustling little reed—
And, with passion and longing and tenderness,
Breathing the forbidden life.

And I droop, noticed by no one,
Into the cold and boggy asylum,
Hailed by the greeting lisp
Of short autumnal moments.

I am happy with the cruel offense,
And in the life resembling a dream,
I envy everyone secretly,
And with everyone I am secretly in love.

I neither know sweetness in torment,
Nor do I search for meaning in it;
But, perhaps, with the imminent ultimate victory
I shall avenge it all.

В огромном омуте прозрачно и темно,
И томное окно белеет;
А сердце — отчего так медленно оно
И так упорно тяжелеет?

То всею тяжестью оно идет ко дну,
Соскучившись по милом иле,
То, как соломинка, минуя глубину,
Наверх всплывает без усилий.

С притворной нежностью у изголовья стой
И сам себя всю жизнь баюкай,
Как небылицею, своей томись тоской
И ласков будь с надменной скукой.

1910

The enormous pool is limpid and dark,
And a longing window is gleaming.
But the heart—why is it so slowly
And so stubbornly growing heavy?

> Now, with all its heaviness, it sinks to the bottom,
> Homesick for the dear silt,
> Now, like a little straw, bypassing the deep,
> It floats up on the top without effort.
>
> Stand, feigning tenderness, at the head of your bed,
> Lull yourself the entire life,
> Languish in your sorrow as if it were a made-up tale,
> And be gentle with the haughty boredom.[65]

In retrospect, one can hardly question the legitimacy of interpreting these poems as meditations of an "assimilated" (and therefore not entirely assimilated) Jew on the conflict of his cultural loyalties. The first indicates an awareness of one's otherness and a sharply felt desire to participate in the "forbidden life," even at the price of pain and humiliation. The second, in which the "pool" figures as a metaphor of a mirror,[66] outlines a strategy for distancing the poetic self from the "actual" ego by transforming it into aesthetic material ("a made-up tale").

What gives such an interpretation added credibility is yet another poem, which, although composed at the same time as the other two, was not published until 1915, and then only in a newspaper.[67] All three poems share a set of images—the pool, the slender stem (the reed and the straw), the deep, the sinking, the heaviness—but it is the particular subject matter of the last poem that serves as a clue to the thematics developed in this cycle. The poem, also a meditation, focuses on Christ's last moments on the cross:

> Неумолимые слова...
> Окаменела Иудея,
> И, с каждым мигом тяжелея,
> Его поникла голова.
>
> Стояли воины кругом
> На страже стынущего тела,
> Как венчик, голова висела
> На стебле тонком и чужом.
>
> И царствовал, и никнул он,
> Как лилия в родимый омут,
> И глубина, где стебли тонут,
> Торжествовала свой закон.
>   1910

> The implacable words...
> Judea became petrified,
> And, heavier with every moment,
> His head drooped.

> Warriors stood guard
> Around the cooling body.
> His head, like a corolla, hung
> On a slender and alien stem.
>
> And He reigned, and He drooped,
> Like a lily into its native pool,
> And the deep where stems sink
> Was celebrating its law.⁶⁸

One way of grasping the meaning of this "triptych" is to relate it to two poems by Fedor Tiutchev on which Mandelstam drew both for the vocabulary (the "reed") and for the conceptual framework, that is, the insoluble contradiction of belonging to two conflicting worlds. One of these allusions, as Kiril Taranovsky has pointed out, goes back to Tiutchev's reversal of Pascal's definition of man as a "thinking reed."⁶⁹ For Pascal, the ability of the human "reed" to think was the highest asset; for Tiutchev, it represented the fatal liability, the cause of human alienation from the harmony of nature: "Why does the soul sing not what the sea sings and why does the thinking reed grumble?" It is this latter "reed" that serves as a metaphor for the protagonist of Mandelstam's poem. Tiutchev's second poem, too, contains a paraphrase from Pascal, this time a definition of man as a "citizen of two worlds" (Tiutchev's "The soul is an inhabitant of two worlds"). One is the daylight of reason; the other is the deep night of irrational desire that threatens to tear the soul apart unless it, "like Mary [Magdalene], presses forever against the feet of Christ."⁷⁰ In both cases, the Tiutchevian subtext reinforces Mandelstam's theme of the rift between the "native pool" and the "forbidden life," and, as in Mandelstam's cycle, attempts to bring about a resolution of the eternal conflict by reiterating the ultimate resolution that took place at Calvary. This similarity between the two poets brings into sharper focus the central difference in their use of the name of Christ. Whereas for Tiutchev, Christ alone can give peace to the unsettled soul, for Mandelstam, he is subject to the same, if more intense, divisions that afflict the poet's own self.

Another approach to the triptych is to examine how each of its members realizes the plot that they all share—a protagonist caught between two conflicting value systems in a way similar to the protagonist caught between two equidistant bales of hay in Buridan's paradox. The first poem, "Out of an evil and miry pool," is so rife with tension between the "pool" and the "forbidden life" that it hardly makes logical sense. How, for example, can one be at the same time "happy with the cruel offense" and "neither know sweetness in torment nor . . . search for meaning in it" while planning imminently to "avenge it all" with the "ultimate victory"? Removing the last stanza, as Mandelstam (or his editors) did in the 1928 edition, helps matters considerably, though at the expense of the original intensity of this cultural double bind.

The second poem, "The enormous pool is limpid and dark," may at first appear to be a picture of tranquility and reconciliation, but the bitterness of the last quatrain makes this initial impression misleading. Mandelstam's "confession" here seems to run as follows: the choice of lyric poetry as one's vocation involves a particular concentration on one's self, which is what occupies the poet as he is examining the split in his "heart" before the "enormous pool" of the mirror. So far so good, but the poem concludes on a sinister note. The poet qua poet does not like the reflection he sees ("feigning tenderness"); he commands himself to deny or conceal his anguish ("as if it were a made-up tale") and to be "gentle with the haughty boredom," a personification, I believe, of an affected Petersburg snob.

The third poem presents the most telling account of frustration stemming from a divided loyalty. Here is a poet's essay in measuring his self against the figure of Christ. As with any consistent comparison, this one focuses on a set of shared features that establishes a relationship of similitude and contrast between the two terms. Taken in random order, these features are the experience of ordeal; affinities to two contradictory orders, one of origins and the Law (Judaism), the other of the new faith and Grace (Christianity);[71] the simile of the "stem" (the "reed," the "straw"); and, finally, the "pool" which, because it is "native," has the irresistible power to draw back into itself what has once issued from it.

The last poem provides a decisive clue for the elucidation of the cycle precisely in the unexpected metaphoric shift from the "petrified Judea" to the deep "pool" of the Law. As far as the poet is concerned, this pool is associated not only with the painful ordeal of seeing one's face in the mirror of the "host culture" but also, and here the similarity ends, with the comfort of return to the native realm. In Russian, the "silt" for which the poet feels nostalgic (the second poem) is emphatically "dear" thanks to the paranomastic play on the two words: *mily il*. The Judaic, therefore, can manifest itself both as something "petrified," hard, emotionally unresponsive, "implacable" (its association with God the Father and the Law) and as something receptive and "dear," a home that can be "missed." This duality lends an air of legitimacy to the otherwise surprising choice of attribute, "native and dear" (*rodimyi*), qualifying the "pool" in the poem about Christ. After all, Mandelstam wrote these lines with the full awareness of the "satanic" connotation that the word "pool," *omut,* has in Russian usage: "In a quiet pool—that's where devils live."[72]

Another near contrast between the two subjects rests on a shared vegetative metaphor: whereas Christ is likened to a complete and specific flower, the poet appears as a generic "reed" and "straw"—lifeless, infertile stems devoid of corolla—which sink into the deep as quickly as they float up to the surface. The name "lily," given to Christ, signifies a completeness on yet another level—the plenitude of the divine androgyne[73]—similar to the one attributed to Christ in Blok's *The Twelve.*[74] As Vladimir Solov'ev once asserted, "One way or another, all true poets knew and sensed this 'feminine shadow' [of God]."[75] To develop the parallelism further, the transcendent plenitude of Christ, which allowed him to "reign" *and* to return to his origin in Judaism, has its mortal analogue in the poet's anguish, his doubts whether he would be able to reconcile his desire to breathe the air of the "forbidden life" with the clinging "silt" of his inherited identity. Recalling Annenskii's remark and Mandelstam's choice of metaphor for poetry, "the breathing of the mystery of marriage,"[76] this analogy may be safely extended into the realm of eros, not the physical variety, but the displaced, mystical, Platonic and Manichean eros that Russian Symbolists had preached, beginning with Vladimir Solov'ev.[77] The frequency with which the common lexical attributes of the erotic appear in the cycle offers an additional justification for a reading of this sort. Consider: "with passion and longing and tenderness," "in love," and "sweetness," or even "voluptuousness" [*sladost'*] in the first poem; the "heart," "heaviness," "tenderness," in the second; and "heavier," the "lily," and "native," or "dear,"[78] in the third. A curious mythic narrative begins to emerge from the "pool" of these early poems—a specific mythology of the poet's self, his poetry, and his milieu.

Existing in a state of tension, these three elements are integrated into a pattern where attraction and repulsion define their place in the world. In the first poem, the "pool" that gave birth to the poet is "evil and miry," a "cold and boggy asylum," while the "forbidden life" outside elicits feelings of "passion and longing and tenderness." The "cruel offense" that the poet hopes to "avenge" is ambiguously defined—as either an offense to a victim of anti-Semitism, or of a man despairing of having been born to Jewish parents—and the ambiguity suggests the not uncommon coexistence of these sentiments, something that one encounters often enough. Yet the coexistence, too, is antagonistic and conflict-ridden. A similar relationship of attraction and repulsion determines the poem's coda, where the disclaimer of the first two lines is negated in the conclusion.

Mysteries of Breathing: 1909–1912

As if such a piling up of negatives were not enough, the second poem offers an opposite view of the predicament. Here, Mandelstam is wearied by the necessity of "feigning tenderness" when what he feels is self-hate or of being "gentle" when confronted with the "haughty boredom." Furthermore, what prompted a bitter outburst in the preceding poem is given a tender treatment in this one: the "silt" is "dear," and there is nothing to prevent the poet from either going down to the bottom or floating up to the surface of the "pool." It would appear that Mandelstam was at least of two minds on the subject of his identity, and with the last poem this ambivalence acquired an even greater intensity as the theme took the form of a meditation on the "historical" origins of his confused state.

As often happens with meditations of this sort, which create a god in one's own image, Mandelstam imputed to the Event and to Christ the features of his own predicament. But where the reflection of the self came out different from the image of God, Mandelstam was able, albeit indirectly, to formulate his fundamental notions of the mythic narrative centered around himself as a poet. It should not appear surprising, although one need not take it for granted, that Mandelstam chose to present himself in terms of the Christian doctrine according to which the New Testament superseded the old faith based on Mosaic Law. After all, he might as well have chosen the teachings of Marx or Nietzsche. These two popular and powerful ideological constructs of the time could have provided him with an equally intricate grammar and a capacious vocabulary. Yet he did not choose them even though he was adequately familiar with both.[79]

Among the many reasons for choosing as he did, two stand out as important: his sensitivity to his "otherness" and his commitment to the art of poetry. They were by no means unrelated, if only because being a *Russian* poet made Mandelstam feel alien all the more. The Symbolist vocabulary, its set of values and its myths, although not properly Christian in any orthodox sense, were permeated with conceptualizations and imagery for which Christianity served as the ultimate source and reference point. No doubt experienced as a necessary condition, this aspect of contemporary poetic culture could not be ignored unless Mandelstam was willing—and he was not—to remain on the margins of Russian letters. What is more, Russian Christian culture had to be accepted and internalized, and, for obvious reasons in Mandelstam's case, reformulated so that it might suit the poet's particular and still unusual situation. This reformulation took the form of a more archaic integrative myth that was capable of organizing into a distinct and highly evocative narrative pattern the disparate elements of the poet's view of the world and of the self.

What I have in mind is the myth of incest. This myth offers an economical model for the analysis of Mandelstam's poetry, as it helps to keep track of the twists and turns in his own life story without obscuring the persistent patterns holding together the complete narrative of this "poète et martyr de son temps."[80] Since his career as a poet has been perceived as a charismatic performance (a characteristic to which much of Mandelstam scholarship testifies),[81] this myth, one of transcendence, may also help to account for the effectiveness with which Mandelstam relied on patterns of verbal magic and, consequently, for the intensity of his charismatic appeal.[82] But most important, the myth of incest apparently provided Mandelstam with an archetypal framework capable of supporting the symbolic vocabulary of his native Russian culture while giving him an opportunity to exploit his problematic relation to it. One is indeed hard put to come up with another universal myth, popular in Mandelstam's milieu, that could have accommodated a conflict of this nature and magnitude.

III

Le Nouvel Hippolyte and Phaedra-Russia: 1915–1916

THE THEATER OF THE LYRIC

And how simple everything was! Art was called tragedy. Just as it should be called. The tragedy was called Vladimir Maiakovskii. *The title concealed a brilliantly simple discovery that a poet was not an author but a subject of lyric poetry who addressed the world in the first person. The title was not the name of the writer, it was the name of the content.*
                    BORIS PASTERNAK, Safe Conduct

    What will you do in the theater of half-words
    And half-masks, heroes and kings?
          OSIP MANDELSTAM, "There is an unshakable scale of values" (1914)

As the French Revolution drew nearer, the pseudo-antique theatricalization of life and politics was gaining ever greater ground, and by the time of the revolution, the practical leaders had already been forced to move and struggle in a dense crowd of personifications and allegories, in the narrow wings of an actual theater, on stage in the scenes of a revived antique drama. When the real Furies of antique ravings descended into this pathetic cardboard play house. . . .
                OSIP MANDELSTAM, "The Nineteenth Century" (1922)

An October (1913) issue of a left-wing newspaper, *Den'*, carried Mandelstam's review of the central dramatic work of Innokentii Annenskii, *Thamyra the Cithara Player*.[1] Even if the assignment of this "Bacchic drama," as the play was subtitled, to Mandelstam was a matter of accident (which was unlikely), it was one of those coincidences that in retrospect seem to have left nothing to chance. For the main protagonist of the drama was an artist, and the action pivoted around the connection Annenskii saw between art and eros, in this case specifically, incest and poetic art. Mandelstam was deeply moved by the play, and his brief review may serve as an introduction to his mythologies of self-presentation circa 1913.[2] The questions I want to ask are what it meant for the *poet* Mandelstam to be a poet, and what, if anything, being a poet had to do with incest, culture's most fundamental taboo.

Annenskii's play (for the younger generation, a welcome relief from Wagnerian ponderousness) centered around a legendary musician, Thamyris, who had the reputation of being a dreamy and withdrawn ascetic among artists, a reputation not very different from the poetic persona in Mandelstam's *Stone*. Indeed, Thamyris's dictum, "I play not for women, I play for stars," might well have become Mandelstam's if we allow for the different vocabularies: the "stars" of the scorned Symbolists[3] would take the place of the "women," and the Acmeist architectural élan the place of Thamyris's "stars." Consider this 1912 programmatic incantation:

> Я ненавижу свет
> Однообразных звезд.
> Здравствуй, мой давний бред —
> Башни стрельчатой рост!
>
> Кружевом, камень, будь,
> И паутиной стань:
> Неба пустую грудь
> Тонкой иглою рань.
>
> I hate the light
> Of uniform stars.
> Welcome my ancient dream—
> A Gothic tower's height!
>
> Stone, turn into lace,
> A cobweb thou shalt be;
> The slender spire pierce
> The empty breast of the sky.[4]

To return to Annenskii, the other protagonist is Thamyris's mother, the nymph Agriopé, who has not seen her son since she gave birth to him twenty years earlier. The action is propelled forward by what might be called a passion to possess—for Thamyris, divine beauty, and for Agriopé, Thamyris—until the grapes of Dionysus turn sour with the tragic irony of a fulfilled wish. All that Thamyris wants is to have the Muse Euterpe perform for him (he even fancies marrying her), and all that Agriopé wants is for her son (a replica of his father) to respond to her intense and rather unsettling affection. Both wishes are eventually granted through the good offices of the jovial drunkard "papa Silenus,"[5] although not in a way that the protagonists could anticipate. To have the Muse perform for him Thamyris enters into a competition with her, only to lose and be punished for his presumption. Having realized that he has become tone-deaf, he blinds himself in despair. His mother, who had once involuntarily offended Zeus, is transformed into a tamed bird, to serve as guide for her listless son. She can have him now. From time to time, as the stage directions indicate, one could see the delicate and enigmatic smile of Zeus fleeting faintly across the cloudless heaven.[6]

What did Mandelstam make of it? "Annenskii," he wrote,

> transformed the theme of a mother in love with her own son into a tormenting feeling of a *lyric infatuation*. . . .
>
> While Thamyris was in communion with music, he was torn between women and stars. But when his cithara refused to serve him and the music of rays grew dark in the eyes burnt out with charcoal, he—so terribly indifferent to his fate—became alien to tragedy, like the bird sitting on his outstretched hand.[7]

Let us take a close look at this passage. As a programmatic anti-Symbolist insistence on wonderment before the irreducible mystery of the universe, the review worked well, echoing the still-fresh Acmeist manifestos,[8] but as an interpretation of Annenskii's "Bacchic drama," it could have fared better. The first item to strike anyone familiar with *Thamyris* is Mandelstam's insistence on conflict, on being "torn between women and stars," as a necessary condition for being an artist. In fact, it is very difficult to conclude this from Annenskii's text. After all, Thamyris had achieved great renown well before the appearance of his ever-youthful nymph mother, who confronted him with the fatal choice. The conflict itself, therefore, was not of Thamyris's making. He merely wished to attain otherworldly perfection, and it was his mother, Agriopé, who fixed the transgression of the incest taboo as the price he would have to pay for his hubris. A man possessed by an idée fixe can hardly be presented as torn by a conflict, and indeed, Thamyris appeared to be indifferent to the ways the gods, including his mother, might put his obsession to use.

At least in one important respect, the review served Mandelstam as a pretext for a declaration of his own, rather than Annenskii's, idea of the poet. If you wish to be a poet, he suggests, you must be torn— whether between "women and stars" (ultimately, your "mother" and the stars) or between a given and a desired identity. As soon as this conflict is resolved, you cease to "hear music," becoming as an artist both deaf and blind. Reverse this picture, and you get Mandelstam's poet. He is one who is blessed (or cursed) with this tormenting state—a fulcrum of "tragedy," a hero who in this particular case is forced to choose between succumbing to his mother's advances or giving up his dream of being a bridegroom to the Muse. Although it should not be taken for granted, Mandelstam's insistence on a close kinship between the mask of a tragic hero and the persona of a lyric poet could hardly be called idiosyncratic. Two months after the publication of Mandelstam's review, Maiakovskii was playing the protagonist in *Vladimir Maiakovskii: A Tragedy,* a work that Pasternak would find emblematic of the modern attitude to verbal art.[9]

Apart from the association of tragedy with the central drama of Christianity, something that many contemporaries took as a matter of course,[10] the "tragic" metaphor qualifying lyric poetry suggests the presence of the cathartic function in the lyric and, significantly for us, presupposes a theatrical pattern of interaction between the poet, who is a "tragic hero," and his "audience," namely, the *listener,* even if he were the reader.[11] The tradition of public recitals, needless to say, provided a natural environment for this metaphor,[12] but it also brought into sharper focus the unsettling questions concerning the nature of the interaction between the poet and his audience. Was the public to be entertained, was it to dictate to the poet what it wished to listen to? And if the poet scorned its advice or command, who was it, then, that served him as the addressee of his poem? These were questions with a long history in Russian letters,[13] and the changing fortunes of modern poetry made it imperative that they be addressed once again.

The epoch of "eternal recurrence"[14] laid bare the archaic roots of art and especially drama, so that for Viacheslav Ivanov or for any younger, fairly educated poet, the origin of tragedy in a communal ritual of sacrifice[15] was almost self-evident.[16] In some cases what was self-evident became transparent, as happened with the modernist actress and director Vera Komissarzhevskaia (1864–1910), who died in the bloom of her career, extending the metaphor of ritual sacrifice into real life.[17] By superimposing the tragic mask on the persona of a lyric poet, Mandelstam was not merely broadening the boundaries of the genre but nudging the lyric, as it had evolved in modern Russia, in the direction of the archetypically central aspect of his culture—a ritual, redeeming sacrifice of the poet.[18] Granted, Mandelstam was speaking only of art, of action taking place in aesthetic imagination, but to the extent that the convention of art demands a suspension of disbelief, what he was saying represented a matter of high seriousness. In the ultimate sense, the audience that came to see the performance of such a poet sought to participate in a reenactment of the drama of salvation.

One who experiences the command of a leader as an inner compulsion or duty, Weber maintained, has recognized the "charisma" of the leader.[19] In the case of a "charismatic" poet, just about the only command involves a request to the audience to remain in their seats and to accept the intimate association between the poet's drama and its other, loftier counterpart. These bonds of "recognition of charisma" between the poet, who "imitates" Christ, and the reader, who does not even wince at it, did, no doubt, exist in Mandelstam's time. "Who does the poet speak to?" he wrote in 1913, and in partial answer to his own question he outlined the "juridical aspect, so to speak, of the interaction accompanying an act of [a poet's] speech": "I speak, therefore people listen to me, listen not just because they have nothing better to do, or out of politeness, *but because it is their duty*" [italics are mine].[20] Alone, these words could not enforce what Weber called "devotion born out of distress and enthusiasm,"[21] but the very fact that they were uttered testifies to a firm belief in the possibility of an ideal charismatic bond uniting the author with his audience.

LE NOUVEL HIPPOLYTE

Anyone familiar with Mandelstam's first two collections would be likely to find even a minor emphasis on the myth of incest a little forced. Especially in the "Acmeist" period (1912–15), Mandelstam's poetry appears devoid of overt mention of incest. Indeed it hardly develops the erotic theme in any conventional manner. This strange fastidiousness cannot be explained away as the pose of an Acmeist poet, for neither Akhmatova, Gumilev, Gorodetskii, or for that matter Zenkevich or Narbut (the five "original" Acmeists) scorned the common thematic material of lyric poetry. The absence of this common lyric currency in the early Mandelstam therefore looks suspicious; it indicates, in the heuristic sense, that a certain mythic taboo played a powerful role in his poetic self-presentation.

A particular configuration of the incest myth, one with a long tradition in European literature, seems to have suited Mandelstam particularly well during his involvement in the younger generation's "Apollonian" revolt against the Symbolist mentors. Following the pattern the Formalist critics would later valorize as a law of literary evolution,[22] the younger poets consistently downplayed their dependence on the more prominent Symbolist figures, particularly the very influential

Viacheslav Ivanov, choosing their allies among those poets who either did not belong to or wished to separate themselves from the theurgist axis (Ivanov, Belyi, Blok). One of these allies, although not to the extent that the Acmeists expected, was Valerii Briusov,[23] who had laid down the theurgist wreath in 1910 to assume the powerful but charismatically thankless position of the literary editor at the eminent liberal journal *Russkaia mysl'*.[24] The other was Innokentii Annenskii, an outsider in the mainstream of Russian Symbolism but an increasingly important figure among the poets associated with the *Apollon*.[25] An essay he wrote as an introduction to his translation of the *Hippolytus* offers a clue to Mandelstam's choice of a specific version of the myth.

Mandelstam's poem (1909–10?), discussed in chapter 2 in connection with Annenskii, contains another allusion to this introduction. I have in mind the first two lines, a description of a poet's state before, as Pushkin put it, "Apollo calls him to a sacred ordeal."[26] I shall cite the entire first stanza:

> Как облаком сердце одето
> И камнем прикинулась плоть,
> Пока назначенье поэта
> Ему не откроет Господь.

> The heart is clothed, as though in a cloud,
> And the flesh pretends to be stone
> Until the vocation of a poet
> Is revealed to him by the Lord.

Compare this with Annenskii's description of Hippolytus, as he enters the stage in the Prologue, following Aphrodite's promise to destroy him (italics are mine):

> After the Cyprian disappears from her balcony, Hippolytus enters the stage in the company of his retinue. But we learn about his imminent approach earlier from the words of the goddess, and this is why the radiant image of Hippolytus excites in the audience a particular feeling. "He does not know," says the goddess, "that the gates of Hades are wide open and that this is his last sun." And behold, *it is as if a cloud clothes* Hippolytus as he steps onto the stage. The goddess's threat would not have produced in us such a subtle aesthetic impression if we saw a man, triumphant, proud, and noisily merry. But we see only a calm, pure, and radiant youth around whom there wafts the aroma of a flowering field and the fresh breath of life.

Annenskii's subsequent characterization of Hippolytus further confirms its relevance for the poet of Mandelstam's "The Heart." Neither was a spontaneous and simple child of nature who follows every stirring of his instinct, but an initiate in the most profound and esoteric mysteries of the word (italics are mine):

> People *sincere by nature* were alien to Euripides—and the first words uttered by Hippolytus make it clear that we have before us not an athlete full of life, not a passionate hunter, and not a boy unconsciously drawn by the voice of Artemis. Behind the appearance of *naive sincerity*, we discern an *adept*, if not a *creator*, of *a new faith*. The meadow where he gathers flowers is not only a preserve of the temple, it is a sacred meadow of the initiated into the mysteries [of the Orphic cult]. . . . Modesty [*stydlivost'*] alone quenches the thirst of its flowers, and only those whose chastity lies in their very nature, who have not yet been touched by passions, who have no need to conceal behind the external decorum the soul darkened by passion, [only those] may gather the sacred flowers on this meadow.[27]

Not for the poet, as Mandelstam wrote in "The Heart," to fall into the temptation to respond to the "yearnings of things:"

> Как женщины, жаждут предметы,
> Как ласки, заветных имен,
> Но тайные ловит приметы
> Поэт, в темноту погружен.
>
> Он ждет сокровенного знака,
> На песнь, как на подвиг, готов:
> И дышит таинственность брака
> В простом сочетании слов.
>
> [1909–10?]

> Like women yearning for a caress, objects
> Yearn for cherished names,
> But grasping at mysterious omens,
> The poet is submerged in darkness.
>
> He is awaiting the secret sign,
> Ready for the song as for an ordeal:
> And the conjugal mystery is breathing
> In a plain conjunction of words.

Against the background of Annenskii's entire essay and Mandelstam's later "Acmeist" poetry, these coincidences begin to reveal a striking similarity between the haughty devotee of Artemis, Hippolytus, and the decorous, self-styled "Roman," the "marble fly" Mandelstam.[28] Needless to say, the poet who wrote "I shall not see the famous *Phèdre*" could not have been unaware of Racine's version of the tragedy. *Phèdre* may have seemed especially appropriate, for example, because

Le Nouvel Hippolyte

Racine identified the Amazon mother of Hippolyte as a "Scythian" (act 2, scene 2), presenting the protagonist as a graft of the wild and primitive hinterland on the civilized Theban stock of Theseus. In a literary milieu in which the early Futurists referred to themselves as "Hylaeans"—an ancient Greek name for the Scythian Crimea—and in which the early Acmeists stressed their identification with the Romance heritage, the paradoxical ancestry of Racine's Hippolyte could easily function as a powerful symbol of an "eternally recurrent" myth.[29] Indeed, "Scythians" and "Romans" were the terms frequently used by the members of the Poets' Guild to designate the "Asiatic," or native and untamed, and the European and "civilized" elements in Russian culture—one characterized by a Dionysian excess, the other by the Apollonian sense of measure and equilibrium.[30] Nevertheless, for the generations of readers and spectators who, like Annenskii, were brought up on A. W. Schlegel's *Comparaison entre le Phèdre de Racine et celle d'Euripide* (1807), a classic proclamation of romantic authenticity, Euripides was the winner hands down, especially if one were to compare the characters of Hippolytus and Hippolyte. Racine's young man, happily in love and soon to be happily married (how conventional, sighed A. W. Schlegel), lacked the obligatory complexity of a modern hero when compared with his Greek counterpart—an intensely partisan and militantly chaste worshipper of Artemis. Finally, and Annenskii stressed this point, Hippolytus was an initiate into the Orphic mysteries, a mystagogue, and therefore someone with whom a Russian poet of the early twentieth century could feel an immediate kinship.[31] The Greek tragedy, especially in Annenskii's subtle and pointedly contemporary interpretation, offered Mandelstam a convenient pattern on which to embroider his own narrative of a poet's fate. Its protagonist, the modernized Hippolytus of Euripides-Annenskii, possessed just about all the attributes Mandelstam might have required for constructing a poet's identity. It remains to be determined now whether these attributes were actually appropriated by the persona of the poet Mandelstam, and if they were, under what circumstances, when, and how.

First, the fatal flaw. For Annenskii, it was a matter of poetic justice that a misogynist like Hippolytus, who wished to disdain the "other half of humanity," as Annenskii put it, should meet his fate exactly where he considered himself to be at his most invulnerable—in his dealings with a woman. Mandelstam's misogyny, implied in "The Heart" and in his filtering out of erotic verse from his first two collections,[32] has a character similar to the ironic trap that tragedians set up for their protagonists. Second, there was the matter of the generational conflict that Annenskii identified in the relations between Theseus and Hippolytus:

> Theseus, with slight modifications, could exist in every century; and for us, the sarcasms that the offended father casts at his peculiar son [*original-syn*] sometimes take the long-familiar form of wholesale accusations against the "young people," now as "Freemasons and Carbonari," now as "nihilists," or as something even more terrifying and contemporary.[33]

For "more terrifying and contemporary," read political terrorism, with which the sixteen-year-old Mandelstam wished to have more than a passing association.

In one sentence, Annenskii presented the three "crisis" generations of Russia in the nineteenth century: men of the Pushkin generation, who grew up during the war of 1812, those whose youth was shaped by the Crimean War and the emancipation of the peasants, and those who were born around 1881 when Alexander II was assassinated and who were now reviving the terror. As a combative member of a particularly restive generation,[34] a terrorist manqué, a poet nurtured on the Symbolist conceptions of a sacred calling, a young man whose father "disapproved,"[35] and, finally, an active member of a new literary movement bent on debunking its immediate predecessors and mentors, Mandelstam could take comfort in Annenskii's commentary. Had he written these words in 1910, and not in 1902, Annenskii would have included the "beautiful and twenty-two-year-old" generation of Maiakovskii, Khlebnikov, Akhmatova, Pasternak, Tsvetaeva, and Mandelstam.[36] Mandelstam was twenty-two in 1913, the year his first collection was published, the last year before the Great War when, according to the Acmeist retrospective lore (Akhmatova's *Poem without a Hero*) the Petersburg poets could sense the "real twentieth century approach along the legendary Neva embankment."[37]

Third, the intentional, almost fastidious chastity of Hippolytus is precisely the quality that the Acmeists accused the Symbolists of lacking. "The Unknowable, as the meaning of the word indicates, cannot be known," wrote Gumilev in 1912, "and all the attempts in this direction are unchaste." Developing the metaphor further, he accused the Symbolists of "cowardly peeking" behind the "curtain of death" in order to see "what would happen next."[38] Mandelstam echoed him a few months later when he compared the Symbolists to an "ungrateful guest who lives at the host's expense, takes advantage of his hospitality and all the while disdains him in his heart of hearts, constantly trying to figure out how to cheat him."[39] (The analogy of the "host," incidentally, was with God.) For Mandelstam, however, all that this lack of "chastity" meant—an offense against good taste and ethical values and a lack of appropriate deference to the Creator—pivoted on a formula resembling a violation of the incest taboo. Before long, this formula began to encroach on other topics, extending beyond the realm of poetry into a phenomenon of a different order, the question of Russian national identity. (I am using the words "incest taboo" largely as a "grammatical" category, namely, a distillation of usage into a set of narrative rules according to which some things can go together and some cannot).

Two important essays that Mandelstam composed in 1914, "Petr Chaadaev" and "On the Interlocutor," may serve as illustrations. "On the Interlocutor" develops a curious theory of a "true" poem as a letter addressed to a "providential" future reader. Mandelstam expressed his contempt both for those poets who are anxious to meet the expectations of the familiar contemporary as well as for those who would imprint the reader with particular expectations in order to have them expeditiously satisfied. In either case, Mandelstam maintained, poetry would be stifled by the familial predictability, and the act of reading, which breathes life into a poem—always new in the unpremeditated encounter of the poet and the reader—would result in a stillborn or monstrous déjà vu, not unlike, one might add, the fruit of an incestuous marriage.

> It is not the acoustics that we have to worry about: they will take care of themselves. Rather, we have to worry about *distance*. It is dull to whisper into the ear of one's neighbor. It is infinitely tedious to bore into one's own soul (Nadson). But to exchange signals with Mars—of course, without indulging in fancy—is a task worthy of a lyric poet.[40]

This emphasis on the "distance"—a feature of his own poetry but hardly by choice alone—could provide the sense of moral and aesthetic superiority, especially within the framework of the incest myth and especially for the poet who was bound to perceive what was foreign as native and what was native as foreign.

In "Petr Chaadaev," Mandelstam followed the same reasoning and praised the country's first philosopher of history for discovering true Russia and becoming the first true Russian—in the Catholic West:

> There is unity—in the West! From the moment that these words ignited in Chaadaev's consciousness, he ceased to belong to himself and forever abandoned the "kinfolk" people and their interests. . . .

Le Nouvel Hippolyte: 1915–1916

> Chaadaev was the first Russian who had truly, ideally, been to the West and found the way back. Contemporaries felt it instinctively and valued terrifically Chaadaev's presence among them. . . .
>
> Having endowed us with inner freedom, Russia has offered us a choice, and those who have made this choice are true Russian people—no matter what their allegiances may be. But woe unto those who, having circled around the native nest, faintheartedly come back.[41]

Finally, in 1915, Mandelstam made his own, first-person declaration proscribing propinquity to "kinfolk":

> Посох мой, моя свобода,
> Сердцевина бытия —
> Скоро ль истиной народа
> Станет истина моя?
>
> Я земле не поклонился
> Прежде, чем себя нашел;
> Посох взял, развеселился
> И в далекий Рим пошел.
>
> Пусть снега на черных пашнях
> Не растают никогда,
> Но печаль моих домашних
> Мне попрежнему чужда.
>
> Снег растает на утесах,
> Солнцем истины палим.
> Прав народ, вручивший посох
> Мне, увидевшему Рим!
>
>   1914

> My staff, my freedom,
> The core of being—
> How long will it be before my truth
> Becomes the people's truth?
>
> I have not bowed to the earth
> Before I found myself;
> I have picked up my staff, rejoiced
> And left for distant Rome.
>
> May the snow on the black furrows
> Never melt,
> Still, the grief of my kinfolk
> Is as alien to me as ever.
>
> The snow shall melt on the mountaintops,
> Burned off by the sun of truth.

Le Nouvel Hippolyte

> Right are the people who have entrusted the staff
> To me, who has seen Rome.[42]

Even if Mandelstam had been successful at making an essayistic virtue out of a temperamental necessity, the central paradox of his plot remained unresolved. That he accepted the terms of contemporary discourse on poetry, namely, the notion of the mystical marriage between the poet and the land, signified an acceptance of the central premise that the notion implied—a confrontation of a poet-bridegroom with bride-Russia. It is one thing to emphasize "distance" when one can take advantage of the culture's preference for intimacy and proximity; it is another when one cannot. The advocacy of cultural distance, then, appears too much like a reversal of desire for an intimacy that had to be held in check for fear of rejection. What better, more resonant pattern could a poet have chosen for a narrative rationalization of this dilemma than the taboo of incest? Whether one predicated poetry on the metaphor of "marriage," as Mandelstam had done in "The Heart," or on the implied metaphor of "incest," as the three 1914 examples above suggest, the desire for the "conjugal mystery" that animates these two antithetical metaphors should become, if anything, more intense. A careful reader of Mandelstam, or any other master of the "seven types of ambiguity" (to borrow Empson's phrase) knows better than to think otherwise.[43] But here, too, Euripides-Annenskii might have lent Mandelstam a helping hand.

Following a tradition that goes back to A. W. Schlegel and Wilamowitz-Moellendorff,[44] Annenskii concluded his essay on *Hippolytus* by giving the tragedy a Christian interpretation. However, unlike Wilamowitz and Schlegel, who had pointed to Hippolytus alone as a hero prefiguring Christian martyrdom, Annenskii extended "sanctity" to Phaedra. She, too, was a noble ascetic soul who fell victim to the vengeance of the "vegetative" goddess Aphrodite. What is more, Annenskii was able to lend the "incest scenario" of Euripides the air of Christian redemption and transcendence. In the fictional sense, Phaedra and Hippolytus played a role similar to that of John the Baptist (Annenskii was no doubt familiar with Wilde's *Salome*), including the moment when the Precursor's head was brought on a charger before the famous virgin. I quote:

> Both Hippolytus and Phaedra perished by their striving to free themselves from the bonds of sex, the yoke of the vegetative form of the soul.
>
> The more I think about this, the more it seems to me that the philosopher of the stage who created, that is, experienced both

Le Nouvel Hippolyte: 1915–1916

Phaedra and Hippolytus was, indeed, one of those few Hellenes who "prepared the way of the Lord." Only he dreamed not about the sentimental Christianity of saints' vitae but about the dream and the philosophical idealism of the Gospels.

In Chapter 22 of the Gospel according to Matthew, we read Christ's conversation with the Sadducees. . . . "For in the resurrection they neither marry, nor are given in marriage, but are as the angels of God in heaven."

Can it be that this lofty conception of heavenly life, as some premonition, rises before us in the tragic hecatomb of *Hippolytus*?[45]

The statement, its assumptions, and its implications seem to have been designed with Mandelstam's dilemma in mind. The mythology of a mystical marriage between the poet and his culture could serve as a foundation of Mandelstam's poetic enterprise even if he did not follow in Blok's footsteps. For the armor of haughtiness and reserve that distinguished the protagonist of *Stone* had its rightful place in the Euripidean scenario: a counterbalance to the indecorous ravings of a Mother-Russia laying a claim on her chaste poet-stepson. But most important, what otherwise would have remained a matter of coincidence—a Jew choosing the vocation of a Russian poet—acquired the necessary character of fate as soon as it became integrated into the poetic master-plot fashioned after *Hippolytus*. Especially in Annenskii's mythic interpretation of the drama, the suffering endured by the poet qua poet could be promoted from the lowly status of pain in love to the much higher rank of martyrdom and redemption.

That the mantle of Annenskii's Hippolytus was a good fit does not, of course, mean that Mandelstam had to wear it. But wear it he did, and not once or twice but throughout his career—according to a plan outlined in "Pushkin and Skriabin," an essay composed sometime in the winter of 1915–16 and intended for delivery to the Petersburg Religious-Philosophical Assembly.[46]

PHAEDRA-RUSSIA AND THE NIGHT SUN

Surviving only in fragments, "Pushkin and Skriabin" is the most enigmatic, the most telling, and the most "dated" piece of Mandelstam's prose. Written in a tone of apocalyptic stridency, not out of keeping with the wartime rhetorical repertoire, it brings to mind the lofty and ponderous pronouncements of the senior Symbolists, "godseekers," and various prophets of Russian messianism who had packed the Religious-Philosophical Assembly since the beginning of the war.[47] As a credo that would be mocked but not renounced,[48] "Pushkin and

Skriabin" shows that Mandelstam, too, was afflicted by the contemporary passion for symbolic overinterpretation, that "dropsy of grand themes" as he would later diagnose the condition.[49] Indeed, in this essay Mandelstam shared both the subject matter and the assumptions of the work of his older mentors—namely, Viacheslav Ivanov's oration "Skriabin's View of Art"[50] and a pamphlet, *Pushkin and Christianity*, written by the veteran of Russian Symbolism, V. V. Gippius, who had taught Mandelstam at the Tenishev School.[51] Not that Mandelstam limited himself to these two sages[52] or merely gathered their statements under one roof. Rather, he used them as a catapult from which to launch his own "philosophy of art," informed, like theirs, by the apocalyptic pathos of the Great War.

Gippius's pamphlet, an expression of the burgeoning Pushkin cult, belonged to the genre of "figural" appreciation, the purpose of which was to revise the reputation of a hero in order to make it conform to and legitimize the values and practices of the current day. In this sense, Pushkin's life and work could be seen as prefiguring the views of a revisionist. To be more specific, Gippius endeavored to win Vladimir Solov'ev's Pushkin, representing amorality, and the early Russian Nietzschean's Pushkin, representing an incarnation of the Greek ideal,[53] to a more recent cause: the "Christianity of the Spirit" or the "Third Testament"—the name given to this new spirituality by its premier prophet, Dmitrii Merezhkovskii.[54] "As far as I know," wrote Solov'ev about the cult of the poet at the close of the nineteenth century, "even the most ardent authors of panegyrics to Pushkin have not recalled Golgotha in connection with his duel."[55] A dozen or so years later, Gippius crossed the Rubicon.[56] Avoiding the temptation to read into Pushkin what could have passed for religious belief, he turned to a more sophisticated strategy, presenting the poet's work and career as a figural and symbolic representation of "this new faith which alone encompasses Christianity and is [all-]accepting."[57] A few brief quotations suffice to convey the tenor and, more important, the flavor of Gippius's treatment of Pushkin:

> If Christianity is truth, it is the truth of movement, not stasis. . . . and if [life's irreconcilable] contradictions obtain, and they do indeed obtain, then Christianity, being the truth of life that is moving in the direction of God, is the truth of transcendence, not rejection: a transfiguration, not a rejection of the world. . . .
>
> A passionate man lives by passions—and they burn him. Should he deny them and run away? [No.] . . . One cannot escape them unless they enter into one and develop into a different kind of fire. A fiery asceticism is possible—a rejection in which passion turns

> into its opposite and, burning this flesh, creates, sets fire to new flesh—just as the graveyard fire of putrefaction, decomposing the corpse, burns for the sake of resurrection. . . .
>
> If one were to define Pushkin's soul, which manifested itself in his poetry, it should be defined as a Christian soul in its main element—[namely,] sin that desires holiness. . . . The depth of his human sinfulness was in sensuality, and to the extent that this sensuality was a suffering sensuality, it was the passion of the Christian sense of God [*bogooshchushchenie*]. And it was in this way that the relationship between sensuality and passion was understood by the Greeks, who in their tragic consciousness identified passion and suffering—*pathos*. We, too, say passion in the sense of suffering—the Lord's Passion.[58]

Gippius went so far as to proclaim Pushkin a microcosm of the present stage of history. This he understood as a progressive transfiguration of flesh into spirit by thermal means (sublimation, in the etymological sense). Whether intentionally or not, Gippius's formulation, especially where it relied on the rhetoric of sensuality and the metaphor of "burning," must have sounded quite pertinent during the "Skriabin Weeks," their heightened atmosphere further intensified by the repeated performances of the orgiastic "Poem of Fire."

> [Pushkin] was merely knocking on the door of the new religious being, where religion and social issues fuse in one concept, in one sensibility—of the kingdom of the Spirit coming into this world. . . .
>
> Pushkin represents our organic Christian life in its longing for sin and holiness, in its swaying of all the fateful antinomies, in its struggle between the flesh and the spirit. Puskhin is our all, including the borderline of religious consciousness which accepts actual social activism in its striving toward the resurrection of all flesh. Pushkin is the highest symbol of our cultural vow, because no one has been able to transform sensuality into passion [*pathos*] so powerfully and instinctively.
>
> This is our longing flesh, being transcended, transfigured.[59]

Viacheslav Ivanov, too, pitched high his memorial speech on Skriabin, with which he toured Russia in the winter and spring of 1915–16. In a lugubrious mystical legato, Ivanov outlined Skriabin's theosophy within the framework of Ivanov's own Orphic hermeticism. In particular, he proposed a place for Skriabin in the historical and cosmic scheme of things, which he, Ivanov, understood as "a mutual desire of the male and the female essences" or as a "divinely aesthetic phenomenon" that "in its actual basis is a divinely erotic process." Speaking about Skriabin's plan to have the Apocalypse commence as a result of the performance of his *Mysterium*—Skriabin's fantastic

Gesamtkunstwerk that remained unfinished[60]—Ivanov went to some length to explain to his audience that such a pandemonium was, more or less, in the nature of matter and spirit:

> As for the mythic Orpheus, music for him [Skriabin] was the primal essence moving and constructing the world. It had to flower with words and evoke images of any and all kinds of beauty. . . . For how could the World Soul, if it exists—and it does—and living Nature, if it is alive—and it is—not respond with a heteroglossal Amen to the symphonic call of mankind, [a call] consonant with [nature's] longing?... Such was the holy madness of Skriabin—that madness out of which everything living is born. For all that is alive is born out of ecstasy and ravings. Such was the illuminating energy of this solar artist who had forgotten that he was only an artist, just as the sun, melting and oozing its life-giving force, seems to forget that it is a heavenly stellar object and not a stream of flowing flame.

More important for Ivanov, Skriabin's death was also fateful because it occurred at the critical juncture in the history of the Spirit:

> But the appointed hour of fragmentation is coming to an end; the point when matter was furthest from the Spirit is past; the ways of "involution," that is, sinking into the depth of matter, have been traversed; "evolution" of man and the world has begun—man's ascent toward God. From now on, universal union is the task of theurgy, and hence symphony [*sobornost'*, symphonic union] as well, as the foundation of the theurgist action. The entire work of Skriabin becomes universal integration, the gathering together of fragments into a single whole, a pure and exceptional synthesis.[61]

Compared to these incantations of Gippius and Ivanov, Mandelstam's claims for art and artist appear far less extravagant, and certainly less heterodox. For Mandelstam as for his mentors, the art of the Christian age was "always action based on the great idea of redemption." But to achieve redemption one did not need to go beyond Christianity into the esoterics of Skriabin's theosophy, Ivanov's recondite religious syncretism,[62] or the "Third Testament" of Merezhkovskii. "The world, together with the artist, had been redeemed," and all that "remained" was to have humanity recall and internalize this Event, that is, "imitate Christ," follow in the footsteps of the Redeemer. Imbued with this singular purpose, wrote Mandelstam, Christian art constituted

> "imitation of Christ," infinitely varied in its manifestations, eternal return to the singular creative act that laid the foundation of our historical era. Christian art is free. It is, in the full sense of the word, "art for art's sake." Not a single necessity, however lofty, over-

shadows its radiant inner freedom, for its prototype, that which it imitates, is the very redemption of the world by Christ. Thus, not sacrifice, not redemption in art, but the free and joyful imitation of Christ—this is the cornerstone of Christian aesthetics.[63]

Unlike Ivanov, Mandelstam drew a sharp distinction between "imitation of Christ" (as in martyrdom)[64] and "sacrifice" (as in ecstatic cults and their latter-day counterparts). For Mandelstam, the promise of redemption had been fulfilled, and therefore imitation of Christ, including martyrdom, could become part of the aesthetic sphere—that is, imitation of Christ for imitation's sake, and not in order to achieve a purpose, such as redemption, lying outside the Christian mimesis. By contrast, Ivanov's position, though ancient in origin and grounded in Christianity, was predicated on a new revelation, which, until it became manifest, could offer no guarantees that an ordeal, aesthetic or otherwise, would have any "serious" redemptive value. Apparently Mandelstam was not entirely impressed by Viacheslav Ivanov's catechism of dying and reviving priest-poets.[65] This same distinction between imitation of Christ and sacrifice had far-reaching implications for a poet's charismatic "project" as well. There is, after all, a world of difference between proclaiming oneself "holy" within the framework of the familiar, established notions of the sacred and being declared "holy" according to a new religious sensibility à la Merezhkovskii's "Third Testament" or Viacheslav Ivanov's syncretic pot-au-feu—a heavy burden indeed. If anything, an "imitator" of the Savior could radiate the sacred with greater intensity than one imitating Orpheus or Frazer's "Priest of Nemi," not to speak of other more ecstatic precursors from Ivanov's catalog.[66]

Finally, Mandelstam had to contend with a dualistic view advocated by Vasilii Rozanov, according to which art represented vitality entirely incompatible with the mortifying beauty of "the sweetest Jesus."[67] The Apostle Paul, Rozanov argued by analogy, was not a Judean Saul to whom some extra qualities were added. Rather, Saul had to die altogether before Christian Paul could come into being. In a similar way, the beauty of the world (art, music, the Greeks) could not coexist with the beauty of Jesus—if one was holy, the other was demonic, and vice versa. Mandelstam found a solution for this Manichaean dilemma in his rather ingenious, though not unheard of, stress on death as an act imitative of Christ's Passion.[68] The Greeks, who had realized the ideal of beauty, were unaware of the beauty and special significance of death known to Christians.[69] Trying to combine the best of both worlds, Mandelstam defined Christianity as "Hellenism fertilized by dying."[70] Thus a Christian artist, or rather, his projected persona, followed the fate of a "Hellene"—mortal but redeemed and assured of a martyr's blessing in a kenotic act of dying. More important, such a death, imitating Christ's Passion, had the power of an innocent's self-sacrifice, that is, the power of "extrapersonal" redemption. It did not matter what had preceded this act of martyrdom, since it alone defined the ultimate meaning of an artist's fate. Surely Mandelstam, who presented death as the ultimate creative act,[71] did not differentiate between an artist's fate and the fate of his creations. On the one hand, according to this anthropology, an artist's career was imbued with the most serious meaning, a capacity to redeem a collectivity that had fallen into sin. On the other, it represented a purely aesthetic, "imitative" phenomenon—a recapitulation of the Savior's life and, with it, the history of humanity culminating in his revelation. To quote "Pushkin and Skriabin," Christian art (and the life it imitated) consisted of a

> joyous communion with God, a game of hide-and-seek of the spirit, as it were, played by the Father with His children! The divine illusion of redemption contained in Christian art stems precisely from the Deity's playing with us, allowing us to wander along the paths of mystery so that we, as if on our own, could run into redemption, having experienced catharsis in art.[72]

Once again, Mandelstam took "the stone that the builders had rejected" and made it the foundation of his view of art. But there were, of course, other stones he did not mind sharing with his senior fellow masons, as this quotation from Viacheslav Ivanov's aphorisms (c. 1908) demonstrates (italics are mine):

> When Hellenic philosophers began to speak about the "phenomena," all they revealed, as was always the case in Hellenism, was religious truth. The concept of the phenomenon [*iavlenie*, or manifestation] had long been familiar to the worshippers of the god of appearances (*epiphaniai*) and disappearances (*athanizmoi*)—the priests of Dionysus. Before it could become the covering over the noumenon, the phenomenon had to be understood as the mask of the god *playing the game of hide-and-seek*, or, as the uninitiated would have been told, the game of life and death. Only in Hellenism was the phenomenon as such considered sacred.[73]

Mandelstam's fundamental assumption about Pushkin was not radically different from that of Gippius or Rozanov;[74] nor was his view of an artist unrelated to Ivanov's Orpheus participating in the "divinely erotic process." Where he differed from them was in his pattern for presenting Pushkin's "passion" or "pathos." Developing his main thesis that the death of an artist "from a fully Christian point of view" represented his ultimate and central creative act, Mandelstam recalled the government's shameful concealment of the place and time of Pushkin's funeral service:

> Pushkin's funeral was held in the night. It was a secret funeral. The marble St. Isaac's—a magnificent sarcophagus—waited in vain for the solar body of the poet. It was at night that the sun was placed into the coffin, and it was in freezing January that the sleds creaked, taking the poet's remains to an out-of-the-way church.
>
> I am recalling the picture of Pushkin's funeral in order to evoke in your memory the image of the night sun, the image of the last Greek tragedy created by Euripides—the vision of the unfortunate Phaedra.[75]

It has been noted that Euripides' Phaedra had no such vision,[76] but the meaning, at least in the most immediate sense, is not hard to come by. Whatever else Mandelstam may have had in mind, the image of the "night sun," although most likely borrowed from the vocabulary of Viacheslav Ivanov,[77] is emblematic of Hippolytus, who in chastity and innocence had to suffer for the most unchaste of crimes. Taking his cue in part from Gippius and in part from Annenskii's interpretation of Euripides, Mandelstam presented Pushkin as a martyr to the cause of sublimating sensuality into Passion (the "fiery asceticism" of Gippius) and freeing humanity from, in Annenskii's words, "the yoke of the vegetative form of the soul." Furthermore, as in Euripides, the one who set the fatal trap for Hippolytus was herself an innocent and tormented victim. Now, in 1915, Phaedra's vision had returned once again: "In the fateful hours of purgation and storm, we have raised Skriabin over our heads, his sun-heart burns over us; but—alas!—this is not the sun of redemption, but the sun of guilt. Affirming Skriabin as her symbol in the hour of a world war, Phaedra-Russia . . ."[78]

The extant manuscript breaks off at this point, but the overall context allows one to reconstruct with some certainty the symbolic meaning that "Phaedra-Russia" was meant to convey: Hippolytus was to Phaedra what Pushkin and Skriabin were to Russia. Although Mandelstam may have intended to be no more than suggestive, his analogy between the relationship of Hippolytus to Phaedra in Euripides and that of the two symbolic figures of Russian art to their country was quite deliberate. Indeed, the enigmatic and unexpected Phaedra is invoked in the essay four times, whereas the Orpheus of Viacheslav Ivanov, who provided Mandelstam with the image of the "sun-heart,"[79] appears only once, and in a negative context at that.

How can we describe the tenor of "Phaedra" in Mandelstam's usage? The first aspect is rather obvious: the drama of Euripides was projected onto the myth of mystical marriage, perhaps the central myth in the Russian Symbolist tradition.[80] Thus, it was not the consummation of the marriage at the price of some extraordinary ordeal that was to resemble a redemptive act (as in Vladimir Solov'ev and, later on, in Blok and Ivanov), but the opposite: the marriage, though an important element, was incestuous and therefore "costly." The heavy toll it exacted could be redemptive only if the protagonist were chaste and innocent. According to Annenskii, both Phaedra and Hippolytus, their minor failings notwithstanding, fitted this bill, presaging the central event and the revelation of Christianity: "Can it be that this lofty conception of heavenly life, as some premonition, rises before us in the tragic hecatomb of *Hippolytus?*"[81] In 1915–16, the second winter of the Great War, Annenskii's words, especially "hecatomb" (a ritual sacrifice), must have sounded well-nigh prophetic. Was not Phaedra-Russia committing suicide while her hitherto "proud" Hippolytus (his other names constitute the newspaper "catalog" of dead heroes) was carried to his battlefield grave on a "black stretcher"?

> Бессонница. Гомер. Тугие паруса.
> Я список кораблей прочел до середины:
> . . . .
> . . . Когда бы не Елена,
> Что Троя вам одна, ахейские мужи?
>
> Insomnia. Homer. Taut sails.
> I've read the *catalog* of ships to the middle.
> . . . .
> . . . If not for Helen,
> What would Troy mean to you, Achaean men?
>
> Человек умирает, песок остывает согретый,
> И вчерашнее солнце на черных носилках несут.
>   1920
>
> Man dies. The sand warmed by him cools,
> And *yesterday's sun is carried away on a black stretcher.*[82]

The second aspect of Phaedra relates specifically to "incest" or its symbolic, exegetic meaning for Mandelstam. Polemicizing with his contemporaries who had abandoned the notion of *imitatio Christi* in favor of "Buddhism and Theosophy" or latter-day Orphism,[83] Mandelstam emphasized the quality of historical reversal evident in this heterodoxy. The turning away from Christianity constituted an unwelcome trend, threatening the progress of Christian humanity toward the Civitas Dei in general and the possibility of free art in particular:

> Time can go backward: the entire course of late modern history, which, with such terrifying force, turned away from Christianity toward Buddhism and Theosophy, testifies to this fact. . . .
> *Time is no more!* Christian chronology is in danger, the fragile count of years of our era is lost—time is rushing back, noisy and hissing like a dammed stream—and the new Orpheus is throwing his lyre into the seething foam: art is no more.[84]

This reversal of the stages of spiritual history "superseded" by Christianity was tantamount to going back to the bottom of the "evil and miry pool" of Judaism, to the "fainthearted" return to Russia of those who rejected the West ("Petr Chaadaev"), to writing one's poetry for the familiar contemporary ("On the Interlocutor"), and finally, to breaking the metaphysical incest taboo. In "Pushkin and Skriabin," Mandelstam made this exegesis explicit, but later he crossed out the passage, perhaps considering its attack on Rome (in fact his own earlier identification with it) too personal and cryptic and its anti-Jewish tone (what with the current anti-Semitism and pogroms)[85] in bad taste. Elaborating on the metaphysical choice between the Roman and the Greek paths facing Christian humanity, Mandelstam modified Nietzsche's "Rome against Judea, Judea against Rome"—the emblem of the drama of history (italics are mine):[86]

> This is what is happening: *Rome has surrounded Golgotha with an iron ring:* [as in the Gospels,] it is necessary to liberate this hill that has become Greek and universal. *A Roman soldier is guarding the Cross* and his lance is at the ready: now the water will begin to flow: it is necessary to remove the Roman guard. The infertile, ungraced part of Europe has revolted against the fertile and the graced—Rome has revolted against Hellas... It is necessary to save Hellas from Rome. Rome [sic] shall be vanquished by Rome—vanquished not even by it but by Judaism—in general, Judaism stands behind its back and only awaits its [Judaism's] appointed hour, and a terrifying, perverse course of history shall *triumph*[,] a reverse flow of time—worse than the sun[?] of Phaedra.[87]

Those who would commit such an abomination—that is, allegorically respond to Phaedra's ravings induced by Aphrodite—were unworthy of the title of Hippolytus; even more, they betrayed their Phaedra-Russia, who, despite her criminal entreaties, was innocent—herself a martyr unwittingly preparing the way for the historical Christ.

Yet the historical reversal—or "recurrence," to use Nietzsche's term—offered an opportunity encountered only at the most crucial juncture in history, when the "Judeo-Roman" world faced its "Greek and universal" counterpart at Golgotha. And in order to describe this aspect of the "return," Mandelstam once again reverted to the allegory of Phaedra, this time in conjunction with the other essential myth of incest, the Oedipus cycle of Sophocles: "The spirit of Greek tragedy awakened in music. Music had run its course and returned whence it issued: once again Phaedra is calling for her nurse; once again Antigone demands a burial and libations for her brother's dear body."

Applying Nietzsche's famous formula to the chiliastic sensibility of Russia, Mandelstam extended this construct in a way that doubtless would have displeased the German author: tragedy, born out of the spirit of music, was not supposed to culminate in the revelation of Christ. As it had over two millennia before, this cycle, according to Mandelstam, now approached its final stage. Possessed by the demonic Aphrodite, Phaedra—to follow Mandelstam's anagogic code—was meant to prevent this cycle from completing itself, even against her will and virtue. But Providence works in mysterious ways, and instead of subverting the course of history, Aphrodite's stratagem served to promote it, anticipating in the "tragic hecatomb" the redemptive love, chastity, and humility of Christ. The new faith, however, was destined not merely to supersede the old but to absorb and integrate it as well—to retain the old in its memory through a proper burial, whatever the price, as Antigone had done for "her brother's dear body."

Of course, although the "spirit of music had returned," the world was not identical to the world of the last centuries before the Revelation. That world lay in ignorance and could aspire only to anticipating Christianity. This world, Mandelstam was convinced, was aware of the Revelation but had ceased to value it and pretended to be ignorant of the archetypal sacrifice (italics are mine):

> Long, too long, have we been playing with music, not suspecting the danger it conceals, and while we were, perhaps from boredom, trying to invent a myth in order to beautify our existence, music threw to us, *not an invented one*, but one that was born, foam born, crimson-born, of royal lineage, a lawful heir to the myths of the ancients—a myth about forgotten Christianity.[88]

Following Viacheslav Ivanov's view of true art as theurgy—from symbol to myth, to revelation or recollection of revelation[89]— Mandelstam outlined a version of this aesthetic program to suit his own temperament and needs. In the context of the "amnesia," the imitation of Christ that he considered central to the art of the Christian era was to take a specific form—anamnesis of the Revelation: both as a personal drama, as in martyrdom, and as a collective act, as in the progressive realization of the Spirit in history. More precisely, out of the "infinitely varied manifestations" of *imitatio Christi,* Mandelstam selected his own repertoire of masks: Phaedra and Hippolytus of Euripides, together with Antigone and, one assumes, Oedipus of Sophocles. These two complementary versions of the incest myth (he may have known that Antigone meant "instead of mother") constituted, in his mind, a historical anticipation of Christianity.

The refusal to acknowledge the truth of Christianity that he perceived in contemporary Russia (and he was not alone in this)[90] was relevant in yet another sense, for it provided one more parallel with Mandelstam's personal dilemma: the amnesia of Russia's elite was analogous to the blindness of the Jews to the appearance of the Messiah. Accordingly, Petersburg-Petrograd, as Nadezhda Mandelstam indicated,[91] assumed the role of a new Jerusalem,[92] the place where the Revelation would be *recollected,* if not revealed. And to take the analogy one step further, the one to perform the act of recollection would be the poet himself—an imitator of Christ even in those instances when he was wearing the mask of his pagan "premonitions." Thus Christian Russians became Jews, and Osip Mandelstam, a Jew among them, assumed the role of a precursor in reverse, one who, instead of announcing the imminent arrival of the Savior, reminded people that he had already arrived, had died on the cross, and had risen. In a poem about a "young Levite" composed in November 1917, he made this identification explicit. The poem's "priests" are most likely the high priests of the contemporary "mystery religions," like the theosophist Andrei Belyi or even Viacheslav Ivanov and V. V. Gippius, who were trying to reconstruct the "destroyed Temple," unaware that the new one had already been built. The poem's dedication to A. V. Kartashev, an Orthodox theologian who had been active in the reform of the Russian Orthodox church and who had not "forgotten" Christianity, speaks in favor of such a reading.[93] The "black-yellow" is associated in Mandelstam with the color of the Jewish prayer shawl, with Judaism,[94] and, quite appropriately, with the Russian Empire, black and yellow being the colors of her flag.[95]

> Среди священников левитом молодым
> На страже утренней он долго оставался.

> Ночь иудейская сгущалася над ним
> И храм разрушенный угрюмо созидался.
>
> Он говорил: небес тревожна желтизна.
> Уж над Ефратом ночь, бегите, иереи!
> А старцы думали: не наша в том вина;
> Се черножелтый свет, се радость Иудеи.
>
> Он с нами был, когда на берегу ручья
> Мы в драгоценный лен Субботу пеленали
> И семисвещником тяжелым освещали
> Ерусалима ночь и чад небытия.
> 1917

> A young Levite among priests,
> He tarried during the morning vigil.
> The Judean night grew thicker around him,
> And on went the sullen rebuilding of the destroyed Temple.
>
> He was saying: the yellow of the skies is alarming,
> Night has already fallen over the Euphrates, run, hierarchs!
> But the elders thought: It's not our fault;
> The color is black-yellow, it is a joy to Judea.
>
> He was with us when, at the bank of a stream,
> We were swathing the Sabbath in precious linen
> And were illuminating with a heavy menorah
> Jerusalem's night and the vapor of nonbeing.[96]

To transpose this scheme into the "Hellenic" idiom, the poet would imitate Christ by assuming the personae of Hippolytus (and Phaedra) and of Oedipus (and Antigone). In short, he would be the muse Mnemosyne of the "myth of forgotten Christianity."

> [Amid] the vineyards of the old Dionysus: I picture *closed eyes and a light, solemn small head, somewhat thrown back.* This is the Muse of recollection, the light Mnemosyne, the eldest in the round dance [italics are mine].[97]

Compare this with Mandelstam's semi-ironic "Self-Portrait" (1913):

> В поднятьи головы крылатый
> Намек. Но мешковат сюртук.
> В закрытьи глаз, в покое рук
> Тайник движенья непочатый.
>
> Так вот кому летать и петь
> И слова пламенная ковкость,

Le Nouvel Hippolyte: 1915–1916

> Чтоб прирожденную неловкость
> Врожденным ритмом одолеть.
> 1913

> In the lifting of the head,
> A promise. But the coat is baggy.
> In the shutting of the eyes, in the calm of the hands,
> An undiscovered treasure trove of movement.
>
> So, that's the one destined to fly and sing,
> And master the flaming malleability of the word
> In order to overcome the congenital unease
> With inborn rhythm.[98]

Poetry inspired by such a muse is not merely the learned, recondite poetry of an Acmeist Brahmin, it is also a form of the imitation of Christ—in the symbolic and anagogical sense, it is the poetry of resurrection. In this art form, unlimited by representation, such an indisputable fact as death endows one's art with the ultimate meaning and sanction. From Mandelstam's Christian perspective, history, too, conformed to this pattern, for it received its meaning from the singular Event in whose light all that had preceded it appeared to have been leading to it.[99] The phylogeny of God's creation was recapitulated in the ontogeny of Christ.[100] This was the kind of recollection that the poetry inspired by Mandelstam's Mnemosyne—a Christian cousin of Nietzsche's "eternal recurrence"—could provide. He continued:

> A mask of forgetfulness falls from the light, fragile face, the features grow more distinct; memory triumphs—even at the price of death: to die means to recall, to recall means to die... To recall whatever the price! To vanquish forgetfulness—even at the price of death: this is Skriabin's motto, this is the heroic thrust of his art! This is what I meant when I said that Skriabin's death was the highest manifestation of his creativity, that it illuminated [his art] in a blinding and unexpected light.[101]

Vladimir Solov'ev, following the tradition of Vasilii Zhukovskii,[102] gave a similar interpretation to the death of "wayward" Pushkin; and so did Annenskii, following A. W. Schlegel and Wilamowitz-Moellendorff, in his essay on Euripides' *Hippolytus*. But Mandelstam went further: an artist's progress and the culmination of this progress in death could be a means of imitating the Savior both on a personal level and on a far grander, extrapersonal, historical scale. How Mandelstam set out to realize the program of "Pushkin and Skriabin" will be the subject of the next chapter, following a brief note on the circumstances of Mandelstam's life during the First World War.

MANDELSTAM BETWEEN *STONE* AND *TRISTIA*

The Great War was only one landmark of Mandelstam's early literary career. The Poet's Guild, that cradle of Acmeism which at first functioned as a nonpartisan Acmeist workshop dedicated to discussions of modern poetry, underwent an important transformation in 1913–14, when it was abandoned by several young poets, including Khlebnikov,[103] who did not wish to be associated with the new movement. This split within the younger generation of poets brought into focus the main theses of Acmeism—for Mandelstam, the "poetics of origins," contrasted with the poetics of "beginnings"[104] and made clearer the difference between the generation's Acmeist and its Futurist cohorts.[105] In March 1914, Akhmatova published her second collection, *Chetki,* and soon afterward Mandelstam began to prepare for publication his second *Kamen'* (1916), which was released in December 1915.[106] If the publication of a second book marked a coming of age for Mandelstam, the outbreak of the First World War did so for his entire generation of poets, who entered the literary scene around 1910. As Pasternak wrote in *Safe Conduct,* the rhythm of history coincided with the rhythm of individual fate, and one could hardly find a better moment either for taking stock of one's past accomplishments or for setting out in a new direction.

Mandelstam greeted the war very much a Russian patriot, believing, as did many of his contemporaries, that it signaled the fulfillment of the nation's historical destiny.[107] On October 30, 1914, he delivered a paper, "A Few Words Concerning Civic Poetry," and although it has not survived, it is quite certain that Mandelstam hailed the verbal war effort of his fellow poets, even if he might not have welcomed some of its particular manifestations.[108] Judging by "Puskhin and Skriabin," he tended to see the country's mission as the establishment of a universal church based on the "symphonic" Helleno-Christian ideal (*sobornost'*),[109] a cause the Russian Orthodox nation, the first among the heirs of Hellas,[110] would naturally champion. It was then that Mandelstam began to stray from his "Catholicism" in the direction of a "catholicity" more compatible with his view of Russia's role in the world.[111] The one gushy patriotic poem—"In a white paradise, a hero reposes" (1914)—and his choice of "Hagia Sophia" (1912) for public recitals[112] (made suddenly topical by Russia's design to seize the Dardanelles) reveal that he viewed the war through the prism of the Russian messianic tradition, internalized by Russian intellectuals since the writings of the Slavophiles.[113] To the extent that "In a white paradise" indicates the poet's thinking at the beginning of the war, it merits a brief discussion here.

To present a picture of a Russian warrior fallen in battle, Mandelstam conflated two motifs: the "white shirts" Tolstoy's peasants put on before the battle of Borodino in *War and Peace,* and his own association of white with an epiphanic ecstatic state experienced by artists and martyrs:[114]

> В белом раю лежит богатырь:
> Пахарь войны, пожилой мужик.
> В серых глазах мировая ширь:
> Великорусский державный лик.
>
> Только святые умеют так
> В благоуханном гробу лежать;
> Выпростав руки, блаженства в знак,
> Славу свою и покой вкушать.
>
> Разве Россия не белый рай
> И не веселые наши сны?
> Радуйся, ратник, не умирай:
> Внуки и правнуки спасены!
>
> декабрь 1914

> In a white paradise, a hero reposes:
> A ploughman of war, an elderly peasant.
> In his gray eyes lies the expanse of the world:
> The face of the Great Russian power.
>
> Only saints can so repose
> In a fragrant coffin—
> Hands folded calmly, a sign of bliss—
> Partaking of their glory and peace.
>
> Is not Russia a white paradise,
> And are not our dreams a joy?
> Rejoice, soldier, do not die:
> Your grandchildren and great-grandchildren are saved![115]

As in the other poetry of Mandelstam's generation, the overtones of saintly militarism disappeared in the course of a year or so, following Mandelstam's abortive attempt to serve as a volunteer nurse on the Polish front.[116] But the "Dionysian-symphonic" pathos, as Mandelstam referred to Beethoven's Ninth in "Pushkin and Skriabin," proved to be more lasting. It animated his pacifist poem "Bestiary. A Dythyramb to Peace,"[117] which concluded on the following note:

> В зверинце заперев зверей,
> Мы успокоимся надолго,
> И станет полноводней Волга,
> И рейнская струя светлей —
> И умудренный человек
> Почтит невольно чужестранца,
> Как полубога, буйством танца
> На берегах великих рек.
>
> Январь 1916

> Having locked up the beast in the bestiary,
> We will calm down for a long time,
> And the Volga will grow fuller,
> And the Rhine stream brighter still—
> And the wizened man
> Will instinctively greet a foreigner,
> As if he were a demigod, with the frenzy of dance
> On the shores of great rivers.

The first year of the war was important for Mandelstam in yet another respect. In late 1915 or early 1916, Mandelstam's romance with another poet, Marina Tsvetaeva, began a relationship that, according to Nadezhda Mandelstam, helped cure the poet of his "congenital unease."[118] Finally, the most decisive argument for treating "Puskhin and Skriabin" as a turning point and a symbolic landmark of Mandelstam's career concerns his poetry proper, which underwent a profound thematic and stylistic change precisely in 1915, the last time we see Mandelstam as a poet of highbrow, "stony" decorum. What he could only timidly begin to express in his second book of poetry, concluding it with a nostalgic meditation on Racine's *Phèdre,* became the stuff of his third collection, *Tristia,* which appropriately commenced with a "Hellenized" version of the myth, a collage made up of bits and pieces of Euripides, Racine, and Mandelstam's own poetry.[119]

IV

Setting the Stage: Prolepsis in Tristia, 1915–1917

What else? Death appears to me sometimes as a magical afternoon dream, which sees far—its gaze frozen—and brilliantly. But death may and must be beautiful in a different way, too, because it is the only child of my will, and in the harmony of the world, it will be, if I so wish, another golden sun.
                INNOKENTII ANNENSKII, "Lermontov's Humor"

THREE BOOKS

A book of poetry should be not a random collection *of heterogeneous poems but precisely a* book, *a self-contained whole united by a single idea. Like a novel, like a treatise, a book of poetry reveals its theme consistently from the first page to the last. . . . Parts in a book of poems are nothing more than chapters, one clarifying another, which cannot be randomly rearranged.*   VALERII BRIUSOV, Urbi et orbi (1903)

We have before us a book, like a song—not a word can be taken out of it.
                ALEKSANDR BLOK (1904)

Mandelstam used the "biographical" principle for plotting his narrative, and thus the order of poems in a collection is almost as important as the order of chapters in a *Bildungsroman* or of themes and parts in a musical composition. This is not to say that Mandelstam's poems cannot be read in isolation. After all, many were first published in newspapers and magazines. But placing an individual piece within a specific context and a fixed order endows both the poem and what surrounds it with a "narrative" meaning that they would not otherwise possess.[1] I shall examine the poems I discuss here and in subsequent chapters as parts of such a hypothetical narrative. I use the word *hypothetical* for two reasons: first, because a narrative line of a collection of lyric poetry is suggested or implied (in the manner of the Formalists' *fabula* or Wagner's leitmotiv)[2] and therefore cannot be precisely defined; and second, because the reader's identification of a poet with the chief protagonist of such a narrative inevitably defers understanding until the book of poems comes to an end. What is more, these rules of a contemporary lyric narrative were intimately related to their archetypal referent point in the Gospels—a link made apparent, for example, in Pasternak's "The Garden of Gethsemane," where Christ speaks about his destiny in almost narratological terms ("But the book of life has come to the page that is dearer than everything holy. Now what has been written shall come to pass, so let it come to pass. Amen").[3] In this sense, both the opening and the closing of any but that last "book" are forever contingent. At the moment of its appearance, however, every new collection has the finality of a testament, and it can remain the last. I shall examine Mandelstam's writings of the post-*Stone* decade from this perspective.

During the period 1915–28, Mandelstam published four books of poetry. All of them included some poetry composed after the publication of the second *Stone* in 1916 (printed in December 1915). Each of the books began and ended in a different way, and each was a significant landmark in the narrative of the poet's fate. I shall discuss them in the order of their appearance, but before doing so I offer this brief bibliographical note. After *Stone* II, the first collection of new poetry to be published was *Tristia*. This book, issued by a Russian publisher in Berlin in 1922, consisted mostly of new poetry but included a number of earlier pieces. Unlike the poems composed in 1915–20, these were interspersed throughout the collection and bore no date, blending with the chronological drift of the later cycles. Because of difficulties in communicating with his Berlin publisher, Mandelstam, who had intended to call the book *The New Stone,* had little to do with this edition except to supply copies of poems. Even its title, echoing the eponymous 1918 poem, is reputed to have been invented by Mikhail Kuzmin.[4]

A few of the poems of the 1915–21 period, as well as one 1923 poem, "He Who Found a Horseshoe," were included in the third *Stone,* subtitled *The First Book of Poetry* (1923). This *Stone* was issued by the State Publishing House (a certain measure of Mandelstam's reputation as being sympathetic to the regime)[5] and was devoted on the whole to the 1908–15 period. Once again, the sequence of poems, all undated, was not strictly chronological. The only collection of

Prolepsis in Tristia: *1915–1917*

post-1915 verse Mandelstam is known to have designed himself, *The Second Book* (1923), was published by Krug, a state-sponsored press headed by A. K. Voronskii that was meant to compete with privately owned presses for the work of fellow travelers.[6] Similar to *Tristia*, *The Second Book* included in addition eleven poems composed during 1921–23. As in *Stone* III, poems here followed a more or less chronological order and were undated—another sign that the author wished to stress an implied (rather than chronological and therefore random) integrity of his book.

The last edition published in Mandelstam's lifetime, the 1928 *Poems,* came out in the middle of a five-year period when he wrote virtually no poetry. The most complete edition, *Poems,* encompassing most of what he had produced since 1908, consisted of three parts: "Stone," the poetry of 1908–15; "Tristia," 1915–20; and "1921–1925," a self-explanatory and meaningful title for an author who had previously avoided dates. The order of poems, too, was significant. Both *Stone* III and *The Second Book* concluded with Mandelstam's longest and latest poems: one with the wistful and retrospective "He Who Found a Horseshoe," the other with the forward-looking, oratorical resolution for the future, "The Slate Ode." By contrast, *Poems* ended with a short, ambivalent, perhaps embittered meditation of an exhausted "aging" poet. This piece, echoing the "cruel romances" of Apollon Grigor'ev and Pushkin's sarcastic parody of Dante's *Inferno,* conveyed an ironic mixture of hope and resignation, indicative of Mandelstam's uncertainty about his future as poet:

> И только и свету — что в звездной колючей неправде,
> А жизнь проплывет театрального капора пеной,
> И некому молвить: «из табора улицы темной»...
>
> 1925

> And what is left of the light is in the starry, prickly untruth,
> And life will float by like the froth of a theater bonnet,
> And I have no one to whom to say: "Out of the gypsy camp of a
>   dark street"...[7]

According to the memoirs of his widow, Mandelstam exercised no control over the 1928 *Poems*. Nevertheless, it is hard to believe that he literally had no hand in dividing the book into parts and choosing the opening and closing poems.[8] However heavily censored and error-ridden this book might be, it was Mandelstam himself who divided his legacy into three periods, 1908–15, 1915–20, and 1921–25; acknowledged his paternity over the 1922 *Tristia*, christened though it was by Mikhail Kuzmin; and invited his readers to accept the collection as legitimate, reservations notwithstanding.⁹ I shall treat it accordingly.

In light of this history, how are we to interpret Mandelstam's choice of the "overture" to the poetry of 1915–20? This body of poems was introduced by what I shall refer to as "Phaedra II" and "Bestiary." Both editions of *Tristia* (1922 and 1928) opened with "Phaedra II" followed by "Bestiary," the order conforming to the chronology of their composition, which *The Second Book* nevertheless reversed. Although both poems were patterned on the familiar Nietzschean dichotomy of Apollo and Dionysus, each set a distinct tone for the collection. Indeed, a book of poems opening with a monologue on "unfortunate Phaedra" produces a beast entirely different from the one that emerges following a poem echoing Schiller's chiliastic "Ode to Joy" and Beethoven's Ninth.

From the vantage point of late 1922, the second year of the New Economic Policy, "Bestiary" could resonate powerfully with the desire for peaceful "work and constancy" in Russia and the world ("A Decembrist," 1918), and as a political statement it could support Mandelstam's "Hellenistic" program for rebuilding postwar Europe as a nonpolitical commonwealth—a sort of a grand-scale *mir*, Russia's celebrated peasant commune.¹⁰ The choice of "Bestiary" may have been determined by commercial reasons as well. Following on the heels of *Tristia, The Second Book* had to look, feel, and be different (despite the fact that two-thirds of *The Second Book* had been printed in the Berlin edition) if it were to sell more than a few copies. This Valerii Briusov understood well when, in an act of particular biliousness, he pronounced *The Second Book* to be identical with *Tristia*.¹¹ Be that as it may, *The Second Book* offered a different periodization and a somewhat different narrative of self-presentation, one that was at odds with the editions of 1922 and that had ceased to be viable by the time the collected *Poems* came out in 1928.

Unlike "Bestiary," "Phaedra II" was essentially an ambiguous poem, capable of serving a greater repertoire of "plots" generated by the "myth of forgotten Christianity" that Mandelstam outlined in "Pushkin and Skriabin." As it did in *Tristia* (1922), "Phaedra II" could function as a metonym of the fate of man before the Christian revelation, which was to be contrasted with the Christian regeneration of the last poem, where the Hagia Sophia and St. Peter's are described as "granaries of universal good."¹² Or, as it did in the 1928 edition, the poem could formulate an inner conflict that would find its ironic resolution in "I intruded into the round dance of shades" ("Ia v khorovod tenei"), a poem that makes light of the earlier "petrified" timidity of the author of *Stone* when he was confronted with eros.[13] Finally, placing it at the head of a collection immediately following *Stone* could emphasize both the continuity and the change in Mandelstam's poetic persona—a theme that preoccupied him all through the 1920s. Indeed, *Stone* (1916 and 1928) concluded with another "Phaedra," a nostalgic yearning for the forever-gone theater of Euripides and Racine, whereas *Tristia* opened with a scene in which both Phaedra and her time, as Mandelstam had insisted in "Pushkin and Skriabin," came back to recapitulate the Christian drama of history. Indeed, the ending of *Stone* II and the beginning of *Tristia* constitute a most remarkable case of asymmetrical anaphora, its two members represented not by words, lines, or even poems but by two large collections of poetry. Behind this oversized rhetorical figure was the overwhelming sense of historical catastrophe, at once a break with the past and a recurrent apocalypse à la Nietzsche and Vico.[14] In Russia's Christian culture, Mandelstam, of course, was not the only poet to predicate the outcome of recent events on the ability of his countrymen to recollect "forgotten Christianity," a process in which a poet was to play a central role. What was specifically Mandelstamian about this mnemonic *imitatio Christi* was the plot around which it revolved, namely, the myth of incest. Such are the reasons prompting me to rely on *Tristia* for the periodization of Mandelstam's work.

AN ENDING AND A BEGINNING: 1915–1916

The wake counters death with birth and rebirth and—joined with the beliefs in afterlife and the world of the night sun—creates the whole of the dual idea of the deity. Sexual union is the polar opposite of death, and the wedding corresponds to the funeral.
        VIACHESLAV IVANOV, "Religion of Dionysus"

Un coup de dés jamais n'abolira le hasard.   STÉPHANE MALLARMÉ

> *Life is without beginning or end.*
> *Chance stalks us all;*
> *Over us hangs the unavoidable gloom*
> *Or brightness of God's face.—*
> *But you, artist, believe firmly*
> *In beginnings and ends.*
>   ALEKSANDR BLOK, Retribution

Mandelstam's progress during the period spanned by the first two collections may be seen as a continuous working through of the implied myth, with the ultimate aim of finding a more adequate expression for it within contemporary poetic conventions and beliefs. After he had interpreted the incest myth in terms of Christian martyrdom, the screen concealing it from the reader lifted, exposing a different stage whose existence had been only suspected by a few initiates into the mysteries of modernist hide-and-seek.[15] Let us consider these two poems that marked the crossroads in Mandelstam's career.[16] I shall cite them here in full, based on a translation by Clarence Brown.[17]

> Я не увижу знаменитой «Федры»,
> В старинном многоярусном театре,
> С прокопченной высокой галереи,
> При свете оплывающих свечей.
> И, равнодушен к суете актеров,
> Сбирающих рукоплесканий жатву,
> Я не услышу обращенный к рампе
> Двойною рифмой оперенный стих:
>
> — Как эти покрывала мне постылы...
>
> Театр Расина! Мощная завеса
> Нас отделяет от другого мира;
> Глубокими морщинами волнуя,
> Меж ним и нами занавес лежит.
> Спадают с плеч классические шали,
> Расплавленный страданьем крепнет голос
> И достигает скорбного закала
> Негодаваньем раскаленный слог...
>
> Я опоздал на празднество Расина!
>
> Вновь шелестят истлевшие афиши,
> И слабо пахнет апельсинной коркой,
> И словно из столетней летаргии —
> Очнувшийся сосед мне говорит:
> — Измученный безумством Мельпомены,
> Я в этой жизни жажду только мира;
> Уйдем, покуда зрители-шакалы
> На растерзанье Музы не пришли!
>
> Когда бы грек увидел наши игры...
>
> 1915

> I shall not see the famous Phaedra
> In the old, many-tiered theater
> With its high smoke-blackened gallery
> By the light of melting candles.
> And, indifferent to the vanity of actors
> Gathering the harvest of applause,

Prolepsis in Tristia: *1915–1917*

> I shall not hear it—directed at the footlights,
> The verse feathered with the coupled rhyme.
>
> "How repellent and fatiguing are these veils to me..."
>
> Racine's theater! A powerful screen
> Separates us from the other world;
> Stirring with its deep folds,
> A curtain lies between it and us.
> Classical shawls are slipping from shoulders;
> A voice, melted by suffering, is gathering strength,
> And, forged in indignation, the style
> Achieves the tempering of grief...
>
> I've missed the festival of Racine!
>
> Again the worn-out posters rustle,
> And, faintly, orange peel emits its scent,
> And, as though awakened from an age-old lethargy,
> My neighbor speaks to me:
> "In torment from the madness of Melpomene,
> In this life, all I am thirsting for is peace,
> Let us leave before the jackal spectators
> Arrive to tear the Muse apart!"
>
> What if a Greek should see our games...

Even for such a master of ambiguity as Mandelstam, this poem was unusual. Constructed around a nostalgic topos—a Russian reader will readily recall Tiutchev's "Blessed is he who visited this world in its fateful moments"[18]—the text nevertheless belies the nostalgic protestation by all available Acmeist means. The unrhymed iambic pentameter, emblematic of the high romantic drama of Pushkin's *Little Tragedies* or *Boris Godunov,* the intricate alternations of feminine and masculine endings, a rising crescendo of the thrice-repeated feminine ending and the falling intonation of the masculine line (3 + 1, 3 + 1), and finally its dazzling alliterative play on the liquids [r] and [l] (consider Racine, Phaedra, Melpomene, gallery) betray the kind of mastery and control that Racine himself might have envied.

Thematic ambiguity, too, is apparent. What the poet bemoans not to have seen is described with such gusto that one wonders whether the original could have lived up to Mandelstam's imaginary copy. In fact, the first stanza functions rhetorically as an antithetical incantation, creating the presence it affirmatively denies. Hence the appearance of what passes for the actual text of Racine (*Phèdre,* act 1, scene 2) in the line following the stanza:

An Ending and a Beginning

Que ces vains ornements, que ces voiles me pèsent.

If only for a moment, Racine's theater had indeed returned.

The incantation reaches an almost Maiakovskian level of intensity[19] in the second stanza. Remarkably, Mandelstam was able to maintain Acmeist equilibrium while the antithetical aspects of the poem were pulling it apart like two linked locomotives going in opposite directions. One powerhouse was the force of historical and metaphysical concealment, the Apollonian "heavy curtain" hiding that "other world"; the other was the Dionysian elimination of all boundaries that made the "classical shawls" slip and confessions fly. Add to this the archetypal, spellbinding potency of Juvenal's "indignant verse" (*fecit indignatio versum*) and you have a striking Mandelstamian brew in which fiery poisons were mixed with an equal measure of cooling antidotes. As soon as the Bacchic element (lines 15–18) began to overwhelm the classical stoicism of the preceding quatrain, the poet, terrified by the power he himself conjured up, pulled back with the rather unconvincing but nevertheless deflating line "I've missed the festival of Racine!"

The last stanza, written in a minor key, completes the poem's two central and antithetical paradigms: one elegiacally nostalgic and full of irretrievable loss, the other ample and restorative. What screened the past from the present in the first stanza[20] yielded to transparency in the second, where nothing separated the "games" played in Petrograd in 1915 from those played in the France of Racine or the Rome of Juvenal, or, of course, from the Greek "sacrificial feasts that gave birth to Melpomene, the favorite muse of Dionysus," in the words of Viacheslav Ivanov. In this context, the words of the "lethargic" aesthete who wished to close his eyes to *this* world must appear vacuous indeed. Unlike him, the poet could appreciate his own implicit analogy between those ancient games and the contemporary sacrificial ones. The war, the "symbolic" death of Skriabin, and the Skriabin "vigils"[21]—all could be classified as that "game of hide-and-seek . . . played by the Father with His children"; thus they, as if by themselves, might stumble across the idea of redemption and God.[22] This was how Mandelstam put it in "Pushkin and Skriabin."

After the pressured atmosphere of this concluding poem of *Stone II*, we read the far more somber second "Phaedra," which opens *Tristia*, almost with a sigh of relief. For here the reader, wearied by nostalgia for Racine, is transported to the still center of tragedy, that archetypal sphere whence the divine "idea" of Phaedra and Hippolytus sprang forth to be "imitated" by Euripides and Seneca, Racine and Mandelstam.

Prolepsis in Tristia: *1915–1917*

— Как этих покрывал и этого убора
Мне пышность тяжела средь моего позора!

    — Будет в каменной Трезене
    Знаменитая беда,
    Царской лестницы ступени
    Покраснеют от стыда,
    . . . .
    . . . .
    И для матери влюбленной
    Солнце черное взойдет.

— О если б ненависть в груди моей кипела —
Но видите — само признанье с уст слетело.

    — Черным пламенем Федра горит
    Среди белого дня.
    Погребальный факел чадит
    Среди белого дня.
    Бойся матери ты, Ипполит:
    Федра — ночь — тебя сторожит
    Среди белого дня.

— Любовью черною я солнце запятнала…
. . . .

    — Мы боимся, мы не смеем
    Горю царскому помочь.
    Уязвленная Тезеем
    На него напала ночь.
    Мы же, песнью похоронной
    Провожая мертвых в дом,
    Страсти дикой и бессонной
    Солнце черное уймем.

                               1916

"O the splendor of these veils and this attire—how
Heavy it is to me amid my shame!"

—In stone Troezen, there will come to pass
A famous misfortune,
The steps of the royal stairs
Will turn red from shame.
  . . . .
  . . . .
And for the enamored mother
A black sun will rise.

"O if only it were hatred seething in my breast—
But, you see, the confession of itself flew from my lips."

> —With a black flame Phaedra burns
> In bright daylight.
> The funeral torch smolders
> In bright daylight.
> Fear your mother, Hippolytus:
> Phaedra-night is stalking you
> In bright daylight.
>
> "I have stained the sun with black love...
> . . . ."
>
> —We fear, we dare not
> Relieve the royal grief.
> Stung by Theseus,
> The night assaulted him.
> But, following the dead home
> With our funeral song,
> We shall appease the black sun
> Of wild and sleepless passion.

This version of the poem, completed in January 1916, differed from the earlier drafts (1915) in showing less narrative fidelity to Racine.[23] The poet eliminated lines in the earlier drafts and replaced some of them with the far more meaningful suspension points.[24] Obviously Mandelstam wished to put considerable distance between this poem and Racine, a wish made further apparent by his inclusion in *Stone* III (1923), right after the first "Phaedra," of a fragment from Racine's tragedy in his own much later rendering.

The second "Phaedra" had to appear as a collage, not a pastiche, and its bonds with its sources had to be considerably weakened to accommodate as much of the present-day meaning as possible, shaped in the image of this proleptic imitation of the kenotic Christ. In this respect, the Acmeist Mandelstam did nothing different from what, say, the Futurist Maiakovskii did with a greater abandon and less equivocation. Consider the concluding lines from Maiakovskii's "The Backbone Flute" (1915):

> В праздник красьте сегодняшнее число.
> Творись,
> распятью равная магия.
> Видите —
> гвоздями слов
> прибит к бумаге я.
>
> Into a holiday paint today's date.
> Arise,

Prolepsis in Tristia: *1915–1917*

> Magic equal to the Crucifixion.
> See—
> With words, nails,
> I have been nailed to paper.

Compared to this Christ figure, Mandelstam's martyrs *avant la lettre*, even when their oppressive shawls were slipping, appeared overdressed. And in fact we can read Mandelstam's opening quotation from Racine as a confession of a poet who felt burdened by the "well-balanced" Acmeist shawls. Nevertheless, "Phaedra II," though still "classical,"[25] owes far more to the contemporary discourse on the primitive archaic culture of Ancient Greece (according to Nietzsche and Frazer) than to the style of Louis XIV, and as such it shares an emphasis on the unbridled and primitive with the works of Russian Futurists, whom Mandelstam, polemics aside, deeply respected.[26]

"What if a Greek should see our games," wrote Mandelstam in concluding *Stone*—and the second "Phaedra" does answer this wistful rhetorical question. The poet had resolved the conflict posed by the taboo and the attraction of "incest" by interpreting it as martyrdom, and there was no longer any need to erect elaborate screens concealing either the theme or the myth itself. More important, in the context of war and anticipation of civic cataclysm, the "Hellenized" and primitive version of the myth possessed the expressive potential that its earlier "distant" counterpart could not begin to rival. On the "personal" level, too, the myth could give a far more "open" expression to the theme of eros, aligning the poet's narrative of self-presentation with the convention of the "mystical marriage" between the poet and his land. Finally, to look at "Phaedra II" through the prism of Viacheslav Ivanov's theory, this perversely nuptial poem was a sign of the poet's "descent" from the heights of his individual communion with the world spirit; it symbolized his return to earth, to the famous metaphysical "soil" of Dostoevsky, in which he would plant himself as the proverbial "corn of wheat," redeeming the people with his self-imposed martyrdom and hastening the realization of the "symphonic" ideal.[27] In this respect, the opening poem of *Tristia* was a turning point, and it served as an introduction to Mandelstam's poetry after *Stone*, defining it as a record of ordeals and bringing together various masks of the suffering "bridegroom" to form a totality of a martyr's fate. Let us focus on a few specifics of the second "Phaedra."

First a word about the structure of the poem. As with its counterpart in *Stone*, "Phaedra II" falls into three parts. Unlike the first "Phaedra," however, it contains no authorial speech. Instead we hear only two voices: Phaedra, who, as Clarence Brown has shown, speaks the words of Racine's Phèdre; and the chorus, which is Mandelstam's own invention. Thus each of the three parts consists of a fragment of Phaedra's monologue, written in refined Alexandrines, and the commentary of the chorus, written, as befits a *vox populi*, in "primitive" rhymed trochaics (a "folk song" meter in the Russian tradition) full of ominous, incantatory repetitions.

After Phaedra had complained about the constraints imposed by her marriage and royal station, the chorus issues its first prolepsis, addressed indirectly to Phaedra: "In the *stone* Troezen, there shall come to pass a famous misfortune, the steps of the royal stairs will turn red from shame... And for the enamored mother a black sun will rise" [italics are mine]. How can one read these words in the context of Mandelstam's "narrative"? A poet who had named two of his previous collections *Stone* and was planning to issue the third, *Tristia*, under the title *New Stone*[28] was, no doubt, fully aware that "stone" connoted a metonym of the poet Mandelstam. Indeed, it is hardly possible to think of this epithet except as a metonym referring the reader to Mandelstam's earlier poetry, with its ambience of highbrow, petrified decorum. Taken together with the "stone" modifying Troezen, the "veils" oppressing Phaedra in both poems also become transparent, no longer an impassive facade concealing the flame of unrequited passion. Of course, such "confessions" do not suddenly "fly from one's lips," and indeed, Mandelstam began to prepare the reader for a change of course as early as 1914. "A *flame* is destroying my dry life" are the first words of his 1914 poem; "and now I am singing, not a stone, but a tree."[29] In "Phaedra II," to use a Jamesian formula, he was no longer "telling" but "showing," and the "classical shawls" that began "slipping from shoulders" in the last poem of *Stone* were very nearly cast off in the "confessional" overture to the poems of 1916–21.

"Phaedra II" could also be interpreted as effective apocalyptic prophecy: the "enamored mother" connoted Russia, oppressed by her imperial "splendor amid the shame" of injustice and slaughter, and the "stone Troezen" pointed to the imperial capital, Petrograd. The "royal stairs" of this city had already once turned "red from shame" over the famous "Bloody Sunday" that set off the 1905 revolution. And as many then suspected, it might be put to shame again. This view of the poem becomes less farfetched if we consider the essay Mandelstam composed six years later commemorating the event. The telling title of the essay, "The Bloody Mysterium of January 9," and the central simile of the roving crowd of demonstrators as a leaderless Greek chorus[30] make it possible for us to view as related the opening poem of *Tristia*,

Prolepsis in Tristia: *1915–1917*

"Pushkin and Skriabin," and Skriabin's unfinished apocalyptic *Mysterium,* as well as the contemporary discourse on tragedy as a form originating in sacrificial rituals of mystery religions that paved the way for the advent of Christianity. These two readings—the self-referential and the social—are not mutually exclusive; they are complementary and interdependent, like a microcosm and a macrocosm and, most important, like Christ's Passion and the suffering of humanity in the Christian mystery of the world redeemed.

The drama of Hippolytus and Phaedra, two innocents entrapped by Aphrodite and both eventually submitting to their fate, received in Mandelstam a Christian, kenotic interpretation. In "Pushkin and Skriabin," the "black sun"—the "sun of guilt" when it connoted the composer's death—had become the "sun of redemption" for Russia's archetypal poet, Pushkin—the double meaning itself recapitulating the ambiguity of Christ's Passion as it was understood by Mandelstam. For the very ambiguity of the word *passion,* which denotes either eros or the torment of martyrdom, suggests a link between sexual desire and a martyr's acceptance of pain and death in imitating Christ.[31] V. V. Gippius made much of this ambiguity in his *Pushkin and Christianity,*[32] and his "etymological" usage, typical of Mandelstam's milieu, associates the "incest" plot with the Christian aura enveloping Mandelstam's poem. The table of symbolization to which this vocabulary belonged was apparently so fixed that Phaedra's "black sun," its incestuous connotation notwithstanding, could reappear in Mandelstam's poem about his mother's funeral and function there as an unequivocal metonym of Christ's death on the cross.

Эта ночь непоправима,
А у вас еще светло.
У ворот Ерусалима
Солнце черное взошло.

Солнце желтое страшнее —
Баю баюшки баю —
В светлом храме иудеи
Хоронили мать мою.

Благодати не имея
И священства лишены,
В светлом храме иудеи
Отпевали прах жены.

И над матерью звенели
Голоса израильтян.

An Ending and a Beginning

> Я проснулся в колыбели,
> Черным солнцем осиян.
>
> 1916

> This night cannot be undone,
> But you still have light.
> At Jerusalem's gate,
> The black sun has risen.
>
> The yellow sun is more terrifying.
> Lulla-lulla-by,
> In a light temple, Judeans
> Were burying my mother.
>
> Not possessing grace
> And deprived of sanctification,
> In a light temple, Judeans
> Were holding a wake over the remains of a woman.
>
> And over the mother, rang
> The voices of the Israelites.
> —I awoke in my cradle,
> Illuminated by the black sun.[33]

Evidently, for the poet's mother, death under the aegis of the Jewish "yellow sun" was just that, death, whereas for her poet son, born under the black rays of Christianity, it was an occasion potentially full of sanctity and grace (*blagodat'*, charisma) as in the kenotic *imitatio Christi*.

To continue with "Phaedra II," why did Mandelstam use the word *mother*, when *stepmother* would have been far more appropriate ("Fear *your mother*, Hippolytus: Phaedra-night is stalking you in bright daylight")? This was inexactness uncharacteristic of the Acmeists. More striking, for one who was intimately familiar with the myth of Hippolytus, a substitution of one kinship term for another could not be a matter of indifference, all the more so since in Russian the words for "mother" and "stepmother" are identical prosodically when used in the genitive singular: *boisia materi, boisia machekhi*. If one cannot dismiss this confusion of terms as a casual slip, what was the significance of this substitution? Most likely Mandelstam, who, like every poet before him, felt free to embroider on the classical pattern, wished to emphasize the specifically "incestuous" aspect of the myth, fearing it would otherwise appear contaminated by a folkloric topos: the proverbial enmity between stepmother and stepchild.

And the final question: how do we locate the poet's self in a poem that generically represents a dramatic fragment? To appeal to the authority of T. S. Eliot, a lyric poet's choice of dramatic form implies a dispersal of the "I" among the cast of characters,[34] in this case the chorus, Phaedra, and Hippolytus, whose presence is implied in the warning to him spoken by the chorus. A conflict in Mandelstam's narrative of self-presentation could either take the "lyric" (or inner) form or, as in this poem, become dramatized. Here, the dramatization was performed in an emphatically "archaic" manner. An appeal to Greek tragedy—a genre of sacred drama embodying the synthesis of religion and art[35]—had a particular significance in Mandelstam's milieu. For a contemporary, then, the poem-fragment referred not merely to an ancient dramatic form but also to a genre comparable to a liturgy celebrating the gods and uniting and purifying the community. (Needless to say, the ritual notion of "catharsis" had not yet acquired the rational psychoanalytic meaning it has in our day.) The author of "Pushkin and Skriabin," who described himself as a true "Hellene," that is, one who combined in one person the tragic and the Christian essences, could not have thought otherwise. Aiming beyond Euripides at the very origins of tragedy, Mandelstam set up a clash between the lines from Racine's *Phèdre* and the song of the chorus, which, although composed by Mandelstam himself, possessed a more "ancient" and "primitive" air than either *Phèdre* or *Hippolytus* taken alone.

The thrice-repeated refrain in the chorus's second entry is not a feature found in Euripides but one belonging more properly to the epic, to folk laments, and to incantations.[36] The poem's closure, the concluding lines of the chorus, suggests the nature of Mandelstam's usage: "But . . . with our *funeral song, we shall appease* the black sun of wild and sleepless passion." In Euripides, on the contrary, the chorus expresses no such intentions; it merely broadcasts the story about the great grief of royalty. For Mandelstam, then, the chorus's song, and perhaps song in general, served a healing, purifying function, not so much as a narrative with which the audience could identify but as an incantation and an exorcism—a catharsis achieved by means of verbal magic.[37] Hence the incantatory refrain "in bright daylight"—or, more precisely, "in white daylight" (*sredi belogo dnia*)—which has two connotations: the topos of Russian folk poetry on the one hand, and the mystical high noon that blinds the soul in a passionate afflatus before endowing it with the ultimate vision of divine light on the other.[38]

A conflation of several referents, Mandelstam's "Phaedra" was meant to present the myth in an archetypal, distilled fashion, to interpret it as an instance of martyrdom, to locate the dramatic action in mystical time at the point of epiphany, between Darkness and Light, and, no less important, to exorcise the spirit of the "famous misfortune." (Clearly this "mystical" and "magical" interpretation was coextensive with "erotic" and "social.") In short, Mandelstam endeavored to recreate an archaic, syncretic, undifferentiated ritual in which art and eros were fused with the sacrament. According to one of the most authoritative comparativists of the time, A. N. Veselovskii (1838–1906), whose writings Mandelstam must have studied at the university, such were the conditions of modern drama at its very origins, when it was as yet unseparated from the primitive sacral "games":

> When the most primitive animistic view of the world evolved in the direction of the more definite concepts of the deity and the framework of myth, [then] ritual took a more stable form of a *cult*, and this development found its expression in the stability of choric action: there appeared religious games [*sic*] in which the element of prayer and sacrifice was supported by symbolic mime. . . .
> Drama[, then,] was an exorcism in personae.[39]

As it functions in the *Tristia*, the second "Phaedra" sets up a mythic pattern, a frame to be imposed on the poems that follow. In them, to paraphrase Mandelstam's remarks about Villon, the poet plays the roles of both the perpetrator and the victim of "incest," martyred in a proleptic *imitatio Christi*, a prophet of the imminent "famous misfortune" that makes the "steps of the royal stairs . . . turn red from shame"; and finally, he is a mourner, even a chorus of mourners, accompanying those who have passed away in order to make the way straight for the coming new and yet unknown age. And while there is no proof that Mandelstam had the entire *Tristia* outlined in his mind as he was composing the second "Phaedra," the poems of 1916–20 followed the script of "Pushkin and Skriabin" and its companion, "Phaedra II." In the poetry of 1915–16, Mandelstam entered a new thematic and stylistic period in which the Blokian myth of the poet and his mystical bride would be transformed into the Mandelstamian poet-Hippolytus and Russia-Phaedra. These two or, including the chorus, three roles formed a basic design for a patchwork of masks—the primary colors of Joseph's coat.

EXCHANGING GIFTS: TSVETAEVA AND MANDELSTAM

Dis manibusque sacrum.

It was in Moscow, in the spring of 1916, and I was giving him, instead of myself, the gift of Moscow.   MARINA TSVETAEVA, Letter to Bakhrakh (1923)[40]

But False Dmitrii viewed himelf quite differently: his deportment was that of a legitimate, natural tsar, completely certain of his royal origin. . . .

Prolepsis in Tristia: 1915–1917

How he came to believe this about himself has remained a mystery, historical as much as psychological.
        V. KLIUCHEVSKII, *Lectures on Russian History*

The Latin phrase above, a frequent inscription on Roman tombs, was chosen by Innokentii Annenskii as an epigraph to his "bacchic drama" *Thamyris the Cythara Player*. The words mean roughly, "A place sacred to gods and shades," and as a verbal frame of the play they served as a metaphor for Annenskii's view of the origin and function of art. In short, art was a tomb—a human monument associated with the ordeal of death and functioning as a place where the exchange between the gods above and the spirits below was effected.

Dis manibusque sacrum is interesting in yet another respect. For an ear attuned to folk etymology, it may evoke a gesture of outstretched hands (*manus*) holding out a gift or, in the context of funeral rites, an offering for a deity (which is, perhaps, why the 1957 edition of Annenskii translated it as "For gods and the shades of the dead this offering"). The gesture itself, whether sacred or not, remains the same, and even in its modern form can be traced to the religious and social rituals of exchange that establish or maintain bonds among all the members of a community, including the dead, the living, and the gods they worship.[41] For gods also give, not only receive, gifts. From them come misfortunes (the box of the "all-giving" *Pan-dora*), or they can make a person unusually "gifted," that is, endowed with a special *charisma*, for which one must give thanks in the hope of avoiding hubris—for gods, a singularly offensive sin.[42] As the story of Pandora suggests, gifts also carry an aura of surprise, mystery, indeterminacy. This aspect of gift-giving found its counterpart in Weber's ideal type of a charismatic figure, who has to prove to his followers that he possesses the special gift as much as he is possessed by it.[43]

Receiving a coveted gift (etymologically, gifts are hortatory, venal, and venomous as well as charismatic)[44] often leads to unanticipated consequences. We do well to fear the Danaeans bearing gifts, even though we cannot do much about it, since we are not supposed to look a gift horse in the mouth. These jack-in-the-box surprises, combining the freedom of gift-giving with the compulsion to give and receive in order to appease, occur not only in exchanges among people or among gods (Hades and Persephone) but also in those involving gods and mortals. Annenskii's Thamyris learned about the price of gods' gifts, just as Zeus eventually learned about the generous-looking and savory but, in fact, mean sacrifices offered him by mortals on the advice of the trickster Prometheus. All of this serves to introduce a poem composed as part of a *poetic exchange*—a conventional genre whose ritual origins were laid bare by the modernists Mandelstam and Tsvetaeva. That is to say, the traditional form of an "epistolary" exchange between two poets (hence, poems may be *addressed*) took the form of a more archaic, and therefore supremely modern, ceremonial exchange of gifts, a Russian potlatch of sorts.

In this exchange Osip Mandelstam courted Marina Tsvetaeva, who, "instead of herself," offered the Petersburg Hippolytus a "gift of Moscow," a city as emblematic of native Russia as St. Petersburg was of the country's turn to the West. Prompted as it was by a "foreigner's" visit to the ancient capital city, the exchange was conducted for the most part in the native key. The poems centered around stylistic and thematic emblems of Russia: "folksy" vocabulary and occasionally syntax, set epithets, churches and icons. Most important for Mandelstam, the exchange revolved around significant junctures in Russia's relations with the West, those tangible symbols, or synecdoches, of the country's ambiguous self-image: the Time of Troubles, the Schism, and, of course, the reign of Peter the Great. The historical drama of Russia's lasting encounter with the West, presented as a national-historical identity crisis, was reenacted by the two poets; or, to rely on a different vocabulary, the macrocosm of history, itself a recapitulation of Christian revelation in Mandelstam's scheme ("Pushkin and Skriabin"), had "returned" to be embodied in the microcosm of the romance between the two poets.

Whoever first set these terms for the exchange, both Mandelstam and Tsvetaeva adhered to them faithfully. Let us now take a look at Tsvetaeva's part, particularly her adumbration of the *Boris Godunov* script. Styling herself *Maryna* Mniszek, the Polish wife of the first pretender, and Mandelstam, False Dmitrii, *Marina* Tsvetaeva produced the following "Nativity" scene:

> Над темной твоею люлькой,
> Димитрий, над люлькой пышной
> Твоею, Марина Мнишек,
> Стояла одна и та же
> Двусмысленная звезда.

> Over your dark cradle,
> Dmitrii, over the luxurious cradle
> Of yours, Maryna Mniszek,
> There stood one and the same
> Ambiguous star.[45]

Prolepsis in Tristia: *1915–1917*

Composed twelve days before the beginning of Easter, this poem points to the two fundamental and related themes of the exchange: the ordeals of martyrdom that a poet must endure to fulfill his mission (which consists of redemptive ordeals) and the ambiguity involved in presenting oneself in terms of another (False Dmitrii) pretending to be someone else (St. Dmitrii the Tsarevich) who, if he had indeed been murdered, died in imitation of Christ, who had died on the cross in order to redeem all. (Analogies of this sort are better grasped in the twilight rather than the light of reason.) To make it less confusing, if the son of Ivan the Terrible, Tsarevich Dmitrii (later canonized), had indeed been assassinated on the orders of Boris Godunov (allegedly in 1591, at the age of nine), then the first False Dmitrii was indeed a pretender, even though his mother (by then, nun Martha) claimed to have recognized in him her son. But what if the pretender's claims were genuine? Then the False Dmitrii was the true Dmitrii, his violent death acquiring the attributes of martyred saints. Tsvetaeva continued with her essay in extended historical analogy:

> В марфиной черной келье
> Яркое ожерелье
> — Солнце в ночи! — горит.
>
> Памятливыми глазами
> Впилась — народ замер.
> Памятливыми губами
> Впилась — в чей — рот.
>
> Сама инокиня
> Признала сына!
> Как же ты — для нас — не тот!

> In Martha's black cell,
> A bright necklace
> —The sun in the night!—burns.
>
> With remembering eyes,
> She thrust—people froze.
> With remembering lips,
> She thrust—into whose?—mouth.
>
> The nun herself
> Recognized her son!
> How, then, can you—for us—not be the one!

Over the "Bethlehem" of their view of poetry and history there indeed hung the same "ambiguous star." Those born under it were subject to its astral influence and vacillated between holiness and damnation,

Exchanging Gifts: Tsvetaeva and Mandelstam

though avoiding at all costs what generations of Russian intellectuals since Herzen had avoided—the "bourgeois European" *juste milieu*.

It is tempting to hear in these lines the echo of possible confessions offered to Tsvetaeva by Osip Mandelstam (can a Jew be a Russian poet, rather than just pretend to be one?), just as one can discern in them an echo of Mandelstam's second "Phaedra" (the "sun in the night," the mother's ambiguous kiss of no less ambiguous recognition). I shall yield to this temptation only so far as it helps substantiate the theme of ambiguity—a poet's uncertainty about his mission, about his self and his country, in short, about everything. Uncertainty is among the oldest afflictions—as old, at least, as the world's first visionary, unsure of the nature of his vision. In prerevolutionary Russia, however, a country ill equipped for the modern age yet rushing into it, uncertainty reached epidemic proportions. Now it manifested itself in social and economic crises, now in mysticism, now in a sudden crop of political agents-provocateurs like Degaev, Azef, and Malinovskii, who maintained a dual allegiance to the police and to the revolution. (Andrei Belyi's *St. Petersburg* [1912] comes readily to mind.) A barely "emancipated" middle-class Jew with a vocation rather than a safe profession, one whose mission was to "remind" Christian Russians of the Resurrection of Christ, was bound to suffer from uncertainty most acutely. Why else would he have insisted with such ardor on the poet's "sense of inner rightness?"[46] Hence the motif of the pretender, central to the exchange between Tsvetaeva—herself in need of inventing less "prosaic" origins[47]—and Mandelstam.

In another poem offered to Mandelstam, Tsvetaeva (this time casting off the mask of Maryna Mniszek) presented herself as a sort of *bonne soeur sans merci,* conferring on her "brother" a very special and complex gift. In part a blessing, this was a gift one could not get enough of, but as an offer of a new identity, it conferred on the recipient an obligation to risk everything for the cause to be pursued under the protection of this same blessing. This was, as Tsvetaeva put it, the "gift of Moscow"—unlike St. Petersburg, a city "not wrought by hands"[48]—a present that imposed a very specific historical framework on the vocation of poet. And Mandelstam felt compelled to respond to the "call." I shall cite Tsvetaeva's poem in toto:

Из рук моих — нерукотворный град
Прими, мой странный, мой прекрасный брат.

По церковке — все сорок сороков
И реющих над ними голубков;

Prolepsis in Tristia: *1915–1917*

И Спасские — с цветами — ворота,
Где шапка православного снята;

Часовню звездную — приют от зол —
Где вытертый — от поцелуев — пол.

Пятисоборный несравненный круг
Прими, мой древний, вдохновенный друг.

К Нечаянныя Радости в саду
Я гостя чужеземного сведу.

Червонные возблещут купола,
Бессонные взгремят колокола,

И на тебя с багряных облаков
Уронит богородица покров,

И встанешь ты, исполнен дивных сил...
— Ты не раскаешься, что ты меня любил.
        31 Марта 1916

Out of my hands—this city not wrought by hand—
Accept, my strange, my beautiful brother.

All the forty times forty churches—one by one,
And the little doves hovering over them;

And with flowers the [Kremlin's] Savior's Gates,
Where a Russian Orthodox man takes off his hat;

The starry chapel—a haven from evils—
Where the floor is worn by kisses.

The incomparable five-cathedral ring—
Accept, my ancient, my inspired friend.

To the Unhoped-for Joy, which stands in a garden,
I shall lead my guest from a foreign land.

The red cupola will begin to shine,
The sleepless bell will begin to chime,

And from the crimson clouds, the Mother of God
Will let her shroud fall over you,

And you will rise, full of wondrous strength...
You won't regret that you've loved me.[49]

To have loved her, even without reciprocity as the closing implies, meant to receive "Russianness" as a gift, including the protection of the Mother of God and her fortifying blessing—a "charisma" that could assure the success of the poet's pursuit. And if he persisted in his unwelcome wooing, the following poem warns him, he would be wise to light a candle at the Iverskaia church and pray to the Mother of God to shield him from the evil spells issuing from the other corner of Marina's mouth:

> Мой — рот — разгарчив,
> Даром что свят — вид.
> Как золотой ларчик,
> Иверская горит.
>
> Ты озорство прикончи
> Да засвети свечу,
> Чтобы с тобой нонче
> Не было — как хочу.
> 31 Марта 1916
>
> My mouth is fiery,
> Even if holy the looks.
> Like a golden box.
> The Iverskaia is shining.
>
> You'd better snuff out your pranks
> And have a candle lit
> Not to have now happen to you—
> What I wish would happen.[50]

The silver of divine magnanimity lined a wrathful cloud.

Mandelstam wrote four poems that can be considered part of this exchange of gifts. All four of them appeared only in *Tristia* but, significantly, not as a single cycle; two followed "Phaedra II" and "The Bestiary," and the other two were inserted in different places in the collection. The one least relevant for the exchange develops the theme of native Russia's ambiguity: her tendency to unbridled turmoil, as in the emblematic *Smutnoe vremia* (Time of Troubles), and the blessed Hellenic "fire" of Orthodox Christianity, Dionysus made meek,[51] embodied in the Kremlin cathedrals.

> О этот воздух, смутой пьяный
> На черной площади Кремля!
> Качают шаткий «мир» смутьяны,
> Тревожно пахнут тополя.
>
> . . . .
>
> Архангельский и Воскресенья
> Просвечивают как ладонь —
> Повсюду скрытое горенье,
> В кувшинах спрятанный огонь...

Prolepsis in Tristia: *1915–1917*

> O this air, drunk with trouble[!]
> In the black square of the Kremlin,
> The troublemakers are rocking the shaky "peace,"
> The linden trees smell alarming.
>
> . . . .
>
> The [cathedrals of the] Archangel and the Resurrection
> Are translucent like the palm of your hand—
> Concealed burning is everywhere,
> Fire hidden in the jugs...[52]

Of the two poems placed together, "In the Diaphony of a Maidenly Chorus" and "In a Peasant Sledge Lined with Straw," the first seems to record Mandelstam's settling into the unfamiliar environment of Moscow. Here is an Acmeist unpacking his bags to surround himself with dear reminders of "European" identity (if not ancestry). Viewed through the forest of such *lares* and *penates,* the Kremlin became the Acropolis (a justifiable transposition etymologically); the Dormition Cathedral, built by Fioravanti, led to Florence (perhaps via Tsvetaeva's name, meaning "of flowers");[53] and the addressee herself blended with the five-cupola cathedrals, Homer's "rosy-fingered Eos," and what looks like an eighteenth-century Russian painting in the classical idiom, "reminding" the poet of

> . . . явление Авроры,
> Но с русским именем и в шубке меховой.
> 1916
>
> . . . the appearance of Aurora,
> But with a Russian name and in a coat of fur.

For her part, Tsvetaeva insisted that Mandelstam accept *her* Russia, one unmediated by the Acmeist catalog of Europe's "great works." This offering Mandelstam—a precursor in reverse[54]—could not refuse in spirit, even if the flesh was hesitant and wanting. The poem that followed the "diaphonic maidenly chorus" of the "tender" and "Florentine" Moscow cathedrals accounted for both his hesitancy and his willingness to accept Tsvetaeva's flattering, challenging, and apparently terrifying gift. I would like to read this poem with special care.

> На розвальнях, уложенных соломой,
> Едва прикрытые рогожей роковой,
> От Воробьевых гор до церковки знакомой
> Мы ехали огромною Москвой.
>
> А в Угличе играют дети в бабки,
> И пахнет хлеб, оставленный в печи.

Exchanging Gifts: Tsvetaeva and Mandelstam

По улицам меня везут без шапки,
И теплятся в часовне три свечи.

Не три свечи горели, а три встречи —
Одну из них сам Бог благословил,
Четвертой не бывать, а Рим далече, —
И никогда он Рима не любил.

Ныряли сани в черные ухабы,
И возвращался с гульбища народ.
Худые мужики и злые бабы
Переминались у ворот.

Сырая даль от птичьих стай чернела,
И связанные руки затекли;
Царевича везут, немеет страшно тело —
И рыжую солому подожгли.

                                        1916

Barely covered with fateful sackcloth,
We were riding in a peasant sledge lined with straw,
From the Sparrow Hills to the familiar little church
Across enormous Moscow.

And in Uglich, children are playing dice,
And it smells of bread left in the oven.
They are carting me through the streets without a hat,
And in a chapel, three candles are flickering warmly.

It wasn't three candles burning, but three encounters—
One of them blessed by God himself,
A fourth there shall not be, and Rome is far away,—
And never did he love Rome.

The sledge was diving into black potholes,
And the folk were returning from their revelries.
Thin muzhiks and their angry women
Were nibbling at sunflower seed by the gates.

The wet yonder turned black with flocks of birds,
And the tied hands have swollen.
They are carting the tsarevich, the body is growing terribly numb,
And the rust-colored straw has been set on fire.[55]

No other Russian poet of this century could represent both the historical and the tangible, material nature of a scene in a single sweep of the eye with as much mastery as could Mandelstam. The principle of composition here is similar to that of the preceding "Moscow-Florence" piece: to set up a network of correspondences between "this" world and the "other". Ever since Baudelaire, the symbolists had been educating the European reader to make sense of these puzzles, but Mandelstam's *correspondences* had a particular Acmeist bent to them. They involved (1) the choice of other worlds to correspond to this one, and (2) a "balanced" relationship among them.

With regard to the first characteristic, Mandelstam linked in this poem present-day Moscow to the landmarks of Russia's past: the seventeenth-century Schism and Alexander Herzen; Tsarevich Dmitrii and the son of Peter the Great, Tsarevich Aleksei; the messianic doctrine of the Muscovite State and the brutal mass executions accompanying the reign of the two most fateful Russian tsars, Ivan the Terrible and Peter. All of these were highly potent and highly ambiguous historical symbols, and at first glance Mandelstam's use of them seems to have nothing in common with the Symbolists' preference for the more abstract and mystical "higher reality"—the *realiora* of Viacheslav Ivanov.[56] Yet we need only recall the historical view that Mandelstam shared with many of his contemporaries—eternal recurrence and the historical cycles of Nietzsche and Vico in a christological, chiliastic interpretation—to realize that the poet's "history" was as evocative of the angelic or infernal spheres as anything that a Symbolist guru could appropriate or coin.

The difference lay, rather, in the role that major historical events played in the formative years of the older and younger generations. Nothing that transpired in the last two decades of the nineteenth century could measure up to the Revolution of 1905–7, when Mandelstam was in his teens; to the tumultuous 1912, when he was barely twenty; or, of course, to the Great War, whose full brunt fell on the men of his generation. Combined with the "classical," decorous world of St. Petersburg (architecturally as much as politically and socially), these circumstances help explain why the Petersburg-dwelling Acmeists felt they could settle for a seemingly modest program, one calling for an Apollonian balance between the one and the "other" world. This one, surrounded by the sea of an uncouth, "Scythian" Russia, had already come to the edge of the precipice,[57] and unlike the Futurists, these *Petersburg* poets were satisfied with the dramatic contrast and disinclined to give it another push.[58]

Perhaps of greater relevance to poetry, the network of correspondences accumulated in the Romantic tradition (including the Symbolists) had condensed and become routinized.[59] Even if unmentioned, this network was always taken for granted, just as the astral meaning of the zodiac was in the back of the mind of a medieval astronomer charting a planet's course. To dwell on these basics of contemporary consciousness, to spell them out, was, to follow the Acmeists' Petersburg parlance, ethically "unchaste" and in aesthetic "bad taste."[60]

But there is a volume of difference between not mentioning an a priori assumption and suggesting that it does not exist. The Symbolists' critical investment—the years of hammering into the brain of the Russian reader the ABCs of magic, mysticism, and myth—was beginning to pay off, even if the Acmeists and the Futurists were now collecting most of the profits. For the more "tangible" the Acmeists' descriptions (specifically Mandelstam's) and the more "vulgar" and streetwise the poetry of Maiakovskii, the greater must be the weight of the angels and devils sitting on the other *invisible* pan of the scale. After all, even such a vintage Acmeist as Mandelstam of the *Stone* period could be pronounced by a sympathetic and knowledgeable observer to be a "philosophical poet in the manner of Aleksandr Blok."[61] A similar equilibrium existed between a poem's "actual" detail and the corresponding historical "symbol." In the poem preceding "In the Sledge," "Muscovy" was in perfect equilibrium with "Florence"; with "In the Sledge" the balance may have shifted toward the symbolic, but still not enough to upset appreciably the Acmeist scale. "Things are what they appear to be" and "things are never what they appear to be." For Mandelstam and the poets of his generation, who did not need to waste their breath pointing out "correspondences" to the unsophisticated reader, these were complementary rather than mutually exclusive statements.

Briefly, how is one to read this poem? Mocking the Symbolists in the early 1920s, Mandelstam wrote that in their world no single thing could be itself, that their "every broom" refused to sweep but asked instead to be taken to a witches' Sabbath.[62] But Mandelstam's new Acmeist broom was no more designed for sweeping, in however inventive a manner, than was that of the Symbolists. Reading this poem, we wonder whether the "fateful sackcloth" or the "straw" or the "peasant sledge" had much to do with actual sacks, stuffing, or transportation, or only with those of the mind (even though there exists undoubtedly a greater immediate kinship between the two parallel series of signifiers and signifieds than between flying and brooms). Rather, these objects remind a Russian reader of the famous painting by Vasilii Surikov, *Boiarynia Morozova*, which portrays with great emotional intensity a disciple of the Schismatic archpriest Avvakum as she is being *carted to the stake in a peasant sledge lined with straw*. (It is worth noting that Avvakum's *Vita* was purported to be one of Mandelstam's "companion books.")[63] The somber tones of public humiliation, death, and mourning that Surikov had conveyed with color and line were condensed by Mandelstam in the highly alliterative *rogozhei rokovoi* (fateful sackcloth),⁶⁴ with all the melancholy and sinisterness that these two veteran words of human misfortune connote. The poem thus opens thematically in the "martyrdom" key, and stylistically in the key of native, hard-core Russia. The challenge of Tsvetaeva's gift was accepted.

Given these two tonalities, the Sparrow (now Lenin) Hills also perform a double duty: first as a landmark, the high point of Moscow, and second as a synecdoche of Mandelstam's other "companion book," *My Past and Thoughts,* by the father of Russian socialism, Alexander Herzen. For Herzen, as for his friend the poet Nikolai Ogarev, these were the "holy hills," where the two of them (mere boys then) stood "leaning against each other and, having suddenly embraced, . . . made a vow, in the sight of the whole of Moscow, to sacrifice our lives to the cause of our chosen struggle."⁶⁵ The cause of political struggle for Herzen and Ogarev was for Mandelstam the mission of a Russian poet. In 1923, in an essay devoted to Pasternak's *My Sister—Life,* he once again resorted to this Russian synecdoche of "sacred cause" and "struggle," this time in order to praise the talent of the Moscow poet for conveying the revolutionary élan and—the highest praise for Mandelstam—for upholding Russia's "Hellenic spirit":

> Of course, Herzen and Ogarev, when in their youth they were standing at the top of the Sparrow Hills, experienced the physiologically sacred enthusiasm of space and a bird's flight. Pasternak's poetry has spoken to us about those moments: this was the glittering *Nike* translated from the Acropolis to the Sparrow Hills.⁶⁶

Although it may not be readily apparent, Herzen and Avvakum went well together. Herzen was the first to present modern Russian authorship as martyrdom,⁶⁷ and Avvakum, seen in this light, was Russia's first martyred author,⁶⁸ completing his autobiography shortly before he was burned at the stake. So much for the Sparrow Hills, the origin of the poet's journey through Moscow.

The destination of this journey is much harder to determine. In fact, there is no reason to believe that the poem refers to any specific church. But even as an anonymous item, the "familiar little church," as the opposite of the "holy hills," defines the coordinates of the entire "Moscow" gamut: from fiery "revolutionary" martyrdom to the meek and diminutive Russian Orthodox piety. In fact, since the mention of this church introduces the theme of Uglich, the town where Tsarevich Dmitrii was murdered (or was he?), it might be related to the first pretender (or was he the true Dmitrii?). Another possibility, if we use

Tsvetaeva's blessings and warnings as a clue, might be the famous church of the miracle-working Iverskaia icon of the Mother of God, the protectress of Moscow.[69] In any case, the "familiar little church" is no more (nor less) an actual church than the "straw," the "sledge," the "sackcloth," and the "Sparrow Hills" are their realistic counterparts. For what we have in this stanza, and in the poem at large, is a palimpsest of *corresponding* and mutually transparent historical layers that allows the reader to see the present as a return of the past. What makes these layers correspond thematically is a complex polyvalent motif of uncertainty about the nature of one's mission: for Dmitrii (or Dmitriis), sainthood and royalty or damnation; for Avvakum, sainthood or infernal heresy; for Russia, a "Western" or "Eastern" way; for Herzen, the illegitimate son of a Russian nobleman, who spent most of his life in European exile, a commitment to the grand scale of "Russian" values or the "just milieu" of the bourgeois West;[70] for the poet Mandelstam, the degree to which the "charisma" of his vocation was genuine. Although the formula was lucid, its "terms" were barely sketched out, thus enabling the reader to project his own terms onto the poet's persona,[71] which would then reflect them back in a condensed form. Tsvetaeva's gift tested Mandelstam's "charisma," that is, his ability to carry out his mission. Mandelstam responded by trying on the masks lying close at hand—all compatible with the ambiguous martyrdom of Hippolytus and Phaedra.

As the poem continues, the masks become limited to an indeterminate, generic tsarevich, in fact, a conflated image: the true Dmitrii of Uglich, a child of nine who accidently fell on a knife and died (or was murdered, or was wounded and survived); the pretender (if that is indeed what he was); and finally, the son of Peter the Great, Tsarevich Aleksei, whom his father (was he really the father, or was he some infinitely more infernal impostor, the Antichrist?)[72] ordered executed for conspiring against him.

Even without Tsvetaeva's vaguely folkloric "gift" poem, it is obvious that Mandelstam was measuring himself against the figure of a folkloric prince who had just been given or promised the Moscow crown. In Russian the words for Christian marriage and for being crowned king are the same, and in fairy tales the tsareviches frequently combine the two exploits (an etymological and folkloric justification for Tsvetaeva's offering Moscow in place of herself), as did Hippolytus and Oedipus, if in a peculiar sense, in Euripides and Sophocles. This "peculiar sense" Mandelstam conveyed through his choice of masks: his tsareviches, like those of Troezen and Thebes, came to an ambiguous end. As heroes of fairy tales, they ended badly, but as tragic figures,

Prolepsis in Tristia: *1915–1917*

especially in Mandelstam's christological sense, like Morozova and Avvakum, they died the redeeming death of a martyr. This requires further elaboration.

According to the official report, Tsarevich Dmitrii was playing the game of *tychka* or *svaika* when he had an epileptic seizure and fell on a knife.[73] The game Mandelstam had children play in Uglich was a form of dice played with bones, *babki*[74]—a substitution that endowed a well-known story with a powerful symbolic meaning. One of Heraclitus's more famous aphorisms, translated literally from its Russian rendering into English, reads: "Eternity is a child playing dice [*kosti*]—a child's kingdom."[75] In these specific historical circumstances, this obscure aphorism of the Eleatic philosopher functions as a prolepsis, recalling the two famous prophecies about the child who would rule over the peaceful world (Isa. 11:6) or the *pax romana* (Virgil's Fourth Eclogue).[76] Does the "babe" have to be sacrificed again and again? Mandelstam's focus on martyrdom begged the question.

Later on, in the early 1920s, looking back at the years of the Great War and the revolution, he would return to the image of the child "playing dice," once again puzzling over why people could not settle for the one all-redeeming sacrifice. In "The Age" (1922), he wrote:

> Век мой, зверь мой, кто сумеет
> Заглянуть в твои зрачки
> И своею кровью склеит
> Двух столетий позвонки?
>
> My age, my beast, who shall be able
> To look into your eyes
> And glue together with his own blood
> The vertebrae of the two centuries?

And further on:

> Словно нежный хрящ ребенка —
> Век младенческой земли,
> Снова в жертву, как ягненка,
> Темя жизни принесли.
>
> Like a tender cartilage of a child,
> Is the age of the infant earth,—
> Again, as if it were a lamb,
> The crown of life has been sacrificed.

In the 1923 "He Who Found a Horseshoe," the image became part of Mandelstam's melancholy apocalyptic prophecy:

Дети играют в бабки позвонками умерших животных.
Хрупкое летоисчисление нашей эры подходит к концу.

Children are playing dice [*babki*] with the vertebrae of dead animals.
Our era's fragile count of years is coming to an end.

In the "Slate Ode" (1923), Mandelstam assumed a more upbeat attitude when speaking about history reaping the mature harvest of time:

Плод нарывал. Зрел виноград.
День бушевал, как день бушует.
И в бабки нежная игра,
И в полдень злых овчарок шубы;
Как мусор с ледяных высот —
Изнанка образов зеленых —
Вода голодная течет,
Крутясь, играя, как звереныш,

The fruit was swelling. The vine maturing.
The day was raging as a day can rage.
And the tender game of dice [*babki*],
And the fur of vicious sheepdogs at high noon;
Like rubbish coming down from the icy heights—
The other side of verdant images—
Hungry water is rushing,
Swirling, playing, like a baby beast.[77]

This "sacrificial" context of "In the Sledge" makes less enigmatic the smell of the "bread left in the oven." Broadly evocative of the peasant, native Russia, it brings to mind the sacramental bread of the Eucharist—in apposition to the human sacrifice of the preceding line. For a reader belonging to the Russian Orthodox culture, for one who had lived through the first year and a half of the world war and had seen recruits, some as young as seventeen, go to the front, these thoughts and associations would not appear unusual. The last two lines of the stanza sharply focus this juxtaposition of actual victimization with the "bloodless sacrifice." Written in the immediate present indicative, as is the rest of the stanza, the third line introduces the speaker directly, in the first person, and in a state—transported hatless—that traditionally signified the public humiliation of a criminal condemned to die.[78] A man in this predicament would do well to have a candle lit (and three would be better) before the miracle-working Icon of Our Lady. These alternations between the spirit and the letter of history (the Eucharist and the ongoing slaughter)[79] spill over into the next stanza via what A. N. Veselovskii termed "negative parallelism." This device, inti-

Prolepsis in Tristia: *1915–1917*

mately associated with magic spells and riddles, is characteristic of Russian folk poetry and may be classified as an intermediary trope, standing somewhere between simile and metaphor, at once differentiating between and bringing together a trope's vehicle and tenor.[80]

This negative (*not* candles *but* encounters) parallelism (*three* of both) introduces a thematic alternation from the motif of protection, intercession, and "bloodless sacrifice" to the motif of the "reason of state." Part of the stanza invokes the famous messianic political formula that assigned to the Muscovite state, after the fall of Constantinople in 1453, the role of the third Rome. Its author, monk Filofei (Philotheus), wrote to Basil III, the father of Ivan the Terrible:

> Hear this, oh pious Tsar! Two Romes have fallen, the third—Moscow—stands, and a fourth there shall not be. In Your powerful Tsardom, our catholic [*sobornaia*] Church alone shines, under the heaven, with its piety brighter than the sun; all the Orthodox tsardoms have gathered together in Your one Tsardom; on the whole earth, You alone are a Christian Tsar.[81]

The wistful "and Rome is far away" (an evocation of Pushkin)[82] that follows Filofei's formula contrasts sharply with the stern and solemn reminder of one's loyalty and suggests that the speaker of the poem might have wished to be nearer the Eternal City. The melancholy tone of this line is in turn drowned in another categorical statement, which concludes the stanza: "And never did he love Rome." Three voices are discernible in this patchwork of quotations: the harsh and accusing voice of the state, the small and wistful voice of one who seems to have been contemplating betrayal, and finally, the voice coming in the latter's defence.

This classification of voices assumes that the "wistful" speaker functions here as the antecedent of the one who "never did love Rome." If Mandelstam had in mind God, as has been suggested,[83] he would surely have capitalized the personal pronoun, as the Russian orthography then required.[84] Because he did not, the reader has no choice but to locate the antecedent among the poet's many masks. One of them, Mandelstam himself, was not entirely without blame, for only six months before his trip to Moscow he had published an essay, "Petr Chaadaev," in which he called Filofei's doctrine "a sickly invention of Kievan [*sic*] monks."[85] To add insult to injury, the penultimate poem of *Stone* (1916), its print barely dry when "In the Sledge" was composed, contained a poetic birth certificate that hardly accords with the claim of an ordinary Russian Orthodox poet: "I was born in Rome and Rome has returned to me."[86] But then the False Dmitrii, too, was a Catholic (secretly converted) who, as tsar of Russia, attended Orthodox services in Moscow. And yet another unfortunate tsarevich might fit the bill: Aleksei, the miserable, scheming son of Peter the Great, who had taken refuge from his father in Italy and was tricked into coming back.

The text that mediates between Tsarevich Aleksei as an actual historical personage and Mandelstam's "tsarevich" seems to be none other than D. S. Merezhkovskii's novel, *The Antichrist: Peter and Alexis* (1905), part of a trilogy with the very serious title *Christ and the Antichrist*.[87] Its two previous parts, *The Death of the Gods: Julian the Apostate* (1896) and *Gods Resurrected: Leonardo da Vinci* (1901)—a "home university" for the contemporary Russian reader, in the words of D. S. Mirsky[88]—served as the novelistic credo of an advocate of Hellenistic, pagan antiquity, of its sensibility, sensuality, and worldview, both in their historical realm and during their rebirth in Renaissance Europe. *Peter and Alexis,* however, was written after Merezhkovskii had switched from his Nietzschean worship of the Greeks to advocacy of the Third Testament that would produce a synthesis of Hellenic corporeality and Christian spirituality, a new humanity of spiritualized flesh.[89] More important, the novel rested on two basic patterns: marriage, in both the specific and the most general sense, and the mission of a kenotic *imitatio Christi* culminating in the martyr's transubstantiation.[90] Tsarevich Aleksei and the author's alter ego, the wanderer Tikhon, participate in both these patterns.

I do not mean to suggest that Mandelstam would have been otherwise unaware of the life history of the tsarevich, particularly that he died under torture before he was to be executed on his father's orders. His education was too good for that. Nevertheless, Merezhkovskii's novel popularized this period of Russian history and, more important, presented it using the historiosophical, mystico-religious vocabulary on which Mandelstam and his generation had been weaned. Dealing with the time of great religious and civil dissension, the novel transformed this period into an elaborate historical metaphor for modern Russia, which was undergoing an equally profound crisis marked by dislocations, civil strife, and the rapid collapse of notions defining the individual and the collective self. According to Merezhkovskii, the beginning of the eighteenth century and the beginning of the twentieth both offered Russia a historical opportunity for the ultimate religious synthesis, and the pathos of *Peter and Alexis* aimed at taking advantage of history's generous second "throw of the dice." It showed the present-day players how their predecessors had not only missed their chance but also suffered to clear the way for *the* game in the country's future.

Finally, for Merezhkovskii—if we follow the implications of the

Prolepsis in Tristia: 1915–1917

trilogy's title—the history of Europe, including Russia, could be read as a symbolic record of the struggle between the Antichrist (the ultimate "pretender-tsarevich") and the one authentic "tsarevich," Christ the Savior. Recall Nikolai Stavrogin of Dostoevsky's *The Possessed*. This novelistic incarnation of the Antichrist had the name of "Ivan-Tsarevich" bestowed on him by Peter Verkhovenskii, the Devil's unambiguous emissary, who was trying to arrange a marriage between the charismatic Stavrogin and "Maria-Tsarevna," Russia the bride in a revolutionary pandemonium. Neither Peter nor Alexis, nor any other specific actor in Merezhkovskii's narrative, filled the bill of Christ or Antichrist completely. But their aspects, taken in isolation, do fall rather neatly into the dual, and essentially Manichaean, scheme, suggesting that all that was required for the desired redemptive synthesis was to break off the tsarevna's engagement to the impostor and arrange for her betrothal to the true tsarevich. Mandelstam—not to speak of Blok, Viacheslav Ivanov, Belyi, and his cohorts Maiakovskii and Tsvetaeva—was, of course, also partial to gnostic nuptials, and judging by "Pushkin and Skriabin," he shared in the chiliastic pathos of the novel's author. For Mandelstam's poet, however, this tsarevna appeared as a femme fatale, a version of the "unfortunate Phaedra." For this reason, among others, Mandelstam chose as a mask Tsarevich Aleksei, who had to compete with his father for the possession of Mother-Russia and whose defeat in the competition could be interpreted as kenotic martyrdom.

Three brief quotations from Merezhkovskii's novel will help invoke the contemporary meaning of the figure of Tsarevich Aleksei. The first involves the metaphor of marriage implied in the tsarevich's musings about his father's program of Westernization:

> The Tsarevich . . . recalled a picture that his father brought home from Holland: the Tsar dressed in sailor's garb embracing an enormous Dutch girl. Alexis smiled involuntarily, thinking to himself that this red-skinned girl was as unlike the [story's] Princess of Florence—"shining like the uncovered sun"—as the whole of Russian Europe was unlike the real one.[91]

The second quotation involved the tsarevich's betrayal, so to speak, of the doctrine of Moscow the Third Rome. Homesick for Russia, he is moved by two songs, one Russian, one Italian:

> The Tsarevich could hardly suppress his tears. It seemed that he had never loved Russia as much as he did now. But he loved her with a new, universal love, together with Europe; he loved the alien land as if it were his own. And his love for the native and his love for the alien

land, like these two songs, were fusing into one. . . . That the third Rome, as the old men called Moscow, had a long way to go before it could be compared with the first true Rome, as long a way as the Petersburg Europe had to go before it could be compared with the real Europe that he had seen with his own eyes.[92]

The third quotation comes from the end of the story, after Aleksei had been tortured and interrogated, and describes the tsarevich's last communion, which is administered by the otherworldly "John the Son of Thunder"—apparently the apostle of the Third Testament, and as such a composite of St. John of the Apocalypse and the son of Zeus's thunderbolt, Dionysus.[93]

It seemed as though John was holding in his hands the sun: this was the Chalice with the Flesh and the Blood. "In the name of the Father, the Son, and the Holy Ghost."

He administered the Eucharist. And the sun entered him [the tsarevich], and he felt that there was neither grief, nor fear, nor pain, nor death, but only eternal life, the eternal sun—Christ.

In the morning, while examining the sick [tsarevich], Dr. Blumenthrost was very surprised: the fever had ended, the wounds were healing; the improvement was so sudden that it seemed miraculous.[94]

The acceptance, indeed the incorporation, of these "gifts" by Tsarevich Aleksei (the Russian word for the Host is "holy gifts," a calque from the Greek *eucharistia*), obligated him to give of himself to Christ accordingly, to recapitulate the original sacrifice. Thus there emerges a fundamental similarity between this pattern and the one followed by Mandelstam's poet when he committed himself to an obligation by accepting Tsvetaeva's "gift."

I do not mean to suggest that one should put Merezhkovskii's label on Mandelstam's tsarevich. The novel is only one of the poem's referents, but one fully in accord with its kenotic, and implicitly mysticoerotic, thematics. By the end of the poem, what began as a sightseeing tour, having passed through the prism of Russian history, became the road to Calvary. The possibly romantic "we" of the first stanza yielded to the first or third person singular, just as the innocuous straw became the sinister burning kindling of the poem's ending. It is worth noting that the fourth stanza, the one least weighed down by allusions, presents a picture of Moscow that was as characteristic of the city in 1718, when Aleksei was executed, as in 1916, when Mandelstam had to contend with Tsvetaeva's generosity. That immutable quality only emphasized the inevitability of the route the "peasant sledge" takes in the poem. But then, the cards had already been stacked in the opening

Prolepsis in Tristia: *1915–1917*

poem of *Tristia,* and the reader should not be surprised that Mother-Russia treated her tsarevich in the same manner as Phaedra-Russia had treated her Hippolytus.

According to Marcel Mauss, the recipient of a gift is compelled not only to accept it—thereby coming into possession of, and becoming possessed by, it—but also to *return* it in the form of a token, however big or small. To do otherwise would reinforce the spell that the gift's spirit maintains over the beneficiary—to remain indebted, to lose face, to offend the giver—indeed, to cause a catastrophe.[95] In June 1916, after he had left the village where he was visiting Tsvetaeva and had gone on to the Crimea, Mandelstam produced his thanksgiving poem. The courtship was over, and for the most part the poem consisted of recollections and mementos presented in a slightly distanced and ironic light. It opened with the following stanza, in which the poet's suspension points leave plenty of room for the reader's ironic fancy.

> Не веря воскресенья чуду,
> На кладбище гуляли мы.
> — Ты знаешь, мне земля повсюду
> Напоминает те холмы
> . . . .
> . . . .
> Где обрывается Россия
> Над морем черным и глухим.

> Incredulous of the miracle of resurrection,
> We were strolling in a graveyard.
> "You know, land everywhere
> Reminds me of those hills
> . . . .
> . . . .
> Where Russia breaks off
> Over the black and muted sea."

The actual thanksgiving takes place at the end:

> Нам остается только имя —
> Чудесный звук, на долгий срок.
> Прими ж ладонями моими
> Пересыпаемый песок.
>
> 1916

> All we are left with is the word:
> A miraculous sound, long-lasting.

118

Exchanging Gifts: Tsvetaeva and Mandelstam

> Do take [this] sand I am pouring back and forth
> From one palm to the other.[96]

The motif of the hands offering a gift, *manibus sacrum*, at once sacred ("not wrought by hand") and personal ("Out of *my* hands"), had begun to reflect back upon itself as a verbal construct. Initially, the motif of *manibus sacrum* might have been prompted by the modernist fascination with the primitive and archaic (common to both scholarship and poetry), functioning as a purposeful imitation of an indeterminate ancient rite. The underlying pattern, in the Saussurian sense of *langue,* could be alienated from the "practice," that is, *parole,* and subjected to a reflective modernist scrutiny—a poetic anthropology of sorts. If I understand the poem correctly, this is what Mandelstam did in juxtaposing the uncertain "miracle of resurrection" of the first line with the "miraculous sound, long-lasting"[97] in the penultimate couplet. The poem focused on the word, the phenomenon of representation, rather than the noumenal Word; on the "nominalist" recollection rather than the "realist" resurrection. The poem's closure was also self-reflective. A formulation of Mandelstam's poetic credo, it deserves a more detailed examination.

The closing two lines, consisting of what was literally at hand on a Crimean beach—sand and the poet's two hands—may be read as an ideogram of time and gift-giving. From one perspective, the lines form an allegory of time, an hourglass. From another, hands function as a synecdoche of gift-giving and -receiving. In his *The Gift* (1925), Mauss suggests that since the institution of the gift involves compulsive reciprocation, one of its central functions is the creation of time (when was the gift given, or a challenge issued, and when is the time for the return, and the return of the return, and so forth). In the most immediate sense, time is relevant here because the exchange between Tsvetaeva and Mandelstam did involve historical projections. Tsvetaeva gave Mandelstam the gift of Muscovite history and historical milieu, and Mandelstam's poem of acceptance was a response worthy of the challenge. But in a more profound sense, the particular gift of poetry and the poetry of gift-giving produced by Tsvetaeva and Mandelstam relied on allusions to other poets and poetry, most obviously the classical Russian authors Derzhavin and Pushkin and their reworkings of Horace's "Exegi monumentum." What Mauss calls the state of "prestation," a never-ending exchange of gifts characteristic of primitive societies,[98] obtained also in poetry, with the authors of the same and different tribes, centuries, or generations involved in perpetual thanksgiving, or, as the Greeks called it, *eucharistia.* Which brings me to the final point—the relationship between the gift in this exchange and the poet's "charisma," the gift of Mandelstam's Christian Mnemosyne ("Pushkin and Skriabin").

As in the "pretender" poem, Mandelstam juxtaposed two ways of celebrating Christ, two ways of acknowledging him in the "Russian" milieu: bloodless sacrifice—the sacrament of the Eucharist; and imitation of the kenotic Christ, or martyrdom. However different they may be, both are a form of a return gift, a fulfillment of the obligation incurred at the first communion when a communicating member of the church takes possession of and, in a manner of speaking, becomes possessed by the Host (recall the Pentecost). What makes the Eucharist a unique gift is the very special eternal clock the ritual creates. And just as the Eucharist imitates and in a mysterial way reenacts the Christ event by the ever-repeated giving of thanks, so poetry approaches eternity and "imitates" Christ by following the pattern of "thanksgiving."[99] "To die means to remember, to remember means to die," Mandelstam wrote in "Pushkin and Skriabin," and we can also interpret this polemical thrust at Viacheslav Ivanov[100] as a complex periphrasis of the two forms of *imitatio Christi:* martyrdom and the Eucharist.[101] All we need do to unpack this periphrasis is to replace "to die" with the more transparent "to return the gift of life in a form worthy of this gift" (as a martyr does), and replace "to remember" with the notion of thanksgiving, or the Eucharist, which liturgically in fact includes "remembering," in the term *anamnesis*.[102]

Returning to Mandelstam's closing ideogram, we can read this as an allegory of the immutable archetype of the gift and the mutable time that forever passes through it—two images that in combination constitute an allegory of poetry. An analogous image from his 1932 poem "Batiushkov," one of the last published in his lifetime, may illustrate. This poem, too, was a thanksgiving, an homage to the nineteenth-century poet who, like Mandelstam, was inspired by the Italian muse. The closing exhortation reads:

> Вечные сны, как образчики крови,
> Переливай из стакана в стакан...
>
> Pour back and forth from one glass to another
> Eternal dreams like samples of blood...[103]

Although this may not be apparent at a chronological, ethnic, and linguistic distance, Mandelstam's poetry was saturated with the most sacred symbolism of the Russian Orthodox culture. One would be hard put to account for the effectiveness, even the meaning, of these two lines without relating them to the central, phenomenally suggestive Christian sacrament.[104] This poem was composed in 1932, a time when the European rationalist tradition and the absurdly bloated police apparatus dictated a skeptical attitude toward all religion. Hence, an allusion to the Eucharist that was capable of escaping the censor of both the mind and the state must have been experienced by the reader with at least as much satisfaction as one is supposed to derive, according to Sigmund Freud, from a clever joke.

I conclude this discussion by quoting another poem, composed in the summer of 1915, which itself represents a celebration of the Eucharist. Significantly, Mandelstam's usage of the poem's central term, *daronositsa* (a case holding the viaticum), is neologistic and based on transparent etymology: that in which the consecrated Host, *dary* (gifts), is carried or contained. Obviously, it was important for Mandelstam to emphasize the twofold nature of the symbol, its mutable time ("July") and permanent time ("outside time") united in a single representation. Thus, in rendering the poem into English I chose to translate *daronositsa* not as Host (from the Latin *hostia,* sacrifice) or Monstrance (a distant kin to Mnemosyne), but as Gift, with its multiplicity of connotations.

Вот дароносица, как солнце золотое,
Повисла в воздухе — великолепный миг,
Здесь должен прозвучать лишь греческий язык:
Взять в руки целый мир, как яблоко простое.

Богослужения торжественный зенит,
Свет в круглой храмине под куполом в июле,
Чтоб полной грудью мы вне времени вздохнули
О луговине той, где время не бежит.

И Евхаристия как вечный полдень длится —
Все причащаются, играют и поют,
И на виду у всех божественный сосуд
Неисчерпаемым весельем струится.

Here is the Gift, like the golden sun,
Suspended in the air—a glorious moment.
Greek speech alone must here ring:
Oh, to hold the entire world in your hands—like a plain apple.

The solemn zenith of the liturgy,
The light under the cupola in the round temple in July
So that we may breathe a deep sigh outside time
About that pasture where time does not fly.

And the Eucharist lasts like the eternal noon—
All are taking communion, playing, singing,

Prolepsis in Tristia: 1915–1917

> And in the sight of all, the divine vessel
> Is streaming an inexhaustible stream of gaiety.[105]

It should not be surprising that this poem, too, was part of an exchange. As Omry Ronen has pointed out, it was composed in response to Mikhail Lozinskii's apocalyptic "That year was the last," dated July 1914, on the very eve of the Great War.[106]

In the essay "Petr Chaadaev," composed in 1914 but not published until the summer of 1915, Mandelstam reproduced Chaadaev's expression of reverence and awe before the idea of the pope: "Is he not an omnipotent symbol of time—not that which flies, but that which is motionless, through which everything passes, but which itself stands impassively and in which and by which all comes to be?"[107]

In the "Eucharist" poem above, a similar formulation became a vessel containing, for a Christian, the gift of gifts. This ability of the "miraculous sound, long-lasting," to convey and define different time-bound contents while remaining the same made poetry resemble the institution of the gift. Even apart from the Christian kenotic thematics and poetics of "Pushkin and Skriabin," poetry for Mandelstam represented a substance imbued with charismatic spirit, for its vehicle was the inherently charismatic word—the medium and the message of the never-ending poetic exchange,[108] or what Mauss would call poetic "prestation." Mandelstam's thanksgiving poem to Tsvetaeva suggested as much. In fact, we can suppose that in one form or another this view of poetry (in part, underlying the poetics of Acmeism)[109] was shared by Mandelstam's generation, including the trendsetters among the readership. Consider the appearance in 1914 of another emblem of verbal prestation: one of the earliest statements of Formalist criticism, Viktor Shklovskii's pamphlet *The Resurrection of the Word*. Better still, consider a passage from Mauss: "The themes of the gift, of freedom and obligation in the gift, of generosity and self-interest in giving, reappear in our own society like the *resurrection* of the dominant motif long forgotten." [italics are mine].[110]

The self Mandelstam presented in his poetry of the early *Tristia* period appears to have originated a conflict, both cultural and psychological, which duplicated the relational pattern of complementarity and antagonism that was, as he and his contemporaries saw it, a fundamental pattern of Russia's "identity." The outcome of such a strategy of self-presentation was not a metaphoric relation between the "poet" and his land (a relation based on similarity) but rather a synecdochic one,[111] with the self functioning as a microcosm of its broader historical and cultural environment, which in its turn was the source and the cause of this very self. Conversely, Mandelstam's "Russia" appropriates from the "poet" the psychological dilemmas of the myth of incest. She is Phaedra-Russia, who stalks her Hippolytus in the night and who in her debasement might pay a high ransom to redeem her own transgression.

Even the poet's "execution," his martyrdom ("In the Sledge"), is within this framework. Indeed, it functions in the poem as a counterpart of yet another hypostasis of Russia: a messianic nation, a savior of humanity, who in her proverbial suffering and humiliation had been imitating the redemptive kenosis of Jesus Christ.[112] This association of the self with the world recalls Kafka's "Penal Colony," a story in which a machine executes a convict by carving into his body the laws he ought not to have transgressed. Similarly in Mandelstam, the "phylogeny" of Russian historical consciousness was recapitulated, or rather inscribed, on the ontogeny of the poet's self.

Whether intentional or involuntary, partial or complete, this was an effective strategy for one engaged in a charismatic project. Mandelstam combined in his figure not only the features of a martyr and the image of Russia that occupied a privileged position in the imagination of Mandelstam's fellow countrymen but also the very terms of the nation's reflections upon her destiny. In the realm of letters, it is hard to think of a more complete identification with what was "serious" and "central" in Mandelstam's milieu. "My poor Tsarevich," Nadezhda Mandelstam wrote in her memoirs, recalling "In the Sledge"; "he remembered that his blood was burdened with the 'heritage of the shepherds, patriarchs, and kings.'"[113] In more than one sense, this was an offer of a *gift* of one's self.

V

The Question of Return: Themes and Variations, 1918–1920

Je t'apporte l'enfant d'une nuit d'Idumée!
STÉPHANE MALLARMÉ, "Don du poème"

We know in fact what ravages a falsified filiation can produce, going as far as the dissociation of the subject's personality when the constraint of the environment is used to sustain its error. They may be no less when, as a result of a man having married the mother of the woman of whom he has had a son, the son will have for a brother a child who is his mother's brother. But if he is later adopted . . . , he will find himself once again the half-brother of his foster mother, and one can imagine the complex feelings with which he will await the birth of a child who will be in this recurrent situation his brother and his nephew at the same time.
JACQUES LACAN, "The Empty Word and the Full Word"[1]

FLIGHT FROM ILIUM

Among the *Tristia* poems is one on which Mandelstam interpreters differ most widely. An important link in Mandelstam's narrative of self-presentation, "Return to the incestuous womb"[2] is particularly significant both as a rare text that develops the theme of incest overtly and as a striking example of Mandelstam's use of the "incest" vocabulary, perhaps even as a model for it.

"Return" was composed sometime in 1920 during Mandelstam's stay in the Crimea, where he had gone after a few months' sojourn in

Kiev. The prototype for the addressee of the poem was Mandelstam's future wife, Nadezhda Khazina, then a twenty-year-old avant-garde painter working at the studio of Alexandra Exter. The biographical and historical background is particularly important in understanding "Return," not only because the poem was composed in a densely "contextualizing" epoch of the revolution and civil war or because it explores the Jewish theme explicitly (a rarity in Mandelstam's poetry),[3] but also because this background has become inseparable from readings of the poem in the literature on Mandelstam. I shall sketch this background briefly.

Situated on the border of the Pale of Settlement, a circumscribed area within which the empire's Jews were required to reside, Kiev was a foremost urban center in the Ukraine and as such had a high concentration of Jewish intelligentsia even before the revolution. We can assume that when he arrived in this city in the spring of 1919, Mandelstam found himself for the first time in an emphatically, if not predominantly, Russian Jewish milieu of leftist artists, writers, and intellectuals, many of whom, like Mandelstam, considered themselves sympathetic to the revolution. Since February, Kiev had been in the hands of the Reds. It was still affluent and hospitable, untouched by the current turmoil and devastation that drove southward the natives of the northern capitals, including many prominent members of the country's cultural elite.[4] It was there that Mandelstam and Nadezhda Khazina (according to her, the only Jewish woman in his life) met and, their romance commencing on May 1, 1919,[5] spent a few months together. By late summer, however, the situation in Kiev had substantially deteriorated. Food was becoming scarce, and in anticipation of an imminent retreat the Bolshevik authorities began to carry out a brutal housecleaning.[6] Although Nadezhda Mandelstam is ambiguous on this point, we can imagine that this environment, growing grimmer by the day, prompted Mandelstam to contemplate departing the city for the seemingly more inviting Crimea.

On August 31, 1919, Kiev was occupied, first by the Ukrainian nationalists and a few hours later by the Denikin Army—a double changing of the guard which, in the words of one historian, the population of the city "celebrated by murdering a large number of Jews."[7] Shortly afterward, Mandelstam managed to board a train bound for Khar'kov, leaving behind Nadezhda Khazina, who as a woman ran a greater risk traveling under conditions of civil war.[8] A few weeks later Mandelstam arrived in the Crimea, where he stayed until July 1920; he then departed for Georgia, moving on from there to Moscow and, finally,

The Question of Return: 1918–1920

Petrograd.⁹ He and Nadezhda Khazina were reunited in Kiev early in 1921, a year and a half after they had separated and a few months after Mandelstam's romance with a Petersburg actress, Ol'ga Arbenina, which had yielded the largest single cycle of love poetry in *Tristia*, had come to an end.¹⁰

In the fall of 1919, the Crimea was controlled by the Whites (Denikin, followed by Wrangel). Although Mandelstam's sojourn there was less dangerous than his crisscrossing front lines would have been, the area was no safe haven for an educated Jew from the north, especially a former official of the People's Commissariat of Culture.¹¹ The operation of the Wrangel counterintelligence, if not directed specifically at Jews, left no doubt that the designations "Jew" and "Red" were treated with ominous frequency as coextensive or synonymous.¹² As might be expected, Mandelstam, who could boast neither a Slavic appearance nor the demeanor of a respectable citizen, was arrested on suspicion of being a Bolshevik spy. As his friends later recalled, once incarcerated, Mandelstam banged on the cell door and shouted that he "was not made for prison," but to no avail.¹³ He would surely have been executed had it not been for the intervention of Maksimilian Voloshin and a certain Colonel Tsygal'skii, who managed to arrange the poet's release.¹⁴ Combined with the news of the Kiev pogroms, which must have reached him in the Crimea, this terroristic atmosphere was no doubt sufficient to stir up some questions relating to the "Jewish theme." These found expression—by however circuitous a route¹⁵—in this poem:

> Вернись в смесительное лоно,
> Откуда, Лия, ты пришла,
> За то, что солнцу Илиона
> Ты желтый сумрак предпочла.
>
> Иди, никто тебя не тронет,
> На грудь отца в глухую ночь
> Пускай главу свою уронит
> Кровосмесительница-дочь.
>
> Но роковая перемена
> В тебе исполниться должна:
> Ты будешь Лия — не Елена, —
> Не потому наречена,
>
> Что царской крови тяжелее
> Струиться в жилах, чем другой —
> Нет, ты полюбишь иудея,
> Исчезнешь в нем — и Бог с тобой.
>
> 1920

> Return to the incestuous womb
> Whence, Leah, thou hast issued,
> Because over the sun of Ilium
> Thou hast preferred the yellow gloom.
>
> Go, no one shall touch thee;
> Onto her father's bosom, into deep night,
> Let the incestuous daughter
> Drop her head.
>
> But a fateful transformation
> Is to be fulfilled in thee:
> Leah thou shalt be, not Helen,
> Called, not because
>
> It is harder for royal blood
> To course in veins than for any other—
> No, thou shalt come to love a Judean,
> Disappear in him—and God be with you.[16]

What are we to make of this poem? Let us first follow the suggestions of the alleged addressee of "Return": Nadezhda Mandelstam.

THE ADDRESSEE AS READER

Mandelstam has one strange poem he wrote in the Crimea when he was thinking about me. He did not reveal to me the meaning of these verses at once: in my youth I would have rebelled if I had found out what fate he had foretold for me. . . .

People should not think that we had a cult of poetry and work. Nothing of the sort: we lived ardently, intensely, made noise, played, had fun.

NADEZHDA MANDELSTAM, Hope Abandoned

As the poem's addressee, or more precisely, as the prototype of one, Nadezhda Mandelstam interpreted "Return" as a verbal spell cast upon her by her lover who wished that she undergo certain changes before becoming his life's companion. Although she did not describe "Return" in so many words, her discussion strongly implies that she experienced the poem, even if unconsciously, as a magic spell: "Once during our Kievan days, Mandelstam mysteriously informed me: when I compose poetry, nobody refuses me anything."[17] And toward the middle of her second volume of memoirs, she spoke about the poem in a way strongly suggestive of verbal magic. The spontaneous, unbidden composition of "Return," she maintained, endowed it with the credentials of a communication *de profundis*—those mysterious depths where human destiny takes shape. In effect, her own fate was determined by the poem (italics are mine):

The Question of Return: 1918–1920

The verses about Leah who has fallen in love with a Jew emerged from the very depth of consciousness [and] were a surprise for Mandelstam himself, who, it would seem, sought in me only tenderness, and *he simply did not want to understand that they had predetermined my fate.* Always and in every detail, he expected from me what he expected from himself and was incapable of separating my fate from his own.[18]

As her future husband came to know her in Kiev in 1919, this avant-garde painter (at twenty, eight years his junior) seemed too independent, perhaps even unreliable, and because of this not exactly a suitable mate for one devoted to a poet's vocation.[19] Not that she believed in any hard-and-fast rule for a poet's choice of companion; rather, Mandelstam's demand for a complete fusion (that she "disappear in him") may have affected the way he perceived his vocation in the first place—a charismatic mission involving ordeals and therefore requiring not submission to a person but a total identification with the mission itself. Reflecting on her eventual choice to follow his "cruel" call (as she put it), she hesitated to attribute it to love alone and spoke particularly about the "incredible intensity" projected by Mandelstam. This signified her acknowledgment of Mandelstam's charismatic gift. To use the terminology of Edward Shils, it was the "centrality" of poetry in contemporary culture, coupled with the poet's "intensity," that made Mandelstam "extraordinary," a bearer of charisma—provided, of course, that his intensity was recognized.[20] And recognized it was (italics are mine):

> There did not and could not exist a separate Leah. Living with him was difficult, but also easy. Difficult because he lived his life with an *incredible intensity* and I always had to run to catch up with him. And easy because it was *him*; and to me, our life together was never boring. Perhaps, because I loved him. I can't be sure.[21]

Hence, the faithful, completely devoted "Leah," and "not Helen." After all, the wife of Menelaus, unlike Jacob's "second best" wife, had taken an extended leave from her conjugal and royal duties.

> Куда плывете вы? Когда бы не Елена,
> Что Троя вам одна, ахейские мужи?
>
> Where are you sailing? If not for Helen,
> What would Troy mean to you, Achaean men?[22]

The Russian Ol'ga Arbenina, with whom Mandelstam became involved while he was separated from his future wife, was definitely a "Helen." For the sake of her kind, men go to war, deceive, murder, and tremble like leaves while sitting in the belly of the wooden beast before leading an assault on the enemy city. One of the poems addressed to Arbenina speaks of the torment awaiting a man who had imprudently abandoned Leah while pursuing the unattainable feminine ideal. For such a man, the morning shall be like a gray swallow beating against the window pane (a harbinger of death in Russian folklore)[23] and his days slow and barren like an ox (hardly a symbol of virility) who is clumsily stirring, trying to shake off the remnants of a long night's slumber:

За то, что я руки твои не сумел удержать,
За то, что я предал соленые нежные губы,
Я должен рассвета в дремучем акрополе ждать.
Как я ненавижу плакучие древние срубы.

Ахейские мужи во тьме снаряжают коня,
Зубчатыми пилами в стены вгрызаются крепко,
Никак не уляжется крови сухая возня,
И нет для тебя ни названья, ни звука, ни слепка.

Как мог я подумать, что ты возвратишься, как смел!
Зачем преждевременно я от тебя оторвался!
Еще не рассеялся мрак и петух не пропел,
Еще в древесину горячий топор не врезался.

Прозрачной слезой на стенах проступила смола,
И чувствует город свои деревянные ребра,
Но хлынула к лестницам кровь и на приступ пошла,
И трижды приснился мужам соблазнительный образ.

Где милая Троя? где царский, где девичий дом?
Он будет разрушен, высокий Приамов скворешник.
И падают стрелы сухим деревянным дождем,
И стрелы другие растут на земле, как орешник.

Последней звезды безболезненно гаснет укол,
И серою ласточкой утро в окно постучится,
И медленный день, как в соломе проснувшийся вол
На стогнах шершавых от долгого сна шевелится.
                                        Декабрь 1920

Because I knew not how to hold on to your hands,
Because I've betrayed your lips, salty and tender,
I must wait for the dawn in a wild and primeval Acropolis.
How I hate the odoriferous, ancient logs of this woodwork.

The Achaean men are outfitting the horse in the dark,
The many-toothed saws sinking deep into timber,
The dry bustling of blood just wouldn't come to rest,
And for you, there is no name, no sound, no imprint.

The Question of Return: 1918–1920

How could I think that you would return, how dared I!
Why did I wrench myself away before it was time!
The dark has not yet dispersed and the cock has not yet crowed,
The hot battle-axe has not yet been plunged into wood.

A transparent tear, resin oozing from the walls,
And the city is sensing its ribs made of timber,
But blood rushed to the ladders and went on the assault,
And the men dreamed three times an alluring image.

Where's dear Troy? where's the royal, where's the maidenly home?
It shall be destroyed, the high roost of Priam.
And arrows fall in a dry, wooden rainfall,
And other arrows shoot from the earth like a grove of nut trees.

The painless sting of the last star is almost extinguished,
And a gray swallow, the morning, will knock on the window pane.
And the slow day, like an ox awakened on his straw bed,
Is stirring on rough streets after a long sleep.[24]

A desire for the "incredibly" intense kinship projected in "Return" could, of course, easily spawn a motif of incest. Hence the conflation of Leah's story and that of Lot's daughters. There was another reason, however: Mandelstam, his wife noted, believed Jews to be all interrelated[25]—a notion fairly consistent with the poet's anti-incestuous, "assimilationist" ethos. In "Pushkin and Skriabin" he spoke eloquently about this abomination on a worldwide historical scale.

The interpretation offered by Nadezhda Mandelstam, even though it does not present an exhaustive reading of the poem, renders "Return," for all intents and purposes, transparent. She accounts for the enigmatic incest motif by asserting Mandelstam's idiosyncratic conviction that all Jews were related, by pointing out the addressee's Jewishness, and finally, by suggesting a momentary lapse in Mandelstam's biblical recall, his confusing the nameless daughters of Lot with Laban's Leah and Rachel.[26] The juxtaposition of "Leah . . . , not Helen" is elaborated as a typology of the stable "workhorse" quality of the one and the essential unreliability (the *Trojan* horse, Helen of *Troy*) of the beautiful other. We understand the tone of the poem, particularly Mandelstam's use of the imperative, once the function of "Return" is implicitly defined: it is a binding conjugal spell that the poet casts on his future wife in order to make her identify with him completely.[27]

Finally, the biographical context suggests that the poem may also represent an elaboration, in a sense, of the forms of address that Nadezhda Khazina and Osip Mandelstam used with each other in their correspondence, and perhaps on other occasions. Her only surviving letter, written in Kiev in 1919 when the two were separated, begins with the puzzling salutation "My dear little brother."[28] Similar echoes of this poem in a letter written by Mandelstam have already been noted in scholarship[29] but are worth citing here nevertheless (italics are mine):

> My dear little child!
> There is almost no hope [*nadezhda*] that this letter will reach you. Tomorrow, Kolachevskii is going to Kiev via Odessa. *I pray to God that you may hear what I shall tell you: my dear little child, I cannot and do not want to be without you,* you are my entire joy, you are my dear [*rodnaia;* literally, my close kin]. You have become so close to me [*rodnaia*] that I speak to you all the time, call you, complain to you. . . . You are a "kinechka" [Ukrainian for "dear little daughter"] for your mother, and you are my "kinechka," too. I am rejoicing and *praising God for giving you to me.* With you, nothing will be frightening, nothing will be heavy. . . . *My dear daughter, my sister,* I smile with your smile and hear your voice in the silence. . . .
> I cannot forgive myself that I left without you. Goodbye, my friend! May God preserve you! My little child! Goodbye![30]

The poem stands in an inverse relation to the letter in that its author wishes to return and be with the addressee rather than the other way around, as seems to be the case with the poem.

TWO MORE READERS READING

Leah is wedded to me in the night.   ST. GREGORY THE GREAT

Personal circumstances, even if convincingly demonstrated, rarely tell a poem's entire story. Both Kiril Taranovsky and Omry Ronen chose in their interpretations to treat "Return" as an important juncture in Mandelstam's writings, the point at which he paused to look at himself both as a Jew and as a Russian poet.

Writing in 1973 for the *Encyclopaedia Judaica Yearbook,* Ronen offered the following interpretation of "Return" (italics are mine):

> Mandelstam's realization that the Jewish predicament cannot be escaped by turning to alien cultures and religions was expressed with greatest force in his 1920 poem addressed to Leah, *the exegetic symbol of creative life.* Here he predicts the eventual return of his muse to the bosom of Judaism, a reunion that he describes as "incestuous."[31]

As yet unaware of Nadezhda Mandelstam's second volume of memoirs (1973), where the personal connotations of "Return" were discussed in detail, Ronen succeeded in providing a convincing and therefore legitimate interpretation of the poem, especially in view of Mandelstam's later writings with their occasionally strong affirmation of his Jewish heritage.³² Using this concise and rather cryptic statement (it was, after all, written for an encyclopedia) as a point of departure, how would one go about interpreting "Return"? Let us start with Leah as an exegetic symbol.

In one of the obituary poems composed after Andrei Belyi's death in 1934, Mandelstam drew on Dante's use of exegetic symbolism to compare his own work with the heritage of the foremost mystical theoretician of modern Russian letters:

> И европейской мысли разветвленье
> Он перенес, как лишь могущий мог:
> Рахиль глядела в зеркало явлений,
> И Лия пела и плела венок.

> The crowds of intellects, influences, impressions—
> He experienced [them] as only a mighty one might.
> Rachel was looking into the mirror of the phenomena,
> But Leah sang and wove her wreath.³³

Compare this with Dante's Leah, who appeared to the Pilgrim in his sleep as he was resting near the summit of Mount Purgatorio (*Purgatorio* 27:91–109; italics are mine):

> . . . *cantando* dicea:
> 'Sappia qualunque il mio nome dimanda
>   ch' i' mi son Lia, e vo movendo intorno
>   le belle mani *a farmi una ghirlanda*.
> . . . .
> *ma mia suora Rachel mai non si smaga
> dal suo miraglio*, e siede tutto giorno.
> . . . .
> lei lo vedere, e me l'ovrare appaga.'

> . . . she *sang*, saying: 'Know, whoever asks my name, that I am Leah, and I go plying my fair hands here and there *to make me a garland*; . . . *but my sister Rachel never leaves her mirror* and sits all day. . . . She with seeing and I with doing am satisfied.'³⁴

Assuming that Mandelstam was aware in 1920 of Leah's symbolic, even anagogical, meaning in medieval exegetic literature (*vita activa*, hence, I assume, Ronen's "creative"), he must also have been aware of the meaning of her counterpart, Rachel—*vita contemplativa*, a life devoted to the contemplation of God in mystical plenitude. Furthermore, he must have known also that the two were treated in this same literature as Old Testament prefigurations of Martha and Mary, a parallelism that Dante developed in the *Divine Comedy* by producing his own two counterparts: Matilda (Leah and Martha in *Purgatorio*) and Beatrice (Rachel and Mary in *Paradiso*).[35] Matilda introduced Dante's pilgrim to Earthly Paradise, whereas with the help of Beatrice he was able to contemplate the celestial spheres and the abode of the godhead. Within this framework, Mandelstam's Helen would replace Rachel, Mary, and Beatrice, who, on the anagogic level, the level of divine meaning, were figures dearer in the sight of God than their counterparts, Leah, Martha, and Matilda. To say the least, the poet's choice of Leah—and the terse syntax of "Return" supports this—was ambivalent.

In his earlier poetry, particularly in the early *Tristia,* Mandelstam preferred to keep a distance between himself and all those who were "thirsting for special names," as he put it in one of his first surviving poems. In the famous diptych "Solominka" (a play on Salome and the Russian word for "a straw"), the addressee was scorned because she had betrayed the icy perfection of her literary namesakes (St. Mark's and Mallarmé's)[36] by showing "tenderness" and even "breaking."[37] In a sense, she had failed her first name, and if the poet was prepared to offer her recompense, it was only by recontextualizing her: he would enter her new, private name, *Solominka,* in the catalog of famous and *fictional* women, which itself seems to have come from either Théophile Gautier or Walter Pater (or both):[38]

> Я научился вам, блаженные слова —
> Ленор, Соломинка, Лигейя, Серафита.
> В огромной комнате тяжелая Нева,
> И голубая кровь струится из гранита.
>
> I have learned you, blessed words:
> Lenore, Solominka, Ligeia, Seraphita.
> The heavy Neva in the enormous room,
> And blue blood is coursing out of the granite.

As to *solominka*'s palpable, "tender" hypostasis, it was no longer welcome. Indeed, it was a disappointment for one who wished to play a literary, Acmeist version of the precursor's role:

> В моей крови живет декабрьская Лигейя,
> Чья в саркофаге спит блаженная любовь,
> А та соломинка, быть может Саломея,
> Убита жалостью и не вернется вновь.
> 1916
>
> In my blood, there lives the December Ligeia
> Whose blessed love sleeps in a sarcophagus.

The Question of Return: 1918–1920

> And that one, a *solominka*, perhaps Salome,
> Is killed by pity and shall never return.[39]

There can hardly be a worse fate for a Mandelstam protagonist than banishment from literary "prestation," never to return as a slightly altered item in the never-ending literary exchange.

Yet it was precisely such a fate that violation of the incest taboo signified in Mandelstam's writings. Why, then, did Mandelstam settle on Leah—this truncated version of the "December Ligeia," phonetically and otherwise? Could he have hoped, if we follow the exegetic usage, that the earthly paradise she might open to him would serve as a passage to the higher bliss of the Christian celestial Paradiso? Perhaps. After all, Jacob's unloved wife, by the sheer number of her progeny, laid a sound foundation for the future glory of Israel, her fecundity abundantly compensating for her looks, an area in which she could not compete with Joseph's mother, Rachel, her sister.

"I am drinking Christianity's cool mountain air." This line from Mandelstam's 1919 poem, together with the opening exclamation, "How precipitous is this crystal pool!" suggests that he might have had something of the sort in mind as he cast his spell on the obstreperous *vita activa*. This hypothesis is not farfetched, especially if one considers his earlier sharp discrimination between the fixedly "Jewish" connotation of the "pool"[40] and the decidedly Christian connotations of verticality he seems to have derived from Chaadaev.[41]

Finally, in trying to escape the Jewish predicament, as Ronen put it, Mandelstam took an unusual tactic: rather than denying his origins, he integrated them into a specific historiosophical scheme—as his 1911 poems about the "pool," the "reed," and the "straw" convincingly demonstrate. Together with the related use of the incest motif, they indicate that Mandelstam's view of himself as a Jew was fundamental to his very Christian lyric narrative, in which the "predicament" became part of the pattern of kenotic *imitatio Christi*. The historical succession of Judaism by Christianity, "fertilized" by the tragic world view of the Greeks ("Pushkin and Skriabin"), constituted for Mandelstam that universal phylogenetic pattern that the ontogeny of self-presentation in his poetry was supposed to recapitulate.

Kiril Taranovsky's reading of "Return" proceeds from the same basic premise as Ronen's, but his conclusions conflict with Ronen's and complement Nadezhda Mandelstam's reading. (Unlike Ronen, Taranovsky had the benefit of her memoirs.) Tracing the image of the "incestuous daughter" to, on the one hand, a superimposition of two biblical referents—Laban's daughters who became Jacob's wives and

Lot's truly incestuous but nameless daughters—and, on the other, Mallarmé's "Don du poème" in Annenskii's translation, Taranovsky interprets "Return" in terms of Mandelstam's long-standing discomfort with his ethnic and religious origins.[42] He summarized his arguments as follows: "If my assumption is valid, and the incestuous daughter is Mandelstam's Muse, then the poem seemingly says that the victory of the Judaic element in his philosophy and his poetry would lead the poet to silence. This is, I strongly believe, the 'deep meaning' of the poem."

These conflicting interpretations need not be considered irreconcilable, for there are many "types of ambiguity" essential to poetry. But even less theoretically, these readings are consonant both with the fundamental multiplicity of Mandelstam's projections and with the deeper pattern of conflict on which he drew repeatedly in the composition of his poetry and prose. To the extent that the interpreters identified the basic elements of the poem, their readings are compatible. Where they differed, as any reader would,[43] is in the frame they imposed on the poem. For Nadezhda Mandelstam, it was her personal involvement with the poet and the relationship between her fate and his. For Omry Ronen, it was Mandelstam's coming to terms with the Jewish aspect of his identity, something that Ronen treats as a process of progressive reconciliation; and Mandelstam's poetry can amply support such a view. Taranovsky, too, approaches the poem as a dynamic entity, but he sees in it an outgrowth of the poet's earlier attitude, his often harsh attacks on "Judaism" that came to be interspersed with the expression of "Jewish pride" in his later years.[44]

EXTENDED FAMILY

And with a firm hand he led blind Leah into Jacob's bridal chamber.
ANNA AKHMATOVA, "Rachel" (1921)

But alarm spoke loudly to the woman:
It's not late, you can still look

At the red towers of the native Sodom,
At the square where you sang, the yard where you spun,
At the empty windows of the tall house
Where you bore children for your dear man.
ANNA AKHMATOVA, "Lot's Wife" (1924)

"Return" clearly has some significance as a report filed by Mandelstam in the middle of his life's way. But I am also concerned here with the generative principle of the poem's composition that emerges when "Return" is approached as a "dream"—not an ordinary dream, but an oracular, commanding dream, a supernatural communication already verbalized by a divinely ordained mouthpiece, a Joseph for instance. Not at all a private affair, this sort of dream possesses a social significance (it is, after all, addressed to someone other than the speaker), and to be effective, it must be recognized as an omen transcending the immediate context and cause. Concentrating on the code and generative formulas on which "Return" appears to rest, I shall treat this poem-prophecy as if it were an epiphenomenal dream interpretation, that is, a text mediating between antecedent phenomena and the catalog of cultural patterns capable of organizing these facts and events in a meaningful and open way.

Let us first examine the poem on its own terms—as a prophecy conveying a set of commands. Thematically it is most remarkable in being both a divine sanction and a divine order to violate the incest taboo. So far, this most fundamental of all prohibitions had been the animating force of Mandelstam's poetry, motivating the ambiguous position of his lyric protagonist in the plot of mystical marriage between the poet and his country. As a Hippolytus or a Joseph,[45] as a tsarevich or a Jokanaan ("Solominka"), that protagonist had so far been able to remain chaste and to benefit, as a charismatic persona, from the high value Christian culture places on the redemptive energy released (as it intensifies the sense of guilt) when an innocent is sacrificed.[46] Nothing short of divine intervention would suffice for lifting the hitherto heroically observed taboo. We may therefore conclude that the voice of the poem's speaker emanated from a divine presence and signaled a switch from one register of the incest myth (Phaedra and Hippolytus) to another, in which the violation of the prohibition had on balance a salutary effect. The well-known versions of this myth are the Oedipus cycle of Sophocles and, directly relevant to "Return," the story of the former citizen of Sodom and the progenitor of the Moabites and the Ammonites, Lot, whose daughters "went unto him" in order to prevent the termination of the family line and, as one dictionary of the Bible (McKenzie's) maintains, to fulfill their destinies as women.

Now, if the speaker has a divine voice, how are we to treat the two characters directly affected by the prophecy: the bridegroom, referred to as father and a Judean, and the bride, who is both Helen of Troy and Leah? Students of folklore ordinarily distinguish between two parts of a magic spell: the so-called epic part, which establishes a background; and the spell itself, often (as in "Return") an imperative construction.[47] The epic part of this particular spell tells us that the central commandment is less an order than a sanction to fulfill the incestuous wish manifested in Leah's preference for the "yellow gloom" (the color of Judaism in Mandelstam)[48] over the Hellenic "sun of Ilium." As to the "father's" role in this scenario—the context implies this strongly—he was not supposed to object. Once again, in Mandelstam's repertoire of dramatic situations, the two do not appear foreign to the basic misogynist plot of Euripides. The difference is that their roles, gender, and kinship status have been reversed, for now a female youth wishes to commit incest with a willing father.[49] In interpreting his patients' dreams, Freud noted that the presence of reversal in one element of dream work signals its presence elsewhere in the dream,[50] and in a poem where this operation is so pervasive we would do well to take this heuristic advice to heart. Indeed, the "father" whom Leah is to wed performs two functions at once. As a father involved in incest, he is Lot, and as husband of Leah, he is Jacob, the father of Joseph.[51] Where the maternal line is continuous with the filial line (Leah is wife *and* daughter), the son's role may be made continuous with that of the father. Mandelstam did not identify Leah's bridegroom by name but only by his kinship status and religion, leaving plenty of room for elasticity in kinship relations.

The relationships established as a result of these operations, though flexible, were by no means random, corresponding to the plot lines basic to Mandelstam's earlier poetry. There, too, the relationship between the sexes was identified with the relationship between mother and son and presented in terms of Phaedra's desire for Hippolytus. Now, with kinship and gender reversed, it was identified with the relationship of daughter to father according to the story of Lot and his daughters: what Lot's daughters were to Lot, daughters were to fathers, wives to husbands, and women to men. Gender overrode filiation, and the female figures, whether mothers, daughters, or wives, formed one class—perpetrators of incest.

For the sake of illustration, this part of Mandelstam's kinship scheme may be tabulated as follows ("===" indicates the point of reversal):

Reversal 1

$$\frac{Phaedra}{Hippolytus} = \frac{mother}{son} === \frac{Lot's\ daughters}{Lot} = \frac{daughters}{father} = \frac{wife}{husband}$$

The other part accounts for the extension of the reversibility of kinship relations to the male line, making it possible for the son to assume the other male roles and function with respect to his mother as father, husband, and son. It followed that gender polarity in the incest drama would now be reversed.

The Question of Return: 1918–1920

Reversal 2

$$\frac{Jacob}{Leah} = \frac{husband}{wife} = \frac{father}{daughter} = \frac{Joseph}{Leah\ (Rachel)} === \frac{mother}{son}$$

That Rachel, not her sister Leah, was Joseph's mother further "overdetermined," or overmotivated, the incest theme: the mother still remained inaccessible, the highest object of desire, despite the prodigious "kinship flexibility."

To follow the exegetic tradition, Mandelstam's Helen of Troy was in this regard identical to Rachel. The two easily blended into one conflated image—Helen-Rachel—encapsulating the essentials of the incest myth and myth in general, namely, its capacity for a narrative realization of the paradox of identity between irreconcilable relational patterns: taking one's own mother for a bride or marrying far outside one's own tribe.[52] Significantly, because it is cast in the rhetoric of a divine commandment, the act of incest the poem's speaker advocates must be seen as a lesser of two evils. It would have been a greater abomination for Helen-Rachel to resist such powerful rhetoric and to prefer the illicit "sun of Ilium" to the "yellow gloom." The implications of "Return" for Mandelstam's mythology of self-presentation were considerable. Previously, his master narrative propelled itself by the protagonist perpetually resisting the temptation of incest. Now a way was found to incorporate the violation of the taboo without diminishing dramatic tension. On the one hand the choice of Leah as the bride of Jacob-Joseph greatly attenuated the incestuous aspect of the theme of marriage; on the other the poem greatly intensified the power of the taboo, which alone motivated the inaccessibility of and continued striving for Leah's ideal counterpart—the sister-daughter-mother-bride Helen-Rachel.

This is the pattern that "Return," as a mediating text, establishes for the reader, and the meaning of the poem depends on the perspectives that it mediates between. In this sense, the three conflicting interpretations presented above are fully reconcilable. Confronted with a different set of perspectives, a poem would yield a different set of results. Let us examine it through the eyes of Mandelstam's contemporary—say, a woefully incomplete version of Mandelstam himself in 1919, somewhere in Koktebel', a tiny mountain village on the shore of the Crimean peninsula.

For a man like Mandelstam, who was accustomed to apocalyptic vocabulary, the association of Petersburg and Petersburg Russia with Sodom came naturally, perhaps even inevitably, when, amid revolution and civil war, he found himself away from his native city and in a mountain retreat resembling Lot's rocky hideout. The association was a rhetorical commonplace, a symbol of the times waiting for a poet capable of elaborating its meaning in the form of a mythic narrative. Mandelstam's turning to the story of Lot, however, had also been determined by his earlier mythic schemata: the abomination of Petersburg,[53] and Phaedra-Russia's ("history running backward") perverse claim on the poet-Hippolytus.

Now that Imperial "stepmother Russia" was no more, Phaedra's role in the script was taken over by the wife of the sole virtuous citizen of Sodom, and that of Hippolytus by her husband, Lot. The mystical, potentially incestuous union of Phaedra and Hippolytus, which had never been consummated, was replaced by an act of incest by the two daughters of the widowed father fleeing the sulphur and brimstone raining down on their native Sodom. Or could it be that, viewed from afar, Phaedra-Russia had become transformed into Helen of Troy–Petersburg, and the poet who had fled the "Ilium" of the "night sun" of St. Petersburg was now forced to settle for a Jewish girl from Kiev[54] and the "yellow gloom" of the Crimean sun? Or was "Return" simply an objectified expression of the fear of having perpetually to look back, a passéistic petrification combined with the realization that the previous life had been irretrievably lost and that now one had to learn to make do even at the price of poetic silence? Or finally, what if "Return," like a talisman, could spell future fecundity and attract the astral influences of the exegetic Leah?

Obviously, as a prophecy-oracle, "Return" could have been all this and more. Certainly, like the opening poem of *Tristia*, it constituted a fundamental revision of the basic "plot," which, although modified, still revolved around the incest taboo. Moreover, as no other poem had done before, it spelled out the symbolic grammar and vocabulary Mandelstam had been developing all throughout *Tristia*. Some rudiments of this lexicon and grammar can be tabulated, if in an adumbrated form, along the paradigmatic (vertical) and the syntagmatic (horizontal) axes. A basic statement in this language—that is to say, a poem—would consist of one or, more often, several items taken from each of the three columns. Later on, I shall examine several "variant" versions of Mandelstam's fundamental "mythology."[55]

The City	*The Groom*	*The Bride*
Petersburg	Hippolytus	Phaedra
Troezen	Oedipus	Antigone [Jocasta]
Thebes	Lot	Lot's daughters
Sodom	Jacob	Leah and Rachel

The Question of Return: 1918–1920

The City	The Groom	The Bride
Venice	Odysseus	Helen
Troy	Orpheus	Eurydice
Ithaca	Joseph	Penelope
Moscow	Venetian Doge	Venetian Dogaressa
Rome	Tsarevich	Susanna
		Maryna Mniszek

The elements in this table represent members of an algebraic formula of sorts and can assume a whole series of compatible values that the poet or the reader might choose to assign. At its most condensed this "formula" produces two contradictory statements: (1) because of the incest taboo, what you want most you cannot have, and (2) for the same reason, what you absolutely cannot have is what you most want. In either case, the penalty for possessing it is an ordeal, perhaps silence or death. Of course, this interpretation, suitable in the structural study of myths, is inadequate for the hermeneutics of poetry, in which the embroidery, the poet's *and* the reader's, has far more value than the cloth or the pattern itself.[56] For this reason I have emphasized the significance of Mandelstam's vocabulary and grammar in the contemporary context as much as I have focused on his "myth," the lowest common denominator of his poetry. This play with the incest myth and the specific form that it took in his art (for example, the redemptive martyrdom of "Pushkin and Skriabin") has been correlated with the turn-of-the-century Christian revival, Russian Nietzscheanism, comparative mythology, and the historiosophical, social, and political issues of Mandelstam's time. Nevertheless, this "mythological" analysis helps to grasp, to use Roman Jakobson's formula, the grammar of Mandelstam's poetry and the poetry of his grammar,[57] without which the meaning of his poetry would be hard to define.

The "symphonic" (*sobornyi*) pathos of Mandelstam's writings led him to establish ever more intricate metonymic and synecdochic links among the significant aspects of such cultural entities as Greece, Russia, the West, Rome and Italy, and, of course, Judaism—the compass of his intellectual universe. On the one hand, these cultural complexes acquired a paradigmatic equivalence. That is, although both the "syntax" and the predicate of Mandelstam's statements on culture remained the same, the subject could be represented by any one of these "analogous" sets. In short, they were progressively interchangeable, allowing Mandelstam, for example, to project the legend of Helen of Troy onto the Hebrew story of Jacob's wooing of Rachel. Not only was Mandelstam a good student of comparative mythology à la James Frazer,

Aleksandr Veselovskii, Tadeusz Zielinski, and Viacheslav Ivanov, but he also could put this knowledge to good use. Like a squirrel preparing for winter, he shelled the cultural ideological formulas of his time to extract from them kernels of similarity to be stored for future use as elements of the poet's expressive vocabulary. These stockpiles then provided Mandelstam for years to come with highly complex, intensely allusive images of the Russian condition.

On the other hand—and here the incest archetype may have been especially helpful—the analogies and similarities reinforced the sense of kinship among disparate elements of the world, the kinship that Mandelstam had always sought and that he believed had to obtain in the "real," if not the actual, universe. In this respect, he, like many of his contemporaries in Russia, proved a faithful heir to the utopian thought of Chaadaev, Herzen, and Dostoevsky. In his famous "Pushkin speech," Dostoevsky described the archetypal Russian poet (Mandelstam's proverbial "sun") as a genius of metamorphosis who could imitate the essences of all cultures and, as such, represented a prefiguration of the eventual universal union of humanity that Russia was destined to champion.[58] Mandelstam's plethora of poetic identities, his "coat of many colors," also could function as such a prefiguration.

This implied for the grammar of his poetry and the poetry of his grammar that the analogies and similarities were not only mutually interchangeable but also interrelated. As such, they were members of a single family and could be manipulated along synecdochic-metonymic and metaphoric lines.[59] The Hebrew Rachel could be "displaced" onto the Greek Helen, Leah could become the sister of the proverbial toast of Troy, and both could serve as "condensed" representations of their respective cultures. The poetic function, wrote Roman Jakobson, consists of the projection of the principle of similarity (or of metaphor) from the axis of selection (the paradigmatic axis) onto the axis of combination (the syntagmatic, metonymic axis).[60] Thanks to the incest archetype that Mandelstam employed in his writings, the reverse—the projection of the principle of contiguity from the axis of combination onto the axis of selection—also held true. Thus, a poem in which these two operations were performed could serve not only as poetry, or to use the definition of Northrop Frye, as a "hypothetical verbal statement imitating action or thought," but also as metapoetry—as an inscription in which the principle of "imitation" was encoded. I shall return to this subject in the next chapter.

"Return," in keeping with Mandelstam's eloquently expressed desire to "Hellenize the world," established kinship bonds (albeit not free of antagonism) between two of these cultural complexes, the Hellenic and the Jewish, which hitherto seemed separated by a wide gulf. The tension of the incest conflict was becoming attenuated. After all, was not the marriage, however incestuous, ordered by the highest authority for both Christian and Jew? Likewise, the notion of "return"—which constituted a "dear" but nevertheless abominable act in the earlier "pool" poem and took the form of the "black sun" in "Pushkin and Skriabin" and the second "Phaedra"—had become progressively acceptable.

VARIATIONS

In a 1914 essay, "Petr Chaadaev," Mandelstam had already sanctioned the "return home," provided that one took an extended tour of distant and alien, and therefore "electively" related, lands. He himself had done so in his "pilgrim" poem ("The Staff"). At first, however, taking a grand tour turned out to be far easier than coming back, to judge by the poem about the unfortunate tsarevich ("In the Sledge," 1916). But in 1917, when Mandelstam found himself in a Crimea that was far more hospitable under Kerenskii than it would be under Wrangel, the return had a much sweeter taste:

Золотистого меда струя из бутылки текла
Так тягуче и долго, что молвить хозяйка успела:
Здесь, в печальной Тавриде, куда нас судьба занесла,
Мы совсем не скучаем — и через плечо поглядела.

Всюду Бахуса службы, как будто на свете одни
Сторожа и собаки — идешь, никого не заметишь —
Как тяжелые бочки, спокойные катятся дни:
Далеко в шалаше голоса — не поймешь, не ответишь.

После чаю мы вышли в огромный коричневый сад,
Как ресницы на окнах опущены темные шторы,
Мимо белых колонн мы пошли посмотреть виноград,
Где воздушным стеклом обливаются сонные горы.

Я сказал: виноград как старинная битва живет,
Где курчавые всадники бьются в кудрявом порядке.
В каменистой Тавриде наука Эллады — и вот
Золотых десятин благородные, ржавые грядки.

Ну, а в комнате белой как прялка стоит тишина.
Пахнет уксусом, краской и свежим вином из подвала.
Помнишь, в греческом доме: любимая весеми жена —
Не Елена — другая — как долго она вышивала?

Золотое руно, где же ты, золотое руно?
Всю дорогу шумели морские тяжелые волны,

Variations

И покинув корабль, натрудивший в морях полотно,
Одиссей возвратился, пространством и временем полный.
                                             1917

Golden, a stream of honey was flowing from a jar,
So viscous and slow that the hostess could utter:
Here, in the sad Taurida where our destiny brought us,
We don't feel bored at all—and then glanced behind her.

Everywhere Bacchus is celebrated, as if there were only
A shepherd and dogs—as you walk, not a soul around you—
Quiet days, like heavy wine barrels, calmly rolling along:
Voices from a faraway tent—you cannot understand or answer.

After tea, we walked out into a garden, brown and large,
Like eyelashes, dark blinds in the windows had been drawn down.
Past white columns, we went on to look at the vines
Where sleepy mountains bathe in the liquid glass of the air.

I spoke: the vines, like the battle of yore, are alive,
Where the curly-haired horsemen engaged in a curlicued combat.
The science of Hellas in the rocky Taurida—and behold,
The noble rusty rows of golden acres and acres.

Now, in the white room like a spinning wheel silence stands.
Scents of vinegar, paint, and young wine from the cellar.
Remember the Greek house: the wife so loved by them all—
No, not Helen, the other—oh how long she embroidered.

Golden fleece, where are you at last, golden fleece?
All along sea waves heaved and heavily rumbled,
And after leaving the ship with its canvas worked over at sea,
Odysseus returned, filled with space and time.

Ostensibly, "The Vine" deals with the return to the Crimea, not Russia, but nevertheless a return.[61] Because the poem ingeniously shows that absence can make presence—Odysseus's absence from home yields Penelope's tapestry (or "embroidery," in Mandelstam's pointedly Russified version)—the poem may legitimately be read as Mandelstam's reply to those critics who had despaired of finding a Russian subject in his poetry.[62] But it is equally tempting to read it as a counterpart, indeed as a Hellenic precedent, that legitimized the return of Mandelstam's Leah to her father's bosom. Like Leah, who had spent years pursuing the elusive image of Helen before returning to her "Judean" bridegroom-father, Odysseus returned to his wife. Did he not, after all his adventures, prefer the modest daylight of Ithaca to the "sun of Ilium"? A reader may be justified in "projecting the principle of similarity" from the poem about Leah and Helen onto the poem about

The Question of Return: 1918–1920

Helen and Penelope. Following Dante's example of complementing the proverbial Leah-Martha and Rachel-Mary with the poet's own Matilda and Beatrice, Mandelstam elaborated on the "exegetic sisters," but he did so by drawing on the storehouse of tradition for his own "blessed names."[63]

If in "Return" Leah takes second place to Helen, does not Helen take second place to Penelope in the poem about Odysseus's return? The answer is yes and no.[64] As we have seen, displacement and condensation—or, in tropological terms, metonymy and synecdoche—often imply in Mandelstam a possibility for identification on the basis of similarity. To put it differently, the contiguity or proximity of characters stemming from their kinship breeds likeness among them. In this sense the poet's attitude toward the symbolic sisters appears ambivalent and indeterminate. There is, in fact, a 1931 "occasional" poem in which the name of Mary, also an allusion to an "easy woman" from Pushkin's *Feast During the Plague,* plays the role of Martha or Leah, and Helen is mentioned as Mandelstam's exegetic Mary. Nadezhda Mandelstam assumed that here, too, she was forced to play second fiddle to the beautiful Helen.[65]

Я скажу тебе с последней
Прямотой:
Все лишь бредни, шерри-бренди,
Ангел мой!

Там где эллину сияла
Красота,
Мне из черных дыр зияла
Срамота.

Греки сбондили Елену
По волнам,
Ну, а мне соленой пеной
По губам!

По губам меня помажет
Пустота,
Строгий кукиш мне покажет —
Нищета.

Ой-ли, так ли, — дуй ли, вей ли, —
Все равно —
Ангел Мэри, пей коктейли,
Дуй вино!

I shall tell you as directly
As I can:

Variations

All is bunk. Drink, angel Mary,
Drink again!
Where the beauty-bedazzled Hellas
Saw its bliss,
There stared at me shame from
Her abyss.

With their Helen sailed the Greeks
Across the waves,
All I got was salty foam,
Just a taste!

Just a taste of nothing ever
On my lips,
Ancient poverty will wave at me
Her fists.

Hither-thither, up or down,
Yours or mine—
All is bunk—so sip your cocktails,
Gulp your wine!

But if in this much later poem Mandelstam drew a sharp line between the celestial, unreachable Helen and the profane angel Mary, accessible and close at hand, the picture he offered in the poem that preceded "Return" in *The Second Book of Poetry* was far more indeterminate. There, the archetypal two sisters appeared as a paradoxical pair of nonidentical twins:

Сестры — тяжесть и нежность — одинаковы ваши приметы.
Медуницы и осы тяжелую розу сосут.
Человек умирает, песок остывает согретый,
И вчерашнее солнце на черных носилках несут.

Ах, тяжелые соты и нежные сети,
Легче камень поднять, чем имя твое повторить!
У меня остается одна забота на свете:
Золотая забота, как времени бремя избыть.

Словно темную воду я пью помутившийся воздух.
Время вспахано плугом, и роза землею была.
В медленном водовороте тяжелые нежные розы,
Розы тяжесть и нежность в двойные венки заплела.

Коктебель, март 1920

Sisters—heaviness and tenderness—your tokens are the same.
Bees and wasps suck on a heavy rose.
Man dies, sand warmed by him cools,
And yesterday's sun is borne away on a black stretcher.

The Question of Return: 1918–1920

> Oh, heavy honeycombs and tender snares,
> Lifting a stone is easier than repeating your name!
> In this world, all I have is but one care:
> A golden care—to be rid of the burden of time.
>
> I am drinking, like dark water, this air growing turbid.
> Time has been ploughed under, and the rose, too, once was earth.
> In a slowly turning whirlpool, heavy, tender roses,
> Rose's heaviness and tenderness she wove into a double wreath.

According to Nadezhda Mandelstam, *The Second Book* was the only one of Mandelstam's post-1916 collections that he personally supervised.[66] The order, therefore, is both significant and important. Indeed, juxtaposing the poem above with "Return" helps to bring into sharper focus the meaning of the "sisters—heaviness and tenderness,"[67] because the phrase becomes part of Mandelstam's poetic vocabulary and subject to his grammar.

The first striking feature of the poem is its capacity for echoing the earlier Mandelstam. Just as in the second "Phaedra," the poet alludes here, perhaps nostalgically, to the architectural simplicity of his first two collections (*Stone* I and II). "Lifting a stone," he puns, turned out to be much easier than speaking in the name of love—the invocational fulcrum of *Tristia* and, of course, lyric poetry in general (hence, Mandelstam's "to repeat"). And it is love, a feminine noun in Russian, that weaves the double wreaths in the classical *vortex amoris* of the poem's closure. Although it retains the mysterious aura of a taboo subject, it is love that combines the crown of thorns with a flower garland.[68] The "golden care" also becomes comprehensible. To establish bonds of kinship between Russia and alien cultures, between the distant past and the present—the very essence of Mandelstam's poetic project—meant to create proximity where there was distance, similarity where there was difference, and simultaneity where time brought about a chronological gap. The latter served him—as it did countless other poets, if rarely with such intensity—as a synecdoche of verbal art. This is not surprising in a "mythological" poet, because in myth, space and time can be made equivalent and interchangeable (isomorphous). Inscribing his own narrative on an ancient tradition allowed him to have his forefathers, as N. Fedorov would have put it, come alive, or as a Freudian might say, to resolve the Oedipal crisis—or, to bring the poem closer to "Pushkin and Skriabin," to defeat, to "Hellenize," death, to "imitate playfully" the mystery of the Resurrection.

Which brings me to the first stanza of the poem. According to Akhmatova, Aleksandr Pushkin served as the referent for the poem's "yesterday's sun."[69] Indeed, Pushkin's nighttime funeral was a key scene in Mandelstam's symbolic vocabulary ("Pushkin and Skriabin"), but it is my sense (and also Nadezhda Mandelstam's) that the image is not a specific one. The poet was casting a wider net, meditating on the paradox of life, love, death, and resurrection. The rose, after all, is the traditional image of the Virgin and the all too traditional symbol of love;[70] the sun, particularly in Mandelstam, is often the sun of redemption and as such might refer to any "martyred redeemer," including the "canonized" Pushkin, who imitated Christ. As to Pushkin—not the historical poet, but the focus of the Pushkin cult—Mandelstam had already linked his death with the Crucifixion. But even with these two clear referents, the image is indeterminate enough to allow for the "sun" of any reader who happens to be shaped by Christian culture. "Man dies." So Mandelstam begins the third line of the first stanza. The universal spareness of the statement speaks for itself. All the more significant, then, was Akhmatova's refusal to see in the image anything but another relic of Pushkin worship. For Mandelstam, it seems to have been far more important to formulate the paradox than to clutter the Russian literary pantheon with yet another haloed bust.

Let us not forget the time and place of the poem's composition: March 1920, the last months of the civil war and three years after the revolution, in the Crimea under Wrangel. Death quite literally stared one in the eye, out of the empty sockets of corpses strung up on the lampposts of Crimean cities.[71] How can a new life be born out of this hecatomb? Intellectuals everywhere, especially those with leftist sympathies, were asking this question. The poem offers a rationalization, not an answer, to this paradox. "Except a corn of wheat fall into the ground and die, it abideth alone: but if it die, it bringeth forth much fruit."

Mandelstam's poem is an elaboration on this parable from the Gospel according to John (John 12:24),[72] an elaboration based also on the parable of the two sisters, Martha and Mary, and their by now numerous cousins: Leah and Rachel, Leah and Helen, Matilda and Beatrice, the two hypostases of the mystical Aphrodite, Helen and Penelope, Helen and Pushkin's wayward Mary, as well as heaviness and tenderness, the bees and the wasps, the earth and the rose. And, to do justice to their other counterparts: the heavy rose, yesterday's sun, turbid air, dark water, heavy honeycombs, tender snares, golden care, and, of course, the double wreath. And is not the slowly turning whirlpool with the floating double wreaths a conflation of the still pool and the forbidden air of the early "twin" poems? The list goes on almost indefinitely. Far more important, all of these twin oxymorons consti-

The Question of Return: 1918–1920

tute, not a parliament of warring and compromising parties (an evil assembly to some Russian eyes), but a harmonious chorus (or is it polyphonic?) in the manner of the universal "symphony," the *sobor* or *mir* of Russian Orthodox theology and social thought. As it proceeds from the dominant differentiation of the first two stanzas to the harmonious unity in the closure of the last two lines, the poem in a sense imitates the progress toward that cherished goal. Mandelstam had traveled a long way from the simple antagonisms of the early *Tristia*, but not long enough to prevent them from resonating with a powerful force in this "symphonic" meditation.

What could be the significance of these seemingly endless variations? I suggest that the poem actually represents a form of semantic incantation, a verbal exorcism of the demons of division, who have to be cast out by an invocation of angels reconciling the opposites.[73] The device Mandelstam employs is sympathetic magic, which is supposed to work by attracting the like with the like.[74] Hence the hypnotically magical repetitions[75] of the paradigm of Martha and Mary as well as that of the "corn of wheat," and hence the binary alternations (rhyme, rhythm, semantics) enclosed in a ternary overall structure that may vaguely allude to the Trinity. Intoned over and over again, this is, nevertheless, a sophisticated prayer in which each repetition invokes its own particular angel, or angels, or patron saint—all of them celebrating the god of love. Gertrude Stein, the author of a similar magic spell—"A rose is a rose is a rose"—cast from the anagram EROS-ROSE, might have appreciated the refined complexity of Mandelstam's incantation, which, curiously, echoes a 1920s Fats Waller hit, "Honeysuckle Rose." Considering the task Mandelstam set himself—"to be rid of the burden of time"—he could hardly ignore the power of verbal magic.

I conclude this chapter with "Venetian Life," a poem that must be seen as part of the Crimean "cycle." Its implicit kinship with "Return" reveals one way Mandelstam came to treat the incest motif after the "Leah" poem.

Веницейской жизни мрачной и бесплодной
Для меня значение светло.
Вот она глядит с улыбкою холодной
В голубое дряхлое стекло.

Тонкий воздух кожи. Синие прожилки.
Белый снег. Зеленая парча.
Всех кладут на кипарисные носилки,
Сонных, теплых вынимают из плаща.

Variations

И горят, горят в корзинах свечи,
Словно голубь залетел в ковчег.
На театре и на праздном вече
Умирает человек.

Ибо нет спасенья от любви и страха:
Тяжелее платины Сатурново кольцо!
Черным бархатом завешенная плаха
И прекрасное лицо.

Тяжелы твои, Венеция, уборы,
В кипарисных рамах зеркала.
Воздух твой граненый. В спальне тают горы
Голубого дряхлого стекла.

Только в пальцах роза или склянка —
Адриатика зеленая, прости!
Что же ты молчишь, скажи, венецианка,
Как от этой смерти праздничной уйти?

Черный Веспер в зеркале мерцает.
Всё проходит. Истина темна.
Человек родится. Жемчуг умирает.
И Сусанна старцев ждать должна.

1920

Venetian life, so dark and barren—
For me, its meaning is bright.
Here she is, looking with a cold smile
Into a blue and decrepit mirror.

The subtle scent of skin. Blue veins.
White snow. Green brocade.
All are placed on cypress-wood stretchers,
Warm, sleepy, removed from their capes.

And candles in baskets keep on burning,
As if a dove flew into the ark.
On stage and in idle assembly,
Man dies.

For there is no salvation from love and fear:
Heavier than platinum is Saturn's ring!
Executioner's block, draped in black velvet
And a beautiful face.

Heavy, Venice, are your adornments,
Mirrors are framed in cypress wood.
Your air is faceted. In the bedroom
Mountains of blue, decrepit glass melt.

> But what's in her fingers: a rose or a vial?
> Green Adriatic, do forgive!
> So why are you keeping silent, tell me, Venetian donna,
> How does one escape this festive death?
>
> Black Vesper is flickering in the mirror.
> Everything passes. Truth is dark.
> Man is born. Pearl dies.
> And Susanna must await the elders.

Like "Return," "Venetian Life" may be read as a complex version of the story of Joseph. Indeed the two poems are linked not only by the theme of a doomed city, with the dying "pearl of the Adriatic" replacing the moribund Troy, or by the common air of sinfulness, implicit violence, and intrigue, but also by a "wandering motif" of slandered innocence familiar from the Joseph legend. Not until the last line of the poem does the reader realize that the collage of emblems constituting "Venetian Life"[76] is framed in a story of the entrapment and eventual vindication of a virtuous woman who—like Joseph when he declined the entreaties of Potiphar's wife or like Hippolytus with Phaedra—preferred to accept the consequences of a false accusation rather than betray her primary loyalties. I have in mind the final line, with its transparent allusion to "Susanna and the Elders" by Tintoretto. Some of the visual allegories of this painting are echoed in Mandelstam's verbal puns: a broken necklace of *pearls* placed between the diaphanous, Venus-like Susanna and the mirror she is staring at, unaware of the presence of two pink-clad and decrepit-looking old men.[77] By no means the last[78] instance of the "Joseph" motif in Mandelstam, "Venetian Life" greatly attenuates the earlier emphasis on conflict. As a result, it resembles not so much the second "Phaedra," with its drama of intense polarization, as the kenotic reconciliation of opposites in "Sisters—heaviness and tenderness," whose "tokens are the same."

The poem's sense appears to emerge from the oxymoronic, in part folk etymological, associations prompted by the word *Venice* (*Venetsiia*): *venok* (wreath or garland), *venets* (crown), Venus, venerial, and, of course, venal and *venum*.[79] As the poem develops the *Tristia* theme of the "double wreath," its key images, such as "Saturn's ring," join the vocabulary that already includes Leah and Rachel,[80] a crown of thorns, a lover's flower garland, a laurel wreath, love and death, and, in art, the eternal expectation of a resurrection. The flickering *black* Vesper plays the role of an etymologically and therefore, in Mandelstam, magically justified astral guide of Venice, the city of beauty and death. As a "fraternal" counterpart of this oxymoronic play,[81] "Saturn's ring" brings a greater emphasis to the "Saturnian" aspect of Mandelstam's myth of mystical marriage. As a result of this accumulation of analogous images, the fabric of allusion becomes dense enough to ensure that the reader associates the name of the city with the ambivalent object held in a "Venetian donna's" hand—a rose? or poison, *venum?*—recalling both Pushkin's *Feast During the Plague* and Blok's cycle "The Dances of Death":

> И девы-розы пьем дыханье, —
> Быть может... полное Чумы.
>
> Пустая улица. Один огонь в окне.
> Еврей-аптекарь охает во сне.
>
> А перед шкапом с надписью *Venena*,...

> And I drink the breath of maiden-rose,
> Perhaps...filled with Plague.
> (Pushkin)

> An empty street. One light in a window.
> A Jew chemist moans in his sleep.
>
> And before the cabinet with a sign *Venena*,...[82]
> (Blok)

Nor can the reader avoid recalling the tradition by which the Doge of Venice is symbolically bound to his city (hence the "ring").[83]

In the late fall of 1920, Mandelstam's Petrograd audience no doubt appreciated this cluster of images. It was to them an open-ended emblem of their own attitude about the "death" of the old Petersburg ("Venice of the North") and the old Russia, which, now that they were no more, could be recalled with nostalgia. Many of them had not yet had time to form an opinion about whether the revolution and the civil war signaled a regeneration or a national suicide. To borrow an allusion from "Venetian Life," the chaos of the revolutionary "flood" had not yet receded (the dove returning to Noah's ark), and the future was still in darkness. Thus understood, the question of the penultimate stanza could have been asked by any of Mandelstam's Russian readers. And in the interval between the penultimate and the final stanza, the poet of "Venetian Life" transformed himself from a man a reader could easily identify with to a mouthpiece issuing the answer in the staccato of an enigmatic Pythian oracle. But lest his readers miss his political points, Mandelstam inserted into the otherwise rarified and pointedly European vocabulary not only the up-to-date, topical *nosilki,* or "stretcher" (as he did in "Sisters"), but also the old Russian *veche,* a term designat-

The Question of Return: 1918–1920

ing the popular assembly in preautocratic Russia, which, beginning with the Decembrists, served as a shibboleth for the intelligentsia disinclined to recognize the legitimacy of the tsar's rule.

The density of allusions and the collage structure of the poem allow multiple readings of "Venetian Life." To some, the poem may even have sounded perilously close to self-parody. In a review of an almanac containing the poem, Briusov could write (and, given the format, convincingly): "Everything that the Petersburg poets offer is all too familiar, customary; [such poetry] used to be read and written long ago. . . . 'For there is no escape from love and fear' or 'Why did I tear myself away from you before it was time.'"[84] The poem's oracular closure, however, offers a hint of how Mandelstam wanted his poem to be perceived, if not of how it was actually understood by his readers, even though we know that Mandelstam assumed the appearance of a visionary as he was reciting "Venetian Life."[85] Considering the "narrative" drift of *Tristia* and the Pythian introduction of the Susanna legend in the final line, we can hardly argue that the previously unreconciled opposites, including Mandelstam's Rachel and Leah, became fused here into *Venice*, a "wreath" (*venok*), a "crown" (*venets*), and a looking glass, while the pair Phaedra-Russia and Hippolytus became transformed into the single figure of Tintoretto's Susanna, who "must await" forever the advances and the slander of the "elders" to be vindicated at the appointed time. We discern here a voice similar to the one that had ordered the "return" of Leah to the incestuous womb.

The chairman of the Petrograd Union of Poets, Aleksandr Blok, who could appreciate the pun "Venice-Venus-Venum," happened to be in the audience at the Poet's Club in Petrograd on October 21, 1920, when Mandelstam publicly recited "Venetian Life." Judging by Blok's response, the recital was a success. Above all, Mandelstam convinced Blok that his poetry did indeed arise out of the generative center of humanity's dreams, even if these dreams were strictly circumscribed by the boundaries of art. Nor did Blok miss the principle the poem was constructed on, namely, the paronomastic, folk-etymological "sprouting" of verse from a key word, which he pondered with the help of Gumilevian commentary. The day after Mandelstam's recital, Blok wrote in his diary:

> The focus of the evening was I. Mandelstam, who came [to Petrograd] after having spent time in a Wrangel prison. He has grown enormously. At first it is unbearable to hear the sing-song common to the Gumilevists. Gradually you get used to it... The artist is there to see. His verses emerge out of dreams—very particular—that lie in

the sphere of art alone. Gumilev defines his way thus: from the irrational to the rational (the opposite of mine). His [Mandelstam's] "Venice." According to Gumilev, everything is rational (including both love and being in love), the irrational lies only in language; in its roots, it is ineffable. (In the beginning was the Word, out of the Word emerged thoughts, words that no longer resembled the Word but that nevertheless had It as their source; and everything will end with the Word—everything will disappear; It alone will remain.)[86]

Osip Mandelstam, Kornei Chukovskii,
Benedikt Livshits, and Iurii Annenkov (Petersburg, August 1914).
Photograph courtesy of Iurii Annenkov.

Osip Mandelstam: a portrait by P. Miturich (1915).
In *Vystavka sovremennoi russloi zhivopisi* (1915).

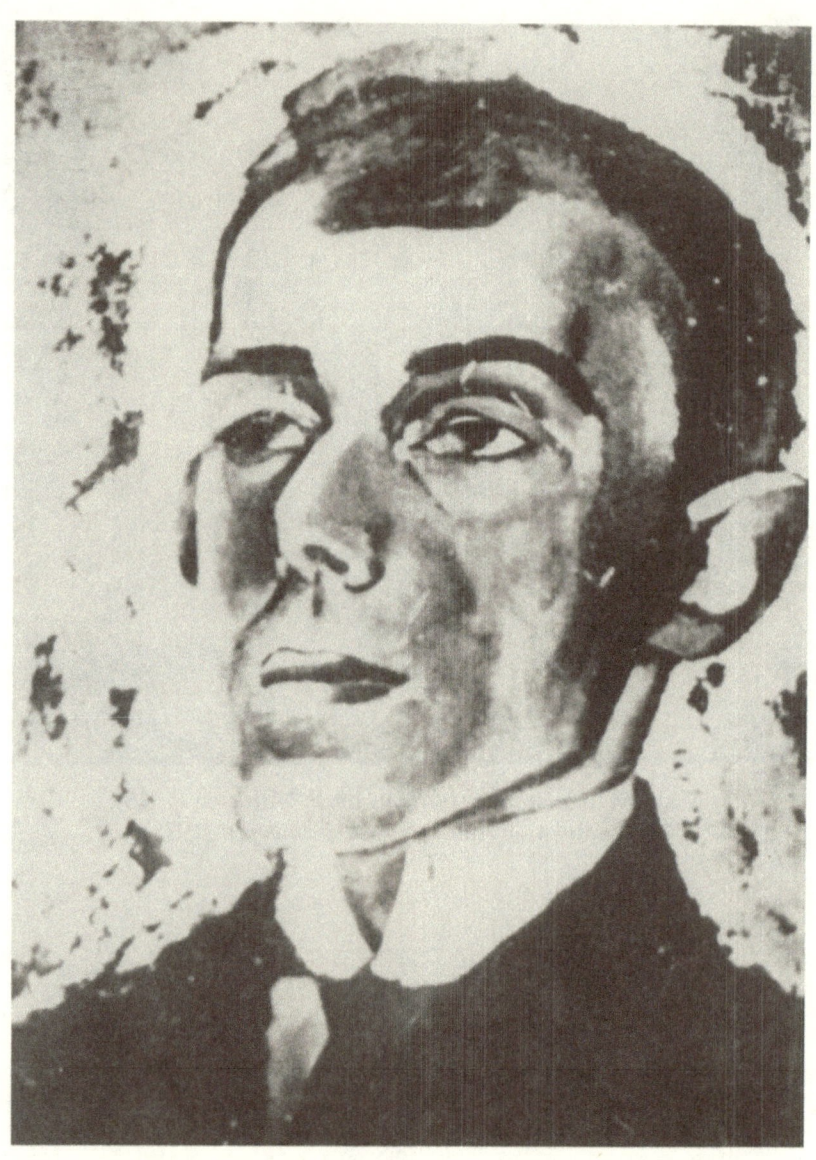

Osip Mandelstam: a portrait by Lev Bruni (c. 1917).

Osip Mandelstam (1923).

Osip Mandelstam (mid-1930s).

Autograph of "Slate Ode," stanzas 7–9 (1923).

VI

Revolutions and the Poetics of a Dying Age

The magical decree is implicit in all language; for the mere act of naming an object or situation decrees that it is to be singled out as such-and-such rather than as something-other. Hence, I think that an attempt to eliminate magic, in this sense, will involve us in the elimination of vocabulary itself as a way of sizing up reality.
   KENNETH BURKE, The Philosophy of Literary Form: Studies in Symbolic Action

Form is nothing but a product of religious creativity. And a literary device is an external expression of a living confession of faith.
   ANDREI BELYI, "The Present and the Future of Russian Poetry" (1907)

HISTORY'S WHEELS

Death is a structural principle.   NADEZHDA MANDELSTAM, Hope Abandoned

Few would doubt that modern poetry in the Western tradition has thrived on myth. But myth, too, can owe a debt to poetry, especially in a culture like that of early-twentieth-century Russia, where poets and poetry were a prized possession shared and cherished by the entire literate urban milieu. With the other institutions unsettled or destroyed in the catastrophic war and the social revolution, poetry, for a while, took the pride of place among the muses of the mobilized society, feeding its seductively "magical" verbal structures to the lexicons of the political "magicians" who were busy naturalizing their own version of the emerging, unfamiliar world. Chthonic narratives, or the mythology of death and revival, are among the verbal structures most suited for the exceptional circumstances in a nation's or an individual's life,[1] and one encounters them again and again in the poetry of the years of war and revolution.[2] In this respect Mandelstam was little different from other contemporary poets, although his background positioned him better than many to make poetic sense out of catastrophic events. As a beginning poet, he had passed through the rigorous "chiliastic-chthonic" academy of Viacheslav Ivanov, where he received his training in Nietzschean aestheticism, Frazer's mythology, Russian populism, and the latest versions of Russian Orthodox Christianity—all required disciplines of Russian modernism that in one form or another account for the essence of what we have come to know as Osip Mandelstam.

"Your seeds," he wrote to Ivanov in 1909, referring to the knowledge dispensed at the famous night vigils at the Tower, "have lodged themselves deep in my soul, and I take fright as I look at their enormous shoots."[3] The disciple's choice of an organic, in fact chthonic, metaphor—hence the "fright," appropriate for an initiate into a chthonic cult—prompts one to imagine some Petersburg version of the Eleusinian mysteries during which the priestly Ivanov or the professorial Tadeusz Zielinski planted their seeds in the poetic soul of Osip Mandelstam. After a period of dormancy that commenced with the strained relations between the "older" and the "younger" generations of poets (the formation of the Poets' Guild and the Acmeist Sturm und Drang of 1912–13), these seeds were revived, grew, and began to blossom—naturally stimulated by the blood-letting of the great European war. The 1916 poem that follows may be counted among these wartime asphodel flowers:

> В Петрополе прозрачном мы умрем,
> Где властвует над нами Прозерпина.
> Мы в каждом вздохе смертный воздух пьем,
> И каждый час нам смертная година.
> Богиня моря, грозная Афина,
> Сними могучий каменный шелом.
> В Петрополе прозрачном мы умрем,
> Где царствуешь не ты, а Прозерпина.
>
> 1916

> In Petropolis, translucent, we shall die
> Where Proserpine reigns over us.
> With each breath we drink the mortal air,
> And each hour is for us death's hour.
> Oh Sea Goddess, formidable Athena,
> Take down your mighty stone helmet.

Revolutions and a Dying Age: 1920–1923

> In Petropolis, translucent, we shall die—
> Here reigns over us, not you, but Proserpine.[4]

Certainly, poets who live in a crisis-ridden country (and especially those of draft age) are inspired to produce darker visions. For Mandelstam and his contemporaries, however, the specter of an apocalypse or an Armageddon (notwithstanding Rozanov's *Apocalypse of Our Time*[5] or some of the Futurist narrative poems)[6] was not the only pattern for constructing the image of the age. The more frequently preferred patterns were associated with the "eternal recurrence"[7] (of Vico, Schopenhauer, Nietzsche, and later, Spengler) or Bergson's *durée,* both positing a historical rhythm as well as simultaneity and both nurturing a vague belief in some form of a collective or individual immortality—at least as they were received in Russia.[8] For it is significant that the poem's prophesied demise of Petersburg does not have the finality of Christian eschatology but is based on the agricultural cycle of the Persephone (or, to use Frazer's generic name for the Queen of the Underworld, the "Corn Goddess") cult. A manifestation of nineteenth-century historical relativism, this view of humanity's past not only guarded against superimposing modern values on chronologically and culturally distant phenomena but also allowed the children of that century (as Mandelstam referred to his contemporaries)[9] to perceive themselves as a recurrent echo of an earlier period and to assume the identity of the original actors of a long-gone age.[10] This is why, in "Pushkin and Skriabin," Mandelstam could inveigh against his contemporaries' lapse into "Buddhism"[11] and speak about the incest-like abomination of "history turning back" while welcoming the "return of the spirit of tragedy," with Phaedra and Antigone once again facing their dreadful dilemmas.

The ideas of cyclicity and the related chthonic mythology so permeated the thinking of the age that it seems it was impossible to discuss the past without making it immediately relevant for the present and future. The pattern cropped up everywhere, and its recurrence itself served frequently as a subject for discussion. Consider this impassioned passage from an essay by Mikhail Kuzmin on the passing of the eighteenth century (italics are mine):

> At the threshold of the nineteenth century, on the eve of the complete change of life, everyday customs, feelings, and social relations, all Europe was gripped by a feverish, enamored, tremulous striving to transfix that fleeting life, the trifles of everyday existence condemned to disappear, the charms and the bric-a-brac of peaceful living, home comedies, "bourgeois" idylls, feelings, and thoughts whose day had just about passed. It was as though people were trying to stop the *wheel of time.*[12]

Apparently, *then* was very much like *now*, and the cycle between the two measured a neat one hundred years. In this rhetorical universe, the cyclical metaphor, whether organic or astronomical, could not be avoided. "Poetry," Kuzmin wrote elsewhere, "like history, can have a wheel."[13] Be it man, epoch, culture, or literary genre, these social phenomena, like the revolutions of planets around their sun or the cycles of vegetative life, had their spring, summer, fall, winter, and, who could tell, perhaps another spring. What effect did this mind-set have on Mandelstam's poetic strategy in the early 1920s? I shall start with an extended example.

THE INNER FORM OF FIN DE SIÈCLE

One of the more distinct patterns etched on the cyclical consciousness of Mandelstam and his contemporaries was the expression *konets veka* (fin de siècle), perhaps the most common symbolic idiom on which a poet could embroider his narrative of a "dying and reviving" age.[14] The English "turn of the century" also is explicit about the circularity of time, but it was the Russian language—where the word *vek* means both *saeculum* and "century," that is, a hundred years—that was particularly suited for a Mandelstamian "etymological" mythologizing. We can imagine that originally the expression provided a powerful resonance to the classical catastrophic myths known to every European schoolchild raised on Hesiod and Virgil, but we can be certain that by the early 1920s its evocative intensity was weakened and largely dispersed. The ambiguous expression had done its work: it had given a certain shape to the thought of the age and retreated into the background of common usage. In his powerfully influential *Symbolism*, Andrei Belyi described this process as "putrefaction," as the "death of the word."[15] The neologisms, the trans-sense, and the wild hyperbolization of the Futurists were meant to inoculate verbal art against this recently discovered disease.[16]

Mandelstam had cautioned the Futurists as early as 1913 against abandoning "the conscious meaning of the word, Logos."[17] He chose a related strategy, related especially to the Futurists' paraphrasing of the old Symbolist precept: "We consider the word to be the creator of myth; as it dies, the word gives birth to myth and vice versa."[18] Hence, rather than discard the "dead word" altogether, Mandelstam approached it as an internalized mental pattern that a speaker of the language accepts a priori and that therefore could serve as an effective vehicle for conveying the poet's narrative "message." By no means a new technique for poetry (witness puns and riddles),[19] it had become especially popular among the post-Symbolist generation, who tended to "secularize" the heavily hieratical myth-making of their mentors so inclined to the "dropsy of grand themes." But since the "myth-making" and "theurgy," or verbal magic, belonged to the sacral sphere a priori, the resulting "secularization" often entailed, and still has the effect of, a sacralization of humble life.[20]

In the vocabulary of the 1920s, this treatment was considered a form of "charade,"[21] a parlor game for members of a society set that functioned, not unlike its ancient cousin the riddle, as a test of initiation. If we turn to a different, perhaps more familiar discourse, Mandelstam's procedure for reanimating the "dead word" begins to resemble a psychoanalyst's construction of the etiology of a neurotic symptom, or, to turn to Roland Barthes, as the emergence of a hegemonic myth mystifying an exploitative power struggle.[22] For the poet, however, who in this respect followed Viacheslav Ivanov's recastings of the comparative-historical theories (e.g., A. N. Veselovskii), the existence of an idiomatic locution such as fin de siècle called for the creation of an explanatory lyric narrative of origins that could eventually be accepted by the culture as a true myth—a crystallization of the nation's character or, as Mandelstam's contemporaries would have put it, the people's communal soul and its destiny. A passage from a 1904 essay by Viacheslav Ivanov may be used verbatim to elaborate Mandelstam's technique in a historical perspective:

> But if symbols are ineffable and inexplicable and we are helpless before their wholesome secret meaning, they reveal one aspect of their nature to a historian—he uncovers them in the petrifications of ancient faiths and deifications, the forgotten myth and abandoned cult. So the corns of wheat of the Pharaohs' granaries have survived even to our suns under the shrouds of the mummies.

A modern poet, according to Ivanov, was to resemble such a historian, but he was also to be more. He was, Ivanov continued,

> unconsciously submerged in the elemental life of folklore. Atavistically, he perceives and stores in himself the reserves of the living past, which colors all his representations, all the combinations of ideas, his inventions in image and expression. . . . An organ of popular self-consciousness, he [the poet] is at the same time an organ of the popular remembrance. It is through him that the people recalls its live soul and restores the powers dormant in it.[23]

These declarations lend themselves particularly well to a comparison with A. N. Veselovskii's seminal monograph, "Psychological Parallelism and Its Forms from the Perspective of Poetic Style."

The Inner Form of Fin de Siècle

The visible world gradually becomes accessible to our consciousness in those spheres that have hitherto seemed lacking in life, incapable of yielding analogies, but now appear full of meaning, humanly suggestive. They [analogies, parallelisms] may also produce those complexes of vital features which we call myth; at this point, I will only recall the description of the steam engine in Zola and Garshin. Clearly, this complex will unconsciously assume the shape of the traditional mythic imagination; it will become a *new form* [*novoobrazovanie*] which can serve not only the goals of poetry but the goals of religion as well. In a similar manner, new religions have given a vital meaning to symbols and legends that had been circulating among the people for centuries without prompting an analogy until there appeared an appropriate object to which they could be applied.[24]

What Mandelstam understood to be the poet's vocation came fairly close to these notions—whether in the scholarly version of Veselovskii or the enchanting pronouncements of Ivanov. In 1922, perhaps in response to the Formalists' fashion for demystifying literary creation, Mandelstam produced a hybrid discourse that joined the rationalizing terminology of scholarship to the enchanting riddle style of the Symbolist and post-Symbolist oracular prose. The occasion was the first anniversary of Blok's death, when the erstwhile authority of Blok's name, which began to decline during the civil war, was not merely revived but intensified tremendously. Now perhaps more than ever before, this name could lend legitimacy to a discourse with which it was associated. Mandelstam's essay, "The Badger's Hole," whatever its other merits and functions, was intended as a claim on the power of this name for defining the terms of discussion for contemporary poetry. To put it bluntly, Mandelstam attempted to translate the relics of the Symbolist Blok, who abhorred Acmeism, to the shrine of the Acmeist aesthetic program. Hence, Blok's legacy was presented by Mandelstam in terms of the poet's cultural genealogy, key myths, and reliance on "migratory motifs." These were the features Mandelstam shared with Blok thanks to their mutual, but of course unequal, affinity with Viacheslav Ivanov's "archetypal" recipe for poetry and the historical-comparative studies of A. N. Veselovskii.[25] Praising "The Steps of the Commendatore" as the "summit of Blok's historical poetics," Mandelstam engaged his reader in a genealogical charade, tethering Blok's *poetry* with the barely visible line to Acmeism through the acknowledgment of a common paternity in the academic learning of Veselovskii's *Historical Poetics:*

> The freedom with which Blok treats the thematics of this poetic tradition [the nineteenth century] makes one think that some plots, in-

dividual and accidental till recently, have earned civic equality with myth. Such are the themes of Don Juan and Carmen [in Blok]. The condensed and exemplary story of Mérimée was fortunate: the light and militant music of Bizet, like a combat bugle, has broadcast across all the backwaters the message about the eternal youth of the Romance race. Blok's poetry offers the last refuge to the narrative-myth that is the youngest in the European family. But what constitutes the summit [read: Acmeism] of Blok's historical poetics [read: Veselovskii], the triumph of the European myth, which moves freely in the traditional forms but is not afraid of an anachronism of modernity, is his "Steps of the Commendatore."[26]

The verbal lore that Mandelstam mined for his poetry was often even less distinguished—"secularized," as he referred to it[27]—than the tale of Don Juan or Mérimée's "Carmen." His world, having collapsed so recently, could provide him with a mountain of salvageable material produced by tradition but no longer attached to it. Moreover, the windowpane through which a poet living in a more placid age could see the world only darkly had been wiped clean (or so it seemed) by the revolutionary wave; the dross of custom, institutions, and everyday drudgery that the Russians call *byt* were no more. "Now," wrote Mandelstam in "Word and Culture," a 1921 essay in which he celebrated the bare minimalism of pre-NEP urban life,

> it is as if the phenomenon of glossolalia were taking place. In a sacred frenzy poets are speaking the languages of all times and cultures. Nothing is impossible. Just as the door of a dying man's house is open to everybody, so the door of the old world is flung open before the crowd. Suddenly everything has become common property. Go and take it. Everything has become accessible: all the labyrinths, all the secret hiding places, all the secret passages. The word has become, not a seven-, but a thousand-reed pipe, animated by the breath of all the ages.[28]

Indicative of Mandelstam's resolve to engage in this revival project (animating the "thousand-reed pipe") was his repeated insistence that the fusion of "joy of recognition" and "wonderment" before novelty must be the central criterion for modern poetry. "Not only can his poems be memorized easily," he wrote about Mikhail Kuzmin in 1916, "but they can be, as it were, recalled (the impression of recall at first reading); they emerge out of forgetfulness (classicism)."[29] Velemir Khlebnikov—another former disciple of Ivanov who, like Mandelstam, was "submerged in the elemental life of folklore"—left a similar definition of poetic speech. He called his neologisms, new words formed on the basis of existing roots, "an unknown man with a familiar face."[30]

But unlike Khlebnikov's neologisms, which were indeed new and could not be easily thematized without a new narrative elaboration, Mandelstam's poetry and prose functioned as an aggregate of "word-themes," each one capable of projecting or implying a *familiar* narrative. Poem-myths produced according to this scheme, Mandelstam was saying, would be something new, for the verbal pattern they elaborated—however deeply it was etched on the linguistic consciousness of contemporaries—was made to appear in a new light. Or, conversely, as verbal structures based on a pattern already internalized, these poems could also be "recognized," "recollected," "remembered"—in the manner of Plato's recollection of primordial knowledge, "anamnesis" (as Ivanov had pointed out in the essay cited previously). In the course of such a "mnemonic" elaboration, the word—the expression itself—became "disautomatized," "revived," indeed, "resurrected" (see Shklovskii's *The Resurrection of the Word*).[31] And just as Mandelstam's etymological principle ran parallel to the Formalists' conceptions ("art as device"), so his insistence on the *charismatic* trance of a modern poet—the Pentecostal "glossolalia"—amplified Shklovskii's own, if less apparent, indebtedness to the ecstatic theories of artistic creativity:

> We can say one thing: it was the fate of many literary phenomena to appear for the first time in the creations of ecstatics. . . . Religious ecstasy has already prefigured the appearance of new forms. What constitutes the history of literature is that poets canonize and introduce into it those new forms which have long been the property of the shared poetic linguistic consciousness.[32]

In his essay, "Word and Culture," Mandelstam laid bare this aspect of his poetics: an "etymological," seemingly ecstatic play on words.[33] In part alluding to the recently minted Russian Imagism, with which he seemed to have had an association,[34] he gave the following advice to poets:

> Write imageless verse, if you can, if you are capable of it. A blind man [*slepoi*] will recognize the dear face, barely touching it with his seeing fingers, and the tears of joy, a true joy of recognition, will burst out of his eyes after a long separation. A poem lives with the inner image, with that ringing cast [*slepok*] of the form that predates the written poem. There is not a single word yet, but the poem is already ringing. What rings is the inner image, this is what the poet senses with his hearing.[35]

In English, the passage loses its effectiveness as simultaneously a statement concerning a technique and an illustration of that technique at work. In Russian, however, where the words *slepoi* (a blind man) and *slepok* (cast) are orthographic paronyms, the etymological or, as the case may be, folk-etymological wordplay is apparent to anyone who can visualize the spelling of these two words. We shall return to this mythology of blindness in the discussion of the "Oedipus" poem.

A literate contemporary would have picked out another interesting item (and one is on record as having done so),[36] namely, a part of the famous term of Alexander Potebnia, the "inner form of the word." Indeed, Mandelstam's treatment of "image" (a double entendre, meaning both icon and trope) was a transparent allusion to Viktor Shklovskii and his critique of Potebnia's unimaginative disciples who insisted that trope represented a sine qua non of poetry.[37] More than one road was leading to Potebnia, the eminent Russian philologist.[38] He applied the term *inner image* to that aspect of the word that represented the word's "closest etymological meaning, namely, the means by which its content is conveyed"; that "content," meanwhile, constituted the word's current referent.[39] To put it simply, the "inner form" is the etymon of the word with respect to which its current usage functions as a metaphor. For Potebnia, this was the essence of language development as well as of poetic creativity—"the word with a live inner form"[40]—which made it doubly appropriate for Mandelstam to turn to the philologist's formulations and to ground his practice in reactivating the "inner form" of the word. Poetry, after all, was language, and Mandelstam's understanding of it as such ran parallel to that of the Formalist school of criticism, with its own linguistic orientation. Finally, and this is a decisive element for Mandelstam's poetics of anamnesis, Potebnia traced this basic linguistic principle to primordial verbal magic and, by implication, to the "ecstatic" states:

> And indeed, both language and poetry contain *positive* proof that according to the beliefs of all the Indo-European nations, the word is thought, the word is truth and justice, wisdom, poetry. Together with wisdom and poetry, the word was considered to be one with the divine principle. There are myths deifying the word itself. Not to mention the Divine Word (Logos) of the Hellenistic Jews. . . . The word is the thing itself which is demonstrated by the etymological kinship of the two words designating the word and the thing. . . . As the essence of things, the word receives power over nature in action and in prayer, etc., etc.[41]

To illustrate this complex of poetic principles, the core of which constitutes the revival of the "inner form of the word" by means of etymological mythologizing, I shall juxtapose a passage from a 1923 overview of Russian literature with one of the more important poems by Mandelstam, "No, never have I been anybody's contemporary," which was composed sometime in January 1924.

Commenting on the dramatic changes in Russian letters, the recent turning away from poetry to prose, I. N. Rozanov characterized the efflorescence of poetry since the turn of the century as a phenomenon comparable to the "blossoming of Pushkin's pleiad," which took place, he added in amazement at history's chronological neatness, "exactly one hundred years ago."[42] Thanks to this awe of round numbers (based, it seems, on some deep-seated numerological superstitions), we sometimes refer to Russian literature of the early twentieth century as the "Silver Age." Mandelstam, who was proverbially "untopical" and "uncontemporary," appealed to the same belief in a hundred-year cycle of return in designing his sarcastic—or, to be precise, enantheopathically magical[43]—response to the offending relevance-minded critics.[44] I shall cite the entire poem:

>Нет, никогда ничей я не был современник,
>Мне не с руки почет такой.
>О как противен мне какой-то соименник,
>То был не я, то был другой.
>
>Два сонных яблока у века-властелина
>И глиняный прекрасный рот,
>Но к млеющей руке стареющего сына
>Он, умирая, припадет.
>
>Я с веком поднимал болезненные веки —
>Два сонных яблока больших,
>И мне гремучие рассказывали реки
>Ход воспаленных тяжб людских.
>
>Сто лет тому назад подушками белела
>Складная легкая постель,
>И странно вытянулось глиняное тело, —
>Кончался века первый хмель.
>
>Среди скрипучего похода мирового
>Какая легкая кровать.
>Ну что же, если нам не выковать другого,
>Давайте с веком вековать.
>
>И в жаркой комнате, в кибитке и в палатке
>Век умирает — а потом
>Два сонных яблока на роговой облатке
>Сияют перистым огнем.
>
>   1924

> No, never have I ever been anybody's contemporary,
> I wouldn't know what to do with such honor.
> Oh, how repulsive to me is that mere namesake,
> That one was not I, that one was another.
>
> Age the master has two sleepy apples
> And a beautiful mouth of clay,
> But to the languid hand of the aging son
> He will fall down as he is dying.
>
> Together with the century, I raised my painful eyelids—
> Two large sleepy orbs,
> And the rumbling rivers related to me
> The course of the fevered disputes of men.
>
> A hundred years ago, its pillows gleaming white,
> A folding light bed;
> Behold the clay body stretched out strangely—
> The age's first intoxication was coming to an end.
>
> Amid the world's creaking nomadic march,
> What a light bed!
> Well, if we cannot hammer out another,
> Let us age with this age.
>
> And in a warm room, in a kibitka, in a tent,
> The age dies—and afterward,
> Two sleepy apples on a corneous *oblatum*
> Blaze with a feathered flame.[45]

The poem has been analyzed superbly by Omry Ronen,[46] and I shall not discuss it here at great length. Although it is enigmatic, even an unprepared reader, especially among Mandelstam's contemporaries, would realize that the eyes of the dead age—with which the poet is identified and which, in turn, is identified as the father of the poet—became the flaming, Phoenix-like host (*oblatum*) illuminating the successor age. Pushkin's Tatyana sealed her letter to Onegin with an "oblatka"—"A pink *oblatka* is drying / On the *fevered* tongue." These lines had long imprinted themselves on the consciousness of the gymnasium-educated Russian reader—or, as the Russian idiom would have it, it was "on everyone's tongue," an "automatic" locution. The word *oblatka* had come to denote a mere sealing stamp, but in his poem Mandelstam revived the "inner form" of the word, restoring its etymological history—as a communion wafer, the medium as well as the message of sacramental communication between a Christian and the Savior and, by extension for Mandelstam, between the modern poet addressee and his predecessor poet, the sacred Pushkin, the medium and the message of the Russian tongue. In Mandelstam's narrative context, this etymological play might be imagined dramatically as a form of the holy communion with the speech of the original, or archetypal, poet being placed on the "fevered tongue" of the aging successor, who, too, was the son of his century-age.[47]

Mandelstam's etymological mythologizing emerges most clearly in the link established between the "age" and the "eyes," a link offering a narrative justification for the paronymy VEK-VEKO (age/century–eyelid). In this manner the expression "the end of the century" received a narrative elaboration: it became a story about the *death* of a *personified* Age, and more, about the glazing over of the Age's *eyes* as he passed away on one of his many deathbeds. The visual motif and the motif of the poet-witness are further supported by the invocation of Gogol's Vii, a monster with *heavy* eyelids whose eyes were so frightful that he killed by looking,[48] and of Maiakovskii's angry, spell-like pun issuing from the poet's mouth: "Lift for me my eyelids of ages [*Podnimite mne vekov veki*]."[49] In a 1922 poem, "The Age" ("Vek"), Mandelstam presented the poet as a martyr who must look straight into the Vii-like eyes of the age, reading in them the mortifying record of its terrors—all in order to establish the continuity of culture between the dead old Russia and the new Russia of his own day. In Gogol's story, Vii's victim was a young man, the reluctant plaything of a witch whom he later murdered and over whose dead but still animated body the witch's father forced him to read the *Psalter* in the hope that her soul would be spared the fires of hell. Thus, Gogol's evil *panochka,* too, was drawn into Mandelstam's mythologies of Hippolytus-poet and Phaedra-Russia.

> Век мой, зверь мой, кто сумеет
> Заглянуть в твои зрачки
> И своею кровью склеит
> Двух столетий позвонки?
> Кровь-строительница хлещет
> Горлом из земных вещей,
> Захребетник лишь трепещет
> На пороге новых дней.

> My age, my beast, who shall be able
> To look deep into your eyes
> And glue with his own blood
> The vertebrae of the two centuries.
> Blood the builder is gushing out of the throat
> Of earthly things,
> Only a parasitic fence-sitter is trembling
> On the threshold of the new days.[50]

Linked to these motifs was the popular "astral mythology," so popular, in fact, that the five-pointed star (the "pentagram" of Pil'niak's witchdoctors)[51] became one of the emblems of the new Soviet state. In Mandelstam, the astral usage can possibly be traced to another mythic elaboration of the "stars-eyes" metaphor ("stars looking down")—according to which the stars in heaven represented the all-seeing eyes of immortal souls, including those of poets (and soon, movie actors) who had left the earth. For the poets of Mandelstam's generation, this was a shared mythology. Recall Maiakovskii's "Still More Petersburg":

> А с неба смотрела какая-то дрянь
> величественно, как Лев Толстой.

> And some kind of rubbish was staring from the sky
> grandly, like Leo Tolstoy.

Or Maiakovskii's "farewell" to Esenin:

> Вы ушли,
>   как говорится,
>   в мир иной.
> Пустота...
>   Летите,
>   в звезды врезываясь.

> You have gone,
>   as the saying goes,
>   into the other world.
> Emptiness...
>   You're flying,
>   slicing into stars.[52]

In Pasternak's no less famous "Hamlet," stars are soul-spectators watching Hamlet through opera glasses aimed at the protagonist out of the dark theater of the night sky:

> Гул затих. Я вышел на подмостки.
> Прислонясь к дверному косяку,
> Я ловлю в далеком отголоске
> Что случится на моем веку.
>
> На меня наставлен сумрак ночи
> Тысячью биноклей на оси.
> Если только можно, Авва Отче,
> Чашу эту мимо пронеси.

> The rumble has died down. I've entered the stage.
> Leaning against the door frame,

The Inner Form of Fin de Siècle

> I am catching in the far-off echo
> What will happen in the course of my age.
>
> The dark of night is aimed at me
> With a thousand binoculars on their axes.
> If only you could, Abba Father,
> Let this cup pass me.[53]

The appeal to stars was in fact so "overworked" that it elicited the following parodic lines from the enfant terrible of Russian modernism, Vadim Shershenevich, who concluded his 1919 "Skyscraper of Images Minus Conjugation" thus:

> В небес голубом стакане
> Гонококки звезд.
>
> In the blue glass of heaven,
>   the gonococci of stars.[54]

Mandelstam himself outlined a partial genealogy of this "myth" (Dante-Goethe-Lermontov-Viacheslav Ivanov) in his "Slate Ode," where stars were ostensibly the stars of classical Russian poetry:

> Звезда с звездой — могучий стык,
> Кремнистый путь из старой песни,
>
> A star and a star is a mighty conjuncture
> The flinty way out of an old song.[55]

And not unexpectedly, the "conjuncture" with which the "Ode" ended, and which echoed the first two lines, also turned out to have something to do with Christ and, by implication, with Mandelstam's incessant thematization of the Eucharist:

> И я хочу вложить персты
> В кремнистый путь из старой песни,
> Как в язву, заключая в стык
> Кремень с водой, с подковой перстень.
>   1923
>
> And I, too, wish to thrust my fingers
> Into the flinty way from the old song
> As into the wound, locking into a conjuncture
> Flint and water, the horseshoe and the signet ring.

The myth based on a pun involving the character of Gogol's "Vii"—Khoma Brut, or Thomas Brute—came full circle, drawing into its complex of implied narratives (for example, the "horseshoe"—*Hippo*-

ytus) the story of the doubting Apostle Thomas and the names of the father-age, "Brute" or "beast" ("My age, my beast").[56]

By expanding this scopoastral myth to include the Host (the "oblatum" of the cornea of the dying age), Mandelstam could ascribe to the practice of poetry the attributes of a transcendent vow—not unlike the vow of a priest who recites the Mass and administers communion and the last rites—a vow monitored by the all-seeing eyes in heaven. As a result of this sacral contextualization, poetic anamnesis came to represent a poet's duty; and for Mandelstam in those years, this meant the duty of a lyric poet, obligating him to a revival of the word. This project, itself an imitation of the Eucharist, could be seen as a mimetic revival of Logos.[57] The "age" and his "son" were dying, and on the narrative level Mandelstam seems to have accepted this "fate"; that is, he put it to use in his poetry by thematizing it in his narratives of self-presentation.

How effective could this verbal filigree be in conveying Mandelstam's "narrative" to contemporaries? Details aside, the general sense of the poems could hardly have been missed by cultivated readers. They were nurtured on the myth of the poet-martyr, poet-prophet, and poet-redeemer; they could readily recognize allusions to classical Russian poetry and the Scripture and were constantly assaulted by such political metaphors as *styk* ("conjuncture" or "joint," a word that originally denoted the space between two contiguous rails)[58] and such politically potent invocations as the story of doubting Thomas applied over and over again to the proverbially "Hamletian" intellectuals.[59] These "words for one day" (*odnodnevki*)—Mandelstam's term for the street argot used by Blok in his *The Twelve*[60]—were no less common or familiar to the contemporary than to the still-vigorous survivor of the shock of the twentieth century, the fin de siècle. Finally, the majority of Mandelstam's readers had gone through the university, where, like the poet, they must have learned from Potebnia's theories that "myth represented a verbal structure,"

> that is (in its simplest form, one word) which combines in a single entity an image (= predicate), representation (*tertium comparationis*), and meaning (= the psychological subject, i.e., that which has to be explained). . . . The existence of myth without the word is as unthinkable . . . as the emergence of the subsequent myth without the existence of the preceding myth-word.[61]

POETICS, SCHOLARSHIP, IDEOLOGY

The years immediately preceding and following the Revolution of 1917 were not only some of the most productive in the development of Russian literature, and especially poetry, but they also constituted a period of extraordinary verbal intensity, which permeated every aspect of Russian life. The relaxation of censorship after the Revolution of 1905 and the growing professionalism and education of urban Russia created an enormous and highly diversified market whose demands, thanks to modern means of communication, were well catered to. Originally a rather esoteric group with a minor circle of readers, Russian modernist poets profited immensely from this development. Whether they sought it or not, by 1910 they had become a highly visible and, where public sensibility was concerned, influential group. Indeed, it was during this period that the literary culture of the Russian intelligentsia, without losing its frame of reference in the elite educational tradition, began to acquire features we associate with the popular culture of our own time: the institution of the celebrity, emphasis on performing arts, and the attendant large-scale public exposure. Tolstoy was perhaps the first man of letters to be processed into an international star by the most modern forms of mass media, including the phonograph and film. Among the earlier modernists, Aleksandr Blok, the exemplar for the post-Symbolist generation, was to benefit from this duality the most. He was the "tragic tenor of the epoch," as Akhmatova called him, combining in a concise formula a reference to the atemporal high mimetic genre, a popular idol's acute sensitivity to the mood of the present, and the celebrity status of the stage star. It should come as no surprise, then, that Blok's appearance was replicated in the dandified lover protagonist in a whole series of films produced around 1910.[62]

The First World War, which brought into being the modern propaganda machine, gave a decisive push to the already-expanded print medium, turning it into a powerful tool of mass exhortation and appeal on a historically unprecedented scale.[63] The revolution inherited this legacy of the war years, and the Bolsheviks, gaining control of the public sphere, including the press, were able to use the new tool with great skill and effectiveness. Supported by the apparatus of violence, language—in its institutional aspect as the medium of mass communication—became the primary means of binding together in a new way a society that had undergone a complete disintegration. And it was the propaganda machine, relying almost exclusively on the verbal medium, that took the pride of place among the institutions empowered to shape the new society and state.

Revolutions and a Dying Age: 1920–1923

Those whose association with the word was a matter of professional interest or vocation—the critics, poets, and writers of fiction—were no doubt threatened by the increasing politicization of language, but they were also encouraged by the implied and explicit acknowledgment of the power of the word. For them, it served as a great source of strength despite (and in part because of) the Soviet government's continued effort to assert total control over the print medium, indeed all forms of public expression. By 1928–29 the last nongovernment presses, including the writers' cooperatives, were shut down for good.[64] Together with the verbal creativity and the enormously productive innovations in linguistic and literary scholarship of the preceding decades, this verbal intensity contributed to the achievement of the Formalists, who produced some of their most interesting work in the decade following the revolution. On friendly terms with many of them and at times a participant in their discussions, Mandelstam absorbed their ideas, using them to substantiate his "philosophy of the word," just as the Formalists themselves relied on his pronouncements, and particularly his poetic practice, for their own theoretical formulations.[65] Since much of Mandelstam's poetic program is incomprehensible outside the context of this exchange, I shall consider it here briefly.

Mandelstam interpreted both the "arbitrariness of the sign"[66] and Potebnia's ideas on poetic image (the "inner form" of the word)[67] as a unique, "Hellenistic" property of the Russian language. These two theories, only partly compatible, appeared to lend philological authority to Mandelstam's own poetic practice. Saussure assured him freedom in the choice of the signifier, and Potebnia vouched for the word's ability to retain the history of its use, which a poet would eventually "resurrect" in an epiphany of simultaneity. This was the "word-Psyche," which "hovered over things as a soul hovers over the body that it has abandoned but has not forgotten."[68] Put another way, poetry could reactivate the word's etymology and unfold in the present the history of its usage. When these two theoretical perspectives combined with Mandelstam's religious and historiosophical thinking and what he had borrowed from the philosophy of Henri Bergson, the resulting mixture produced a full-blown, word-centered weltanschauung. Even the existence of the nation was predicated on the protective power of verbal art and, by implication, the verbal artist.

> We have no Acropolis. Our culture, to this day, wanders around and cannot find its walls. And yet, every word of Dal's dictionary is the kernel of the Acropolis, a little Kremlin, a winged fortress of nominalism equipped with the Hellenistic spirit for an indefatigable struggle

with the formless elements, with nonbeing, which threatens our history from all sides.[69]

This passage could be Mandelstam's credo. But while it is emblematic of his faith in the power of the word, the faith itself was something that he shared with many Russian intellectuals. A little over half a century before him, Alexander Herzen, too, the St. Paul of the Russian intelligentsia, discerned an augury of Russia's future glory in the literary phenomenon by which the artistry of authors combined with their readiness to sacrifice themselves in the name of liberation.[70] This flattering (for a writer) view of literary authorship acquired a special poignancy in the wake of the revolution, as the other, no less tenuous, aspects of Herzen's scheme were miraculously coming true. Thus Mandelstam, who had seen the old regime vanish without a trace, could safely proclaim, echoing Herzen's view of Russia as an eager raw youth of history, that Russia was yet to reach her acme, that she was yet to produce her Acropolis—for an Acmeist, a symbol of a national destiny fulfilled. Even more uncanny than the radical political renewal of Russia was the realization of Herzen's key prediction that Russia would become the leading champion of socialism. Wrapping himself in the mantle of Herzen's certified clairvoyance, Mandelstam could augur with considerable authority that the Russian language (he meant her *belles lettres*) would be the cornerstone of the new nation and the main vehicle for her mission in history.

There was hardly anything idiosyncratic or arcane in this implicit appeal to Herzen. Herzen's writings as well as his biography had become part of the rhetoric of intellectual legitimation for the members of the intelligentsia as they were trying to define their stand vis-à-vis the new regime. Furthermore, the game of locating prophecies was a popular one in those uncertain times, and judging by the press, nothing could please the intelligentsia reader more than finding in Herzen's voluminous writings passages that could be used verbatim as commentary on the very latest issue.[71] In this regard, Mandelstam was no different from his contemporaries. To appreciate his difference we must look at his paean to the Russian language with the eyes of a reader of poetry. Then the dry bones of the messianic scheme, all too familiar to students of Russia, will begin to come alive as a historically and individually unique expression.

The apposition of the Acropolis and the Kremlin brings to the surface the etymological kinship of the two synecdochic emblems of Greek and Russian culture. Their association with the dictionary of Vladimir Dal, the dictionary, as its title states, of the "*living* Great Russian language," gives substance to the "live" presence of the spirit of Hellas in the poet's native tongue. In a context of this sort, we would do well to search for the presence of the other guardian angel of the Russian language, Pushkin, and if I am not mistaken, the image of the "kernel" (*oreshek*) alludes to him here, via the fabulous singing squirrel cracking golden nuts in his "Tale About Tsar Saltan."[72] Pushkin's tamed squirrel lived in a well-guarded crystal house where she sang songs, all the while cracking golden nuts with emerald kernels, from which the treasury minted the kingdom's gold coin. The allusion provided Mandelstam, if only implicitly, with one of the controlling images of the essay—a metaphor of a poet or, broadly, an author who can never sing enough songs or shell enough golden nuts (with their kernels of the "nominalist spirit" of the Russian language) but who, as he continues with his unending task, enriches the nation's treasury with the gold reserve of cultural value. This was a vocabulary easily understood by every educated Russian in the early years of the revolution and the NEP, when the paper currency as well as the promise of a new and just society often seemed secured only by faith (see Mandelstam's "Humanism and the Present").

To return to Mandelstam's declaration, the "winged fortress of nominalism" represents yet another complex metaphor-metonymy of the word, developing further the apposition of the Kremlin-Acropolis. Homer's heroes spoke "winged words," whereas the essential role of the Russian language as guardian of the country's identity endows the word with the character both of a military fortification and of wings, an attribute both of Nike, the protectress of victories, and Psyche, the Greek soul who migrates from body to body.[73]

Nor should one take Mandelstam literally when trying to understand what he meant by "nominalism." Moscow linguists became aware of the Saussurian notion of the "arbitrariness of the sign" as early as 1918,[74] and by 1922, when Mandelstam's essay came out, it already figured prominently in the discussions of modern Russian poetry. It did, for example, in Jakobson's *Noveishaia russkaia poeziia,* a work Mandelstam appears to have been familiar with even before its publication.[75] Not indifferent to the authority that science commanded among his contemporaries, Mandelstam must have derived particular satisfaction from the fact that the latest linguistic theory confirmed his own poetic practice. For Mandelstam's "word-Psyche," his metaphor for the word in poetry, was as arbitrary in her attachments as any semiotic sign.[76] Further, by choosing to refer to the Saussurian concept as "nominalism," Mandelstam was pointing to its association with the philosophical trends he had relied on in legitimizing the Acmeist creed. I have in mind medieval nominalism as well as its revival in the work of the neo-Kantian Freiburg school[77] and, most important, in the intuitivism of Henri Bergson, perhaps the most popular philosophical system of the early twentieth century.[78] But of course, Mandelstam was not a philosopher, and it would be a mistake—all of this genealogy notwithstanding—to hold his terminology to a rigorous test. For his nominalism, and no doubt that of many of his contemporaries, tended to cross rather easily into the realist domain insofar, at least, as he believed in the power of the word over the essential world. Mandelstam's frequent appeals to Potebnia, seen through the symbolist, magical prism, indicate as much.

On the one hand, the never-complete identity between the verbal sign and what it signified, or, as Mandelstam put it in his essay, "the eternal cracking of the nut because it can never be quite cracked,"[79] points to the nominalism of Roscelinus and William of Ockham,[80] Bergson, the theory of Saussure, and the Tiutchevean nominalist theme of the ineffable poetic thought[81] (almost a standard refrain in contemporary discussions of poetry). On the other hand, the intensely "etymological" context, permeated with Potebnia's ideas on language, prompts an etymological reading of "nominalism" as the capacity for magical nomination (*nomen est omen*), for affecting the world with the word. This subject was addressed in relation to poetry in scholarly terms by Potebnia and Veselovskii and, later, in theurgical terms by Viacheslav Ivanov, Blok, and Belyi.[82] Of course, the understanding of poetry Mandelstam advocated in "Word and Culture" did not replicate a naive belief in verbal magic. Nevertheless, the two were not unrelated, as the explicit identification of the word with the good luck charm Nike demonstrates.

Like Belyi in his "The Magic of Words," Mandelstam considered the word to be capable of, as he put it, an "indefatigable struggle with the formless elements, with nonbeing."[83] The essay "Word and Culture" began with praise for Henri Bergson for "considering phenomena outside of their chronological order."[84] And although Mandelstam's interpretation was rather unusual,[85] there is little doubt that some of his formulations are incomprehensible without reference to the work of the French philosopher. Using Bergson as a departure point (in this respect, too, like Belyi),[86] he proposed a view of poetry as an organ that intuitively apprehends and interacts with the world free of any mediation. Like Bergson's intuitive wasps, a poet in this scheme would perceive and convey the plenitude of living matter in both space and time and would thus function as the creative memory of the human race—an active, continuous, ever-present memory "gnawing into the future."[87] The terms may have been new, but the message differed little from the one proclaimed in "Pushkin and Skriabin."

Some of the poet's lecture notes from his days at the University of St. Petersburg, preserved in the Mandelstam archive at Princeton, demonstrate his familiarity with medieval nominalists. They, like Bergson, considered intuition to be the main intellectual faculty that enabled an individual not only to perceive objects truly but also (and here one is reminded of Saussure's synchronic linguistics) to perceive immediately the *relation* among objects within a totality.[88] Mandelstam's apparent reliance on this philosophical tradition helps us understand his critique of the Symbolists' poetics for its Realism, which, in extreme form, tended to deny reality to individual differences, treating them instead as a manifestation of immutable forms. For the medieval Realists, just as for the Symbolists of Mandelstam's critique, everything became everything else, or, as he put it, "nothing wanted to be itself." Speaking of the Acmeist reaction to this "contredanse of correspondences," he offered a new formulation reminiscent of Abelard's nominalist understanding of the word: "Away from Symbolism, long live the live rose."[89]

For Mandelstam, who yearned for the possibility of preserving every moment in its individual fullness from the time of his earliest thoughts in "François Villon," the "realism" of the Symbolists must have appeared at the very least misguided and at worst abhorrent:

> Man is no longer a master of his house. He has to live in some place, a kind of a church or a sacred grove of the Druids. The eye of a master of things has nothing to rest itself on, it has no respite. All utensils are in rebellion. The broom is asking to be let go to the witches' Sabbath, the pot no longer wants to cook but demands for itself some kind of absolute significance (as if cooking had no absolute significance). The master has been chased out of the house, and he no longer dares to step inside.[90]

In terms of Mandelstam's "Hellenistic" understanding of language, the "ringing and speaking flesh," a cooking pot did indeed possess both a singular and an absolute significance, but, of course, only insofar as it was the word.

The Futurists' valorization of the "word as such," the "self-generated word," and the Formalists' related understanding of poetic language as a discourse "oriented toward the mode of expression" (*ustanovka na vyrazhenie*)[91] constituted the coordinates for Mandelstam's insistence on the reality of the word. In terms of Kantian aesthetics, which were discernibly present in contemporary critical thought,[92] the word in poetry came closest to being "the thing in itself" and could therefore claim reality with at least as much authority as any material object. In this respect, Mandelstam's "nominalism" affirmed the independence of the word from its referent, contingent or universal; at the same time, it presented the word as an entity satisfying the foremost condition of materiality, as a force capable of "indefatigable struggle with the formless elements, with nonbeing, which threatens our history from all sides." Put differently, the poetic word, no longer a mere sign of a referent, was understood by him as a sign that, remaining a sign and therefore free and "arbitrary," *was* a referent, a thing, as well. Polemicizing with the Formalists (ostensibly Shklovskii), Leon Trotsky wrote in his *Art and Revolution:*

> The Formalist school represents an abortive idealism applied to the question of art. The Formalists show an untimely ripening religiosity. They are followers of St. John. They believe that "in the beginning was the Word." But we believe that in the beginning was the deed. The word followed, as its phonetic shadow.[93]

To this Viktor Shklovskii responded: "But the word is not a shadow. The word is a thing."[94]

Arguments about this issue had, of course, preceded the polemical exchange between Trotsky and Shklovskii. Indeed, its origins go back to Plato, but in more recent times its rhetoric can be traced to N. Gumilev's "The Word," which quotes the beginning of the Gospel according to St. John, and to Mandelstam's famous polemical aphorism about "word-Psyche" in "Word and Culture" (1921).[95] What was only sketched out in that essay received elaborate treatment in the lengthy and programmatic "On the Nature of the Word," which Mandelstam published as a pamphlet a year before Trotsky's *Literature and Revolution* and almost simultaneously with Trotsky's articles on the "Non-October Literature," which appeared in *Pravda* in the late summer and fall of 1922.[96] Mandelstam's stance in "On the Nature of the Word" had much in common with the earlier pronouncements of the Formalists, but unlike the Formalists, who wished to distance themselves from the political agenda of the moment, Mandelstam combined his "nominalism" with an insistence on the social significance of art for the revolution. There obtained, he argued, an essential fraternity and teleological kinship between those engaged in material production and the artisans of the word. Alluding to Michelangelo's "Creation of Adam," he concluded:

> To replace the romantic, the aristocratic dreamer about the pure symbol, about the abstract aesthetics of the word, to replace Symbolism,

Futurism, and Imagism, there came the live poetry of the word-thing, and her creator is not the idealist dreamer Mozart, but the severe and exacting artisan Salieri, who stretches out his hand to the master of things and material values, the builder and the producer of the world of things.[97]

If we wonder which of these two "artisans" was Adam and which was God, "Adamism," the alternate name of Acmeism,[98] may answer the question. In the 1923 "Slate Ode," Mandelstam went even further, presenting the poet as one who—like the doubting Thomas "placing his fingers" into Christ's "wound" upon the transfiguration—wished to feel and experience the miracle of Russia's revolutionary "rebirth."

Thus Mandelstam was carving out for himself an ethical-aesthetic program. The ethics were those of a Russian *intelligent* who was willing to go along with the Bolsheviks insofar as their program appeared to fulfill the vaguely populist, Herzenist agenda; and in this regard, Mandelstam's stand did not differ much from the "change of landmarks" mentality or the earlier populism of Viacheslav Ivanov and Blok.[99] In his aesthetics, he drew a line between himself and the Symbolists, whose poetics were based on the perception of the word as a contingent manifestation of a universal; between himself and the Futurists, who in their "anxiety of influence"[100] tended to view the past as an ossified entity; between himself and the Russian Imagists, with whom he had associated briefly[101] and who considered a particularly striking image the essential feature of poetry; and finally, between the Formalists' rigorous nominalism and his own rather impure version. At the same time, his essays of the period are incomprehensible without the theory and practice associated with these four schools. He owed them some of his most significant ideas: Viacheslav Ivanov's "archetypal" memory of the word and myth as a narrative elaboration of word-symbol (after all, Max Müller, A. A. Potebnia, and A. N. Veselovskii were not poets); the Futurists' pathos of "beginnings," their orientation toward the future;[102] and even the Imagists' particular skill at deflating and debasing all-too-serious assumptions about Russian poetry.[103] Clearly, the eclecticism of Mandelstam's response to the contemporary discourse on poetry was intentional. Coming from the poet who quoted with approval Velemir Khlebnikov's

> Крылышкуя золотописьмом
> Тончайших жил
> Кузнечик в кузов пуза уложил
> Прибрежных много трав и вер.

> Winging its goldscript
> Of most subtle veins,
> A grasshopper has stuffed his gut's trunk
> With blades of so many kinds of grass and faiths

this response fit well with Mandelstam's view of himself as a Verlaine-like, naive, "synthetic poet of modernity."[104]

Poetry constituted the condensed essence of language, and by virtue of its extraordinary density, it could serve as a guarantor of the identity of the race, whereas the poet, although stripped of the more individualistic romantic paraphernalia, continued to wear the prophetlike mask of one who mediated between the most sacred core of the culture and the profane masses—between the *center* of the nation's linguistic consciousness and the popular periphery, the people, whose verbal garden he was *called* to cultivate. Without the poet's green thumb, Mandelstam was saying, not only the state ("Word and Culture") but the nation itself ("On the Nature of the Word") would surely wither away.

THE WORD'S SUFFERING AND MAGIC

> *Classical poetry—this is the poetry of revolution.*
> OSIP MANDELSTAM, "Word and Culture" (1921)

> *The double truth of invention and recollection is needed like bread.*
> OSIP MANDELSTAM, "The Birth of the Plot" (1922)

The pathos of the two essays "Word and Culture" (1921) and "On the Nature of the Word" (1922), which were intimately associated with the poems of *Tristia* and *1921–1925,* was meant to demonstrate the central formative function of poetry in a society sailing into unknown waters. As early as 1913 Mandelstam had proclaimed the power of the poetic word to "hypnotize," to hold spellbound the "empty space"[105] that seems to have been gaping at humanity everywhere in prewar Europe. Now, less than a decade later, when the frame of reference sustaining him in the old world had entirely fallen apart, he found both himself and the corner of the universe he used to inhabit buried under the rubble of the war and the disintegrated state. He was, to sum up the complex metaphor of the later *Tristia,* a young man buried alive. The task of poetry—or, more modestly, his own task—was to preserve that departed world (now cleansed by death of all objectionable accretions) in the form of a living memory, a kind of spiritual culture that was unsullied by the ever-compromising business of life:

Yes, the old world is "not of this world," but it is alive more than ever. Culture has become church. What happened was the separation of culture-church from state. Society life does not have anything to do with us any more. We take not food, but refection, live not in a room, but in a monastic cell, we wear not clothes, but vestments. At last, we have acquired inner freedom, true inner joy. . . . A Christian—and now every man of culture is a Christian—does not know a purely physical hunger. For him, the word is flesh and simple bread is merriment and mystery.[106]

The passage vibrates with the asceticism of the first postrevolutionary years, and while it could not have made the front page of *Pravda,* it certainly should not be taken as proof of Mandelstam's alienation from the revolution. Like his 1918 "Twilight of Freedom," a somber poem which he quoted in "Word and Culture" and one in which he had called on the "brothers" to "glorify the twilight burden of power assumed in tears by the people's leader" (meaning Lenin), this essay, too, represented an offer of moral support to the new regime.[107] It came from a poet who appreciated the "cultural" tolerance of the revolutionary state. But, as one who had been expecting a speedier emergence of an ideal community under the guidance of the new state,[108] Mandelstam was expressing a certain discomfort with and puzzlement over the state's current nonactivist role in cultural affairs.[109] In this respect, the Russian revolution, he concluded in the same essay, went further than the French and separated "culture" from "state," apparently not satisfied with merely severing ties between the state and ecclesiastical authority. To situate Mandelstam within the Russian intellectual tradition, we could say that he looked at the revolutionary government through the prism of Slavophile political theory (particularly Khomiakov),[110] his outlook shaped further by the intense camaraderie and intimacy that dominated the atmosphere of the writers' commune in the Petrograd House of Arts during the last months of War Communism. Indeed, if we make proper allowance for scale, Mandelstam's ideal society begins to resemble closely the society in the House of Arts (maintained by the "tolerant" state) so fondly remembered by many of its veterans, among them Ol'ga Forsh, Viktor Shklovskii, and Vladislav Khodasevich.[111] Whatever else we may say about Mandelstam's declarations in favor of poetic anamnesis, it cannot be construed as a harking back to the "good old days," unless, of course, we decide to contextualize these words in the rhetoric and ideology of our own epoch. What Mandelstam wished to revive was the memory of that now old, and therefore purified, culture, to make it, in Bergson's words,[112] "immediately given" to the consciousness of his time and ours. He believed—and as the Mandelstam scholarship of the recent decades has shown, justifiably—that his poetry could preserve a system or, better still, a patchwork of verbal referents that defined the identity of his generation and, in a more local sense, Mandelstam's Petersburg cohort and its milieu.[113] His famous 1920 poem spells out splendidly both his intent and his method as he attempted to assume the identity of his generation's Mnemosyne.

> В Петербурге мы сойдемся снова,
> Словно солнце мы похоронили в нем,
> И блаженное, бессмысленное слово
> В первый раз произнесем.
> В черном бархате советской ночи,
> В бархате всемирной пустоты,
> Всё поют блаженных жен родные очи,
> Всё цветут бессмертные цветы.
>
> Дикой кошкой горбится столица,
> На мосту патруль стоит,
> Только злой мотор во мгле промчится
> И кукушкой прокричит.
> Мне не надо пропуска ночного,
> Часовых я не боюсь:
> За блаженное бессмысленное слово
> Я в ночи советской помолюсь.
>
> Слышу легкий театральный шорох
> И девическое «ах» —
> И бессмертных роз огромный ворох
> У Киприды на руках.
> У костра мы греемся от скуки,
> Может быть века пройдут,
> И блаженных жен родные руки
> Легкий пепел соберут.
>
> Где-то грядки красные партера,
> Пышно взбиты шифоньерки лож;
> Заводная кукла офицера;
> Не для черных душ и низменных святош...
> Что ж, гаси, пожалуй, наши свечи
> В черном бархате всемирной пустоты,
> Всё поют блаженных жен крутые плечи,
> А ночного солнца не заметишь ты.
>
>   25 ноября 1920

> We shall gather again in Petersburg,
> As if we had buried the sun in it,
> And the blessed, senseless word

> We shall utter for the first time.
> In the black velvet of the Soviet night,
> In the black velvet of universal emptiness,
> The dear eyes of blessed women are still singing,
> Immortal flowers are still blossoming.
>
> A wild cat, the capital is hunching,
> A patrol is standing on the bridge,
> A lone vicious auto dashing through the darkness,
> Crying out its coo-coo.
> I don't need a night pass,
> The sentries don't give me fright:
> For the blessed, senseless word
> I shall say my prayer in the Soviet night.
>
> I hear the light rustle of the theater
> And a maidenly "Ah"—
> And behold—an enormous bunch of immortal roses
> In the Cyprian's hands.
> We are warming ourselves by a bonfire from boredom,
> Perhaps ages will pass,
> And the blessed women's dear hands
> Will gather the light ash.
>
> Somewhere, the red flowerbeds of orchestra seats,
> The upholstery of the boxes, splendiferously whipped;
> The winding doll of an officer;
> Not for the black souls or base hypocrites...
> Well, perhaps you should blow out our candles.
> In the black velvet of universal emptiness,
> The high shoulders of blessed women are still singing,
> But you won't notice the night sun.[114]

"They," namely the members of the poet's old Petersburg cohort, will gather *again* and will pronounce the blessed and senseless word *for the first time*.[115] The conjuncture of these two contrary adverbs of time expressed the paradox of the "word as such" ("The Morning of Acmeism"),[116] the all-generating Logos that all words imitate in their imperfect capacity to convey new meanings as well as retain old ones (the "inner form" of Potebnia). This principle the poem recapitulated doubly, in intention and in method: first, by organizing its material so that the detail of the present alluded to a like detail in the past; second, by presenting a plot in which passing away was deprived of the finality of oblivion by repeated recollections and, ultimately, by a periphrastic invocation of Orpheus, the "night sun." Even the more elementary repetitions (whole phrases, words, and the dense paronymy)[117] reenact

The Word's Suffering and Magic

the principal operation of the "blessed and senseless word"—by being unloosed from their immediate signification through repetition, a process that reminds us of a shamanistic performance or the much-talked-about ecstatics (Shklovskii, Mandelstam), or of the prewar controversies on Mt. Athos concerning the autonomous divinity of the name of the Lord.[118] "Every magical procedure," Max Weber noted about more primitive cultures,

> which has been "proved" efficacious is naturally repeated strictly in the successful form. That is extended to everything that has symbolic significance. The slightest departure from the approved norm may vitiate the action. All branches of human activity get drawn into this circle of symbolic magic.[119]

With a few allowances for Mandelstam's "modernism," this "universal" of magic may help account for the poet's preoccupation with iteration. What had been proven to be "efficacious," that is, poems that had survived, must be repeated to endow the "new" with their "influence." To be perceived, however, the iteration had to be made apparent, moved into the foreground.

The transparent allusions to Pushkin's Parny-like youthful poem "Krivtsovu,"[120] with its precious chthonic eroticism, and to Blok's "The Steps of the Commendatore"[121] are reinterpreted in the poem: one by having its topoi (the Cyprian, ashes) replaced by the *realia* of 1920 Petrograd (bonfire), the other by making it possible to read Blok's theme of retribution as the vengeance of the revolution visited on the old world for its many sins.[122] As a result, the poem begins to resemble "an unfamiliar man with a familiar face," forcing the reader into a mnemonic recapitulation in the course of which the "inner form of the word," the constructive principle of poetry, is itself rejuvenated.[123] Because such a recollection can never be assuredly complete, the reader, at least for a while, finds himself suspended in recollection, experiencing a trancelike "magical" state that is the prerogative of the shamanistic poet. This electricity of allusion generated in the mind of the reader by the mnemonic attraction between a given poem and its possible "interlocutors" helps to account for the special hypnotic effect of Mandelstam's art.

The "prayer for the blessed and senseless word," strategically placed in the middle of the poem, performs a similar function. By subtly baring the device (as the Formalists would have put it), Mandelstam offered a script for recollecting the origins of poetry. For the poem is as much about composing a prayer as it itself is a prayer of remem-

181

brance. Better still, it is an incantation (the two genres were frequently confused)[124] based on sympathetic homologies of the past, the present and the future that unfold around the all-inclusive center of the "blessed and senseless word."[125] Recall in this connection Blok's record of Gumilev's theory of the Word: "In the beginning was the Word, out of the Word emerged thoughts, words that no longer resembled the Word but that nevertheless had It as their source; and everything will end with the Word—everything will disappear, it alone will remain."[126] Mandelstam treated this Word, which resided in every word, as a force possessing magical, healing power[127] at the same time that it itself required intercession and support from the poet. Hence only after the poet's prayer for the "word," which is "senseless" and strongly erotic in connotation (*blazhENNoe—zhENy*), does the hypnotic recollection begin. One after another there follow the synecdoches of the prerevolutionary, perhaps even prewar, life associated with the theater,[128] with the cult of Pushkin, and with the belief that the generation of Mandelstam was recapitulating Pushkin's epoch.[129] In fact, in the penultimate stanza Mandelstam thematizes a common detail of Petrograd life in winter, a street bonfire,[130] into a funeral pyre and, further, into the ashes from Pushkin's poem "For Krivtsov."[131]

This interweaving of the poetic speech of different epochs into a single verbal fabric accounts only for a portion of Mandelstam's design. By aligning the poem's homologies (the poems of Pushkin, Blok, and Mandelstam himself) as a shaman would do, according to A. N. Veselovskii,[132] Mandelstam both created and imitated a magical verbal structure based on sympathetic attraction—a structure capable of transferring attributes of one object to another presented as its look-alike. Conveying a desire for a future recapitulation of the contemporary Pushkin cult in a similar cult of Mandelstam's own generation, such a structure imitated both belief in the power of the word, or the Word, and the magical practices associated with this power.

Once this act of "magical" anamnesis had been initiated, including the inscription of newer memories (Mandelstam) into the older ones (Pushkin and Blok), the "candles" of those who would gather again in the *capital of Petersburg* (in 1920, Moscow was the capital and Petrograd was the city's name) could be blown out. They no longer had anything to fear, for having effected a communion with the "blessed and senseless word," they were assured of remaining in the memory of poetry. They would certainly "gather again," even if in the form of scattered "ashes" being "gathered" by the "dear hands" of "blessed women." In death, they will remain invulnerable, sustained in Elysium by the rays of the indestructible "night sun," Orpheus, the archetypal poet, whose head was *still singing* after it had been severed from his body.¹³³ In a later version of the poem, mention of Orpheus was more explicit. The first four lines of the last stanza read:

> Где-то хоры сладкие Орфея
> И родные темные зрачки,
> И на грядки кресел с галереи
> Падают афиши-голубки.

> Somewhere—the sweet choruses of Orpheus
> And the dear dark eyes,
> And over the flowerbeds of the seats,
> Dovelike playbills are falling.

That this poem by Mandelstam was not a stylization of Orphic mysteries but a fully modern poem is indicated by the presence of the chilling "perhaps," which qualified the poet's hope for immortality. Without this offhand reminder of the tenuousness of verbal constructions, we would have had a well-rounded metaphysics à la Viacheslav Ivanov, such as Mandelstam criticized as a young man,¹³⁴ and not a script for a martyr-poet subjecting himself to the ordeals of incestlike recollection in order to redeem his time and himself. The polemics he echoed in his letter to Ivanov alert us to the meaning this "perhaps" had for those who constituted the poet's "we":

> In the deepest essay of the second *Book of Reflections* [by Innokenti Annenskii], one can barely discern—but still discern—the mighty dark rays of one weltanschauung whose influence over our time cannot be denied. I am speaking about Leo Shestov and his "philosophy of tragedy" [*Nietzsche and Dostoevsky*]. . . . It was precisely the philosophy of tragedy that had taught Annenskii to look so clearly into abysses together with Shestov. . . . Where Viacheslav Ivanov [*Across the Stars*] possesses the certainty and the synthesis of one who has found [the solution], there Annenskii shows the hopelessness and the analysis of one who is seeking. One is flying "across the stars," peacefully contemplating the *realia*. For the other—the stars, no matter how much they gleam and glitter, cannot always bring peace. Because in the "suspicious little corners" and at the bottom of the seductive, ironically gaping abysses, there sometimes suddenly flash and burn out such suns, such suns...¹³⁵

The poet, who at the age of eighteen was prepared to look at the world through the eyes of Shestov and Annenskii, was not about to dismiss a far wider and deeper "abyss" gaping at him in revolutionary Russia when he was twenty-nine.

Indeed, behind the poem's local concern for the "immortality" of those in whose name the poem's speaker "prayed" or "cast his spells," there stood an express desire to secure the present and to safeguard the new community that might otherwise be overwhelmed by change. Insistence, as Nietzsche put it, on the advantages of history for life was not a particularly original position, but as I tried to demonstrate earlier, the less one's common sense was capable of resisting, indeed, of noticing the internalized *vehicle* on which Mandelstam based his constructions, the more successful was the vehicle itself at delivering the assigned *tenor* at the emotional doorstep of an unsuspecting reader. What this tenor was should become apparent once we consider this, one of Mandelstam's most striking rhetorical flights (I have glossed the text for the sake of immediate reference):

> The life of the word has entered a heroic era. The word is flesh and bread. It shares the fate of bread and flesh: suffering. People are hungry. The state is hungrier. But there is something still hungrier: time. Time wants to devour the state. Like the sound of the trumpet [of the archangel] does the threat that Derzhavin scribbled on his slate board resound in our ears. ["The river of time in its course washes away all the deeds of men.... And if anything remains thanks to the sound of the Lyre or the Trumpet of fame—that, too, shall be devoured by the maw of eternity and shall not escape the common fate."] He who shall lift up the word and show it to time as a priest lifting up the Host—shall be the second *Jesus Navin* [i.e., Joshua]. There is nothing hungrier than the modern state, and a hungry state is more terrifying than a hungry man. Compassion for the state that denies the word— this is the civic goal and the martyrdom to be sought by a modern poet.[136]

For us, as for the contemporary reader, the passage invokes one or more of the countless poetic elaborations of the pagan and Christian allegories of devouring time (Kronos-chronos and his children, and so on). But for the reader raised on the imaginative literature of high social and spiritual seriousness *and* living in constant fear for his life, squeezing the last drop out of a starvation ration—for that reader, Mandelstam's verbal enthusiam was thoroughly in tune with day-to-day experience. That was, after all, a "hungry time" (*golodnoe vremia*), and on the basis of this expression Mandelstam reconstructed the mythology of, say, Kronos, recalling N. G. Chernyshevskii's famous comment concerning the revolution's insatiable appetite for those born to it. Mandelstam's mythic elaboration of the innocuous "hungry time"—in the course of which the meagerness of the diet and a common belief in the power of verbal appeal became transformed into a simile of the Eucharist—possessed an edifying meaning, lending a sacramental aura to that reader's weekly allotments of the barely edible daily bread.

To have accepted that much of Mandelstam's metaphor meant also to have accepted some or all of the rest of his package, namely: (1) the potential identification of the essay's author with Joshua, whose word could stop the sun in its course and whose prefiguration of Christ is transparent in his Russian name; (2) the identification of the poet with a priest, and his word with the bread and wine of the Eucharist; (3) the transformation of the reader into a member of the poet's congregation, if not indeed his church; and finally (4), the view of the poet as a martyr who imitated the voluntary passion of Christ by composing a form of civic poetry that would show *com-passion* for the state, thereby redeeming it and society from future oblivion. Few of Mandelstam's poems develop the civic theme in a conventional manner, but most pieces in the late *Tristia* and *1921–1925* do present the poet (whatever his guise) as a martyr undergoing ordeals according to the archetypal script of death and rebirth.

This concept of a poet, in a sense related to the teaching of Paul,[137] had an eminent history in Russian modernism, going back to Vladimir Solov'ev's "You are the priest, the altar, and the sacrifice"[138] and its recodification by the "theurgist" Symbolists, particularly in Viacheslav Ivanov's Dionysian aesthetics:

> The Dionysian original principle [*nachalo*], antinomial by nature, can be variously described and formally defined, but it reveals itself in its plenitude only in experience, and one will look in vain for an understanding in analyzing what constitutes its vital components. Dionysus both accepts and denies any predicate; in his understanding, *a* is not-*a;* in his cult, the sacrifice and the priest are united in a relation of identity.[139]

Where Mandelstam parted ways with this lofty and still-powerful tradition was, first, in the intense "secularization" of the "ringing and speaking flesh," as he referred to poetic speech ("despite all its complexity, modern poetry is naive").[140] Second, and no less significant, he added to the archetype of dying and reviving the principle of existential uncertainty, the "perhaps," whose rhetoric he and his contemporaries had absorbed from Annenskii, Shestov, and, ultimately, Nietzsche.[141] The "perhaps" constituted one pole of his poetry; the other was a radical, almost fundamentalist, adherence to the sacramental, chthonic, and ultimately Eucharistic narrative. These were the alpha and omega of Mandelstam's poetic paradigms. Although virtually identical to his formulations in "Pushkin and Skriabin," they were now ordering a new, postrevolutionary experience. What remains to be examined is the repertoire of identities these paradigms projected in the period of the late *Tristia* and *1921–1925*.

VII

Dying as Metaphor and the Ironic Mode: 1920–1930

> *O. Mandelstam, the author of* Tristia . . . *is mournfully singing a funeral dirge over a romantic, an idealist, an aristocratic dreamer yearning after a pure symbol and an abstract aesthetics of the word, because [writes Mandelstam]* "to replace Symbolism, Futurism, and Imagism there has come the live poetry of the word-thing, and its creator is not the idealist-dreamer Mozart, but the somber and severe master-craftsman Salieri, who is extending his hand to the master-craftsman of things and the material world."
>
> P. D. ZHUKOV, "The Left Front of the Arts" (1923)[1]

> *I am—perhaps—the last poet...* VLADIMIR MAIAKOVSKII

MANDELSTAM'S AND THE COMMUNE'S TRAIN

In the early 1920s, even the informed and well-disposed critics identified Mandelstam's poetry with what in the postrevolutionary nomenclature was called the past. The lone antiphonal voice was that of Viktor Zhirmunskii. By 1921 he had twice declared that the Acmeists, including Mandelstam, "had overcome" Symbolism, implying that they, too, played the role of the avant-garde in the dialectics of literary history.[2] The rest preferred to see in Mandelstam a poet who, like the characters in the *Inferno*, marched forward with his head turned back, albeit "along his own way."[3] To cite one example, Gollerbakh, a prominent Petersburg critic of the old school, praised Mandelstam's poetry for its alleged fidelity to the traditions of Russian Symbolism.[4] The Formalists, too, tended to locate Mandelstam in a niche reserved for extant antiquities. Thus Eikhenbaum, with little regard for Zhirmunskii's dialectics, classified Mandelstam and Akhmatova as "guardians of tradition," their relation to Symbolism as reformist, not revolutionary, and their poetry as a "deepening" of Symbolism, faithful to the aestheticism of Annenskii and Mallarmé.[5] Perhaps most remarkable, Mandelstam joined the chorus in 1922, when he referred to the Acmeist cohort as the "younger Symbolists" (see "On the Nature of the Word").

This identification with the past was a complex matter and could have had unpredictable consequences even among the most ardent avant-gardists. Nikolai Punin, a Futurist art critic associated with the Left Front of Arts, could write a superlative, enthusiastic review of *Tristia*—all the while nudging Mandelstam, if ever so slightly, toward the ditch into which modern history was supposed to deposit a new generation every five or so years.[6] Punin's brief review, especially his rhetoric, can be considered exemplary for the Mandelstam criticism of the 1920s, and as it is little known, I shall cite it here almost in its entirety:

> May the specialists whose names are known only because there are such poets as Akhmatova and Blok figure out how these wonderful poems are made. Why don't you, critics, you theorists of the psychological and formal method, write something about the most remarkable poet of your (preceding ours) generation? He is your poet—a humanist. . . .
>
> *Tristia* is a very luxuriant and solemn collection, but this is not the Baroque, this is, as it were, the night of form.
>
> None of us could have participated in this poetry—which is why it stands apart from our generation. I, too, would like in full stupidity to deny the existence of any form except the one in whose construction I participate; but each school, even a mighty one that covers the compass of its time, possesses "shameful loners." . . . These truly strange people are capable of resurrecting Raphael during the years of the most outrageous persecution for things of this sort. Like them, Mandelstam is shaking the "swaying world" of the troublemakers, re-shuffling history's cards. . . .
>
> If tomorrow, as we can expect, we become capable of substituting formulas of language for [verse] stanzas, he will still be praying for words as before: "For the blessed, senseless word I shall pray in the Soviet night." . . .
>
> Let us make a compact, then, never to forget him, no matter how silent the literary criticism around him might be. Over its head, we shall be speaking with the poet, the most remarkable thing that the old world bequeathed to us as it was passing away.[7]

(The author of the review was actually a few years older than Mandelstam).

When it came to the aggressive, party-minded critics, Mandelstam's proverbial association with the "old world" became cause for verbal attacks that were menacing in their tone. Whereas the more sympathetic critics tempered their view of Mandelstam's anachronism with an examination of his poetic genealogy or admiration for his uniqueness and mastery, never disputing his claim on the reader in the present, the intolerant ones tended to dismiss him as a contemporary poet with unequivocal bluntness, using his own confessional meditations as literal evidence of his harmfulness or irrelevance. In 1925, G. Lelevich, a critic and poet associated with the journal *On Guard,* which advocated strict party control in literary affairs, elaborated on Mandelstam's "A Concert at the Railroad Station," interpreting the poem as proof that the poet, as well as his admirers and publishers, had overstayed their welcome on the Soviet literary stage. Without denying Lelevich's political motives, could it be that Mandelstam himself had written a script for his critics, a script that separated contemporaries into the living and the dead but left no distinguishing marks?

Нельзя дышать, и твердь кишит червями,
И ни одна звезда не говорит,
Но, видит Бог, есть музыка над нами,
Дрожит вокзал от пенья аонид
И снова, паровозными свистками
Разорванный, скрипичный воздух слит.

Огромный парк. Вокзала шар стеклянный.
Железный мир опять заворожен.
На звучный пир в элизиум туманный
Торжественно уносится вагон.
Павлиний крик и рокот фортепьянный —
Я опоздал. Мне страшно. Это сон.

И я вхожу в стеклянный лес вокзала,
Скрипичный строй в смятеньи и слезах.
Ночного хора дикое начало,
И запах роз в гниющих парниках,
Где под стеклянным небом ночевала
Родная тень в кочующих толпах.

И мнится мне: весь в музыке и пене
Железный мир так нищенски дрожит,
В стеклянные я упираюсь сени;
Горячий пар зрачки смычков слепит.

Dying as Metaphor: 1920–1930

Куда же ты? На тризне милой тени
В последний раз нам музыка звучит.

1921

> It is impossible to breathe, and the firmament is teeming with
>   worms,
> And not a single star is speaking.
> But, God is my witness, there is music above us.
> The railroad station is trembling from the singing of the Aonides.
> And again, having been torn by the steam engine whistles,
> The violin air is flowing, is fused.
>
> The enormous park. The glass sphere of the station.
> Again, the iron world is spellbound.
> To the feast of sound in the misty Elysium,
> A railroad car is flying with solemn pomp.
> A peacock's scream and the piano's rumble—
> I am late. It's frightening. I'm in a dream.
>
> And I am entering the glass forest of the station,
> The harmony of the violins is in tears and confused.
> The savage origin of the night chorus;
> And the scent of roses from the rotting hot houses
> Where, under the glass sky, nights have been spent by
> The dear shade among the crowds of nomads.
>
> Behold I have a vision: all in music and froth,
> The iron world is trembling so miserably,
> I am steadying myself against the glass walls;
> The hot steam is blinding the eyes of the boughs.
> Where are you off to? At the funeral feast for the dear shade,
> Music sounds for us for the last time.[8]

What is important in this poem is not the laughable naiveté with which Mandelstam manages to transpose into the centers of modern technology the images of Antiquity. What is important in him is the sense of the collapse of the real world, the sensation of the terrifying terminus, the borderline beyond which there begins agony, the sensation of the approaching end. Mandelstam is right: music sounds for them for the last time. For the poets of *The Russian Contemporary*, as for Hamlet, time is out of joint.[9]

The polemical harshness aside, it is clear that both the poet and his critics, sympathetic as well as hostile, were working within the confines of a single metaphoric cluster: agony, followed by death, followed by interment. Not only did Mandelstam countenance such stereotyping of himself, but he was, in fact, the one to suggest it as early as the 1916 "We shall die in the translucent Petropolis," elaborating the theme further with virtually every subsequent poem. Certainly he must have discerned even in Lelevich an echo, albeit with different accents, of his own dictum about the necessity for poetry (for some poetry) to be like the "Egyptian funeral barque." In his programmatic "On the Nature of the Word" (1922), where this simile appears, Mandelstam offered the following elaboration:

> The noise of [our] age will die down, [our] culture will fall asleep, the people [*narod, das Volk*] who has given its best efforts to the new social class will be regenerated, and this whole current will carry in its tow the fragile barque of the human word, [carry it] into the open sea of the future, which lacks sympathetic understanding and where dull commentary supplants the fresh breeze of the hostility and empathy of contemporaries. How, then, can we prepare this vessel for its long journey and not supply it with everything necessary for the reader, so alien and dear? Once again I shall compare a poem to the Egyptian barque of the dead. In this barque everything [necessary] for life has been stored, nothing has been forgotten.[10]

Let us examine more closely this controlling metaphor of Mandelstam's poetic paradigms of the late 1910s and 1920s—a floating sepulcher from which the poet's self repeatedly emerged, only to return to it at the end of another poem.

In "A Concert at the Railroad Station," Mandelstam used for a setting the beautiful iron-and-glass Victorian building that served as both railroad station and concert hall for Pavlovsk, the fashionable suburb of Petersburg. A chapter of his autobiographical prose, *The Noise of Time*, is devoted to the tradition of these Pavlovsk concerts.[11] What was particular about this setting was its potential for symbolic signification: it was a place where the new "iron" world (faint echoes of Hesiod's "ages"), the steam engine, and the old world, "music," predictably clashed. But Mandelstam managed to endow this explosive emblem—which, incidentally, could not help echoing a contemporary revolutionary song ("Our steam engine, fly forward. The commune is the next stop. We have no other road. We've got rifles in our hands")—with a far more complex meaning. Weaving into the poem transparent allusions to Lermontov and Tiutchev, he virtually saturated it with the prose and poetry of Blok, or more precisely, with the familiar symbolic taxonomy created by and associated with the recently deceased poet: the nineteenth century as the "iron age" (*Retribution*), and Nietzschean "music" as the elemental force of popular will manifesting itself in gypsy romantic abandon ("Carmen"), verbal magic ("Poetry of Spells and Incantations"), natural calamities (the comet, the earthquake), and social explosions.

Dying as Metaphor: 1920–1930

В партере — ночь. Нельзя дышать.

In the orchestra—it's night. Impossible to breathe.
(A. Blok, from the "Karmen" cycle)¹²

В последнии раз — опомнись, старый мир!
  На братский пир труда и мира,
В последний раз на светлый братскийй пир
  Сзывает варварская лира!

For the last time—come to your senses, old world!
  To the fraternal feast of labor and peace,
For the last time—to the bright fraternal feast
  The barbarian lyre is calling.
(A. Blok, "The Scythians," 1918)

The nineteenth century is the age of iron. The age is a convoy of heavy carts rushing over the cobblestones, drawn by exhausted horses whipped by people with yellow, pale faces; these people are edgy from hunger and poverty; their mouths are open, yelling obscenities; but one cannot hear their swearing . . . because the iron strips with which their carts are loaded are making a deafening noise.

And the nineteenth century is all trembling, all shaking and rumbling like these iron strips. People intimidated by this civilization are trembling. (A. Blok, "The Lightning Flashes of Art," 1909, 1918)[13]

We used to love those dissonances, those roars, that ringing, those unexpected transitions . . . in the orchestra. But if we *truly loved them* and did not merely tickle our nerves in a fashionable concert hall after dinner—then we must listen and love the same sounds now when they fly out of the universal orchestra; and as we listen, we must understand that this is about the same thing, the very same thing.

Music, after all, is no toy; and that beast who used to think music a toy—let it now behave like a beast: tremble, grovel, and hoard your own wealth! (A. Blok, "Intelligentsia and the Revolution," 1918)[14]

For those of us who have the benefit of hindsight, Mandelstam's certainty of the death of the old world, which, he admitted, had once been so ominous, deceitful, and cruel, seems perfectly reasonable: "But your spine is broken, my cruel, dear age" ("Vek," 1922). If a little more obliquely, "A Concert at the Railroad Station" (dated 1921 but first published in 1924)[15] conveys the same message. Not everyone, however, shared his views; and some, like Lelevich, found even a funeral oration over the dead "age" threatening and, implicitly, counterrevolutionary. We should keep in mind therefore that Mandelstam's position, however harmless it may appear now and however loyal it in fact was, could serve as fuel in contemporary controversies.[16] The position itself may be summarized as follows: purified by death and therefore no longer threatening, the old world could continue to exist, in the form of memory, in the Schillerian Elysium of culture that would become part of contemporary consciousness and would make every word vibrate with the entire historical compass of its meaning. This exemplary program the poem set before the reader.

Having appropriated Blok's "music," Mandelstam restored to the word its other, ordinary usage of the concert-going years. Yet he accomplished this in such a way that the word *music* could not fail to display what it had meant in Blok, or, for that matter, in Nietzsche's *Birth of Tragedy out of the Spirit of Music*. For music here was still "the wild origin of the night chorus"—an obvious periphrasis of the title of Nietzsche's book. What represented an aggregate for Blok (his "music" being somehow coextensive with the revolution, the people, and so on) underwent in Mandelstam a process of differentiation followed by a fusion on a different tropological level: a heterogeneous image of the miserably trembling iron world surrounded by music and covered with froth—resembling a horse in lather.[17] The strata of meaning unfolded like petals around a powerfully suggestive emblem, or to use Mandelstam's own simile, like the sections of a Bergsonian "fan-time" opening around the immediate consciousness of the present.[18] At the same time, the oxymoronic, tension-ridden emblem of the past, in which the "iron world" and the "concert music" were inseparable, was pushed into the present.

A reader of Mandelstam in the 1920s no doubt noticed that the poem had absorbed the latest usage: the "naive" mixture consisting of the steam engine of history from a contemporary revolutionary song as well as N. Gumilev's highly popular "ballad" about the "wayward tramcar" that could transport one into the "India of the Spirit."[19] Tiutchev's line ("For the last time faith shall be put to a test")[20] as paraphrased by Mandelstam in the closure transformed the poem into a vow of anamnesis and a plea for a pause at the "funeral feast for the dear shade." Even Lermontov, the archetypally "late" Russian poet and hence a model for the "latecomers" of Mandelstam's generation ("Lermontov, our tormentor"),[21] could not imagine such an ordeal. When he walked out alone onto the road, nature was in harmony and stars did speak.[22] The same stars greeted the poet of Mandelstam's "Concert" with silence. Yet his suffering, too, paid off, for in the course of it he succeeded in exhuming both himself ("the dear shade") and a powerful strand in the tradition of Russian poetry, linking both to the language of the day. The poem's function was to effect the return.

> Время вспахано плугом, и роза землею была.
>
> Time is turned up by the plough, and a rose, too, once was earth.[23]

The interpretation can become more specific if we read the poem against the background of Mandelstam's program for poetry in "Word and Culture." There Mandelstam called for the appearance of a poet who would be powerful enough to stop time and whose word would be capable of freezing the moment in recollection in the same way that the lifting up of the Host during the Mass suspends temporality and produces anamnesis. The Host is atemporal and the priest transfers its attribute to time itself. Likewise the word, transformed into a node of memory by the poet, can operate according to the principle of sympathetic magic and tame the devouring time (a eucharistic anamnesis).[24] A claim to this sort of charismatic endowment required proof, and Mandelstam showed that he could accomplish the impossible when in "Concert" he managed to hitch the Pullman of memory—scheduled for Elysium—to the commune's train even as he was celebrating a funeral feast for his own departing shadow.

In the critical language of the day, this form of sympathetic magic bore another name, a principal term of the early Formalism: "making strange." "A poet," wrote Mandelstam's friend Viktor Shklovskii, "tears a concept out of that semantic series where it had already settled and transfers it with the aid of the word (a trope) into a different semantic series."[25] What Mandelstam was attempting to do, then, may be rephrased as the "making strange" of time by transferring onto it the attributes of objects, including the word, that resemble time in amnesia and obscurity of origins but are now capable of memory and regeneration. In this respect, "A Concert at the Railroad Station," the opening poem of the collection *1921–1925*, was built on the legacy of *Tristia*, a book of poetry that one critic, paraphrasing Mandelstam, qualified as a "funeral dirge over the romantic, the idealist, the aristocratic dreamer yearning after the pure symbol, after the abstract aesthetics of the word."[26] That dreamer, of course, was the poet's own mask, a martyrlike figure who both in *Tristia* and in *1921–1925* died in order to remember, and remembered in order to die—quite in keeping with the formula for kenotic *imitatio Christi* in "Pushkin and Skriabin": "To die means to remember [i.e., redeem], to remember means to die."[27]

The comparison of a poem to the consecrated Host apparently possessed a profound formal, tropological, and religious motivation. The Formalist critics, as Trotsky once pointed out, displayed an "untimely ripening religiosity," and the compatibility of the central Formalist term with Mandelstam's religious discourse indicates that he was not far off the mark. Only the qualifier "untimely" seems inappropriate. Verbal magic, A. N. Veselovskii wrote at the turn of the century apropos literary modernism, tends to be revived precisely during periods of social turmoil, "when the difference between what is and what is desired ripens, when faith in the stability of the present religious and social order grows weak, and the yearning for something new and better is felt more acutely."[28]

Consonant with the global transformation that his country had just undergone, Mandelstam's poetry was to remember "everything necessary for life" ("On the Nature of the Word"). The selection criterion depended on Mandelstam's interpretation of universal *brotherhood*, the express purpose of the revolution. As with the other topoi of the day, this one received a narrative elaboration based on the "inner form" of the word: a brotherhood as a metaphor of a large family, really. Hypothetically, the associative chain implied in this "myth" ran as follows: since "brotherhood" was the aim, then the society established as a result of the revolution would be a *family*, a community of siblings and the opposite of the old society whose life culminated in a global *fratricidal* strife. Such a literalist interpretation was not uncommon in the atmosphere of revolutionary enthusiasm, much of it nurtured on the ideals of the peasant commune as it was understood by the Russian populists. An Anglophobe, Mandelstam had no more sentimental feelings about a constitutional democracy and its institutions than did his contemporary Ezra Pound.[29] A passage from Mandelstam's 1922 essay "Humanism and the Present" helps to bring into focus the poet's political stance.

Mandelstam began his essay by implying a similarity between nineteenth-century Europe and the slave society of Egypt and Assyria, for they held in common a penchant for mammoth projects and an indiscriminate use of mass labor. By contrast, Russia was destined to inaugurate a new type of society:

> There is a different social architecture; its scale, its measure, too, is man, but it builds, not out of man, but for man; it builds its grandeur, not on the insignificance of a single individual, but in conformity with the highest purpose and according to its needs.
>
> We all feel the monumental character of the approaching social architecture. We cannot yet see the mountain, but it casts its shadow over us already. We who are no longer used to the monumental forms of social life, who have grown accustomed to the flatness of the

nineteenth-century state and legalism, we move in this shadow in fear and puzzlement, not knowing what it is: the wing of the approaching night or the shadow of a native city that we are to enter. . . .

The monumental nature of the approaching social architecture is determined by its vocation to organize the world economy according to the principle of universal homeliness, for the good of man, expanding the compass of its home freedom to the borders of the universe, fanning the flame of man's individual hearth until it becomes the universal flame.[30]

The "Hellenistic" thematism of *Tristia* further limited the choice of the "necessary objects" to those of the "golden age" of European culture, which was to make its comeback on a world scale (*v mirovom masshtabe*), opening to all, in the words of Mandelstam's 1919 "nuptial poem," the "tender tombs of the Archipelago."[31] This helps to explain Mandelstam's otherwise enigmatic slogan: "classical poetry is the poetry of revolution." "Not because David reaped the harvest of Robespierre, but because the earth wished it so," he went on to explain his paradox, appealing at the same time to the archetypal authority of the French revolution. The "earth," the Russian *zemlia*, has connotations of the will of all people, a "symphony," as well as the cyclical nature of the agriculture: two meanings that suited both Mandelstam's "eternal recurrence" and the populist oratory of the revolutionary years.[32] Indeed, few in Mandelstam's intellectual milieu would have disagreed, including the Russian Orthodox thinker, Pavel Florenskii, as well as the Symbolist Andrei Belyi, who said: "Orthodoxy is universal, and heresy, in its essence, is partisan. . . . The cause of the Orthodox, symphonic mind is to gather together all the fragments, their entire plenitude. . . . 'One needs to possess many strings in order to play on the lyre of eternity.'"[33]

Finally, because the invocation of the "necessary objects" in poetry was meant to facilitate the "highest goal" of universal brotherhood, their selection was determined on the basis of their compatibility with the daily life with which they were to resonate—the humble, ascetically bare environment of postrevolutionary Russia. Otherwise poetry would not have the effect of "sympathetic magic" and would fail to encourage the processes of recollection and recurrence. This helps to explain why Mandelstam's choice of special objects and beings in *Tristia* and *1921–1925* fell on bees, honey, clay jugs, swallows, grasshoppers, mint, honeysuckle, homespun linen (*kholst*), salt, a loaf of bread, a barrel, a cock in a cooking pot, a knife, a lantern, and, of course, the green bough.[34] These were the words with which Mandelstam, a practitioner of sacramental poetry, proposed to cast a spell on time.

AN OFFERING OF DEAD BEES

Two poems from the later *Tristia* are exemplary of a central theme of Mandelstam's poetry, what he called the "golden care to lighten the burden of time" ("Sisters—heaviness and tenderness"). The first centers around a simple—but, in the Petrograd of 1920, precious—gift of honey. This poem (belonging to the "Arbenina" cycle)[35] is written in an approximation of Dante's terzina: an endecasyllabic line, even though all the endings are feminine and unrhymed.

> Возьми на радость из моих ладоней
> Немного солнца и немного меда,
> Как нам велели пчелы Персефоны.
>
> Не отвязать неприкрепленной лодки,
> Не услыхать в меха обутой тени,
> Не превозмочь в дремучей жизни страха.
>
> Нам остаются только поцелуи,
> Мохнатые, как маленькие пчелы,
> Что умирают, вылетев из улья.
>
> Они шуршат в прозрачных дебрях ночи,
> Их родина — дремучий лес Тайгета,
> Их пища — время, медуница, мята.
>
> Возьми ж на радость дикий мой подарок,
> Невзрачное сухое ожерелье
> Из мертвых пчел, мед превративших в солнце.
>
> Ноябрь 1920

> Take for the sake of joy out of my hands
> A little sun and a little honey,
> As the bees of Persephone have commanded us.
>
> Not to untie the untied barque,
> Not to hear the sound of a fur-shod shadow,
> Not to overcome, in life's thicket, fear.
>
> All we are left with is kisses,
> Furry, like little bees
> That die, flying out of the beehive.
>
> They rustle in the transparent thicket of the night,
> Their native home is the thick forest of Taygetos,
> Their nourishment is time, honeysuckle, mint.

> So take for the sake of joy this wild gift of mine,
> This plain dry necklace
> Of dead bees who turned their honey into the sun.[36]

There is no single aspect of the poem that determines its effectiveness, whether we look at it through the eyes of the contemporary reader living in fear and hunger and excitement in the world of civil war Petrograd (late fall or winter 1920) or through the eyes of a modern admirer of Mandelstam who is aware of the century's subsequent history and who experiences a particular modern fascination before the erotic, literary, mythological, and biographical suggestiveness of a poem composed by a "martyred" poet. As a structuralist critic might tersely put it, "Take for the Sake of Joy" works on many levels. I would like to discuss it from a particular angle—as an instance of Mandelstam's use, or imitation, of sympathetic magic. I will look at it as a verbal structure in which the theme of transformation and rebirth is recapitulated in the paronymic play with the magical effect of transferring the mnemonic attributes of the word, its capacity to reactivate the "inner form," onto the mortal, "amnesiac" aspect of living.[37]

Thematically, the poem is transparent. Its mere juxtaposition with the opening declaration in "Pushkin and Skriabin," where Mandelstam compared the symbolic significance of a poet's death with the shining "sun," should suffice to contextualize the paradox elaborated in the poem. But let us take a closer look, as readers unaware of "Pushkin and Skriabin" (which Mandelstam never made public anyway). Whatever deep and hidden meanings the poem might possess, it is apparently about love, death, and rebirth (Persephone), and of course about poetry (bees and honey as traditional topoi of verbal art). But above all, the poem is about gift-giving, which supplies not only a theme but also a pattern enclosing the other thematic items in a frame of perpetual return, or "prestation," to use Marcel Mauss's term (see Chapter 4).

The gift of this poem becomes transformed in substance in the course of the poem, which itself represents an offering: the gift of "a little sun and a little honey" becomes in the end a "wild gift" (intimations of primitivism, violence, and ordeals) consisting of an unprepossessing "dry necklace," in fact, a string of "dead bees."[38] A decoration, this necklace is also an amulet, a more common object then, perhaps, than now.[39] Its magical power has been generated in the course of the poem, and, like the poet's gift, it will be able to transform "honey" into "the sun" in the hands of the recipient. The power itself seems to derive from its likeness to and association with other magically endowed objects, and ultimately from its mythic origins—in the

An Offering of Dead Bees

underworld, in the "elemental soul of the kingdom of bees"[40]—which set in motion the pattern of rejuvenation and eternal recurrence. According to Jakobson, the process by means of which an object magically absorbs the properties of other objects (sympathetic and contagious magic) corresponds to the basic tropological operations: metaphor and metonymy.[41] Mandelstam's "necklace of dead bees" combines both operations. It is circular; it is an artifact composed of dead matter and therefore is *like* the cyclical kingdom of the Corn Goddess (metaphoric "magic"); and it is *part* of and originated in that kingdom and relates to it as microcosm to macrocosm (synecdochic "magic"). I am not implying that a poetry reader, contemporary or modern, would analyze the poem in this fashion; rather, the method of analysis produced by Jakobson, Mandelstam's contemporary, had to be roughly compatible with the range of readings possible at that time. Indeed, it was then that the theory itself was being formulated.[42]

To make all of this magic at least minimally effective, the Shamanistic poet Mandelstam had to design his poem so as to establish a string of homological situations fitting his description of the rites of Persephone's bees, namely, the reversal of the linear flow of time by its repatterning according to the archetype of death and revival. As a result, the ordinary progression, "the sun—herbs—bees—honey—death of bees," was enlarged to include "honey—death of bees—the sun," becoming cyclical rather than linear. One who accepts this amulet will *have* to participate in, indeed perpetuate, this reversal, as the rules of gift-giving dictate.

The poet's "magic" was especially effective in its paronymic play, for the poem was skillfully orchestrated around such clusters as pchol*y*—pots*elui*—sol*n*ts*e* (bees—kisses—the sun). The penultimate tercet ends with a tour de force of such wordplay, encompassing paronymic, folk-etymological, and allusive homologies: *vre*m*ia,* m*edunitsa,* m*iata* (time, honeysuckle, mint). The first two homologies speak for themselves. The last, particularly the seemingly out of place "mint," had a powerful allusive and "magical" significance. Not only was it an herb sacred to Persephone and Adonis (Mentha),[43] but more important, it also pointed to the programmatic declaration of modernism, Verlaine's "Art poétique," where it played the role of an amulet of true poetry (italics are mine):

> Que ton vers soit la *bonne aventure*
> Eparse au vent crispé du matin
> Qui va fleurant la *menthe* et le thym...
> Et tout le reste est littérature.[44]

Dying as Metaphor: 1920–1930

But who was the speaker of the poem, and who the recipient of his magic gift?

Whatever the personal history surrounding this poem, Mandelstam no doubt intended it for the reader unaware of the details of the poet's love life. That is, the first-person plural of the poem places the reader on an equal footing with the speaker. The common denominator that the poem defines for the two is most vividly expressed in the second stanza, where death, life, and love are fused: the erotic "untying" combines a topos of wedding folklore with Charon's barque, the shadow of death, quiet as a thief in the night, and the fear that cannot be escaped in a life resembling Dante's "selva oscura."[45] It is mortality, the proximity of death—or, in the intense expressiveness of the poem, the underworld itself, where eros, regeneration, and death are as inseparable as they are in the myth of Persephone.[46] Mandelstam, of course, is stressing the somber, chthonic aspect of life's paradox, positioning both the speaker and the reader to admit a resigned acceptance of death and forcing them to look at life itself through the eyes of a departed soul. That intense awareness of death, that Shestovian "perhaps," is what prepares the climactic resolution with its sudden paradox of immortality achieved through dying. "With death, He has vanquished death": so goes a formula of the Russian Orthodox Easter liturgy, an important item in the contemporary reader's repertoire, from which the closure drew much of its power.[47] Thus, the recipient of the magical amulet was obligated to recapitulate not only the Mandelstamian "mnemonic" poetry but the Gospel drama as well. He was to reproduce in the future what the speaker of the poem had already accomplished.

The magic of "Take for the Sake of Joy" should be most effective among those who had been nurtured on "great Russian literature" and had no particular trouble maintaining on occasion that "everything began with the Word and would end with the Word" (N. Gumilev) or that the "Russian language was the ringing and speaking flesh" (Mandelstam) or, on a less shrill note, that all the material needed for the biography of a Russian *intelligent* was a history of his reading:

> I have never been able to understand the Tolstoys, the Aksakovs, the Bagrov grandchildren enamored of family archives with their epic recollections of home life. I repeat—my memory is hostile, not loving, and its purpose is to distance, not reproduce, the past. A middle-class *intelligent* [*raznochinets*] needs no memory; for him, it will suffice to tell us about the books he has read—and his biography is done and ready.[48]

Those who happened not to share these views and were insensitive to the multiple versions of Mandelstam's "poetics of the Eucharist" might have found suggestive the endecasyllabic tercets in which the poem was composed. This feature was enough to associate the poet with Dante—*the* poet, and one whose very name means *charis*, or gift. Those familiar with contemporary Russian poetry would relate "Take for the Sake of Joy" to Gumilev's "Word" and, beyond that, to the many "bees and honey" poems by Konstantin Bal'mont, Viacheslav Ivanov, and Maksimilian Voloshin. Those more at home with French Symbolist poetry would make enough sense of Mandelstam's "gift" by recalling Mallarmé's "Don du poème" and especially Verlaine's "Art poétique." Opera lovers would find subtle references to Wagner's *Tristan*, admirers of Nietzsche to Zarathustra's "honey sacrifice." Finally, a reader unversed in any of these areas but aware of the comparative study of myth could find considerable satisfaction in being admitted into the chthonic world of Mandelstam's poem with the aid of Frazer's "golden bough." In short, many roads led to Rome and its environs. In this sense, Mandelstam's very modern poem, his reputation as a difficult poet notwithstanding, was as simple as it was complex—"as intricate as it was naive," in Mandelstam's own words—or, if we compare it to dream work, "overdetermined." Because it had something for everyone, the poem's "magic"—even when much of the poem remained murky—could not be missed by a reader willing to accept the poem's gift. If anything, the murkiness itself, as Russian modernists believed, constituted a major factor in the effectiveness of a verbal charm, whether a folk spell or a sophisticated riddle-incantation produced by a Symbolist, a Futurist, or an Acmeist poet.[49]

OEDIPUS, ANTIGONE, AND THE FORGOTTEN WORD

No other poem pulls together the main thematic and stylistic strands of *Tristia* as well as "I Have Forgotten the Word I Wanted to Say." Even this first line of the poem can be taken alone as an example of Mandelstam's "secular" revision of Symbolism. With *word* inserted into it, the colorless colloquial phrase—a Russian version of "What was it I wanted to say?"—becomes a potent "symbol" capable of summoning from the depths of time a rich and intricate mythology. For in the poem are invocations of the Oedipus cycle, Plato, Virgil, the Orphics, Hans Christian Andersen, Mallarmé, and Frazer, not to mention the Russian poetic tradition stretching from Derzhavin to M. Lozinskii's verses adressed to Akhmatova.

Dying as Metaphor: 1920–1930

Я слово позабыл, что я хотел сказать.
Слепая ласточка в чертог теней вернется,
На крыльях срезанных, с прозрачными играть.
В беспамятстве ночная песнь поется.

Не слышно птиц. Бессмертник не цветет.
Прозрачны гривы табуна ночного.
В сухой реке пустой челнок плывет.
Среди кузнечиков беспамятствует слово.

И медленно растет, как бы шатер иль храм,
То вдруг прокинется безумной Антигоной,
То мертвой ласточкой бросается к ногам
С стигийской нежностью и веткою зеленой.

О если бы вернуть и зрячих пальцев стыд,
И выпуклую радость узнаванья.
Я так боюсь рыданья Аонид,
Тумана, звона и зиянья.

А смертным власть дана любить и узнавать,
Для них и звук в персты прольется,
Но я забыл, что я хочу сказать,
И мысль бесплотная в чертог теней вернется.

Всё не о том прозрачная твердит,
Всё ласточка, подружка, Антигона...
А на губах как черный лед горит
Стигийского воспоминанье звона.

Ноябрь 1920

I have forgotten the word that I wanted to say.
A blind swallow will return to the palace of shadows,
Her wings clipped, to play with the transparent ones.
The night song is sung in amnesiac madness.

Birds can't be heard. The immortelles aren't blooming.
In night's herd, the horses have transparent manes.
In a dry river, an empty barque is floating.
Among the grasshoppers, the word is raving mad.

And grows slowly, as if a tent or a temple,
Now a mad Antigone, it rushes past me,
Now a dead swallow, it dashes to my feet
With Stygian tenderness and a green bough.

Oh, if only to regain the shame of seeing fingers,
And the salient joy of recognition.
I so fear the wailing of the Aonides,
The mist, the ringing, and the hiatus agape.

> But the mortals have been given the power to love and recognize,
> For them, even sound will pour into fingers,
> But I've forgotten what I want to say,
> And the incorporeal thought will return to the palace of the shadows.
>
> Transparent, it keeps intoning not what I want,
> A swallow still, a girlfriend, an Antigone...
> And on my lips, like black ice, burns
> The memory of Stygian ringing.[50]

The poem may have been composed as an extended pun of the kind that often sustains stories about verbal magic, in which forgetting a word—a usual occurrence by ordinary standards—can spell a real calamity.[51] This is, indeed, the mental space in which the poem operates. A mere memory slip is amplified on a hyperbolic scale, becoming the loss of that one and only word, the chthonic "open sesame," the password to rebirth and immortality. The poem's plot,[52] then, may be summarized as a search for the forgotten word in the course of which the speaker undergoes an ordeal of descent into the underworld. Paradoxically, the death of the poet recovers the word. Without undermining the principle of eternal recurrence, the closure describes that phase of the cycle when the speaker's sojourn in the Avernus has become a memory of one who had died and through death was reborn.

Whether the immortality thus achieved was to be secular-poetic, Orphic, Eleusian, Platonic, or Christian would depend on the reader's preference. We can be certain, however, that the secular-poetic and the Christian perspectives had a particularly powerful significance for Mandelstam, the author of "Pushkin and Skriabin" and "Word and Culture," as well as for the contemporary reader. That the poem was couched in the "Orphic," or, in any case, the Hellenistic mythological idiom does not change matters in the least, since Greek antiquity had long before been assimilated to "modern" Christianity by the Russian Nietzscheans, D. Merezhkovskii, Viacheslav Ivanov, and, indeed, Mandelstam himself. Two passages from Ivanov's early treatise on Dionysus offer some idea of the knowledge of antique religious practices available to Mandelstam (italics are mine):

> The mask here [in Hellenistic funeral rites] is an apotropaic object guarding the soul of the departed from hostile forces of the underworld that are capable of destroying him. Gold tablets with Orphic verses found in the graves in Southern Italy have similar meaning. They give the soul, or a substitute in its place, the ready-made for-

mulas of answers, which the soul, the "daughter of the Earth and the starry Heaven," has to pass on, at the crossroads and during the ordeals, to the guardians of the underworld in order to reach the place of peace and to drink of "the cold water flowing out of the lake of Memory," that is, in order to safeguard for herself immortality. The halos adorning the heads of our own dead as well as the *texts of prayers placed in their hands* originated apparently in the distant past.[53]

Most of the poem's allusions have been well documented,[54] and it would add little to point out that, for example, the second stanza follows a Virgilian pun from Book 6 of *The Aeneid,* wherein *Avernus* is derived from the Greek *a-ornos,* or "birdless."[55] I shall concentrate instead on Mandelstam's choice of the protagonist-vehicle and its relation to the poem's main theme: the recovery of memory or, simply, the establishment of continuity between the present and the past—in the terms of Mandelstam's Bergsonian utopia, the omnipresence of the past.[56] How, indeed, does this preoccupation relate to the figure of the blind Oedipus, who would rather return to his prior state with its unbearable shame than join the immortals? For that matter, how is Antigone to be associated with the search for the forgotten word? Finally, how does this twice-invoked incest motif fit in with Mandelstam's earlier "mythologies" of self-presentation associated with the mother-stepmother Phaedra and Leah, the poet's erstwhile daughter-bride?

I would like to suggest a view of the poem that makes it emblematic of Mandelstam's entire "mnemonic" enterprise. The self-reflective nature of modernism—and the Acmeists were perhaps the most self-reflective poets of their generation[57]—and the charismatic view of Russian literature common in Mandelstam's milieu created conditions under which it was possible and, from a certain reader's point of view, laudable to predicate one's identity on a reading list (see *The Noise of Time*). The whole of Soviet Russia went through a similar experience in the 1930s, when, in its turn toward nationalism, the state forcefully encouraged a cult of the nineteenth-century classics (minus Dostoevsky) in an attempt to create a new national identity built on Russia's past.[58] Yet no matter how intense the charisma of literature may have been, the self-referentiality of modernism, its awareness of the contingent nature of art (not to speak of the propaganda power of the modern state), tended to make problematic any sweeping claims to art's ultimate seriousness. Indeed, this ambiguity in the Russian literary culture served as a structuring principle in the presentation of self in Mandelstam's poetry.

In the years immediately following the revolution, when the Russian language seemed to provide the only "institution" of historical continuity, identity based on letters grew in symbolic force, and so did the doubts concerning its actual power and relevance in the revolutionary epoch.

> Выстроили пушки по опушке,
> глухи к белогвардейской ласке.
> А почему
> не атакован Пушкин?
> И прочие
> генералы классики?
>
> You've set up cannons at the edge of the wood.
> You are deaf to the caresses of the White Guards.
> But why
> Haven't you launched an attack on Pushkin?
> And what about the other
> Classic-Generals?[59]

Maiakovskii's lines present a good example of the opposite contemporary attitude toward continuity. It is ironic that, although diametrically opposed to Mandelstam's program, the poem ascribed to the word the same extraordinary power over the determination of the nation's identity.[60]

> Словно нежный хрящ ребенка —
> Век младенческой земли,
> Снова в жертву, как ягненка,
> Темя жизни принесли.
>
> Чтобы вырвать век из плена,
> Чтобы новый мир начать,
> Узловатых дней колена
> Нужно флейтою связать.
>
> Like the tender cartilage of a babe
> Is the age of the infant earth,—
> Once again, like a lamb on the altar,
> The tender crown of life has been sacrificed.
>
> In order to tear the age out of captivity,
> In order to begin the new world,
> The joints of gnarled days
> With a flute one must bind.[61]

This was Mandelstam's reply to Maiakovskii's nihilist stance as well as a specific chastisement of him as a poet. Was Maiakovskii not betraying his own earlier declaration, in "The Backbone Flute" (1915), of a poet's kenotic destiny?

Dying as Metaphor: 1920–1930

Я сегодня буду играть на флейте,
На собственном позвоночнике.

Today I shall be playing the flute,
My own backbone.

That flute Mandelstam now picked up and was proposing to "play." There was no need to break again the already-broken backbone of the "beast-age." Rather, it was the poet's duty to offer himself as a sacrifice, that is, to devote his poetry to a "memorial service" for the past epoch. The steam engine of the new epoch was moving forward at a fast pace, and Mandelstam's dedication to memorial thematics that ran "against the nap of the world" ("Ia po lesenke pristavnoi," 1922)[62] did indeed represent an ordeal and a sacrifice. If one wishes to be literal, he may have been sacrificing popularity among contemporary readers. In terms of Mandelstam's logo-ethical discourse, then, the word possessed tremendous redemptive power because it, too, was capable of supreme suffering. This was a matter of profound belief and of equally profound anxiety and doubt. For the word, the "pure joy, a cure from grief," could become lost, could "die" or be forgotten.

A quintessential, if rather frail, shell of protective identity for many exemplary protagonists, Russian literature was doubly so for the figure of a poet cultivated by Mandelstam—a character whose ancestors, to paraphrase an often-quoted passage from *The Noise of Time,* spoke in Hebrew and Yiddish rather than in the "epic hexameters" of such Russian noblemen as Aksakov or Tolstoy. He was a poet who set out to redeem Russia in the persona of a Hippolytus, presenting the country's predicament as the ordeal of Phaedra behind whom there stood the image of historiosophical incest: Russia, as baptized Jew, lapsing back into the religion that Christianity had already superseded (see chapter 3). Even now, after "Phaedra-Russia" had been dead at least three years (that is, in 1920, when "I Have Forgotten the Word" was composed), the vocation of a poet was still perceived by Mandelstam's protagonist in terms of a drama of incest. However, an important change had taken place.

The protagonist was no longer the innocent and haughty Hippolytus; it was Oedipus—the savior of Thebes, the *son* and *husband* of Jocasta (Jocasta-Russia?), the murderer of Laius, the "century" or "age" ("1 January 1924")—one who blinded himself and was now cared for by his daughter-sister Antigone (the name means "in place of a mother"). Better still, he wore both masks at once: that of an Oedipus who had recognized his true identity and transgressions;

and that of a daughter of an incestuous marriage, who was therefore doubly a member of her family and doubly faithful to her duty of caring for her kin both in life and in death. The essential narrative pattern was echoed in poem after poem throughout *Tristia* and *1921–1925*. The mask of Oedipus epitomized crime inadvertently committed, that of Antigone inadvertent guilt. Each was "a blameless victim as well as the most beloved child of the gods," as Viacheslav Ivanov once described them.[63] In assuming both masks, Mandelstam's poet was expressing a sentiment typical for a sizable segment of the intelligentsia, especially writers, who, outpaced by events, tried to regain their position in society even if it meant presenting themselves as protagonists in narratives of fate and retribution.[64] This often-quoted statement by Andrei Belyi may serve as an elaboration:

> We, humanists, free philosophers, exhausting ourselves with complaints about violence, we *are:* the subtlest perpetrators of violence, executioners and tyrants; the state monopoly on thought is our mirror image: we are the "guard sleeping at the doorway [of power]"; and—yes, we *are* "Bolsheviks," too.[65]

In a similar way, Mandelstam's poet went about reclaiming for himself a place at the culture's center, where he could present himself not merely as a victim of the times but as a son of the "age the master" ("1 January 1924") who had inadvertently absorbed the abomination of his epoch and could therefore, poetically speaking, offer himself as an innocent redemptive sacrifice. The death of Oedipus was, after all, a "good-luck charm" for the city from which he passed into the other world, and his daughter Antigone (buried alive for burying the dead) had far more favor in the eyes of the gods than had the statesman Creon.

This substitution of one incest myth for another enabled Mandelstam to maintain continuity in the narrative pattern of self-presentation—a necessary condition for producing a protagonist-consciousness capable of focusing onto itself Mandelstam's view of "culture" as an omnipresent and ever-present memory of the race. Hence the hypostases of the word in the third stanza, each ringing more than one bell: the "tent" calls up the theme of the "tabernacle" (which Mandelstam repeatedly "secularized" as "tent");[66] the "temple" brings up his early poems about the exemplary masterpieces of world architecture ("Hagia Sophia," "Notre Dame"); Antigone develops further the theme of poetry as a redemptive ordeal of incest and parthenogenesis (as in Mallarmé's "Don du poème"), serving as an emblematic nexus for the main thematic threads of *Tristia:* "exile," "return," "incest," "retribution" and "innocence," "funeral rites" and "self-interment."

Finally, the "blind swallow with a green bough," perhaps the richest of the chthonic word-myths in Mandelstam, possessed both the paronymic suggestiveness of an image with a transparent "inner form" (LAS*tochka*-LAS*ka*-SL*epoi*-PAL*'tsy*) and prodigious evocative power with regard to the previous uses of the word in Mandelstam and other poets.[67] A frequent protagonist in the folklore and folklore-inspired narratives of death and revival, the swallow, *lastochka,* can easily summon up its etymon—*laska,* a common Slavic word for "love." Given contemporary poetic practice, the "inner form" revealed itself with virtual inevitability, both because of the thematics, associated with the mythology of eros and death, and because *lastochka* simply happened to be a word with an easily retrievable etymology. The swallow's attribute "blind," *slepoi,* transferred to the word an aspect of "incest" (Oedipus) and provided the paronymic motivation for the Oedipus "narrative": sL*epoi*—paL*'tsy*—*vypukL*aia (blind—fingers—salient), the tactile metaphor for the "recognition" of the "inner form of the word," which in Mandelstam constituted a process both resembling and related to resurrection.[68] The "green bough," then, betrayed a close kinship to the "golden bough" of Virgil and Frazer. All of these aspects of the "swallow" are then recapitulated in the poem's "Oedipus narrative."

To the extent that the identity of the poet's figure was predicated on literature, it was likely to be presented ultimately in the form of the Word, and to the extent that this identity (bound with eros) happened to be fundamentally problematic, it was likely to find its expression in the century's central myth of uncertainty and differentiation, the myth of incest. The pervasive eroticism of modern Russian poetry and the centrality of the theme of the "mystical marriage," as well as a general cult of sensuality common to Mandelstam's generation,[69] made the choice of the incest myth well-nigh inevitable. Although there was no way of predicting this development in advance, when viewed in retrospect, Mandelstam's choices lack neither consistency nor internal coherence. The myth of incest functioned as a tightly woven narrative of self-presentation meant to recapitulate the redemptive suffering of the *Word.* What better mythology can one imagine for the charismatic aspect of Russian literature at this time of great stress and, for the people of Mandelstam's intellectual background, of profound social atonement?

Oedipus, Antigone, and the Forgotten Word

The poet Mandelstam, a man in his late twenties who had previously fashioned himself a haughty Hippolytus, assumed the persona of a decrepit Oedipus, a Hippolytus who had become tolerant and accepting in his old age. In his earlier poetry, the familiarity of close kin (whatever the metaphor was intended to signify) was a taboo never to be breached: "And the grief of my kinfolk is alien to me as before" (1914).[70] Needless to say, an Oedipus or an Antigone was not prone to such discriminations; they were far more likely to conceive of the world (recall Mandelstam's essay "Humanism and the Present") as a home, and of humanity as a family gathered around a radiating universal hearth.[71] Indeed, *Tristia* is concluded with a somber, almost liturgical declaration of love for the spirit of Russia, a funeral service at Petersburg's St. Isaac's, with some apologies for the more universal symbols that had hitherto preoccupied Mandelstam:

> Люблю под сводами седыя тишины
> Молебнов, панихид блужданье
> И трогательный чин, ему же все должны,—
> У Исаака отпеванье.
>
> Люблю священника неторопливый шаг,
> Широкий вынос плащаницы
> И в ветхом неводе Генисаретский мрак
> Великопостныя седмицы.
>
> Ветхозаветный дым на теплых алтарях
> И иерея возглас сирый,
> Смиренник царственный: снег чистый на плечах
> И одичалые порфиры.
>
> Соборы вечные Софии и Петра,
> Амбары воздуха и света,
> Зернохранилища вселенского добра
> И риги нового завета.
>
> Не к вам влечется дух в годины тяжких бед,
> Сюда влачится по ступеням
> Широкопасмурным несчастья волчий след,
> Ему ж вовеки не изменим:
>
> Зане свободен раб, преодолевший страх,
> И сохранилось свыше меры
> В прохладных житницах, в глубоких закромах
> Зерно глубокой, полной веры.
>
> 1921

Under the bridal veil of milky whiteness, St. Isaac's
Stands like a pigeon house capped by a graying head,

And its staff is stirring the gray silence
And the airy ritual clear to one's heart.

The wandering ghost of age-old funeral rites,
The fanning out of the procession with the Shroud,
And, in the ancient net, the Genisareth gloom
Of the week of High Lent.

The Old Testament incense rising from warm altars
And a priest's unassuming call,
His royalty so humble: pure snow on his shoulders
And his crimson robes gone wild.

Eternal cathedrals of Sophia and Peter,
The granaries of air and light,
The storehouses of universal weal,
And the threshing floors of the New Testament.

Not to you is my spirit drawn in these times of hardship,
It's to this place [where], dragging themselves up the steps,
Broad and gloomy, stream wolf tracks of misfortune;
We shan't betray them ever:

For the servant who has overcome fear is free again,
And the grain has survived in amounts beyond measure—
In the cool stores and in deep silos—
The grain of profound, wholesome faith.[72]

THE IRONY AND PROSE OF THE NEP

They will throw you out, Parnok, they will definitely throw you out.
OSIP MANDELSTAM, The Egyptian Stamp (1928)

In Mandelstam's poetry, Iurii Tynianov once wrote, "as in Schiller, 'sober concepts dance a Bacchic dance' (Heine)."[73] To illustrate his point he proceeded to quote from "I Have Forgotten the Word." Apparently, Mandelstam's allusive technique was contagious, infecting the critic himself. Instead of addressing Mandelstam's poetic project directly—either his desire for a pandemic anamnesis or his emphasis on the "familial" unity of cultures and words—Tynianov chose a playfully oblique reference to Schiller's "Ode to Joy," Beethoven's Ninth, and Mandelstam's own "Ode to Beethoven"—all seen through one of the most ironic romantic prisms, the eyes of Heinrich Heine.[74] Tynianov's review was entitled "The Space Between" ("Promezhutok") and appeared in 1924, the "transitional" time when the enthusiasm of the civil war years had become diluted with the ironies and the pragmatism of the NEP period. This loss of "intensity," "centeredness," and a clearly defined direction, so characteristic of the social and cultural life of the country, could not be conducive to Mandelstam's poetic enterprise. For it is not the nature of a martyr or a prophet—a model for Mandelstam's "poet"—to thrive on pluralism, irony, and the general fatigue with grand questions and global themes, including the metaphysics of the fin de siècle and the dawning of a new era. "At the end of an age," Mandelstam wrote in *The Noise of Time,* indulging in gentle self-parody, "abstract concepts stink of rotten fish."[75] Spoken by the author of the somber and solemn "1 January 1924," a poem meant to provide a cure from self-doubt, these words expressed a sentiment closely resembling, in fact anticipating, Tynianov's friendly sarcasm.[76] Be that as it may, for over five years following "The Space Between," Mandelstam would not be writing any poetry. For even his lifestyle, that of a literary laborer (he was supporting himself and his wife by translating), became incompatible with "charismatic" expectation. According to Weber,

> Modern charismatic movements of artistic origin represent "independents without gainful employment" (in everyday language, *rentiers*). Normally such persons are the best qualified to follow [and be] a charismatic leader. This is just as logically consistent as the medieval friar's vow of poverty, which demands the very opposite.[77]

Accordingly, even though Mandelstam did not disengage from the poetic enterprise altogether, the poems he included in his 1928 edition (most of his work since 1909) were arranged in a new pattern. The reader was presented with a different design of a "poetic career," one subtly reflecting the emphatically unheroic character of the NEP.

Unlike the 1922 collection, the *Tristia* of the 1928 *Poems* (Stikhotvoreniia) concluded with an ironic recapitulation of the career of Mandelstam's poet—from the naive chastity and solemnity of *Stone* to the lighthearted wisdom one associates with the love poetry of Ovid, Catullus, the early Pushkin, and Pushkin's eighteenth-century French model, Parny. Composed in 1920 but included in *The Second Book* (1923) rather than *Tristia,* the poem characteristically relied on the "subtext" provided by two famous poems by Pushkin. The youthful and blasphemous *Gabriliad* (about the seduction of the Virgin by the Archangel Gabriel) informed the closure, and the somber and serious "The Prophet" (a reworking of Isaiah's call to prophecy) supplied such key lexical items as the "Seraphim" and the burning "coals."[78] Fortuna's "wheel," too, had gained in levity, imparting its pattern not to the ponderous cycles of historical recurrence but to the course of the poet's amorous exploits. Indeed, it would be hard to find another

Dying as Metaphor: 1920–1930

poem by Mandelstam that could better demonstrate the coexistence and mutual reinforcement of two such diametrically opposed sentiments: an enthusiastic belief in the Word and a deep suspicion that its power might, in fact, be quite tenuous.

> Я в хоровод теней, топтавших нежный луг,
> С певучим именем вмешался,
> Но всё растаяло, и только слабый звук
> В туманной памяти остался.
>
> Сначала думал я, что имя — серафим,
> И тела легкого дичился,
> Немного дней прошло, и я смешался с ним
> И в милой тени растворился.
>
> И снова яблоня теряет дикий плод,
> И тайный образ мне мелькает,
> И богохульствует, и сам себя клянет,
> И угли ревности глотает.
>
> А счастье катится, как обруч золотой,
> Чужую волю исполняя,
> И ты гоняешься за легкою весной,
> Ладонью воздух рассекая.
>
> И так устроено, что не выходим мы
> Из заколдованного круга.
> Земли девической упругие холмы
> Лежат спеленутые туго.
>
> 1920

> Into the round dance of shadows trampling a tender meadow,
> I intruded with a tender name,
> But everything dissolved, and only a feeble sound
> Remained in misty memory.
>
> At first, I thought: the word is Seraphim,
> And I shied away from the light body,
> Not many days had passed, and I entwined with it
> And dissolved myself in the dear shadow.
>
> And again, the apple tree loses its wild fruit,
> And the secret image fleets before me,
> And blasphemes, and curses itself,
> And swallows the coals of jealousy.
>
> And happiness rolls like a golden hoop,
> Fulfilling the will of another,
> And you are chasing after the light spring,
> Your hand cleaving the air.

> And it is set up so that we do not leave
> The magic circle.
> The taut hills of maidenly earth
> Lie tightly swaddled.[79]

The last poem of *1921–1925*, the third and final part of *Poems*, reiterated the same theme (if in a more somber key) in the form of a pledge—a rhetorical pattern encountered throughout *1921–1925*.[80] Even if the word was fragile, even if the poet had no audience, he would still remain faithful to his thematic and ethical allegiances—the mnemonic funeral for the dying and the dead. A branch of bird-cherry that had figured next to the moving piston of a steam engine in an early Futurist declaration[81] and had served as a synecdochic reminder of death-in-love for the Mandelstam of *Tristia*[82] now had a different "frame": a sleek black carriage of bygone days undulating to the "outmoded" tune of Schubertian sentiments:

> I shall be dashing about the gypsy camp of a dark street
> After a branch of bird-cherry in a black well-sprung carriage,
> After a snow bonnet, after the eternal, the water mill noise.
> . . . .
> And I have no one to whom to say: "Out of the gypsy camp of a dark street."[83]

Here was a declaration of fidelity to the poetics of revival—combined with irony (two parts bitter, one part sweet). Even though the sense of mission was growing increasingly vague—a common occurrence in the unstable "charismatic" universe[84]—the main themes of Mandelstam's poetic career could not be easily abandoned.

Like the collected *Poems*, *The Egyptian Stamp* appeared in 1928. It was a novella containing, among other things, a cruel parody on the very self that had animated some of Mandelstam's loftiest poetry in the *Tristia* period. To the extent that the style is the man, what Mandelstam tried to accomplish in his only essay in narrative prose was to parody the particular mythologies and the related symbolic vocabulary of his self-presentation. To offer one example, the revival of the "inner form of the word," the delicate symbolism of poetic communion and revival of the departed, the journeys through Persephone's domain of memory—the stuff of *Tristia* and *1921–1925*—now supplied the food for a silly pun: "Tele*phone* has not yet been installed at Proserpine's and at Perse*phone*'s."[85] Another central feature of Mandelstam's poetic project, the gradual "accumulation" of attributes by the protagonist-poet, became the subject of parody in the concluding pages of the novella. "Oh God, do not make me resemble Parnok," the clever narrator of stories of Parnok's misfortunes was praying in mock despair,

> Grant me strength to distinguish myself from him. For I, too, have stood in that terrifying patient line, which crawls to the little yellow window of the box office—at first in the freezing cold outside, then under the low bathhouse ceilings of the Alexandrinka. For I, too, am terrified by the theater, frightening like a peasant hovel without a chimney, like a village bathhouse in which someone was brutally murdered for the sake of a cutaway fur coat and a pair of felt boots. For I, too, am sustained only by Petersburg, concert-going, yellow, ominous, its feathers ruffled, wintry.[86]

Mandelstam was flaunting before the reader the exorbitant resemblance between himself and his alter ego—the "mosquito-prince" protagonist, the "Collegiate Assessor for the city of Thebes"[87]—who in turn was modeled on a friend: like Mandelstam, a Petersburg Jew, Valentin Parnakh.[88] A poet, a dance critic, the pioneer of jazz in Russia, Parnakh also happened to be the brother of Sophia Parnok, whom Mandelstam had once tried to replace in Tsvetaeva's heart. This "genealogy" should give some idea of how appropriate the metaphor of incest was for the Russian literary milieu of Mandelstam's generation.[89]

Curiously, the story was set in Petrograd in the summer of 1917. This most "pluralistic" summer in Russia's entire modern history was chosen by Mandelstam as a backdrop for a string of events associated with Parnok, events with but one thing in common: grievous injustice. Even in her best hour of true democracy and freedom (one would like to impute such sentiments to Mandelstam), the old Russia could not pull her own weight, nor could Parnok adjust to the new environment. Neither, the author was suggesting, possessed the equipment to cross the seas of history. Like an actual Egyptian stamp, which was designed to become effaced if ever reused,[90] Parnok was unable to preserve his "face" in the world that had replaced the familiar "Egypt." Apart from its obvious Josephian connotations, the choice of the novella's title (it was Parnok's school nickname) echoed Mandelstam's abiding preoccupation with preserving the memory of oneself for future generations: as a mariner does when he throws into the sea a bottle with a message—an emblem for poetry in Mandelstam's 1914 essay "On the Addressee" ("O sobesednikie"). By 1928, the seal had sprung a leak.

Nothing worked for Parnok. His attempt to save a man from a lynch mob ended in failure. His evening coat, "kidnapped" at the very outset "like a Sabine woman," was now owned by a certain junior officer with a hyper-Christian last name, Krzyzanowski—"man of the Cross." To add insult to injury, the woman he had been assiduously courting "according to the conventional rules of romance" (for "Parnok was a victim of received concepts concerning the course of a romance")[91] fell prey to another plot. She was last seen boarding what might be called the "Anna Karenina Express," bound from Petrograd to Moscow, in the company of the junior officer Krzyzanowski. Petersburg, the magnificent Petersburg of Mandelstam's early poetry, too had gone bad. It now resembled "Nero eating a soup of crushed flies," and the narrator, the creation of the "right fellow traveler Mandelstam,"[92] was now blaming it for the torments of the unfortunate Parnok:

> Petersburg, you are responsible for your poor son! For all this confusion, for the pathetic love of music, for every jelly bean in the little paper bag held by a girl from the Bestuzhev College sitting in the top tier of the Noblemen Assembly Hall—you shall answer, Petersburg![93]

Could such a place deserve to survive, let alone be resurrected in the poet's memory? Despite Nadezhda Mandelstam's assertions to the contrary, *The Egyptian Stamp* was neither a momentary lapse nor an uncommon phenomenon.[94] Together with Iu. Olesha's *Envy* (1927), K. Vaginov's *Goat Song* (1928), M. Zoshchenko's *Mishel' Siniagin* (1930), and B. Pasternak's *Spektorskii* (1924–1931), it belonged to the genre of *samokritika,* or self-mockery, that many intellectuals practiced at the fin de siècle for the NEP.[95]

For Mandelstam, the malaise was not entirely new. In 1923 he was already showing signs of weariness, even impatience, with the tight network of correspondences that he, the latter-day Russian Joseph-Hippolytus, had so painstakingly woven. Consider these lines, full of skepticism and disenchantment, from what is the longest poem by Mandelstam, the 1923 "He Who Found a Horseshoe":

> С чего начать?
> Всё трещит и качается.
> Воздух дрожит от сравнений.
> Ни одно слово не лучше другого,
> Земля гудит метафорой,
> И легкие двуколки,
> В броской упряжи густых от натуги птичьих стай,
> Разрываются на части,
> Соперничая с храпящими любимцами ристалищ.

Dying as Metaphor: 1920–1930

> Where to begin?
> Everything creaks and sways.
> The air is vibrating with similes.
> Not one word is better than another,
> The earth tolls with metaphor,
> And the light two-wheelers,
> In the gaudy harness of bird flocks, dense from tension,
> Are torn to pieces,
> Competing with the snorting favorites of the races.[96]

Keeping in mind the subtitle of the poem, "A Pindaric Fragment," it is not hard to recognize in the "snorting favorites" a metonymy of the horses pulling the charioteers of the new state (Pindar used to extoll their predecessors in Hellas) as well as those who followed the mood of the spectator crowd. A Hippolytus, one who used to harness poetry's "swallows into military legions" ("Twilight of Freedom," 1918), was now finding it very hard to keep up with the other athletes, let alone compete to win. All he could hope for was that one day a future reader would come across the old horseshoe lost by his Pegasus and, having shined it with a piece of wool, nail it—a talisman—over the entrance of his house for good fortune.[97] The narrator of *Egyptian Stamp* closely resembled this poet: the loss of the coat by his protagonist was not very different from the poet's broken chariot and his expiring Pegasus overstressed by modern poetry's race. Both works originated in the sense of loss, and both made this loss productive. After all, Hippolytus became a hero only after his chariot crashed, Joseph achieved fame only after he had been stripped of his beautiful coat, and the proverbial overcoat of Gogol's Akakii Akakievich—only because it had been stolen from him—was able to serve as womb for Dostoevsky's art.

WHAT HAPPENED TO THE COAT

It is one of the more remarkable coincidences of literary history that the man who in November 1928 accused Mandelstam, however rashly, of plagiarizing his translation of Coster's novel should have used a simile that went to the very heart of Mandelstam's monument of self-presentation: "When I, as I am walking through a flea market, recognize, even in its altered state, my coat which yesterday hung in my antechamber, I have the right to say: 'Look here, this is a stolen coat.'"[98]

Much of the story of this incident has been related before (although largely from Mandelstam's perspective), and I shall not dwell on it here at length.[99] Suffice it to say that through a production error, the title page of the new edition credited Mandelstam with translating

Légende de Uylenspiegel, whereas he had in fact only revised a popular 1916 translation by Arkadii Gornfel'd. The translator had every reason to be outraged. A well-known literary figure who began his career in the previous century, Gornfel'd was in 1928 going through a particularly difficult time. In a literary establishment becoming increasingly dominated by new people, his once respectable credentials of talented publicist and an associate of Korolenko and the populists were close to being irrelevant and certainly were outdated. His manuscripts, he wrote to one of his friends, had been gathering dust at the Leningrad State Publishing House for several years, and journals that had previously welcomed his work were no longer soliciting his contributions. For this severely disabled man (he could not move without assistance), the progressive loss of income must have been frightening. To add insult to injury, neither the publisher of Coster, who bore the legal responsibility, nor Mandelstam, who could have been more sensitive to the rights of a fellow author, informed Gornfel'd of the plans to reissue his translation. Despite the publisher's public apology and Mandelstam's public admission of his moral responsibility as well as his offer to compensate Gornfel'd with "all his literary income," the affair dragged on and on. This tormenting stream of accusations and counteraccusations nearly unhinged Mandelstam, and finally, after firing a parting shot at the cursed writers' establishment in the form of *The Fourth Prose,*[100] he went on a long journey to Armenia, not returning to Moscow until the spring of 1931.

In Gornfel'd's bitter letter to the editor of Leningrad's *Krasnaia gazeta* (November 28, 1928), cited previously, the elaboration of the Joseph metaphor had come full circle. Now, rising to the surface, it began to figure as an emblem of Mandelstam in such literary landmarks of 1930–31 as Pasternak's narrative poem *Spektorskii* and Zoshchenko's *Mishel' Siniagin,* a mock biography of a mock Symbolist nonpoet. A member of the intelligentsia, argued the two authors, using an allusion to Mandelstam's trials and litigations as one illustration, had to accept these minor discomforts of Soviet life, if for no other reason than to atone for the social injustice by which he, a former member of the former bourgeois class, had had the good fortune to benefit before the people's revolution.

Indeed, how could Mandelstam, proud of his oath of allegiance to the course of the "fourth estate" ("1 January 1924"), be so upset about a few stains on his "coat of many colors" (SPEKTOR*skii* called for such a pun) when the entire country was offering itself as a sacrifice in an attempt to reverse the millennia of injustice. Musing to himself on the nature of the revolution (not without a mention of incest, which should prepare us for the appearance of Mandelstam),[101] the narrator of Pasternak's poem treated with sarcasm the people like himself—in fact, like Mandelstam, considering the sartorial metaphor—whose avowed identification with the fate of Russia and commitment to the people's cause could not withstand the test of a little dirt thrown up by the wheel of history:

> Тогда ты в крик. Я вам не шут! Насилье!
> Я жил как вы. Но отзыв предрешен:
> История не в том что мы носили,
> А в том, как нас пускали нагишом.

> Then you scream. I won't be your buffoon! Brutality!
> I've lived like you. But the retort is predestined:
> History is not in what we used to wear,
> It is—in how we've been paraded in the nude.[102]

A year later Mandelstam would taunt Pasternak by sporting his latest version of the coat of many colors, warning those who found his identification with Russia's destiny presumptuous and his treatment of the "people's revolution" indelicate that they might suffer the same fate as "eloquence" in Verlaine's "Art poétique" ("Prends l'éloquence et tords-lui son cou!"):

> Пора вам знать, я тоже современник,
> Я человек эпохи Москвошвея,
> Смотрите, как на мне топорщится пиджак,
> Как я ступать и говорить умею!
> Попробуйте меня от века оторвать! —
> Ручаюсь вам, себе свернете шею!

> It is high time you learn: I, too, am a contemporary,
> I am a man of the epoch of the Moscow Garment Trust,
> See how my coat bunches,
> How I can do my step and speak!
> Just try to tear me away from the century!—
> I guarantee, you'll break your own neck![103]

Zoshchenko, who would soon be writing stories about the successful reeducation of convicts at the construction site of the White Sea Canal),[104] put Mandelstam's travails to similar use, if not as tactfully as Pasternak. He transferred the "coat allegory" to his character Siniagin, a caricature of a post-Symbolist poet who would rather beg and pilfer, even steal a coat from the house of the narrator—a relative of the protagonist!—than do an honest day's work.

> The author must add that he himself was in serious need, and his assistance to the relative [Siniagin] was insignificant. However, on many occasions the author gave him small sums, which Michel accepted haughtily and without gratitude.[105]
>
> But once, in the absence of the author, Michel took from the coat hanger somebody's coat with a monkey-fur collar and sold it literally for pennies, after which he simply stopped visiting the author and did not even respond to his greetings.
>
> Of course, the author appreciated his sad state and did not so much as mention the theft, but Michel, sensing his own guilt, would just turn away from the author, not wishing to enter into any conversations with him.
>
> The author is relating this with an extraordinarily, so to speak, embarrassed feeling and even with the consciousness of his own sort of guilt, even though he himself wasn't at all to blame.[106]

Even these two fellow writers whom Mandelstam admired could not fully empathize with his demands for the restoration of his personal dignity. The "historical moment," in the dialectical argot of the day, did not make provisions for such individualistic self-indulgence.

Deprived of his protective attire, his honor in question, Mandelstam reached into the wardrobe of identities and wrapped himself in that ineffable nongarment of Russian literature's humiliated and wronged. A mere trace, really, it was no more part of an overcoat than a hole is part of a bagel or a scrivener is part of literature—because the overcoat in question, which once did indeed belong to the fictional government copyist and amateur calligrapher Akakii Akakievich, had been stolen once and for all. Not for him the oppressive warmth of opulent furs meant to adorn the shoulders of the ranking Russian authors:

> I, a furrier of precious furs, who has nearly been stifled by literary peltry, carry a moral responsibility for having suggested to the Petersburg scoundrel a desire to quote like a slanderous joke Gogol's hot coat of fur torn in the middle of the night from the back of the oldest Komsomol member—Akakii Akakievich. I myself tear down the literary fur coat and stamp on it with my feet. In a minus-thirty freezing cold, wearing a thin little jacket, I shall run three times around the boulevard ring of Moscow.[107]

He himself had never been comfortable wearing this sort of expensive attire. In a 1922 essay, "Fur Coat," he compared his sense of puritan unease at the first "abundance" of the NEP period with the shame he felt wearing a secondhand coat acquired at a flea market.

Dying as Metaphor: 1920–1930

The same symbolic image forms the closure of the last vignette in *The Noise of Time* (1925). Such "lordly fur coats" were "above" a Russian writer's "station," however coveted or even worn they might have been. A Russian author, Mandelstam was suggesting, if he wished to be true to the spirit of Russian literature, would be far better off wearing the kenotic hair shirt of an Avvakum or a cape lined with the proverbial "fish fur," as did the "aging son of the century" in "1 January 1924."[108] Better still was to have one's coat stolen in the middle of the freezing Russian winter.

Just as many poems by Mandelstam have so-called companion pieces, so *The Egyptian Stamp* finds its double in *The Fourth Prose* (because it was the fourth, and also by analogy with the "fourth estate" and the "fourth Rome"). The former parodied and debased the mythologies of Joseph in Egypt and of Hippolytus (Parnok's feet were like the *hooves* of a sheep); the latter raised them to the heroic level in the image of a proud poet-martyr racing around the boulevard ring of Moscow, exposing himself to the metaphysical cold of the Russian state in the manner of a demonic Akakii Akakievich who returned from the dead to assault again and again the fur-clad literary generals. That Mandelstam, who in 1929–30 worked for the aggressively anti-NEP newspaper *Moskovskii komsomolets*,[109] should present his new alter ego, Akakii, as the first member of the Komsomol speaks volumes about the way he placed himself and the scandal in the political map of the day.

The self-mockery of *The Egyptian Stamp* signified an attempt at reconciliation with the regime; the self-abasement of *The Fourth Prose* spelled alienation from society and utter disdain for the literary fraternity. In *The Fourth Prose,* the narrator tried to save lives, whereas his literary "brother" hounded people to death;[110] he "composed from voice," whereas they, "the canine rabble, scribbled"[111] (cf. Christ's "It is written, but I say unto you"); they dressed in luscious furs, whereas he was dying of exposure with the wronged and the humbled; he was the innocent Susanna whom they, the "thin-necked" lecherous elders, pawed; he was Dante's Pilgrim in the "selva oscura," and they, the satanic beasts trying to sidetrack him from his appointed way.[112] And while they were fighting over a bagel like the fatuous, bourgeois "clean ones" in Maiakovskii's *Mystery-Bouffe* (1918), he, like one of the "unclean," luxuriated in the possession of a "bagel's hole." "The dough part may be gobbled up," he wrote with the glee of the Underground Man, "but the hole will always be there."[113]

It comes as no surprise that this indictment culminated in something closely resembling the French revolutionary call to arms, *aux armes*. For a poet who wrote a poem on the Tennis Court Oath, in which he assured his reader that "the language of cobblestone" (that is, street fighting and the sound of a galloping Pegasus of civic poetry) was more comprehensible to him that the cooing of "the dove,"[114] the following string of paronyms could not have been accidental:

> In Red Square, Vii is reading a telephone book. Raise my eyelids... Connect me with the Central Committee.
>
> ARMEnians from Erivan are walking around with green painted herrings. *Ich bin* ARM—I am poor.
>
> And the coat of arms of ARMavir proclaims: all bark, no bite.[115]

Ending his jeremiad on a self-deprecating note may have deflated what began to sound like an appeal to a revolt. But not to puncture his swelling indignation with the saying would have meant to replay the predictable script produced by the same literary universe that had jeered, mocked, and, in effect, cast him out. Literature no longer offered Mandelstam what Pasternak called "safe conduct."

Nevertheless, to be forsaken by a literature in which an author's charismatic appeal was associated with a kenotic *imitatio Christi* constituted, perhaps, the ultimate proof of the charismatic nature of an author's mission. In "Pushkin and Skriabin," Mandelstam was preparing himself for a different set of rules, with death alone capable of transforming one's art into a martyr's vita. Now all of a sudden he was playing for keeps—a great irony in a period when the "literature of fact" was enjoying a fashion.[116] Everything we know about Mandelstam at the time indicates that his persona and the person were becoming coextensive. After all, it was Osip Mandelstam, not the biblical Joseph or Gogol's Akakii Akakievich, who responded to Gornfel'd's allegory of the "coat" and the ensuing accusations of plagiarism and underhanded wheeling and dealing. The generic indeterminacy of *The Fourth Prose* matched the interpenetration of literature and life, rendering Mandelstam's *Dichtung* and *Wahrheit* mutually transparent.

VIII

History and Myth: 1930–1938

> Весь горизонт в огне, и близко появленье,
> Но страшно мне: изменишь облик Ты.
> ALEKSANDR BLOK, 1901

> As a Russian or a Hellene understands it, truth is directly related to every individual, whereas for a Roman and a Jew it is mediated by society.
>
> FATHER PAVEL FLORENSKII, The Pillar and the Affirmation of Truth (1914)

> And now came the sudden end of that tragedy: motivated by the entire development, the stage death turned out to be real. And we are shocked like a spectator before whose eyes, in the fifth act of a tragedy, an actor is losing real blood. The boundary between theater and life has been demolished.
>
> BORIS EIKHENBAUM, "Blok's Fate" (1922)

BETWEEN THE WOLFHOUND AND THE WOLF

> Ma poi ch'i' fui al piè d'un colle giunto,
> là dove terminava quella valle
> che m'avea di paura il cor compunto,
> guardai in alto, e vide le sue spalle
> vestite già de' raggi del pianeta
> che mena dritto altrui per ogni calle.
> DANTE, *Inferno*, canto 1

Not the production error, or the failure to contact the original translator, or the subsequent insinuations, lawsuits, and counterlawsuits, not even the arbitration by the Federation of Soviet Writers could have added up to the nightmare that the Gornfel'd affair ultimately became for Mandelstam had it not coincided with the outset of the Stalin revolution. The pressures caused by this "great break," as the late 1920s came to be known, were crushing and omnipresent. The entire society was on the move, and in the frenzy of the mass dislocations, construction, and terror of the First Five-Year Plan, every event of note resonated to the beat of the political struggles. Little wonder, then, that literary controversies—involved since 1917 invariably with power—grew so uncompromising and sharp that a local incident, as Mandelstam's certainly was, erupted into a serious scandal with grave political implications. The "affair" became one more test of political agility for the warring factions of the literary establishment, whose own power ebbed and flowed with the changes in the political fortunes of their patrons and allies at the top.

Mandelstam was not above the fray. When I. I. Ionov, the publisher who replaced Mandelstam's friend Narbut as a manager of the translation industry, vowed to deny Mandelstam any future contracts (ostensibly because he had violated one contract by translating Meyne Reed from the French rather than the original English),[1] Mandelstam did not accept his fate meekly. For him, as for many authors who could earn a living by their own writing, translation work represented an equivalent to employment in the proverbial "satanic mills": a backbreaking, alienating labor with pay barely sufficient to sustain life. The strategy he chose was to declare war on the entire translation establishment. The opening salvo was a lengthy article entitled "Streams of Slapdash," for which Mandelstam borrowed heavily from the arsenal of contemporary cannibalistic rhetoric. Fired in the middle of the government campaign to purge the Soviet apparatus of undesirable elements, it fit neatly on the third page of the April 7, 1929, issue of *Izvestiia*. Consider this passage:

> Poisoning of wells, wreckage and pollution of sewers and water mains, poor maintenance of caldrons in communal kitchens are all crimes liable to prosecution by the courts. But the ugly, unbelievable to the point of indignation, state of the shops in which world literature is produced for our reader, the wreckage of the transmission belts that connect the mind of the mass Soviet reader with the aesthetic production of the West and the East, of Europe and America, indeed of the whole of mankind in its past and its present—all this unheard-of wreckage has thus far gone unpunished, has been treated as something innocent, as a matter of course.[2]

Judged on merit, Mandelstam's outrage should seem fully justified. But in the wake of the Shakhty trial (one of the first exemplary prosecutions of "bourgeois specialists"), to describe the literary hacks as "wreckers" (or "pests," *vrediteli*) and to demand criminal prosecution for those whose only crime was an atrocious translation job amounted to more than an indulgence in a rhetorical pastiche. Understandably, the party under attack was quick to respond to Mandelstam's accusations, if not with heavy guns, then at least with field artillery of poisonous innuendo, suggesting that it was not the business of authors caught plagiarizing to promulgate publishing reforms.[3] The eventual result (see Appendix I for details) was Mandelstam's effective alienation from the literary community. Another author might not have survived, as author, the hardships of being an outsider, but Mandelstam, whose reputation had recently been buttressed by the simultaneous publication of three collections (one of poetry, one of essays, and one of prose—all in 1928) managed to make do, thanks in part to the patronage of the still powerful Nikolai Bukharin.[4]

More important, the "affair," its scale magnified by the rapid politicization of the entire society, led Mandelstam to assume once again, as in the years of *Stone,* the proud and heroic stance of a literary Hippolytus. "'The sick son of the century,'" wrote Nadezhda Mandelstam, paraphrasing one of the poet's mythologies and suggesting an almost miraculous cure-conversion, "suddenly realized that it was he who was, in fact, quite healthy."[5] Indeed, some of Mandelstam's poems of the early 1930s indicate that he was abandoning, albeit gradually, the irony and self-parody of Parnok and his creator[6] in favor of his earlier master plots.

One of the more programmatic encounters with the restored poet occurs in "Lamarck." Although it may seem abstract now, this 1932 poem bears the unmistakable marks of its time, associated as it was with perhaps the most important symbolic project of the early 1930s— the "heroic" construction of the Moscow Metro. The prominent "moving ladder," a reference to the subway escalator, binds the poem unequivocally to the industrialization under the First Five-Year Plan. Obviously Mandelstam, who had proposed to steer the Egyptian funeral barque of the old culture into the future, thought it significant that his compatriots were now measuring the progress of the new state by the speed with which the mining crews burrowed deep into the earth. After all, they were moving back in time—in the archaeological, biological, and geological sense—in order to construct the first Russian and socialist underground. This is why I propose to interpret "Lamarck" as a meditation on the place of Mandelstam's poet in the heroic labors of the First Five-Year Plan.

ЛАМАРК

Был старик, застенчивый как мальчик,
Неуклюжий, робкий патриарх...
Кто за честь природы фехтовальщик?
Ну, конечно, пламенный Ламарк.

Если все живое лишь помарка
За короткий выморочный день,
На подвижной лестнице Ламарка
Я займу последнюю ступень.

К кольчецам спущусь и к усоногим,
Прошуршав средь ящериц и змей,
По упругим сходням, по излогам
Сокращусь, исчезну, как Протей.

Роговую мантию надену,
От горячей крови откажусь,
Обрасту присосками и в пену
Океана завитком вопьюсь.

Мы прошли разряды насекомых
С наливными рюмочками глаз.
Он сказал: природа вся в разломах,
Зренья нет — ты зришь в последний раз.

Он сказал: довольно полнозвучья, —
Ты напрасно Моцарта любил:
Наступает глухота паучья,
Здесь провал сильнее наших сил.

И от нас природа отступила —
Так, как будто мы ей не нужны,
И продольный мозг она вложила,
Словно шпагу, в темные ножны.

И подъемный мост она забыла,
Опоздала опустить для тех,
У кого зеленая могила,
Красное дыханье, гибкий смех...

       7–9 мая 1932

Lamarck

There was an old man, shy like a boy,
An awkward, timid patriarch...
Who is the swordsman fighting for the honor of nature?
But, of course, the fiery Lamarck.

If all that's alive is but a slip
Made in a short heir-less day,

History and Myth: 1930–1938

> On the moving stair of Lamarck
> I shall take the very last rung.
>
> I'll descend to the annelids and the arthropods,
> Rustling by the lizards and the snakes,
> Down the hanging bridges, into the breaches
> I will shrink, disappear like Proteus.
>
> I shall put on a corneous mantle,
> My hot blood I shall give up,
> Grow suckers all over and into the froth
> Of the ocean shall bore like a curl.
>
> We have passed the category of insects
> With filled shot-glasses for eyes.
> He said: "Breaks are everywhere in nature,
> The sight is no more—you've seen your last."
>
> He said: "Enough of sonority,
> You have loved Mozart in vain,
> Now begins the spiders' deafness,
> Here comes a breach beyond our strength."
>
> And nature stepped back away from us
> As if she needed us no more,
> And she slid the oblong brain,
> Like a sword, into a dark sheath.
>
> And she forgot the drawbridge,
> Was too late to lower it for those
> Whose grave is green,
> Whose breath is red, and laughter limber...[7]

Descending the mineshaft of time, the poet is guided by the scientist, who in his patriarchal appearance bears some resemblance to the author himself. The journey itself is mapped according to the Lamarckian evolutionary scheme, which in turn is traced over the subterranean cosmology of Dante. Particularly noteworthy, Mandelstam superimposed the two schemes onto a third: the social, ethical, and kenotic tradition of the Russian intelligentsia, the history of its identification with the people's cause. Hence the tour becomes also a movement down the ladder of social class, evoking the intelligentsia's past commitment to the liberation of the humblest, those who, like the lower forms of life, were deprived of the pure pleasures of music, visual art, and thinking. The poem's wordplay makes the journey even more specific. The humble Dostoevskian offspring of the Decembrist nobility, the clumsy "mosquito prince" and the self-effacing Egyptian postage stamp, MARKa, although they remain outside the poem proper, nevertheless serve as genealogical antecedents, as the "inner form" of the shy and awkward LaMARK. They invest the name with an elaborate cumulative meaning, including the convention of tracing the origins of the intelligentsia in the nobility's revolt of 1825 that motivates the particular presentation of the Swiss naturalist. A scientist, an *intelligent* in the Russian sense, he is a noble "swordsman fighting for the honor of nature" down to its lowest forms.[8] The alternative route, discarded by the poet, would have meant supporting the "mutation" theory of history, in which the present forms owe no loyalty to past memories and commitments, dismissing them as *poMARki* of the past—slips, mutations, mistakes of youth.

This use of science for a discourse on the ethics of history begs a comparison with Albert Einstein's refusal to believe that God could play dice with the universe. But perhaps more apposite is Dostoevsky's famous wager on Christ. Like him, Mandelstam declares in "Lamarck" a permanent loyalty to a world based on a form of *imitatio Christi*, the kenotic tradition of the intelligentsia, even if the idea of such a world has been refuted as false or, closer to the sense of the poem, irrelevant.

Like many poems of *Tristia*, "Lamarck" was also about a descent into the underworld, but unlike them it involved neither an Oedipus wracked by guilt nor a member of a prematurely dead generation meekly assisting in his own interment. A Dantean pilgrimage, this descent was undertaken by a hero of the old intelligentsia faith, unwavering in his principles. Even after he had found himself separated from the present by the unbridgeable breach of a historical death, he was still alive: his gravesite was covered with verdure, he could still laugh like a youth, and his breathing, or spirit, was as red as ever—in harmony with his past commitment and the present times.

Mandelstam's intelligentsia contemporaries, who had lived through the "great break" (or was it a breach?) and witnessed the collectivization of agriculture, the debates in the biological sciences, as well as the construction of the Moscow subway, which then was the symbol par excellence of progress and urban modernity, could no doubt see in the poem a meditation on Russia's recent history. Like them, Mandelstam was groping for a solution to the riddle of the revolution, trying to find a formulation for two contradictory theses: (1) that the revolution was justified historically and ethically and therefore had to be accepted; and (2) that it was hard or impossible to countenance morally its cruelty and indifference toward individual human beings, especially members of the outmoded intelligentsia. And although the breach in ideology caused by this contradiction could not be transcended by Mandelstam intellectually, the poet Mandelstam succeeded in making it appear natural by merging it with the analogous phenomena in two authoritative texts: a scientific theory and the foremost masterpiece of Christian art. This was Mandelstam's contribution to the theory of evolution, and as in the biological debates of those days when neo-Lamarckism was gaining official sanction,[9] the picture that emerged out of Mandelstam's otherwise loyal poem was paradoxical and complex.

It would thus be wrong to reduce Mandelstam's writings to a romantic notion of a David fighting the Goliath of the Soviet state. Mandelstam's commitment to the "revolution," however naive and utopian his expectations may appear to us now, was long-standing and entirely serious. It is worth recalling that he sided with the Reds in the civil war; relegated those who followed the Wrangel army into exile to the Antechamber of the Inferno, where the souls of the undistinguished, or "neutral," fall like leaves from the Tree of Life;[10] praised Lenin as "the people's leader assuming in tears the fateful burden" of state power;[11] and finally ridiculed his own humanistic affinities in *The Egyptian Stamp*.[12] He lived in an ambiguous epoch, and his attitudes were shaped by it accordingly. Even in *The Fourth Prose* (1930) we see Mandelstam appealing to some sort of revolutionary puritanism and asceticism. Visited by a lame girl, a member of the "light cavalry" on an ideological search-and-destroy mission, the narrator Mandelstam, who was on the staff of this "cavalry's" newspaper, *Moskovskii komsomolets*, managed to recognize the devil's hoof[13] and began to behave accordingly in order to guard himself against this pathetic emissary of Beelzebub (italics are mine):

> We mooch cigarettes from one another and continue our Chinese games, *encoding into the formulas of animal cowardice the great, powerful, forbidden concept of class*. Animal fear is banging on typewriters, animal fear is doing copy editing on sheets of toilet paper, it rattles off denunciations, hits those who are lying down, demands execution for prisoners.[14]

A man who had given up on his former commitment to the revolution would hardly have appealed to the "great, powerful, forbidden concept of class," even if he despised, as did Mandelstam, the atmosphere of animal fear engendered by the "accelerated socialist construction." Nor would he have mocked the "trembling innocent bourgeois" and the party members reposing in their comfortable company.

> I have always wondered where the bourgeois get their fastidiousness, their so-called decency. Decency is what establishes kinship between the bourgeois and the animal. Many party members rest in the com-

pany of the bourgeois for exactly the same reason that the adults require the company of pink-cheeked children.[15]

Even taking into account Mandelstam's distraught state following the episode with Gornfel'd (he consulted a psychiatrist in 1930)[16] and the contradictory (polyphonic?) nature of the text itself, *The Fourth Prose* represented a savage satire—an "idealistic" indictment of Soviet society and the state reminiscent of Maiakovskii's "committed" attacks on the *homo soveticus* in both poetry and drama. The decision to conclude *The Fourth Prose* with a transparent allusion to the 1918 *Mystery-Bouffe* (an emblem of the revolution's enthusiastic infancy) can be interpreted as a nostalgic invocation of the monastic simplicity and "incorruptibility" of the years of War Communism, which contrasted sharply with the growing terror interlarded, as it were, with the "bourgeois vestiges" of NEP. "Who needs this soiled and pawed socialism anyway?" Mandelstam reportedly wrote in one of the destroyed drafts of *The Fourth Prose*.[17] Maiakovskii and Mandelstam were not alone in looking back to the puritanical aura of War Communism, so different, it seemed, from the perceived putrefaction of Soviet society and state at the close of the NEP and the beginning of the Stalin epoch. Such sentiments were not uncommon in the intelligentsia milieu, and it is a sad historical irony that it happened to be Stalin and his allies who used these sentiments and the civil war rhetoric that went with them as the foundation of a society very different from what the two poets could have had in mind.[18] All of this is to suggest that the "parting of the ways" between the state and the members of the intelligentsia elite took a few years to develop.

Indeed, many of Mandelstam's poems of 1931–32 display an ambiguous attitude to the Stalin revolution. Although much of what he saw he found repulsive, he was nevertheless unwilling to declare himself squarely against the changes then taking place. In poem after poem he projected the image of a man torn between his commitment to the cause of the "fourth estate"—which he identified with the continuing revolution—and his growing amazement, and later, horror, at its violent and distorted form:

> Чур! Не просить, не жаловаться! Цыц!
> Не хныкать!
>   Для того ли разночинцы
> Рассохлые топтали сапоги, чтоб я теперь их предал?
> Мы умрем, как пехотинцы,
> Но не прославим ни хищи, ни поденщины, ни лжи!

History and Myth: 1930–1938

> Guard me! No begging, no complaints! Hush!
> No whimpering!
>   Did the *raznochintsy*
> Tramp in their cracked boots for me now to betray them?
> We shall die like foot soldiers,
> But shall praise neither theft, nor toil, nor lies![19]

This poem, "Midnight in Moscow," which contained a sharp retort to Pasternak, was published in *Literaturnaia gazeta* in November 1933. At that time, when newspapers were full of loyal affirmations of social transformation, the poem could not be interpreted as a sign of dissent, despite the complexity and ambiguity of much of its imagery. After all, it began with midnight and ended on the optimistic note of the 1930s, as Moscow's "Buddhist," ahistorical slumber came to an end in the new Petrine Westernization (hence the Renaissance paintings), carried out by the latter-day Peter the Great, Joseph Stalin:

> Я говорю с эпохою, но разве
> Душа у ней пеньковая и разве
> Она у нас постыдно прижилась,
> Как сморщенный зверек в тибетском храме, —
> Почешется и в цинковую ванну —
> Изобрази еще нам, Марь Иванна!
>
> Пусть это оскорбительно — поймите:
> Есть блуд труда, и он у нас в крови.
>
> Уже светает. Шумят сады зеленым телеграфом.
> К Рембрандту входит в гости Рафаэль.
> Он с Моцартом в Москве души не чает —
> За карий глаз, за воробьиный хмель.
>
> И словно пневматическую почту
> Иль студенец медузы черноморской
> Передают с квартиры на квартиру
> Конвейером воздушным сквозняки,
> Как майские студенты-шелапуты…
>   Май–4 июня 1932

> I speak with the epoch, but is
> Its soul cheap and has
> It been a shameful hanger-on among us,
> Like the shriveled little creature in a Tibetan temple—
> It'll scratch itself and hop into a zinc bath—
> More tricks for us, please, Mar' Ivanna!
>
> Even if it's offensive, you ought to understand:
> There is lust for labor, and it's in our blood.

It is already sunrise. The parks' green telegraph is humming.
Rembrandt has just arrived to visit Raphael.
Neither he nor Mozart can get enough of Moscow—
Charmed by her brown eye, her sparrow drunkenness.

And like the pneumatic mail
Or the aspic of the Black Sea medusa,
From flat to flat,
Drafts, like a conveyer belt, pass on,
Like wayward students gone a-maying...[20]

The May 1932 issue of *Novyi mir* contained a poem by Pasternak that expressed similar sentiments with the aid of a similar Petrine metaphor—if more bluntly (I cite only part of it):

Но лишь сейчас сказать пора,
Величьем дня сравненье разня:
Начало славных дней Петра
Мрачили мятежи и казни.
. . . .
Итак, вперед, не трепеща
И утешаясь параллелью,
Пока ты жив, и не моща,
И о тебе не пожалели.

But only now the time has come to say,
Marking the difference by stressing today's grandeur:
The beginning of Peter's glorious days
Passed under the pall of revolts and executions.
. . . .
Hence forward, without trembling,
And drawing on the parallel for solace,
While you are still alive and not a relic
For whom one should feel sorry.[21]

The ideological frame of reference that Mandelstam had absorbed in the course of his life left him and many of his contemporaries with a limited choice: either to accept the "march of history" or to join those whom Mandelstam presented in a 1922 poem as parasites "trembling on the threshold of the new days."[22] His inability to reject this procrustean dilemma altogether, to substitute for it another, more varied discourse, helps to explain why he found it necessary in 1931 to reaffirm his pledge (indeed a spell—*Chur,* "Guard me!") of allegiance to the fourth estate, to insist on his fundamental alienation from the Imperial world that had reared him, his sentimental attachments notwithstanding, and even to doubt—a rarity in Mandelstam—his own rectitude.

History and Myth: 1930–1938

С миром державным я был лишь ребячески связан,
Устриц боялся и на гвардейцев смотрел исподлобья —
И ни крупицей души я ему не обязан,
Как я ни мучил себя по чужому подобью.

Январь 1931

With the Imperial world my connection is no more than childish.
Fear of oysters, and a furtive glance at the guardsmen,
Not a speck of my soul I owe it,
As much as I tortured myself to look like another.[23]

Я с дымящей лучиной вхожу
К шестипалой неправде в избу:
Дай-ка я на тебя погляжу —
Ведь лежать мне в сосновом гробу!
. . . .
Тишь да глушь у нее, вошь да мша,
Полуспаленка, полутюрьма.
— Ничего, хороша, хороша!
Я и сам ведь такой же, кума.

Москва, 4 апр. 1931

Holding a smoldering chip, I walk into
The hut of the six-fingered untruth:
Let me take a look at you—
For I shall be lying in a pine coffin!

. . . .

It's still and deep at her place, lice and moss,
It's half-bedroom, half-jail
—It's all right, you are good, you are good!
I myself am like this, my cousin.[24]

His close friend B. S. Kuzin (whose friendship "awakened" Mandelstam "like a shot," as he put it in his poem "To the German Tongue") wrote about the poet's state of mind in the early 1930s:

> In particular, it seems he had a strong temptation to acquire faith in our official ideology, to accept all the terrors for which it served as a screen, and to join the ranks of the active fighters for the great ideas and for the beautiful socialist future. . . . But whenever he would begin his loyal twitter—and I used to respond to it with tempestuous anger—he did not get hotly polemical, did not ardently insist on his position, but only begged me to agree with him: "Tell me, Boris Sergeevich, tell me, isn't this really good?" And in a day or two: "Did I really say this? What nonsense!"[25]

The famous "wolf" poem exemplifies, perhaps better than any other poem of the period, the state of mind Mandelstam wished to project in his poetry (and apparently projected in life, too) at the beginning of the 1930s. It merits closer consideration.

> За гремучую доблесть грядущих веков,
> За высокое племя людей
> Я лишился и чаши на пире отцов,
> И веселья и чести своей.
>
> Мне на плечи кидается век-волкодав,
> Но не волк я по крови своей,
> Запихай меня лучше, как шапку, в рукав
> Жаркой шубы сибирских степей, —
>
> Чтоб не видеть ни труса, ни хлипкой грязцы,
> Ни кровавых костей в колесе,
> Чтоб сияли всю ночь голубые песцы
> Мне в своей первобытной красе.
>
> Уведи меня в ночь, где течет Енисей,
> И сосна до звезды достает,
> Потому что не волк я по крови своей
> И меня только равный убьет.
>
> 17–28 марта 1931

> For the sake of the thundering glory of the coming ages,
> For the sake of the lofty tribe of men,
> I have been deprived of the cup at the feast of my fathers,
> Of merriment and honor.
>
> The age-wolfhound jumps on my shoulders,
> But I am not a wolf by blood,
> Better stuff me, like a hat, into the sleeve
> Of the hot fur coat of the Siberian steppes.
>
> So as not to witness the quaking, or the slushy filth,
> Or the bloody bones in the wheel,
> So as the blue lynxes shone all night
> In their primeval beauty,
>
> Take me into the night where the Yenisey flows
> And the pine reaches out to the star,
> Because I am not a wolf by blood
> And only by an equal shall I be killed.[26]

The bill of particulars the poem presents to the epoch is approximately as follows: the revolution that has sacrificed the present for bombastic future glory has deprived the poet of "the cup at the feast of

[his] fathers, of merriment and honor," has wrongfully assaulted him ("The age-wolfhound jumps on my shoulders"), and finally, has created a world so violent, filthy, and scared that the sight of it has become unbearable for the poet. His only wish now is to be led away by some unnamed master of his fortune—as far away as possible from this scene, even to Siberia. The last stanza contains an invocation of the Lermontovian "magic tokens," a star and a pine tree,[27] which are to assure poetry's eternal "prestation," a spell-like repetition in which the poet once again protests the attack by affirming that he is not "a wolf by blood." This particular formulation, I hardly need point out, had a powerful significance for a poet who had repeatedly inscribed himself in incest narratives (the Russian for "incest" is literally "polluting or mixing blood"). The poem ended in a folkloric formula of conditional invincibility—a sort of Achilles' heel.

The curious phrase by which the poet expresses his preference for Siberia (better to be a hat stuffed into the sleeve of a *coat*) requires pause and elaboration. It echoes Mandelstam's polemic with a recent poem by Pasternak, where poetry was compared with a ticket to a concert of "roots and wombs" and, more important, with the token (*nomerok*) one received in exchange for one's topcoat and hat, which according to the still new rule had to be checked before the performance. Apparently Pasternak's poem was seen by Mandelstam as part of the earlier polemic.[28]

> А в рифмах умирает рок,
> И правдой входит в наш мирок
> Миров разноголосица.
>
> И рифма не вторенье строк,
> А гардеробный номерок,
> Талон на место у колонн
> В загробный гул корней и лон.
> . . . .
> И рифма не вторенье строк,
> Но вход и пропуск за порог,
> Чтоб сдать, как плащ за бляшкою,
> Болезни тягость тяжкую,
> Боязнь огласки и греха
> За громкой бляшкою стиха.
>
> And in the rhymes, one's fate dies,
> And the heteroglossia of worlds
> Enters our little world as truth.

> And the rhyme is not an echoing of lines,
> But a cloakroom token,
> A voucher for a place at the columns,
> A pass into the underworld of roots and wombs.
>
> . . . .
>
> And the rhyme is not an echoing of lines,
> But an entry and a pass [admitting] beyond the threshold
> Where you check in, like a raincoat in exchange for a token,
> The burdensome burden of [love]sickness,
> The fear of exposure and sin—
> In exchange for the loud token of verse.[29]

Mandelstam interpreted this therapeutic view of verbal art as a trivialization of the poet's sacred calling to bear witness to and identify with one's age. Checking in one's coat of quotidian existence in order to gain admission to art—a sort of concert hall of life, to unpack Pasternak's metaphor—was not an acceptable narrative for the poet who fashioned himself a Joseph or, more recently, as Gogol's Akakii Akakievich. His coat could not be checked in—for it was not a thing but a token signifying a void that could never be filled.

Mandelstam's rejoinder to Pasternak's seemingly innocent variation on an ancient theme was composed in the form of snatches of conversation, as if overheard in a crowd of spectators fighting for their coats after a performance. Those who followed Pasternak's concept of poetry—"upper-class lies"—were soon to mingle with the snorting and unrefined citizenry (burghers, *gorozhane,* that is, *meshchane*). But those who followed Mandelstam would recall the heroism of War Communism, the exemplars of tragic loyalty (Lermontov's *Masquerade*), and the historical suffering of the dispossessed who, like Nekrasov's peasants, dared not enter magnificent buildings. A poet, Mandelstam is insisting, should not forget what century he lived in—the century of the wolfhound destined to rid the world of the wolf that had preyed on people since the beginning of time. Mikhail Zoshchenko's 1927 story "Pleasantries of Culture," in which the cloakroom rule is identified with the NEP and its absence with War Communism, amply justifies such a reading.[30] Bearing the demeanor of kenotic resignation emblematic of the Russian peasant ("hat in hand"), such a poet should remain outside and share his fate with the humble, who are shoved unceremoniously, like a hat into a coat's "sleeve" by a rude cloakroom attendant. For the poet, who chose a martyr's way, prayer was the only hope.

History and Myth: 1930–1938

Ночь на дворе. Барская ложь!
После меня — хоть потоп.
Что же потом? — храп горожан
И толкотня в гардероб.

Бал-маскарад. Век-волкодав.
Так затверди ж на зубок:
С шапкой в руках, шапку в рукав —
И да хранит тебя Бог!

Москва, Март 1931

It's night outside. What upper-class lies!
Après moi le déluge.
But then what?—The snorting of citizens
And pushing and shoving in the cloakroom.

A ball-masquerade. The wolfhound-age.
You've got to remember this well:
With hat in hand, hat into the sleeve—
And may God preserve you![31]

Although this was a poem militant in tone and animated by the poet's empathy with the humiliated and the wronged, particularly the peasants victimized by collectivization, its companion piece, "For the Sake of the Thundering Valor," displays a different and far more ambivalent set of accents. Indeed, contrary to the traditional view,[32] a closer, more contextual scrutiny reveals a picture in which the poet's aversion to the brutality of the epoch is combined with a historical and moral justification of the very cause of his distress.

As with a number of Mandelstam's poems, this one is constructed around an allusion to Dante, specifically Virgil's prophecy in canto 1 of the *Inferno,* which helps to identify the prototypes of the protagonists in Mandelstam's poem. Thus, behind the "age-wolfhound" of Mandelstam, one discerns Dante's *Veltro* (the Hound) who, according to Virgil, will rid Italy of the covetous and corrupt *lupa* (the she-wolf). It was this she-wolf who terrified Dante's Pilgrim as he was trying to find his way out of the "selva oscura." Virgil's prophecy also helps explain Mandelstam's metaphor "I am not a wolf by blood," since Virgil predicted that before the Hound's appearance many creatures would have mated with the she-wolf (an appropriate allegory for Mandelstam's "incest" mythologies). Finally, the Hound himself embodied the ideals of social justice that in Mandelstam's time were associated with the revolutionary messianic class, which, to use the prophetic words of Dante's Virgil, "shall not feed on land or pelf but on wisdom, and love, and valor." Against this background, the repulsive sights of Mandelstam's poem might constitute a good enough reason for the poet to withdraw, indeed be exiled, like Dante. Still, however repulsive, these "excesses"—as the "quaking," the "slushy filth," and the "bloody bones in the wheel" might have been qualified at the time—do not justify for the poet a wholesale rejection of the revolution. So, at least, the allusion to Dante's righteous *Veltro* seems to suggest.[33]

HIPPOLYTUS AND HEPHAESTUS

There someone powerful is singing alone.
OSIP MANDELSTAM (from a 1931 fragment)

By late 1932, alternative viewpoints begin to appear in Mandelstam's writings. First came the transparently cryptic lines about King Arshak in *Journey to Armenia* (1932), published in *Zvezda* in 1933. The passage had been excised by the censor, but the magazine's editor, Tsezar' Vol'pe, managed to "smuggle it through," even at the risk (his fear was shortly thereafter justified) of losing his position:[34]

1. Arshak's body is unwashed and his beard has gone wild.
2. The King's nails are broken, and centipedes are crawling over his face.
3. His ears have grown stupid from silence, but there was a time when they listened to Greek music.
4. His tongue has become wretched from the prison food, but there was a time when it pressed grapes to the palate and was sly like the tip of a flautist's tongue.
5. Arshak's seed has gone weak in his scrotum and his voice is thin like the bleating of a sheep...
6. King Shapukh, so thinks Arshak, has vanquished me, and—even worse—he has appropriated my air.
7. The Assyrian is holding my heart.
8. He is the chief over my hair and my nails. He grows my beard and swallows my saliva, so used he is to the thought that I am here, in the fortress.[35]

The passage ostensibly concerns an Armenian king from the Arshak dynasty (A.D. 63–453), but no special imagination is required to see Stalin's features in the "Assyrian." In August 1933, Mandelstam received an ultimatum to remove *Journey* from the projected two-volume edition and to renounce it altogether.[36] He refused, and soon (August 30) found his name denounced in *Pravda* together with some of the best names in Russian letters: Viktor Shklovskii, Konstantin Vaginov, and Nikolai Zabolotskii.

History and Myth: 1930–1938

But he did not heed the warning. The epigraph he chose for his *Conversation About Dante* (1933) offers a concise definition of the poet's contemporary stand: "Così gradai con la faccia levata." The words are taken from a telling passage in canto 16 of the *Inferno* (the dialogue with Farinata), in which the Pilgrim delivers one of his invectives against his native city: "'The new people and the sudden gains have begot in thee, Florence, arrogance and excess so that already thou weepest for it.' *This I cried with lifted face*" [italics are mine]. Anyone familiar with Mandelstam's iconography will recognize the poet in this pose; indeed, Mandelstam actually recorded it in an early poem entitled "Self-Portrait":

> В поднятьи головы крылатый
> Намек. Но мешковат сюртук.
> В закрытьи глаз, в покое рук
> Тайник движенья непочатый.
>
> In the tilt of the head, there is a winged
> Hint. But the coat's a bit baggy.
> In the closing of the eyes, in the stillness of the hands,
> An untapped treasure trove of movement.[37]

The poet, it seems, was prepared now to pit himself against the whole world, very much in the manner of his Florentine mentor. Indeed, the voice one hears in a series of poems composed in 1933 is neither muted nor twisted by doubt. One poem composed at the same time as the *Conversation* speaks, with a supreme clarity not often encountered in Mandelstam, about the devastation of the countryside in the terror of forced collectivization.

> Природа своего не узнает лица,
> А тени страшные — Украины, Кубани...
> Как в туфлях войлочных голодные крестьяне
> Калитку стерегут, не трогая кольца.
> Старый Крым, май 1933
>
> Nature does not recognize its own face,
> And the terrifying shadows—the Ukraine, the Kuban'...
> So the hungry peasants in felt boots
> Stand by the gate, not daring to touch the latch.[38]

Another poem overflows with anger at what most other Muscovites would have considered, in those days of catastrophic shortage, a stroke of the most incredible luck: the receipt of a flat in 1933 with the help of patrons in high places. There was, however, an undeniable logic to this anger. As a poet of "prestation," Mandelstam understood very well that such a gift, coming from an all-too-powerful donor, represented a sign of domination and thus obligated him to reciprocity.[39] For a poet with the self-image of an outcast, one who had long nurtured the charisma of a Dostoevskian dervish, governmental largesse represented a sign of his own unfreedom—a duty of the beneficiary to repay the authorities in poetic coin.

Against this "mythological" background, Pasternak's perfectly innocent congratulations ("Well, you've gotten yourself an apartment—now you can write") had the sound of a steel trap closing.[40] Taking offense at Pasternak's remark, Mandelstam went on to compose this poem, a parodic pastiche of the famous "Ballad" by V. Khodasevich (poetry redeeming the misery of material existence) tuned to the Nekrasov key—a poetic idiom of civic invective, a genre perfected by one of Dostoevsky's great contemporaries.[41] In one of his more remarkable "journalistic" poems, "About the Weather," Nekrasov told of a clever trick that some carriage owners devised to discourage street urchins from hitching rides: they simply studded the back of the carriage with concealed sharp nails. Mandelstam endowed this socioeconomic mythology with a new sociopolitical elaboration:

Квартира тиха, как бумага
Пустая без всяких затей —
И слышно, как булькает влага
По трубам внутри батарей.

Имущество в полном порядке,
Лягушкой застыл телефон,
Видавшие виды манатки
На улицу просятся вон.

А стены проклятые тонки,
И некуда больше бежать —
А я как дурак на гребенке
Обязан кому-то играть...

Наглей комсомольской ячейки
И вузовской песни наглей,
Присевших на школькой скамейке
Учить щебетать палачей.

Пайковые книги читаю,
Пеньковые речи ловлю,
И грозное баюшки-баю
Кулацкому паю пою.

Какой-нибудь изобразитель,
Чесатель колхозного льна,

History and Myth: 1930–1938

Чернила и крови смеситель
Достоин такого рожна.

Какой-нибудь честный предатель,
Проваренный в чистках, как соль,
Жены и детей содержатель —
Такую ухлопает моль...

И столько мучительной злости
Таит в себе каждый намек,
Как будто вколачивал гвозди
Некрасова здесь молоток.

Давай же с тобой, как на плахе,
За семьдесят лет, начинать —
Тебе, старику и неряхе,
Пора сапогами стучать.

И вместо ключа Ипокрены
Давнишнего страха струя
Ворвется в халтурные стены
Московского злого жилья.

     Москва, Фурманов переулок
       Ноябрь 1933

The flat is still like a sheet of paper—
Empty. Amenities? None.
And you hear the gurgling of liquids
Inside the radiator pipes.

Possessions are in complete order,
The telephone has frozen like a frog,
Belongings that have been around
Are pleading to get outside.

And the cursed walls are thin,
And there is no longer any escape—
And, like a buffoon playing on a comb,
I've got to perform for someone...

More brazen than a Komsomol cell,
More arrogant than a college song,
Perched for a while on a school bench
Sit executioners whom I've got to instruct in the twitter.

I read rationed books,
I catch cheap phrases,
And a terrible lullaby
I sing to the kulak baby boy.

Only some sort of depictor,
A comber of the kolkhoz flax,

Hippolytus and Hephaestus

> An incestuous polluter of ink and blood
> Deserves to be so impaled.
>
> Only some sort of honest traitor,
> Boiled through and through in the purges, like salt,
> A keeper of his wife and children
> Will rattle off twaddle like this...
>
> And so much tormenting viciousness
> Is hidden in every hint,
> As though concealed nails have been hammered
> Here by Nekrasov's hammer.
>
> So let us, you and I—as if on a scaffold,
> Past seventy,—begin again:
> It's time for you, old man and slob,
> To go tramping in your boots.
>
> And in place of the Hippocrene's stream,
> A stream of the old fear
> Shall burst into the slapdash walls
> Of an evil Moscow flat.[42]

The poem shows Mandelstam reasserting the combative persona of Hippolytus, who is rejecting, as once before, the incestuous advances of what was now the *Soviet* Russia-Phaedra. The time of acceptance of guilt, of the poet's resignation to being buried alive, had passed. He was now fitting the mask of the incestuous Oedipus on the young brood of Soviet poets whom, in exchange for the "slapdash . . . Moscow flat" (recall "The Streams of Slapdash"), the aging Hippolytus was obliged to coach in poetic diction. They, not the poet Mandelstam, would be engaged in the incestuous "polluting" of "ink" and blood (cf. *chernila i krovi smesitel'* and *krovosmesitel'*), whereas he, a HIPpolytus, whose rightful place is at the "spring of the horse," HIPPOcrene, will have to make do with the "stream of the old fear."[43]

Sometime in November 1933 Mandelstam finally pointed the accusing finger at Stalin, the demonic "other" of a true charismatic Russian poet, producing a searing epigram[44]—to my knowledge the only contemporary document of its kind—that a few months later would result in his arrest, with its profound psychological trauma, and subsequent exile.

> Мы живем, под собою не чуя страны,
> Наши речи за десять шагов не слышны,
>
> А где хватит на полразговорца, —
> Там припомнят кремлевского горца.

History and Myth: 1930–1938

Его толстые пальцы, как черви, жирны,
А слова, как пудовые гири, верны.

Тараканьи смеются усища,
И сияют его голенища.

А вокруг его сброд тонкошеих вождей,
Он играет услугами полулюдей.

Кто свистит, кто мяучит, кто хнычет,
Он один лишь бабачит и тычет.

Как подковы кует за указом указ —
Кому в пах, кому в лоб, кому в бровь, кому в глаз.

Что ни казнь у него, — то малина
И широкая грудь осетина.

Ноябрь 1933

We live, sensing no country under our feet,
Our words can't be heard beyond ten paces,

And where there is enough for half a chat—
There the Kremlin mountaineer is mentioned.

His greasy fingers are, like worms, fat,
And his words, like big dumbbells, correct.

His roach mustachios grin,
The tops of his jackboots gleam.

Around him is the rabble of thin-necked leaders,
He toys with the favors of these half-humans.

This one whistles, that one meows, that one whimpers,
He alone is gruff and familiar.

He forges ukases one after another, like horseshoes—
One gets it in the groin, one in the head, one in the brow, one in the eye.

Each execution for him is a treat,
And the broad chest of an Ossete.[45]

    This poem becomes a representation of the poet's "other" through one of the key metonyms of Mandelstam's narrative of self-presentation, the "horseshoe," which enters into complex relationship with the central mythologies of his poetry: Hippolytus (incest, poetry, honor) and Joseph in Egypt (exile, slander, and injustice). The formulas are not cleanly delineated, but their entire complex may be defined as a hypothetical set of associations: poetry—Pegasus—Hippocrene—Hippolytus-and-Phaedra—the Bronze Horseman—history (Maiakovskii's "nag of history")[46]—the horseshoe good-luck charm (Verlaine's

Hippolytus and Hephaestus

bonne aventure)—poetry. This approximation of the complex of motifs is colored by chastity, ordeal, virtue, activity. The corresponding complex of "Oedipal" homologies is colored by the sense of guilt and resignation, an acceptance of the sentence of death pronounced by history. It was apparently the former set, characteristic of Mandelstam's *Stone* and the early *Tristia*, that was resurfacing in the early 1930s after Mandelstam's five years of poetic silence came to an end. Not surprisingly, his poetry displays a wealth of equestrian and racing imagery that is essentially focused on the poet's self:

> Держу пари, что я еще не умер,
> И, как жокей, ручаюсь головой,
> Что я еще могу набедокурить
> На рысистой дорожке беговой.
> . . . .
> Не волноваться. Нетерпенье — роскошь,
> Я постепенно скорость разовью —
> Холодным шагом выйду на дорожку —
> Я сохранил дистанцию мою.
> Москва, 7 июня 1931

> I'll bet with you that I haven't died yet,
> And, like a jockey, I bet my head
> That I can still do pranks
> At a fast race track.
> . . . .
> Stay calm. Impatience is too costly.
> I'll gradually build up speed—
> We'll enter the track at a cool trot—
> I have preserved my distance.[47]

> Вы помните, как бегуны
> В окрестностях Вероны
> Уже разматывать должны
> Кусок сукна зеленый?
>
> Но всех других опередит
> Тот самый, тот — который
> Из книги Данта убежит,
> Ведя по кругу споры.
> Москва, май 1932–
Воронеж, сентябрь 1935

> Do you remember how the race runners
> Outside Verona,
> Had to unroll
> A piece of a green runner?

History and Myth: 1930–1938

> But ahead of them all
> Will be that one, he who
> Will run away from Dante's book,
> Arguing in circles.⁴⁸

> Когда покой бежит из-под копыт,
> Ты скажешь —
>   Москва, Май–июнь 1931

> When peace slips away like earth under hooves,
> You'll say . . .⁴⁹

Or consider these few lines, the last of which, it is now obvious, is a pun on the name of Phaedra's stepson, Hippolytus.

> Мне с каждым днем дышать все тяжелее,
> А между тем нельзя повременить —
> Ведь рождены для наслажденья бегом
> Лишь сердце человека и коня...
>   Лето 1932

> With every day, it is more difficult for me to breathe,
> And yet, I can't postpone—
> For it is for the pleasure of the race
> That the heart of man and the heart of horse are born...⁵⁰

"He who found the horseshoe" of Mandelstam's poetry received the good-luck charm of memory and the right of entry into the poetic "prestation," the poets' eternal exchange. To come across one of the horseshoes manufactured in Stalin's smithy was quite another matter. But the lofty horseman flying to Mount Parnassus could not do without the base and ridiculous Hephaestus. In the charismatic tradition to which Mandelstam belonged, the two tended to benefit from one another.

HOOFPRINTS IN THE BLACK EARTH

> *I am in the heart of the age, the way's uncertain*
> *The road to the goal lengthens with time—*
> *And my staff with its fatigued ash,*
> *And my brass with its impoverished color.*
>   OSIP MANDELSTAM (December 14, 1936)

It would be gratifying to think that Mandelstam, once he perceived the inexcusable brutality of the new state, never relinquished his insight. The record speaks otherwise. The poems of 1933 discussed previously are the exception rather than the rule. At least judging by the poetry composed in Voronezh, Mandelstam once again was reaching for the rationalizations familiar from his writings of the 1920s and early 1930s, expanding them to include the grievously offended party. The figure of Stalin now came to haunt his verse, confronting him over and over again with the transgression for which the "Assyrian holding his heart," that other king, had nearly destroyed him but then had magnanimously granted a semireprieve.[51]

Mandelstam wrote a number of poems beginning in 1935 that deal with Stalin either directly or indirectly—as an expression of the poet's remorse and his desire to atone for his offense. In a 1935 poem, Mandelstam already calls himself a "nonparty Bolshevik, like all [my] friends [and] like this foe."[52] "I must live, breathing and bolshevizing myself (*bol'sheveia*)," are the words from another 1935 poem, in which he refers to the causes of his present predicament—his bourgeois social origins and the epigram—as "the damned seam, the clumsy prank" that had rendered him a pariah among people.

> Я не хочу средь юношей тепличных
> Разменивать последний грош души,
> Но, как в колхоз идет единоличник,
> Я в мир вхожу, и люди хороши.
> . . . .
> Проклятый шов, нелепая затея
> Нас разлучили. А теперь пойми —
> Я должен жить, дыша и большевея,
> И перед смертью хорошея
> Еще побыть и поиграть с людьми.
>   Воронеж, Май–июнь 1935

> I do not wish, among the hothouse youth,
> To change the last coin of my soul,
> But, as a farmer joining the kolkhoz,
> I come into the world, and people are good.
> . . . .
> A damned seam, a clumsy prank,
> Have separated us. So now keep in mind:
> I must live, breathing and bolshevizing myself,
> And, bettering myself before I die,
> Be with people and play with them a little more.[53]

He even accepted the "corrective" nature of his exile. The poems that follow are a mythic Mandelstamian elaboration of a common sartorial-agrarian metaphor for socialist reeducation: *repatterning,* as in altering an old piece of clothing or an agrarian map. For Mandelstam,

History and Myth: 1930–1938

whose poetic wardrobe contained Joseph's coat of many colors as well as the ephemeral Gogolian overcoat, this metaphor was doubly significant. It was placed, together with the first Soviet "talkie," *Chapaev*, a film about a heroic civil war *cavalryman*, in the service of Mandelstam's mythologies of pride and ordeal (Hippolytus) and eventual resurrection:

> Измеряй меня, край, перекраивай, —
> Чуден жар прикрепленной земли! —
> Захлестнулась винтовка Чапаева —
> Помоги, развяжи, раздели!
> Воронеж, Май–июнь 1935

> Measure me, my land, *repattern* me—
> How miraculous is the heat of attached earth!—
> Chapaev's rifle choked and sank—
> Help me, untie the knot, pass a fair judgment! [54]

> Поезд шел на Урал. В открытые рты нам
> Говорящий Чапаев с картины скакал звуковой —
> За бревенчатым тыном, на ленте простынной
> Умереть и вскочить на коня своего!
> Воронеж, Июнь 1935

> The train was going to the Urals. Into our open mouths
> The talking Chapaev was galloping from a sound film—
> Behind a log fence, on a bedsheet tape—
> To die and to spring back on your horse! [55]

Stalin, or rather his iconic features, begin to appear early in 1937, either simultaneously with the "Ode to Stalin" or shortly after it was finished. In "Sleep Defends My Don Drowsiness," one finds Stalin's metonyms pulled out of a propaganda poster: "The brow and the head of the militant armor are lovingly combined with the eyes."[56] Another poem alludes directly to the plea for mercy represented by the "Ode," and to its addressee: "It is to him—into his very core—I came, entering the Kremlin without a pass, tearing the canvas of distance, bowing my head heavy with guilt."[57] In still another Voronezh poem, "Had our enemies captured me," Mandelstam refers to Stalin by name.[58] Stalin even enters a love poem, addressed to a singer, Elekonida Popova: "My black-browed glory, tie me up with your thick brow, you, who are ready for life and death, who utter lovingly the thunderous name of Stalin with the tenderness of a vow, with love." This and a companion poem, both addressed to the "black-browed" admirer of Stalin, are tucked away in the Addenda of the fourth volume of Mandelstam's *Collected Works*.[59]

I do not intend to represent here the entire spectrum of the Voronezh poems, not even those that deal with the theme of exile. Many are politically neutral. Some have nothing to do with exile. Among those that do, several are free from official rationalization, as are the "little demon" poems where the Pushkinian-Gogolian-Dostoevskian trickster gets to be the "fall guy" in Mandelstam's misfortune. These poems show clearly that Mandelstam's "poet" would have been glad to withdraw from civic concerns. Nevertheless, they too belong to the "Ode" cycle.[60]

Elaborating once again on his central equestrian and eucharistic metaphors of poetry (properly speaking, synecdoches), Mandelstam was trying to separate his vocation as a poet from his preoccupations as a citizen, which had led to his arrest (the two "affairs" of the second stanza). The poem below, the first draft of this subset, shows how difficult it was for Mandelstam to give up the identity of a combative Hippolytus:

> Дрожжи мира дорогие —
> Звуки, слезы и труды —
> Словно вмятины, впервые
> Певчей полные воды,
> Подкопытные наперстки —
> Бега сжатого следы —
> Раздают не по разверстке:
> На столетья — без слюды...
>
> Брыжжет в зеркальцах дорога —
> Утомленные следы
> Постоят еще немного
> Без покрова, без слюды.
> И уже мое родное
> Отлегло, как будто вкось
> По нему прошло другое
> И на нем отозвалось...
>
> Воронеж, 12 января 1937

> The dear leaven of the world—
> Sounds, tears, and labors—
> Almost like impressions for the first time
> Filled with singing waters,
> Underhoof thimbles—
> Traces of a condensed race—
> They grant not by rations:
> Enough for centuries—not covered by mica...
>
> The road is bursting, inlaid with little mirrors,
> The tired imprints

History and Myth: 1930–1938

> Will stay like this a little longer—
> Unshrouded, not covered by mica.
> And my native and dear affair
> Has slipped as if over and across it
> There rode another one
> And echoed itself in it…

The apparent conflict between the two stanzas intensifies in the next, somewhat later, version. Following the "eucharistic" first stanza, Mandelstam's funereal duo of resignation, the blind Oedipus and his guide Antigone, make their melancholy appearance. The water filling the hoofprints has now been changed in color to copper:

> Дрожжи мира дорогие —
> Звуки, слезы и труды —
> Ударенья дождевые
> Закипающей беды
> И потери звуковые
> Из какой вернуть руды?
>
> В нищей памяти впервые
> Чуешь вмятины сырые,
> Медной полные воды —
> И идешь за ними следом,
> Сам себе не мил, неведом —
> И слепой и поводырь.
>   Воронеж, 12–18 января 1937

> The dear leaven of the world—
> Sounds, tears, and labors—
> The rainbeats
> Of misfortune coming to the boil
> And the sonorous losses—
> Out of what ore can they be reextracted?
>
> In the impoverished memory for the first time
> You sense raw holes,
> Full of coppery water—
> And you follow them,
> Unhappy with yourself, unknown to yourself—
> Both a blind man and a blind man's guide.[61]

Finally the blame is laid at the doorstep of the "little demon with wet fur," famous for egging on Dostoevsky's proud misfits (like *Ippolit*, with whom Mandelstam on occasion identified)[62] to commit the ever more embarrassing gaucheries. Equally important was the admission in the last stanza that the poet's civic honesty sidetracked and destroyed him—"kicked off the axle." This pun ("axle"—*os'*—*os*ip Mandelstam) recalls not only the poet's name but also, of course, the crash of Hippolytus's chariot at the conclusion of the eponymous tragedy. Couched in language imitating the dialect of rural Russia, these refined Petersburg "mythologies" make for bitterly ironic reading:

> Влез бесенок в мокрой шёрстке —
> Ну, куда ему? куды?
> В подкопытные наперстки,
> В торопливые следы —
> По копейкам воздух версткий
> Обирает с слободы.
>
> Брыжжет в зеркальцах дорога —
> Торопливые следы
> Постоят еще немного
> Без покрова, без слюды.
> Колесо стучит отлого —
> Улеглось — и полбеды!
>
> Скучно мне — мое прямое
> Дело тараторит вкось:
> По нему прошлось другое,
> Надсмеялось, сбило ось!
>
> Воронеж, 12–18 января 1937

> The little demon, his fur wet, has climbed in—
> What's he doin' here? Where's he goin'?
> Into the underhoof thimbles,
> Into the rushed imprints.
> It's the kopeck tax on the rationed air
> That he is collecting from the town folk.
>
> The road is bursting, inlaid with little mirrors—
> The rushed imprints
> Will stay like this a little longer
> Unshrouded, not covered by mica.
> The wheel bangs, slipping from its axle—
> The affair is settled—it's not half-bad!
>
> I am bored—my straight
> Affair [and/or criminal case] is clanging, slipping from its axle:
> Another one rode over it,
> Had a laugh, kicked out the axle!

This harmlessly apolitical verse notwithstanding, the *other* poems do represent a coherent entity, demonstrating that Mandelstam was more of a man of his times than either he[63] or many of those who have written about him have been willing to admit. Even Nadezhda Mandelstam, with her canonical image of the poet, has insisted: "All of us led a double existence, and no one could avoid that fate." For Mandelstam's "poet" this was a double existence in yet another sense: he could not disentangle himself from a poetics in which the charisma of the author was predicated on the authority of a supreme ruler assigned the role of the poet's other. The "Ode to Stalin" shows how intimately intertwined these *four* aspects of the poet's existence actually were.

THE STORY OF THE "ODE"

If manuscripts do not burn, as Mikhail Bulgakov once suggested, they at least get hot sitting in the fire, which is more or less what happened to the "Ode to Stalin." The first indication that Mandelstam might have written something like the "Ode" came from Anna Akhmatova's recollections of Mandelstam and had the effect of a minor literary bombshell.[64] Two years later, in 1967, the issue was taken up by Clarence Brown, who had been working on Mandelstam for nearly a decade.[65] To determine whether Mandelstam had actually written the "Ode," Brown analyzed some twenty-four poems composed during the Voronezh exile (1935–37), relating them to what he had been able to find out about the poet's life at that time. The conclusion of this first thorough, and still timely, study of the later Mandelstam was largely negative. Hard as he tried, Mandelstam—it would seem—was unable to twist the arm of his muse, even though he knew very well that a panegyric to Stalin might assure him continued existence.

There was, however, evidence to the contrary, including Akhmatova's authoritative statement and a number of powerful poems composed in Voronezh exile. Among the most remarkable is a poem that does as much justice to Mandelstam's poetics of anamnesis (it ranges from the *Lay of Igor's Campaign* to Rembrandt's *Night Watch,* to Pushkin's "Monument," to Pasternak's cycle "Artist") as it does to the nightmares of anticipated imprisonment and the paranoid enthusiasm gripping the nation in 1937 in a double Stalinist embrace.

Если б меня наши враги взяли
И перестали со мной говорить люди;
Если б лишили меня всего в мире —
Права дышать и открывать двери
И утверждать, что бытие будет,
И что народ, как судия, судит;
Если б меня смели держать зверем,
Пищу мою на пол кидать стали б, —

The Story of the "Ode"

Я не смолчу, не заглушу боли,
Но начерчу то, что чертить волен,
И раскачав в колокол стан голый,
И разбудив вражеской тьмы угол,
Я запрягу десять волов в голос
И поведу руку во тьме плугом,
И, в океан братских очей сжатый,
Я упаду тяжестью всей жатвы,
Сжатостью всей рвущейся вдаль клятвы,
И в глубине сторожевой ночи
Чернорабочей вспыхнут земли очи,
И промелькнет пламенных лет стая,
Прошелестит спелой грозой — Ленин,
Но на земле, что избежит тленья,
Будет будить разум и жизнь — Сталин.

Воронеж, 1937

Had our enemies captured me
And had people stopped speaking to me;
Had I been deprived of everything in the world—
The right to breathe, and to open doors,
And to assert that "being" means "shall be,"
And that the people, like the judge, judges;
Were I to be kept like a beast,
My food thrown on the floor,—
I wouldn't be silent, I wouldn't suppress the pain,
But I shall draw pictures I wish to draw,
And rocking the bell of the naked walls,
And having awakened the corner of the enemy darkness,
I shall harness my voice to ten bullocks,
And cleave the dark with my hand like a plough,
And in the depth of the watchful night,
The eyes of the common laborer earth shall flash
And, into the united legion of fraternal eyes,
I shall fall with the weight of the whole harvest,
With all the denseness of an oath tearing into distance,
And the flock of the flaming years will come, flying,
Like a ripe thunderstorm, will rustle past—Lenin,
And on the earth that will avoid decay,
Reason and life will be kept awake by Stalin.[66]

Pieces like this kept the puzzle unresolved. And since they did not fit the otherwise satisfying picture of a poet incapable of violating the integrity of his talent, Brown decided to defer his final judgment, hoping that more conclusive evidence might eventually turn up.

The problem was resolved by Nadezhda Mandelstam. In the first book of her memoirs, published in 1970, she acknowledged Mandelstam's composition of the "Ode," adding that she had preserved the complete text of it for fear it would otherwise have survived in the "wild versions circulating in 1937."[67] It was not until 1975 that the poem itself, albeit seven lines short of complete, made its first appearance in print, published in the *Slavic Review* by an anonymous contributor.[68] A few months later a fuller version was included in a brief essay by Bengt Jangfeldt. In one important respect, Jangfeldt's account complemented, if not contradicted, that of the poet's widow. He cites an unnamed friend of the Mandelstams who, contrary to Nadezhda Mandelstam's assertion, maintained that the poet "was not at all ashamed of the 'Stalin verses' . . . and read them on several occasions after his return from the Voronezh exile." A complete version of the "Ode," presumably supplied by Nadezhda Mandelstam herself, had to await the publication of the fourth volume of Mandelstam's *Collected Works*, issued in Paris in 1980.[69]

What we know about the events surrounding the composition of the "Ode to Stalin" comes from the poet's correspondence and the memoirs of Nadezhda Mandelstam, who, alone among her husband's companions in Voronezh, has chosen to make her recollections public.[70] Following is a brief account, based essentially on her story.

The poem was composed sometime in January 1937, which places it in the middle of the *Second Voronezh Notebook*,[71] when Mandelstam's exile in Voronezh was coming to an end. Increasingly apprehensive—indeed, desperate—about his future, Mandelstam decided to buy his way out by paying Stalin in poetic kind, that is, by composing a paean in his honor. This was a realistic response to a situation growing grimmer by the day. Mandelstam's fellow exiles whom he befriended in Voronezh were being rearrested one by one.[72] The Voronezh Theater that had previously offered Mandelstam an opportunity to earn a meager income no longer wanted anything to do with him. Graver still, the Voronezh section of the Writers' Union, supposed to supervise the poet's ideological reeducation, had ceased to respond to his requests for work or assistance.[73] But perhaps worst of all for Mandelstam, the fear of dealing with a poet in disgrace was now threatening to sever the last links connecting him with the literary community on the "mainland."[74] Reading Mandelstam's correspondence of those months, it is especially painful to realize that many of his pleas, not just for financial assistance or intercession but merely for an acknowledgment of his existence, went unanswered. This social isolation, intense to begin with, was made doubly unbearable by Mandelstam's health, which was

The Story of the "Ode"

deteriorating rapidly under the stress of continuous harassment. The suddenness with which Mandelstam was reduced to these most minimal circumstances, too, must have caused considerable pain.

A letter to K. I. Chukovskii, written early in 1937 after the "Ode" had been finished and while his wife was either in or on her way to Moscow, testifies to Mandelstam's desperate state at the end of his term of exile:

Dear Kornei Ivanovich!

What is happening to me—cannot continue any longer. Neither my wife nor I is capable of enduring this horror any longer. Moreover, we have come to a decision to terminate all of this by whatever means. This is not a "temporary residence in Voronezh," an "administrative exile," etc. Here is what it is: a man who has gone through a most acute psychosis (more precisely, exhausting and grim madness)—right after this illness, after an attempt at suicide, physically crippled—this man took up work. I said—my judges are in the right. I have found all of this historically meaningful. All right. I worked at breakneck speed. In return I got beatings. I was ostracized. I was morally tortured. Still, I went on working. I thought it a miracle to have access to work. I gave up pride. I thought our entire life a miracle. A year and a half later, I became an invalid. By that time, without any guilt on my part, everything had been taken away from me: the right to live, to work, to medical care. I have been reduced to the status of a dog, a cur... I am a shadow. I do not exist. All I have is the right to die. My wife and I are being prompted to commit suicide. Turning to the Writers' Union is no use. They will wash their hands of it. There is only one man in the world who can and must be appealed to with this matter. People write to him only when they consider it their duty to do so. I cannot give guarantees for myself, I cannot put a value on myself. I am not speaking about my own letter. If you want to save me from an unavoidable end—to save two people—help, plead with others to write [on my behalf]. It is ridiculous to think that this may "hit back" those who would agree [to write]. There is no other way out. This is the only historical way out. But do understand: we refuse to delay our agony. Each time I let my wife go away, I become psychologically ill. It is dreadful to look at her—she is so sick. Just think: WHY is she going [to Moscow]? What does our life hang on? I will not serve another term of exile. I can't.

O. Mandelstam

My illness. I cannot remain "alone" for a moment. Now my wife's mother, an elderly woman, has come to stay with me. If I am left alone—I'll be placed in a madhouse.[75]

History and Myth: 1930–1938

Even after his arrest in May 1934, Mandelstam still had the stature of a major literary figure whose misfortune could encourage a number of prominent writers to express their "concern." It was ostensibly on their behalf that N. Bukharin, though unaware of the exact nature of the accusation against Mandelstam, petitioned Stalin. Stalin, in turn, grew sufficiently alarmed about the negative publicity in the writers' community to take it upon himself personally to counteract it by telephoning Boris Pasternak, who, it was rumored, was being groomed for the position of "first Soviet poet."[76] The story of their conversation has been told more than once,[77] but it is so characteristic of the special relationship between the state authority and literary authorship in modern Russia that it deserves more than a passing mention here.

Sometime in 1934 the great leader, whose cult was already in full bloom, telephoned one of the top members of what Solzhenitsyn called Russia's "second government," who happened to be living in a communal apartment. After assuring Pasternak that he did not need to worry about Mandelstam—that Mandelstam's case was under review and would be favorably settled—Stalin, it appears, decided to stage a little provocation, to force Pasternak to admit his friendship with Mandelstam and, by implication, his knowledge of the offending poem. "Why did you not appeal to me directly?" he is reported to have said. "I would have been climbing walls if I'd known that my friend had been arrested. He *is* your friend, isn't he?" Pasternak parried the question by suggesting that "poets, like women, feel jealous of each other." Without pausing for a transition, Stalin went on to his next question: "But he is a master, a master?" It would seem he was worried that the offending epigram might stick if Mandelstam was indeed a great poet.[78] "This is beside the point," Pasternak replied. "And why are we talking about Mandelstam and only Mandelstam? I've wanted to meet with you for a long time and have a serious discussion." "What about?" "About life and death." Stalin hung up. His attempt at diffusing the concern of the literary community marked the beginning of Mandelstam's transformation from a poet of the first magnitude into a nonperson—a forgotten author denied even the offensive effectiveness of his gift. By 1937, this process was very nearly complete.

Loss of face, disease, fear, financial ruin—any one of these might serve as a good excuse for bowing to the authorities, and in combination they no doubt justify an outward display of contrition and awe before an almighty tyrant. Yet the circumstances under which the "Ode" was composed appear to be more complex, and Nadezhda Mandelstam went further to suggest that her husband for a while (but how long?) assumed the mentality of the contemporary crowd. "In order to write such an 'Ode' it is necessary to tune oneself like a musical instrument, to consciously yield to the common hypnosis, to cast a spell over oneself with the words of the liturgy, which, in our day, muffled all human voices."[79] The tone of profound sincerity in the "Ode" and the consummate skill of its composition demonstrate that the poet's perfect pitch worked, even in this instance, without fail.

But perhaps the word "even" is inappropriate here, for there is hardly anything unusual in a poet's (or anybody's, for that matter) fascination with an omnipotent leader who has enjoyed a litany of praise for almost a decade. Poetry of the Napoleonic era abounds in such examples. Nor is it unusual for a victim to identify with his tormentor, especially if the tormentor happens to be exalted and the victim either physically or psychologically isolated. Bruno Bettelheim's analysis of the "Heil Hitler" salute and the effect of its adoption by anti-Nazi Germans is instructive in this regard,[80] as are the pleas of Ovid, the archetypal exile for poets and especially for Mandelstam. It is also worth recalling that Dostoevsky's political conversion occurred under similar circumstances (or so it seems). The composition of the "Ode," then, as that of any significant work of art, appears overdetermined. Fear, misery, practical considerations, and, most important, the tradition of projecting the attributes of an autocrat onto the "archetypal" poet (Pushkin and Alexander I and Nicholas I; Lermontov and Nicholas I) must all have been at work as Mandelstam was "tuning himself" for the composition of this magnificent paean. But even more than that was involved.

For the "Ode" to come into being, the emotional state of the poet had to be objectified, had to locate itself in that ideological space where contemporary consciousness overlapped with the "mythologies" the poet superimposed onto the world: his poetics, his myths, his beliefs—in sum, the ideology with which he made sense of the world.[81] Without such objectification, Mandelstam's expressive resources would have remained untapped, and the "Ode," had it come into existence at all, would not have risen above the Stalin doggerels of the kind that Akhmatova produced after the Second World War, when the noose around her neck was once again beginning to tighten.[82] Was there anything in Mandelstam's frame of reference capable of accommodating such an enterprise?

History and Myth: 1930–1938

TWO JOSEPHS

You are king. Live by yourself.
ALEKSANDR PUSHKIN, "For a Poet"

1

Когда б я уголь взял для высшей похвалы —
Для радости рисунка непреложной, —
Я б воздух расчертил на хитрые углы
И осторожно и тревожно.
Чтоб настоящее в чертах отозвалось,
В искусстве с дерзостью гранича,
Я б рассказал о том, кто сдвинул мира ось,
Ста сорока народов чтя обычай.
Я б поднял брови малый уголок,
И поднял вновь и разрешил иначе:
Знать, Прометей раздул свой уголёк, —
Гляди, Эсхил, как я, рисуя, плачу!

2

Я б несколько гремучих линий взял,
Все моложавое его тысячелетье,
И мужество улыбкою связал
И развязал в ненапряженном свете,
И в дружбе мудрых глаз найду для близнеца,
Какого не скажу, то выраженье, близясь
К которому, к нему, — вдруг узнаёшь отца
И задыхаешься, почуяв мира близость.
И я хочу благодарить холмы,
Что эту кость и эту кисть развили:
Он родился в горах и горечь знал тюрьмы.
Хочу назвать его — не Сталин, — Джугашвили!

3

Художник, береги и охраняй бойца:
В рост окружи его сырым и синим бором
Вниманья влажного. Не огорчить отца
Недобрым образом иль мыслей недобором,
Художник, помоги тому, кто весь с тобой,
Кто мыслит, чувствует и строит.
Не я и не другой — ему народ родной —
Народ-Гомер хвалу утроит.
Художник, береги и охраняй бойца:
Лес человечества за ним поет густея,
Само грядущее — дружина мудреца
И слушает его все чаще, все смелее.

Two Josephs

4

Он свесился с трибуны как с горы
В бугры голов. Должник сильнее иска.
Могучие глаза решительно добры,
Густая бровь кому-то светит близко,
И я хотел бы стрелкой указать
На твердость рта — отца речей упрямых
Лепное, сложное, крутое веко, знать,
Работает из миллиона рамок.
Весь — откровенность, весь — признанья медь.
И зоркий слух, не терпящий сурдинки,
На всех готовых жить и умереть
Бегут играя хмурые морщинки.

5

Сжимая уголёк, в котором все сошлось,
Рукою жадною одно лишь сходство клича,
Рукою хищною — ловить лишь сходства ось —
Я уголь искрошу, ища его обличья.
Я у него учусь не для себя учась.
Я у него учусь — к себе не знать пощады,
Несчастья скроют ли большого плана часть,
Я разыщу его в случайностях их чада...
Пусть недостоин я еще иметь друзей,
Пусть не насыщен я и желчью и слезами,
Он все мне чудится в шинели, в картузе,
На чудной площади с счастливыми глазами.

6

Глазами Сталина раздвинута гора
И вдаль прищурилась равнина.
Как море без морщин, как завтра из вчера —
До солнца борозды от плуга-исполина.
Он улыбается улыбкою жнеца
Рукопожатий в разговоре,
Который начался и длится без конца
На шестиклятвенном просторе.
И каждое гумно и каждая копна
Сильна, убориста, умна — добро живое —
Чудо народное! Да будет жизнь крупна.
Ворочается счастье стержневое.

7

И шестикратно я в сознаньи берегу
Свидетель медленный труда, борьбы и жатвы

History and Myth: 1930–1938

Его огромный путь — через тайгу.
И ленинский октябрь — до выполненной клятвы.
Уходят вдаль людских голов бугры:
Я уменьшаюсь там, меня уж не заметят,
Но в книгах ласковых и в играх детворы
Воскресну я сказать, что солнце светит.
Правдивей правды нет, чем искренность бойца:
Для чести и любви, для доблести и стали.
Есть имя славное для сжатых губ чтеца —
Его мы слышали и мы его застали.

январь 1937

1

Were I to take up the charcoal for the sake of supreme praise—
For the sake of the eternal joy of drawing—
I would divide the air into clever angles
Both carefully and anxiously.
To make the present echo in his features
(My art bordering on audacity),
I would speak about him who has shifted the world's axis
Honoring the customs of one hundred and forty peoples.
I would lift a small corner of his brow
And lift it again, and redraw it differently:
Oh, it must be Prometheus blowing on his coal—
Look, Aeschylus, how I weep as I am drawing.

2

I would take a few thunderous lines,
His youthful millennium entire,
And would bind his courage with his smile,
And let it loose again, illuminated softly.
And in the friendship of his wise eyes, I shall find for the twin
(I won't say who he is) that expression, drawing close to
Which, to him—you suddenly recognize the father
And gasp, sensing the proximity of the world.
And I want to thank the hills
That have shaped this bone and this hand:
He was born in the mountains and knew the bitterness of jail.
I want to call him, not Stalin,—Dzhugashvili!

3

Artist, cherish and guard the warrior:
Surround him entire with a damp blue forest
Of moist concern. Do not upset the father
With an unwholesome image or an inferior thought.
Artist, help him who is with you completely,
Who is thinking, feeling, and building.

Two Josephs

Not I, no, not another—his dear people—
The Homer-people will offer him a triple praise.
Artist, cherish and guard the warrior:
The forest of mankind growing ever denser is singing behind him,
The future itself is this wise man's retinue,
And it heeds him more and more often, with ever greater daring.

4

He is bending over a podium as if over a mountain
Into the hillocks of heads. A debtor stronger than any claim.
His mighty eyes are decisively kind,
His thick eyebrow is glaring at somebody,
And I would like to mark with an arrow
The firmness of his mouth—the father of stubborn speeches;
His eyelid, sculpted, complicated and abrupt,
Projects, verily, out of a million frames.
He is—all sincerity, he is—all brass of fame.
And his farsighted hearing is intolerant to muffling.
His careworn little wrinkles are playfully stretching
To reach out to all who are ready for living and dying.

5

Grasping the charcoal, the focus of everything,
Summoning with a greedy hand the likeness alone,
With a rapacious hand—to catch only the axis of likeness—
I shall make the coal crumble, searching out his features.
I am learning from him, but learning not for my own sake,
I am learning from him to be merciless to myself.
Should even a part of his great plan be hidden by misfortunes,
I'll seek him out in the fumes of these accidents...
Granted, I am still unworthy of having friends,
Granted, I have not yet been sated with gall or tears,
Still, I sense his presence: in his military coat and cap
He is standing in the miraculous square, his eyes happy.

6

The mountain came apart under Stalin's eyes,
And the plain is squinting into the distance.
Like a sea without wrinkles, like tomorrow out of yesterday—
The furrows of a colossal plough reach to the sun.
He is smiling with the smile of a harvester
Of handshakes in the conversation,
Which once began and has continued since, without end
On the expanse of his six oaths.
And each threshing-floor, and each sheaf
Is strong, fit, and clever—living wealth—

People's miracle! May life be large.
The axle of happiness keeps on tossing and turning.

7

And six times over I cherish in my mind—
A slow witness of labors, struggles, harvests—
The enormous distance he has traversed across the taiga,
And from the Leninist October—to the fulfilled oath.
The hillocks of people's heads are growing more distant:
I am diminishing in them, won't even be noticed,
But in tender books and in children's games,
I shall be resurrected to say that the sun—shines.
No truer truth exists than a warrior's sincerity:
For honor and love, for valor and steel,
There is a glorious name made for the taut lips of a rhapsode—
We've heard it, we lived to see him.

No other Stalin-related poem has the scope of the "Ode." It is the second longest poem ever composed by Mandelstam (after "He Who Found a Horseshoe"), and its thematic breadth offers a unique entry into the conceptual and mythic world of his later poetry. Mandelstam's idea of himself and his art, his view of his "crime" and approaching death, his vision of Stalin and the posthumous life of his poetry—all are contained in the "Ode" and are presented with a skill that would have been appreciated in the Greece of the tyrants or Augustan Rome and should, therefore, be of aesthetic value in our own day. To judge by formal features alone, the poem belongs to one of the most difficult genres of panegyric poetry, the Pindaric ode. The exuberant imagery framed in the rhetoric of praise, triadic divisions within stanzas that follow the pattern of strophe, antistrophe, and epode, and finally the lines of unequal length combining hexameter, pentameter, and tetrameter conform to the basic scheme of the ancient genre of glorifying a supreme leader.[83] Such a strict adherence to the Pindaric rules is unknown to the mainstream of the Russian odic tradition, which may in part explain why the editors published the poem under a provisional title, "Verses on Stalin." It is safe to assume that Mandelstam, who must have been aware of his priority in the genre, wished to produce something unique—a fitting tribute from a great master of verbal art to a great master of political power.

Among the letters he wrote upon finishing the "Ode" is one addressed to the authority on the genre, a critic who had praised Mandelstam's poetry as "philosophical odes," Iurii Tynianov. The poem, although it was not mentioned explicitly, served as a hidden focal point of the letter—a subtle, implicit tuning of the reader to the wavelength of the "genre." Alluding to the now sinister-sounding words of Trotsky, "In the beginning was the deed [*delo,* also a criminal case], and the word followed as its phonetic shadow," Mandelstam was appealing to literary loyalties of the 1920s, seeking to convince one of the foremost literary scholars, novelists, and screen writers of the decade that he deserved the attention afforded the dead classics of Russian literature:

> Dear Iurii Nikolaevich!
>
> I want to see you. What can I do about it? It's a legitimate wish.
>
> Please, do not consider me a shadow. I still cast one. But of late I am becoming comprehensible decisively to all. This is menacing. For a quarter of a century now, mixing the serious with trifles, I have been flowing into Russian poetry; but soon my verse will fuse with it, having altered certain elements in its structure and composition.
>
> It is easy not to answer my letter. To justify abstaining from writing a letter or a note is impossible. You shall do according to your wishes.
>
> Your O.M.[84]

The "oceanic" metaphor of poetry here[85] represents, in fact, a double entendre, since the word *naplyvat'* (to flow, as in "ebb and flow") denotes also the technique of a cinematic closeup, and thus it refers both to Mandelstam's poetics of metapoetry (the Formalist foregrounding of the device) and to the cinematic perspective realized in the "Ode." Tynianov, who used cinematic techniques in his own novels,[86] was one of a small number of people on whom such prompting would not have been lost.

The poem begins with a traditional poetic conceit for expressing the ineffable: if only the poet possessed the limitless power of representation, he would sketch with a charcoal across the firmament of heaven the portrait of the one who had "shifted the world's axis" (or axle). The purpose of this conceit was to convert the poet's confessed inadequacy into an affirmation of his creative gift at a higher rate of exchange. In an unspoken competition, Mandelstam invited Aeschylus to watch him "weep as [he is] drawing"—with the flaming coal of Prometheus. Transcending pain, the poet will offer a pictorial tribute to Stalin in the form of a long-overdue atonement for the transgression of Prometheus that had once angered Stalin's counterpart in the pantheon of Greek deities. The second stanza, as it continues the theme of representation, introduces another conceit central to the "Ode": a rapturous search for Stalin's likeness.

His aim will be achieved, Mandelstam says enigmatically, after he produces a twin (*bliznets*) whose identity he pointedly refuses to disclose. Yet in his features one would recognize the face of the "father" and "gasp" from the closeness of the essence of the world, a feeling Aleksandr Blok had once, resorting to identical rhetoric,[87] associated with the revolution. The third stanza exhorts artists not to misrepresent the leader, now called the "warrior" (*boets*) and again the "father" (*otets*). The main part of the poem begins with the fourth stanza, again canvaslike or cinematographic in quality: Stalin is addressing the "hillocks of heads" from a mountainlike podium. Remarkably, this portrait appears to derive from a newsreel of Lenin addressing a crowd in Sverdlov Square on May 5, 1920—a prototype for many a Lenin poster. This substitution is doubly significant: first because Stalin was not known for his oratorical skill, and second because Lenin, who was a skillful speaker, is missing from the "Ode" (except by attribute and implication). In 1937 such an omission was rare and therefore meaningful even in the unabashedly worshipful Soviet folklore of those days.[88]

In the fifth stanza, Mandelstam returns to the subject of his craft and speaks about the technique he employs in drawing the portrait of Stalin. Only in this section does Mandelstam disclose the nature of his relation to his subject, whose portrait is once again composed from bits and pieces of propaganda placards.

In the sixth stanza, Mandelstam goes on to describe the transformation of the earth under the power of Stalin's vision (a trompe l'oeil, one is tempted to say): Stalin's eyes make a mountain come apart, opening to view a cultivated plain with furrows stretching into the sunset. The "sixfold oath" that describes this field of plenty refers to Stalin's funeral oration for Lenin: "We vow to thee, Comrade Lenin," and so forth, six times and, possibly, Stalin's "six conditions for industrialization."[89] In order to emphasize the magical, or miraculous, nature of the transformation, Mandelstam suddenly shifts to trochee—*Chudo narodnoe!* (People's miracle!)—creating a metrical equivalent of the Greek spondee. Although not unusual for the Russian iambic, such a shift, as Mandelstam may have learned from Viacheslav Ivanov, served to mark an epiphany in sacred Greek poetry.[90] Appropriately, this line also contains an element of an archetypal verbal formula with which God brought forth the universe: *Da budet zhisn' krupna* (Let there be large life, or Let life be large).

The poem's coda (stanza seven) has three distinct parts. In the first, the poet recalls Stalin's life six times, partly in reference to the sixfold oath and partly in allusion to the six days of Creation. He then expresses the hope that his own art will survive him and will benefit future generations, and finally, he thanks fate for having allowed him to be a contemporary of the man who embodies honor and love, valor and steel-like firmness. Not surprisingly, the last rhyme is a paronym of Stalin (*stali, zastali*), prompting a few thoughts on magic spells and riddles that paronymically encode names of deities or spirits to whom an enchanter makes an appeal.

Intended in part as a masterful example of official Stalinist literature, the "Ode" had to absorb contemporary official rhetoric with all its maniacal verbosity. Consider, for example, the following greeting to Stalin, "telephoned" to Moscow by the Congress of Iakutian Soviets who had just finished debating the project of the Stalin constitution:

> And our first thought, our first word, is addressed to you, our dear leader and teacher, father and friend Iosif Vissarionovich! We have no words to express our gratitude and love for you, the creator of the new Constitution—this charter [Magna Carta?] of the socialist peoples. . . . You have made a vow over Lenin's sepulcher to fulfill Lenin's commandment. . . . Have the Iakutian people ever dreamed that they would have in abundance, not only bread, meat, and butter, but vegetables whose massive growth has until recently been considered a miracle. . . . We vow a holy vow: to cherish, to preserve, . . . to broaden further the Stakhanovite movement that you have brought forth.[91]

In fact, the Promethean motif, too, was a commonplace among the paeans to the great Socialist construction, as "Prometheus Unbound" by a Belorussian poet Iakub Kolos should indicate (it appeared in the same October issue of *Izvestiia*):

> Расправляет плечи-крылья
> Прометей на воле.
> Стали дни поэмой-былью,
> Сказочною долей.
>
> Кто, откуда те герои —
> Демченко, Стаханов,
> Что идут победным строем,
> Шагом великанов?
>
> Stretching his shoulder-wings,
> Prometheus is free.
> Days have become an epic poem,
> A fairy tale come true.
>
> Who and where from are these heroes—
> Demchenko, Stakhanov—

History and Myth: 1930–1938

> That are marching in a triumphant formation
> At the pace of giants?

Stakhanov, it may be recalled, was a miner, whence his association with the Titans—one of them the father of Prometheus—imprisoned in the bowels of the earth.[92] Indeed, as Mandelstam was complaining to Tynianov, his poetry was becoming comprehensible.

Viewed from an intrinsic perspective, the "Ode to Stalin" functions as a keystone in a cycle consisting of some twenty-four poems written between December 1936 and February 1937.[93] Some of them, such as the "twin" poems dealing with a statue of a Buddha-like deity residing inside a mountain,[94] are barely comprehensible without the "Ode," whereas others acquire a new, fuller meaning that would otherwise have been lost. For example, one is tempted to see features of Stalin in the "cat" from the "Kashchei" poem.[95] A particularly striking insight is produced when the "Ode" is juxtaposed with the "wasps" poem. Clarence Brown suspected a link between this poem and the "Ode,"[96] and Nadezhda Mandelstam, who unlike him had access to both texts, pointed out that the two have a central image in common: the "axis," or *os'*.[97] In the "Ode," Stalin is called the one who "had shifted the world's axis" (stanza 1), and the word appears once again in stanza 5, where Mandelstam develops the theme of his relation to Stalin. Attempting to "catch the likeness" of his subject, the poet isolates the essence of Stalin's appearance, the core, which he refers to as the "axis of likeness" (*skhodstva os'*). The nature of this latter axis is broached in the second stanza, where Mandelstam introduces a mysterious "twin" of his subject in whose features one is bound to recognize the father.

The choice of the word "twin" for the poet's representation of Stalin was far from random. To begin with, it resonated with Pasternak's choice of an equivalent image in his "Stalin" poem, one of the two published in the first January issue of *Izvestiia* in 1936.[98] Like Mandelstam's, Pasternak's "twin" (Pasternak used the more colloquial *dvoinia*) was a mysterious creature whose identity was nowhere explicitly defined but whose attributes suggested a christological image—shared by poets, precursors, and leaders alike. Below are the first five stanzas of the poem, as it appeared in the newspaper (italics are mine):

> Я понял: все живо.
> Векам не пропасть,
> И жизнь без наживы —
> Завидная часть.

Two Josephs

Бывали и бойни,
И поед живьем,
Но вечно наш двойня
Гремел соловьем.

Глубокою ночью
Загаданный впрок,
Не он ли, пророча,
Нас с вами предрек?

Спасибо, спасибо
Двум тысячам лет,
В трудах без разгиба
Оставившим свет.

Спасибо предтечам,
Спасибо вождям,
Не тем же, так нечем
Отплачивать нам.

И смех у завалин,
И мысль от сохи,
И Ленин и Сталин,
И эти стихи.

I have realized: all's alive.
Centuries won't perish,
And life without accumulated wealth
Is an enviable fortune.

There have been slaughters before,
And the devouring of the living,
But *our twin* forever
Thundered like a nightingale.

In the deep night,
Thought up to last a long time,
Wasn't it he who, prophesying,
Predicted you and me.

Thanks and thanks again
To the two thousand years
That, laboring without unbending,
Have left this world.

Thanks be to the precursors,
Thanks be to the leaders,
If not in the same kind,
We'll have nothing to repay with.

> And the laughter outside peasants' huts
> And thought coming from the plough,
> And Lenin and Stalin,
> And these verses.

One can imagine that Pasternak's "idea," fundamental to the charismatic mission of a Russian poet, struck Mandelstam as highly appropriate when he was "tuning himself" for the composition of the "Ode." An equally pertinent suggestion was contained in the other of Pasternak's *Izvestiia* poems, "Obstreperous Temperament Is to My Liking." I quote the conclusion:

> И этим гением поступка
> Так поглощен другой поэт,
> Что тяжелеет, словно губка,
> Любою из его примет.
>
> Как в этой двухголосной фуге
> Он сам ни бесконечно мал,
> Он верит в знанье друг о друге
> Предельно крайних двух начал.

> And this genius of action
> Is so absorbing for the other poet,
> Who fills himself heavy, like a sponge,
> With any of his features
>
> However small he himself is
> In this double-voiced fugue,
> He believes in the mutual awareness of each other of
> These infinitely diametrical essences.

This motif of "doubling" resonated powerfully with Pasternak's earliest collection, *Bliznets v tuchakh* (The Twin in Storm Clouds, 1914), the title of which yielded easily to a narrative elaboration: a fellow-poet (Pasternak's "twin") drafting in the stormy sky that had gathered over his head the "thunderous" outlines of his other "twin," the "fatherly" Joseph Stalin.[99] In a letter to Pasternak written on January 2, 1937, when the "Ode" was almost or entirely completed, Mandelstam appears to allude to this borrowing via a "contiguous" citation of the key word in Pasternak's first line: "Thank you for *all* and for the fact that 'all' is 'not all yet.'"[100]

In the third stanza, the "father" and the twin are presented in their martial aspect, emphasized by the rhyming scheme: *otets-bliznets-boets*. In the fourth stanza, where the first real portrait of Stalin appears—a posterlike image of Stalin addressing the crowd—Mandelstam refers to his subject as a "debtor stronger than any claim" (*dolzhnik sil'nee iska*) and, once again, as "father." The insistence on the paternity of Stalin echoes the Old Testament with its paternalistic symbolism, and we indeed encounter a similar "debtor" formula in Psalms: "The Lord hath sworn and will not repent,"[101] or "My covenant will I not break . . . Once I have sworn by my holiness that I will not lie unto David." The formula itself, however, stands at the core of Mandelstam's conception of poetic "prestation," poetry as an ever-continuing exchange of gifts, which here manifests itself as a transcendent contractual agreement between the supernatural figure of the "father," whose gifts are inexhaustible, and his "children," whose "claims" could never exceed *his* magnanimity—a potlatch in which the father always triumphs.

But how does the poet define himself in relation to Stalin the father? The answer is found in stanza 5, which becomes transparent when juxtaposed with Mandelstam's 1937 "wasps" poem:

> Вооруженный зреньем узких ос,
> Сосущих ось земную, ось земную,
> Я чую все, с чем свидеться пришлось,
> И вспоминаю наизусть и всуе.
>
> Armed with the eyesight of slender wasps
> Sucking the earth's axis, the earth's axis,
> I sense all that I have ever encountered
> And recall by heart and profanely.[102]

Even though the choice of "wasps" may have been determined by Mandelstam's reading of Bergson, who considered these insects the paragons of intuitive perception,[103] the poem's "poetics" are defined by paronomasia, in this case a play on the phonetic similarity between the genitive plural of *osa: os;* the accusative singular of the word *axis: os';* the ending of the verb signifying an unpremeditated encounter: *prishlos';* and, of course, the vocative form of his own first name Osip: *Os',* a contraction of "Joseph," the name he happened to share with Stalin.[104] "Solominka," a famous poetic declaration of the earlier Mandelstam, is constructed on such a play on first names,[105] and in the "Ode" the poet exploited the potential of the remarkable coincidence, transforming it into a likeness. A careful reading of the fifth stanza demonstrates that Mandelstam made the coincidence work for him with supreme mastery.

IMAGE AND LIKENESS

The similitude that Mandelstam sought with such fervor as he was sketching in the air the portrait of Stalin, as he was creating the "twin," involved not only the morphological essence of Stalin's face (a portrait arranged around the axis of facial symmetry) but also—indeed, primarily—the identity between his famous tormentor and himself. This identification of the poet's persona with the subject of his poetic portrait is common in poetic iconography [106] and is related to confessional literature, both medieval and modern. [107] But it had a special significance for the tradition in which an author's place in the culture was in large measure predicated on his capacity to project onto himself, by means of challenge, the aura of the focused, charismatic authority of the supreme ruler.

The authority of one both undermined and supported the authority of the other in a relation of mutually reinforced rivalry. This conflict the "Ode" was meant to resolve by drawing on the paternalistic vocabulary of the Stalin cult [108] while making the Aeschylean version of the myth of Prometheus coextensive with the sacred narrative about the Son and the Father. [109] Consider the fifth stanza: "Granted, I have not been sated with gall or tears" (line 10). Here, the poem's artist with a burning coal in his hand (recall Prometheus, Pushkin's "The Prophet," and the calling of Isaiah) wore the transparent mask of the one who accepted the bitter cup predestined for him by his Father. [110] To leave no doubt about the parallelism—a kenotic *imitatio Christi*—Mandelstam offers a prophecy concerning his own resurrection in the final stanza: "in tender books and in children's games, I shall be resurrected to say that the sun—shines." But what can this imitation of Christ's voluntary submission to an ordeal have to do with the pagan myth of Prometheus that opens the poem?

The conjuncture of the two narratives bore the unmistakable signature of Mandelstam, "the last Helleno-Christian poet," [111] who had once imagined that a poet's life resembled a "game played by the Father with His children" ("Pushkin and Skriabin"). This view of "Christian art" defined the use of the Aeschylean myth in the "Ode to Stalin." The story of Joseph the dreamer who was once Pharaoh's prisoner was also summoned up to effect the transition from a relationship of conflict to one of indispensable service and ultimate identification (neither of the namesakes was an ethnic Russian). Prometheus of Aeschylus, recalled at the outset, passed almost imperceptibly into another mythic register where the guilty poet, his once-misused creative gift, and the Zeus of the Soviet Olympus could be presented as, respectively, Christ and God the Father. After all, Prometheus, like Christ, was a transgressor with respect to established authority. But his offense, even though beneficial for mankind, served to set the tragic cycle in motion, whereas Christ's much later violation of the Law and his subsequent Crucifixion put the tragic cycle to rest. Mandelstam's personal misfortune thus recapitulated the religious and moral evolution of humanity—or, to put it differently, the phylogeny of history was recapitulated in the ontogeny of Mandelstam.

Emphasizing the dynamic aspect in the development of the "Ode's" central myth, that is, by having the Christian view supersede its Greek counterpart, Mandelstam was pleading for a different interpretation of his predicament, integrating it into the framework of universal Christian redemption and forgiveness. "Where is the bound and nailed-down groan, Where is Prometheus—the rock's support and likeness? . . . That is not to be—tragedies cannot be brought back," wrote Mandelstam shortly after completing the "Ode," almost in an attempt to exorcise the tragic pattern from his own life.[112]

The "Ode to Stalin," too, seems to have been meant as an exorcism, at least to the extent that it bore some features of an elaborate magic spell. The coincidences of the first name of the poet and his addressee and the talismanic "charcoal" point to such a pattern. Before Mandelstam, the burning coal of the archetypal rebel had touched the lips of the prophet Isaiah, replaced the heart of Pushkin's Prophet, and in more recent times—and mined in fabulous quantities—earned a singular fame for Stakhanov (one can expect an Acmeist Mandelstam to outline his paradigms with this kind of precision). Such a history is bound to confer transcendent powers on the mineral, transforming it, by contagion,[113] not only into a magical tool with which to fashion a fitting image of Stalin but also into a talisman that would grant the poet his wishes. This was not the first time Mandelstam had occasion to recall Pushkin's "talismanic" words: "Guard me in the days of persecution, / In the days of remorse and agitation: / You were given me on the day of sorrow."[114]

Finally, the structure of the poem provides an even stronger indication of a magical subtext, for the "Ode" follows the twofold formula of a homeopathic spell,[115] that is, one based on analogy or comparison.[116] The first part of such a spell recounts a phenomenon that has already taken place—here the development of tragedy into the Christ event—and the second contains a wish for a similar outcome with respect to an unrelated but in some ways comparable situation—Mandelstam's desire to have his predicament interpreted within the Christian rather than the Promethean or Old Testament framework.

History and Myth: 1930–1938

Thus the initial analogy with Prometheus would yield to the desired *imitatio Christi,* the "stolen fire" to the magnanimity of the "debtor stronger than any claim," and the angry Zeus-Stalin to God the Father.

This Helleno-Christian myth, tragic and heroic as well as kenotic and redemptive in its specific generation in the "Ode," became the foundation (a concealed one, as myths require)[117] of a book that more than any other work contributed to Mandelstam's revival: the two volumes of Nadezhda Mandelstam's memoirs. There, of course, Stalin was revealed as a false god, but the "Ode"'s pattern of self-presentation, the "twins," could function well without him: the "prodigal son" could practice his divine gift and even return to his Father.[118] The very first paragraph of her memoirs defines the reader's frame of reference, tuning him to the correct "mythology," once again imperceptibly, as myths require, and establishing a theme that will inform the entire narrative like a Wagnerian leitmotiv:

> Having slapped Aleksei Tolstoy [the author of the famous *Road to Calvary*], O. M. without delay returned to Moscow and there telephoned Anna Andreevna [Akhmatova] every day, pleading with her to come to Moscow. She tarried; he was getting angry. With her ticket purchased and ready to go, she paused by the window and became pensive. "Praying that this cup may pass you?" asked Punin, an intelligent, bilious, and brilliant man. It was he who suddenly said to Akhmatova, as they were strolling through the Tretiakov Gallery: "And now let us look how you are going to be conveyed to the execution" [reference to Surikov's "Boiarynia Morozova"]. This prompted the poem "And afterwards, on a peasant cart . . ." But she was not fated to make this journey: "They are saving you for the very end," Nikolai Nikolaevich Punin would say, and his face would become distorted by a tic. But at the very end, they forgot about her and did not arrest her.

The scandalous slap belongs to the Dostoevskian tradition of unmasking an antichrist in a sudden breakdown of social conventions (viz. scandals in *The Possessed*). Here, the slap exposes the "other" Tolstoy as a false prophet. By implication, his famous trilogy *Khozhdenie po mukam* is a diabolical perversion of the *Road to Calvary* or the apocryphal story of the Virgin's Descent into Hell (the Russian title alludes to both), which will be set aright in Nadezhda Mandelstam's own narrative.[119] As befits an imitator of the one who prayed at Gethsemane, Mandelstam pleads with his friend Akhmatova to come and keep vigil with him; and as befits one assigned the role of the poet's apostle, she delays. An allusion to the prayer at Gethsemane follows, and Punin's biliousness once again reminds the reader of the "bitter cup" (*zhelch* is bile or gall). Christ's Passion is implicit in Punin's comparison of Akhmatova with a martyred disciple of the archpriest Avvakum, the archetype for Russia's martyred authors. Without any apparent motivation, the narrator finally focuses on Punin's nervous tic. In part a mimetic ploy, this isolated detail begins to generate its own associations in a densely allusive context. Punin, formerly a militant Futurist, is represented by a feature that he shares with Mikhail Bulgakov's Pontius Pilate as he is interrogating Ieshua, and with Dostoevsky's Tikhon as he is listening to the most inspired portions of Stavrogin's confession.[120] Like most other "intelligent and brilliant" people one encounters in the memoirs, Punin bears the mark of possession—or so the context seems to suggest.

The symbolism of Gethsemane would once again reappear in the chapter devoted to the "Ode," where the poem itself would be referred to as the "prayer of the cup."[121] Few of the things that happened to Mandelstam are excluded from this scenario. The key event was the death of the poet in a transit concentration camp, so important also because it had at once converted into prophecy all the kenotic topoi of Mandelstam's oeuvre. What remained was to align the facts of the poet's life with the mythologies of his writings. "My goal," explained Nadezhda Mandelstam, "was to justify Mandelstam's life by means of preserving what constituted its meaning."[122] If what she had in mind was a demonstration of the poet's identification with the values and concerns of the Russian intelligentsia, her mission could not have been better served. Enveloped in another's speech, he has become a letter, an intoxicating line, a book that we are now dreaming.

APPENDIX I

The Mandelstam–Gornfel'd Affair

Although Mandelstam did not participate in the literary world's factional struggle of the late 1920s, his friendship with V. Narbut, together with N. Bukharin's patronage, placed him, if only by association, in tentative alliance with the head of RAPP (the Russian Association of Proletarian Writers) and the editor of *On Literary Guard*, L. Averbakh, who was at that time at war with A. Voronskii and his *Red Virgin Soil*. Vl. Narbut, one of the original Acmeists and now a party functionary in charge of the publishing house Land and Factory, was also active in the campaign against Voronskii. Defeated, Voronskii was removed from the editorship of his journal and expelled from the party (1927–28) (see Maguire, *Red Virgin Soil*, pp. 181–182). Then he fought back. With the help of Maxim Gorky, he managed to engineer the downfall of Narbut (accused of denouncing his party affiliation when a captive of the Whites in the civil war). Narbut was removed from Land and Factory and expelled from the party in July–August 1928 (see NM 2, p. 64).

The incident with A. G. Gornfel'd's (1867–1941) translation of Coster began in the fall of 1928. On November 13, 1928, Land and Factory made a public apology and accepted full responsibility for not having informed Gornfel'd of their plans to reissue his 1916 translation in a heavily edited form and for putting Mandelstam's name on the title page as the translator. Needless to say, this removed much of the blame from Mandelstam. The apology notwithstanding, Gornfel'd—whose generational affinities and dyed-in-the-wool populist credentials earned him little respect or notice among the people of the new literary establishment—took the opportunity to strike back. Implicitly identifying Mandelstam with the unscrupulous literary bosses, Gornfel'd compared his conduct with that of a friend stealing a fur coat from the hanger in his host's house (letter to the editor, *Evening Red Gazette*,

Appendix I

November 28, 1928). On December 10, 1928, Mandelstam published a rejoinder in which he pointed an accusing finger at the translation industry and traded insults with Gornfel'd. How dared this mere "critic," Mandelstam wondered indignantly, accuse of theft "a Russian poet and man of letters." It is hard to say whether the attribute "Russian" was meant to cast aspersions on the authority of Gornfel'd, who, like Mandelstam, was a Jew. In *The Fourth Prose,* however, the narrator did subject Gornfel'd to a barrage of anti-Semitic rhetoric (whether facetiously or not is beside the point).

In January 1929, the new head of Land and Factory, I. I. Ionov, broke all contractual agreements with Mandelstam and his friend the poet Benedikt Livshits, ostensibly after discovering that the two had translated Meyne Reed from the French rather than from the original English, as their contract had specified. Whether for professional or factional reasons (or both), Ionov refused to collaborate any further with the two translators, effectively depriving Mandelstam of his main source of livelihood (see Mandelstam's letter to Ionov, *SS* 4, pp. 121ff.).

Unsuccessful in his conciliatory attempts to restore a working relationship with the publisher, Mandelstam attempted a frontal assault on the translation industry (mostly Land and Factory) in *Izvestiia* (April 7, 1929). A counterattack took the form of a thinly veiled innuendo by D. I. Zaslavskii, "Modest Plagiarism or Shameless Slapdash" ("Skromnyi plagiat ili razviaznaia khaltura," *Literaturnaia gazeta* 3 [May 7, 1929]). The next issue of *Literaturnaia gazeta* published an indignant letter in defense of Mandelstam signed by fifteen prominent literary figures, including L. Averbakh. Both the presence of Averbakh's name and the striking intensity of the polemics over a decidedly local matter indicate that the scuffle, whatever its origin, may have had strategic implications for the questions of policy and leadership in culture and ideology that were then being reshaped.

APPENDIX II

A Note on Pasternak

Boris Pasternak represented the absent Mandelstam at one of the meetings of the so-called Conflict [arbitration] Committee of the Federation of Soviet Writers, which was convened on Mandelstam's request. Subsequent to the meeting, Pasternak wrote to Nikolai Tikhonov: "Mandelstam, for me, will become a perfect enigma if he does not learn an edifying lesson from what has happened to him recently. What a trifling gramophone-newspaper [noise], indigestible nonsense he is making out of this lucky ordeal which has fallen into his hands and which might have been a source of renewed strength and youthful, new dignity—if only he had resolved to admit his guilt [*sic*]. But he has preferred perfect trifles such as 'public protests' and 'persecution of writers' to the bitter charm of such an admission. . . . He [Mandelstam] was absent from the meeting, and I, his defender, was the first to admit that he was guilty, merrily and in a comradely manner; and in the same tone, I reminded the audience how difficult it is sometimes to read newspapers (the campaign to reveal the 'former people' [*byvshie liudi*] etc., etc.); and in general, to the limit of my ability, I have tried to give a push to the avalanche of public opinion whose loud and expansive landing purged the air, so appropriate for and deserved by the accused. Now the question remains: will Osip Emilievich take advantage of this purity, and will he want to appreciate it?" (*LN* 93, pp. 678ff., letter of June 14, 1929; portions cited anonymously in "Zametki" [1981]).

NOTES

ABBREVIATIONS

LN	*Literaturnoe nasledtsvo*
NM 1	Nadezhda Mandelstam, *Vospominaniia*
NM 2	Nadezhda Mandelstam, *Vtoraia kniga*
PiR	*Pechat' i revoliutsiia* (Leningrad)
RL	*Russian Literature* (Amsterdam)
RM	*Russkaia mysl'* (Moscow)
SH	*Slavica Hierosolymitana*
SS	*Sobranie sochinenii* (Collected Works)
VRSKhD	*Vestnik russkogo studencheskogo khristianskogo dvizheniia* (*Le Messager*)

I

1. V. L'vov-Rogachevskii, *Russko-evreiskaia literatura* (Moscow, 1922), pp. 103–129.

2. P. Brown, "The Saint as Exemplar in Late Antiquity," *Representations* 1, no. 2 (1983): 19 ff.

3. See the chapter entitled "Knizhnyi shkaf" (The Bookcase) in Mandelstam's *Shum vremeni* (The Noise of Time), *SS* 2, pp. 56 ff. See also C. Brown's discussion of the poet's father, Emilii Veniaminovich Mandelstam, in *Mandelstam* (Cambridge, 1973). See further the discussion of the poet's family in NM 2, pp. 568–578.

4. Cf. Gogol's "The Overcoat," specifically the scene of Akakii's birth and christening.

5. Cf. also Marina Tsvetaeva's frequent fashioning of herself as Maryna Mniszek. For name symbolism in Pasternak's *Doctor Zhivago* and a polemic concerning its significance, see E. Wilson, "Legend and Symbol in Doctor Zhivago," in his *The Bit Between My Teeth: A Literary Chronicle of 1950–1965*

(New York, 1965), pp. 447 ff.; M. F. Rowland and P. Rowland, *Pasternak's Doctor Zhivago* (Carbondale, Ill., 1967), pp. 10 ff.; and H. Gifford, *Pasternak: A Critical Study* (Cambridge, 1977), pp. 191 ff. See also N. Iu. Griakalova, "Fol'klornye traditsii v poezii Anny Akhmatovoi," *Russkaia literatura* 25, no. 1 (1982).

6. In this way, Joseph distinguished himself from the "wise men magicians" (Gen. 41:8) for whom Egypt remained famous into the Renaissance (viz. *Hermes Tristmegistus*). See F. A. Yates, *Giordano Bruno and the Hermetic Tradition* (London, 1964), pp. 1–20. By implication, professional diviners did not attribute their skill to the "spirit of God" (Gen. 41:16 and 38) but to themselves or some minor demons. Nevertheless, the whole hermetic thematism of the Joseph legend seems related to the Egyptian culture of the occult, since the divinatory motifs are in general underplayed in the Old Testament. Apparently God addressed his chosen people directly, thus obviating the need for divination. See "Divination" in *Encyclopaedia of Religion and Ethics*, ed. James Hastings (New York, 1961).

7. In Weber's classification system, charismatic authority represents a power related to and distinguished from the other two "ideal types," namely, *traditional* authority, based on the "eternal yesterday" ("Politics as a Vocation") and the *rational-legal* type characterized by systematic regularity and professionalism. I have relied on the following editions of Max Weber: *From Max Weber: Essays in Sociology*, ed. H. H. Gerth and C. Wright Mills (New York, 1958); and *Max Weber on Charisma and Institution Building*, ed. S. N. Eisenstadt (Chicago, 1968); hereafter referred to as *Essays* and *Charisma*, respectively. I have also found helpful the exposition of Weber's thought by R. Bendix, *Max Weber: An Intellectual Portrait* (New York, 1960).

8. Weber, *Charisma*, p. 49. For a discussion of a symbiosis of the traditional and charismatic types of domination, see R. Bendix, "Max Weber's Sociology Today," *International Social Science Journal* 17 (1965): 19–20. See also note 11.

9. Weber, *Charisma*, p. 48.

10. I have in mind Durkheim's distinction between the "sacred" and the "profane" as fundamental to any form of religion and, therefore, to all cultures. See E. Durkheim, *Elementary Forms of the Religious Life* (New York, 1915), pp. 52–63. "Sacredness," in whatever form, is attributed to the "central." See E. Shils, *Center and Periphery: Essays in Macrosociology* (Chicago, 1975), p. 263. For a discussion of this confluence of the Weberian and the Durkheimian frameworks, see S. N. Eisenstadt's introduction to *Charisma*, pp. xli–xlv.

11. In developing Weber's thinking, Edward Shils writes: "The need for order and a fascination of disorder persist, and the charismatic propensity is a function of the need for order. The generator or author of order arouses the charismatic responsiveness. Whether it be God's law or natural law or scientific law or positive law or the society as a whole, or even a particular corporate body of institutions like the army, whatever embodies, expresses or symbolizes the essence of an ordered cosmos or any significant sector thereof awakens the disposition of awe and reverence, the charismatic disposition. Men need an

order within which they can locate themselves, an order providing coherence, continuity, justice" (Shils, "Charisma, Order, and Status," in *Center and Periphery*, p. 261). For case studies making use of Shils's theory, see C. Geertz, "Centers, Kings, and Charisma," in *Culture and Its Creators*, ed. J. Ben David and T. N. Clarke (Chicago, 1977), pp. 150–171; and P. Brown, "The Saint as Exemplar." For a discussion of the contribution made by Shils and Geertz to the concept of charisma, see S. N. Eisenstadt's introduction to *Charisma*, pp. xxii–xli.

12. Shils, *Center and Periphery*, pp. 3–16 and 257 ff.

13. Weber, *Charisma*, pp. 49 ff.

14. Cor. 12:8–11; Rom. 12. Related and sometimes virtually identical terms in the Bible include "favor," "grace," and "the spirit of God." All are divine gifts. For a more detailed discussion, see "Grace" in *The Oxford Dictionary of the Christian Church*, 2d ed. (London, 1977). Max Weber's own notion of charisma, as he repeatedly acknowledged (*Essays*, p. 246), originated in a discussion of charismatic leadership and organization in the early Christian Church by Rudolph Sohm, *Kirchenrecht*. See Bendix, *Max Weber*, p. 325 n.

15. Shils, *Center and Periphery*, pp. 258 ff.

16. Weber, *Essays*, p. 49.

17. Ibid., pp. 248–250.

18. Ibid.

19. On estrangement as a condition of holiness in the late Antique society of the Mediterranean, see P. Brown, "The Rise and Function of the Holy Man in Late Antiquity," in *Society and the Holy in Late Antiquity* (Berkeley and Los Angeles, 1982), pp. 115–129. The experience was not irrelevant to the Russian Orthodox institution of "starchestvo" (ibid., p. 152), as any reader of Dostoevsky would readily recognize. In fact, one of the first Russian Symbolists, Aleksandr Dobroliubov (1876–1944?), a legendary and important figure, became one such "holy man." In the late 1890s he became a novice at the Solovetskii Monastery and later founded a sect of "Free Christians" among the Volga peasants that was known as "Dobroliubovtsy." See A. Belyi, *Nachalo veka* (Moscow and Leningrad, 1933), pp. 363–364; and P. Pertsov, *Literaturnye vospominaniia* (Moscow and Leningrad, 1933), pp. 237–240. Dobroliubov was a major influence in the early career of Briusov and an old friend and spiritual guide of Mandelstam's teacher of Russian literature, V. V. Gippius. See E. V. Ivanova, "Valerii Briusov i Aleksandr Dobroliubov," *Izvestiia Akademii nauk SSSR. Seriia literatury i iazyka* 40, no. 3 (1981): 255–273; and V. V. Gippius's autobiographical narrative poem *Lik chelovecheskii* (St. Petersburg and Berlin, 1922), canto 3:28 ff. and 40 ff.

20. This recollection refers to Mandelstam's recital of his poetry in Petrograd in the winter of 1920. See N. Pavlovich, "Vospominaniia ob Aleksandre Bloke," in *Blokovskii sbornik. Trudy nauchnoi konferentsii, posviashchennoi izucheniiu zhizni i tvorchestva A. A. Bloka* (Tartu, 1964), p. 472. Cf. the impressions of Vladimir Veidle (Weidlé), who found Mandelstam's manner of recitation "ridiculous" ("O poslednikh stikhakh Mandel'shtama," *Vozdushnye puti* 2 [1961]: 70).

21. Blok, *SS* 7, p. 371. Significantly, "Venetian Life," the poem that particularly struck Blok, has discernible echoes of the Joseph legend. See chapter 5.

22. "O sovremennom sostoianii" was reprinted in 1918. Blok's usage of the word *artist*, which in Russian has the ambivalent connotation of a performing artist, was a mark of high praise and appreciation of a poet's talent for conveying the "serious" ineffable (hence my use of the French *artiste*). Cf. also: "Thoughtful and careful, he [Blok] called the poem read by Mandelstam 'artistic'" (V. A. Zorgenfrei, "A. A. Blok," *Zapiski mechtatelei* 6 [1922]: 148). In "Iskusstvo i revoliutsiia" (Art and Revolution, 1918), Blok wrote that history would "destroy the age-old lie of civilization [the profane versus the sacred "culture"] and elevate people to the height of artistic mankind" (*SS* 6, p. 22). See P. P. Gromov, *Blok. Ego predshestvenniki i sovremenniki* (Moscow and Leningrad, 1966), p. 380. For a different reading of this characterization, see NM 2, p. 378; and note 85, chapter 5.

23. S. Adrianov, professor of Russian literature at the University of St. Petersburg, cited Blok's drama, *Roza i krest*, as convincing evidence of Russia's spiritual recovery. See his "'Roza i krest' A. Bloka," *Vestnik Evropy* 11 (1913): 385. A similar view was expressed by Viacheslav Ivanov (see *LN* 92 [1983], bk. 3, p. 397). See also S. Bernshtein, "Golos Bloka" (1920), in *Blokovskii sbornik*, vol. 2 (Tartu, 1977).

24. S. T. Aksakov, *Istoriia moego znakomstva s Gogolem*, in *Gogol' v vospominaniiakh sovremennikov*, ed. S. Mashinskii (Moscow, 1952), pp. 119 ff.

25. "Maiakovskii recited [his poem] once again but toward the end, he again slid into the shamanistic incantations [*shamanskie zaklinaniia*]." From the diary of A. Lazarevskii (June 21, 1915), cited in V. Katanian, *Maiakovskii: Literaturnaia khronika* (Moscow, 1961), p. 72.

26. Regarding the response of Mandelstam's contemporaries, see note 65.

27. O. Mandelstam, "Utro akmeizma" (The Morning of Acmeism, 1913), *SS* 2, p. 321. See also Mandelstam's invocation of glossolalia in "Slovo i kul'tura" (1921), *SS* 2, p. 227.

28. A juxtaposition of poetry recitals in Russia with the tradition of magical healing, soothsaying, and transcendent communication relying on trance states will make an instructive study. See F. D. Goodman, *Speaking in Tongues: A Cross-Cultural Study of Glossolalia* (Chicago, 1972); and her *Trance, Healing, and Hallucination* (New York, 1974). See also note 65.

29. Quoted in C. Brown, *Mandelstam*, p. 129. For an interpretation of Pasternak's remark, see L. Fleishman, *Pasternak v dvadtsatye gody* (Munich, [1981]), pp. 327 ff. See also H. Gifford, "Mandelstam and Pasternak: The Antipodes," in *Russian and Slavic Literature*, ed. R. Freeborn, R. R. Milner-Gulland, and C. A. Ward (Cambridge, Mass., 1976), pp. 376–386.

30. L. Ginsburg, "Iz starykh zapisei," in *O starom i novom* (Leningrad, 1982), p. 354 ("Poety").

31. Cf. a similar characterization of another poet, this time during the "bourgeois" NEP period (1926): "She [Akhmatova] has the demeanor of an ex-queen at a bourgeois resort" (L. Ginzburg, *O starom i novom*, p. 373). And further, after having been greeted by a slight nod from Akhmatova: "Her ges-

ture came out well, it corresponded to that historico-literary need for adulation [*blagogovenie*] that I experience in relation to her" (ibid.).

32. Nadezhda Mandelstam, despite her sober attitude to Khlebnikov, makes a point of relating how Mandelstam, hardly a pragmatist himself, had once taken care of the otherwordly, helpless Khlebnikov by demanding that Nicholas Berdiaev (then the chairman of the Writers' Union) provide a room of "at least six square meters" for "the world's greatest poet before whom all world poetry pales" (NM 2, pp. 107 ff.). This anecdote suggests that Pasternak's characterization of Mandelstam in 1932 as the "second Khlebnikov" did not emerge altogether spontaneously but had been cultivated for a long time and had wide currency.

33. On the institution of the "fools in Christ," *iurodivye*, which commenced in seventh-century Byzantium with St. Symeon the Holy Fool, see, among the more recent works, N. Challis and H. W. Dewey, "The Blessed Fools of Old Russia," *Jahrbuch für Geschichte Osteuropas* 22 (1974): 1–11.

34. R. Jakobson, "On a Generation That Squandered Its Poets" (1931), in *Major Soviet Writers: Essays in Criticism*, ed. E. J. Brown (Oxford, 1973), p. 9. Jakobson's essay made a deep impression on Mandelstam, eliciting from him the exclamation "It is written with a biblical might [*Ona napisana s bibleiskoi moshch'iu*]!" (see H. McLean, "Smert' Vladimira Maiakovskogo" [review], *Slavic Review* 36, no. 1 [1977]: 155). Biblical might, indeed, and not in the figurative sense alone. See also Iu. Tynianov, "O Khlebnikove" (1928): "Khlebnikov's biography—a biography of a poet outside the literature of books and magazines, who is happy in his own way, in his own way unhappy, complex, a 'recluse' and an extrovert—ended terribly. It [the biography] is associated with his poetic persona." See Iu. Tynianov, *Problema stikhotvornogo iazyka* (Moscow, 1965), p. 298.

35. Based on unpublished memoirs of Pavel Miturich. Among other things, Miturich believed that Khlebnikov was victimized by the Maiakovskii-Brik ménage.

36. "Avtoportret." See also the memoir portraits of Mandelstam in Il'ia Erenburg (1961), Nikolai Chukovskii (1964), Vsevolod Rozhdestvenskii (1958), Sergei Makovskii (1962). For a discussion of the memoir record of Mandelstam's appearance, see C. Brown, *Mandelstam*, pp. 49–52.

37. O. Mandelstam, *The Egyptian Stamp* (1928).

38. M. Tsvetaeva, *Poema kontsa* (1924, 1926), end of pt. 12. See S. Karlinsky, *Marina Cvetaeva* (Berkeley and Los Angeles, 1966), pp. 212–214.

39. NM 2, p. 34.

40. SS 1:141 ("Net, nikogda nichei ia ne byl sovremennik"). Line four is a periphrasis of Lermontov's: "No I am not Byron, I am another one, / A chosen who is yet unknown, / Like him, a wanderer being chased by the world / But one with a Russian soul" (cf. Byron's "I was born for opposition"). The second stanza is based on a complex allusion to Gogol's story "Vii" about an iron demon of retribution with giant eyelids whose gaze brought death to those in his view. The poem is discussed in chapter 7.

41. Few people note when citing these ghoulishly pleasing words that

Gumilev's tragic execution—whether or not he participated in the so-called Tagantsev conspiracy—had nothing to do with his poetry. On the contrary, his best chance for surviving the summary justice of the Cheka rested on his fame as one of Russia's foremost poets.

42. This attitude, which goes back to Nikolai Gogol's short essay on Pushkin ("Neskol'ko slov o Pushkine," *Arabeski*), was "codified" in Dostoevsky's "Pushkin Speech." In Mandelstam's time, its proponents included Viacheslav Ivanov ("Poet i chern'") and, the poet who both cultivated it and benefited from it most, Aleksandr Blok (see his "Sud'ba pisatelia," "O naznachenii poeta," "Katilina"). The Formalist critics began discussing the problem of a "poet's biography" as a "literary fact" following the death of Aleksandr Blok. See Iu. Tynianov, "Litso" (1921), in *Poetika. Istoriia literatury. Kino* (Moscow, 1977); B. Eikhenbaum, "Sud'ba Bloka" (1921), in *Ob Alekasandre Bloke* (Petrograd, 1921); and B. Tomashevskii, "Literatura i biografiia," *Kniga i revoliutsiia* 4 (1923): 6–9. Jakobson's essay on Maiakovskii, "O pokolenii, rastrativshem svoikh poetov," may be seen as a culmination of this discussion insofar as it combines both the "religious" and the "scholarly" aspects of the traditional cult of the poet. More recently, the problem was addressed by L. Ginzburg in her study *O lirike* (Leningrad, 1974), specifically in chapter 3, "Problema lichnosti."

43. My thinking on this issue has been influenced considerably by R. Girard, *Violence and the Sacred* (Baltimore and London, 1977); see especially chapter 10, "The Gods, the Dead, the Sacred, and Sacrificial Substitution."

44. Vl. Maiakovskii, "Sergeiu Eseninu" (1926).

45. L. Fleishman, "O gibeli Maiakovskogo kak 'literaturnom fakte.'" *SH* 4 (1979): 126–130.

46. "On a Generation That Squandered Its Poets" (1931), p. 9.

47. Iu. Tynianov, "O literaturnom fakte." Nadezhda Mandelstam recalled that Tynianov had once suggested to her that she "organize" Mandelstam's biography according to the principle he had outlined in "O literaturnom fakte" (NM 2, p. 368). If such a conversation did indeed take place, it must have been on that rare occasion when her sense of humor happened to abandon her.

48. "Vek" (1923), *SS* 1:145. The poem is discussed in detail in chapter 6.

49. Nadezhda Mandelstam was alluding to O. Mandelstam, "Chetvertaia proza."

50. Durkheim, *Religious Life*, pp. 236 ff., 465.

51. Geertz, "Ideology as a Symbolic System," in *Interpretation of Cultures* (New York, 1973).

52. Durkheim, *Religious Life*, p. 237.

53. Ibid., p. 238.

54. *SS* 2, p. 320. See the epigraph at the beginning of this section.

55. "In the first place, it is easy to see that the elements by which the wish-fulfillment is expressed are represented with *special intensity*" (S. Freud, *The Interpretation of Dreams* [New York, 1965], p. 365). In terms of Freud's en-

ergetics, the locus of the greatest repression is the locus of the greatest intensity ("damming up" in need of "discharging"). The ultimate, paradigmatic intensity is associated with the Odeipus complex: "the beginnings of religion, morals, society and art *converge* in the Oedipus complex" (*Totem and Taboo* [1913], *Standard Edition,* vol. 13, p. 156). I have added the emphasis to point to the Oedipus complex as a symbolic nexus, not a cause—a caveat in keeping with Freud's own stated intention (see his opening to chapter 4 of *Totem and Taboo*). Note that Freud used Durkheim's *Elementary Forms of the Religious Life* when composing the last chapter of *Totem and Taboo* (*Standard Edition,* vol. 13, p. 147).

56. Cf. Khlebnikov's numerology cum astrology in *Doski sud'by;* and N. Gumilev's "Slovo" (1920; italics are mine): "A dlia nizkoi zhizni byli chisla, Kak domashnii pod"iaremnyi skot, Potomu chto vse ottenki smysla *umnoe chislo* peredaet."

57. Cf. Max Weber's fear of rationalization of social life in his "Politics as a Vocation," in *Essays*.

58. This metaphor comes from Thomas Carlyle's characterization of Voltaire, which was used as an epigraph to one of the first modernist declarations in Russia, N. M. Minskii's treatise *In the Light of Conscience* (*Pri svete sovesti,* 2d ed. [St. Petersburg, 1897], p. 130). Comparing a hero to a star, Carlyle maintained that if egoism were the only driving force of human action and interaction, people "would, by and by, diffuse themselves over space, and constitute a remarkable Chaos, but no habitable solar or stellar system."

59. C. Geertz, "Ideology as a Symbolic System," pp. 193–233, esp. pp. 207, 220, 231.

60. I do not mean to suggest that literature "reflects" or even "refracts" anything in society, or that it relates to society as the icing on the cake relates to its base, or that it is an autonomous, self-generated, and self-consuming endeavor. Rather, at least as far as the Mandelstam phenomenon is concerned, I approach literature as one of many significant forms of communal symbolic activity (institutional religion and political ideology are examples of others). Together and more or less mutually defined, they make up a society's symbolic culture—its view and sanction of itself. See Geertz, "Art as a Cultural System," in *Local Knowledge* (New York, 1983), pp. 94–120, esp. p. 99; and his "Centers, Kings, and Charisma: Reflections on the Symbolics of Power," ibid., pp. 121–146. A stimulating discussion of this issue may also be found in Kenneth Burke's *The Philosophy of Literary Form: Studies in Symbolic Action,* 3d ed. (Berkeley and Los Angeles, 1973), pp. 1–137. For a review of approaches to the problem of literature and society, particularly as it relates to Russia, see W. M. Todd's introduction to his *Literature and Society in Imperial Russia: 1800–1914* (Stanford, 1978), pp. 1–5.

61. S. N. Bernshtein is reputed to have been the first to deliver a paper on Saussure's *Cours.* See A. A. Kholodovich, "O 'Kurse obshchei lingvistiki' F. de Sossiura," in F. de Saussure, *Trudy po iazykoznaniiu,* trans. and ed. A. A. Kholodovich (Moscow, 1977), p. 28n.

62. S. N. Bernshtein, "Golos Bloka," prepared for publication by A. Ivich and G. Superfin, *Blokovskii sbornik II. Trudy Vtoroi nauchnoi konferentsii, posviashchennoi izucheniiu zhizni i tvorchestva A. A. Bloka* (Tartu, 1977), pp. 454–527 (quotation is from p. 458). The article was to be included in a posthumous collection of essays on Blok, *Ob Aleksandre Bloke* (Petrograd, 1921), but the collection appeared without it because the accompanying charts and diagrams required better printing facilities than were available at the time. Since then, fragments of the study, as Ivich and Superfin note, have been appearing in publications of the author and his students.

63. E. J. Brown, *The Proletarian Episode in Russian Literature: 1928–1932* (New York, 1953).

64. "Mandelstam's 'holy foolishness' [*iurodstvo*] is a sacrifice of the everyday appearance of a human being. This means that not a single granule of the effort of his will is spent outside his poetic work.... Everything has gone into it, and for the realm of everyday life, there has remained an eccentric man with unregulated desires, a 'madman'" (L. Ginzburg, "Iz starykh zapisei," in *O starom i novom*, p. 413).

65. Contemporaries were attuned to Mandelstam's reliance on attributes of verbal magic, describing his poetry as "shamanistic," "exorcist," "prayer-like," or "spellbinding" (in the etymological sense). "Osip Mandelstam used to come here [the Petersburg bohemian cabaret "The Wandering Dog"], with his narrow head of an aged youth thrown back; he used to pronounce the lines of his verse as though he were an apprentice who had learned a mighty spell" (V. Shklovskii, *Zhili-byli*, in *SS*, vol. 1: *Rasskazy i povesti* [Moscow, 1973], p. 84). "He sang like a shaman possessed by visions"—this about Mandelstam's reading at the "Prival komediantov" in 1917 (E. Tager, "O Mandel'shtame," *Novyi zhurnal* 85 [1965]: 184). "Mandelstam's nostalgic spells: 'Remain foam, Aphrodite'" (B. Livshits, *Polutoroglazyi strelets* [New York, 1978]). Similar statements may be found in Vl. Piast, *Vstrechi* (Moscow, 1929), p. 157; and G. Ivanov, *Peterburgskie zimy* (New York, 1952), p. 120. Blok's well-known impression of Mandelstam's performance in 1918 belongs to the same genre and resembles closely a description of a shamanistic performance. Cf. E. R. Dodds, *The Greeks and the Irrational* (Berkeley and Los Angeles, 1951), pp. 140 ff. See also A. Welsh, *Roots of Lyric: Primitive Poetry and Modern Poetics* (Princeton, 1978), chapters 6 and 7; and R. C. Elliott, *The Power of Satire: Magic, Ritual, Art* (Princeton, 1960), esp. chapter 5. For a discussion of verbal magic as an element of Mandelstam's poetics, see O. Ronen, "Osip Mandel'štam: An Ode and an Elegy" (Ph.D. diss., Harvard University, 1976), pp. 8 ff. and elsewhere. See also his "An Introduction to Mandel'štam's *Slate Ode* and *1 January 1924*: Similarity and Complementarity," *SH* 4 (1979): 214–222. There was nothing idiosyncratic in this aspect of Mandelstam's poetry. Among his contemporaries, Sologub, Bal'mont, Belyi, and Blok, not to speak of Gumilev and Khlebnikov, took a special interest in the "magic of words." Scholarly interest in the problem, too, was quite intense. For a review of contemporary scholarship on the folk uses of verbal magic, see V. P. Petrov,

"Zagovory," in *Iz istorii russkoi sovetskoi fol'kloristiki*, ed. A. A. Gorelov (Leningrad, 1981), pp. 77–142.

66. Discussed in W. A. Meeks, *The First Urban Christians: The Social World of the Apostle Paul* (New Haven, 1983), pp. 172–174.

67. E. J. Brown, *Mayakovsky: A Poet in the Revolution* (Princeton, 1973), pp. 12 ff.; and V. Katanian, *Maiakovskii: Literaturnaia khronika* (Moscow, 1961), pp. 417 ff. For a report of the meeting, see N. V. Reformatskaia, ed., *Maiakovskii v vospominaniiakh sovremennikov* (Moscow, 1963).

68. See Elliott, *The Power of Satire;* Welsh, *Roots of Lyric.*

69. "I Shubert na vode, i Motsart v ptich'em game," *SS* 1:281.

70. "10 January 1934" (1934), *SS* 1:289.

71. "Barsuch'ia nora" (The Badger's Hole), *SS* 2, p. 275.

72. D. Fanger, *The Creation of Nikolai Gogol'* (Cambridge, Mass., 1979), pp. 69 ff.

73. N. V. Gogol', "Neskol'ko slov o Pushkine" (A Few Words about Pushkin), *SS* 8, p. 50.

74. E. A. Shtakenshneider, *Dnevnik i zapiski* (Moscow and Leningrad, 1934), pp. 423 ff.; and A. I. Faresov, "Literator-muchenik," in his *Protiv techenii: N. S. Leskov. Ego zhizn', sochineniia, polemika i vospominaniia o nem* (St. Petersburg, 1904), p. 405. On "starchestvo," in particular, see N. Arseniev, *Holy Moscow* (London, 1940), esp. chapter 9; I. Smolitsch, *Russisches Mönchtum: Entstehung, Entwicklung und Wesen, 988–1917* (Würzburg, 1953); and V. Lossky, "Les startsy d'Optino," *Contacts* 33 (1961): 163–176.

75. P. Brown, "Eastern and Western Christiandom in Late Antiquity: A Parting of the Ways," in *Society and the Holy in Late Antiquity*, pp. 166–195.

76. J. B. Dunlop, *Starets Amvrosy: Model for Dostoevsky's Starets Zossima* (Belmont, Mass., 1972).

77. H. McLean, *Nikolay Leskov: Man and His Art* (Cambridge, Mass., 1977), "The Prolog," pp. 596–610.

78. Cited in P. Florenskii, *Stolp i utverzhdenie istiny: Opyt pravoslavnoi feoditsei v dvenadtsati pis'makh* (Moscow, 1914), p. 684 n. See also E. Vytorpskii, *Istoricheskoe opisanie Kozel'skoi Optinoi pustyni, vnov' sostavlennoe* (Troitse-Sergievskaia Lavra, 1902), p. 128; and P. Matveev, "L. N. Tolstoi i N. N. Strakhov v Optinoi pustyni," *Istoricheskii vestnik* 4 (1907): 151–157.

79. Iu. M. Steklov, *N. G. Chernyshevskii* (Moscow and Leningrad, 1928), vol. 2, p. 216 (kindly suggested by I. Paperno).

80. N. Valentinov [N. V. Vol'skii], *Encounters with Lenin* (London, 1968), pp. 66–68; and L. H. Haimson, *The Russian Marxists and the Origins of Bolshevism* (Cambridge, Mass., 1955), pp. 97–103.

81. N. Riasanovsky, *A Parting of Ways: Government and the Educated Public in Russia, 1801–1855* (Oxford, 1976); and M. Raeff, *The Origins of the Russian Intelligentsia* (New York, 1966) (traces alienation to the end of the eighteenth century). See also M. Malia, *Alexander Herzen and the Birth of Russian Socialism, 1812–1855* (Cambridge, Mass., 1961).

82. Cf. W. M. Todd III, "Institutions of Literature," in *Fiction and Society*

in the Age of Pushkin: Ideology, Institutions, and Narrative (Cambridge, Mass., 1986).

83. Note that Pushkin referred to the authors of the eighteenth century *Summa* as "the skeptical priesthood of the *Encyclopédie*" (*Entsiklopedii skepticheskii prichet*). See also Todd, "*Eugene Onegin:* 'Life's Novel,'" in *Literature and Society in Imperial Russia.*

84. See V. R. Leikina-Svirskaia, *Russkaia intelligentsiia v 1900–1917 gg.* (Moscow, 1981), particularly her discussion of the Union of Unions in chapter 7 ("Intelligetsiia v revoliutsionnoi bor'be"), where she deals with the issue of exfoliation. See also J. C. McClelland, *Autocrats and Academics: Education, Culture, and Society in Tsarist Russia* (Chicago, 1979).

85. "While Tolstoy is alive, walking behind his plough, behind his white little horse along the furrow, the morning is dewy, fresh, unfrightening, the vampires are asleep—and thank God. Tolstoy is coming—this is the sun coming. And if the sun sets, Tolstoy dies, *the last genius passes away*—what then? May God grant Lev Nikolaevich a long life among us. May he know that *all* contemporary Russian citizens, without distinction . . . have absorbed with their mother's milk at least a small measure of his great vital force" (quoted in A. Blok, "The Sun over Russia: The Eightieth Birthday of Lev Nikolaevich Tolstoy" [Solntse nad Rossiei, 1908], *SS* 5, p. 302); italics are mine.

86. For a contemporary review of opinions concerning the effect of the "differentiation" on Russian literature, see N. Shapir, "Uchitel'stvo literatury," *RM* 34, no. 4 (1913), pp. 1–37 (4th pagination).

87. A. Blok, "O sovremennom sostoianii russkogo simvolizma" (On the Present State of Russian Symbolism, 1910), *SS* 5, p. 433.

88. Ibid.

89. A. Blok, "Otvet Merezhkovskomu" (1910), *SS* 5, p. 444.

90. On the pathos of the Acmeist school as a justification of poetry, see R. Timenchik, "Tekst v tekste u akmeistov," in *Tekst v tekste. Trudy po znakovym sistemam XIV* (Tartu, 1981).

91. O. Mandelstam, "Gumanizm i sovremennost'" (1922), *SS* 2, p. 352.

92. *The Prose of Osip Mandelstam* (Princeton, 1967); and C. Brown, *Mandelstam.* On Mandelstam's early years, see also A. Morozov's publication of the diary of S. P. Kablukov, Mandelstam's older friend: A. Morozov, "Mandel'shtam v zapisiakh dnevnika S. P. Kablukova," *VRSKhD* 129, no. 3 (1979): 131–155.

93. Note that the main protagonists in Pasternak's prose are never Jewish. Pasternak's attitude may be glimpsed in the name of one of Iurii Zhivago's satellites, Gordon, whose name conveniently breaks into two parts, *gord* and *on,* meaning "he is proud"—an attribute at the very bottom of the scale of values in Pasternak's famous novel. One is tempted to suspect that Mandelstam, not known for his humility, was a prototype of Gordon. Cf. Pasternak's attitude to Mandelstam's handling of the Gornfel'd affair in "Zamechaniia o peresechenii biografii." On Pasternak's attitude to Jews, see also the record of his conversations with Sir Isaiah Berlin after World War II in Berlin's *Personal Impressions* (New York, 1981).

94. O. Mandelstam, *The Noise of Time* and "The Bloody Mysterium of January 9." See also "The Age" (1922) and "He Who Found a Horseshoe" (1923).

95. Exceptions included skilled craftsmen, professionals with higher education, and merchants whose businesses had a turnover exceeding one hundred thousand rubles. Mandelstam's father most likely belonged to either the first or the third category. See E. V. Vainshtein, *Deistvuiushchee zakonodatelstvo o evreiakh: Po svodu zakonov s raziasneniiami* (Kiev, 1911). See also G. N. Vetlugin, *Polnaia spravochnaia kniga o pravakh evreev: S raziasneniiami, opredeleniiami i resheniiami Pravitelstvuiushchago Senata* (St. Petersburg, 1913); L. Greenberg, *The Jews in Russia: The Struggle for Emancipation* (New York, 1976); and S. W. Baron, *The Russian Jews Under Tsars and Soviets* (New York and London, 1975).

96. *Ves' Peterburg na 1909 g. Adresnaia i spravochnaia kniga g. S.-Peterburga* (St. Petersburg, 1909). See also Mandelstam's descriptions of the recitals in the Tenishev Hall in *The Noise of Time*.

97. *The Noise of Time*.

98. For an *S-R,* not an incompatible combination (consider the leader of the party, V. M. Chernov).

99. Morozov, "Mandel'shtam v zapisiakh dnevnika Kablukova."

100. D. S. Mirskii, *A History of Russian Literature* (New York, 1973), p. 435. *The Scales* (*Vesy*) ceased publication in 1909, yielding its role to the new *Apollon*.

101. See S. N. Bulgakov, "Geroizm i podvizhnichestvo," in *Vekhi: Sbornik statei o russkoi intelligentsii,* ed. M. O. Gershenzon, 3d ed. (Moscow, 1909), pp. 23–96. For a recent discussion of the notion, see P. Henry, "Imagery of *Podvig* and *Podvizhnichestvo* in the Works of Garshin and the Early Gor'kii," *Slavonic and East European Review* 61, no. 1 (1983): 139–159.

102. B. Savinkov, *Vospominaniia terrorista,* 2d ed. (Kharkov, 1926), pp. 34, 36, 97, 103. In a private letter of May 1905, E. K. Metner, who at the time served as a government censor for Nizhnii Novgorod, declared that "Kaliaev and his kind were right" and that Kaliaev struck him as a man of "very subtle character, Blok-like." See N. V. Kotrelev and R. D. Timenchik, "Blok v neizdannoi perepiske i dnevnikakh sovremennikov (1898–1921)," *LN* 92 (1983), bk. 3, p. 224.

103. See Viacheslav Ivanov's "O nepriiatii mira" (1906), an introduction to Georgii Chulkov's brochure *O misticheskom anarkhizme* (St. Petersburg, 1906).

104. *The Prose of Osip Mandelstam,* pp. 83–85.

105. O. Mandelstam, "Pushkin i Skriabin" (1915), *SS* 2. Cf. Viacheslav Ivanov's major two-volume collection of poetry, *Cor ardens* (1910–12).

106. *The Noise of Time* and NM 1. See also B. Kozmin, ed., *Pisateli sovremennoi epokhi. Bio-bibliograficheskii slovar' russkikh pisatelei xx veka,* vol. 1 (Moscow, 1928).

107. Mandelstam's letter to his mother (April 20, 1908), *SS* 4, pp. 115 ff. See also M. Karpovich, "Moe znakomstvo s Mandel'shtamom," *Novyi zhurnal* 49 (1957). In Paris, Mandelstam met Nikolai Gumilev, a fact, as R. Timenchik

has noted, that happened to be recorded in Mandelstam's humorous lines "I v Peterburge akmeist mne blizhe, chem romanticheckii Pierro v Parizhe."

108. M. Karpovich, "Moe znakomstvo," pp. 258–261. Cited here from C. Brown, *Mandelstam,* p. 34.

109. Cf. the description of Mandelstam's recital in Khardzhiev's letter to B. Eikhenbaum, quoted earlier in this chapter.

110. Mandelstam was brought to Ivanov's salon, the Tower, on May 16, 1909, by a poet, Viktor Gofman. Here the two attended the eighth and last meeting of the "Academy of Poetry" (Poeticheskaia akademiia), a series of lectures on the history of poetry and versification that Ivanov had been delivering to the young poets who gathered at his salon. From that time on Mandelstam was a frequent visitor, especially during 1911, the last year before the younger poets broke away from Ivanov's tutelage. For a history of Mandelstam's relations with Viacheslav Ivanov, see A. A. Morozov, "Pis'ma O. E. Mandel'shtama V. I. Ivanovu," in *Gosudarstvennaia publichnaia biblioteka SSSR imeni V. I. Lenina. Zapiski Otdela rukopisei,* vol. 34 (Moscow, 1975), pp. 258–274. For a recent controversy surrounding Ivanov's influence over Mandelstam, see K. Taranovsky, *Essays on Mandel'štam* (Cambridge, Mass., 1976), pp. 83 ff.; and NM 2, pp. 30 ff.

111. Viach. Ivanov, "Avtobiograficheskoe pis'mo," *SS* 3, pp. 16 ff. Ivanov studied with Mommsen (beginning in 1886), it appears, at the same time as Max Weber.

112. Sociological implications of Ivanov's "mission" would make an interesting dissertation topic. The present study addresses this question only as it touches on Mandelstam. For a critical appraisal of Ivanov's work, see J. West, *Russian Symbolism: A Study of Vyacheslav Ivanov and the Russian Symbolist Aesthetic* (London, 1970). For a brief overview, see also S. Averintsev's introduction to Viach. Ivanov, *Stikhotvoreniia i poemy* (Leningrad, 1976).

113. Viach. Ivanov, "Religiia Dionisa: Eia proiskhozhdenie i vliianie" (The Religion of Dionysus: Its Origins and Influence), *Voprosy zhizni* 6, 7 (July 1905): 185–220, 122–148. For the examples of the uses of Erwin Rohde's *Psyche,* see ibid., p. 196; and Frazer's *New Golden Bough* (New York, 1959), p. 216.

114. Viach. Ivanov, "Poet i chern'" (The Poet and the Rabble, 1904), *SS* 1, p. 713.

115. "O russkoi idee" (On the Russian Idea, 1909), *SS* 3, esp. pp. 331–333. Cf. also A. Belyi in *Vesy,* nos. 2 and 3 (1909). For contemporary debates concerning *Vekhi* and the role of religion and "obshchestvennost'," the godbuilders and the god-seekers, see Vl. Kranikhfel'dt, "Literaturnye otkliki," *Sovremennyi mir* 8 (1909); V. A. Bazarov, "Bogoiskateli i bogostroiteli," *Vershiny* (1909); D. Filosofov, "Druz'ia ili vragi," *RM* 8 (1909); P. B. Struve, "Religiia i sotsializm," *RM* 8 (1909); and N. M. Minskii (Vilenkin), "Narod i intelligentsiia," *RM* 9 (1909). See also J. Scherrer, *Die Petersburger Religiös-Philosophischen Vereinigungen: Die Entwicklung des religiösen Selbstverständnisses ihrer Intelligencija-Mitglieder (1901–1917),* vol. 19 in *Forschungen zur Osteuropäi-*

schen Geschichte (Berlin, 1973); and C. Read, *Religion, Revolution, and the Russian Intelligentsia, 1900–1912* (London, 1979).

116. For a critique of the "philosophy of [ethical] norm" from a Nietzschean position, see Lev Shestov's introduction to *Apofeoz bespochvennosti* (Moscow, 1905), reprinted in 1911. For a contemporary reading of the book, see A. Remizov, "Po povodu knigi L. Shestova 'Apofeoz bezpochvennosti,'" *RM* 7 (July 1905), p. 204 (3d pagination). Mandelstam was referring to Knut Hamsun's *Pan* (1894). Anna Akhmatova recalled the enormous impact Hamsun had on her in 1907–8; together with Ibsen, he was the *vlastitel' dum*. See E. L. Mandrykina, "Iz rukopisnogo nasolediia Akhmatovoi," *Neva* 6 (1979): 198. See also M. N. Raudar, "Obrazy severa i severnoi kul'tury v tvorchestve Anny Akhmatovoi," in *Skandinavskii sbornik* 24 (1981): 208–224. In his programmatic "O poezii i zaumnom iazyke" (1919), V. Shklovskii chose to draw on Hamsun's authority to legitimize the use of trans-sense language. On Minskii: Mandelstam was referring to N. M. Minskii (Vilenkin), *Pri svete sovesti* (1897), one of the tamer versions of Russian Nietzscheism. The central postulates of Minskii's philosophy, which he called Maeonism (from Plato's *me on* [nothing]), defined "maeons," or those thoughts that are supposed to liberate humanity from the burden of contradictions, as "concepts that are absolutely opposite to experience and therefore completely negative conceptions" (pp. 188 ff.). Minskii was a prominent figure in the intellectual life of St. Petersburg (in 1905 he even edited the Bolshevik paper *Novaia zhizn'*). See also his *Religiia budushchego: Filosofskie razgovory* (St. Petersburg, 1905); and a review by Vasilii Rozanov, "Odna iz russkikh poetiko-filosofskikh kontseptsii," *Zolotoe runo* 7–9 (1906). For a response by Minskii, see his "Zabvennaia dusha (otvet V. Rozanovu)" in *Na obshchestvennye temy* (St. Petersburg, 1909).

117. Both letters are published in *SS* 2. See also A. Morozov, "Pis'ma Mandel'shtama Ivanovu."

118. See Mandelstam's letter to Ivanov of August 13, 1909 (*SS* 3), in which the young poet attempted a mild critique of the mentor from a Nietzschean, existentialist position, at that time identified with Innokentii Annenskii and Lev Shestov, and opposed to the well-balanced books of Ivanov's metaphysics. See K. Erberg, "O vozdushnykh mostakh kritiki," *Apollon* 2 (1909): 54–59. See also Morozov, "Pis'ma Mandel'shtama Ivanovu," p. 259.

119. Morozov, "Pis'ma Mandel'shtama Ivanovu"; and idem, "Mandel'shtam v zapisiakh dnevnikah Kablukova."

120. "As to the ideas," wrote Mandelstam in 1922 about the origins of Acmeism, "they came from the very same Viacheslav Ivanov" (Mandelstam, "O prirode slova," *SS* 2).

121. Viach. Ivanov, "Kop'e Afiny" (1904), *SS* 1, pp. 729 ff.

122. Ibid., p. 730.

123. Viach. Ivanov, "Religiia Dionisa," pp. 142–148.

124. Viach. Ivanov, "Poet i chern'," *SS* 1, p. 713.

125. Ibid.

126. Ivanov's cycle *Roza* was based on Veselovskii's *Poetika rozy*, his programmatic poem "Ozero Nemi" on Frazer's *The Golden Bough*.

127. On the legendary Tower, see O. Deshart, "Vvedenie," in Viach. Ivanov, *SS* 1. See also Ivanov's diaries in *SS* 2, pp. 771–807; and V. Piast, *Vstrechi* (Moscow, 1928). For a testimony to Ivanov's great influence on the younger generation, see G. Adamovich, "Viacheslav Ivanov i Lev Shestov," in his *Odinochestvo i svoboda* (New York, 1955), p. 254. For an opposing view, see the not entirely reliable but often verifiable memoirs of Georgii Ivanov, *Peterburgskie zimy* (New York, 1952), pp. 66–67.

128. For the record of the debates, see *Apollon* 8 and 9 (1910). Ivanov read his paper at the Obshchesvto Revnitelei Khudozhestvennogo Slova on March 26, 1910. Blok delivered his response on April 8. See Briusov's "O rechi rabskoi" in *Apollon* 9 (1910); and Belyi's "Venok ili venets" in the following issue.

129. See the annotations to the essay in *SS* 5. See also Bel'kind, "A. Blok i Viacheslav Ivanov," *Blokovskii sbornik II. Trudy Vtoroi nauchnoi konferentsii, posviashchennoi izucheniiu zhizni i tvorchestva A. A. Bloka* (Tartu, 1972), pp. 365–384.

130. G. G. Superfin and R. D. Timenchik, "Pis'ma A. A. Akhmatovoi k V. Ia. Briusovu," *Gosudarstvennaia publichnaia biblioteka SSSR imeni V. I. Lenina. Zapiski Otdela rukopisei* 32 (Moscow, 1972), pp. 272–280; *Aleksandr Blok: Novye materialy i issledovaniia, LN* 92 (1983), bk. 3; and G. P. Struve, *Neizdannyi Gumilev* (Paris, 1982).

131. *LN* 92 (1983), bk. 3, pp. 279–280 and 372.

132. See N. Gumilev on I. Annenskii's "Antichnyi mif v sovremennoi frantsuzskoi poezii," in N. Gumilev, *SS*, vol. 4: *Rasskazy, ocherki, literaturno-kriticheskie i drugie stat'i, "Zapiski kavalerista"* (Washington, D.C., 1968), p. 330 (first published in *Apollon* 1–2 [1914] as "Pis'mo o russkoi poezii").

133. "We consider the word to be the creator of myth; the word, as it dies, gives birth to myth, and vice versa" (from *Sadok sudei* [1913], in Vl. Markov, ed., *Manifesty i programmy russkikh futuristov, Slavische Propyläen*, vol. 27 [Munich, 1967], p. 52).

134. O. Mandelstam, "O prirode slova" (discussed in chapter 6).

135. In her correspondence, Anastasiia Nikolaevna Chebotarevskaia (the wife of Fedor Sologub) reported that Osip Mandelstam, belonging as he did to a "disturbed" generation, publicly predicted the imminent demise of the Symbolists' supremacy at the editorial offices of *Apollon*. See *LN* 92 (1983), bk. 3, pp. 409–410.

136. Kablukov's diary, in Morozov, "Mandel'shtam v zapisiakh dnevnika Kablukova."

137. Ibid.

138. Ibid.

139. Ibid.

140. Certificate of baptism in E. Vagin, "Mandel'shtam—khristianin XX veka," *Novoe russkoe slovo* (New York) 10 (December 1978).

141. R. A. Knox, *Enthusiasm: A Chapter in the History of Religion with a Special Reference to the XVII and XVIII Centuries* (Oxford, 1950), pp. 513–549 and 578–592.

142. Kablukov's diary, in Morozov, "Mandel'shtam v zapisiakh dnevnika Kablukova."

143. "Chuvstvo sobstvennoi pravoty" (the sense of one's own rightness) functions as a crucial ingredient of the poet's biographical myth in Nadezhda Mandelstam's memoirs. Understandably, she was highly critical of *The Egyptian Stamp* (1928), in which the authorlike protagonist indulged in self-mockery, a sentiment quite common among the intellectuals on the eve of the Stalin revolution. By 1927 Mandelstam had earned himself a reputation as one who was "preoccupied with translations and prose" (V. Saianov, "K voprosu os sud'bakh akmeizma," *Na literaturnom postu* 17–18 [1927]), two genres that did not require a pose of haughty self-righteousness.

144. Cited in M. O. Chudakova, *Poetika Mikhaila Zoshchenko* (Moscow, 1979), p. 25.

145. A. Lezhnev: "They [the poets] moved from the foreground of literature into the background and then disappeared in the wings entirely. In 1921 they were published on a large scale, in 1924 on a small scale, in 1926 they ceased being published at all" ("Uzel," *Krasnaia nov'* 8 [1926]: 230). I. Rozanov: "The center of gravity and the dominant interests have shifted from poetry to prose" (*Literaturnye otkliki* [Moscow, 1923], p. 71). B. Eikhenbaum: "The problems of prose are now in the center of literature. The interest in intimate form, and in poetic speech in general, has completely disappeared" ("O Shatobriane, o chervontsakh i russkoi literature," *Zhizn' iskusstva* 1 [1924]: 3). Iu. Tynianov: "Three years ago, prose decisively ordered poetry to clear the premises" ("Promezhutok" [1924], in *Poetika. Istoriia literatury. Kino*, p. 168). Mikhail Kuzmin voiced a contrary opinion: "Poetry, as history, can have a wheel" ("Parnasskie zarosli," *Zavtra: Literaturno-kriticheskii sbornik* [Berlin, 1923], p. 122).

146. NM 1, pp. 177–188 ("Pereotsenska tsennostei"). See a typical warning in B. Ol'khovyi, "O poputnichestve i poputchikakh," *PiR* 6 (1929): 9: "Such a poet [Mandelstam] is no 'fellow traveler,' not even with the 'right deviation,' but a poet who represents an antipode of fellow-travelism."

147. Cf. Olesha's *Zavist'* (Moscow, 1927).

148. NM 1 and 2 on the "plagiarism" affair. See also "Zamechaniia o peresechenii biografii Osipa Mandel'shtama i Borisa Pasternaka," *Pamiat'. Istoricheskii sbornik* 4 (Moscow, 1979; Paris, 1981); and E. B. Pasternak and E. V. Pasternak, "Boris Pasternak: Iz perepiski s pisateliami," in *Iz istorii sovetskoi literatury 1920–1930-kh godov, LN* 93 (Moscow, 1983), pp. 678–680. For a brief chronology of the events surrounding the "affair," see Appendix I.

149. See NM 1 on Bukharin's decision to make Mandelstam a *personal'nyi pensioner*, i.e., a recipient of a special pension including certain nonmonetary but highly valuable privileges such as access to the special food store for high officials and free passage on city transport. See also NM 2, pp. 603 ff.; and A. Grigor'ev and I. Petrova, "Mandel'shtam na poroge tridtsatykh godov," *RL* V-2 (April 1977): 181–192. Thanks to Bukharin, in 1932 (or 1933) Mandelstam was able to sign a contract and receive an advance for a two-volume edition of his works (see NM 2, p. 466).

150. The Mandelstams moved into the apartment after their return from the Crimea (NM 2, p. 466). For a supplementary record of the Mandelstams' peregrinations between the return from Armenia and the arrest and exile in 1934, see the extremely valuable recollections of B. S. Kuzin, "Ob O. E. Mandel'shtame," in *VRSKhD* 140, nos. 3–4 (1983): 116.

151. What makes it especially ironic is that Mandelstam's vituperations in *The Fourth Prose* against A. G. Gornfel'd, who accused Mandelstam of literary theft, had an anti-Semitic flavor. Consider: "This paralytic d'Anthés, this uncle Monia from the Basseinaia Street . . . Uncle Gornfel'd, why did you decide to complain in the *Birzhevka,* that is, *The Red Evening Gazette,* in the Soviet year of 1929? You would have done better to weep in the clean Jewish literary waistcoat of Mr. Propper. You would have done better to relate your misfortune to the banker with sciatic nerve, kugel, and the tallith . . ." (*SS* 2, p. 185). Since it was Mandelstam, not Gornfel'd, who was in the wrong (though not to the extent claimed by Gornfel'd), the passage begins to appear doubly ironic.

152. S. Cohen, *Bukharin and the Bolshevik Revolution: A Political Biography 1888–1938* (New York, 1973), p. 276 (and broadly, chapter 9). See also R. C. Tucker, "Stalinism as Revolution from Above," and Moshe Lewin, "The Social Background of Stalinism," both in *Stalinism: Essays in Historical Interpretation,* ed. Robert C. Tucker (New York, 1977).

153. "Zasnula chern' . . ." *SS* 1:163. According to the diary of S. P. Kablukov (Morozov, "Mandel'shtam v zapisiakh dnevnika Kablukova"), this poem, which Mandelstam included in his *Stone* (1916), was removed by the censor. The "Harlequin" was the nickname given by the courtiers to Emperor Paul I (1796–1801), the eccentric son of Catherine II. Paul was murdered, if not on the orders then with direct knowledge of his son, the poem's other tsar, Emperor Alexander I (1801–1825). In presenting Alexander, Mandelstam was relying on the Pushkinian allegory of the Bronze Horseman seen through the prism of Innokentii Annenskii's "Petersburg" (1910): "He [the Horseman] was both terrible and daring, / But the steed let him down, / The tsar failed to crush the serpent, / And, stepped upon, it became our idol." The "beast," to rely on Mandelstam's usage (e.g., *SS* 3, p. 130, and "The Age"), refers most likely to the steed—Russia—who turned out to be too wild for Alexander's feeble hand. However, the word also echoes the apocalyptic euphemism for Napoleon, current during Alexander's reign. "You, Russia, who rest on stone and blood" is reminiscent of Alexander Herzen's "Petersburg was built on stone and blood" (*On the Development of the Revolutionary Ideas in Russia,* in Herzen, *Sochineniia,* vol. 3 [1956], p. 255).

154. I am using the term in the sense it was used in R. Barthes, *Mythologies* (New York, 1972), esp. pp. 117–121.

II

1. "Dykhanie" (1909), *SS* 1:8. Reviewing *Stone* (1916), Vl. Piast wrote: "Let us see, then, what kind of poetry this eccentric poet finds appropriate to

so weighty a title? [The text of "Dykhanie" follows.] Aha! We begin to guess already that the title of the book has been selected 'ad absurdum' [*ot protivnogo*]" (*Den'* 20 [January 21, 1916]: 5). Piast [Pestovskii], a poet and a close friend of Blok's, knew Mandelstam very well, especially during the so-called dandyism period (1913), when the two frequented the Petersburg bohemian cabaret "Brodiachaia sobaka." See Piast's memoirs, *Vstrechi* (Moscow, 1929).

2. Vl. Piast (see n. 1) found in *neuznavaemyi s nedavnikh por* (line 10) a "certain infantile helplessness." See also C. Brown, *Mandelstam* (Cambridge, 1973), pp. 169–171.

3. Mandelstam's "K iubilieiu F. K. Sologuba" (*SS* 2, pp. 355–357) shows his appreciation of the older poet whose Petersburg salon he frequented in the prewar and war years. One of Mandelstam's descriptions of Sologub, in fact, echoes the poem: "Sologub's poetry presupposes the existence and melting of eternal ice." Or further on: "He was born in nontime and slowly saturated himself with time, learned how to breathe, and taught how to live."

4. The rehearsed artlessness of the poem points, first of all, to Mikhail Kuzmin, an unsurpassed master of this style. The poem combines the simplistic "folk" rhyming pattern, "mismatched" with the iambic rather than the trochaic meter, and made still more unusual by slightly "off" colloquial syntax, with the most intricate internal rhyming and paronomastic play: TELO—DELAT', S NIM—edINYM (first stanza), RADOST'—blagoDARIT', ZHIT'—SKAZHITe (second stanza). On Kuzmin's "handwriting," see Vl. Markov, "Poeziia Mikhaila Kuzmina," in Kuzmin, *Sobranie stikhov,* vol. 3 (Munich, 1977), pp. 336ff., 343ff., 354–358. On Kuzmin and the beginnings of Acmeism, see J. E. Malmstad, "Mikhail Kuzmin: A Chronicle of His Life and Times," in Kuzmin, *Sobranie stikhov,* vol. 3, pp. 132ff. Kuzmin's elevation to stardom (Malmstad, ibid., p. 133), in fact, coincided with Mandelstam's earliest attempts at poetry while still a Tenishev student. The poem's date (1909) also may point to Kuzmin, who in the same year published his novel *Nezhnyi Iosif* in *Zolotoe runo*. A major influence on the Acmeists (see R. D. Timenchik, V. N. Toporov, and T. V. Tsiv'ian, "Akhmatova i Kuzmin," *RL* VI-3 [1978]), Kuzmin exemplified for Mandelstam the most precious principle of poetry—"recollection" ("K vykhodu Al'manakha muz")—and, indeed, some of the more programmatic poems by Mandelstam echo Kuzmin distinctly. Compare Kuzmin's "Smiris', o serdtse, ne ropshchi" (*Apollon* 5 [1911]) with Mandelstam's "Paden'e—neizmennyi sputnik strakha" (1912), "Zverinets" (1916), and "Grifel'naia oda" (1923). This 1911 poem by Kuzmin apparently served as a salon conversation piece in 1911—witness its repeated "appropriation" by Viacheslav Ivanov in his "Huitain" (1911?), where the first four lines serve as the epigraph as well as the first quatrain of Ivanov's poem.

5. The poem might easily have been read as a pastiche of K. Bal'mont's "Zhizn' prokhodit—vechen son": "Zhizn' prokhodit—vechen son. / Khorosho mne,—ia vliublen. / Zhizn' prokhodit—skazki net. / Khorosho mne—ia poet. / Dushen mir,—v dushe svezho. / Khorosho mne—khorosho." Mandelstam included this poem in the never-published *Anthology of Modern Russian Poetry* he was compiling in the 1920s (see the Princeton Archive). An attentive

(and retentive) reader of Bal'mont, Mandelstam displayed his ambivalent attitude toward the older poet by praising his poetry as "translations which prompt one to suspect the existence of an interesting original." One comes across the traces of these "interesting originals" in Mandelstam's poetry of the *Tristia* period. Cf., e.g., "Ia naravne s drugimi / Khochu tebe sluzhit', / Ot revnosti sukhimi / Gubami vorozhit'" (Mandelstam) with Bal'mont's "Eshche neobkhodimo liubit' i ubivat', / Eshche neobkhodimo nakladyvat' pechat'." The similarity between the two poems goes well beyond metrics. Much of Mandelstam's "verbal magic," too, appears to be related to Bal'mont's "magic of words."

6. In a composite review, S. Gorodetskii faulted Mandelstam for his uncertain knowledge of the Russian language. See Gorodetskii, "Stikhi o voine v 'Apollone,'" *Rech'* 3 (November 1914).

7. Casting about for a surefire self-image of youthful poetic innocence, Mandelstam's friend Larisa Reisner (for a while an intimate friend of N. Gumilev) felt free to convert Mandelstam's "Dykhanie" into her autobiographical prose: "There is not in the entire Petersburg a single crystal window covered with virginal hoarfrost and a dense covering of snow that Hafiz [N. Gumilev] has not made opaque with his breath, forever leaving a gaping opening into emptiness in the clear frosty patterns." This autobiographical novel (1919–21), which remained unfinished, was published as *Avtobiograficheskii roman* in *Iz istorii sovetskoi literatury 1920–1930-kh godov*, *LN* 93 (Moscow, 1983), p. 205.

8. G. Ivanov, *Peterburgskie zimy* (New York, 1952), pp. 115 ff.

9. This last is all the more striking, since it appears not in the last poem (as a self-congratulation for work well done) but in the first poem of the book. By comparison, even the lapidary arrogance in the lines ending the first *Stone* ranks as a tentative understatement:

> Но чем внимательней, твердыня Нотр Дам,
> Я изучал твои чудовищные ребра,
> Тем чаще думал я: из тяжести недобой
> И я когда-нибудь прекрасное создам.

> And the more carefully, o firmament Notre Dame,
> I have been studying your monstrous ribs,
> The more frequently I thought: out of the unkindly heaviness,
> I, too, shall create the beautiful someday.

("Gde rimskii sudiia sudil chuzhoi narod" [Where the Roman judge judged an alien people, 1912], *SS* 1:39).

10. Reliance on the pattern of Andersen's tales was no more unusual than reliance on the patterns of Greek myths. Echoes of "The Snow Queen" can be heard in Aleksandr Blok's "Vtoroe kreshchenie" (1907), in *Snezhnaia maska,* and of course, in Andrei Belyi's *Kubok metelei* (Moscow, 1908). For the poets of Mandelstam's generation, too, "The Snow Queen" functions as an important motif. For example, in Marina Tsvetaeva's cycle "Podruga" (1914–15), ad-

dressed to Sofiia Parnok: "Segodnia, chasu v vos'mom" and "Mogu li ne vspomnit' ia" (see S. Poliakova, *Zakatnye ony dni: Tsvetaeva i Parnok* [Ann Arbor, 1983], p. 119 n. 7). Consider also Stravinsky's contemporary ballet, "Le baiser de la Fée," based on "The Snow Queen" (suggested by Robert P. Hughes).

11. NM 2, pp. 544 ff.

12. I. Annenskii, "O sovremennom lirizme," *Knigi otrazhenii* (Moscow, 1979), pp. 342 ff. Annenskii had in mind Briusov's poem "No pochemu temno? Goriat bessil'no svechi," from the collection *Vse napevy*.

13. J. Lacan, "La relation d'objet et les structures freudiennes," *Bulletin de psychologie* 10, no. 10 (April 1957): 602–605; and idem, "La signification du phallus: Die Bedeutung des Phallus," *Ecrits* (Paris, 1966), pp. 685–695. R. Barthes, *S/Z. An Essay* (New York, 1974), e.g., pp. 106 ff. For Derrida, see his discussion of Rousseau's "Essay on the Origin of Languages" in J. Derrida, *Of Grammatology* (Baltimore, 1976), esp. pp. 263–268.

14. "Viacheslav Ivanov, as a poet and a theoretician, came forth during a transitional epoch for literature. One such epoch found its distinct embodiment in the ancient 'Alexandrianism.' . . . We are close to their epoch" (A. Blok, "Tvorchestvo Viacheslava Ivanova" [1905], *SS* 5, pp. 7 and 8). M. Kuzmin's famous cycle *Aleksandriiskie pesni* (The Songs of Alexandria) came out in 1906 and was "extremely well received by critics and public alike" (see Malmstad, "Mikhail Kuzmin"). See also P. P. Muratov, "Stil' epokhi," *RM* 31, no. 1 (1910), pp. 94–99 (14th pagination), for parallels between the 1900s and the Alexandrian epoch. This subject and the general kinship between antiquity and the present are discussed at length by V. Buzeskul, *Antichnost' i sovremennost': Sovremennye temy v antichnoi Gretsii*, 2d ed. (St. Petersburg, 1914); for a review of this book, see *Zavety* 2 (1913): 196–198.

15. Cf. A. V. Lunacharskii: "The root of art is eros even among animals" ("Taneev i Skriabin," *Novyi mir* 6 [1925]: 116).

16. Annenskii's 1909 article, seminal for the subsequent development of Russian poetry, served in retrospect as a critical declaration of the new *Apollon*, where it was published in the first three issues (*Apollon* [1909] 1:12–42, 2:3–29, and 3:5–29). In particular, Annenskii's emphasis on the effectiveness of subtle poetic allusions to other poets had far-reaching implications for the poetry of Akhmatova and Mandelstam (see his treatment of Sologub). Not only was Annenskii's view substantially different from much of the Symbolist criticism, but his impressionistic manner of presentation, his emphasis on craft rather than message, and his broad scope set the tone for some of the more important essays on poetry, such as Iu. Tynianov's "Promezhutok" (1924), which would appear in years to come. See the annotations to *Knigi otrazhenii*, pp. 630–632. Mandelstam thought highly of Annenskii's criticism. His "Literaturnaia Moskva" and "Literaturnaia Moskva. Rozhdenie fabuly" (1922), as well as "O sovremennoi poezii. K vykhodu 'Al'manakha muz'" (1916), demonstrate his affinity with Annenskii's famous essay (the latter even in its title).

17. "Kak oblakom serdtse odeto," *SS* 2:457. The poem was composed no later than August 1910, when Mandelstam sent it, together with nine other

poems, to Viacheslav Ivanov. See A. A. Morozov, "Pis'ma O. E. Mandel'shtama V. I. Ivanovu," in *Gosudarstvennaia publichnaia biblioteka SSSR imeni V. I. Lenina. Zapiski Otdela rukopisei,* vol. 34 (Moscow, 1975), pp. 270–273.

18. N. Gumilev, "Pis'mo o russkoi poezii," *Apollon* 1–2 (1914): 126.

19. N. Gumilev, "Pis'mo o russkoi poezii" (*Apollon* 1–2 [1914]), in *SS* 4 (Washington, D.C., 1968), p. 327.

20. V. Khodasevich, "Literaturnyi subbotnik—o novykh stikhakh," *Utro Rossii* 30 (January 30, 1916): 5. My gratitude to the late G. P. Struve for providing me with this reference to Khodasevich.

21. V. Briusov, "Poetu" ("Ty dolzhen byt' gordym kak znamia"), in *Vse napevy* (1909); first published in *Vesy* 1 (1908). The lines in question read: "Byt' mozhet, vse v zhizni lish' sredstvo / Dlia iarko-pevuchikh stikhov, / I ty s bespechal'nogo detstva / Ishchi sochetaniia slov."

22. O. Mandelstam, "Kak oblakom serdtse odeto," *SS* 2:457. The editors' provisional date for the poem's composition, 1909–10, is indirectly substantiated by the present discussion.

23. Mandelstam and his circle were aware of the etymological reverberations of *akme:* akmon—Adam-kadmon—kamen'—petrus—Petersburg. As G. G. Superfin (noted in "Russkaia semanticheskaia poetika") and O. Ronen have both pointed out, the words *Kamen'* and *Akme* (the publisher of *Stone*), placed one over the other on the title page of Mandelstam's first collection of poetry, were meant to emphasize Mandelstam and the movement's etymological ken. See O. Ronen, "Leksicheskii povtor, podtekst i smysl v poetike Osipa Mandel'štama," in *Slavic Poetics: Essays in Honor of Kiril Taranovsky,* ed. Roman Jakobson, C. H. van Schoneveld, and Dean S. Worth (The Hague, 1973).

24. S. Gorodetskii, "Muzyka i arkhitektura v poezii," *Rech'* 17 (30) (June 1913).

25. The tradition of viewing 1912 as the year of Mandelstam's transition from Symbolism to Acmeism goes back to Nikolai Gumilev's review of *Kamen'* I (*Apollon* 1–2 [1914]: 126). See also Gumilev, *SS* 4, pp. 326 ff.

26. Such words as "the joy of life" and the "acceptance of the world" were used by S. Gorodetskii in "Nekotorye techeniia v sovremennoi russkoi poezii," *Apollon* 1 (1913): 48, and, somewhat more judiciously, by N. Gumilev in his concurrent manifesto "Nasledie simvolizma i akmeizm" (ibid., p. 45). See also R. D. Timenchik, "Zametki ob akmeizme," *RL* 7/8 (1974).

27. *Stone: The First Book of Poems* (*Kamen'* III) came out in 1923, that is, a year or so after *Tristia* (1921) and *The Second Book* (*Vtoraia kniga,* 1922). Consisting primarily of poems composed between 1908 and 1915, it opened with "The sound, cautious and hollow" (1908, *SS* 1:1), and closed with the 1923 "He Who Found a Horseshoe," a penultimate poem of *The Second Book.* Furthermore, it contained "Not believing in the miracle of the Resurrection" (1916, *SS* 1:90), "That evening, the lancet forest of the organ did not rumble" (1917, *SS* 1:96), and "In Petersburg, we shall gather again" (1920, *SS* 1:18)—all already published as part of *Tristia.*

28. See E. Said, *Beginnings: Intention and Method* (New York, 1975), pp. 6 and 174 ff.; and Nietzsche's concepts of "origin versus purpose," central to

Notes to Pages 40–41

Said's critical enterprise, in Nietzsche, *On the Genealogy of Morals* (New York, 1969), pp. 77–78. In contrast to the Acmeist "epic" of Mandelstam and (later) of Akhmatova (*Poema bez geroiia*), which conform to the pattern of "origins," the Futurist verse narratives of Khlebnikov and Maiakovskii (epics of "beginnings," in Said's terms) may be seen as an inversion of the Symbolist conception of the genre, which was largely based on the mythological poetics of Viacheslav Ivanov and which found its ultimate expression in the "trilogy" of Aleksandr Blok.

29. See, for example, A. Blok's "Dusha pisatelia" (A Writer's Soul), *SS* 5, pp. 369–370. This notion provides the conceptual framework for a 1972 study of Blok by D. Maksimov, "Ideia puti v poeticheskom mire Al. Bloka," in *Poeziia i proza Al. Bloka* (Leningrad, 1981), pp. 6–152.

30. "Barsuch'ia nora" (1923), *SS* 2:270 ff.

31. As it was advertised in *Giperborei* 2 (November 1912), the upcoming edition of Mandelstam's poetry was to be named after his 1911 poem "Rakovina" (*SS* 1:26).

32. Cf. D. M. Segal's term for a specifically Mandelstamian trope, *ambivalentnaia antiteza* (an ambivalent antithesis), in Segal, "O nekotorykh aspektakh smyslovoi struktury 'Grifel'noi ody' O. E. Mandel'shtama," *RL* 2 (1972).

33. Cf. Mandelstam's criticism of Viacheslav Ivanov's weltanschauung in *Across the Stars* as excessively smooth: "Even ecstasy is not dangerous—because you foresee the outcome. Only the breathing of the cosmos wafts about your book, imparting to it a charm it shares with *Zarathustra*—compensating for the astronomical roundness of your system, which you yourself shake in the best passages of your book, indeed, shake continuously. One more feature your book shares with *Zarathustra*—is that each word in it fulfills its purpose with fiery hatred and hates sincerely its own place and its own neighbors" (letter to Viach. Ivanov of August 13, 1909, *SS* 2, pp. 486 ff.).

34. A note on translation. According to Dal''s *Dictionary* (St. Petersburg and Moscow, 1905), the word *korabel'shchik* means "owner of a merchant ship," which conforms to Pushkin's usage in *Skazka o Tsare Saltane:* "Korabel'shchiki v otvet." The word may, however, mean simply a seafarer, a mariner—an acceptable usage supplied by D. N. Ushakov's *Dictionary* (Moscow, 1935), where it is illustrated by the same line from Pushkin. *Zastrel'shchik,* which I translate as "vanguard soldier," constitutes, according to Dal', a term for a specially designated front-line soldier who fires the first shot at the enemy, thereby signaling to others that the battle has begun and that it is time to commence firing. In civilian usage after World War I, it designated a social, political, or industrial "activist" (Ushakov, 1935).

35. "Vysokii dom postroil plotnik diuzhii" in "Na kamennykh otrogakh Pierii" (1919), *SS* 1:105. Cf. Sappho's Fragment 148 in J. M. Edmonds, ed., *Lyra Graeca,* vol. 1 (London, 1928). For a discussion of Mandelstam's reworking of Sappho, see R. Przybylski, "Arcadia Osipa Mandelsztama," *Slavia Orientalis* 13, no. 3 (1964): 243–262; K. Taranovsky, *Essays on Mandel'štam* (Cambridge, Mass., 1976), pp. 83–114; and G. Levinton, "'Na kamennykh otrogakh Pierii' Osipa Mandel'shtama: Materialy k analizu," *RL* V-2 and V-3 (1977).

36. Cf. Mandelstam's "Sestry—tiazhest' i nezhnost'—odinakovy vashi primety" (1920, *SS* 1:108), one version of which reads: "It is easier to lift a *stone* than to utter the word—*to love*." See *Tristia* (1922).

37. Myth-making by nominations goes back to the "mythological" school of Russian folklore, A. N. Afanas'ev and F. I. Buslaev, and further back to the theories of Max Müller. See, for example, F. I. Buslaev, "Dogadki i mechtaniia o pervobytnom cheloveke," *Sochineniia,* vol. 1 (St. Petersburg, 1908), p. 111. Closer to Mandelstam, see Viach. Ivanov, "Zavety simvolizma" (1910), *SS* 2, pp. 593–594; and A. Belyi, *Simvolizm* (Moscow, 1910), p. 70 ("Emblematika smysla") and p. 448 ("Magiia slov"). Cf. also N. Gumilev: "Bozhestvennye naimenovan'ia tebe daruiutsia, poet" (Divine names are given thee, poet).

38. "Na pesn', kak na *podvig*, gotov." It is enlightening to juxtapose Mandelstam's *podvig* (ordeal) with the definition of *podvizhnichestvo* (an act of engaging in ordeals) offered in the Russian theological dictionary: "a type of spiritual and external exercise based on self-abnegation with the purpose of Christian self-improvement. It characterized the ascetic monks, who were not subject to specific external rules.... It grew particularly among the Christians of both sexes in the first and second centuries when these men and women... remained chaste for their entire life" (*Polnyi pravoslavnyi bogoslovskii slovar'*, vol. 2 [St. Petersburg, 1913], cols. 1820–1821). Unlike a heroic feat, *podvig* or *podvizhnichestvo*, especially in a stylistically or thematically sacred context, owes little to the tradition of pagan, godlike heroism with its promotion of the self. Rather, it represents essentially an act of humility before, and in the service of, a higher communal ideal. As such, it is intimately connected to the notion of *sobornost'* (symphony), one of the central tenets of the Russian Orthodox culture. See S. N. Bulgakov, "Geroizm i podvizhnichestvo," in *Vekhi: Sbornik statei o russkoi intelligentsii,* ed. M. O. Gershenzon, 3d ed. (Moscow, 1909), pp. 23–96. For a recent discussion of the notion, see P. Henry, "Imagery of *Podvig* and *Podvizhnichestvo* in the Works of Garshin and the Early Gor'kii," *Slavonic and East European Review* 61, no. 1 (1983): 139–159.

39. Viach. Ivanov, "Poet i Chern'" (The Poet and the Rabble, 1904), *SS* 1; reprinted in *Po zvezdam* (1909), which Mandelstam read carefully a few months before he sent the poem under discussion to Viacheslav Ivanov. Mandelstam offered a critique of the collection in his letter to Ivanov written on August 13/26, 1909 (*SS* 2, pp. 468–488). For a discussion of this letter, see chapter 1; and Morozov, "Pis'ma Mandel'shtama Ivanovu." The "wafting of the subtle cool" as a sign of approaching poetic afflatus eventually appeared in Mandelstam's poem "Na kamennykh otrogakh Pierii" (1919)—another example of his customary use of Ivanov. On the contemporary usage of "thoughtful action" [*umnoe delan'e*], see P. Florenskii, *Stolp i utverzhdenie istiny: Opyt pravoslavnoi feoditsei v dvenadtsati pis'makh* (Moscow, 1914), p. 108.

40. A. Blok, "Khudozhnik" (1912).

41. Cf. another passage from Viacheslav Ivanov: "Let us, finally, take a closer look at the process during which out of erotic ecstasy there emerges a mystical epiphany; out of this epiphany, a spiritual conception accompanied

by a clear calm of an enriched, gladdened soul; out of this calm, a new musical stirring, drawing the spirit toward engendering a new form of transfiguration; out of this musical stirring, a poetic dream in which memories serve only as material for the contemplation of the Apollonian image that is to reflect itself in the word as a harmonious body of rhythmic creation; until finally, out of the desire, inflamed by the contemplation of this Apollonian image, there emerges the verbal flesh of a sonnet" (Viach. Ivanov, "O granitsakh iskusstva" [1912], *SS* 2, pp. 630 ff.).

42. I am using the word *sacred* in the Durkheimian sense (E. Durkheim, *Elementary Forms of the Religious Life* [New York, 1965], pp. 356 ff.).

43. Significantly, in discussing Viacheslav Ivanov's "Poet i Chern'" (The Poet and the Rabble, 1904), Blok emphasized the "ordeal" as central to the experience of a modern poet, who, being an "Alexandrian," represents, as it were, an anticipatory imitator of Christ: "During the period of the concealed rebellion, which made silence even deeper and in which the Word was destined to be born—could literature (itself the word) not burn itself to ashes with the inner flame?" ("Tvorchestvo Viacheslava Ivanova," *SS* 5, p. 7). See also Ivanov's programmatic poem "Sloki" in *Prozrachnost'. Vtoraia kniga liriki* (Moscow, 1904).

44. G. Levinton noted a possible connection between Blok's essay on spells and incantations and Mandelstam's poem. See Levinton's "Zametki o fol'klorizme Bloka," in *Mif, fol'klor, literatura* (Leningrad, 1978), p. 184n.

45. "Poeziia zagovorov i zaklinanii" and "Stikhiia i kul'tura" in A. Blok, *SS* 5.

46. "'Obolokus' ia obolokom, obtychus' chastymi zvezdami',—govorit zaklinatel'; i vot on uzhe mag, plyvushchii v oblake, opoiasannyi Mlechnym Putem" (A. Blok, "Poeziia zagovorov i zaklinanii," *SS* 5, p. 48). Cf. Levinton, "Zametki o fol'klorizme Bloka," pp. 175 and 183 ff. See also Blok: "[The poet] must possess that singular word of incantation [*zaklinanie*] which has not yet become a 'lie'" ("Tvorchestvo Viacheslava Ivanova," *SS* 5, pp. 9 ff.).

47. G. Ivanov (*Novyi zhurnal* 43 [1955]: 276) noted Mandelstam's early interest in theosophy (*zaigryval s teosofiei*), which makes Mandelstam similar to Gumilev in this respect (see V. Nevedomskaia, "Vospominaniia o Gumileve," *Novyi zhurnal* 38 [1954]: 190); Gumilev's poetry often makes use of the metempsychosis formula and astral symbolism (e.g., "Zabludivshiisia tramvai" and "Zvezdnyi uzhas"). In the early 1920s Mandelstam became a harsh opponent of theosophy as a "vulgar materialism," echoing Vl. Solov'ev's critique, which in turn invoked Hegel's *schlechte Unendlichkeit*. See "O prirode slova," *SS* 2, p. 243. See also O. Ronen, "Osip Mandel'štam: An Ode and an Elegy," (Ph.D. diss. Harvard University, 1976), p. 18n.

48. Noted by I. Annenskii, "O sovremennom lirizme" (1909), in *Knigi otrazhenii* (Moscow, 1979), p. 361.

49. Mandelstam, *SS* 2, pp. 302, 305. Written in 1910, perhaps as a term paper, the essay was published in the fourth issue of *Apollon* for 1913 and must be seen as a serious, declarative statement, since the preceding issue contained the Acmeist manifestos of the poet's two comrades-in-arms, Nikolai Gumilev

and Sergei Gorodetskii. Very close to them in letter and spirit but composed much earlier, it may have served as the Acmeist answer to the Futurists' backdating of their "birthday." On this anxiety of priority among the younger generation, see V. Markov, *Russian Futurism: A History* (Berkeley and Los Angeles, 1968), p. 135; and R. D. Timenchik, "Zametki ob akmeizme," *RL* 7/8 (1974): 25 n. 7. The essay concludes the 1928 collection of Mandelstam's critical prose (*O poezii*), which indicates that the poet assigned it a programmatic significance even at that late date.

50. Viach. Ivanov, "Kop'e Afiny" (1904, 1909), *SS* 1, p. 733.
51. A. Blok, "Na pole Kulikovom." Cf. the common "Mother-Russia."
52. S. Greenblatt, *Renaissance Self-Fashioning* (Chicago: 1980).
53. V. Khodasevich, "Literaturnyi subbotnik," p. 6.
54. D. Vygodskii, "Poeziia i poetika: Iz itogov 1916 g.," *Letopis'* 1 (1917): 251–252. The one poet Vygodskii singled out for praise was V. Maiakovskii ("Prostoe kak mychanie"). See also a review of *Stone* II in *Letopis'* 5 (1916): 288–289, where *Stone* was described as "a lifeless jewel." *Vestnik znaniia* reviewed *Stone* together with *Lyrika,* by Grigorii Aronson, arriving at the conclusion that the two books "were equal before the Muse": "Those who like subtle poetry designed to impress with its style, abstract feelings, salon sophistication, humor *du belle esprit* will prefer the artistry of Mandelstam; those who are more captivated by the tender melancholy of autumnal landscapes and the elegiac voluptuousness of autumnal skies will prefer the sensitive Aronson" (anonymous reviewer, *Vestnik znaniia* 5–6 [1916]: 379).
55. V. Zhirmunskii, "Preodolevshie simvolizm" (1916), in *Voprosy teorii literatury* (Leningrad, 1928), p. 305.
56. "Ia vzdragivaiu ot kholoda" (1912), *SS* 1:28; "Ia nenavizhu svet" (1912), *SS* 1:29; and "Otravlen khleb i vozdukh vypit" (1913), *SS* 1:54.
57. V. Gal'skii (Vadim Shershenevich, the future leader of the Russian Imagists) wrote in 1916: "One supposes that O. Mandelstam has something to say; but for some reason he does not want to be convincing. In order to affect the reader, *to force him to submit,* one of two things is necessary: you have to be either *sincere* or powerful. Mr. Mandelstam lacks *sincerity;* as to power, he does not have it yet" ("O. Mandel'shtam. Kamen'. Stikhi" [review], *Novaiia zhizn': Literaturno-obshchestvennyi al'manakh* 4 [Moscow, 1916]: 188).
58. A. Blok, "Pis'ma o poezii" (1908), *SS* 5, pp. 277–302, esp. pp. 277 ff. Note that the poet whom Blok selected as a negative example of the value of "sincerity" in poetry was N. M. Minskii, a Symbolist of the older generation and, like Mandelstam, a Jew. One can only wonder how Blok, who was prone to anti-Semitism, would have reacted to Minskii's "confessions." Mandelstam's letter to V. V. Gippius (April 9/27, 1908) reveals that the young poet took special care not to be identified with Minskii for reasons that perhaps had less to do with Minskii's philosophy than he wished to suggest: "Oh, do not worry, this is not 'maeonism,' and, in general, I have nothing in common with Minskii" (*SS* 2, p. 484).
59. W. M. Todd III, "*Eugene Onegin:* 'Life's Novel,'" in *Literature and Society in Imperial Russia: 1800–1914,* ed. W. M. Todd III (Stanford, 1978),

pp. 203–236. See also his "Pushkin, Aleksandr Sergeevich," in *The Handbook of Russian Literature*, ed. Victor Terras (New Haven, 1985).

60. As viewed by the Symbolist theurgists, poetry was to bring a new religion into the world, a task hardly compatible either with deception or with a conventionalized attitude toward verbal art.

61. "Ia znaiu, chto obman v videnii ne myslim" (1911), *SS* 4:507.

62. Zinaida Gippius, after the initial cool reception, promoted Mandelstam in the early 1910s, to which the unfortunate nickname amply testifies (NM 2, p. 34). See also A. Morozov, "Mandel'shtam v zapisiakh dnevnika S. P. Kablukova," *VRSKhD* 129, no. 3 (1979): 137–139.

63. Blok's letter to Belyi (June 6, 1911), *SS* 8, p. 344.

64. First pointed out by O. Ronen in "Mandel'shtam, Osip Emilyevich," *Encyclopaedia Judaica: Year Book 1973* (Jerusalem, 1973).

65. "Iz omuta zlogo i viazkogo" and "V ogromnom omute prozrachno i temno" (1910), *SS* 1:17 and 18. The last stanza of the first poem appeared in the 1911 *Apollon* (no. 5) selections from Mandelstam but was omitted in subsequent publications.

66. The central image may be traced to Viacheslav Ivanov's translation of Baudelaire's "Les phares," "Maiaki" (1905), which reads in part: "O Vinchi— zerkalo v ch'em omute bezdonnom / Mertsaiut angely, ulybchivonezhny, / Luchem bezglasnykh tain, v zatvore, ograzhdennom / Zubtsami gornykh l'dov i sumrachnoi sosny. . . ." (Viach. Ivanov, *Stikhotvoreniia i poemy* [Leningrad, 1976], p. 14). Mallarmé's "Hèrodiade" may have served as an additional source, judging by Mandelstam's use of the famous poem in his "Solominka" I and II.

67. *Golos zhizni* 25 (June 17, 1915). The text of the poem was recorded in the 1910 entry in Kablukov's diary (Morozov, "Mandel'shtam v zapisniakh dnevnika Kablukova"), which was published after the appearance of the articles by Omry Ronen ("Mandel'shtam, Osip Emilyevich") and Kiril Taranovsky ("The Black-Yellow Light: The Jewish Theme in Mandel'štam's Poetry," in *Essays on Mandel'štam*). As a result, the two scholars used the journal publication as the date of the poem's composition. What seems to have prompted Mandelstam to "resurrect" the poem in 1915 was the death of Skriabin in April of that year. Mandelstam associated the event with a whole complex of ideas concerning "Christian culture." Some of the poem's images, such as the ring of the Roman Guard around the Cross, resurfaced in drafts of Mandelstam's essay "Pushkin i Skriabin" (1915). See *SS* 4, p. 100.

68. "Neumolimye slova... Okamenela Iudeia," *Stikhotvoreniia* (Leningrad, 1973). The American edition of Mandelstam has "Neutolimye," which carries a different meaning—"unquenchable," rather than "implacable." The version printed in *Stikhotvoreniia* coincides with the autograph copy of the poem in Kablukov's diary. See Morozov, "Mandel'shtam v zapisiakh dnevnika Kablukova."

69. F. Tiutchev, "Pevuchest' est' v morskikh volnakh." K. Taranovsky, *Essays on Mandel'štam*, p. 53.

70. F. Tiutchev, "O veshchaia dusha moia." On the uses of Tiutchev in

Mandelstam, see E. Toddes, "Tiutchev i Mandel'shtam," *International Journal of Slavic Linguistics and Poetics* 17 (1974).

71. In Russian Orthodox culture, the distinction between the Old and the New Testament as between "Law" and "Grace" (based on Paul's Epistle to the Galatians and later developed by Augustine) goes back to the famous twelfth-century sermon by the Metropolitan Hilarion, "Slovo o zakone i blagodati," and, further, to the so-called Paul's Epistle to the Hebrews. Mandelstam was no doubt familiar with Hilarion's "sermon" from his days at the Tenishev School.

72. V. Dal' lists yet another Russian saying under the *omut* entry: "In a pool—that's where the water demon [*vodianoi*] lives." In 1919 Mandelstam reversed the image, using it in a positive association with Christianity, this time as a religion not opposed to "the Law" but encompassing it (hence the sheepdogs and the shepherd-kings of the Old Testament). This poem, "V khrustal'nom *omute* kakaia krutizna!" (How precipitous is this crystal pool! *SS* 1:106), is obviously related directly to the triptych and, even more specifically, to "V ogromnom omute prozrachno i temno" (The enormous pool is limpid and dark).

73. Cf. Mandelstam's "feminine" self-presentation as a "shell without pearls" in "Rakovina" (1911, *SS* 1:26), a poem under whose title Mandelstam's first book of poetry was originally advertised in *Giperborei* 2 (November 1912).

74. "In a white corolla of roses, ahead [of them] is Jesus Christ." Mandelstam uses *venchik* (corolla) in a similar context in a poem dedicated to S. P. Kablukov and written at the same time as the cycle under discussion. See "Ubity med'iu vechernei," *SS* 2:457kh. For an analysis of this image in Blok, see S. Hackel, *The Poet and the Revolution: Alexander Blok's "The Twelve"* (Oxford, 1975), pp. 118–143. As Hackel points out (p. 119n. 3), the "femininity" of Blok's Christ had been noted in earlier criticism by R. Poggioli, A. E. Gorelov, and R. Przybylski. See also L. Dolgopolov, *Poema Aleksandra Bloka "Dvenadtsat'"* (Leningrad, 1979), pp. 66–72. Pavel Florenskii's *Stolp i utverzhdenie istiny* contains a learned digression—including a bibliography of literature on the subject—on the nature of the nimbus (pp. 672–674).

75. Vl. Solov'ev, "Poeziia Ia. P. Polonskogo. Kriticheskii ocherk" (1896), *SS* 7, p. 330. The subject is discussed more fully in "Zhiznennaia drama Platona" and "O smysle liubvi," where Solov'ev, relying on Genesis 1:27 ("Male and female created he them"), attempts to demonstrate the androgynous nature of God (*SS* 9). Solov'ev's theory of eros became a matter of public discussion precisely in 1910. See S. N. Syromiatnikov, "Liubov' u Vladimira Solov'eva," *Novoe vremia* (May 9, 1910).

76. "Kak oblakom serdtse odeto," *SS* 2:457ts. Cf. also "Dykhanie" (1909, *SS* 1:8), the opening poem of the first *Kamen'* (1913).

77. Vl. Solov'ev, "Zhiznennaia drama Platona," *SS* 9, pp. 226–228. Much of Solov'ev's discussion is based on Diotima's speech in Plato's *Symposium*, and it is worth mentioning that Viach. Ivanov's wife, Zinovieva-Annibal, was known to the family's acquaintances by the name of Socrates' wise teacher.

78. The Russian *rodimyi* carries both connotations and is frequently used as an adjective of endearment. Cf. Tiutchev's usage in "Vetr nochnoi," with which Mandelstam was thoroughly familiar and which he employed in "Khaos iudeiskii," a chapter in *Shum vremeni*.

79. Cf. Mandelstam's "Erfurtskaia programma," a chapter in *Shum vremeni*. One of many examples of Mandelstam's familiarity with Nietzsche is found in his letter to Viacheslav Ivanov, written on August 13/26, 1909 (*SS* 2, pp. 486–488).

80. See "Le destin: Mandelstam poète et martyr de son temps," chapter 1 of N. Struve, *Ossip Mandelstam* (Paris, 1982). The two parts of this title do go very well together.

81. See, for example, G. Levinton and R. D. Timenchik, "Kniga K. F. Taranovskogo o poezii O. E. Mandel'shtama," *RL* VI-2 (1978). Very interesting in this regard are the recently published memoirs of Mandelstam's 1930s friend B. S. Kuzin. He wrote: "Had I continued my acquaintance with N. Ia. [Mandelstam], then I would have inevitably come in contact with those who are creating—I can't find a better word—the cult of Mandelstam. I like neither salons nor cults. I want to retain my memory of O. E. [Mandelstam] as my dearest friend. The object of a cult, *ipso facto*, is not a friend" (Kuzin, "Ob O. E. Mandel'shtame," *VRSKhD* 140, nos. 3–4 [1983]: 128).

82. Weber defined the sentiment experienced by followers of a charismatic personality as "devotion to the extraordinary and unheard-of, to what is strange to all rule and tradition and which therefore is viewed as divine" (*Essays in Sociology*, ed. H. H. Gerth and C. Wright Mills [New York, 1958], p. 249).

III

1. The review may have been arranged by Vladimir Piast, a frequent contributor to the newspaper and at that time a close friend of Osip Mandelstam. See Vl. Piast, *Vstrechi* (Moscow, 1929). See also Blok's diaries for October 26, 1911: "In the evening we are having tea at 'Kvisiani'—myself, Piast, and Mandelstam (the eternal) [*sic*]" (A. Blok, *SS* 7, p. 78; see also p. 150).

2. For biographical information on Mandelstam circa 1913, see Kablukov's "Diary" (A. Morozov, "Mandel'shtam v zapisiakh dnevnika S. P. Kablukova," *VRSKhD* 129, no. 3 [1979]); Piast's *Vstrechi*; Kuzmin's *Plavaiushchie-puteshestvuiushchie*; Tager's "Vospominaniia"; and Timenchik's "Zametki ob akmeizme" (*RL* 7/8 [1974]).

3. Cf. Viacheslav Ivanov's first book of poetry, *Guiding Stars* (1901), and his first book of essays, *Across the Stars* (1909). See also the polemics around the closure of *The Divine Comedy* in *Trudy i dni* (1912). On the stars as an ambivalent image in Mandelstam, see NM 1, p. 215; and L. Ginzburg, "Poetika Osipa Mandel'shtama" (1966), contained in both *O lirike*, 2d ed. (Leningrad, 1974), and *O starom i novom* (Leningrad, 1982). Cf. further Maiakovskii, "Na smert' Esenina"; Akhmatova, "Vse dushi milykh na vysokikh zvezdakh" (1921); or Mandelstam, "Mne v serdtse dlinnoi bulabkoiu opustitsia vdrug

Notes to Pages 57–59

zvezda" ("Ia vzdragivaiu ot kholoda," 1912); "Zolotye zvezdy v koshel'ke" ("Zolotoi," 1912); "No razve tak zvezda mertsaet" ("Na strashnoi vysote bluzhdaiushchii ogon'," 1918); "Grifel'naia oda" (1923); "1 ianvaria 1924" (1924); "Stilhi o neizvestnom soldate" (1937). Omry Ronen deals extensively with the star symbolism in Mandelstam's poetry. See his ("K siuzhetu 'Stikhov o neizvestnom soldate' Mandel'shtama," *SH* 4 [1979], pp. 214 ff.), where he links Mandelstam's early usage of the image to H. G. Wells's story "The Crystal Egg." See also Wells's *The Star*. For a more extensive treatment of the theme, see O. Ronen, "Osip Mandel'štam: An Ode and an Elegy" (Ph.D. diss., Harvard University, 1976), pp. 108–111; and idem, *An Approach to Mandel'štam* (Jerusalem, 1983), pp. 61–74. I briefly return to this subject in chapter 6.

4. "Ia nenavizhu svet" (1912), *SS* 1:29.

5. Among the Greeks, Silenus, a satyr, was known as a tutor to the young Dionysus—an unequivocal invitation to read the tragedy in the Nietzschean key.

6. This image may have been retrospectively interpreted in terms of the famous painting by Leon Bakst, *Terror antiquus* (1909), and an analysis of it performed by Viacheslav Ivanov in his essay "Drevnii uzhas" (1909).

7. "Innokentii Annenskii, Famira-kifared. Vakkhicheskaia drama" (1913), *SS* 2, p. 416. Mandelstam's comments elsewhere about Annenskii have been used to define Mandelstam's own work. In the same review, insisting that *Thamyris* was for reading rather than seeing, Mandelstam declared incredulously: "Why, indeed, should the cymbals and the flute that had been transformed into words be returned to the primordial state of sound?" In his "Silentium" (1909), Mandelstam called for the opposite in nearly the same words. See also "O prirode slova," where he uses allusions to his own poetry to describe Annenskii (*SS* 2, pp. 252–253), and "Pis'mo o russkoi poezii," where he presents Annenskii as an ideal "organic poet" in order to give historical legitimacy to his own views (*SS* 3, pp. 34–35).

8. N. Gumilev, "Nasledie simvolizma i akmeizm," S. Gorodetskii, "Nekotorye techeniia v sovremennoi russkoi poezii" (both appeared in *Apollon* 1 [1913]); and Mandelstam's "Utro akmeizma" (*SS* 2, pp. 320–325). Mandelstam's essay was written, most likely, around the same time as Gumilev's and Gorodetskii's but was not published until 1919 during the Acmeists' second major attempt to outbid the Futurists for the leading role in poetry.

9. *Okhrannaia gramota*, *SS* 3, p. 273 (quoted in the epigraph to this section). Maiakovskii's *Vladimir Maiakovskii: A Tragedy in Two Acts with a Prologue and an Epilogue* was staged in Petersburg in December 1913. See V. Katanian, *Maiakovskii* (Moscow, 1961), pp. 50 ff.

10. Cf. Ivanov's treatment of the Promethean myth: "Prometheus's hope that he would be redeemed by Dionysus is the hope for the triumph of the Dionysian essence in human nature. Calling forth into being the tribe of man, he (Prometheus) knows that he will be crucified, and nevertheless trusts that he will be saved by it [crucifixion]. Such is his sacrificial humility in rebellion and conflict; such is his self-exhaustion [*samoistoshchenie;* literally, "kenosis"] in hate and in love" (Viach. Ivanov, "O deistvii i deiastve" [On Action and

Agon], *SS* 2, p. 168). The essay was composed in 1919 to serve as a foreword to Ivanov's tragedy *Prometheus*. See also his "O sushchestve tragedii" (On the Nature of Tragedy, 1912), where Ivanov gives a "Pauline" gloss to tragedy; and a postscriptum, "O liricheskoi teme" (On the Lyric Theme), where Ivanov makes a distinction between "triadic" ("Apollonian") and "diadic" ("Dionysian") types of lyric poetry. The Acmeists tended to cultivate the latter type (viz. "vos'mistishiia" octets). See also T. Zielinski (F. F. Zelinskii), *Iz zhizni idei*. Cf. R. D. Timenchik, "Zametki ob akmeizme II," *RL* V-3 (1977).

11. According to Ivanov, a "diadic," Dionysian lyric poet "intentionally avoids the ultimate reconciling harmony in order to achieve a greater effectiveness for his sounds which must for a long time continue to create tension in and overwhelm the soul of the *listener* until by fully experiencing them [the sounds of a poem] he [the listener] perceives their *cathartic* strength" [italics are mine] ("O liricheskoi teme," *SS* 2, p. 204). See also the preceding note.

12. See Piast's essay "O chtenii Blokom stikhov" (in *Ob Aleksandre Bloke* [Petrograd, 1921]), in which he discusses Blok's stage training as well as the interest professional actors showed in Blok's recitals.

13. Writers for whom this issue was crucial include: Pushkin, Lermontov, Nekrasov, Ivanov, Blok, Eikhenbaum, Tynianov.

14. Popularity of Nietzsche's "eternal recurrence" among the Acmeists is noted in Levin et al., "Russkaia semanticheskaia poetika kak potentsial'naia kul'turnaia paradigma," *RL* 7/8 (1974). Mandelstam's interest in Vico's theory of history (see NM 1) should be seen in a similar light.

15. Viach. Ivanov, "O sushchestve tragedii."

16. A. N. Veselovskii, "Tri glavy iz istoricheskoi poetiki," in *Istoricheskaia poetika* (Moscow, 1940).

17. See, for example, Blok's speeches on the death of Komissarzhevskaia and Vrubel' (1910), as well as Mandelstam's "Komissarzhevskaia" (a chapter in his *Shum vremeni* [1925], in *SS* 2).

18. A similar fusion of theatrical convention with the motif of Christian redemption informs "Hamlet," the opening poem of the Zhivago cycle in Pasternak's eponymous novel. On the "theatrical" aspect of Pasternak's "poet," see Michel Aucouturier, "The Legend of the Poet and the Image of the Actor in the Short Stories of Pasternak," *Studies in Short Fiction* 3 (1966): 225–235; see also his "The Metonymous Hero, or the Beginnings of Pasternak the Novelist," *Books Abroad* 44 (Spring 1977): 222–227. See also N. A. Nilsson, "Life as Ecstasy and Sacrifice: Two Poems by Pasternak," *Scando-Slavica* 5 (1959).

19. Such a leader "knows only inner determination and only inner restraint. The holder of charisma seizes the task that is adequate for him and demands obedience and a following by virtue of his mission. . . . If they [the followers] recognize him, he is their master—so long as he knows how to maintain recognition by 'proving' himself. But he does not derive his 'right' from their will, in the manner of an election. Rather, the reverse holds: it is the *duty* of those to whom he addresses his mission to recognize him as their charismatically qualified leader" (Weber, *Essays in Sociology* [New York, 1958], pp. 246 ff.).

20. "O sobesednike" (1914), *SS* 2, p. 234.

21. Weber, *Essays,* p. 249.

22. For example, Iu. Tynianov, "Literaturnyi fakt" (1924) and "O literaturnoi evoliutsii" (1927), in *Poetika. Istoriia literatury. Kino* (Moscow, 1977); or Boris Eikhenbaum's introduction to *Anna Akhmatova: Opyt analiza* (Petersburg, 1923) and his emphasis on the Acmeists' choice of Annenskii as a representative of the earlier, "pure" modernism that was overrun, as it were, by the later offsprings of the movement, the Symbolist theurgists (pp. 25 ff.).

23. Concerning the plans of the Acmeists to enroll Briusov's support for their literary assault, see G. Superfin and R. Timenchik, "Pis'ma A. Akhmatovoi k V. Ia. Briusovu," in *Gosudarstvennaia publichnaia biblioteka SSSR imeni V. I. Lenina. Zapiski otdela rukopisei,* vol. 32 (Moscow, 1972), pp. 272–280. See also N. Gumilev, *Neizdannye stikhi i pis'ma* (Paris, 1980), especially Gumilev's correspondence with Briusov (letters 44 ff.).

24. It is no accident that among the major poets of modern Russia, Briusov was the only one who held a regular, salaried position in publishing—moreover, publishing of fiction and poetry. Money, particularly in the form of a regular salary, together with professional loyalty to a "worldly" literary institution, ran contrary to any pretension to a poet's "prophetic" calling. See Max Weber, *Charisma and Institution Building* (New York, 1968), p. 55, on Stefan George and his circle.

25. On Annenskii and his increasing influence and visibility in the late 1900s, see R. Timenchik, "Zametki ob akmeizme III" *RL* IX-2 (1981); Superfin and Timenchik, "Pis'ma A. Akhmatovoi"; and S. Driver, "Acmeism," *Slavic and East European Journal* 2 (1968).

26. "Poet" ("Poka ne trebuet poeta").

27. I. Annenskii, "Tragediia Ippolita i Fedry" (1902), in *Knigi otrazhenii* (Moscow, 1979), pp. 383–384, reprinted from Annenskii's translations of Euripides (*Teatr Evripida. Polnyi stikhotvornyi perevod I. F. Annenskogo,* vol. 1 [St. Petersburg, 1908], pp. 329–349).

28. "Marble fly" was Velemir Khlebnikov's nickname for the author of *Stone.* See L. Brik, "Maiakovskii i chuzhie stikhi. Iz vospominanii," *Znamia* 3 (1940): 182.

29. B. Livshits, *Polutoroglazyi strelets* (New York, 1978; reprint of the 1933 Moscow edition), pp. 2–34. See also Vl. Markov, *Russian Futurism: A History* (Berkeley and Los Angeles, 1968). Cf. Mandelstam's declaration that Acmeism traces its genealogy to the "Romance soil circa 1200" ("Utro Acmeisma," *SS* 2, p. 325).

30. For example, El. Kuzmina-Karavaeva's book of poetry *Skifskie cherepki* or Mandelstam's poem of the period "O vremenakh prostykh i grubykh" (1914, *SS* 1:60). See V. Galakhov (V. V. Gippius), "Tsekh poetov," *Zhizn',* vol. 5 (Odessa, 1918), p. 12. Cited in R. D. Timenchik, "Zametki ob akmeizme," p. 34.

31. Viach. Ivanov, "Orfei," *Trudy i dni* 1 (January–February 1912): 63.

32. In 1911, Mandelstam produced what appears to be a cycle of love

poems, none of which he included in any of the three editions of *Stone*. See *SS* 1:156, 1:175, 1:241, 4:510, 4:509, and possibly 4:506.

33. Annenskii, *Knigi otrazhenii*, p. 395. In his introduction to *Teatr Evripida* (vol. 1, p. vi), Annenskii wrote that in his prefaces to each tragedy he "sometimes had to touch on social and political themes."

34. See Anastasiia Chebotarevskaia's letter to Viacheslav Ivanov (January 21, 1913) in *LN* 92 (1983), bk. 3, pp. 409 ff.

35. G. Ivanov, *Peterburgskie zimy* (New York, 1952), p. 125. See also Mandelstam's humorous poem "V deviatsot trinadtsatom, kak iabloko rumian" (November–December 1913), which attributes the following sins to the son born of "monstrous parents": pawning family silver and clothes and running up fantastic debts with the "money changers" (*SS* 1:421).

36. Vl. Maiakovskii, *Oblako v shtanakh* (1914–15).

37. A quarter of a century later, these "twenty-two-year-olds" would be parading as gassed soldiers, cripples, convicts, and ghosts in Mandelstam's own final "accounting"—his "Verses on the Unknown Soldier: An Oratorio" (Stikhi o neizvestnom soldate, 1937).

38. N. Gumilev, "Nasledie simvolizma i akmeizm," *Apollon* 1 (1913): 43–44.

39. Mandelstam, "Utro akmeizma" (1912–13?), *SS* 2, p. 232.

40. "O sobesednike" (1914), *SS* 2, pp. 234, 235, 239. Mandelstam's attitude to S. Nadson (1862–87) was not a simple one. The ridicule to which he subjected the "martyr" of the 1880s in *The Noise of Time* contains more than a grain of self-parody, coming as it did from a poet who was accustomed to commanding audiences in a similar way. It is significant that Mandelstam's "Za gremuchuiu doblest' griadushchikh vekov" (1931) was composed in the "key" of Nadson's "Ver', nastanet pora i pogibnet Vaal." In *The Noise of Time* he chose this very poem as an emblem of "Nadsonovism" ("nadsonovshchina s ee idealom i Vaalom"). According to recently published memoirs of S. Lipkin, Mandelstam was aware of the echo (see S. Lipkin, "Ugl', pylaiushchii ognem," in *Vnutrennie protivorechiia* 7 [1984]).

41. Mandelstam, "Petr Chaadaev" (1914), *SS* 2, pp. 290–292.

42. "Posokh" (1915), *SS* 1:69. Cf. Viach. Ivanov, "Lira i os'" (1914); S. Gorodetskii, "Posokh" (addressed to Mandelstam); A. Pushkin, "V evreiskoi khizhine lampada." Mandelstam's "Petr Chaadaev" helps to elucidate many images in this poem. Even though his name is never mentioned, the essay owes much to Alexander Herzen, who was able to transform what was a sad necessity for Chaadaev (Russia's "ferity") into a blessing and a virtue of freedom. See especially Herzen's *From the Other Shore* and *On the Development of Revolutionary Ideas in Russia*. For a Chaadaevian subtext, see G. P. Struve, "Ital'ianskie obrazy v poezii Osipa Mandel'shtama," *Studi in onore di Ettore Lo Gatto e Giovanni Maver* (Rome, 1962).

43. See also S. Freud, "The Antithetical Sense of Primal Words" (1910), *Standard Edition*, vol. 11.

44. *Euripides, Hippolytos*, griechisch und deutsch von U. von Wilamowitz-

Moellendorff (Berlin, 1891); cited in Annenskii, *Knigi otrazhenii*, p. 396. A. W. Schlegel, *Comparaison entre "Phèdre" de Racine et celle d'Euripide* (Oxford, 1962; reprint of the 1807 Paris edition), p. 104.

45. Annenskii, "Tragediia Ippolita i Fedry," in *Knigi otrazhenii*, pp. 296 ff.

46. According to Nadezhda Mandelstam (NM 2, p. 121), this presentation did indeed take place (she is less sure in her first book, NM 1, p. 182). However, according to the list of the meetings of the Assembly compiled by J. Scherrer (*Die St. Petersburger Religiös-Philosophischen Vereinigungen* [Berlin, 1973]), it did not. I find it quite plausible, however, that Mandelstam read the paper for a similar audience in a different gathering. For discussion of the paper, see C. Brown, *Mandelstam* (Cambridge, 1973); NM 1 and NM 2 (especially the chapter "The Young Levite"); N. Struve, *Ossip Mandelstam* (Paris, 1982); and J. G. Harris's introduction and annotations to "Pushkin and Skriabin" (Mandelstam, *Complete Critical Prose and Letters* [Ann Arbor, 1979]).

47. Out of nine sessions of the St. Petersburg Religious-Philosophical Assembly between November 1914 and April 1915, at least eight were devoted to Russian nationalism. The first wartime session (November 26, 1914) centered on two papers, A. A. Meier's "The Religious Meaning of Messianism" (Religioznyi smysl messianizma) and D. S. Merezhkovskii's "On the Religious Lie of Nationalism" (O religioznoi lzhi natsionalizma); the third focused on Zinaida Gippius's "History in Christianity," the fifth on a discussion of the first two sessions. At the sixth session, S. M. Solov'ev read his "On Contemporary Patriotism"; and at the seventh, S. I. Gessen's "The Idea of a Nation" was discussed. The last two sessions were devoted to a reading and discussion of D. M. Koigen's "Gosudarstvo i religiia." The season of 1915–16 dealt with church reform, the "struggle for religious consciousness," the Resurrection, and the issue of church and state. See *Zapiski S. Peterburgskogo* [*Petrogradskogo*] *religiozno-filosofskogo obshchestva* 6 (1915). For a history of the society, see J. Scherrer, *Die St. Petersburger Religiös-Philosophischen Vereinigungen*.

48. For a discussion of change in Mandelstam's prose, see N. Berkovskii, "O proze Mandel'shtama," in *Tekushchaia literatura* (Moscow, 1930); Mirskii's review of *Shum vremeni* in *Blagonamerennyi* (Brussels, 1926); C. Brown, *Mandelstam;* Nadezhda Mandelstam's discussion of *The Egyptian Stamp* in her memoirs; J. G. Harris, "Autobiographical Theory and the Problem of Aesthetic Coherence in Mandelstam's *The Noise of Time*," *Essays in Poetics* 9, no. 2 (1984); C. Izenberg, "Associative Chains in *Egipetskaia marka*," *RL* V-3 (1977); G. Freidin, "The Whisper of History and the Noise of Time in the Writings of Osip Mandelstam," *The Russian Review* 37, no. 4 (1978). See also D. M. West, *Mandelstam: The Egyptian Stamp*, Birmingham Slavonic Monographs, no. 10 (1980), pp. 5 ff., 27.

49. "Buria i natisk" (1922), *SS* 2, pp. 341, 343. What Mandelstam called the "dropsy of grand themes" found an echo in Boris Eikhenbaum's characterization of Russian Symbolism and its affliction as "thematic extensification" (*Anna Akhmatova*, pp. 8 ff., 29 ff.).

50. Viach. Ivanov, "Vzgliad Skriabina na iskusstvo" (*SS* 3, pp. 172–189), where it was published for the first time. The editors cite the author's

Notes to Pages 69–71

note: "Read at concert-assemblies of the Skriabin Society in Petrograd in December 1915, and in Moscow in January 1916, and also in Kiev in April 1916" (*SS* 3, p. 736). In December 1915, Mandelstam was in Petrograd; in January 1916, he was in Moscow, where he had a long visit with Viacheslav Ivanov (see A. Morozov, "Mandel'shtam v zapisiakh dnevnika Kablukova"). There is therefore little likelihood that he missed Ivanov's lecture. Those who like coincidences will appreciate that the fifteen-year-old Nadezhda Khazina attended Viacheslav Ivanov's lecture in Kiev (NM 2, p. 451).

51. V. V. Gippius, *Pushkin i khristianstvo* (Petrograd, 1915). A sympathetic, though not uncritical, review of Gippius by B. Griftsov appears in *RM* 37, no. 1 (1916), pp. 1–2 (3d pagination). For Blok's response to the pamphlet, see Blok's letter to Gippius of October 20, 1915 (Blok, *SS* 8, p. 444). Mandelstam maintained close contact with Gippius, who was a regular participant in the sessions of The Poets' Guild all through the early 1910s, and he could not have remained unaware of this, his teacher's, *profession de foi*. Mandelstam emphasized Gippius's influence on his intellectual development by devoting to him "In a Fur Coat Above His Station," the last chapter of his autobiographical *The Noise of Time*. We can judge the extent to which Mandelstam identified with Gippius by his choice of the synecdoche "fur coat," which he often applied to himself (see chapter 7).

52. V. Rozanov's "O sladchaishem Iisuse i gor'kikh plodakh mira" (1907), a part of *Temnyi lik* (1911), is another important work in the background of Mandelstam's "Pushkin and Skriabin." See V. Rozanov, *Temnyi lik: Metafizika khristianstva* (Würzburg, 1975; reprint of the 1911 St. Petersburg edition).

53. Vl. Solov'ev, "Sud'ba Pushkina" (Pushkin's Fate, 1897). For example, Solov'ev (*SS* 9, p. 36) attributed Pushkin's "untimely" death to the poet's "*rejection* of that moral force which was accessible to him and which he could have used to his advantage without much effort." Solov'ev's essay was, in part, directed against the growing cult of Pushkin among the early Russian Nietzscheans, including, no doubt, D. M. Merezhkovskii's essay on Pushkin in his collection *Vechnye sputniki* (Eternal Companions) (St. Petersburg, 1896).

54. Gippius, *Pushkin i khristianstvo*, pp. 6–7. The reference to Merezhkovskii is explicit: "I believe that Merezhkovskii will accept my understanding of Pushkin, although it differs from the one he had voiced before [in *Vechnye sputniki*], because I shall be speaking about Pushkin as a phenomenon of religious life."

55. Vl. Solov'ev, "Sud'ba Pushkina," *SS* 9, p. 50.

56. V. V. Gippius's 1915 pamphlet *Pushkin i khristianstvo* was based on a lecture, "Pushkin," which he delivered before the St. Petersburg Religious-Philosophical Assembly on November 21, 1911. For Blok's response to the lecture, see Blok's diary for 1911 (Blok, *SS* 7, p. 95).

57. Gippius, *Pushkin i khristianstvo*, pp. 6–7.

58. Ibid., pp. 7–8, 10.

59. Ibid., p. 43.

60. See, for example, Igor' Glebov [B. V. Asaf'ev], *Skriabin. Opyt kharakteristiki* (Berlin, 1923).

61. Viach. Ivanov, "Vzgliad Skriabina na iskusstvo" (1915), *SS* 3, pp. 175, 187.

62. At least at that time, Viacheslav Ivanov, however, considered himself a proper Russian Orthodox believer. See, for example, his "Staraia i novaia vera" (The Old and the New Faith, 1916), in which he criticizes Nicholas Berdiaev from expressly Russian Orthodox positions.

63. Mandelstam, *SS* 2, pp. 314 ff.

64. N. Struve, *Ossip Mandelstam,* pp. 115–130.

65. An early formulation of Viacheslav Ivanov's position may be found in his 1904 poem "Sloki" ("Kto skazhet: 'Zdes' ogon'"—o peple khladnom"): ". . . And learn the power of secret action / A priest's sword is Love; Love is murder. / 'Whence offering?' Whence—THOU and I? / All is an offering and offerer. All is aflame. Be silent." A further elaboration can be found in his essays "Kop'e Afiny" (Athena's Spear, 1904; in *Po zvezdam* [St. Petersburg, 1909]) and "Religioznoe delo Vladimira Solov'eva" (The Religious Cause of Vladimir Solov'ev, 1910; in *Rodnoe i vselenskoe* [Moscow, 1917]), first published in 1911 in *O Vladimire Solov'eve. Sbornik Pervyi.* The formula represents an echo of the famous conclusion from Vladimir Solov'ev's sophiological poem "Blizko, daleko, ne zdes' i ne tam" (1876): "I am the altar, and the sacrifice, and the priest, / Standing before you tormented by bliss" (in *Stikhotvoreniia i shutochnye p'esy* [Leningrad, 1974]).

66. See, for example, Viacheslav Ivanov's poems "Orfei rasterzannyi" (Orpheus Rent, 1904); "Zhrets ozera Nemi: Lunnaia ballada" (The Priest of Lake Nemi: A Lunar Ballad, 1903); or "Serdtse Dionisa" (The Heart of Dionysus, 1910), part of *Cor ardens,* from which Mandelstam borrowed the image of a dying artist as a radiant "sun-heart." Lest I be misunderstood, I am speaking not about the form of religiosity preached by Ivanov at about the time Mandelstam composed the essay (some of his contemporary thoughts were distinctly marked by "sobriety") but about the "ecstatic" Dionysian trend that was firmly associated with his name and his earlier writings.

67. "About the sweetest Jesus and the bitter fruits of the world" (O sladchaishem Iisuse i gor'kikh plodakh mira), in Rozanov, *Temnyi lik.*

68. Death, or rather submission to death, constitutes the ultimate element of a kenotic *imitatio Christi,* insofar as it is analogous to Christ's final, voluntary, self-sacrificial "emptying out." There exist a number of studies discussing the particular emphasis on Christian kenosis in the Russian Orthodox tradition (beginning with sanctification of the eleventh-century Princes Boris and Gleb). One of the most relevant for Mandelstam is N. Gorodetzky, *The Humiliated Christ in Modern Russian Thought* (London and New York, 1938).

69. "Death is the crown of life. Now, at the end of my days, I have realized that there is triumph in death, as Mandelstam once told me" (NM 2, p. 124).

70. "Pushkin and Skriabin," *SS* 2, p. 318.

71. "I want to speak about Skriabin's death as the highest act of his creative career" (ibid., p. 313).

72. Ibid., p. 315. This should also explain Mandelstam's assertion, directed at Rozanov, that "Christianity has not been afraid of music" (ibid., p. 318). For the Greeks, music was associated with tragedy and death (Nietzsche), but for Christianity, which "naturalized" dying, there was no need to fear music.

73. Viach. Ivanov, "Sporady" (c. 1908), *SS* 3, p. 117. This particular section ("Sporady III: O ellinstve") was first published in *Po zvezdam* (1909), a collection of Ivanov's critical prose that Mandelstam read with great care. See his letter to Ivanov (August 13, 1909) in *SS* 2, pp. 486 ff.

74. "If you please, it [Christianity] 'forgives' Gogol, too, and Pushkin, and jam, even a whore and whoredom, without which, incidentally, all the saints, beginning with St. Augustine, would not have wound up in its net. . . . Of course, Gogol could have been 'saved.' But there is salvation and salvation: there are 'heroes' of salvation, . . . there is a poetry of Christian salvation, a 'spiritual novel' of sorts. Only martyrs have passed through this; and Gogol became and had to become a martyr in order to enter the poetry of Christianity" (Rozanov, "O sladchaishem Iisuse i gor'kikh plodakh mira" [1911], in *Temnyi lik*).

75. *SS* 2, pp. 313 ff.

76. In his introduction to *SS* 3, Iurii Ivask suggests that the image of the "black sun" may have been associated with Nerval's "soleil noir" from "El desdichado" (*SS* 3, pp. xxii). Mandelstam was certainly aware of Nerval, whose work appeared in translations in Russia in early 1910, for instance in *Severnye zapiski*, in which Mandelstam was frequently published. Many possible sources of Mandelstam's image are offered by the editors of *SS* 3 (pp. 404–411), from antiquity through the Old and the New Testaments, the Talmud, and early Christian literature to *The Lay of Igor's Campaign* and Avvakum's autobiography. Kiril Taranovsky pointed to Viacheslav Ivanov's poetry as a possible source (*Essays on Mandel'štam* [Cambridge, Mass., 1976], p. 87). Nadezhda Mandelstam gives particular emphasis to Avvakum's *Life* ("a book he was always reading"), *The Lay of Igor's Campaign*, Gogol's words about Pushkin's death, and, finally, the eclipse during the Crucifixion in Matthew and Luke (NM 2, pp. 127–128). As she has also pointed out, the association of Pushkin with the sun being buried may go back to Gogol's lamentation after Pushkin's death (NM 2, p. 127). Contrary to her assertion, however, a careful perusal of Annenskii's critical prose yields no instances of "black" or "night sun." The image, however, was common enough in contemporary poetry, and it appears in a Briusovian poem by Mikhail Lozinskii, "Vest'" (1908; in *Gornyi kliuch*, 2d ed. [Petrograd, 1922], p. 73). I have narrowed my discussion to the sources that help define the "trajectory" of Mandelstam's usage without attempting an exhaustive catalog of possible allusions.

77. Cf. Viach. Ivanov's "Serdtse Dionisa" (The Heart of Dionysus, 1910) from *Cor ardens*: "Oh Parnassus, . . . offering a sacrifice, thou concealed in the *solar sepulcher* the heart of the ancient Zagreus . . . the *heart of Sun-Dionysus*." Or consider his "Orfei rasterzannyi" (Orpheus Rent) from *Prozrachnost'* (1904):

"O night sun, sing to thy dark music the testament of day in the tears of darkness." A more recent relevant text: "The lyre-player [Orpheus], both as Phoebus and as the creator of rhythm [Eurhythmos], sang in the night the harmony of the spheres, setting them in motion and thereby calling out the sun. He himself was *the night sun,* like Dionysus, and, like him, he was a martyr. The mystical Musagetes is Orpheus, the *sun of the dark depths,* the logos of the profound, internally empirical knowledge" (Viach. Ivanov, "Orfei," *Trudy i dni* 1 [January–February 1912]: 63). Taranovsky suggests Racine's *flamme funeste* and limits Mandelstam's usage in "Fedra" to the "black sun of *wild and sleepless passion*" (*Essays on Mandel'štam,* p. 150n. 6). Note that a good key to Mandelstam's usage of the image may be found in Vladislav Khodasevich's "Ballada," which thematizes the same usage in reverse: a sixteen-watt bulb of prosaic and meager existence is replaced by the lyre-playing astral Orpheus.

78. Mandelstam, *SS* 2, p. 314.

79. Ivanov, "Orfei," p. 63.

80. Among the prominent figures who paid homage to it were Vladimir Solov'ev, Aleksandr Blok, Andrei Belyi, and Viacheslav Ivanov.

81. Annenskii, *Knigi otrazhenii,* p. 397.

82. "Bessonnitsa. Gomer. Tugie parusa" (*SS* 1:78) and "Sestry—tiazhest' i nezhnost'—odinakovy vashi primety" (*SS* 1:1920). A possible connection between Mandelstam's use of Homer's "catalog of ships" (*The Iliad*) and the lists of war dead published daily in newspapers throughout the war was first noted by N. A. Nilsson ("Mandel'shtam's Poem 'Voz'mi na radost','" *RL* 7/8 [1974]).

83. *SS* 2, p. 314.

84. Ibid.

85. Cf. Viach. Ivanov's "K ideologii evreiskogo voprosa" (1915; in *Rodnoe i vselenskoe* [Moscow, 1917]), a powerful condemnation of current anti-Semitism.

86. "The symbol of this struggle [between the 'ressentiment' and the 'aristocratic' sense of the world], inscribed in letters legible across all human history, is 'Rome against Judea, Judea against Rome—there has hitherto been no greater event than *this* struggle, *this* question, *this* contradiction" (F. Nietzsche, *On the Genealogy of Morals* [New York, 1969], pp. 52ff. [section 16 of pt. I]).

87. The Archive of Osip and Nadezhda Mandelstam at Firestone Library, Princeton University. It seems that the passage was either to precede or to follow the part of the essay where Mandelstam establishes an opposition between the "fertile soil" of Hellas and the "rocky soil" of Rome ("Rome is Hellas deprived of grace") (*SS* 2, p. 318). Cf. also *okamenela Iudeia* (Judea has grown petrified) in the "Christ" poem (*SS* 1:182). In *SS* 4, the same text is published with minor variations. "Hellas will be vanquished by Rome" and "history will reverse the flow of time—the black sun of Phaedra." Although the first of these variants appears closer to what Mandelstam had in mind, the mistake, or rather the slip of the pen, is also meaningful, suggesting that Mandelstam had ambivalent feelings about dismissing his beloved and "native" Rome out of

Notes to Pages 77–80

hand. See especially his 1914 "Posokh" (*SS* 1:69) and "S veselym rzhaniem pasutsia tabuny" (*SS* 1:80), which, according to the commentary by N. Khardzhiev, was composed in August 1915 (*Stikhotvoreniia* [1973], p. 268). Emphasis is added where Mandelstam seems to be quoting his own 1910 poem, "The Implacable Words."

88. "Pushkin and Skriabin," *SS* 2, p. 317.

89. Viach. Ivanov, "Poet i chern'" (The Poet and the Rabble, 1904), included in *Po zvezdam, SS* 1, pp. 709–714.

90. Cf. Mother Maria [E. Skobtsova], "Vstrechi s Blokom (K piatnadtsatiletiiu so dnia smerti)," *Sovremennye zapiski* (Paris) 63 (1937): 211–228. The author, herself a poet, knew Mandelstam and during the early 1910s belonged to the same circle of Petersburg literati.

91. NM 2, pp. 121 ff.

92. S. Monas, in his introduction to Mandelstam's *Selected Essays* (Austin, 1977).

93. A. V. Kartashev (1875–1960) served as a minister of religious faiths in the provisional government. He was arrested following the October coup and released in March 1918. Mandelstam published the poem with a dedication to him in April 1918, but the date in the *Tristia* publication is 1917. According to Nadezhda Mandelstam, the poem was composed in November 1917, perhaps as a response to Kartashev's arrest (NM 2, p. 121).

94. See the editors' discussion of Mandelstam's "black-yellow" symbolism in Mandelstam, *SS* 3, pp. 409 ff.

95. See Mandelstam's 1917 poem "Imperatorskii visson" (*SS* 1:189), which celebrates the fall of the autocracy. In this poem Mandelstam refers to the imperial standard as a "sulking black-yellow rag."

96. *SS* 1:100. Cf. Taranovsky's reading of the poem: "Since the 'Sabbath swathed in precious linen' is . . . the image of the dead Christ, the 'sullen rebuilding of the destroyed Temple' should be explained as a metaphor for the time between Friday night and Sunday morning, the three days in which Christ has promised to rebuild the temple destroyed by him (Matt. 26:61)" (Taranovsky, *Essays on Mandel'štam*, p. 55).

97. *SS* 2, p. 317.

98. "Avtoportret" ("V podniat'i golovy krylatyi"), *SS* 1:164. The poem is dated 1913. According to numerous memoirists, the head thrown back and the eyes closed were the most striking features of Mandelstam's appearance during public readings.

99. Cf. a characterization of Mandelstam by his friend, composer Artur Lur'e: "Most of all, Mandelstam required a *capacity for recurrence* [*povtornost'*]; he thought that a 'beautiful moment,' having fleeted, must repeat again and again. As memory constructs form in music, so history constructed form in Mandelstam's poetry" ("Detskii rai," *Vozdushnye puti* [New York, 1963], p. 170).

100. The same formula of phylogenetic-ontogenetic recapitulation can be found in P. Florenskii, *Stolp i utverzhdenie istiny* (Moscow, 1914), pp. 62 ff.

101. *SS* 2, pp. 317–318.

102. V. S. Solov'ev, "Sud'ba Pushkina," *SS* 9, p. 59. Zhukovskii's letter to S. L. Pushkin (February 15, 1837) (V. A. Zhukovskii, *SS* 4, pp. 607, 615).

103. For Khlebnikov's difficulties and his break with *Apollon*, see Vl. Markov, *Russian Futurism;* and idem, *The Longer Poems* (Berkeley and Los Angeles, 1962). Gumilev, not Makovskii, was the focus of Khlebnikov's dissatisfaction with the journal. See also Timenchik, "Zametki ob akmeizme," pp. 30 ff.

104. I am using this word as Edward Said does in *Beginnings: Intention and Method* (New York, 1975).

105. See Timenchik, "Zametki ob akmeizme." The article is doubly valuable, as it both pieces together a history of the Acmeist fraternity and contains valuable and little-known testimony of contemporaries who at one time or another considered themselves Acmeists.

106. Lozinskii's note of April 15 in Morozov, "Mandel'shtam v zapisiakh dnevnika Kablukova," p. 150. The date on Kablukov's copy of *Stone* II is December 15, 1915.

107. "This encounter with the soldiers and officers and this hour spent in a forward trench filled the soul with quiet faith and firm strength for a long time and allowed us, who are weak, to taste of the nourishment of the brave and strong in spirit" (V. M. Zhirmunskii, "Po Vostochnoi Galitsii s sanitarnym otriadom" [July 1915], *RM* 37, no. 2 [1916], p. 62 [2d pagination]). A member of the Poet's Guild and a friend of Mandelstam's, E. Iu. Kuzmina-Karavaeva (subsequently Mother Maria) recalled two decades later: "The soul accepted the war. It was not a question of victory over the Germans; the Germans were, just about, beside the point. It was a question of the people [*narod*], which had suddenly become a unified, live personality; in a sense, with the outbreak of this war, it [the people] began its history. We had been preparing for this sea voyage too long, impatiently expecting change too long, not to rejoice at the arrival of the appointed hour. . . . Especially firm was the awareness that the end was near. The war was the preliminary to the end. Just strain your eye, strain your ear, and you sense the presence of the messengers of transfiguration among us" (Mother Maria [E. I. Kuzmina-Karavaeva], "Vstrechi s Blokom," p. 223).

108. Noted in V. Kniazhin [Ivoilov], ed., *Pis'ma A. Bloka* (Moscow, 1925), p. 213. Reviews of war poetry by another Acmeist, Sergei Gorodetskii, offer some idea of what Mandelstam's paper may have been about (see his "Stikhi o voine v 'Apollone,'" *Rech'* [November 3, 1914]). Gorodetskii was critical of Mandelstam's more interesting war poems ("Evropa" and "Ni triumpha, ni voiny"), detecting in them a pernicious "Futurist influence." Nevertheless, he approved Akhmatova's extended comparisons between the warriors and saints, qualifying her poems as "a religious act, however small." Was Mandelstam's "V belom raiu lezhit bogatyr'" a response to Gorodetskii's praise of Akhmatova? We may assume as much, since at the time, "all conversations [were] about the War and around the War." See Vl. Berenshtam, "Voina i poety: Pis'mo iz Petrograda," *Russkie vedomosti* (January 1, 1915), which describes an evening at the Sologubs at which Mandelstam read his "Reims i

Kel'n" (*SS* 1:181). See also G. Ivanov, "Voennye stikhi," *Apollon* 4–5 (1915): 85. Cf. S. Broyde, *Osip Mandel'štam and His Age: A Commentary on the Themes of War and Revolution in the Poetry, 1913–1923* (Cambridge, Mass., 1975).

109. Although the term itself is not mentioned in the extant fragments, other code names of the concept are the "chorus" (*khor*) and the "round dance" (*khorovod*). Thus Mandelstam contrasted Skriabin's mute chorus in *Prometheus: The Poem of Fire* with the "Catholic joy" of the last movement of Beethoven's Ninth as a "temptation of a siren" with the "triumph of white glory," as he called the famous movement in his "Ode to Beethoven." Schiller's "Seid umschlungen, Millionen" had been emblematic of the "symphonic" ideal in Russia, at least since Dostoevsky's *Brothers Karamazov*.

110. Mandelstam, "O prirode slova" (1921), *SS* 2, p. 245. "[In this essay, there] appears another feature of the times that has become ordinary—Russian messianism" (A. Bem, "O. Mandel'shtam, 'O prirode slova'" [review], *Volia Rossii* 6–7 [1923]: 159).

111. Cf. Morozov, "Mandel'shtam v zapisiakh dnevnika Kablukova," pp. 146–147. Mandelstam's position prior to this switch might be defined in the same words that K. Mochulskii used to define Vl. Solov'ev's stand: "In [*Istoriia i budushchnost' teokratii* (1888)] theocracy takes on a distinct Catholic form: the author declares that it was not the Orthodox but the Catholic church that had been the guardian of the idea of universality [*vselenskaia ideia*]; it was not the West but the East that had rejected the universal unity; its vehicle [universal unity, or catholicity] is the Bishop of Rome, the direct descendant of Apostle Peter" (Mochulskii, *Vladimir Solov'ev: Zhizn' i uchenie* [Paris, 1936], p. 67). There is no doubt that Mandelstam was familiar with this work by Solov'ev either directly or through Sergei Trubetskoi's work.

112. According to a report in *Rech'* (January 26, 1915), during a recital at the City Duma, Mandelstam read two poems: "Hagia Sophia" and "The Reims Cathedral," a poem based on the newspaper reports (exaggerated) of the cathedral's total destruction by German bombardments. See a report in *Rech'*, September 9, 1914, and, in a subsequent issue (September 11), a companion piece by A. Benua (Benois), who characterized the bombardment of the cathedral, this "prayer crystallized in stone," as a "blasphemy against the Holy Ghost." In late December 1914, Mandelstam read "The Reims Cathedral" at a recital held at Fedor Sologub's apartment (Vl. Berenshtam, "Voina i poety").

113. N. Riasanovsky, *Russia and the West in the Teachings of the Slavophiles* (Cambridge, Mass., 1952); see also J. Scherrer, *Die St. Petersburger Religiös-Philosophischen Vereinigungen*.

114. "Belyi ekstaz," in part, goes back to Innokentii Annenskii's eponymous essay on Turgenev, "Belyi ekstaz. Strannaia istoriia, rasskazannaia Turgenevym" (in *Knigi otrazhenii*, pp. 141–146). For Annenskii, this state of ecstasy could be achieved by a chaste personality. Discussed in W. Schlott, *Zur Funktion antiker Göttermythen in der Lyrik Osip Mandel'štams*, in Europäische Hochschulschriften, series 16, vol. 18 in Slawische Sprachen und Literaturen (Frankfurt am Main and Bern, 1981). Schlott, however, ignored the signifi-

cance of Viacheslav Ivanov's notion of Dionysian ecstasy for Mandelstam's use of the image. See also the discussion of Merezhkovskii's *Khristos i Antikhrist* in chapter 4.

115. *SS* 4:511.

116. Mandelstam left for Warsaw in December 1914, returning to Petrograd sometime in January 1915 (see Morozov, "Mandel'shtam v zapisiakh dnevnika Kablukova"). See also *Peterburgskie zimy* by Georgii Ivanov, whose rather fantastic account of this trip has been largely discredited by Anna Akhmatova and Nadezhda Mandelstam.

117. "Zverinets. Oda miru" (January 1916), *SS* 1:82. See a discussion of this poem in Broyde, *Osip Mandel'štam and His Age*. On Mandelstam's 1916 reading of the poem, see E. Tager, "O Mandel'shtame," *Novyi zhurnal* 186 (1965).

118. NM 2, p. 522. See also M. Tsvetaeva, "Istoriia odnogo posviashcheniia," *Oxford Slavonic Papers* 9 (1964), and several discussions of the relationship between the two poets in S. Karlinsky, *Marina Cvetaeva: Her Life and Art* (Berkeley and Los Angeles, 1966); C. Brown, *Mandelstam;* K. Taranovsky, *Essays on Mandel'štam;* and Morozov, "Mandel'shtam v zapisiakh dnevnika Kablukova." Although Mandelstam had met Tsvetaeva before (July 1915, in Koktebel'), the "romance" seems to have begun shortly after they met again, in January 1916, at a party given by the poet L. Kannegisser (a member of the Poets' Guild) during Tsvetaeva's first visit to Petrograd (see Tsvetaeva, "Nezdeshnii vecher," in *Proza* [New York, 1953], p. 280). At the time, Tsvetaeva was breaking up with Sofiia Parnok (see S. Poliakova's introduction to S. Parnok, *Sobranie stikhotvorenii* [Ann Arbor, 1979], pp. 15–18; and S. Poliakova, *Zakatnye ony dni: Tsvetaeva i Parnok* [Ann Arbor, 1983], pp. 61, 110–114 [Tsvetaeva's letter to Mikhail Kuzmin]). Collectors of literary curiosities will appreciate the fact that Sofiia Parnok was not indifferent to Salomeia Andronikova, the addressee of Mandelstam's "Solominka" cycle. Finally, Sofiia Parnok's brother, Valentin Parnakh—among other things a poet, a dance critic, and a musician who was the first to bring jazz to Russia (see F. Starr, *Red and Hot* [New York, 1983])—was a friend of Mandelstam's and a member of the Poets' Guild. He is the prototype for Parnok in Mandelstam's *The Egyptian Stamp*.

119. "Ia ne uvizhu znamenitoi Fedry" (1915, *SS* 1:81) and "Kak etikh pokryval i etogo ubora" (1915, *SS* 1:82). Despite the fact that it was Mikhail Kuzmin who, according to Nadezhda Mandelstam, compiled the third book and gave it its title, Mandelstam did not substantially change the composition of the collection and included it as *Tristia* in his *Poems,* published in 1928 (*Stikhotvoreniia*) (see NM 1; and N. Khardzhiev's annotations to *Stikhotvoreniia* [Leningrad, 1973], p. 251). Perhaps, if Mandelstam had been able to maintain better communication with Berlin, where *Tristia* was being published in late 1920, it would have come out as *Novyi kamen'* (The New Stone), the title, according to Khardzhiev, that Mandelstam originally intended.

IV

1. The "epic" element in the lyric has been discussed by Briusov and Blok (e.g., Blok's review of Briusov's *Urbi et orbi*). For more recent views, see L. Ginzburg, *O lirike* (Leningrad, 1974); D. Maksimov, "Ideia puti v poeticheskom mire Al. Bloka," in *Poeziia i proza Aleksandra Bloka* (Leningrad, 1981), pp. 6–151; N. Mandelstam (e.g., the chapters "Kniga i tetrad'" and "Tsikl" in NM 1); and L. Dolgopolov, *Na rubezhe vekov: O russkoi literature kontsa XIX–nachala XX* (Leningrad, 1977).

2. R. P. Hughes, "Nothung, the Cassia Flower, and a 'Spirit of Music' in the Poetry of Aleksandr Blok," *California Slavic Studies* 6 (1971): 49–60.

3. B. Pasternak, *Doktor Zhivago:* "Gefsimanskii sad": "No kniga zhizni podoshla k stranitse, / Kotoraia dorozhe vsekh sviatyn'. / Seichas dolzhno napisannoe sbyt'sia, / Puskai zhe sbudetsia ono. Amin'." As Omry Ronen ("Osip Mandel'štam: An Ode and an Elegy" [Ph.D. diss., Harvard University, 1976]; *An Approach to Mandel'štam* [Jerusalem, 1983]) has shown, Mandelstam paid particular attention to the poems that other poets composed at the end of their lives (e.g., Derzhavin's "Reka vremen") and that were therefore most intensely "illuminated by the sun" of their death ("Pushkin and Skriabin").

4. NM 1; C. Brown, *Mandelstam* (Cambridge, 1973); N. I. Khardzhiev in *Stikhotvoreniia* (1973).

5. According to NM 2 (pp. 501 ff.), some of Mandelstam's old friends, specifically Shileiko, believed as late as the spring of 1924 that the poet had been abjectly seeking favor with the regime. What prompted these "rumors" is not clear, but it was not hard to consider Mandelstam a sympathetic fellow traveler in view of his substantial contributions to *Red Virgin Soil*, the almanac *Nashi dni*, and *Prozhektor* (all edited by A. K. Voronskii) in 1922–24. Especially "Vek" and "Nashedshii podkovu," both published in the January 1923 issue of *Krasnaia nov'*, may lend themselves to such an interpretation.

6. R. A. Maguire, *Red Virgin Soil: Soviet Literature in the 1920s* (Princeton, 1968), p. 32. See also E. Dinershtein, "A. K. Voronskii: Iz perepiski s sovetskimi pisateliami (Vstupitel'naia stat'ia)," in *Iz istorii sovetskoi literatury 1920–1930-kh godov: Novye materialy i issledovaniia, LN* 93 (1983), pp. 535 ff. Cf. L. Fleishman, *Pasternak v dvadtsatye gody* (Munich, 1981), p. 24n.

7. "Ia budu metat'sia po taboru ulitsy temnoi" (1925, *SS* 1:144). The addressee of the poem is Ol'ga Vaksel'. About her affair with Mandelstam, see NM 1 and 2 and the recently published notes of Ol'ga Vaksel', "O Mandel'shtame. Iz dnevnika," *Chast' rechi* (New York) 1 (1980): 251–254, as well as S. Polianina, "Ol'ga Vaksel'" (ibid., pp. 254–263).

8. NM 1, p. 200. Contradicting Nadezhda Mandelstam's assertion, N. Khardzhiev describes the galleys of the 1928 edition as containing substantial editorial changes in Mandelstam's own hand and the hand of his friend, the poet Benedikt Livshits (see *Stikhotvoreniia* [1973], p. 312 [annotations to no. 276]). In fact, Nadezhda Mandelstam's statements are at times contradictory, and in the chapter devoted to the dating of the poetry of 1920–21 she

maintains that the order of poems in *Stikhotvoreniia* (1928) restores the sequence garbled in *Tristia* (NM 2, p. 68).

9. In 1937, exiled Mandelstam inscribed a copy of the 1928 *Poems* for his Voronezh friend Natasha Shtempel': "For dear Natasha,—I do not know how to inscribe [this]: what joy that I could find [a copy of this] book to give as a gift, however bad it is. I promise not to write such books and obey [her] in everything—under one condition, that [she] obey me too." Signed: O.M., V[oronezh], March 3, [19]27 [*sic*] (Princeton Archive).

10. In the political spectrum of the period, Mandelstam's position came close to that of the "Change of Landmarks" (*Smena vekh,* named after an eponymous collection of essays, 1921), an émigré movement whose goal was to reconcile the Russian intelligentsia with the Bolshevik Revolution (see, for example, M. Aucouturier, "Smena vekh i russkaia literatura 20-kh godov," in *Odna ili dve russkikh literatury?* [Lausanne, 1981]). In early 1922, Mandelstam was actually identified as a "smenovekhovets" (*SS* 4, p. 181). As to his "Hellenistic" program (a kind of a sacralization of everyday life), he spelled it out in both the poetry and the prose of the period, beginning with a poem "Dekabrist" (1918): "But empty heavens do not want a sacrifice—everywhere there is work and constancy." Of particular interest are such essays as "Gumanizm i sovremennost'," "O vnutrennem ellinizme v russkoi literature" (virtually identical with "O prirode slova"), and, most transparent, the recently reprinted "Pshenitsa chelovecheskaia" (The Wheat of Humanity)—all published in the Change of Landmarks newspaper *Nakanune* in 1922–23. On the last of these essays, published in the June 22 issue of the paper, see L. Fleishman, "Neizvestnaia stat'ia Osipa Mandel'shtama," *Wiener Slawistischer Almanach* 10 (1982): 451–459. In "The Wheat of Humanity," Mandelstam recalled Herzen, pointing directly to the origins of his understanding of the future of Russia and Europe. Such uses of Herzen were commonplace in the contemporary press. See, for example, I. Lezhnev, "Velikii sintez," *Novaia Rossiia* 1 (1922): 14–28, where a leader of the Change of Landmarks likewise uses Herzen's "prophecies" to legitimize the Bolshevik Revolution from the "Slavophile" position. On Herzen as an "intense Slavophile nationalist," see K. Levin's *A. I. Gertsen: Lichnost' i ideologiia,* 2d ed. (Petrograd, 1922) (reviewed favorably in *PiR* 6 [1922]: 278–279). See also P. F. Preobrazhenskii, "Al. Gertsen i K. Leont'ev: Sravnitel'naia morfologiia tvorchestva," *PiR* 2/5 (1922): 79–87. Cf. S. Broyde, *Osip Mandel'štam and His Age* (Cambridge, Mass., 1975), pp. 5–6, 9–28, 35–36, 200. On Herzen and Mandelstam, cf. Sydney Monas's introduction to *Osip Mandelstam: Selected Essays* (Austin, 1977), pp. i–xxvi. Herzen's "Buddhism in Science" (noted by Monas) was not the chief source of Mandelstam's appellation "Buddhist." See Vl. Solov'ev, "Buddiiskoe nastroenie v poezii" (1894), *SS* 7, pp. 81–99.

11. V. Briusov, "Sredi stikhov" (review of *The Second Book*), *PiR* 6 (1923): 63–66. The bitterness and unfairness of Briusov's review becomes more comprehensible if we consider his own, compared to Mandelstam's, unsuccessful attempts at introducing high, classical diction into contemporary poetry.

See A. Men'shutin and A. Siniavskii, *Poeziia pervykh let revoliutsii: 1917–1920* (Moscow, 1964), pp. 372–375. Further, Briusov's criticism should be viewed in the context of the savage attack mounted on Briusov himself by the *Lef* critic B. I. Arvatov, who described Briusov's use of classical vocabulary as "counterrevolutionary" ("Kontrrevoliutsiia formy," *Lef* 1 [1923]). "Why did Comrade Arvatov, for polemical reasons, use the argument that he himself does not believe? Is it decent?" (Briusov, "Sredi stikhov," p. 88). Mandelstam could have addressed these words to Briusov. Was Briusov offering *Lef* a substitute victim in the form of Mandelstam? D. S. Mirskii reflected on the incident in a Briusov obituary (*Sovremennye zapiski* 25 [1924]: 414–426). In general, however, Briusov had a high opinion of Mandelstam, "whose poems are always beautiful and well thought out" ("Vchera, segodnia i zavtra russkoi poezii," *PiR* 7 [1922]: 52). Cf. C. Brown, *Mandelstam*, pp. 111 ff.; and Ronen, "Osip Mandel'štam," p. 117.

12. "Liubliu pod svodami sediya tishiny" (1921), *SS* 1:124. Cf. Mandelstam's quotation of M. Lomonosov's ode of 1747 in "Pshenitsa chelovecheskaia": "Tsarei i tsarstv zemnykh otrada / Vozliublennaia tishina." See note 10 (Fleishman, "Neizvestnaia stat'ia Mandel'shtama").

13. "Ia v khorovod tenei, toptavshikh nezhnyi lug" (1921), *SS* 1:123.

14. Nadezhda Mandelstam (NM 1, p. 257) testifies to Mandelstam's owning a volume of Vico's writings in the 1920s. Vico's ideas were frequently discussed in Russia both before the revolution (in connection with Nietzsche) and afterward (often in connection with Spengler). See, for example, V. Pertsev, "V. Buzeskul, 'Antichnost' i sovremnennost'" (review), *Golos minuvshego* 5 (1913); B. Vipper, *Krugovorot istorii* (Moscow, 1923); V. Fridliand, "Krugovorot professora istorii" (review of Vipper's *Krugovorot istorii*), *PiR* 6 (1923); and A. Lunacharskii, "Taneev i Skriabin," *Novyi mir* 6 (1925). On "eternal recurrence" as a specifically Acmeist myth, see Iu. I. Levin et al., "Russkaia semanticheskaia poetika kak potentsial'naia kul'turnaia paradigma," *RL* 7/8 (1974).

15. See the discussion of N. Gumilev's and Vl. Khodasevich's responses to Mandelstam in chapter 3.

16. The first one, "Ia ne uvizhu znamenitoi Fedry" (*SS* 1:81), had been composed by November 18, 1915, when Kablukov sent a copy of it to his friend D. V. Znamenskii. See A. Morozov, "Mandel'shtam v zapisiakh dnevnika S. P. Kablukova," *VRSKhD* 129, no. 3 (1979): 149. Cf. *Stikhotvoreniia* (1973), p. 268. An extant copy of a version of the second poem (*SS* 1:82), recorded in Mandelstam's own hand, bears the date "13 October 1915." This autograph is available at the Mandelstam Archive at Princeton University. According to Khardzhiev, the final draft of the published version (M. L. Lozinskii's archive) was dated 1916. See *Stikhotvoreniia* (1973), pp. 268–269.

17. C. Brown, *Mandelstam*, pp. 208–209, 212–213.

18. "Blessed is he who visited this world in its fateful moments" ("Tsitseron" ["Orator rimskii govoril"]). Cf. further such "apocalyptically" relevant expressions as: "the night of Rome," the "setting of [Rome's] bloody star in all its grandeur," "he [Cicero] was drinking immortality." Cf. "drinking

mortal air" in "V Petropole prozrachnom my umrem" (1916), *SS* 1:89. See also note 51.

19. "Maiakovskii read ["A Cloud in Trousers"] once again, but toward the end slid back into [the manner of] a shaman-conjurer [*shaman-zaklinatel'*]," a June 1915 entry from the diary of B. Lazarevskii (cited in V. Katanian, *Maiakovskii: Literaturnaia khronika* [Moscow, 1961], p. 72).

20. Mandelstam's usage of the "screen" or curtain [*zanaves*] echoes clearly N. Gumilev's words from his Acmeist manifesto "Nasledie simvolizma i akmeizm" (*Apollon* 1 [1913]): "Death is a screen [*zanaves*] separating us, the actors, from the spectators."

21. On "igry" (games) in relation to the "Skriabin Weeks," a series of performances and lectures dedicated to the deceased composer, see A. Morozov's commentary to Kablukov's diary (Morozov, "Mandel'shtam v zapisiakh dnevnika Kablukova"). See also Ronen, *An Approach to Mandel'štam*.

22. Cf. Mandelstam's usage of the word *game* (*igra*) in a 1920 essay "The State and Rhythm": "A conscious creation of history [made possible by the revolution], its birth out of a celebration as a manifestation of the people's creative will, shall be from now on an inalienable right of mankind. In the future, the *social game* will take the place of social contradictions and will become that fermenting agent which assures an organic blossoming of culture" (*SS* 3, p. 126).

23. For a detailed discussion of the uses of Racine and Euripides in these two poems see C. Brown, *Mandelstam*, pp. 213 ff. See also L. Martinez, "Le noir et le blanc. A propos de trois poèmes de Mandelstam," *Cahiers de linguistique d'Orientalisme et de Slavistique* 3–4 (1974): 118–137; and K. Taranovsky, *Essays on Mandel'štam* (Cambridge, Mass., 1976), pp. 150 ff.

24. One 1915 draft differs from the final version as follows. Lines 7–10: "Here she is: what words and how terrible she looks[!] Hippolytus, sensing truth, is avoiding her presence." Lines 13–21: "Like a black torch amid bright daylight, Phaedra ignited with her love for Hippolytus and herself has perished, blaming the son, learning from the old nurse. Forgetting her kin and the royal title, [she] cast a shadow of untruth on the youth, lured the hunter into a trap. You shall be bewailed by the woods, o stag!" Lines 26–29: "But we, following the dead home with a funeral song, are singing the sun of the wild and sleepless passion." The sheet also contains a quatrain that belongs to the "chorus" somewhere at the beginning of the poem: "Let us gather the fruit of the misfortune[,] and for the fatigued Phaedra, the black sun of the wild and sleepless passion shall set." Cf. another draft, one from M. Lozinskii's archive, in *Stikhotvoreniia* (1973), pp. 269 ff.

25. C. Brown, "The Classical in *Tristia*," in *Mandelstam*; V. Terras, "Classical Motives in the Poetry of Osip Mandelstam," *Slavic and East European Journal* 3 (1966); G. Levinton, "'Na kamennykh otrogakh Pierii' Osipa Mandel'shtama: Materialy k analizu," *RL* V-2, V-3 (March 1977, July 1977); N. A. Nilsson, "Mandel'stam's Poem 'Voz'mi na radost','" *RL* 7/8 (1974); and K. Taranovsky, "Bees and Wasps: Mandel'stam and Vjaceslav Ivanov," in *Essays on Mandel'štam*.

26. "Significantly, Mandelstam, when he attempts to legitimize the [notion] of the word independent of meaning, comes close to the Futurists" (I. Gruzdev, "Sovremennaia russkaia poeziia," *Kniga i revoliutsiia* 3 [1923]: 34). See also M. Karpovich, "Moe znakomstvo s Mandel'stamom"; *Novyi zhurnal* 49 (1957); NM 1, p. 377; O. Mandelstam, "Literaturnaia Moskva" (*SS* 2, particular focus on Maiakovskii); R. Timenchik, "Zametki ob akmeizme III," *RL* IX-II (1981); Taranovsky, "A Concert at the Railroad Station," in *Essays on Mandel'štam;* Ronen, "Leksicheskii povtor," "Osip Mandel'štam," and *An Approach to Mandel'štam;* and Vl. Khodasevich, "O Mandel'shtame," *Dni* 65 (1922). See also Khardzhiev's commentary on "Grifel'naia oda" and "Nashedshii podkovu" in *Stikhotvoreniia* (1973); and Vl. Markov, "Mysli o russkom futurizme," *Novyi zhyrnal* 38 (1954). According to Nadezhda Mandelstam (NM 2, p. 514), the original friendship between Maiakovskii and Mandelstam was spoiled by the zealots of the respective movements.

27. Viach. Ivanov, "O niskhozhdenii," *Vesy* 5 (1905), included in his essay collection *Po zvezdam* (St. Petersburg, 1909) under the title "Simvolika esteticheskikh nachal." Cf. Bakhtin's (1920) characterization of Ivanov's theory in Bakhtin, *Estetika slovesnogo tvorchestva* (Moscow, 1979), pp. 375 ff. See also note 40.

28. *Stikhotvoreniia* (1973), p. 251n.3.

29. "Unichtozhaet plamen'," *SS* 1:73. For a fuller version of this poem (1915), which includes the cross as one of the referents for the "tree," see *Stikhotvoreniia* (1973), pp. 266 ff. The poem was polemically pointed in the direction of Viacheslav Ivanov's 1904 poem "Krest zla" (The Cross of Evil): "Kak izrekut, o brat'ia, usta soblazna vest'? / I Grekh—altar' raspiat'ia, / I zla Golgofa est'!"

30. "The lesson of January 9—regicide—is a true lesson of tragedies: life is impossible unless the tsar is killed. January 9 is a tragedy with chorus alone, without the hero, without the shepherd. . . . January 9 is a Petersburg tragedy; it could unfold only in Petersburg: its plan, the network of its streets, left an indelible trace on the nature of the historical event" (*SS* 3, pp. 130, 131). I hardly need point out that the word *shepherd,* as a Russian saying goes, comes from a different opera.

31. Cf. Taranovsky, *Essays on Mandel'štam,* p. 150: "The origin of Mandelstam's image is clear enough: it is the 'black sun of *wild and sleepless passion.*'"

32. See discussion of V. V. Gippius in chapter 3.

33. "Eta noch' nepopravima" (1916), *SS* 1:91. Cf. Aleksandr Blok's development of Tristan's "autobiography" in Wagner's music drama: "Zachatyi v noch', ia v noch' rozhden / . . . Tak tiazhek materi byl ston / Tak cheren nochi zev [Conceived in the night, I was born in the night . . . So heavy was mother's moan, So black the maw of the night]." Cf. *Tristan und Isolde,* act 2, scene 3: "es ist das dunkel / nächt'ge Land, / daraus die Mutter / mich entstand. . . . Ihr Liebesberger war / das Wunderreich der Nacht / aus ich erst erwacht."

34. T. S. Eliot, *The Three Voices of Poetry* (New York, 1954).

35. Viach. Ivanov, "Predchuvstviia i predvestiia" (1906), *SS* 2, pp. 93–

94; "O suchshestve tragedii" (1912), ibid., pp. 192 ff.; and "Drevnii uzhas," in *Po zvezdam*.

36. A. N. Veselovskii, "Epicheskie povtoreniia kak khronologicheskii moment," in *Istoricheskaia poetika* (Moscow, 1940), pp. 93–124.

37. Cf. another 1916 poem, "The daughter of Andronicus Comnenus": "Oh daughter of Byzantium's glory! / Help me this night / To rescue the sun from captivity. / Help me to defeat with a harmonious song / The luxury of mortal flesh. . . ." ("Doch' Andronika Komnena," *SS* 4:512). The implied "Orphic" plot may be formulated as follows: held captive by the dark eros, the sun can be liberated only with a special song, which the poet can produce only if "the Emperor's daughter," in her own turn, helps the poet to defeat the spell of her "luxuriant mortal flesh." Cf. Taranovsky, *Essays on Mandel'štam*, p. 150.

38. For a possible background for Mandelstam's imagery in mystical literature, see a discussion of St. John of the Cross in E. G. Gardner, *Dante and the Mystics* (New York, 1968), esp. p. 302. Dante's Pilgrim, too, is blinded as he contemplates Christ as the Sun in *Paradiso*, 8th Sphere. Consonant imagery may also be found in contemporary writings such as I. Annenskii's essay "Belyi ekstaz," where the image is associated with the ultimate aesthetization of suffering, a pure artistry of life. Mandelstam's "Pushkin and Skriabin" echoes Annenskii's essay, as does his "Ode to Beethoven" (*beloi slavy torzhestvo*). Consider also Annenskii's emphasis on high noon as the time of the fateful action in his preface to the translation of *Hippolytus*. On this subject, cf. W. Schlott, *Zur Funktion antiker Göttermythen in der Lyrik Osip Mandel'štams* (Frankfurt am Main, 1981), pp. 103 ff. In the terminology of Viacheslav Ivanov, "white ecstasy" corresponded to the "ascent," "the individuated *white* break with the verdure." It is a "symbol of that tragic [action] that commences when one of the participants in the round dance of Dionysus comes out of the dithyrambic circle. Out of the impersonal elements of the orgiastic dithyrambic, there arises the lofty image of the tragic hero, prominent in his individual particularity, etc." (Viach. Ivanov, "Simvolika esteticheskikh nachal" [1905], *SS* 1, p. 825). Mandelstam was most impressed by this element of Ivanov's theory. See his letter to Viacheslav Ivanov (August 13/26, 1909, *SS* 2, p. 487), where he cites this passage; his poems "Dano mne telo" and "Silentium" (*SS* 1:8 and 1:14); and the "pool" poems discussed in chapter 2. See also note 27.

39. A. N. Veselovskii, "Tri glavy iz istoricheskoi poetiki" (1899), in *Istoricheskaia poetika*, p. 211.

40. A. Bakhrakh, "Pis'ma Mariny Tsvetaevoi," *Mosty* (Munich) 5 (1960): 299–304.

41. M. Mauss, *The Gift: Forms and Functions of Exchange in Archaic Societies* (Essai sur le don, forme archaïque de l'échange, 1925) (New York, 1967), pp. 1, 52, 67.

42. E. R. Dodds, *The Greeks and the Irrational* (Berkeley and Los Angeles, 1951), chapter 2: "From Shame-Culture to Guilt-Culture," esp. pp. 38 ff. See also D. Panofsky and E. Panofsky, *Pandora's Box: The Changing Aspects of a Mythical Symbol* (New York, 1965).

43. "If proof of his charismatic qualification fails him for long, the leader

endowed with charisma tends to think *his god or his magical or heroic powers have deserted him*" [italics are mine]. Or: "Whenever it [charisma] appears it constitutes a 'call' in the most emphatic sense of the word, a 'mission,' or a 'spiritual duty'" (M. Weber, *Charisma and Institution Building* [Chicago, 1968], pp. 49 and 52).

44. A pledge places one in a dangerous position, both the one who offers it and the one who receives it. "The fact is that the pledge as a thing given spells danger for the two parties concerned. . . . The danger expressed by the thing given or transmitted is nowhere better expressed than in very ancient Germanic languages. This explains the meaning of the word *Gift* as gift and poison" (Mauss, *The Gift,* pp. 61 ff.). Mauss's etymological excursion is most illuminating. Cf. Russian: *iad-eda* (poison-food) with the Latinate pair *poison-potion.* "We compare the uncertainty of the meaning of *gift* with that of the Latin *venenum* and the Greek *filtron* and *fármakon.* . . . Cf. also *venia, venus, venenum—vanati* (Sanskrit, to give pleasure) and *gewinnen* and win" (ibid., p. 127n.). Cf. Mandelstam's poem "Venitseiskaia zhizn'" (1920), which thematizes this etymological ambiguity: *Venetsianka,* "a Venetian woman," is rhymed with *sklianka,* "a vial with poison." The name of the "pearl of the Adriatic" is itself derived from *veneti* (those beloved or *venal*) and *venenum.* One encounters similar thematization in A. Blok's cycle "Pliaski smerti."

45. "Dmitrii! Marina! V mire" (March 29/30, 1916), in Tsvetaeva, *Stikhotvoreniia i poemy,* vol. 1, pp. 213 ff.

46. "Truly, poetry is the consciousness of one's inner rightness" (from "O sobesednike" [1914], *SS* 2, p. 236). The statement is an important one for Mandelstam's reception, and not only in the memoirs of his widow but in those of others as well. See Emil' Mindlin, *Neobyknovennye sobesedniki* (Moscow, 1968), pp. 82–83. On this subject see also chapter 2.

47. "Takova u nas marinok spes', u *poliachek-*to" (That's how fickle we, Marinas, are, we the Polish girls) and "Novoprestavlennoi *boliaryne* Marine" (the just-deceased boayryna Marina).

48. In traditional Russian usage, the term *nerukotvornyi* (not wrought by hand) refers specifically to the miracle central to the Orthodox veneration of icons: the appearance of an imprint of Christ's face on a towel belonging to a painter who was trying unsuccessfully to catch God's likeness on an icon. The imprinted icon, *Spas nerukotvornyi* (Savior not wrought by hand), possessed miraculous healing powers. The Russian Orthodox church celebrates the translation of the icon from Edessa to Constantinople (994) on August 16 together with the celebration (*poprazdnik*) of the Dormition of the Virgin. The echo of this coincidence is evident in Tsvetaeva's poem. On the legend, see N. V. Pokrovskii, *Siiskii ikonopisnyi podlinnik,* vyp. 1 (St. Petersburg, 1895), pp. 49–52. On the liturgical significance, see K. T. Nikol'skii, *Posobie k izucheniiu ustava bogosluzheniia Pravoslavnoi Tserkvi* (St. Petersburg, 1900), pp. 22 ff. (n. 3), 507–508. At least on the lexical level, the legend might represent a thematization of the representation of Christ as the "tabernacle, not made with hands," contrasted to the Old Testament tabernacle (*skiniia nerukotvornaia, to est', ne takovogo ustroeniia,* Heb. 9:11 and elsewhere). The same expression, it

might be recalled, was used by Pushkin in his "Pamiatnik" ("Ia pamiatnik sebe vozdvig *nerukotvornyi*").

49. "Iz ruk moikh—nerukotvornyi grad" (March 31, 1916), in Tsvetaeva, *Stikhotvoreniia i poemy*, vol. 1, pp. 215 ff. The "shroud" (*pokrov*, also meaning "protection") that Tsvetaeva had in mind referred to the vision of St. Andrew the Fool and his disciple Epiphaneus (c. 936) to whom the Mother of God appeared hovering in the air in the company of prophets, apostles, and angels praying for peace and extending a blessing and protection over the Christians with her shroud. The Russian Orthodox church celebrates this holiday, *Pokrov Presviatyia Bogoroditsy*, on October 1. See Nikol'skii, *Posobie k izucheniiu*, pp. 537 ff. See also N. P. Kondakov, *Ikonografiia Bogomateri*, vol. 2 (Petrograd, 1915), pp. 56–62, 93–102.

50. "Mimo nochnykh bashen" (March 31, 1916), in Tsvetaeva, *Stikhotvoreniia i poemy*, vol. 1, p. 216.

51. Cf. "Pushkin and Skriabin," *SS* 2.

52. "O etot vozdukh, smutoi p'ianyi" (April 1916). In *Tristia*, the word *mir* is spelled with the Russian letter "i" (not the "iota"), which is why it is translated as "peace." For another version, see *Stikhotvoreniia* (1973), p. 271. Cf. a later, disdainful view of "Muscovite" Russia in "Vsë chuzhdo nam v stolitse nepotrebnoi" (1917?), *SS* 2, p. 457 ch, pp. 457 ff. An approximate prose translation is as follows: "All's alien for us in the ungainly capital: her dry, stale earth, the riotous trading at the bread Sukharevka, and the terrifying sight of the highwayman Kremlin. // Wild and homely, she rules the whole people [*mir*]. With her million oriental carts—a pull, and on she goes: a peasant woman's girth of her market places oppresses [one] like half a universe. // Her churches' honeycombs are fragrant, like wild honey in the thick of the woods, and flocks of birds in dense migrations alarm her gloomy heavens. // In commerce she's a clever fox, and before the prince a pathetic slave woman. The troubled water of the *udel'naia* river flows, as of old, into dry troughs." The modifier *udel'nyi* refers to the "appendage" Russia of internecine wars before the emergence of the centralized Muscovite state in the fifteenth century (hence the "troubled water" [*mutnyi-smutnyi*] of Old Russia's "river"). The poem undoubtedly influenced the prose of a great admirer of Mandelstam's poetry, Boris Pilniak. See Pilniak's letter to Voronskii (1922) in *LN* 93 (1983), p. 570. Cf. also *SS* 1:102 ("Kogda v temnoi nochi zamiraet," 1918): Moscow—Herculaneum.

53. Suggested by V. Borisov. See Levinton, "'Na kamennykh otragakh Pierii' Mandel'shtama," p. 223. On this poem, see also Schlott, *Antike Göttermythen in der Lyrik Mandel'štams*.

54. The theme will receive a somewhat different rendering in the "Solominka" cycle (1916).

55. "Na rozval'niakh, ulozhennykh solomoi," *SS* 1:85. According to Khardzhiev (*Stikhotvoreniia*, 1973), a final draft of the poem is dated March 1916. On this poem and the exchange, see also S. Karlinsky, *Marina Cvetaeva: Her Life and Art* (Berkeley and Los Angeles, 1966), pp. 38–40, 126; C. Brown, *Mandelstam*, pp. 225–227; Taranovsky, *Essays on Mandel'štam*, pp. 11–120; L.

Ginzburg, "Poetika Osipa Mandel'shtama," in *O lirike* (Leningrad, 1974); Levinton (1977); and Schlott, *Antike Göttermythen in der Lyrik Mandel'štams*, pp. 118–133 (particularly on the poem "V raznogolositse devicheskogo khora," *SS* 1:84).

56. Viach. Ivanov, "Zavety simvolizma." See Mandelstam's polemic in "Utro akmeizma" (*SS* 2). To sum up the differences most succinctly, Viacheslav Ivanov was a true realist, whereas Mandelstam was a nominalist, in the medieval sense of the word—hence the other title of the Acmeist movement, Adamism, suggesting that poets, like Adam, must give things new names. See the Acmeist "manifestos" (Gumilev's "Nasledie simvolizma i akmeizm," Gorodetskii's "Nekotorye techeniia v sovremennoi poezii," and Mandelstam's "Utro akmeizma"). For more specific history, see S. Driver, "Acmeism," *Slavic and East European Journal* 2 (1968); and R. Timenchik, "Zametki ob akmeizme" I, *RL* 7/8 (1974), and III, *RL* IX-II (1981).

57. "Russian history moves along the edge, along the bank, over a precipice, and is ready at any moment to fall off into nihilism, that is, into the [state of being] excommunicated from the word" (Mandelstam, "O prirode slova," *SS* 2, p. 248).

58. Mandelstam's "Notre Dame" (1912) is a good example of this Acmeist formula of dramatic balance: "Next to a reed, an oak, and everywhere the plumb is king." See P. Steiner, "Poem as Manifesto: Mandel'štam's 'Notre Dame,'" *RL* V-3 (July 1977): 239–256.

59. Mandelstam, "O sovremennoi poezii (K vykhodu 'Al'manakha muz')" (1916), *SS* 3, pp. 27–30, deals with the predictability of the Symbolist poetic vocabulary. See also V. Gofman, "Iazyk simvolistov," in *LN* 27–29 (1937), pp. 54–105. See especially his discussion of the Symbolists' tendency "to project a verbal utterance onto a ready-made, stable, religious-mystical background which colors the consciousness of people of certain epochs" (pp. 66 ff.). Note that in his essay Gofman generously quotes from Mandelstam's critique of the Symbolists.

60. Manifestos of Mandelstam and Gumilev, respectively.

61. Vl. Piast's speech at the Tenishev School on December 7, 1913 ("Poeziia vne grupp," *Rech'* [December 9, 1913]).

62. Mandelstam, "O prirode slova," *SS* 2, p. 255.

63. NM 2, p. 128. Cf. also the opening paragraph of Nadezhda Mandelstam's memoirs (NM 1, p. 1), a prelude to the poet's arrest and representing a context in which the painting plays a similar, if not identical, role (this time with respect to both Akhmatova and Mandelstam).

64. The expression seems to have been determined by the possibility of paronomasia: RAgózhii, "sackcloth," as a synecdoche of kenotic humiliation, and RAkavoi, "fateful," alluding to a martyr's tragic fate.

65. A. Herzen (Gertsen), *Byloe i Dumy: chasti 1-3*, in *Sochineniia*, vol. 4 (Moscow, 1956), p. 80.

66. "Zametki o poezii," *SS* 2, p. 265.

67. A. Herzen, *O razvitii revoliutsionnykh idei v Rossii* (On the Development of Revolutionary Ideas in Russia), in *Sochineniia*, vol. 3, p. 454.

68. On the reception of Avvakum in the nineteenth century, see E. I. Mamimin in *Trudy Otdela drevne-russkoi literatury Instituta russkoi literatury Akademii nauk SSSR (Pushkinskogo doma)* 13 (1957). See also V. I. Malyshev, "Bibliografiia sochinenii protopopa Avvakuma i literatury o nem 1917–1953 gg.," in *Trudy Otdela drevne-russkoi literatury* 10 (1954): 435–446.

69. N. Struve (*Neizdannyi Gumilev* [Paris, 1982]) believes that Mandelstam had in mind the Iverskaia Church. It would certainly be an important item on any traveler's list of famous sights. The pivotal mention of the Virgin in two poems of the Tsvetaeva cycle, one of them specifically of the Iverskaia Virgin, points to the Iverskaia Church, the shrine of the fabulous icon. Taranovsky (*Essays on Mandel'štam*) identifies the "church" as one in which Maryna Mniszek and the Pretender were married. See also N. A. Skvortsov, *Arkheologiia i topografiia Moskvy. Kurs lektsii* (Moscow, 1913).

70. Discussed in M. Malia, *Alexander Herzen and the Birth of Russian Socialism, 1812–1855* (Cambridge, Mass., 1961), pp. 497ff. For a history of the Russian intelligentsia based on this premise, see R. V. Ivanov-Razumnik, *Istoriia russkoi obshchestvennoi mysli* (St. Petersburg, 1907).

71. Cf. W. Iser, *The Act of Reading: A Theory of Aesthetic Response* (Baltimore and London, 1978), pp. 118–129.

72. D. S. Merezhkovskii, *Petr i Aleksei*, vol. 3 in *Khristos i Antikhrist* (St. Petersburg, 1907). Cf. Iu. M. Lotman and B. A. Uspenskii, "Rol' dual'nykh modelei v dinamike russkoi kul'tury (do kontsa XVIII veka)," *Trudy po russkoi i slavianskoi filologii* 28 (Tartu, 1977).

73. Godunov's investigators determined that Tsarevich Dmitrii fell on a knife during an epileptic seizure while playing the game of "svaika." Similar to darts, this game is played with a knife (or a large nail) which is thrown at the target on the ground (Dal''s *Dictionary*, s.v. "Svaika" and "Tychka"). See S. F. Platonov, *Ocherki po istorii smuty v Moskovskom gosudarstve* (St. Petersburg, 1910), and, a no less likely source, his *Sokrashchennyi kurs russkoi istorii dlia srednei shkoly* (St. Petersburg, 1914), pp. 156ff. A student at the University of St. Petersburg, Mandelstam could have attended Platonov's lectures on the Muscovite state. He might have also been familiar with more specialized literature, such as N. Ustrialov, *Skazaniia sovremennikov o Dmitrii Samozvantse* (St. Petersburg, 1859).

74. According to Dal''s *Dictionary* (s.v. "Baba"), "babki" was played with vertebrae, or with objects of a similar design that had one protruding side called *khrebetik* (i.e., a little spine, or the "spinous process of the vertebra"). Therefore, the translation of *babki* as "knucklebones" (C. Brown, *Mandelstam*, p. 222; Broyde, *Osip Mandel'štam*, pp. 177, 189; and Taranovsky, *Essays on Mandel'štam*, p. 119) might be misleading. Iu. M. Lotman suggested that the substitution may be attributed to the two poems by Pushkin with almost identical titles: "Na statuiu igraiushchego v babki" and "Na statuiu igraiushchego v svaiku" (Lotman, "O sootnoshenii zvukovykh i smyslovykh zhestov v poeticheskom tekste," in *Semiotika teksta. Trudy po znakovym sistemam* 11 [Tartu, 1979], p. 119). For another view, see L. Ginzburg, *O lirike*, p. 281. Mandelstam resorted to the former in "Boris Sinani," where his S-R populist friend

Notes to Pages 112–114

who *died young* is compared to the statue for which Pushkin composed his inscription (in fact one of the last poems composed by him). This constellation of referents is discussed in Ronen, *An Approach to Mandel'štam,* pp. 154–156.

75. The aphorisms of Heracleitos, translated into Russian by Vladimir Nilender (a one-time fiancé of Tsvetaeva and a friend of Mandelstam), were published in Moscow by the Symbolist publishing house of Musaget: *Geraklit efesskii, fragmenty* (Moscow, 1910). This particular fragment reads as follows: "Vechnost' est' ditia, igraiushchee kostiami—tsarstvo ditiati." Mandelstam's "babki" is merely an archaic and uniquely Russian word for casting dice.

76. The "precursor" theme becomes more pronounced when this poem is juxtaposed with Mandelstam's description of his friend Boris Sinani, who *died* shortly after graduating from the Tenishev: "His movements, when necessary, were large and possessed a swagger, like those of the boy playing *babki* in the sculpture of Fedor Tolstoi; . . . his stride, astonishingly light, was the stride of a barefooted man. He would have looked right with a sheepdog at his feet and a tall staff: he had golden animal fuzz on his cheeks and chin. [He looked] either like a Russian boy playing *svaika* or like the Italian John the Baptist with a barely noticeable bump on his nose" (*The Noise of Time, SS* 2, p. 89). In her "Poetika Osipa Mandel'shtama," Lidiia Ginzburg noted a connection between Pushkin's "Na statuiu mal'chika, igraiushchego v babki" and Mandelstam's "In the Sledge."

77. On this image (*igra v babki* and/or *kosti*), cf. D. Segal, "O nekotorykh aspektakh smyslovoi struktury 'Grifel'noi ody' O. E. Mandel'shtama," *RL* 2 (1972), p. 65; Broyde, *Osip Mandel'štam,* pp. 189–190; Taranovsky, *Essays on Mandel'štam,* p. 119; Levinton, "'Na kamennykh otragakh Pierii' Mandel'shtama," p. 234 n. 210; and Ronen, *An Approach to Mandel'štam,* pp. 154–156.

78. Cf. Pushkin, *Istoriia Pugacheva, SS* 4, p. 497: "Suddenly everything began to stir and grew noisy; there were shouts: they are carting him, they are carting him! Following a detachment of the Cuirassiers, there passed a sledge with an elevated platform. On it sat Pugachev, bare-headed."

79. One of the poems Tsvetaeva recited at the "otherworldly evening" at the Kannegissers, where she made friends with Mandelstam (they had met before in Koktebel'), was the stridently pro-German "Ty miru otdana na travliu" (1914). The poem had such lines as "O Germany, my madness! O Germany, my love!" ("Nezdeshnii vecher," in Tsvetaeva, *Proza* [New York, 1953], pp. 277 ff.). The poem must have impressed Mandelstam deeply, for its echoes are heard not only in his 1916 "Bestiary" but also in the 1932 "K nemetskoi rechi."

80. A. N. Veselovskii, "Psikhologicheskii parallelizm i ego formy v otrazhenii poeticheskogo stilia" in *Istoricheskaia poetika,* pp. 164 ff., 173–175, and 185–194. On the use of Veselovskii in the poetry of Russian modernism (particularly Mandelstam), see also Levinton, "'Na kamennykh otragakh Pierii' Mandel'shtama," p. 207. Not only was Mandelstam familiar with this term, but he used it in his own criticism, identifying one of the characteristic features of Anna Akhmatova's poetry as "asimmetrichnyi parallelizm narodnoi pesni" (*SS* 3, p. 34).

81. Cited in V. O. Kliuchevskii, *Kurs russkoi istorii*, vol. 3 (Moscow, 1937), p. 315.

82. Cf. Pushkin (the last stanza of *Eugene Onegin*): "Some are gone already, and those [i.e., the Decembrists in exile] are far away, as Saadi has once said" (*Inykh uzh net, a te daleche, kak Sadi nekogda skazal*). Note the quoting of another poet's quotation—the transparency of the Acmeist *palimpsest*. Cf. C. Brown, *Mandelstam*, p. 224, which identifies the allusion to Pushkin.

83. C. Brown, *Mandelstam*, p. 223; and Taranovsky, *Essays on Mandel'štam*, p. 119.

84. The pronoun was capitalized neither in the Berlin *Tristia*, printed in the old orthography, nor in the poem's first publication in *Al'manakh muz* (St. Petersburg, 1916), p. 113. By contrast, it *was* capitalized in "Neumolimye slova" (*SS* 1:182).

85. *SS* 2, p. 286.

86. "S veselym rzhaniem pasutsia tabuny," *SS* 1:80.

87. "Tsarevich alone was brought from Moscow under guard" (*Tsarevicha odnogo privezli iz Moskvy pod karaulom*) (Merezhkovskii, *Petr i Aleksei*, p. 515). For the "carting of the tsarevich through Moscow," see ibid., p. 413. One can find a more conventional interpretation of the story in "O tsareviche Aleksee," a ballad by K. K. Sluchevskii, who followed the interpretation of S. M. Solov'ev (*Istoriia Rossii s drevneishikh vremen*, vol. 17, chap. 2).

88. D. S. Mirsky, *A History of Russian Literature* (New York, 1973), p. 417.

89. G. Florovskii, *Puti russkogo bogosloviia* (Paris, 1981), p. 457.

90. These two patterns were well within the Schellengian tradition and, in Russia, well within the millenarian scenario of Vladimir Solov'ev. See his "Smysl liubvi" (*SS*, vol. 9) and the philosophical magnum opus *Opravdanie dobra*.

91. Merezhkovskii, *Petr i Aleksei*, p. 316. The reference is to the eighteenth-century Russian tale, "A Story About a Russian Sailor, Vasilii Kariotskii, and About the Beautiful Princess [*korolevna*] Irakliia of the Florentine Land" (see *Russkaia proza XVIII veka*, ed. G. P. Makogonenko and A. V. Zapadov, vol. 1 [Moscow and Leningrad, 1950], pp. 22–41).

92. Ibid., pp. 306, 315.

93. This probable genealogy of Merezhkovskii's John was kindly suggested to me by Simon Karlinsky.

94. Merezhkovskii, *Petr i Aleksei*, p. 545. Those interested in literary parody will appreciate juxtaposing this passage as well as other instances of contemporary fascination with the image of the black or night sun with Kornei Chukovskii's narrative poem for children, "Crocodile," in which the beast swallows the sun.

95. "The obligation of worthy return is imperative. Face is lost forever if it is not made or if equivalent value is not destroyed" (Mauss, *The Gift*, p. 41).

96. "Ne veria voskresen'ia chudu," *SS* 1:90. See also *Stikhotvoreniia* (1973). Interesting observations concerning this poem may be found in Levinton, "'Na kamennykh otragakh Pierii' Mandel'shtama," p. 237 n. 236.

97. Cf. Derzhavin's Horatian "Pamiatnik": "I have erected a monument to myself, *miraculous* [*chudesnyi*], eternal."

98. Mauss, *The Gift*, pp. 6 ff.

99. Cf. H. Bloom, "Kenosis or Repetition and Discontinuity," in *The Anxiety of Influence: A Theory of Poetry* (New York, 1973).

100. Cf. Viach. Ivanov, recalling the mysteries of ancient speech: "na iazyke feurgov 'umeret'' znachilo 'rodit'sia,' 'rodit'sia' znachilo 'umeret''" ("to die" meant "to be born," "to be born" meant "to die"), in "Zavety simvolizma" (1910).

101. Cf. O. Ronen, "The Dry River and the Black Ice: Anamnesis and Amnesia in Mandel'štam's poem 'Ia slovo pozabyl, čto ia xotel skazat','" *SH* 1 (1977): 184.

102. N. Zernov, *Eastern Christiandom: A Study of Origins and Development of the Eastern Orthodox Church* (New York, 1961), p. 444. Another part of the liturgy of the Eucharist bears the name "anaphora" (a familiar rhetorical term), which literally signifies "a return gift" and is used here to mean an offering (ibid.). The Russian word for "Host" is *Sviatye dary* (Holy Gifts). See also D. G. Dix, "The Meaning of the Eucharist" (particularly "The Eucharist as Anamnesis," pp. 243–247), in *The Shape of the Liturgy* (London, 1945).

103. "Vechnye sny, kak obrazchiki krovi, perelivai iz stakana v stakan" ("Batiushkov" [1932], *SS* 1:261). It was published in *Novyi mir* 6 (1932).

104. Cf. Levinton, "'Na kamennykh otragakh Pierii' Mandel'shtama," p. 223.

105. "Vot daronositsa kak solntse zolotoe" (1915), *SS* 1:117.

106. O. Ronen, "An Introduction to Mandel'štam's *Slate Ode* and *1 January 1924:* Similarity and Complementarity," *SH* 4 (1979), p. 148n. In visual terms, Mandelstam's fascination with the "daronositsa" may be related, and not without reason, to the tomb, the sepulcher, and to him who rose from it. The image bears a further comparison with Merezhkovskii's novel, in which the actual *daronositsa* is juxtaposed with the black crate that carried a statue of Aphrodite into Russia from Rome on the order of Peter the Great. Mandelstam's "black sun" and the related images, although highly condensed, echo this juxtaposition. I shall examine them at greater length later on. The "apple" metaphor may be traced both to the "orb," the Byzantine symbol of autocratic power, and to the monstrance, since both objects are crowned with the cross.

107. "Petr Chaadaev," *SS* 2, p. 286.

108. Mauss, *The Gift*, p. 6.

109. Cf. one of Mandelstam's earliest poems: "In the informality of a creating exchange, tell me, who would be able to combine artfully the severity of Tiutchev with Verlaine's infantile jest?" (1908, *SS* 4:498). A central principle of Acmeist poetics of allusion, "creating exchange" was first discussed by Taranovsky and Ronen. See also C. Brown, "On Reading Mandelstam," in O. Mandelstam, *SS* 1, p. xiv ff.

110. Mauss, *The Gift*, p. 66.

111. See N. Berkovskii, "O proze Mandel'shtama," in *Tekushchaia literatura* (Moscow, 1930). Cf. M. Aucouturier, "The Legend of the Poet and the

Image of the Actor in the Short Stories of Pasternak," *Studies in Short Fiction* 3 (1966): 225–235; and idem, "The Metonymous Hero, or the Beginnings of Pasternak the Novelist," *Books Abroad* 44 (Spring 1977): 222–227. Cf. also Roman Jakobson's pioneering "Randbemerkungen zur Prosa des Dichters Pasternak," *Slavische Rundschau* 7 (1935); N. A. Nilsson, "Life as Ecstasy and Sacrifice: Two Poems by Pasternak," *Scando-Slavica* 5 (1959).

112. The topic has been explored in N. Gorodetzky, *The Humiliated Christ in Modern Russian Thought* (London and New York, 1938). See also G. P. Fedotov, *The Russian Religious Mind* (Cambridge, Mass., 1946). On the use of the notion in Blok, see S. Hackel, *The Poet and the Revolution* (Oxford, 1975), pp. 98–103. For a discussion of its relevance in Pasternak's *Doktor Zhivago*, see M. F. Rowland and P. Rowland, *Pasternak's Doctor Zhivago* (Carbondale, Ill., 1967), pp. 173–194.

113. The last words are a citation from Mandelstam's auto-descriptive *Fourth Prose*.

V

1. J. Lacan, *The Language of the Self: The Function of Language in Psychoanalysis* (New York, 1968), pp. 40 ff.

2. "Vernis' v smesitel'noe lono" (1920) has most frequently, and in my opinion incorrectly, been translated as "Return to the incestuous *bosom*" (see, for example, O. Ronen, "Mandelstam, Osip Emilyevich," in *Encyclopaedia Judaica: Year Book 1973* [Jerusalem, 1973]). Although the most frequent poetic usage of the Russian *lono* ("bosom" or "womb," according to the dictionaries of Dal' [Moscow, 1903–9] and Ushakov [Moscow, 1935]) warrants its translation as "bosom" or "lap" (e.g., *na lone prirody*, "in the lap of nature"), this is so because the word is preceded by the preposition *na*, which signifies exteriority. By contrast, Mandelstam uses the preposition *v*, which signifies interiority or, in the case of motion, a movement terminating in a confined space—hence the womb as the terminus of Leah's return. Indeed, the womb is a far more appropriate place for the "pollution of blood" (the literal meaning of the Russian *krovosmeshenie*, "incest") than the bosom.

3. For a survey, see K. Taranovsky, *Essays on Mandel'štam* (Cambridge, Mass., 1976), esp. chapter 3.

4. "Guests from the North" (NM 2, p. 20). See also I. Erenburg, *Liudi, gody, zhizn': Kniga pervaia i vtoraia* (Moscow, 1961), pp. 455, 469–470.

5. NM 2, p. 20.

6. P. Kenez, *Civil War in South Russia, 1919–1920: The Defeat of the Whites* (Berkeley and Los Angeles, 1977), p. 159.

7. Ibid., p. 154. See also N. I. Shtif, *Pogromy na Ukraine: Period Dobrovol'cheskoi armii* (Berlin, 1922); and Erenburg, *Liudi, gody, zhizn'*, pp. 476–477.

8. NM 2, p. 27.

9. See Mandelstam's recollections of the civil war in the Crimea in his

Feodosiia (Thedosia) and "Men'sheviki v Gruzii" (Mensheviks in Georgia), *SS* 2, pp. 111–128 and 195–200.

10. The following *Tristia* poems were addressed to Arbenina: "V Peterburge my soidemsia snova," "Chut' mertsaet prizrachnaia stsena," "Voz'mi na radost' iz moikh ladonei," "Za to, chto ia ruki tvoi ne sumel uderzhat'," "Mne zhalko, chto teper' zima," "Ia naravne s drugimi." See G. Dal'nii (G. G. Superfin), "Po povodu trekhtomnogo sobraniia O. Mandel'shtama," *VRSKhD* 97 (1970): 140–144, and N. Khardziev's annotations to these poems in Mandelstam, *Stikhotvoreniia* (Leningrad, 1973).

11. On Mandelstam's service in the People's Commissariat, see C. Brown, *Mandelstam* (Cambridge, 1973), p. 79, and NM 2, p. 451. It appears that even in Kiev, Mandelstam held a government post that enabled him to live at the Hotel Continental and hire Nadezhda Khazina as his secretary (C. Brown, *Mandelstam,* p. 76). We shall never know why this information was not included in Nadezhda Mandelstam's memoirs. Why did Mandelstam, whose sympathies, at least since the middle of 1918, lay with the Bolshevik Revolution, choose to travel to the Crimea, the stronghold of the Whites? Even assuming that politics influenced Mandelstam's travel plans, it was safer for him to go to the Crimea, specifically to M. Voloshin's pension, than to either Moscow or Petrograd, which would have involved a far more dangerous adventure of crossing the front lines. Voloshin enjoyed a reputation as a man who could save his friends from both the Reds and the Whites, to which Nadezhda Mandelstam testifies in her memoirs (NM 2, p. 21). One can find a plausible explanation—by analogy—in Erenburg, *Liudi, gody, zhizn',* p. 477. See also M. Voloshin, "Vospominaniia (April 1932)," *SH* 5–6 (1981): 501–522. As to Mandelstam's political views during his stay in the White south, they do not seem to have changed at all. Two poems, "Gde noch' brosaet iakoria" and "Akter i rabochii," composed while he was still in the Crimea, provide ample testimony of his leftist leanings. On the former poem, see O. Ronen, "Osip Mandel'štam: An Ode and an Elegy" (Ph.D. diss., Harvard University, 1976), p. 76 ff. (n. 57); see also chapter 8, this volume.

12. "The results of the trials [under Wrangel] were determined in advance. All the accused were condemned to death. . . . In the city center, there were usually ten to fifteen half-naked corpses hanging from the tram poles with the shameful sign 'A Communist.' This made a shocking impression even on the petty bourgeois public [*meshchanskaia publika*] and created a chilling paralyzed atmosphere in the city. It was then . . . that *Tavricheskii golos* . . . began enumerating the evils that the executed had committed against the Russian Army, crudely emphasizing their Jewish extraction. 'A Jew by nationality, also a Jew, of course, a Jew'" (P. Novitskii, "Iz istorii krymskoi pechati v 1919–1920 gg.," *PiR* 1 [1921]: 59). See also Kenez, *Civil War in Russia,* p. 175 and elsewhere; D. Maslov, "Pechat' pri Vrangele," in *Antanta i Vrangel': Sbornik statei* (Moscow and Petrograd, 1923); and V. Obolenskii, "Krym pri Vrangele," *Na chuzhoi storone* (Berlin and Prague) 9 (1925).

13. Erenburg, *Liudi, gody, zhizn',* p. 495.

14. On Tsygal'skii, see E. Mindlin, *Neobyknovennye sobesedniki* (Moscow, 1968), p. 7. Whether Mandelstam was picked up because of his passing contact with the Bolshevik underground (as Nadezhda Mandelstam maintains) or for his dervishlike appearance, or simply for no reason at all, remains a mystery. See testimonials in C. Brown, *Mandelstam,* p. 80, as well as Mindlin's memoirs. Passages relating to Mandelstam's stay in the Crimea, including the story of the arrest, are reprinted in Mandelstam, *SS* 2, pp. 511–529. Mandelstam broke with Voloshin after the latter had accused him of stealing a volume of Dante (*SS* 2, pp. 522ff.). Voloshin's role in this affair and the subsequent arrest is unclear: his own account of the events, still unpublished, is reported to be different from what we know now. See A. Morozov, "Mandel'shtam v zapisiakh dnevnika S. P. Kablukova," *VRSKhD* 129, no. 3 (1979), p. 139.

15. Cf. Mandelstam's description of the relation between events and a poetic text in "Conversation about Dante" (crossing a Chinese river by jumping from one junk to another; the river has been crossed but it is impossible to trace exactly the route one took crossing it). These are very much Bergsonian images and arguments, concerning the unpredictability of the *élan vital* as it moves through matter, of the intuition as it grasps the universe, and of the memory as it *immediately* presents the past to our consciousness. See especially H. Bergson, *L'energie spirituelle* (Paris, 1976), pp. 31 ff. On Bergson as an aesthetician, see V. Asmus, "Estetika Bergsona," *Na literaturnom postu* 2 (1929): 4–18. See also N. Losskii, *Intuitivnaia filosofiia Bergsona* (St. Petersburg, 1922); R. Arbour, *Henri Bergson et les lettres françaises* (Paris, 1955); and T. E. Hulme, *Speculations: Essays on Humanism and the Philosophy of Art* (London, 1936).

16. "Vernis' v smesitel'noe lono" (1920), *SS* 1:109. The meaning of the last words of the poem has been controversial, since the Russian *i Bog s toboi* may, depending on the situation, signify either "leave me alone" or "so be it," or, literally, "may God be with you." Since it is a patriarchal, God-like figure who is issuing the command in the poem, I have settled on the literal option, but "so be it" might have done as well.

17. NM 2, p. 30.
18. NM 2, p. 264.
19. NM 2, pp. 18 ff.
20. See the discussion in chapter 1.
21. NM 2, p. 265.
22. "Bessonnitsa. Gomer. Tugie parusa" (1915), *SS* 1:78.
23. Mandelstam's swallow here is *gray,* an epithet quite "against nature" in the case of a swallow. One might say that a gray swallow is to a black (ordinary) swallow as an ox is to a bull. On the swallow as a bad omen, see A. N. Afanas'ev, *Poeticheskie vozzreniia slavian na prirodu: Opyt sravnitel'nogo izucheniia slavianskikh predanii i verovanii v sviazi s mificheskimi skazaniiami drugikh narodov* (Moscow, 1865–69), p. 348; and E. Kagarov, *Kul't fetishei, zhivotnykh i rastenii v drevnei Gretsii* (St. Petersburg, 1913), p. 272n.12. According to the Russian sayings in Dal', "lastochka" can function allegorically as a harbinger of spring, a messenger, a harbinger of death knocking on the window of a dying man, and a bird signifying speech impairment, or tongue-tie.

See also "Swallow" in d'Arsy W. Thompson, *A Glossary of Greek Birds* (Hildesheim and Olms, 1966); J. Hastings, ed., *Encyclopaedia of Religion and Ethics* (New York, n.d.), vol. 1, s.v. "Amulets" (a swallow in or trying to get into a room is a death omen). Cf. Taranovsky, *Essays on Mandel'štam,* p. 158 n. 18; and A. D. Hope, "The Blind Swallow: Some Parleyings with Mandelstam," in *The Pack of Autolycus* (Canberra and Norwalk, Conn., 1978).

24. "Za to, chto Ia ruki tvoi ne sumel uderzhat'" (December 1920), *SS* 1:119. For an analysis of this poem, see L. Ginzburg, "Poetika Osipa Mandel'shtama," in *O lirike* (Leningrad, 1974); Ginzburg was the first (in 1966) to discuss the poem's Homeric subtext (*The Odyssey,* bk. 4). Note that the "wild Acropolis" is the horse that is pitted against the pliant, "civilized" Troy. Hence the "city's" sensing of its wooden ribs, which paraphrases Helen's "running her hands over the wood" as she walked around *three times.* "The high roost of Priam" is an echo of the high tower at the Skaian Gates (*The Iliad,* bk. 3, lines 149 ff.) from which the Trojan elders observed the battles. Further, one can discern the echo of another proverbial myth of lust, that of Pasiphaë, Phaedra's mother, who hid in the wooden cow to attract the attention of Poseidon's bull. Apart from the Homeric and Hellenic mythology Mandelstam uses here for his bricolage, the poem is associated with Pushkin's "Vospominanie" and with a number of poems from A. Fet's cycle "Vechera i nochi," especially "Na stoge sena noch'iu iuzhnoi." Mandelstam's last two lines contain a pun on the archaic Russian word for "city streets," *stogna,* and the unspoken word for "hayloft," *senoval,* represented metonymically by the "straw," *soloma.* The effect of this pun is to bring together the poems by Pushkin and Fet (not to speak of Mandelstam's own "straw" verses) and make them serve as background for this particular piece. See also G. Levinton and R. D. Timenchik, "Kniga K. F. Taranovskogo o poezii O. E. Mandel'shtama," *RL* VI-2 (1978): 210 n.

25. NM 2, p. 262.

26. NM 2, p. 263.

27. R. C. Elliott, *The Power of Satire: Magic, Ritual, Art* (Princeton, 1960), p. 68. Cf. Mandelstam's own words as he tried to explain, in 1934 or 1935 following his arrest for the epigram on Stalin, why it was that Stalin had not punished him with the customary severity of those days: "Why is Stalin afraid of 'mastery'?—it's sort of a superstition for him, he is afraid we [poets] can cast a spell [*nashamanit'*]" (NM 1, p. 156).

28. Princeton Archive.

29. E.g., Taranovsky, *Essays on Mandel'štam,* p. 60.

30. *SS* 2, pp. 199 ff.

31. O. Ronen, "Mandelshtam," *Encyclopaedia Judaica.*

32. Ronen, ibid., enumerates the following: "Chetvertaia proza" (1930?) and "Kantsona" ("Neuzheli ia uvizhu zavtra" [1931], *SS* 1:236).

33. "Emu kavkazskie krichali gory" (1934), *SS* 1:292. Kiril Taranovsky was the first to point to this allusion to Dante. See his "Tri zametki o poezii Mandel'shtama," *International Journal of Slavic Linguistics and Poetics* 12 (1969): 169–170. It is unlikely, however, that Mandelstam, as Taranovsky suggests, had Belyi in mind in the case of Leah as well as Rachel. After all, it was he, the

speaker of Mandelstam's poem, who was "singing" and "weaving" the funeral "wreath" for Belyi, who was both a poet *and* a theoretician. Hence the adversative conjunction "but" (*a*). Compare also with A. Fet's poem "K Ofelii": "Ofeliia gibla i pela, I *pela, spletaia venki;* S tsvetami, venkami i pesn'iu Na dno opustilas' reki."

34. *The Divine Comedy of Dante Alighieri,* trans. and comment. John D. Sinclair, vol. 2: *Purgatorio* (New York, 1939), pp. 354 (the original text) and 355 (the translation).

35. "Mary who sits at the Master's feet and 'hath chosen the better part,' is recognized as the type of the contemplative life; and her sister Martha, who is 'careful and troubled about many things,' is the accepted type of the active life. Dante does not make use of these, but of the corresponding Old Testament symbols, Rachel and Leah, as they were interpreted in mediaeval theology from the time of Gregory the Great" (K. Vossler, *Mediaeval Culture: An Introduction to Dante and His Times,* vol. 1 [New York, 1929], p. 183). "St. Gregory the Great, when the office of the Papacy was forced upon him, bewailed the loss of his Rachel, the quiet life of contemplation in his monastery: 'The beauty of contemplative life I have loved as Rachel, barren indeed but clear-eyed and fair, which, although by its quiet it bears less, yet sees the light more clearly. *Leah is wedded to me in the night,* the active life namely, fruitful but blear-eyed, seeing less though bringing forth abundantly'" [italics are mine] (cited in the Sinclair edition of *Purgatorio,* p. 361). "Martha" and "Mary" were common proverbial referents in the Russian of Mandelstam's time. In the words of an American student of Russian spirituality, the allegory of Martha and Mary was "as common in Russia as 'faith without works is dead' is common here. Speaking roughly, Eastern Christianity is associated with Mary's good part and Western Christianity with the way of Martha and service" (S. Graham, *The Way of Martha and the Way of Mary* [New York, 1916], p. v).

36. S. Mallarmé, *Les noces d'Hèrodiade. Mystère* (Paris, 1959), pp. 65, 69 ("Scène"). Mandelstam attended a performance of the Wilde-Strauss *Salome* while still in Paris and, according to Mikhail Karpovich, composed a poem about the danseuse after the performance. See M. Karpovich, "Moe znakomstvo s Mandel'shtamom," *Novyi zhurnal* 49 (1957): 258–261. Cf. Taranovsky, *Essays on Mandel'štam,* pp. 148 ff. Although both Wilde-Strauss and Mallarmé must be in the poem's background, Mallarmé's *icy* heroine—who, incidentally, stares into a mirror to see in its "cadre gelé" "eau froide par l'ennui"—seems to be more relevant to Mandelstam's Solominka-Salome than the "overheated" maiden casting off her seven veils on a sultry Palestinian night in the eponymous music drama.

37. The lines "*Slomalas'* milaia solomka nezhivaia, / Ne Salomeia, net, solominka skorei" represent an obvious (however rare in Mandelstam) play on a vulgar expression for sexual intercourse with a virgin, *slomat' tselku* (literally "to break the wholeness of virginity"). The drafts of the poem (Princeton Archive) are far more suggestive than the final version, indicating that Mandelstam made a special effort to maintain decorum.

38. "What happens with us in the use of certain names, as expressing

summarily, this name for you and that for me—Helen, Gretchen, Mary—a hundred associations . . . which, through a very wide and deep experience, they have power of bringing with them; in which respect *such names are but revealing instances of the whole significance, power and use of language in general*" [italics are mine] (W. Pater, "A Study of Dionysus: The Spiritual Form of Fire and Dew," in *Greek Studies. A Series of Essays* [New York, 1899], p. 35). On Gautier, see Khardzhiev in *Stikhotvoreniia* (1973), p. 272. The poem seems also to be related to one of the more emblematic poems of the young Akhmatova, "Kak solominkoi, p'esh' moiu dushu" (in *Vecher* [St. Petersburg, 1912]), and, as Khradzhiev noted (*Stikhotvoreniia* 1973), Velemir Khlebnikov's burlesque drama *Oshibka smerti*. On Akhmatova, cf. B. Eikhenbaum on this poem and "Kak belich'ia rasplastannaia shkurka" (to which Mandelstam responded later on in *Tristia*) as eminently representative of the post-Symbolist innovative technique (B. Eikhenbaum, *Anna Akhmatova: Opyt analiza* [Petersburg, 1923], p. 56). See also V. A. Piast, *Vstrechi* (Moscow, 1929), p. 156.

39. Mandelstam's friend S. P. Kablukov, a devout Christian, considered the poem blasphemous, reading it, no doubt, as a parody of the Gospel legend. Confronted with the evidence, Mandelstam was contrite, declaring to Kablukov that "sex was especially dangerous for him as one who had left the Jewish milieu, that he was aware of the dangerous road he was on, that his situation was terrible but that he was incapable of changing the course and even of not composing during this erotic madness, and that he saw no way out except a speedy conversion to Russian Orthodoxy" (A. Morozov, "Mandel'shtam v zapisiakh dnevnika Kablukova," p. 153).

40. "Iz omuta zlogo i viazkogo" and "V ogromnom omute prozrachno i temno" (1911), *SS* 1:17 and 1:18; discussed in chapter 2. On this theme of "reconciliation," cf. Ronen, "Osip Mandel'štam," p. 161.

41. "An obelisk, which does not even cast enough shade to give you refuge from the heat of . . . the sun, does not render any useful service but forces you to lift your eyes to heaven; so the great temple of the Christian world, when in the hour of dusk you stroll under its enormous vaulted ceiling and when the deep shadows have already filled the entire ship but the glass panes of the cupola are still burning with the last rays of the setting sun, arouses in you a greater wonderment rather than [merely] charming you with its superhuman scale" (M. Gershenzon, *Petr Chaadaev: Zhizn' i myshlen'e* [St. Petersburg, 1908], p. 276). Cf. Mandelstam's letter to Viacheslav Ivanov: "Does a man, when he enters under the vaulted ceiling of Notre Dame, think about the truth [or falsehood] of Catholicism, rather than becoming a Catholic for the sole reason of being under these vaulted arches?" (August 13/26, 1909, *SS* 2, p. 486). For an opposite view, see Mandelstam's "Paden'e—neizmennyi sputnik strakha" (1912), *SS* 1:34. Cf. O. Ronen, "Leksicheskii povtor, podtekst i smysl v poetike Osipa Mandel'štama," in *Slavic Poetics: Essays in Honor of Kiril Taranovsky*, ed. R. Jakobson, C. H. van Schoneveld, and D. S. Worth (The Hague, 1973), p. 368n.

42. K. Taranovsky, "The Black-Yellow Light: The Jewish Theme in Mandel'stam's poetry," in *Essays on Mandel'štam*, pp. 48–67 (pp. 59–64 deal specifi-

cally with "Return"); the following quoted passage is from p. 63. The question of whether Mandelstam relied on the translation by Annenskii or on the original by Mallarmé, two poets whom he valued most highly (Morozov, "Mandel'shtam v zapisiakh dnevnika Kablukova"), is important, since the choice of one or the other for the subtext will yield a different interpretation. On "Don du poème," see R. G. Cohn, *Towards the Poems of Mallarmé* (Berkeley and Los Angeles, 1965), pp. 47–51.

43. W. Empson, *Seven Types of Ambiguity* (New York, 1947). See also N. N. Holland, *5 readers reading* (New Haven, 1975); and W. Iser, *The Act of Reading: A Theory of Aesthetic Response* (Baltimore and London, 1978), particularly on the relationship among the "theme," the "horizon," and the "repertoire."

44. The vulgar anti-Semitic vituperations against Gornfel'd in "Chetvertaia proza" (1930, 1931?), where Mandelstam accuses this "diadia Monia s Basseinoi" (uncle Monia from the Basseinaia Street) of murdering *Russian* poets in the manner of the French d'Anthes, represents a good example of this strange attitude. For in the same work, Mandelstam proudly declares himself an heir of the biblical "shepherds, patriarchs, and kings."

45. Cf. Mandelstam's "Otravlen khleb, i vozdukh vypit" (1913), *SS* 1:54:

> The bread has been poisoned, the air drunk up:
> How hard it is to tend the wounds!
> Joseph, when sold into Egypt,
> Could not be more aggrieved.

This is the only instance in which Mandelstam compared an Old Testament character with his "poet." In "Kantsona" (1931, *SS* 1:236), he vaguely projected the self onto the "Prodigal Son" (see NM 2, pp. 614–624), a projection that does not exclude the possibility of conflation with Jacob's (Israel's) son Joseph, who, though not by his own will, left his father. In fact, the self in this poem also includes Dante, from whom Mandelstam, using a circuitous metonymic route, derived the "Zeiss binoculars," "the psalmist's gift to the clairvoyant" Zeus. I discuss this poem in chapter 8.

46. Cf. R. Girard, *Violence and the Sacred* (Baltimore and London, 1977), pp. 270, 271.

47. See, for example, N. Poznanskii, *Zagovory: Opyt issledovaniia proiskhozhdeniia i razvitiia zagovornykh formul* (Petrograd, 1917), published as *Zapiski istoriko-filologicheskogo fakul'teta Petrogradskogo Universiteta*, vol. 136, esp. pp. 26 ff. See also A. Belyi, "Magiia slov," in *Simvolizm* (Moscow, 1910), which approaches verbal magic as a sort of *fiat;* and A. Blok's "Poeziia zagovorov i zaklinanii" (*SS* 5), which was based, in the first place, on the writings of Veselovskii and Potebnia, among others.

48. See *SS* 3, pp. 409 ff.

49. One may also interpret Mandelstam's formula as something far more innocent, namely, a paraphrase of the biblical metaphor for Israel, *lono avraamovo* (kindly suggested by B. Gasparov). However, the attribute "in-

cestuous" continues to describe this otherwise commendable decision to return to the ancestral fold.

50. See Freud on reversal in dreams, e.g., *The Interpretation of Dreams* (New York, 1965), pp. 361–363.

51. The element of apogamy (as in Zeus giving birth to Athena) is another feature that links "Return" to Mallarmé's "Don du poème." However, Mallarmé's "enfant d'une nuit d'Idumée" decidedly represents a poem (as it does in Annenskii), and not, like Mandelstam's Leah, the poet's muse or the poet himself. See Mandelstam's essay "François Villon" (written in 1910, when he was nineteen), which he emphatically placed at the conclusion of the 1928 edition of his collected essays, *O poezii*. In that essay, Mandelstam explicitly stated that the "other" of a lyric poet represented an aspect of his "I," an aspect alienated from the whole ego in such a way that a poet may engage in a dialogue with himself. Cf. T. S. Eliot, *The Three Voices of Poetry* (New York, 1954).

52. In an incest myth, the "inability to connect two kinds of relationships is overcome (or rather replaced) by the assertion that contradictory relationships are identical inasmuch as they are both self-contradictory in a similar way" (C. Lévi-Strauss, "The Structural Study of Myth," in *Structural Anthropology* [New York, 1963], p. 216).

53. See his *Tristia* poem "V Petropole prozrachnom my umrem" (We shall die in the translucent Petropolis).

54. If Mandelstam's 1921 "usage" of the image of "heavy blood" is an indicator, the extraordinary density of blood denoted one's predisposition to historical activism. Thus, the "blood" lines in the poem add emphasis to Leah as the allegorical *vita activa*, despite her "return." Cf. "In the veins of each century there courses alien, not its own, blood, and the stronger, the more historically intensive the age, the heavier the weight of this alien blood" (*SS 2*, p. 282). Cf. contemporary usage in Librovich, *Nerusskaia krov' v russkikh pisateliakh*: "In Russia, those who reflect the people's life [*otrazhateli narodnoi zhizni*] are in large numbers, if not primarily, persons of non-Russian or half-Russian origin—persons in whose veins there courses [*v zhilakh kotorykh struitsia*] non-Russian blood, and even where it is Russian it is mixed with the alien" (cited in A. G. Gornfel'd, *Knigi i liudi: Literaturnye besedy I* [St. Petersburg, 1908], pp. 299 ff.).

55. Cf. Claude Lévi-Strauss's understanding of myth as the sum of its variants in "The Structural Study of Myth."

56. "Myth is the part of language where the formula *traduttore, traditore* reaches its lowest truth value. From that point of view it should be placed in the gamut of linguistic expressions at the end opposite to that of poetry, in spite of all the claims that have been made to prove the contrary. Poetry is a kind of speech which cannot be translated except at the cost of serious distortions; whereas the mythical value of the myth is preserved even through the worst translations" (Lévi-Strauss, "The Structural Study of Myth," p. 210). One may wish to add to this rather formidable statement that "serious distortions" occur every time a reader attempts to interpret, indeed merely to read, a

poem, unless, of course, he deals with some other kind of poetry (I can think only of a poem composed and read by God in his privacy) that speaks outside the reader's mind.

57. R. Jakobson, "Poetry of grammar and grammar of poetry," *Lingua* 21 (1968): 597–609.

58. Cf. "Zverinets" (The Bestiary, 1916), *SS* 1:83: "But I am singing the wine of time—the source of the Italic speech—and, in the proto-Arian cradle, the Slavic and Germanic flax."

59. R. Jakobson, "The Metaphoric and Metonymic Poles," in R. Jakobson and M. Halle, *The Fundamentals of Language* (The Hague and Paris, 1956), pp. 90–96.

60. R. Jakobson, "Linguistics and Poetics," in *Style in Language,* ed. T. Sebeok (Cambridge, Mass., 1960), pp. 350–377.

61. "Zolotistogo meda struia. . . ," *SS* 1:92. L. Ginzburg discusses this poem in "Poetika Osipa Mandel'shtama," *O starom i novom* (Leningrad, 1982).

62. Even as late as 1916, Nikolai Gumilev spoke about Mandelstam as a "poet who has had difficulties mastering the Russian language" (N. Gumilev, "Zametki o russkoi poezii," *SS* 4, p. 363). Another Acmeist, Sergei Gorodetskii, writing for an ultranationalist journal, was more explicit about the sources of Mandelstam's allegedly clumsy Russian: "He [Mandelstam] has learned the language. And although no study can serve as a substitute for the language to which one is born, nevertheless, Mandelstam's poetry belongs to literature. True, anyone sensitive to language will notice in it certain shortcomings, which the author skillfully tries to pass for his own, personal style. . . . However, it is a big mistake to consider Mandelstam's private [*uslovnyi*] language some sort of 'Russian Latin,' as do some of his admirers" ("Poeziia kak iskusstvo," *Lukomor'e* 18 [April 30, 1916]). Or consider an opinion of a member of the younger generation associated with the Acmeists: "Undoubtedly, Mandelstam's poetry is beautiful, but this beauty is not his own, it is alien [*chuzaia*]. As to Mandelstam qua poet, he is not of the present (I am afraid, no longer of the present). There is only the solemn grandeur of Ancient Rome and Catholic Rome, the dead beauty of the Admiralty and Tsarskoe Selo" (I. Oksenov, "O. Mandel'shtam. Kamen'. Stikhi. 'Giperborei,' P. 1916" [review], *Novyi zhurnal dlia vsekh* 2–3 [1916]: 74 ff.). A few years later Oksenov would count himself among the admirers of Mandelstam's poetry.

63. See my discussion of "Solominka" earlier in this chapter.

64. Cf. L. Ginzburg's interpretation in "Poetika Osipa Mandel'shtama," *O lirike.*

65. See NM 2, p. 278. Cf. Taranovsky, *Essays on Mandel'štam,* pp. 62 ff.

66. NM 1, p. 200.

67. I am aware of three analyses of the poem: D. M. Segal, "Mikrosemantika odnogo stikhotvoreniia," in Jakobson, van Schoneveld, and Worth, *Slavic Poetics,* pp. 345–405; H. Henry, "Étude de fonctionnement d'un poème de Mandel'stam," *Action poétique* 63 (1975): 21–31; and N. Struve, *Ossip Mandelstam* (Paris, 1982), pp. 181–183.

68. There are two more versions of the second stanza. The variants are telling and speak for themselves. One of them reads: "Lifting a stone is easier than saying: to love" (Princeton Archive). The other: "I have but one care left in this world: A golden care, to *kill* the burden of time" (*Tristia* [Berlin, 1922], p. 55).

69. A. Akhmatova, *Sochineniia*, vol. 2 (Washington, D.C., 1968), p. 177. See also H. Henry, "Étude de fonctionnement d'un poème," pp. 24–25; and N. Struve, *Ossip Mandelstam*, pp. 182–183.

70. B. Seward, *The Symbolic Rose* (New York, 1960), pp. 55–56, 136–137.

71. "The town council [of Novorossiisk] sent a delegation to Wrangel in April [1920] complaining that the parents would not send their children to school because the children were terrified by seeing so many people hanged in the streets" (Kenez, *Civil War in South Russia*, p. 275). For eyewitness accounts, see D. Maslov, "Pechat' pri Vrangele"; and V. Obolenskii, "Krym pri Vrangele."

72. In 1920, Vladislav Khodasevich came out with his *Putem zerna* (The Way of the Grain). Or cf. V. Khlebnikov's "Nasha osnova" (1920): "Slovotvorchestvo uchit, chto vse raznoobrazie slova iskhodit ot osnovnykh zvykov azbuki, zameniaiushchikh *semena slova*. Iz etikh iskhodnykh tochek stroitsia slovo, i novyi *seiatel' iazykov* mozhet prosto napolnit' ladon' 28 zvukami azbuki, *zernami iazyka*" [italics are mine] (Khlebnikov, *SP* 5, p. 228). Once again, this was a common allegory in search of a mythic narrative.

73. Cf. N. Struve's matter-of-fact treatment of this poem as a "formule incantatoire" (*Ossip Mandelstam*, pp. 182–184).

74. For a more-or-less contemporary view of sympathetic magic, different from that of Sir James Frazer, see M. Mauss, *A General Theory of Magic* (London, 1972), pp. 11–12, 98–102.

75. For Mandelstam's contemporaries, such a view of iteration in poetry was commonplace. Cf. B. Larin, "O 'Kiparisovom lartse,'" *Literaturnaia mysl': Al'manakh*, vol. 2 (Petrograd, 1923). For Larin, Annenskii was a poet who "courageously put to a test motives repeated a hundred times." Citing Annenskii's densely iterative poem "Nevozmozhno," Larin echoed the early Futurist declarations and maintained that repetition of a word in a poem empties the word of conventional meaning and endows it with new meaning, creating the axiological "autonomy of the word" (*samotsennost' slova*). "Poetry," he wrote, "is more of a bait, a riddle, than a message, because it must always be a new name [*novoe nazvanie*]. In poetry . . . there is present a power of unmediated suggestion. . . . A poem is the only lyric name [*imia*] which cannot be represented but which is comprehensible like a spell [*vniatno kak navazhdenie*]" (ibid., pp. 152ff.). Larin's essay was written in 1922. On it and on the Formalists' response to Larin's ideas, see the commentary by E. A. Toddes, A. P. Chudakov, and M. O. Chudakova in Iu. Tynianov, *Poetika. Istoriia literatury. Kino* (Moscow, 1977), p. 455.

76. Some of the most astute contemporary readers of Mandelstam found his use of the "collage" technique—that is, the conjoining of self-enclosed

stanzas and even lines—excessive. See S. Bobrov, "O. Mandelstam. 'Tristia'" (review), *PiR* 4 (1923): 259; and L. Lunts, "Tsekh poetov," *Knizhnyi ugol* 8 (1922): 54. As Ronen ("Osip Mandel'štam") has noted, Mandelstam, who often numbered stanzas (see *Tristia*), responded to this criticism by abandoning this essentially graphic emphasis on division numbers and sometimes by removing stanzaic divisions altogether (as in "Iazyk bulyzhnika . . . ," which in a draft was divided into seven numbered quatrains).

77. "And the intricate pattern he [Tintoretto] has thought up to replace the banal drapery serves to bring out that jewelry still-life within which is a broken necklace—symbol as it were of the coming fate of Venice" (A. Malraux, *The Voices of Silence* [Princeton, 1978], p. 439). Cf. also a description of the funeral seen through the child's eye in Mandelstam's *The Noise of Time* (1923–25): "Once, accompanied by my nanny and mother, I was walking along the Moika past the chocolate Italian Embassy. Suddenly—the doors are opened and they allow everybody in, and the place smells of resin, incense, and something sweet and pleasant. *Black velvet* was muffling the entry way and the walls decorated with silver and tropical plants: the embalmed Italian Ambassador was lying very high up. What was this all to me? I do not know, but these were strong and sharp impressions, and I cherish them to this day" (*SS* 2, p. 54).

78. The motif is used again, in a personal context, in *The Fourth Prose:* "And everything was terrifying, as in a child's dream. *Nel mezzo del'cammin di nostra vita*—in the middle of life's way, I was stopped in a wild Soviet forest by robbers who called themselves my judges. They were elders with sinewy necks and small gooselike heads who were unworthy of carrying the burden of age. For the first time in my life, I was needed by literature, and it was squeezing me, pawing and feeling me, and everything was terrifying, as in a child's dream" (*SS* 2, pp. 188 ff.).

79. "Venok ili venets?" was the title of A. Belyi's famous reply (*Apollon* 11 [1910]) to Briusov's "O 'rechi rabskoi' v zashchitu poezii" (*Apollon* 9 [1910], the issue containing Mandelstam's first publication).

80. Together with the motif of the mirror (stanzas 1 and 5), the "wreath" in "Venetian Life" once again returns to the theme of Rachel, contemplating herself in the mirror, and Leah, singing and weaving a wreath.

81. Cf. "Prozrachnaia zvezda, bluzhdaiushchii ogon', Tvoi brat, Petropol', umiraet" ("Na strashnoi vysote . . ." [1918], *SS* 1:101, and *Stikhotvoreniia*, no. 87).

82. A. Blok, "Pliaski smerti" ("Pustaia ulitsa. Odin ogon' v okne," October 1912).

83. M. Voloshin gave the following explication of the Saturn and Vesper symbolism: "Venus is beauty; Saturn is fate. . . . Venus testifies to magnanimity, kindness, expansiveness; Saturn binds lovers with the ring of pride, signifies closure that can be broken only with a passionate, always tragic gesture" ("Liki tvorchestva," *Apollon* 2 [1909]: 1–4 [2d pagination]). Viacheslav Ivanov uses the image "Saturn's ring" in his cycle "Zolotye zavesy" ("Son razvernul ogneiazychnyi svitok," 1907) in *Cor ardens*. Cf. Ronen, "Osip Mandel'štam." Further echoes are found in E. T. A. Hoffmann's "The Doge and the Dogaressa"

(known from Pushkin's unfinished translation). R. Timenchik ("Zametki ob akmeizme," *RL* 7/8 [1974]) suggests a connection with Mikhail Kuzmin's "Venetian" narrative poem, *Novyi rolla*. In contemporary usage, "Saturn's ring" represented instances of an "astrological" reintegration of astronomical knowledge. Cf. C. Flammarion, *Popular Astronomy* (n.p., 1907), p. 432: "The ancient opinion of Saturn has been preserved to our day, even among cultured minds. The marvellous ring which surrounds this strange world, far from effacing this legendary impression, has even further confirmed it." Flammarion's *Dream of an Astronomer* (the English edition of 1923) begins with a description of Venice similar to that presented in the poem.

84. V. Briusov, "'Al'manakh Tsekha poetov,' kn. 2 (Pg., 1921) and 'SOPO. Pervyi sbornik stikhov' (M. 4-yi god 1-go veka [1921])" (review), *PiR* 3 (1921): 270–271.

85. N. Pavlovich. See note 20, chap. 1.

86. A. Blok, *SS* 7, p. 371. In her memoirs, Nadezhda Mandelstam refused to see praise in Blok's qualification of Mandelstam as an *artist*. Although she singled out Blok as the most favorably disposed to Mandelstam of all the Symbolists (certainly an overstatement—Briusov and Ivanov are on record as praising Mandelstam), she wrote that even he "did make an entry in his diary about the Yid and the artist" (NM 2, p. 378). It would seem that she was speaking about this particular entry (the only one in which Mandelstam is called "artist"), suggesting that it was not printed in its entirety. Or was it the entry of 1911 in which Blok referred to Mandelstam parenthetically as "the eternal"? (see Blok, *SS* 7, p. 78). P. Gromov, an authority on Blok and a critic very sympathetic to Mandelstam, treated the same entry as "a high degree of praise in the overall system of Blok's views" (Gromov, *Blok. Ego predshestvenniki i sovremenniki* [Moscow and Leningrad, 1966], p. 380).

VI

1. "In the literature of transitional eras, for instance, we find an especial profusion of rebirth rituals, where the poet is making symbolic passes that will endow him with new identity. Now, imagine him trying to do a very thorough job of this reidentification. To be completely reborn, he would have to change his very lineage itself. He would have to revise, not only his present but also his past" (K. Burke, "Freud—and the Analysis of Poetry," in *The Philosophy of Literary Form: Studies in Symbolic Action* [Berkeley and Los Angeles, 1973], p. 273).

2. See, for example, a composite review by Valerii Briusov in which he discusses the proliferation of such imagery in contemporary poetry ("Sredi stikhov," *PiR* 2 [1922]: 149). A thorough discussion of the subject may be found in B. Jangfeldt, *Majakovskij and Futurism: 1917–1921*, Stockholm Studies in Russian Literature, no. 5 (Stockholm, 1976), esp. chapter 3: "The Revolution of the Spirit."

3. Letter to Viacheslav Ivanov, *SS* 2, p. 485. For the correct date (June 20, 1909, not 1910), see A. Morozov, "Pis'ma O. E. Mandel'shtama V. I. Iva-

novu," in *Gosudarstvennaia publichnaia biblioteka SSSR imeni V. I. Lenina. Zapiski Otdela rukopisei,* vol. 34 (Moscow, 1975), p. 262.

4. Mandelstam, "V Petropole prozrachnom my umrem," *SS* 1:89. This is another instance of Mandelstam's reworking of the Trojan cycle. Here Petersburg is Troy, about which it had been prophesied that its walls could not be breached as long as they contained Athene's Palladium (Apollodorus, *Epitome* 5:10). According to a later, Roman, tradition, Palladium was linked to *palta,* or "things hurled from heaven"—a link Mandelstam must have been aware of. He conflated the *palta*-Palladium with Tiutchev's stone ("Having rolled from a mountain, a stone came to rest in the valley") in his 1912 programmatic poem "Falling is an inevitable companion of fear": "Who hurls stones to us from on high, and does the stone deny the yoke of dust?" The architectural, Petersburg pathos of the early Mandelstam also points in this direction. Further, the poem echoes some of the habitual formulations concerning the nature and "destiny" of St. Petersburg that were current in the 1910s. Nikolai Shapir, who frequently wrote on such matters for *Severnye zapiski,* said the following: "Not Phoebus-Apollo, but Athene, 'the patroness of cities,' and Mars, swelling with power and subordinated to her—these are our gods ("Filosofsko-kul'turnye ocherki," *Severnye zapiski* 9 [September 1913]: 69).

5. V. Rozanov, *Apokalipsis nashego vremeni* (Sergiev Posad, 1917–18).

6. V. Khlebnikov, *Noch' v okope* (1922); Vl. Maiakovskii, *Voina i mir* (1916).

7. Cf. Iu. Levin, D. Segal, R. Timenchik, V. Toporov, and T. Tsiv'ian, "Russkaia semanticheskaia poetika kak potentsial'naia kul'turnaia paradigma," *RL* 7/8 (1974): 47–82.

8. "The life of a historical system leads inevitably to aging . . . , for it carries on its back its entire past, and this heavy burden of past experience grows so big as to become unbearable" (N. O. Losskii, *Intuitivnaia filosofiia Bergsona* [Petersburg, 1922], p. 13). Bergson spoke of the possible eventual victory over death in *L'évolution créatrice* (ibid., p. 92). The similarity between Bergson and Spengler can be traced to their common source in Nietzsche. On this, see H. S. Hughes, *Oswald Spengler: A Critical Estimate* (New York and London, 1952), p. 52. Viacheslav Ivanov's revision of Nietzsche, which involved a Christianization of the self-proclaimed "Antichrist," needs no commentary, but see, for example, his "Nietsshe i Dionis" (1904, *SS* 2) as well as the contemporaneous "Ellinskaia religiia stradaiushchego boga" (*Novyi put'*, 1–3, 5, 8–9 [1904]).

9. "The Nineteenth Century." For Mandelstam's poetic elaboration of this formula, forever associated with Alfred de Musset, see O. Ronen, *An Approach to Mandel'štam* (Jerusalem, 1983), pp. 226, 249–248.

10. On the early twentieth century as an "Alexandrian epoch," see A. Blok, "Tvorchestvo Viacheslava Ivanova" (1905), *SS* 5; M. Kuzmin's collection of poetry "Aleksandriiskie pesni" (1908); and Mandelstam's "Pushkin and Skriabin" (1915). A particularly poignant formulation may be found in P. P. Muratov, "Stil' epokhi" (*RM* 31, no. 1 [1910], pp. 94–99). "The antique world

had turned out to be so intimately related to ours and so close and dear, that the 'dead' culture has at once become revived for us" (V. Pertsev, "V. Buzeskul, 'Antichnost' i sovremennost'" [review], *Golos minuvshego* 5 [1913]: 250). This pathos is, of course, also behind the contemporary classic in the genre, Tadeusz Zielinski's three-volume *Iz zhizni idei*.

11. Cf. "Many of our authors have already found in the Buddhist legends motifs and plots for their own work; but a true representative of the Buddhist *mood* must be a poet who does not apparently take any interest in Buddhism and, in general, strictly guards his Russian verse against the encroachment of all sorts of heterogeneous names and terms" (Vl. Solov'ev, "Buddiiskoe nastroenie v poezii" [1894], in *SS* 7, p. 82). Mandelstam owed to this article his characterization of the psychologically intricate and pessimistic Flaubert as the "Buddhist prayer wheel" (see his essay "Konets romana," *SS* 2).

12. M. Kuzmin, *Uslovnosti: Stat'i ob iskusstve* (Petrograd, 1923), p. 87.

13. M. Kuzmin, "Parnasskie zarosli," in *Zavtra: Literaturno-kriticheskii sbornik,* vol. 1, ed. E. Zamiatin, M. Kuzmin, and M. Lozinskii (Berlin, 1923), p. 122.

14. Cf. B. Pasternak's letter to Mandelstam (January 31, 1925) concerning the planned *Spektoskii:* "The illusion of the extraordinary nature of the epoch is abandoned. The terminal style (the end of the century, the end of the revolution, the end of youth, the death of Europe [Spengler]) recedes, grows more and more shallow and ceases to function. The destinies of cultures, as before, become a matter of choice and good will" ("Chudo poeticheskogo voploshcheniia [Pis'ma Borisa Pasternaka]," *Voprosy literatury* 9 [1972]: 161).

15. A. Belyi, *Simvolizm,* (Moscow, 1910), p. 436. For a discussion of Belyi's impact on the Futurists, see, Dmitrij Tschizewskij's preface to his anthology on Russian Futurism, *Anfänge des russischen Futurismus* (Wiesbaden, 1963), and his preface to a reprint of Belyi's *Glassolaliia,* "Andrej Belyjs 'Glassolalija'—Ein 'Poem über die Lautwelt'" (Munich, 1976). See also Vl. Markov, *The Longer Poems of Velemir Khlebnikov* (Berkeley and Los Angeles, 1962), p. 13. The early Formalist theories were perceived as a direct outgrowth of Belyi's religious *Wissenschaft*. See, for example, D. Filosofov's review of *Sborniki po teorii poeticheskogo iazyka. Vypusk I* (Petrograd, 1916) in *Rech'* (September 26, 1916), which was pointedly entitled "Magiia slov," echoing Belyi's seminal essay (1910).

16. For example, I. V. Ignat'ev, "Ego-Futurizm" (1913): "The word has reached its limit." Or the Futurists' "Poshchechina obshchestvennomy vkusu" (The Slap in the Face of Public Taste, 1912): "And if even in *our* words there have still remained dirty imprints of your 'common sense' and 'good taste,' they are, nevertheless, already illuminated by the *first* Fluttering Dawns of the New Coming Beauty of the Self-Valued (Self-Generated) Word" (in Vl. Markov, ed., *Manifesty i programmy russkikh futuristov,* vol. 27 of *Slavische Propyläen* [Munich, 1967], pp. 45 and 51).

17. Mandelstam, "Utro akmeizma" (The Morning of Acmeism, 1913?), *SS* 2, p. 321.

Notes to Pages 157–158

18. From "Sadok sudei" (Trap for Judges). This was item ten in the program of the Hylaea group (in Markov, *Manifesty i programmy russkikh futuristov,* p. 52).

19. A. Welsh, *Roots of Lyric: Primitive Poetry and Modern Poetics* (Princeton, 1978), pp. 25–47.

20. See Innokentii Annenskii's remark on Fedor Sologub's "howling dog" (*Vysoka luna gospodnia*) as a modern version of the Hecate myth in Annenskii, *Knigi otrazhenii* (Moscow, 1979), "O sovremennom lirizme," p. 350. Or see V. Briusov on Maiakovskii's "Ia sosh'iu sebe chernye shtany iz barkhata golosa moego" ("Kofta-fata," 1913): an elaboration of the colloquial metaphor *barkhatnyi golos* ("velvety voice"), in V. Briusov, "God russkoi poezii," *RM* 5 (1914), p. 30 (4th pagination). In the late 1920s, this obsession with "secularized-sacralized" objects became a matter of parody in the fiction of Konstantin Vaginov. Not unrelated to Mandelstam's milieu and the poet himself (cf. the Unknown Poet in Vaginov's 1928 novel *Kozlinaia pesn'*) were often-pathological collectors: a collector of kitsch and pornography, Kostia Rotikov (*Kozlinaia pesn'*), or the protagonist of the unfinished *Garpagoniada,* who collected clipped fingernails.

21. N. Stepanov, "O. Mandel'shtam, 'Stikhotvoreniia' (1928)" (review), *Zvezda* 6 (1928): 123–124. According to Stepanov, "Word-themes grow enormous labyrinths of meanings that lead one astray and through which the reader must make his way in order to arrive at the story [fabula] of the poem. The result is a poem-charade with a concealed key word." This approach to Mandelstam was quite common at the time. Cf. Stepanov's very similar approach to B. Pasternak in his review "Dve knigi" (*Zvezda* 11 [1927]: 166–68): "One needs a poetic key . . . one solves them as a rebus." A. Lezhnev wrote that Mandelstam's poems "were composed like a rebus" ("Literaturnye zametki," *PiR* 4 [1925]: 151). Cf. Tynianov's formulation in "Promezhutok" (1924): "The semantic series [*smyslovoi riad*] in Mandelstam is such that a *single* image, a single lexical series, colors all the rest—this is the key to the entire hierarchy of images" (Iu. Tynianov, *Poetika. Istoriia literatury. Kino,* ed. E. A. Toddes, A. P. Chudakov, and M. O. Chudakova [Moscow, 1977], p. 188). Stepanov's work was obviously inspired by his teacher, Tynianov. Sergei Bobrov was perhaps the first critic to note and to emphasize this principle when he spoke about Mandelstam's "word-poems." See his review "O. Mandelstam. 'Tristia,'" *PiR* 4 (1923): 261. V. Vinogradov offered a similar analysis of Akhmatova's poetics: "Above all [her poetry] represents a typical example how the development of a verbal series dominating consciousness defines the *general plot pattern* [*kanva fabuliarnogo uzora*] and the character of favored narrative structures [*siuzhetnye skhemy*]. . . . In this manner, in the course of artistic framing of the theme of war and civil strife, what actually takes place is an extension of the sphere of symbols that revolve between love and death [Akhmatova's thematic core, according to Vinogradov]" ("O simvolakh Anny Akhmatovoi," in *Literaturnaia mysl': Al'manakh,* vol. 1 [Petrograd, 1922], pp. 91–138, esp. p. 134).

22. R. Barthes, *Mythologies* (New York, 1972), p. 142.

23. Viach. Ivanov, "Poet i chern'" (The Poet and the Rabble, 1904), *SS* 1, p. 713.

24. A. Veselovskii, "Psikhologicheskii parallelizm i ego formy v otrazhenii poeticheskogo stilia," in *Istoricheskaia poetika* (Moscow, 1940), p. 129. This was the stuff of a lecture course at the University of St. Petersburg. Consider a passage from a collection of articles by A. K. Borozdin, one of Mandelstam's instructors: "The elementary mythological ideas emerged together with poetry, and both verbal creativity and poetry were intimately intertwined with the creation of myths." (*Ocherki po istorii russkoi literatury: Russkaia narodnaia slovesnost' i drevniaia pis'mennost'* [n.p., 1913], p. 2).

25. "Establishing a poet's literary genesis, his literary sources, his *kinship* and origin, takes us at once to firm ground" (Mandelstam, *SS* 2, pp. 270ff.). Cf. Veselovskii, *Istoricheskaia poetika*, p. 47.

26. Mandelstam, "Barsuch'ia nora" (The Badger's Hole, 1921), *SS* 2, p. 273. Cf. G. Levinton, "Zametki o fol'klorizme Bloka," in *Mif, fol'klor, literatura*, ed. V. G. Bazanov et al. (Leningrad, 1978), pp. 171ff. and 175ff.

27. "O prirode slova" *obmirshchenie iazyka*. In "Zavety simvolizma" (The Legacy of Symbolism, 1910), Viacheslav Ivanov wrote about Symbolism's appropriation of the "mysterial" poetry of the ancients: "the renewed symbolic energy of the word which had not been subjugated for long centuries by serving external experience, thanks to the religious tradition and the conservatism of the people's soul" (*Apollon* 8 [1910]: 12). Mandelstam could have subscribed to this statement with only one proviso: his word could be revived even after the "long centuries" of servitude in the cause of external experience. This was the meaning, for him, of the "secularization" of poetic speech.

28. *SS* 2, p. 222. Cf. A. Belyi, *Glassolaliia: Poema o zvuke* (Moscow, 1917).

29. Mandelstam, "K vykhodu Al'manakha muz" (1916), *SS* 2, p. 29. Cf. "Literaturnaia Moskva" (1922), *SS* 2: "The double truth of invention and recollection is required—like bread"; 1922 was, of course, the year of the great famine in the Volga region.

30. Quoted (in connection with a discussion concerning a possible synthesis of Acmeism and Futurism) in I. Gruzdev, "Sovremennaia russkaia poeziia," *Kniga i revoliutsiia* 3 (1923): 35. The idea of the new poetry as a synthesis of the familiar and unfamiliar, however, goes back to Mandelstam's "Utro Akmeizma" (1913), where it found expression in an elaborate pun on the word *kamen'*. The Acmeists, wrote the author of *Stone*, take the "stone" from Tiutchev and make it the cornerstone of their *new* edifice.

31. "[Poetic] images are a given, and in poetry there is much more recollection of images than thinking in images" (V. Shklovskii, "Iskusstvo kak priem," in *Poetika: Sborniki po teorii poeticheskogo iazyka* [Petrograd, 1919], p. 102 [hereafter referred to as *Poetika* (1919); on the "disautomatization," see pp. 104ff.). See also V. Erlich, *Russian Formalism: History—Doctrine* (New Haven and London, 1981), pp. 76ff., 176–178.

32. V. Shklovskii, "O poezii i zaumnom iazyke" (1916), in *Poetika* (1919), p. 26. Shklovskii cited Mandelstam's "Silentium" (1909) as an example of a poet's express wish for the "trans-sense" language: "Remain foam, Aphrodite, and, word, return to music" (p. 22).

33. D. G. Konovalov, *Religioznyi ekstaz v russkom misticheskom sektantstve: Issledovanie*, pt. 1, vyp. 1: *Fizicheskie iavleniia v kartine sektantskogo ekstaza* (Sergiev Posad, 1908). This study provided a wealth of material for the early declarations of the Formalist critics. See V. Shklovskii, "O poezii i zaumnom iazyke"; and L. P. Iakubinskii, "Skoplenie odinakovykh plavnykh v prakticheskom i poeticheskom iazykakh," in *Poetika* (1919), pp. 22n and 57n, respectively.

34. "Deviatnadtsatyi vek" was published in the first issue of the Imagists' magazine *Gostinitsa dlia puteshestvuiushchikh v prekrasnom*, 1922. Mandelstam may have wished to temper the emphasis on the "image" characteristic of the Russian Imagists, in whom he took considerable interest. By late 1923 what could pass for mild criticism became an oblique declaration of rejection when Mandelstam alluded, in "Grifel'naia oda" (*SS* 1: 137), to the founder of Russian Imagism, Vadim Shershenevich: "Kak mertvyi *shershen'* (hornet) vozle sot, den' pestryi vymeten s pozorom." In "O prirode slova" he was less oblique: "Representatives of the Moscow metaphoric school who call themselves Imagists, chafing in their attempts to adapt language to modernity, have been left far behind language, and their fate is to be swept out like paper rubbish" (*SS* 2, p. 247). Cf. Vadim Shershenevich's own words (from "Esteticheskie stansy"): "I remind myself of a piece of paper that someone has thrown into a toilet [*Sam sebe napominaiiu bumazhku, kem-to broshennuiu v klozet*]." However, Mandelstam was not averse to borrowing from Shershenevich, whose poem "Printsip meshchanskoi kontseptsii" is echoed distinctly in the description of the telegraph office in *Egipetskaia marka*. My references to Shershenevich are made according to *Russian Imagism: 1919–1924*, ed. Vl. Markov (Giessen, 1980).

35. *SS* 2, pp. 221–222.

36. A. Bem's review of "O prirode slova," *Volia Rossii* (Prague) 6–7 (1923): 159–160.

37. See V. Shklovskii, "Potebnia" (1916), in *Poetika* (1919), p. 4. For a "revisionist" view of Shklovskii's relation to Potebnia, see Daniel Rancour-Laferrière, "Potebnja, Šklovkij and the Familiarity/Strangeness Paradox," *RL* IV-1 (1976): 174–198. Shklovskii's "suppressed" indebtedness to Potebnia did not escape some of his contemporaries. "The novelty of the Formal method consists solely of the fact that its modern founders have very well internalized [*usvoili*] certain long-forgotten ideas of Potebnia" (E. Gollerbakh, [no title], *Novaia russkaia kniga* 7 [1922], p. 5).

38. Erlich, *Russian Formalism*, pp. 23–26.

39. A. A. Potebnia, *Mysl' i iazyk* (Odessa, 1922), p. 145 ("Poeziia, proza, sgushchenie mysli").

40. A. A. Potebnia, "Iz zapisok po teorii slovsnosti," in *Estetika i poetika* (Moscow, 1976), p. 309: "The elements of the word with a live representation correspond to elements of a poetic work, for such a word, even taken by itself,

is a poetic work. . . . What is representation in the word corresponds to the image (or a certain unity of images) in a poetic work. The terms denoting a poetic image can be the same as those denoting image in the word, that is, sign, symbol, which contains representation, the inner form."

41. Potebnia, *Estetika i poetika,* p. 143.

42. I. Rozanov, "Obzor khudozhestvennoi literatury za dva goda," in *Literaturnye otkliki. Stat'i* (Moscow, 1923), p. 71.

43. Following Sir James Frazer, E. Kagarov (*Kul't fetishei, zhivotnykh i rastenii v drevnei Gretsii* [Petersburg, 1913], p. 88) distinguishes three types of magic: homeopathic, contagious, and *enantheopathic,* the latter based on reversal. It stands to reason that the rhetoric of sarcasm may, in fact, have originated in forms of enantheopathic verbal magic, just as the rhetoric of satire can be traced to forms of magical incantations and spells (see R. C. Elliott, *The Power of Satire: Magic, Ritual, Art* [Princeton, 1960]). Cf. Viacheslav Ivanov: "Word-symbol is produced by magical suggestion which assimilates the auditor to the mysteries of poetry. . . . The task of poetry [in ancient times] was the spellbinding magic of rhythmic speech mediating between the world of divine essences and man" ("Zavety simvolizma," 1910). Cf. also Andrei Belyi: "The sounds of the word are a spell . . . the roots of the word are the result of creative experiments in the art of cognition; they are—magic" ("Zhezl Aarona," *Skify* 1 [1917]).

44. There was hardly a poet, including Maiakovskii, who was spared an accusation of "untopicality," but Mandelstam's Acmeist reputation made him a more frequent target of this unimaginative (and in those days purely verbal) form of criticism. A key to the contemporary reading of the poem may be found in B. Pasternak's letter to Mandelstam regarding the appearance of the 1928 collection of poetry. Trying to humor Mandelstam and, in part, to deflate his pose of a persecuted figure, Pasternak wrote: "I obtained your book yesterday. What a happy man you are, what pride you must derive from being the *namesake* of the author." Yet in the same letter, Pasternak, who was then reworking his earlier poetry, described Mandelstam's verse as extratemporal, "undisturbed in its loftiness and thematic density by the changes in the street"— echoing precisely the accusation he tried to dismiss in the congratulatory portion of the letter. For the full text of the letter, see "Zametki o peresechenii biografii Osipa Mandel'shtama i Borisa Pasternaka," *Pamiat'* 4 (Moscow, 1979; Paris, 1981).

45. "Net, nikogda nichei ia ne byl sovremennik," *SS* 1: 141. My translation of the word *oblatka* as the Latin *oblatum* puts a somewhat greater emphasis on the "communion" referent of the trope in English than it does in Russian. The difference, however, is only one of degree. In Russian, the communion bread (which is *leavened* in the Orthodox Church) is called *prosfora* (a word derived from the Greek), whereas *oblatka,* although etymologically an identical term, refers largely to a thin unleavened wafer or a waferlike piece of paper used to seal letters in place of sealing wax. In Russia, it was not uncommon to seal letters with moistened bread when regular stationery was unavailable or in short supply after World War II, and it was probably no different during the

civil war or in the early 1920s. A good context for Mandelstam's usage of the image may be found in his "Zametki o Shen'e," where he follows the lines from *Eugene Onegin* with a conclusion: "It is thus that national divisions collapse, and the elemental force of one language calls out to another over the heads of space and time, for all languages are united in a fraternal union which rests on the freedom and *Gemütlichkeit* [*domashnost'*] of each; and in this freedom, they are fraternally related and call out to each other like family members" (*SS* 2, p. 300). This passage "dates" "Zametki" as concluded about 1922–23.

46. O. Ronen, *An Approach to Mandel'štam* (Jerusalem, 1983), pp. 331–363.

47. Cf. Mandelstam's "On the Interlocutor" (1914, *SS* 2), which develops extensively a key simile for Mandelstam: a poem is compared to a letter sealed in a bottle that a reader in posterity shall "providentially" discover as something addressed to himself. Note that chapter 3 of *Eugene Onegin,* where the word *oblatka* appears, was composed in 1824, exactly a hundred years before Mandelstam's poem.

48. Gogol's "Vii" (see Ronen, *Approach to Mandel'štam,* pp. 240–241) does, of course, resonate strongly with Mandelstam's "archetypal" narrative of Phaedra and Hippolytus. In both cases, the male protagonists enter against their will into a sexual compact with a woman who ought not be available to them (the taboo of age—the witch first appears as an old woman—and then of social status in "Vii" and incest in *Hippolytus*). The protagonists' demise, too, is effected by an older man—in both cases a father. Cf. also the killing of Andrii by his father in *Taras Bul'ba.* For pertinent and stimulating readings of "Vii," see S. Karlinsky, *The Sexual Labyrinth of Nikolai Gogol* (Cambridge, Mass., 1976), pp. 86–96; and L. Stilman, "The All-Seeing Eye in Gogol," in *Gogol from the Twentieth Century: Eleven Essays,* ed. R. A. Maguire (Princeton, 1974).

49. "Slushaite! Iz menia slepym Viem vremia oret: 'Podymite, podymite mne vekov veki" (Listen! Time is screaming out of me like the blind Vii: 'Lift for me my eyelids of ages.'") (V. Maiakovskii, *Voina i mir* [1916]). "Vygoraia ot liubopytstva, zvezd glaza povylezli iz orbit" (Losing color from curiosity, the eyes of the stars have stuck out of their orbits) (ibid.). See "Gogol' v stikhakh Maiakovskogo" by N. Khardzhiev, part of "Zametki o Maiakovskom," in N. Khardzhiev and Vl. Trenin, *Poeticheskaia kul'tura Maiakovskogo* (Moscow, 1969), p. 188. See also "Gogol' i Maiakovskii," in A. Belyi, *Masterstvo Gogolia* (Moscow, 1934). Cf. also Belyi: "Revolution is an operation of removing the cataracts from the eye of the artist" ("Dnevnik pisatelia," *Rossiia* 2/11 [1924]: 146).

50. "Vek" (1923), *SS* 1: 135. Cf. S. Broyde, *Osip Mandelštam and His Age* (Cambridge, Mass., 1975), pp. 107ff.

51. B. Pilniak, *Golyi god* (Petrograd, Moscow, and Berlin, 1921).

52. "Sergeiu Eseninu" (1926). Maiakovskii dated the poem in a more precise fashion, "January–March," alluding perhaps to Easter. For one who com-

mitted suicide on a Thursday during the Holy Week, this was not an unusual allusion.

53. B. Pasternak, "Hamlet." One encounters the metaphor "stars are the axes of the universe" among the writers of Mandelstam's generation. See, for example, N. Punin, "O. Mandelstam. 'Tristia'" (review) *Zhizn' iskusstva* 41 (October 17, 1922): 3. The early Pasternak, the author of *Bliznets v tuchakh* (1914), was particularly involved with astral imagery.

54. V. Shershenevich, "Neboskreb obrazov minus spriazhenie," in Markov, *Russian Imagism,* p. 42. Cf. V. Shklovskii's characterization of I. Babel''s "principal device": "to speak in the same voice about the stars and the clap" (Shklovskii, "Babel': Kriticheskii romans" [1924], in *Gamburgskii schet* [Leningrad, 1928], p. 80).

55. See A. Fet, "Mezh temi zvezdami i mnoiu / Kakaia-to sviaz' rodilas'" ("Ia dolgo stoial nepodvizhno"), "Odna zvezda nad vsemi dyshit i tak drozhit / Ona luchom almaznym pyshet / I govorit" ("Odna zvezda nad vsemi dyshit"), "Ot liudei utait'sia vozmozhno / No ot zvezd nichego ne sokryt'" ("Ot ognei, ot tolpy besposhchadnoi"). Cf. also Viacheslav Ivanov on Dante's Pilgrim emerging out of the Inferno and his own collection of poetry *Guiding Stars* (1901) and the collection of essays *Po zvezdam* (From Star to Star) (St. Petersburg, 1909). Goethe's lines from *Faust* read: "Erkennest dann der Sterne lauf, / Und wenn Natur dich unterweist, / Dann geht die Seelenkraft dir auf, / Wie spricht ein Geist zum andern Geist." Lermontov's poem "Vykhozhu odin ia na dorogu." V. Khlebnikov: "Let man, who has rested from work, go and read the cuneiforms of constellations. To understand the will of the stars means to unfold before everyone's eyes the scroll of true freedom. They hang over us in this too black a night, these tablets of coming laws, and is it not the meaning of division—to get rid of the wire of governments between the hearing of humanity and the stars. Let the power of stars be wireless" ("Nasha osnova," *SP* 3, p. 242). Most items in this list of possible allusions can be found in Ronen, "Osip Mandel'štam" and *Approach to Mandel'štam,* which contain a most thorough and stimulating analysis of "Grifel'naia oda" and "1 ianvaria 1924." The colloquialism of this astral imagery is further evident in N. Minskii's essay on Blok and Dante ("Blok i Dante," *Sovremennye zapiski* [Paris] 7 [October 5, 1921]: 188–208), in which he presents the two poets as "two stars illuminating each other"(p. 198).

56. Cf. Blok's usage in a commemorative essay on Vl. Soloviev, "Rytsar'-monakh": "Soloviev, alone of this world, struck the enemy with its own weapon: he learned to forget time; he only tamed it, throwing over the shaggy fur of the monster [*kosmataia sherst' chudovishcha*] a light, silvery bridal veil of laughter" (Blok, *SS* 5, p. 450).

57. Cf. A. Belyi's "The ideal of beauty is the ideal of a human being, and aesthetic creation, as it expands, inevitably leads to the transfiguration of human personality; Zarathustra, Buddha, Christ are as much the artists of life as they are life's lawgivers; their ethics merge with aesthetics, and vice versa. *Kant's imperative in [the artist's] heart and starry heaven over his head are here insep-*

arable" ("Problemy kul'tury," in *Simvolizm*, p. 10). Cf. also Khlebnikov's rephrasing: "Let the power of stars be wireless. One of the ways [of achieving it] are the Scales of the Futurist which with one end stir the sky and with the other disappear in the heartbeat" ("Nasha osnova," *SP* 3, p. 243). One can, perhaps, discern in the latter an echo of Tiutchev's "Rainbow."

58. A. Voronskii, *Na styke* (Moscow, 1923). Polemicizing with his opponents from the journal *Na postu*, whose goal was to establish a "class hegemony" in Russian letters, Voronskii, who advocated a more conciliatory, mediating position, wrote: "Where shall we place our guards [i.e., the party activists] . . . at the junction [*styk*] between the Communists and the fellow travelers?" Hence the metaphor's association with the problem of historical continuity in contemporary usage. In part, the expression may be traced to the emblematic revolutionary song of the period: "Our steam engine, fly forward. The next stop is the Commune. We have no other road [railroad]; in our hands we hold a rifle." See also an almanac published by the Moscow "salon," "Moskovskii tsekh poetov," which had existed since the early 1920s (see S. Gorodetskii, ed., *Styk: Pervyi sbornik stikhov Moskovskogo Tsekha poetov* [Moscow, 1925]). Together with representatives of the "fellow-traveling" older groups (the Acmeists Gorodetskii and Zenkevich; the Symbolists Belyi, Briusov, and Piast; the Futurist Pasternak), the contributors included a number of the "proletarian" and "peasant" poets. By the time "Slate Ode" was composed, the word *styk* had also become a term in Formalist poetics. "Coined" by Osip Brik, it denoted an epanoleptic alliteration conjoining two contiguous lines (not dissimilar to Mandelstam's epanoleptic figure formed by the last poem of *Stone* II and the first poem of *Tristia*). See O. Brik, "Zvukovye povtory," in *Poetika* (1919), pp. 83, 87ff.

59. See, for example, E. Zamiatin, "O sintetizme" (1921), in *A Soviet Heretic: Essays by Yevgeny Zamyatin* (Chicago, 1970): "We know that, of the twelve Apostles, only Thomas was not an artist. He alone could see nothing but what he could touch. And we who have been titrated through Schopenhauer, Kant, Einstein, and Symbolism, we know that the world, the thing in itself, reality, are not what is visible to the Thomases" (p. 85). In "Grifel'naia oda," Mandelstam polemicized with this one-sided Futurist apology by declaring himself a Thomas who wishes to synthesize the two opposing trends ("And I, too, wish to thrust my fingers into the flinty way . . . as into the wound, locking into a *styk* flint and water . . ."). Mandelstam's image of the advance scout (*zastrel'shchik*), too, may be traced to Zamiatin's essay: "There is a tactical axiom: every battle requires a group of self-sacrificing scouts doomed to cross a certain dread line, and to pave the earth beyond with their bodies under the cruel laughter of machine guns. . . . The role of these self-sacrificing scouts was taken by the numerous clan of Futurists" (ibid., p. 82).

60. Mandelstam, "Barsuch'ia nora" (The Badger's Hole): "slova-odnodnevki" (*SS* 2, p. 274).

61. A. A. Potebnia, *Iz zapisok po teorii slovesnosti* ("Ob uchastii iazyka v obrazovanii mifov"), in *Estetika i poetika*, p. 444.

62. *LN* 92 (1983), bk. 3, p. 357.

63. For a discussion of the subject, see F. Starr, *Red and Hot* (New York, 1983); and P. Fussell, *Great War in Modern Memory* (Oxford, 1975).

64. On one of the last such cooperatives, "Uzel," see S. Poliakova, "Poeziia Sofii Parnok," in S. Parnok, *Sobranie stikhotvorenii* (Ann Arbor, 1979), pp. 29–31.

65. See the annotations by E. Toddes, A. Chudakov, and M. Chudakova in Tynianov, *Poetika,* e.g., pp. 473nn.7,13, 475n.31.

66. S. Kartsevskii read a paper on Saussure for an audience of Moscow linguists as early as 1919. S. I. Bernshtein read a paper on him in Moscow in 1923. See A. A. Kholodovich, "O 'Kurse obshchei lingvistiki' F. de Sossiura," Foreword to Ferdinand de Saussure, *Trudy po iazykoznaniiu* (Moscow, 1977), p. 28n.4. See also Erlich, *Russian Formalism,* p. 65.

67. Noted in A. Bem's review of Mandelstam's "O prirode slova" (first published as a separate pamphlet), *Volia Rossii* (Prague) 6–7 (1923): 159ff.

68. Mandelstam, "O prirode slova." The formulation appears to have resurfaced in, or even prefigured, the polemics between Trotskii and the Formalists. See note 94. K. Taranovsky (*Essays on Mandel'štam* [Cambridge, Mass., 1976]) traces Mandelstam's formulation to Tiutchev—"Kak dushi smotriat"—and to Orphics in Viacheslav Ivanov, the latter connection resurfacing in Mandelstam's 1917 Crimean poem "Eshche daleko asfodelei" as "shleif vospominanii za kormoi."

69. *SS* 2, p. 251. Cf. Mandelstam's "winged Nike" with Shklovskii's essay "Potebnia" in *Poetika* (1919): "Nike is Nike even without the head as long as she retains her wings."

70. A. Herzen, *O razvitii revoliutsionnykh idei v Rossii,* vol. 3 of *Sochineniia* (Moscow, 1956).

71. On the uses in the 1920s of Herzen as the prophet of the 1917 revolution, see an article by Ivanov-Razumnik, "Gersten o nashikh dniakh," which consisted almost entirely of "pertinent" quotations from Herzen's writings on 1848 (R. V. Ivanov-Razumnik, *A. I. Gertsen: 1870–1920* [Petrograd, 1920]). Cf.: "One of Herzen's prophecies has already come true: 'Russia will never be *juste-milieu*' . . . What is this: the Third Rome or the Third International? Neither. This is the Third Russia" (the anonymous [I. Lezhnev?] leading article in *Novaia Rossiia* 1 [March 1922]: 13). For many Russian intellectuals, particularly those associated with the Socialist Revolutionary party, Herzen's writings virtually possessed the status of a sacred text. Cf. the following "confession" by a former S-R who was planning to repatriate to Russia: "Other people had the Gospels for the holy writ, and for me, this was that little blue issue of Herzen's *The Bell* with a medallion of the Decembrists [on the cover]. . . . You will say that this was religion, too. Yes, yes, exactly so. This, too, was religion . . . We were anticipating our own type of Resurrection of Christ, anticipating the second coming of Christ" (an anonymous letter to the Editor, *Dni* 5 [November 3, 1922]).

72. This Pushkinian image reappears later on—in part as commentary on the posthumous reception of Maiakovskii—in Mandelstam's "Stikhi o russkoi poezii" (July 1932): "I zrachek krovavoi belki krutiat v strashnom kolese" (*SS*

1: 264). Cf. Vl. Maiakovskii, *Pro eto:* "V etoi teme, / i lichnoi / i melkoi, / perepetoi ne raz / i ne piat', / ia kruzhil poeticheskoi belkoi / i khochu kruzhit'sia opiat'."

73. "Winged Nike" is, of course, a tautology, because the wings constitute the "distinctive feature" of the goddess. After all, a statuette without a head but with wings intact can still be identified as Nike, but one without wings, even if everything else is intact, cannot. See note 69. Mandelstam used the image in his essay on Pasternak, "Zametki o poezii," *SS* 2, p. 265.

74. On Saussure, see note 66.

75. Erlich, *Russian Formalism*, p. 65.

76. Cf. R. Jakobson: "The function of poetry is to point out that the sign is not identical with its referent" ("Co je poesie," in *Volné směry* 30 [1933–34]: 229).

77. The Freiburg School was perhaps the foremost representative of the Nominalist tradition in philosophy at the turn of the twentieth century.

78. Many Russians were familiar with Bergson on the basis of N. O. Losskii's *Intuitivnaia filosofiia Bergsona*, which had gone through three editions by 1922. Bergson's philosophy (specifically, *Matter and Memory*) represented, in fact, one of the inspirational sources for the early Formalist theory of poetic speech as "disautomatized." See L. P. Iakubinskii, "Skoplenie odinakovykh plavnykh," p. 52n. The question of Bergson's influence on contemporary Soviet criticism is discussed in R. A. Maguire, *Red Virgin Soil: Soviet Literature in the 1920s* (Princeton, 1968). See also A. Asmus, "Estetika Bergsona," *Na literaturnom postu* 2 (1929): 2–18.

79. *SS* 2, p. 249.

80. Mandelstam may have been familiar with Ockham on the basis of Windelbandt's *Istoriia novoi filosofii* (St. Petersburg, 1904–5).

81. Tiutchev's "A thought verbalized is a lie" ("Silentium"). Cf. Mandelstam's "Silentium" and Blok's programmatic "Khudoznik" (The Artist).

82. "The goal of poetry was the spellbinding magic of rhythmic speech mediating between the world of divine essences and man" (Viach. Ivanov, "Zavety simvolizma," *Apollon* 8 [1910]: 12). For Blok, see "Poeziia zagovor i zaklinanii" (1906, *SS* 5), where the value of modern poetry is predicated on its retention of verbal magic (the "gold dust" in the otherwise valueless ore). Hence S. Gorodetskii's characterization of Blok's central technique as "liromagicheskii priem" (S. Gorodetskii, "Nekotorye techeniia v sovremennoi russkoi poezii," *Apollon* 1 [1913]: 47). For A. Belyi, see "Problemy kul'tury," in *Simvolizm*.

83. *SS* 2, p. 251.

84. *SS* 2, p. 242.

85. The question of this misreading is discussed in my article "The Whisper of History and the Noise of Time in the Poetry and Prose of Osip Mandel'shtam," *The Russian Review* 37, no. 4 (1978): 433 and 433n. For a different view, see N. Struve, *Ossip Mandelstam* (Paris, 1982).

86. A. Belyi, "Problemy kul'tury," in *Simvolizm*.

87. See note 78.

88. For a discussion of Ockham's intuitivism, see M. H. Carré, *Realists and Nominalists* (Oxford, 1946), pp. 107–110.

89. See Abelard: "Could the generic term 'rose' continue to have significance if no particular roses were to exist?" (in B. Geyer, ed., *Beiträge zur Geschichte der Philosophie des Mittelaters*, vol. 21 [1919], p. 8).

90. *SS* 2, p. 255.

91. R. Jakobson, *Noveishaia russkaia poeziia (Nabrosok pervyi). Viktor Khlebnikov* (Prague, 1921), p. 10; and B. Tomashevskii, *Teoriia literatury: Poetika* (Moscow, 1931), p. 9.

92. See Erlich, *Russian Formalism*, p. 210.

93. L. Trotskii, *Literature and Revolution* (Moscow, 1924) p. 183. Reference is to Shklovskii's treatment of the ecstatics in "O poezii i zaumnom iazyke" (1919), published in *Poetika* (1919). Indirectly, the passage is linking Shklovskii with Gumilev's "Slovo," a poem that cites the first verse of the Gospel according to John.

94. V. Shklovskii, *O teorii prozy* (Moscow and Leningrad, 1925), p. 5. Ronen ("Osip Mandel'štam") was the first to point to Trotskii as the object of Shklovskii's polemics.

95. Psyche-soul-shadow in the underworld. Although Trotskii never mentioned Mandelstam by name, it is unlikely that he was ignorant of Mandelstam's critical writings. Far lesser names made their way into his *Literature and Revolution*. What makes this hypothesis even more plausible is that in "Promezhutok," Iurii Tynianov substituted Trotskii's "shadows" for Mandelstam's "word-Psyche" in defining principal features of Mandelstam's poetics: "He has, not words, but shadows of words [*u nego ne slova, a teni slov*]." Coming from a Formalist critic and appearing in 1924, these words could not help referring to Trotskii's self-assured pronouncement.

96. "On the Nature of the Word," finished about February–March 1922, was published in Khar'kov by Rakovskaia's press "Istoki." The epigraph from Gumilev's "Slovo" was inserted by the press (NM 2, p. 86). Then the capital of the Soviet Ukraine, Kharkov was, of course, well supplied with the publications from Moscow and Petrograd. Trotskii's *Literature and Revolution* came out in 1923 (1st ed.). Trotskii was working on a series of articles, "Vne-Oktabr'skaia literatura," for Pravda sometime around August 15, 1922 (L. Fleishman, *Pasternak v dvadtsatye gody* [Munich, (1981)], p. 14). According to I. Howe, Trotskii wrote the bulk of *Literature and Revolution* in the summers of 1922 and 1923 (*Leon Trotsky* [New York, 1978], p. 96).

97. *SS* 2, p. 259. Mandelstam was not the only one to use the Pushkinian allegories of Mozart and Salieri to describe the difference between Symbolism and Acmeism, respectively. This terminology was implied by Valerii Briusov in his earliest characterization of the Acmeists as poets who "check their inspiration with reason [*proverka vdokhnoveniia rassudkom*]" ("Segoniashnii den' russkoi poezii," *RM* 33, no. 7 [July 1912], p. 22 [3d pagination]). See also V. Stanevich, "O Sal'erizme," *Trudy i dni* 7 (1914). More recently, comparing Gumilev and Blok, E. Gollerbakh resorted to the same terms. This approach prompts one to treat Mandelstam's essay—which begins with an epigraph

from Gumilev and concludes with the affirmation of "manliness," a virtual synecdoche of Gumilev—as a form of obituary and a funeral vow of loyalty to the tradition initiated by a fellow Acmeist and friend. In the same review, Gollerbakh singled out Mandelstam from among the Petersburg "passé-ists" as a poet of profound thought who produced a number of "'aphoristic verses' which would survive their author" (E. Gollerbakh, "Peterburgskaia Kamena," *Novaia Rossiia. Obshchestvenno-literaturnyi i nauchnyi ezhemesiachnyi zhurnal* [Petrograd] 1 [1922]: 87–88). See also Nadezhda Mandelstam's essay "Motsart i Sal'eri" (*VRSKhD* 103 [1972]), which carries on the ethico-literary debates begun during the "crisis of Symbolism."

98. See Gumilev's and Gorodetskii's manifestos of Acmeism. For the history of the naming of the school, see R. Timenchik, "Zametki ob akmeizme," *RL* 7/8 (1974): 24–30.

99. As an author, Mandelstam was closely associated with the Change of Landmarks publications such as *Rossiia* and *Nakanune,* and it was indicative of Mandelstam's attitude that the editor of *Sovetskii iug* subtitled Mandelstam's essay "Shuba" as "Zapiski smenovekhovtsa" (Notes of a Change-of-Landmarks-ist). Regarding Ivanov and Blok, among the more recent works that touch on the subject of their ideological allegiances, see Z. G. Mints, "A. Blok i V. Ivanov," in *Edinstvo i izmenchivost' istoriko-literaturnogo protsessa. Uchene zapiski Tartuskogo gosudarstvennogo universiteta,* no. 604. *Trudy po russkoi i slavianskoi filologii. Literaturovedenie* (Tartu, 1983), pp. 97–111. The article contains a bibliography.

100. B. Jangfeldt, *Majakovskij and Futurism,* pp. 51–71.

101. "Deviatnadtsatyi vek" was published in the first issue of the Imagists' magazine *Gostinnitsa dlia puteshestvuiushchikh v prekrasnom* (1922).

102. Compare Mandelstam's "On the Nature of the Word" (*SS* 2) with the more conventional (i.e., not overly involved with numerology) portions of Khlebnikov's "Nasha osnova" (1921).

103. See note 34, and Vl. Markov, Introduction to *Russian Imagism: 1919–1924.*

104. "Literaturnaia Moskva (rozhdenie fabuly)" (1922), *SS* 2, p. 336. "I imagine a synthetic poet of modernity, not as a Verhaern, but as a Verlaine of culture. For him the entire complexity of the world is the same Pushkinian reed-pipe" ("Slovo i kul'tura" [1921], *SS* 2, p. 227). Cf. Mandelstam's earliest poetic declaration: "Who could successfully combine the severity of Tiutchev with Verlaine's childishness, imparting his own stamp to the combination" (*SS* 4, p. 498). In "Slovo i kul'tura," Mandelstam was polemicizing with V. Briusov, the champion of Verhaern in Russia, who had been advocating "scientific poetry," at least since 1909 (see Briusov, "Literaturnaia zhizn' Frantsii: Nauchnaia poeziia," *RM* 6 [1909]). Scientific poetry, as Briusov advocated it in the early 1920s, was ostensibly directed against the use of folkloric "superstition" as practiced by Mandelstam, V. Khlebnikov, Vl. Khodasevich (e.g., "Ballada"), and many others. See Briusov's "Pou sto" (1922), in *Dali, SS* 3, p. 137. See also D. Maksimov, *Valerii Briusov* (Leningrad, 1969), pp. 233–338. Mandelstam followed Briusov's work of those years with serious interest. Rising

above the fray, he praised Briusov's latest Futurist-oriented poetry in the 1923 essay "Buria i natisk." See also E. Zamiatin, "O sintetizme" (1921), in *Litsa* (New York, 1967).

105. Mandelstam, "Utro Akmeizma" (1913), *SS* 2.

106. "Slovo i kul'tura" (1921), *SS* 2, p. 223.

107. L. Ginzburg, "Poetika Osipa Mandel'shtama," in *O starom i novom* (Leningrad, 1982), pp. 257ff.

108. See Mandelstam's "Pshenitsa chelovecheskaia" (*Nakanune* [Berlin], June 7, 1922) and "Gumanizm i sovremennost'" (*SS* 2, pp. 352–54). For Mandelstam's negative attitude to England, as a haughty bourgeois country isolated from the great European tradition, see Kablukov's diary (A. Morozov, "Mandel'shtam v zapisiakh dnevnika S. P. Kablukova," *VRSKhD* 129, no. 3 [1979]). Cf.: "I see nothing organic in a constitutional system—rather, an organic clamp, reflecting the decay of the organism of a people who have lost the religious center. In my convictions, I am no democrat. . . . One should always remember the irrationality of being that gives birth to the ordeal of history [*rozhdaiushchego muku istorii*]" (N. Berdiaev, "K psikhologii revoliutsii," *RM* 29, no. 3 [1908]: 51–71).

109. See M. Lewin, "The Social Background of Stalinism," in *Stalinism: Essays on Historical Interpretation*, ed. R. C. Tucker (New York, 1977); and S. Cohen, *Bukharin and the Bolshevik Revolution: A Political Biography 1888–1938* (New York, 1973), on the "statism" of the first years after the revolution.

110. See S. V. Utechin, *Russian Political Thought: A Concise History* (New York and London, 1963), pp. 78–90.

111. O. Forsh, *Sumashedshii korabl'* (Moscow, 1931); Vl. Khodasevich, *Nekropol'* (Brussels, 1939); V. Shklovskii, *Sentimental'noe puteshestvie* (Berlin, 1923); N. Berberova, *Kursiv moi: Avtobiografiia* (Munich, 1972); I. Odoevtseva, *Na beregakh Nevy* (Washington, D.C., 1967). The list can go on.

112. H. Bergson, *Essai sur les données immédiates de la conscience* (Paris, 1924). As a testimony of Mandelstam's early admiration for Bergson, see Georgii Ivanov's "Bergsona on znal naizust'," in *Peterburgskie zimy* [New York, 1952], p. 113). On this subject, see also N. Struve, *Ossip Mandelstam*, and J. G. Harris's annotations to Osip Mandelstam, *The Complete Critical Prose and Letters* (Ann Arbor, 1979), pp. 615–616.

113. Cf. Mandelstam's poem "Sokhrani moiu rech'" (*SS* 1: 235), addressed to Akhmatova: "Preserve my speech for the sake of its aftertaste of misfortune and smoke." See also G. Levinton and R. Timenchik, "Kniga K. F. Taranovskogo o poezii O. E. Mandel'shtama," *RL* VI-2 (1978): 198.

114. Mandelstam, "V Peterburge my soidemsia snova" (*SS* 1: 118). On this poem, see Broyde, *Osip Mandel'štam and His Age*, pp. 82–102; J. van der Eng-Liedmeier, "Mandel'štam's poem 'V Peterburge my sojdemsja snova,'" *RL* 7/8 (1974): 181–201; and J. E. Malmstad, "A Note on Mandel'štam's 'V Peterburge my sojdemsja snova,'" *RL* V-II (1977): 193–199.

115. The question whether the "we" referred to the poet and his beloved (O. Arbenina, to whom the poem is dedicated) or to the poet's cohort has been a matter of controversy. See, for example, NM 2, pp. 67ff.; Taranovsky, *Essays*

on Mandel'štam, p. 164n.26, who is in agreement with Nadezhda Mandelstam's identification of "we" as the poet's friends; and L. Ginzburg, "Poetika Osipa Mandel'shtama," in *O starom i novom*, p. 271, who makes the perplexing assertion that Mandelstam had in mind a future erotic union (the meaning of the Russian *skhodit'sia*) with Arbenina. On the identification of the addressee of this poem and the so-called Arbenina cycle, see G. Dal'nii [G. G. Superfin], "Po povodu trekhtomnogo sobraniia O. Mandel'shtama," *VRSKhD* 97 (1970), p. 143.

116. "V Peterburge my soidemsia snova" (*SS* 1: 118). It is significant that Mandelstam included the *Tristia* poem in the farewell-to-youth *Kamen': The First Book of Poetry* (1923) but not in the forward-looking *Second Book* (1923).

117. The examples of paronymy: blazhENNoe zhENy ([ë] pronounced as [e], as in the classical tradition); BESSmertnye tsvety—BESSmyslennoe slovo.

118. Mandelstam devoted to them a poem, "Imiabozhtsy" (1915). See note 124.

119. M. Weber, *Wissenschaft und Gesellschaft* 1, p. 230 (cited in R. Bendix, *Max Weber: An Intellectual Portrait* [New York, 1960], p. 89).

120. Pointed out by Ronen, *An Approach to Mandel'štam*.

121. A. Blok, "Shagi komandora" (1910–12). Cf. "Chto tebe tvoia postylaia svoboda, *strakh* poznavshii Don Zhuan," "Proletaet, bryznuv v noch' ogniami, chernyi, tikhii, kak sova, *motor*." The *chastushka*-like lines about the night pass and the fear of a sentry also recall Blok, specifically, *The Twelve*.

122. A. Blok's introduction to *Vozmezdie*. See also Blok's "Intelligentsiia i revoliutsiia" (1918): "We must listen and love the same sounds now that they issue from the orchestra of the world and, as we listen, understand that this [music] is about the same thing, the same thing. Music is no toy; and that *beast* who used to think that music was a toy must now act like a beast: shake, grovel, and guard his things" (*SS* 6, p. 11).

123. This is what N. Stepanov called a "charade." See note 21.

124. A 1912 poem by Mandelstam is a good example of conflation of prayer and incantation: "Thine image, tormenting and vacillating / I could not palpably perceive in the fog. / 'Oh Lord!' I said by mistake, / Without intending to say it. / God's name, like an enormous bird, / Flew out of my breast. / Ahead of me, thick fog is swirling, / An empty cage is behind me" ("Obraz Tvoi, muchitel'nyi i zybkii," *SS* 1: 30). The poem was in Mandelstam's repertoire of public recitals during the civil war. According to Nadezhda Mandelstam (NM 2), he recited it, for example, in Kiev in 1919. The poem, no doubt, is associated with the "Name-of-the-Lord" heresy, which also conflated the notions of incantation and prayer (which are by no means as clearly delineated in the dogmatic literature as one might wish). "The name Jesus predates the god-man Jesus. And this name is a divinity in itself, it is God—'true Jesus'" (from Ilarion [Zelenukhin], *V gorakh Kavkaza*, cited by the Old Believer Bishop Mikhail in "Afonskaia smuta (ob Imiabozhtsakh)," *Rech'*, June 4 (May 22), 1913.

125. Cf. Mandelstam's image of the time of history as a "Bergsonian fan"

unfolding both the present and the future around a center of human consciousness ("Slovo i kul'tura" [1921], *SS* 2, p. 242).

126. See also Viach. Ivanov, "Kop'e Afiny" (1904, 1909): "the psychology of prayer activity, native to the observations of the Brahmins, who knew that out of the energy of the prayer there mysteriously and truly emerges a deity" (*SS* 1, p. 730).

127. One of the central arguments in Ronen, "Osip Mandel'štam."

128. The poem, apart from being part of the Arbenina cycle, also belongs to the theater cycle, associated with the 1920 revival of the famous 1913 production by Mikhail Fokine of Gluck's *Orpheus and Eurydice*. This and the other relevant poem ("Vnov' mertsaet prizrachnaia stsena") are splendidly contextualized in John Malmstad's "Note on Mandel'štam's 'V Peterburge my soidemsia snova.'" Cf. readings of the poem by S. Broyde, *Osip Mandel'štam and His Age*, pp. 82–102; and J. van der Eng-Liedmeier, "Mandel'štam's poem 'V Peterburge my sojdemsja snova.'"

129. Note the use of Mandelstam's poems dealing with the Pushkinian epoch in the historical novels of Iurii Tynianov: "1 ianvaria 1924" and "Net, nikogrda" in *Smert' Vazir'-Mukhtara* (Ronen, "Osip Mandel'štam"); and "Dekabrist" in *Kiukhlia* (A. Men'shutin and A. Siniavskii, *Poeziia pervykh let revoliutsii: 1917–1920* [Moscow, 1964], p. 398).

130. Cf. Mandelstam's 1912 "Peterburgskie strofy": "Heavy is the burden of a northern snob, Onegin's ancient ennui; At the Senate square: a wave of a snow drift, smoke from a bonfire, and the chill of a bayonet." The last three items in the poem's enumeration are synecdoches or, better, emblems of the ordeals that a Russian martyr had to undergo (Konstantin Leont'ev's freeze of the Imperial Byzantine state, the literal and metaphoric burning at the stake, and the bayonet of the government troops dispersing a demonstration or suppressing a rebellion). The Senate Square was the place where the Decembrists took their final stand.

131. The allusion to Pushkin's "For Krivtsov" ("Ne pugai nas, milyi drug," 1817) was first pointed out by Ronen, "Leksicheskii povtor, podtekst i smysl v poetike Osipa Mandel'štama," in *Slavic Poetics: Essays in Honor of Kiril Taranovsky*, ed. R. Jakobson, C. H. van Schonefeld, and D. S. Worth (The Hague, 1973). In an approximate English rendering, the poem reads: "Do not frighten us, dear friend, with the tomb's close house-warming: We have not, believe me, time for this sort of trifling business. Let another slowly draw on the chilling cup of life; as to us, we'll give up our youth only together with our dear life; each of us shall take a seat on the threshold of his own tomb, plead for and receive: a fresh wreath from the Queen of Paphos [Aphrodite], another moment—from our trusty leisure; fill the common cup, and the crowds of our shadows will flee to the calm Lethe; the instant of our death shall be bright: And the beloveds of the playboys shall gather their light ash into the idle urns of feasts."

132. See note 23 and my discussion of Veselovskii in this chapter.

133. Vl. Khodasevich's famous "Ballada" (1921) provides an excellent

gloss to Mandelstam's usage of the "night sun" in this poem, for it is, of course, the astral Orpheus who in Khodasevich replaces the "sixteen-candle-power sun." The poem is equally significant in what it has to say about the "blessed and senseless word": "Bessviaznye, strastnye rechi, Nel'zia v nikh poniat' nichego, No *zvuki pravdivee smysla, I slovo sil'nee vsego.*"

134. Mandelstam's letter to Ivanov of August 13, 1909 (*SS* 2, pp. 486–488).
135. K. Erberg "O vozdushnykh mostakh kritiki," *Apollon* 2 (1909): 61.
136. In Russian the last phrase reads: *obshchestvennyi put' i podvig sovremennogo poeta* ("Slovo i kul'tura" [1921], *SS* 2, pp. 226ff.).
137. E.g., Hebrews 9.
138. Vl. Solov'ev, "Blizko, daleko l'," *Stikhotvoreniia* (1974), p. 63.
139. Viach. Ivanov, "Nietzsche and Dionysus" (1904, 1909), *SS* 1, p. 719. This "identity" should not be confused with Mandelstam's polemics with Ivanov in "Morning of Acmeism" (1913, *SS* 2, p. 324) where he advocated, instead of Ivanov's "a realibus ad realiora," the concept of identity between the work of art and the work of nature, fundamental to the aesthetics of Schiller and, especially, Schelling. Since Mandelstam's essay is full of puns, his "'A = A'—what a beautiful theme for poetry" may also be interpreted as an inversion of Ivanov's *Dionysian* formula by one who at the time identified with the journal *Apollon*. In any case, tracing Mandelstam's declaration to Henri Bergson unnecessarily attributes to the poet a basic misunderstanding of the French philosopher, who used the basic logical formula in *Creative Evolution* in order to show its incompatibility with the true, intuitive, creative consciousness. Cf. N. Struve, *Ossip Mandelstam*.
140. Mandelstam, "Slovo i kul'tura" (1921), *SS* 2, p. 227.
141. Mandelstam, letter to Ivanov of August 13, 1909 (*SS* 2, pp. 486ff.).

VII

1. P. D. Zhukov, "Levyi front isskusstv," *Kniga i revoliutsiia* 3/27 (1923): 41.
2. V. Zhirmunskii, "Preodolevshie simvolizm" (1916, 1921), in *Voprosy teorii literatury* (Leningrad, 1928), pp. 278–333, esp. p. 330, where Mandelstam is compared with Gogol and Maiakovskii.
3. B. Eikhenbaum, *Anna Akhmatova: Opyt analiza* (Petersburg, 1923), p. 26.
4. "There is an unforgivable callousness in our attitude toward the dead—we cross them out, associate them with the past. . . . Infinitely rich is the consciousness that says: 'all is in the present.' . . . The vitality of symbolism, its incessant charm. . . . The reflected light of symbolism [can be seen in the recent work of] Mikhail Kuzmin, O. Mandelstam, Nikolai Gumilev" (E. Gollerbakh, [no title], *Novaia russkaia kniga* [Berlin] 7 [1922], p. 2).
5. Eikhenbaum, *Anna Akhmatova:* "The poetry of symbolism is already behind us. It is no longer possible to speak about Bal'mont, and about Blok—it is already difficult. Before us, there are Akhmatova and Mandelstam on one side and the Futurists and the Imagists on the other" (pp. 7ff.). On the Ac-

meists as elaborators of the Symbolist tradition: "Acmeists expand this area of the [Symbolist] tradition. Mandelstam strengthens the classical line and declares: 'Classical poetry is the poetry of revolution'" (p. 19). Against Zhirmunskii: "Acmeists are not a militant group: they consider their chief mission to be the achievement of equilibrium, smoothing out contradictions, introduction of corrections" (p. 24). Eikhenbaum's position was consonant with Iurii Tynianov's view of Akhmatova in "Promezhutok" (1924) as a poet virtually limited to the theme of Lot's wife.

6. Eikhenbaum, *Anna Akhmatova*, p. 7.

7. N. Punin, *Zhizn' iskusstva* 41 (October 17, 1922): 3.

8. "Kontsert na vokzale" (*SS* 1: 125). For an interpretation of the poem as one developing the "Lermontovian" theme of the poet's way, see K. Taranovsky, "Concert at the Railroad Station: The Problem of Context and Subtext," in *Essays on Mandel'štam* (Cambridge, Mass., 1976). Apart from situating Mandelstam in a particular tradition and showing how Mandelstam managed to encode the tradition in the four stanzas, the essay focuses on the approach to reading Mandelstam that was pioneered by the author and received a further elaboration in the work of his students, Omry Ronen and Steven Broyde. For a discussion of this poem that takes as its point of departure Iurii Tynianov's views, see L. Ginzburg, "Poetika Osipa Mandel'shtama," in *O starom i novom* (Leningrad, 1982). If I am not mistaken, Lidiia Ginzburg was the first to hint at the presence of a Blokian subtext in the poem. For the rich Tiutchevian subtext, see E. Toddes, "Mandel'shtam i Tiutchev," *International Journal of Slavic Linguistics and Poetics* 17 (1974). For a more precise dating as well as a wealth of additional "subtexts," see O. Ronen, *An Approach to Mandel'štam* (Jerusalem, 1983), pp. xvii–xx.

9. G. Lelevich, "Gippokratovo litso" (Hippocrates' mask), *Krasnaia nov'* 1 (1925): 296. The article's title refers to a medical term for the "death mask"— a pall that comes over a dying man's face. Among other poets wearing this "mask," according to Lelevich, were Pasternak and Khodasevich. The mention of Hamlet's famous line refers to Mandelstam's "Vek" (1922, *SS* 1: 135): "In order to tear the age out of captivity, in order to erect the new world, the joints of gnarled days need to be bound together with the flute. . . . But your spine is broken, my cruel, dear age/century." *The Russian Contemporary* was a short-lived journal (only four issues appeared, all in 1924).

10. *SS* 2, p. 258.

11. *Shum vremeni*, "Muzyka v Pavlovske," *SS* 2. According to NM 2, Mandelstam had most of *The Noise of Time* finished in 1923. See the correspondence between Mandelstam and Pasternak in "Zamechaniia o peresechenii biografii Osipa Mandel'shtama i Borisa Pasternaka," in *Pamiat': Istoricheskii sbornik* 4 (Moscow, 1979; Paris, 1981), p. 293. See also letters of Mandelstam and Pilniak to Voronskii in *Iz istorii sovetskoi literatury 1920–1930-kh godov*, *LN* 93 (Moscow, 1983), pp. 570 and 601.

12. Apart from this Blokian subtext, see also David Burliuk's 1913 poem "Luna kak vsha polzet nebes podkladkoi" (noted by Taranovsky, *Essays on Mandel'štam*): "The sky is a corpse!!! Not more! / Stars are worms drunk with fog

... Stars—worms—(pussy, live) rash!" etc. This rather artless imitation of Baudelaire's "Charogne" (or, in general, of the *poètes maudits*) was cited by V. Khlebnikov and A. Kruchenykh in *Dokhlaia luna* (Moscow, 1913). See Vl. Markov, *Manifesty i programmy russkikh futuristov*, vol. 27 of *Slavische Propyläen* (Munich, 1967), p. 54. It is also possible that the "works" had something to do with a now-lost mediating text the echo of which can be heard in the following passage: "Let heaven portend trouble. Let old women pronounce oracles [*prorekaiut*] about the *worm in heaven crawling in refuse*, let them predict wholesale death from hunger" (N. Nikitin, "Kamni," *Zavtra: Literaturno-kriticheskii sbornik*, vol. 1, ed. E. Zamiatin, M. Kuzmin, and M. Lozinskii (Berlin, 1923), p. 36.

13. Blok's imagery here owes much to the "echo" of the railroad at the end of *Madame Bovary*, when Emma's daydreaming in a hotel room is disturbed by the deafening noise of a cart hauling strips of iron. Mandelstam noted this "railroad link" between Tolstoy's *Anna Karenina* and Flaubert's novel about, as he called her, "Anna's younger cousin." See Mandelstam's digression on prose at the conclusion of *The Egyptian Stamp*.

14. The last sentence provides a valuable subtext to Mandelstam's "Vek" (1922): "Only a parasite living off the backs of beasts [*zakhrebetnik*] trembles at the threshold of the new days." Clearly, the poet who wished to be identified with the dead century and offer himself as a sacrificial victim to establish continuity between the new and old age did not wish to be confused with the "parasitic" remnants of that age. That same caution, exemplified also by the "oath of allegiance to the fourth estate" ("1 January 1924"), resurfaces in the 1930s, particularly in "The age-wolfhound leaps on my shoulders" and "Eshche daleko mne do patriarkha."

15. For a different, more precise, dating of the poem as well as a detailed discussion, see Ronen, *An Approach to Mandel'štam*, pp. xvii–xx.

16. The story of Mandelstam's "setting things straight" with one of his friends, Shileiko, who accused the poet of toadying before the new regime, suggests that his position around 1924 (before the publication of "1 January 1924") lent itself to ambiguous interpretations on both sides of the political aisle (NM 2, pp. 500–501).

17. In a polemic with Lidiia Ginzburg, who saw in the image a simile of "a horse in a lather," Taranovsky pointed to the froth (*pena*) as an allusion to Mandelstam's earlier programmatic "Silentium," a poem about the birth of Aphrodite out of the foam of the sea ("Remain foam, Aphrodite, and word, return to music"). I do not consider the two points mutually exclusive, especially in view of Mandelstam's identification of the "age," the nineteenth century, with the "beast" (see his "My beast, my age") and with the steed (see Broyde, *Osip Mandel'štam and His Age* [Cambridge, Mass., 1975], on "He Who Found a Horseshoe").

18. Mandelstam, "On the Nature of the Word," SS 2, p. 242. Cf. N. Struve, *Ossip Mandelstam* (Paris, 1982); and G. Freidin, "The Whisper of History and the Noise of Time in the Writings of Osip Mandelstam," *The Russian Review* 37, no. 4 (1978): 436.

19. N. Gumilev, "Zabludivshiisia tramvai" (1920).
20. Fedor Tiutchev, "Ia liuteran liubliu bogosluzhen'e."
21. Mandelstam, "Stikhi o russkoi poezii" (1933), *SS* 1: 262–264. Echoes of Lermontov's "1 January" ("Kak chasto pestroiu tolpoiu okruzhen") are discernible in Mandelstam's "1 January 1924." The last stanza of "A Concert" alludes to Lermontov's "Dream" ("With lead in my chest, in the valley of Dagestan," 1841): "And I dreamed of a luminescent night feast in my native land" (*I snilsia mne siiaiushchii ogniami Vechernii pir v rodimoi storone*). Note the dedication to Lermontov in Pasternak's *My Sister-Life* (1921). A poignant characterization of Lermontov may be found in Pasternak's article on the Georgian poet Nikolai Baratashvili: "Artists-outcasts [*khudozhniki-otshchepentsy*] like to cross every *t* and dot every *i*. They are unusually specific because they do not believe others to be capable [of discernment]. Lermontov's specificity is insistent and haughty. His details captivate us supernaturally. In their small features we recognize what we ourselves ought to have [imaginatively] completed. This is a magical reading of our thoughts across great distance" (cited in E. B. Pasternak and E. V. Pasternak, "Boris Pasternak: Iz perepiski s pisateliami," *LN* 93, p. 728n.4). Lermontov played a similar role in Maiakovskii's self-image of a kenotic poet-outcast. The "ethical" aspect of Mandelstam's allusive poetics, too, may be traced to a Lermontov poem: "It will encounter no response among the worldly din—the word born out of flame and light. But whether in a temple or amid battle, wherever I am, as soon as I hear it, I shall recognize it. With my prayer unfinished, I shall respond to that sound, and I will dash out of a battle in order to greet it" ("Est' rechi—znachen'e" [1840]).
22. M. Lermontov, "Vykhozhu odin ia na dorogu."
23. Mandelstam, "Sestry—tiazhest' i nezhnost' . . ." (1920), *SS* 1: 108.
24. Cf. the discussion of Mandelstam's poetics of "anamnesis" in Iu. Levin et al., "Russkaia semanticheskaia poetika kak potentsial'naia kul'turnaia paradigma" *RL* 7/8 (1974): 47–82.
25. V. Shklovskii, *Razvertyvanie siuzheta* (Petrograd, 1921), p. 10. Cf. Iu. Tynianov's conception of the "density of poetic/rhythmic series" (*tesnota stikhovogo/ritmicheskogo riada*) developed in *Problema stikhotvornogo iazyka* (Moscow, 1965), p. 76. A periphrasis of this terminology is in Mandelstam's "Ia po lesenke pristavnoi": "I shall tear myself out of the burning series and shall return to my native phonoseries" (*Iz goriashchikh vyrvus' riadov i vernus' v rodnoi zvukoriad*). This wordplay was possible since the Russian *riad*, "series," denotes also "harmony," "rank," "row," and, etymologically, "order" (*poriadok*).
26. See note 1. Zhukov called Mandelstam the second Andreevskii (a nineteenth-century Russian poet who opposed the civic-minded tendentiousness of contemporary art) and quoted with approval the lines of Akhmatova ("Now nobody will listen to songs") and Maiakovskii ("Perhaps I am the last poet") announcing the end of the poetry.
27. Cf. O. Ronen, "The Dry River and the Black Ice: Anamnesis and Amnesia in Mandel'štam's poem 'Ja slovo pozabyl, čto ja xotel skazat,'" *SH* 1 (1977): 177–184.

28. A. N. Veselovskii, "Psikhologicheskii parallelizm i ego formy v otrazhenii poeticheskogo stilia," in *Istoricheskaia poetika* (Moscow, 1940), p. 190.

29. "Oh, Europe, a new Hellas, guard the Acropolis and Piraeus! We do not need *gifts from the island*" (Mandelstam, "Sobiralis' elliny voinoiu" [1914], *SS* 1: 70). In early 1917, Mandelstam's friend Kablukov recorded with strong disapproval Mandelstam's vituperations against the "parliamentary, haughty England" (A. Morozov, "Mandel'shtam v zapisiakh dnevnika S. P. Kablukova," *VRSKhD* 129, no. 3 [1979], p. 154). See also Broyde, *Osip Mandel'štam and His Age*, pp. 23ff.

30. Mandelstam, "Gumanism i sovremennost'" (Humanism and the Present, 1922). See also L. Fleishman's publication of another contemporary essay by Mandelstam, "Pshenitsa chelovecheskaia" (The Wheat of Humanity), which further clarifies Mandelstam's political thinking during the first years of the NEP ("Neizvestnaia stat'ia Osipa Mandel'shtama," *Wiener Slawistischer Almanach* 10 [1982]). As Fleishman noted, there exists a certain symmetry between the pro-Soviet politics of Mandelstam's publicistic writings of the period and Nadezhda Mandelstam's tendency to dismiss them as insignificant trifles produced in one sitting for the sake of meager royalties. The "mountain" casting its shadow in this essay bears fruitful comparison with its counterpart in the "Sermon on the Mount" part of "Slate Ode": "I am night's friend, I am the front soldier of the day. Blessed is he who has called flint a pupil of running water. *Blessed is he who tied the sandal on the foot of the mountains* on firm ground" (*SS* 1: 137). Tying the sandal to the mountain of the approaching social architecture can hardly be construed as an expression of disloyalty to the Soviet regime.

31. Mandelstam, "Na kamennykh otrogakh Pierii" (1919).

32. P. Florenskii, *Stolp i utverzhdenie istiny: Opyt pravoslavnoi feoditsei v dvenadtsati pis'makh* (Moscow, 1914), p. 161. The quotation from Belyi comes from *Simvolizm* (Moscow, 1910), p. 30.

33. Mandelstam, "O prirode slova" (On the Nature of the Word, 1921). For the association of *zemlia* with the Slavophile and populist concept of conciliarity (*sobornost'*), consider: *zemskii sobor, zemstvo*. This is yet another reason not to confuse Mandelstam's "classicism" with the related program by A. Efros announced in 'Vestnik y poroga: Dukh klassiki" (in *Liricheskii krug: Stranitsy poezii i kritiki,* vol.1 [Moscow, 1922]). Significantly, Mandelstam's contribution to this issue consisted of two poems printed in *reverse* chronological order. The first, "Umyvalsia noch'iu na dvore" (1921), a poem signifying resolve in the face of a possible death, was permeated with Russian folklore in terms of both its strongly flavored rural lexicon ("na dvore," "na zamok," "vorota," "topor," "kholst") and its composition, which strongly echoed the two-part structure of incantations: the "epic" (first two stanzas) and the spell proper (N. Poznanskii, *Zagovory* [Petrograd, 1917]). The other, "Kogda Psikheia-zhizn' spuskaetsia k teniam" (1920), ending on a hesitant note, represented the epitome of Mandelstam's "Hellenism" of the *Tristia* period. Cf. O. Ronen, "Anamnesis and Amnesia," and "A Beam upon the Axe: Some Antecedents to Osip Mandel'štam's 'Umyvalsja nočiu na dvore,'" *SH* 1 (1977).

34. The texts in which these images appear are: *SS* 1, nos. 116, 127, 112–114, 108, 126. Cf. O. Ronen's "Osip Mandel'štam: An Ode and an Elegy" [Ph.D. diss., Harvard University, 1976]) productive characterization of such iterative usage as "talismanic" (and/or "magic helpers").

35. G. Dal'nii [G. G. Superfin], "Po povodu trekhtomnogo sobraniia O. Mandel'shtama," *VRSKhD* 97 (1970).

36. "Voz'mi na radost' iz moikh ladonei," *SS* 1: 116. I translate the word *medunitsa* (lungwort) as "honeysuckle" for the sake of retaining Mandelstam's etymological wordplay. Cf. Konstantin Bal'mont's *Sonety solntsa, meda i luny* (Moscow, 1917), which may have served as a source of elementary vocabulary and grammar for this poem, particularly in view of the cycle's Nietzschean and Lermontovian referents. Mandelstam described his poetry as "translations that suggest the existence of a brilliant original," possibly Mandelstam's own verse. On a deeper level, Mandelstam may have been relying on Viacheslav Ivanov, especially *Cor ardens* (e.g., "Kogda vzmyvaet dukh v nadmirnye vysoty" or the cycle "Zolotye zavesy"), and, of course, Nietzsche's "The Honey Sacrifice" in *Thus Spake Zarathustra*. See also Taranovsky, *Essays on Mandel'štam*, pp. 99–110; and N. A. Nilsson, "Mandel'shtam's Poem 'Voz'mi na radost,'" *RL* 7/8 (1974).

37. Skriabin understood this paronymic play (including trans-sense) as a form of orchestration: "In language, there exist laws of [thematic?] development similar to those in music. . . . The word grows more complex, as do the harmonies, by means of inclusion of certain overtones" (L. Sabaneev, *Vospominaniia o Skriabine* [Moscow, 1925], p. 252, cited in N. Khardzhiev, "Maiakovskii i Khlebnikov," in N. Kkardzhiev and Vl. Trenin, *Poeticheskaia kul'tura Maiakovskogo* [Moscow, 1969], p. 98).

38. In his "Notes on Chénier" (1915?), Mandelstam described the poetry of the Romantics as inimical to the sense of continuity of tradition and likened it to a "necklace of dead nightingales," which "will not convey, will not reveal its enigmas," and which "does not know [the concept of] heritage" (*SS* 2, p. 296). The "cyclical" bees of Persephone were, of course, another matter. The dating of this essay is unclear. It may have been begun in 1914–15 but seems to have been finished much later.

39. Cf. Pasternak's *Doktor Zhivago*, where an icon worn as an amulet by a young cadet deflects Zhivago's bullet. Praising the 1940 edition of Akhmatova's poetry, Pasternak mentioned in his letter to Akhmatova "the magical effect of your representational power" (cited in E. B. Pasternak and E. V. Pasternak, "Boris Pasternak: Iz perepiski s pisateliami," p. 661).

40. Viach. Ivanov, "Religiia Dionisa: Ee proiskhozhdenie i vliianie," *Voprosy zhizni* 6 (1905): 193. Cf. further "Here—'at grave's door young life is effervescent,' as Pushkin put it, and 'plenitude overcomes death' (*so überwältiget Fülle den Tod*), as Goethe says in his *Venetian Epigrams*, as he is describing these Orphic sarcophagi" (ibid., p. 196).

41. See discussion of Jakobson's "Metaphoric and Metonymic Pole" in chapter 4.

42. Cf. R. Timenchik: "Acmeist poetics itself created the object of its

striving which only later underwent explication" ("Tekst v tekste u akmeistov," in *Tekst v tekste: Trudy po znakovym sistemam,* vol. 14 [Tartu, 1981]). Similar observations, if related more to Futurism, may be found in V. Erlich's *Russian Formalism: History—Doctrine* (New Haven and London, 1981), and in the essays on the legacy of Roman Jakobson by E. J. Brown ("Roman Osipovich Jakobson 1896–1982: The Unity of His Thought on Verbal Art," *The Russian Review* 42, no. 1 [1983]) and Hugh McLean ("A Linguist Among Poets," *International Journal of Slavic Linguistics and Poetics* 3 [1983]).

43. M. Detienne, *The Garden of Adonis* (Sussex, Eng., 1977), esp. chapter 4, "The Misfortunes of Mint." Among Mandelstam's probable sources are the story of the Nymph Mintha in Ovid (*Metamorphoses* 10: 728n and A. N. Veselovskii's discussion of the myth of Adonis in "Tri glavy iz istoricheskoi poetiki," *Istoricheskaia poetika,* pp. 221ff.

44. Noted by G. Levinton and R. D. Timenchik ("Kniga K. F. Taranovskogo o poezii O. E. Mandel'shtama," *RL* VI-2 [1978]). That Verlaine's "bonne aventure" (a good luck charm, an amulet) was interpreted as verbal magic may be seen from Boris Pasternak's 1938 translation of the poem. The last stanza reads: "Puskai on vyboltaet sduru / Vse, chto, v pot'makh *chudotvoria,* / *Navorozhit* emu zaria . . . / Vse prochee—literatura" (E. Etkind, ed. *Frantsuzskie stikhi v perevode russkikh poetov XIX–XX vv.* [Moscow, 1969], p. 481).

45. *Dremuchii les* is, needless to say, a topos from Russian fairy tales— another instance of Mandelstam's "naiveté" as a modern poet. Dante's *vita* and *selva oscura* underwent a catachresis to become Mandelstam's "dremuchaia zhizn'," just as his Taygetos asks to be "folk-etymologized" as a derivative of the Russian *taiga*. For the unusual elliptical syntax, cf. Vadim Shershenevich's ideas (via Marinetti) on the use of elliptical infinitive construction in "Lomat' grammatiku" (*2 × 2 = 5* [Moscow, 1920]) and his own practice of the rule, for example, in "Agrammaticheskaia statika" (*Loshad' kak loshad'*), which is echoed in Mandelstam's 1922 "Komu—arak. . . ." The opening sonnet of Bal'mont's *Sonety* also is built around infinitive constructions ("Tvorit', . . . uznat', . . . proiti, . . . sledit'").

46. ". . . My, kak pchely u chresl Afrodity, / V'emsia, solnechnoi pyl'iu povity, / Nad ognem zolotogo tsvetka." (M. Voloshin, "Deti solnecho-ryzhego meda" [1910], in *Stikhotvoreniia,* ed. L. A. Evstigneeva [Leningrad, 1977], p. 184).

47. W. Iser, *The Act of Reading: A Theory of Aesthetic Response* (Baltimore and London, 1978), pp. 68–85.

48. Mandelstam, "Komissarzhevskaia," in *The Noise of Time,* SS 2, p. 99.

49. Mandelstam: "Muchit sil'nee, chem liubaia futuristicheskaia zagadka" (on Annenskii). Writing about the power of the word in Slavic mythology, Afanas'ev maintained that the less people understood the incantation, the greater was the incantation's effectiveness (see A. N. Afanas'ev, *Poeticheskie vozzreniia slavian na prirodu,* pt. 1 [Moscow, 1865], p. 355). This was a common point made by the Futurists ("Deklaratsiia slova kak takovogo") and later

on by the Formalists (e.g., V. Shklovskii, "O poezii i zaumnom iazyke" [1916], in *Poetika: Sborniki po teorii poeticheskogo iazyka* [Petrograd, 1919]).

50. Mandelstam, "Ia slovo pozabyl, chto ia khotel skazat'" (1920), *SS* 1: 113. As first published in 1921, it bore the date November 1920. For draft versions, see N. Khardzhiev's annotations in *Stikhotvoreniia* (Leningrad, 1973), p. 278.

51. See Potebnia on the witch who has forgotten the right word.

52. Cf. Taranovsky's assertion concerning the poem's plot (*Essays on Mandel'štam*, p. 77). Cf. also Ronen, "Anamnesis and Amnesia."

53. Viach. Ivanov, "Religiia Dionisa," pp. 199ff. Cf. Mandelstam's "I ponyne na Afone" (1915): "Slovo—chistoe vesel'e, Istselen'e ot toski" (*SS* 1: 75). Or the 1923 "Kak tel'tse malen'koe krylyshkom": "Ne zabyvai menia, kazni menia, No dai mne imia! Dai mne imia! Mne budet legche s nim, poimi menia, V beremennoi glubokoi sini" (*SS* 1: 139). Both poems, thematically as well as stylistically (they imitate incantations), belong to the genre of verbal magic focused on memory or, more specifically, on the antiamnesiac power of the word.

54. V. Terras, "Classical Motives in the Poetry of Osip Mandelstam," *Slavic and East European Journal* 3 (1966): 251–267; Taranovsky, *Essays on Mandel'štam*, pp. 77ff.; and Ronen, "Anamnesis and Amnesia." The poem may be further elucidated if juxtaposed with Pavel Florenskii's "genealogical" (Nietzsche) meditations on the nature of truth: "Truth, as a Hellene understood it, was *alethea*, that is, something capable of abiding in the stream of forgetfulness [*potok zabveniia*], in the Lethean streams of the sensual world—something that overcomes time . . . , something eternally remembering [cf. Mandelstam's "Eucharist"]. Truth is an eternal memory of a consciousness" (Florenskii, *Stolp i utverzhdenie istiny*, p. 18). Likewise, Florenskii's etymology of *styd* (shame) from *sty-‹d›nu, sty-t'* (to grow cold) might have been related to Mandelstam wordplay here ("ice," "burning," "shame"), which conflated the erotic, "mnemonic," and chthonic thematics. "Shame," Florenskii concluded, "is the feeling of spiritual cold that arises from baring that which must be covered" (ibid., pp. 703–704). Cf. the conclusion of Ronen, "Anamnesis and Amnesia."

55. "Aid—bez-vid, govorit Platon (Gorgii, 495b)" (Florenskii, *Stolp i utverzhdenie istiny*, p. 178).

56. Cf. A. Men'shutin and A. Siniavskii, *Poeziia pervykh let revoliutsii: 1917–1920* (Moscow, 1964), p. 400.

57. Among the more recent works dealing with this issue see R. Timenchik, "Tekst v tekste u akmeistov." The article contains an extensive bibliography.

58. The history of this cult and its association with the ideological climate of the 1920s and, particularly, the 1930s still remains to be written, but see M. Friedberg, *Russian Classics in Soviet Jackets* (New York and London, 1962), esp. chapter 5: "Official Attitudes Toward the Russian Classics," pp. 81–147; and chapter 6: "The Russian Classics and the Soviet Readers," pp. 148–166.

59. Vl. Maiakovskii, "Radovat'sia rano" (December 1918).

60. On the formation of attitudes toward the classical heritage in the years

following the revolution, see B. Jangfeldt, *Majakovskii and Futurism: 1917– 1921*, in Stockholm Studies in Russian Literature, no. 5 (Stockholm, 1976), esp. pp. 51–71.

61. Mandelstam, "Vek" (The Age, 1922), *SS* 1: 132. In a general sense, the lines are self-explanatory; still, they require some glosses. The "age of the infant earth" is a metonymic pun based on the metaphors associated with the contemporary discourse on Russian history, the nineteenth century, or post-Petrine Russia (Herzen) as a period of *infancy* for the country. Cf.: "This qualitatively overripe nineteenth century, the century of steel and neurasthenia was, in the life of Russia, *the first century, the century of brilliant infancy*" (N. Shapir, "Filosofsko-kul'turnye ocherki," *Severnye zapiski* 9 [September 1913]: 58–80). As this innocuous passage indicates, the discourse on Russian history was drenched in associations of redemptive sacrifice with the commencement of a new age. At the risk of being literalist, the "crown of life" (literally, the fontanel, soft cartilage at the top of an infant's skull) has to be interpreted as pointing to the high and recent artistic achievement ("Acme") that the revolution had rendered outdated before it could enjoy a period of natural growth. In effect, Mandelstam is talking about himself, attempting to interpret his perceived "premature retirement" in terms of the redemptive sacrifice. Contemporaries could see through the poem easily, and N. Stepanov even found it crude (see his review of Mandelstam's *Stikhotvoreniia* [1928] in *Zvezda* 6 [1928]: 123). Cf. Broyde, *Osip Mandel'štam and His Age*.

62. *SS* 1:132. On this and its companion poem ("Ia ne znaiu s kakikh por"), see Taranovsky, "The Hayloft," in *Essays on Mandel'štam;* and G. Levinton and R. Timenchik, "Kniga Taranovskogo o poezii Mandel'shtama."

63. Viach. Ivanov, "Dostoevskii i roman-tragediia" (pt. 2) *RM* 32, no. 6 (1911), p. 10 (2d pagination).

64. See, for example, Blok's essay "Katilina" (1918) or his preface to *Vozmezdie*. This theme of "retribution," of the artist's responsibility for everything that is happening in the world (echoes of Dostoevsky), runs through Boris Eikhenbaum's "Sud'ba Bloka" (1921). Cf.: "Blok felt the impending tragedy of his generation and his own tragedy as a master of that generation. . . . Blok knew that this life will demand a retribution and will force one to listen to it" (*Ob Aleksandre Bloke* [Petersburg, 1921], pp. 49 and 51).

65. "Guard sleeping at the doorway" is a quotation from Aleksandr Pushkin's "Nedvizhnyi strazh dremal u tsarskogo poroga" (A. Belyi, "Dnevnik pisatelia. Pochemu ia ne mogu kul'turno rabotat'," *Zapiski mechtatelei* 2–3 [1921]: 115).

66. Mandelstam, "Ode to Beethoven" (1914), *SS* 1: 72: "Oh the flame of the grandiose sacrifice! Half the sky is covered in fire—and it is rent over us, the tent of the royal tabernacle." The imagery is based on the Ivanovian identification of Dionysus and Prometheus as prefigurations of Christ, which in its turn leads to the identification of Christ with the High Priest, the Tabernacle, and the Sacrifice in St. Paul's Epistle to the Hebrews (9:11ff.). The same symbolism is used profanely in "Football II" (1913), *SS* 1: 167: "And with the lev-

ity of a heavyweight, the boxer parried the blows... Oh, the defenseless veil, the unguarded tent!..." The 1914 poem, "There is an unshakable scale of values" (*SS* 1: 64) belongs to the same thematic development: "Like the royal staff in the prophets' tabernacle, solemn pain blossomed among us." Cf. the consequently transparent pun based on the expression "the fear of God" in *The Egyptian Stamp,* where the narrator suggests that "mathematicians should build a tent" in which to house "fear": "I like fear. I've almost said: 'With fear I am not afraid.'"

67. On Mandelstam's uses of *lastochka,* see Taranovsky, *Essays on Mandel'štam,* pp. 158ff.; and G. Freidin, "Time, Identity, and Myth in Osip Mandelstam" (Ph.D. diss., University of California, 1979), chapters 4 and 6. For a few additional and valuable observations, see Levinton and Timenchik, "Kniga Taranovskogo o poezii Mandel'shtama."

68. Cf. Ronen, "Anamnesis and Amnesia."

69. S. Poliakova, *Zakatnye ony dni: Tsvetaeva i Parnok* (Ann Arbor, 1983), p. 24. See also the memoirs of Ol'ga Vaksel', who in the mid 1920s was being courted simultaneously by Osip and Nadezhda Mandelstam (O. Vaksel', "O Mandel'shtame. Iz dnevnika," *Chast' rechi* [New York] 1 [1980]: 251–254). See also S. Polianina, "Ol'ga Vaksel'," *Chast' rechi* 1 (1980): 254–262.

70. "Posokh" (The Staff), *SS* 1: 69.

71. The usage of *domashnost'* (domesticity, familiarity) in this context is oxymoronic. Blok is "domashnii," Pasternak is "domashnii," "universitetskii seminarii," too, is "domashnii."

72. A later, "authorized" version of the first five lines (see *Stikhotvoreniia,* 1973):

> Liubliu pod svodami sedyia tishiny,
> Molebnov, panikhid bluzhdan'e
> I trogatel'nyi chin, emu zhe vse dolzhny,—
> U Isaaka otpevan'e.
> Liubliu sviashchennika netoroplivyi shag, . . .

Cf. Viacheslav Ivanov's poem "Molchaniia" (*Cor ardens*): "Soidem pod svody tishiny . . . gde reiut liki proritsanii." The juxtaposition illustrates well what Mandelstam meant by the "secularization" of poetic speech (Ivanov's "proritsaniia" vs. Mandelstam's "vozglas siryi"). Compare this poem with Mandelstam's "Pshenitsa chelovechestva" (1922), published in Fleishman, "Neizvestnaia stat'ia Mandel'shtama."

73. Iu. Tynianov, "Promezhutok," in *Poetika. Istoriia literatury. Kino* (Moscow, 1977), pp. 189ff.

74. Heine was, of course, the most important of the non-Russian authors for Tynianov, who extensively translated him and devoted to him some of his major historical and comparative work (i.e., "Tiutchev i Geine" in *Arkhaisty i novatory* [Leningrad, 1927]; and "Blok i Geine" in *Ob Aleksandre Bloke.* See, for example, L. Ginzburg, "Tynianov-uchenyi," in *Vospominaniia o Iurii Tynianove,* ed. V. A. Kaverin (Moscow, 1983), p. 171. The passage from "Pro-

mezhutok" must also be interpreted in generational terms—another instance of a younger critic making the poet aware that he was, like a classic, "dead." On the uses of Mandelstam in Tynianov's fiction, see Men'shutin and Siniavskii, *Poeziia pervykh let revoliutsii,* pp. 398ff.; and Ronen, *An Approach to Mandel'štam,* pp. 343–345.

75. Cf. Boris Pasternak's letter to Mandelstam (January 31, 1925) concerning the planned *Spektorskii* (cited in note 14, chap. 6). Mandelstam's treatment of these themes in *Shum vremeni* was, indeed, perceived as disdainful. See N. Lerner, "Osip Mandel'shtam. 'Shum vremeni'" (review), *Byloe* 6 (1925): 244.

76. According to the poet's widow, *The Noise of Time* (written for the most part in Gaspra in 1923) developed the problematic of the poem "The Age" (1922), the problematic that found its resolution in "1 January 1924" (a "curative" poem, in the words of Ronen, "Osip Mandel'štam"). See NM 2, p. 482.

77. M. Weber, *Essays in Sociology* (New York, 1958), p. 248.

78. See note 75.

79. "Ia v khorovod tenei, toptavshikh nezhnyi lug," *SS* 1: 123. The poem belongs to the Arbenina cycle. Cf. Pushkin, "The Prophet": "And the six-winged *Seraph* appeared to me at the crossroads. . . . And he cleaved my chest with a sword and removed the trembling heart and placed a *flaming coal* into the rent chest." Pushkin's poem is an elaboration on the call of Isaiah to prophecy. Compare the last two lines with the second stanza of Pushkin's *Gavriliada* (Gabriliad): "Shestnadtsat' let, nevinnoe smiren'e / Brov' chernaia, dvukh devstvennykh kholmov / Pod polotnom uprugoe dvizhen'e."

80. On the pledge pattern, see Ronen, "A Beam Upon the Axe"; see also idem, "Osip Mandel'štam."

81. "We are inviting you to a country where trees speak, where scientific unions resembling waves are, where armies of love are, where *time blossoms like bird-cherry* and goes like a piston, where the trans-man [*zachelovek*] wearing a carpenter's apron is sawing times into boards and, like a turner, treats his tomorrow" [italics are mine] (V. Khlebnikov, "Pust' Mlechnyi put' . . . ," in *Truba marsian* [1916], *Sobranie Proizvedenii,* vol. 5, p. 152).

82. "Chto poiut chasy-kuznechik" (1917), *SS* 1: 98. This poem, part of the "Akhmatova" cycle, echoes meaningfully Blok's "Karmen" verses, together with his essay "Poeziia zagovorov i zaklinanii" (passages on the Herodiade) and the Bizet opera itself. For other subtexts and for a detailed analysis of the poem, see Taranovsky, *Essays on Mandel'štam,* pp. 68–82; and Freidin, "Time, Identity, and Myth."

83. Mandelstam, "Ia budu metat'sia po taboru ulitsy temnoi" (1925), *SS* 1: 144. The meter of the poem, coinciding with Pushkin's pastiche of Dante's *Inferno,* may be echoing some of the more unpleasant episodes in Mandelstam's (or rather, the Mandelstams') courtship of Ol'ga Vaksel'. See Vaksel', "O Mandel'shtame"; and Polianina, "Ol'ga Vaksel'."

84. Weber, *Essays,* p. 248.

85. *SS* 2, p. 20.

86. *SS* 2, pp. 24ff.
87. *SS* 2, p. 38.
88. On Parnakh, see C. Brown, introduction to *The Prose of Osip Mandelstam* (Princeton, 1965); N. Berberova, *Kursiv moi: Avtobiografiia* (Munich, 1972), pp. 251, 656, 674; and R. Timenchik, "Zametki ob akmeizme," *RL* 7/8 (1974): 37ff. One of Parnakh's poems, "Restorany," bears a dedication to Mandelstam (V. Parnakh, *Samum* [Paris, 1919], pp. 4ff.).
89. C. Izenberg, "Associative Chains in *Egipetskaia marka*," *RL* V-3 (1977): 257–276. Most personages in *The Egyptian Stamp* bear the names of Mandelstam's actual friends. See also D. M. West, *Mandelstam: The Egyptian Stamp*, Birmingham Slavonic Monographs, no. 10 (1980), pp. 29–58 ("Characters and Setting").
90. O. Ronen, "Leksicheskii povtor, podtekst i smysl v poetike Osipa Mandel'štama," in *Slavic Poetics: Essays in Honor of Kiril Taranovsky*, ed. R. Jakobson, C. H. van Schoneveld, and D. S. Worth (The Hague, 1973).
91. *SS* 2, p. 13.
92. For a characterization of Mandelstam as a "right fellow traveler," see, for example, B. Ol'khovyi, "O poputnichestve i poputchikakh," pt. 1, *PiR* 5 (1929): 11. See also Nadezhda Mandelstam's petition to V. Molotov for an academic appointment for her husband (December 1930), in A. Grigor'ev and I. Petrova, "Mandel'shtam na poroge tridtsatykh godov," *RL* V-2 (1977): 182–184. The petition was first published in *Pamiat'* 1 (1976).
93. *SS* 2, p. 30.
94. *NM* 2, p. 212.
95. A possible link between *Egipetskaia marka* and Vaginov's *Kozlinaia pesn'* is worth investigating. Mandelstam followed Vaginov's career after at least 1926 (*SS* 3, 232), the time when, according to N. Mandelstam's letter to Molotov, he began work on *Egipetskaia marka*. See Grigor'ev and Petrova, "Mandel'shtam na poroge tridtsatykh godov."
96. "Nashedshii podkovu," *SS* 1: 136. This passage follows—virtually word for word—Pavel Florenskii's meditation on skepticism: "I enter the last circle of the skeptical inferno—into that part where the very meaning of words becomes lost. Words cease to be fixed and abandon their nests [*sryvaiutsia so svoikh gnezd*]. Everything metamorphoses into everything else, every expression [*slovosochetanie*] is equivalent to any other, and every word can exchange places with another. Here intellect loses itself . . . the cold . . . madness." (Florenskii, *Stolp i utverzhdenie istiny*, p. 38).
97. Cf. Broyde, *Osip Mandel'štam and His Age*, pp. 169–199, which offers a far more detailed treatment of the poem.
98. A. G. Gornfel'd, Letter to the Editor, *Krasnaia gazeta* (Leningrad), November 28, 1928. Mandelstam used these words as an epigraph to his public reply in the Moscow *Vecherniaia gazeta* (December 10, 1928).
99. C. Brown, *Mandelstam* (Cambridge, Mass., 1973), pp. 124–125; "Zamechaniia o peresechenii biografii Mandel'shtama i Pasternaka," pp. 307–309; E. B. Pasternak and E. V. Pasternak, "Boris Pasternak: Iz perepiski s pisateliami," in *LN* 93, pp. 679–680. For a description of Gornfel'd's situation in

the late 1920s, see Abram Palei, "Vospominaniia ob A. G. Gornfel'de," in *Al'-manakh bibliofila*, vol. 5 (Moscow, 1978), pp. 242–248. See Appendix 1 for the chronology of events associated with the affair.

100. According to Nadezhda Mandelstam (NM 2, p. 149), Mandelstam was writing it in the winter of 1929–30 and must have completed it some time before May 1930, when the Mandelstams left for Armenia. See Grigor'ev and Petrova, "Mandel'shtam na poroge tridtsatykh godov," pp. 181–182.

101. The motif of incest is developed in the same section, in the stanzas preceding the "sartorial" one, and is interpreted as an all-embracing communality of a society in which every member bears responsibility for another's sin: "Suddenly some girl cries out in the pantry. . . . And the yard is in the smoke of suppressed desires, in the bare feet of dashing flags. . . . Along the way, it turns out that in the world there is not a speck of dust without a small stain of kinship [*piatnyshko rodstva*]" (B. Pasternak, *Stikhotvoreniia i poemy* [Moscow and Leningrad, 1965], p. 335). One of Parnok's nicknames in *The Egyptian Stamp* is "stain remover" (*piatnovyvodchik*). Cf. L. Fleishman, *Pasternak v dvadtsatye gody* (Munich, [1981]), p. 153.

102. Pasternak, *Stikhotvoreniia i poemy*, p. 336.

103. "Polnoch' v Moskve" (May–June 1931), *SS* 1: 260. For the correct date, see J. Baines, *Mandelstam: The Later Poetry* (Cambridge, 1976). Many of Mandelstam's poems following his return to Moscow in the spring of 1931 were polemically directed at Pasternak. See Appendix II and chapter 8. The polemical intent of "Polnoch' v Moskve" was noted by Fleishman, *Stikhotvoreniia i poemy*, p. 150n.46.

104. Together with Gor'kii, N. A. Tolstoi, Valentin Kataev, Vera Inber, and Kornelii Zelinskii, Zoshchenko participated in a volume celebrating the Stalin Canal (linking the White and the Baltic seas), contributing to it his story "Rasskaz pro odnogo spekulianta" (later included in his *Golubaia kniga*). See M. Zoshchenko, *Izbrannoe*, vol. 2 (Leningrad, 1978), pp. 43–46.

105. Cf. I. Erenburg's story about Mandelstam in Theodosia: "He once gathered together rich 'liberals' and said to them strictly: 'On the Judgment Day you will be asked whether you understood the poet Mandelstam; you will answer no. You will be asked whether you have fed him, and if you answer yes, much shall be forgiven you" (Erenburg, *Liudi, gody, zhizn': Kniga pervaia i vtoraia* [Moscow, 1961], p. 497.

106. M. Zoshchenko, *Mishel' Siniagin* (1930), in *Izbrannoe*, vol. 1, p. 498. Note the "monkey-fur collar" as a possible further hint at the "literary" nature of the coat (literature as imitation, "aping," of life). *Siniagin* must have come out after *The Fourth Prose* had been finished (April 1930). Otherwise, Mandelstam, who had the warmest words for Zoshchenko in *The Fourth Prose*, calling his writings "the Bible of labor," would no doubt have withdrawn them.

107. *Chetvertaia proza*, *SS* 2, p. 189.

108. See Mandelstam's "Kharkov" essay "Shuba" (1922), *SS* 4.

109. NM 2, pp. 592–597, and Grigor'ev and Petrova, "Mandel'shtam na poroge tridtsatykh godov," p. 181.

110. Mandelstam, *Chetvertaia proza*, *SS* 2, pp. 177, 184. According to

Nadezhda Mandelstam, the *Prose* was composed in the spring of 1930, shortly before the Mandelstams left for Armenia (in April 1930).

111. Ibid., p. 182.

112. Ibid., pp. 188ff. Some of the pathos of *The Fourth Prose* may be traced to another masterpiece by Gogol, *Notes of a Madman* (kindly suggested by Boris Gasparov). Even though rumors about Mandelstam's "madness" were circulating in literary circles (see B. S. Kuzin's memoirs), I refrain from introducing this other text, as it might overshadow the purposiveness and the Dostoevskian self-affirmation of *The Fourth Prose*.

113. Ibid., p. 191. In Maiakovskii, the lines are "Chego kipiatites'? / Obeshchali i delim porovnu: / odnomu—bublik, drugomu—dyrka ot bublika. / Eto i est' demokraticheskaia respublika." See the annotations in *SS* 2, p. 617. Before leaving for Armenia, the Mandelstams may have attended the first performance of Maiakovskii's *Bath*. See L. Fleishman, "Epizod s Bezymenskim v *Puteshestvii v Armeniiu*," *SH* 3 (1978), p. 195.

114. Mandelstam, "Iazyk bulyzhnika mne golubia poniatnei" (1923), *SS* 1: 138. Apart from Barbier (see Khardzhiev's commentary in *Stikhotvoreniia* [1973]), the poem is based, in part, on the following literary reminiscences: André Chéneir, "Jeu de pomme"; Aleksandr Pushkin, "Andrei Shen'e" (lines 160ff.); Innokentii Annenskii "Buddiiskaia messa v Parizhe"; and Nikolai Gumilev, "U tsygan." It further plays out Mallarmé's definition of poetry as the *jeu suprême*, punning it against "jeu de pomme" and, no doubt, *pomme de discorde*. Cf.: "Again, the frost smells of the apple"("1 ianvaria 1924"); "Oh, to take the world into one's hand like an apple" ("Vot daronositsa"); and "So a child answers: I shall give you an apple, or I shall not give you an apple" ("Nashedshii podkovu"). The allusion to Annenskii is most interesting. Compare Annenskii's "A v vozdukhe zhila neponiataia fraza" with Mandelstam's "I v vozdukhe plyvet zabytaia karinka, I v pamiati zhivet pletenaia korzinka." In *The Noise of Time*, most of which was done in 1923, Mandelstam recalls the delirium of his dying friend Boris Sinani: "Dying, Boris was deliriously speaking about Finland, moving to Raivola, and some ropes for packing the belongings" (*SS* 2, p. 97). This was a memory associated with their attempt to join the Military Organization of the Socialist Revolutionary party. Cf. also the line from a lost poem by Mandelstam composed in Paris (in M. Karpovich, "Moe znakomstvo s Mandel'shtamom," *Novyi zhurnal* 49 [1957]): "podniat' skripuchii verkh solomennykh korzin." On "Iazyk bulyzhnika," see also D. Segal, "Pamiat' zreniia: pamiat' smysla," *RL* 7/8 (1974).

115. *SS* 2, p. 192. Cf. in Mandelstam's "Armenia" cycle: "k oruzhiu zovushchaia, Armeniia, Armeniia." The pun begins even earlier, but it cannot be easily conveyed in English: "Khodit nemets-shARmanshchik s shubertovskim leerkastenom, takoi neudachnik, takoi shARomyzhnik. *Ich bin arm. Ia beden*."

116. See N. Chuzhak, ed., *Literatura fakta. Pervyi sbornik materialov rabotnikov LEF'a* (Moscow, 1929). Mandelstam in fact translated one of the French authors, Pierre Hamp, whom one of the contributors to the volume, S. M. Tretiakov, considered exemplary of the trend (see G. P. Struve, *Russian Literature Under Lenin and Stalin: 1917–1953* [Norman, Okla., 1971], pp. 215–217).

Some of the elements of the program had already been spelled out by Mandelstam in 1923 (see especially his essay on Auguste Barbier, published in *Prozhektor*), when he pointed out that Dante's *Commedia* had the topicality of a newspaper in its day and age. Further, the fact that Mandelstam avoided using invented names for the characters in his prose, including the fictional *Egyptian Stamp*, indicates that he was taking the trend seriously—whatever use he wished to put it to. See also N. Berkovskii, "O proze Mandel'shtama," in *Tekushchaia literatura* (Moscow, 1930), pp. 155–181.

VIII

1. See a draft of Mandelstam's letter to I. I. Ionov, *SS* 4, pp. 121–126. The letter was written sometime in January 1929.

2. "Potoki khaltury" (Streams of Slap-Dash), *Izvestiia* 80 (April 7, 1929), in *SS* 2, p. 428. The same issue contained a lengthy unsigned article with the following impressive title: "To Purge the State Apparatus by Means of the Masses and Together with the Masses." Appearing three months later in *Na literaturnom postu*, no. 13 (July 1929), Mandelstam's "O perevodakh" (On Translations) was a much calmer and more reasoned article.

3. D. I. Zaslavskii, "Skromnyi plagiat ili razviaznaia khaltura," *Literaturnaia gazeta* 3 (1929).

4. NM 1, p. 120.

5. NM 1, p. 186.

6. In a surviving draft of *The Egyptian Stamp*, with the action set in the 1920s rather than during the "Kerenskii summer," the Oedipal theme was much more explicit, as was Parnok's identification with authorship: "Parnok wrote not for himself, not for the critics, but for his dear mustachioed mother who deified him" (Princeton Archive). In the final version, professional authorship is attributed only to the narrator, and the "mustachio" to the "young Greek woman lying in a coffin." Cf. also the "mustachioed silence of the [narrator's childhood] apartment."

7. *SS* 1:254. Bearing the date May 7–9, 1932, the poem was first published in *Novyi mir* 6 (1932). Lamarck is presented here in terms of Mandelstam's "patriarchal" image. Cf. Khardzhiev's letter to Eikhenbaum (discussed in chapter 1) and the 1931 poem "Eshche daleko mne do *patriarkha*" (*SS* 1: 251).

8. One might say that this metamorphosis had been "programmed" in the genetic code of the "mosquito," since it originated in the disguise used by Pushkin's Tsar Saltan (a character whose fate was similar to Joseph's) when he wished to visit the country of his birth incognito. On the "mosquito prince" from Mandelstam's poem "Ia ne znaiu s kakikh por," see K. Taranovsky, *Essays on Mandel'štam* (Cambridge, Mass, 1976), pp. 30ff.; and G. Levinton and R. Timenchik, "Kniga K. F. Taranovskogo o poezii O. E. Mandel'shtama," *RL* VI-2 (1978): 200ff.

9. The poem was composed during Mandelstam's friendship with a biologist, Boris Kuzin (like Mandelstam, an admirer of Bergson and a neo-

Lamarckian), who was involved in the contemporary debates concerning the viability of Lamarckism for Soviet science. See B. S. Kuzin's memoirs of his friendship with Mandelstam ("Ob O. E. Mandel'shtame," *VRSKhD* 140, nos. 3–4 [1983]: 99–129). On the debates, see P. Bondarenko, *Protiv mekhanicheskogo materializma i men'shevistvuiushchego idealizma v biologii* (Moscow and Leningrad, 1931); D. Joravsky, *Soviet Marxism and Natural Science* (New York, 1961); idem, *The Lysenko Affair* (Cambridge, Mass., 1970), pp. 207ff.; and Zh. Medvedev, *The Rise and Fall of T. D. Lysenko* (New York, 1969), pp. 9–17.

10. "Gde noch' brosaet iakoria," *SS* 2: 458. Although he did it without invoking the Dantean subtext (*Inferno* 3: 111ff.), O. Ronen ("Osip Mandel'štam: An Ode and an Elegy" [Ph.D. diss., Harvard University, 1976]) convincingly demonstrates that the subject of the poem, the "dry leaves of October falling off the Tree of Life," was not the Bolsheviks but the Whites fleeing the Crimea in the fall of 1920. Ronen thus disputed the assertion contained in the commentary accompanying the poem in *Novoe russkoe slovo* (New York, April 16, 1971). See also S. Broyde, *Osip Mandel'štam and His Age* (Cambridge, Mass., 1975), pp. 70–73 and 214n.37.

11. "Proslavim, brat'ia, sumerki svobody," *SS* 1: 103. This is another Dantesque poem by Mandelstam—at least insofar as the last stanza recapitulates the story told by Dante's Ulysses about his last journey "beyond the pillars of Hercules" (hence "Take courage, men"). Cf. an analysis of this poem by Broyde, *Osip Mandel'štam and His Age*, pp. 47ff. See also A. Morozov, "Mandel'shtam v zapisiakh dnevnika S. P. Kablukova," *VRSKhD* 129, no. 3 (1979): 134; and N. A. Nilsson, "Ship Metaphors in Mandel'štam's Poetry," in *To Honor Roman Jakobson*, vol. 2 (The Hague, 1967), pp. 1436–1444.

12. Nadezhda Mandelstam described the years 1924–27 as a period when her husband tried to reconcile himself to the regime, *The Egyptian Stamp* being one product of this attempt at reconciliation (NM 2, p. 255). See also her description of their visit to Shileiko in 1924, which suggests that contemporaries were not unaware of these attempts (NM 2, pp. 500ff.). "Mandelstam was one of those who began to see early, but he was not among the first of them, by far" (NM 1, p. 186).

13. "Light Cavalry" was the name of the special Komsomol groups charged with assisting the party in its struggle against bureaucratization and poor economic performance in Soviet enterprises. These groups became especially active following the adoption of the Five-Year Plan in 1928. According to Nadezhda Mandelstam (NM 1, p. 186), "after severing his connections with the writers' organizations, Mandelstam served on the staff of *Moskovskii komsomolets* for almost a year," that is, from the summer of 1929 to the spring of 1930. Cf. the interpretation of the passage below in J. Baines, *Mandelstam: The Later Poetry* (1976).

14. *SS* 2, p. 179. "Chinese games" (*kitaishchina*) most likely is an allusion to Dostoevsky's famous comparison of Russian bureaucracy with the Chinese Imperial state: "I would say that we are just like China only without her orderliness. We are only beginning what the Chinese have already accomplished. Doubtless we will achieve the same accomplishment, but when? In order to

accept a thousand volumes of ceremonies, in order to win the right never to think about anything once and for all, we will have to live for at least another thousand years of pensiveness" (F. M. Dostoevskii, *Polnoe sobranie sochinenii*, vol. 21 [Leningrad, 1980], p. 7). Given this subtext, Mandelstam's invective can hardly represent a wish for the return of the good old days before 1917. Rather, it has much in common with the mentality of War Communism, when one did not have to "encode" into the formulas of "Chinese" servility the "great and powerful concept of class." Compare this with a 1922 essay, "The Fur Coat": "This was a severe and beautiful winter of 1920–21, the last harvest-time winter of Soviet Russia; and I miss it, remember it with tenderness. . . . I feel oppressed by my heavy fur coat, just as the whole of Russia feels oppressed by the fortuitous satiety, fortuitous warmth, the ill-gotten second-hand wealth" (*SS* 4, p. 95). This is about the first glimmer of economic recovery under NEP.

15. Mandelstam, *Chetvertaia proza, SS* 2, p. 178.

16. Sometime in the early spring of 1930, when he was finishing *The Fourth Prose* and about to depart for Armenia, Mandelstam visited a psychiatrist (NM 2, p. 298). See also Nadezhda Mandelstam's petition to V. Molotov (December 1930) requesting a university teaching position for Mandelstam. The request was motivated, in the words of the petition, by the "grievous state of poet Mandelstam," his "serious nervous disorder caused by a trauma (which resulted from the persecution of Mandelstam)" ("Dva pis'ma N. Ia. Mandel'shtam," in *Pamiat': Istoricheskii sbornik* 1 [Moscow, 1976; New York, 1978], pp. 302–307). For additional biographical materials pertaining to the late 1920s and the early 1930s, see A. Grigor'ev and I. Petrova, "Mandel'shtam na poroge tridtsatykh godov," *RL* V-2 (1977): 181–192.

17. NM 2, p. 405. All that Nadezhda Mandelstam remembered from the destroyed section of *The Fourth Prose* were two sentences. One was followed by expletives ("*Komy on teper' nuzhen etot sotsializm zalapannyi* . . ."). The other read: "If citizens suddenly decided to construct a Renaissance, what would have come out of it? A cafe 'Renaissance,' at best."

18. S. F. Cohen, *Bukharin and the Bolshevik Revolution: A Political Biography, 1888–1938* (New York, 1973), pp. 313–315.

19. Mandelstam, "Polnoch' v Moskve," *SS* 1: 260. According to Baines, *The Later Poetry*, the poem was written in May 1931. "1 ianvaria 1924" (*SS* 1: 140) is perhaps the most elaborate of the early representations of this dilemma. On this poem and specifically on the use of the "fourth estate" in Mandelstam, see O. Ronen, "An Introduction to Mandel'štam's *Slate Ode* and *1 January 1924*: Similarity and Complementarity," *SH* 4 (1979): 146–158. See also Ronen, "Osip Mandel'štam," and his "Četvertoe soslovie: Vierte Stand or Fourth Estate? (A Rejoinder)," *SH* 5–6 (1981): 319–324. Ronen's insistence on interpreting the term *chetvertoe soslovie* as "the proletariat" is supported, if indeed it needs additional support, by the following instance of contemporary usage: "Kuskova writes: 'the growing "fourth estate" cannot give up its hope for a distant paradise for labor, for the great promised land where there will be

Notes to Pages 231–233

neither the rifles that shoot nor any inequality'" (A. S. Izgoev, "Na perevale. Zhizni' i publitsistika," *RM* 33, no. 27 [1912], p. 142 [2d pagination]).

20. Responding to Pasternak (see chapter 7 on *Spektorskii*), Mandelstam defended in this poem his right to pass judgment on the epoch. History is not a fragile, cheap (*pen'kovaia dusha*), or fastidious affair that constantly requires a ritual bath like a sacred monkey in a Tibetan temple. L. Fleishman (*Pasternak v dvadtsatye gody* [Munich, (1981)], p. 150n.46) offers a valuable subtext for these lines—Pasternak's 1928 poem "Bal'zak." The "Buddhist" motif, however, points strongly to Mandelstam's intellectual hero, Alexander Herzen, specifically to his characterization of Peter I: "Petr I ne mog udovol'stvovat'sia zhalkoi rol'iu khristianskogo Dalai-Lamy. . . . Petr I predstaet pered svoim narodom slovno prostoi smertnyi. Vse vidiat kak etot *neutomimyi truzhennik, odetyi v skromnyi siurtuk voennogo pokroia,* s utra do vechera otdaet prikazaniia i uchit, kak nado ikh vypolniat'; on kuz-nets, stoliar, inzhener, arkhitektor i shturman" (Gertzen, *O razvitii revoliutsionnaykh idei v Rossii,* in *Sochineniia,* vol. 3 [Moscow, 1956], p. 413). The Petrine metaphor for Stalin (recall his "Mao jacket") and the First Five-Year Plan were, of course, commonplace at the time. On one level, therefore, the poem's message concerns the awakening of Moscow-Russia from its ahistorical "Buddhist" (Herzen's epithet) torpor under the guidance of the "indefatigable laborer in a modest coat of a military cut" who "from morning till night issues orders and teaches how they ought to be carried out." This was not the first time that Mandelstam invoked Herzen's Peter the Great (echoing Pushkin's view) as a measure of modern Russian history. See especially "Nashedshii podkovy." Cf. Broyde, *Osip Mandel'štam and His Age,* pp. 180–182. See also H. Gifford, "Mandelstam and Pasternak: The Antipodes," in *Russian and Slavic Literature,* ed. R. Freeborn, R. R. Milner-Gulland, and C. A. Ward (Cambridge, Mass., 1976), pp. 376–386.

21. B. Pasternak, *Stikhotvoreniia: poemy* (Moscow and Leningrad, 1965), p. 377.

22. "Vek," *SS* 1: 135.

23. "S mirom derzhavnym ia byl lish' rebiacheski sviazan," *SS* 1: 222. First published in *Zvezda* 4 (1931): 113.

24. "Ia s dymiashchei luchinoi vkhozhu (April 4, 1931), *SS* 1: 231. Cf. Baines, *The Later Poetry,* pp. 27–28, 66.

25. Kuzin, "Ob O. E. Mandel'shtame," p. 114.

26. "Za gremuchuiu doblest' griadushchikh vekov," *SS* 1: 227. A number of drafts of this poem may be found in the Mandelstam Archive at Princeton University. They indicate that during the initial stages of composition, Mandelstam was working on a text that would later yield three separate poems: "Za gremuchuiu doblest'"; "Ia s dymiashchei luchinoi vkhozhu," *SS* 1: 227; and "Net, ne spriatat'sia mne ot velikoi mury," *SS* 1: 232. Other lines and whole stanzas belonging to these drafts have been published in *SS* 1: 242–246. The "wolf" poem is dated by Nikolai Khardzhiev as "March 17–28, 1932" (in O. Mandelstam, *Stikhotvoreniia* [Leningrad, 1973], p. 153). The dates for the other two in *SS* 1 are April 4, 1932, and April 1932, respectively. Khardzhiev

also cites four different versions of the concluding stanza of the "wolf" poem (ibid., p. 288). For a discussion of the composition of the poem, see NM 1, pp. 158, 197, 201–202, 204; and Baines, *The Later Poems,* pp. 20–24.

27. M. Lermontov, "Vykhozhu odin ia na dorogu," "Zvezda"; "Na severe dikom stoit odinoko Na goloi vershine sosna."

28. Cf. "Zamechaniia o peresechenii biografii Osipa Mandel'shtama: Borisa Pasternaka," in *Pamiat': Istoricheskii sbornik* (Moscow, 1979; Paris, 1981); the anonymous author of this article was puzzled by Mandelstam's "overreaction" to Pasternak's "perfectly innocent words."

29. B. Pasternak, "Krasavitsa moia, vsia stat'" (1931), part of *Vtoroe rozhdenie* (1932). Cf. a discussion of Mandelstam's polemic in NM 1, pp. 158; and "Zamechaniia o peresechenii biografii Mandel'shtama," pp. 313ff.

30. The story begins: "I have always been in sympathy with the central institutions. Even when they were introducing NEP during the epoch of War Communism, I did not protest. If it's NEP, it's NEP. You know better. But, by the way, during the introduction of NEP, my heart would desperately sink. I somehow envisioned certain radical changes. And indeed, during the War Communism it was really free with respect to culture and civilization. Say, in the theater you were free to sit without taking your clothes off—just sit there in what you had on when you came. That was an achievement. This question of culture is a hard one. Take, for example, that [rule about] taking your clothes off in the theater. Of course, no argument, without their overcoats on the public is better distinguished" (M. Zoshchenko, *Izbrannoe,* vol. 1: *Rasskasy i fel'etony. Povesti* [Leningrad, 1978], p. 168).

31. Mandelstam, *SS* 1: 230. The motif of the coat appears in another poem composed in March 1931, "Zhil Aleksandr Gertsevich," an ironic self-portrait made up of Pushkin's first name, Herzen for a patronymic, and pieces of Schubert's *Lieder* for the family name. The poem recalls Gornfel'd's words perhaps, Zoshchenko's *Mishel' Siniagin,* and definitely Schubert's "Der Krähe" from *Die Winterreise:* "With music-dove, death isn't frightening, and afterward—a crow fur coat—to hang on a hook."

32. "As to the wolf cycle, it did not bode any special hardship—a labor camp at worst" (NM 1, p. 16). See also NM 2, pp. 603ff., which refers to the composition of the "wolf" cycle in the period when the Mandelstams "thought that the screws had been tightened to the limit and it was time to expect an improvement." This ambivalence is, of course, detectable in much of Mandelstam's poetry written after his return from Armenia in the fall of 1930.

33. The last stanza of the third version, cited by Nikolai Khardzhiev (see note 30), contains another allusion to Dante in the second line (*Inferno* 32: 46–48). Mandelstam: "Take me away into the night where the Enisei flows and a tear on the eyelashes is like ice, because I am not a wolf by blood and a human being will not die in me." Cf. Dante: "Their eyes, which before were moist only within, gushed over at the lids, and the frost bound the tears between and locked them up again" (*The Divine Comedy of Dante Alighieri: Inferno,* trans. John D. Sinclair [New York, 1939], p. 397). Dante's description refers to the traitors frozen in the ice of the Caina.

34. NM 2, pp. 460ff.
35. Mandelstam, *Puteshestvie v Armeniiu*, SS 2, pp. 175ff. On it, see Henry Gifford's introduction to O. Mandelstam, *Journey to Armenia* (San Francisco, 1979).
36. NM 2, pp. 466–473.
37. "Avtoportret," *SS* 1: 164.
38. "Kholodnaia vesna. Golodnyi Staryi Krym," *SS* 1: 271.
39. See M. Mauss, *The Gift: Forms and Functions of Exchange in Archaic Societies* (New York, 1967), pp. 41–43.
40. NM 1, p. 157; and "Zamechaniia," pp. 314ff.
41. For a discussion of the several other important subtexts of this poem (B. Pasternak, "V kvartire prokhlada usad'by"; A. Blok, "Druz'iam"; N. Nekrasov, "V. G. Belinskii," "Deshevaia pokupka"), see Ronen, "Leksicheskii povtor," pp. 385ff.; and idem, *An Approach to Mandel'štam* (Jerusalem, 1983). See also V. V. Musatov, "Nekrasov v poeticheskom soznanii Mandel'shtama," in *N. A. Nekrasov i russkaia literatura vtoroi poloviny XIX–nachala XX vekov, Mezhvuzovskii sbornik nauchnykh trudov*, no. 64 (Yaroslavl, 1982), pp. 94–101.
42. "Kvartira tikha, kak bumaga," *SS* 1: 272. A future student of this poem may wish to juxtapose the "still telephone" with the suicide theme in Mandelstam ("samoubiitsa-telefon" in *SS* 1: 194; "k Persefone telefon eshche ne proveden" in *Egipetskaia Marka*); line 10 with the similar line in "1 January 1924"; and line 18 with line 48 in "Polnoch' v Moskve" and with Pasternak's 1928 poem "Bal'zak": "On v'et, kak nitku iz pen'ki, istoriiu sego pritona." See Fleishman, *Pasternak v dvadtsatye gody*.
43. Sometime in the early 1930s, before Mandelstam's arrest, wrote Nadezhda Mandelstam, "The three of us [herself, her husband, and Akhmatova] were standing together when suddenly Mandelstam melted with joy: several little girls ran past us in a single file, imagining themselves to be horses. The first one stopped and impatiently asked: 'Where is the previous horsy?' The 'previous horsy' got bored with stomping its hooves and had fled. . . . I grabbed Mandelstam by his hand to prevent him from joining the kids as the lead horse. Akhmatova, too, was sensing danger. She said to Mandelstam: 'Do not run away from us—you are *our* previous horsy.' And we went to the Punins to have tea" (NM 2, p. 415).
44. For the events surrounding the composition of this poem, see NM 1, pp. 165–167ff. See also Baines, *The Later Poems*, pp. 84–86.
45. Mandelstam, "My zhivem, pod soboiu ne chuia strany," *SS* 1: 286. For another version in which Stalin, in reference to the brutality of the collectivization, is called a "murderer and a muzhikoclast" (*dushegubets i muzhikoborets*), see Baines, *The Later Poems*, p. 84.
46. Vl. Maiakovskii, "Levyi marsh" (Left March): "We shall ride the nag of history to death with our left, left, left." The relation between this poem and Mandelstam's "He Who Found a Horseshoe" is discussed in Broyde, *Osip Mandel'štam and His Age*.
47. "Dovol'no kuksit'sia! Bumagi v stol zasunem," *SS* 1: 247.
48. "Vy pomnite, kak beguny," *SS* 1: 257.

49. "Polnoch' v Moskve . . . ," *SS* 1: 260.
50. "Segodnia mozhno sniat' dekal'komani," *SS* 1: 265.
51. NM 1, p. 101. The other exiles in Cherdyn' turned away from Mandelstam after the news of the commutation had arrived.
52. "Ty dolzhen mnoi povelevat'," *SS* 4: 515.
53. "Stansy," *SS* 1: 312.
54. "Ot syroi prostyni govoriashchaia," *SS* 1: 311.
55. "Den' stoial o pitai golovakh . . . ," *SS* 1: 313.
56. "Oboroniaet son moiu donskuiu son'," *SS* 1: 371.
57. "Sred' narodnogo shuma i spekha," *SS* 1: 361.
58. "Esli b menia nashi vragi vziali," *SS* 1: 372. The correct version of the poem's coda, cited here, appears in a draft copied by Nadezhda Mandelstam (deposited at the Mandelstam Archive at Princeton University). Baines (*The Later Poems*, p. 202), however, follows the poet's widow in insisting that the poem ends instead in "Budet *gubit'* razum i zhizn' Stalin" (Stalin will keep *destroying* reason and life). But, as previously noted by C. Brown ("Into the Heart of Darkness," *Slavic Review* 26, no. 4 [1967]: 601–603) and B. Jangfeldt ("Osip Mandel'štam's 'Ode to Stalin,'" *Scando-Slavica*, 22 [1976]: 39–41), this reading, or version, contradicts the logic of the rest of the poem. The edition of Mandelstam's *Voronezhskie tetradi* prepared by V. Shveitser (Ann Arbor, 1980) follows Brown and Jangfeldt, attributing the other version to "the memory of Nadezhda Mandelstam" (p. 85).
59. *SS* 4: 147–148.
60. Baines, *The Later Poems*, pp. 175ff.
61. This and the two poems to follow are in *SS* 1, nos. 346, 347, and 348. Cf. Baines, *The Later Poems*, pp. 174–178. The word *verstkii* is a play on at least two terms: *prodrazverstka* (grain requisitioning during the War Communism and the collectivization) and *verstka* (galleys).
62. Cf. a passage from *Egipetskaia Marka:* "In the evening, at a dacha in Pavlovsk, these same gentlemen *littérateurs* taught a lesson to a poor youth—Hippolytus. He did not even get a chance to read to them out of his calico notebook. Some Rousseau!" (*SS* 2, p. 27).
63. "Net, nikogda nichei ia ne byl sovremennik," *SS* 1: 141.
64. A. Akhmatova, *Sochineniia*, vol. 2 (Paris, 1968), p. 181. These reminiscences originally appeared in *Vozdushnye puti* 4 (1965).
65. Brown, "Into the Heart of Darkness."
66. Mandelstam, "Esli b menia nashi vragi vziali" (*SS* 1: 372) represents a corrupt version of the poem. I am citing it here in the form it appears in V. Shveitser's edition of Mandelstam's *Voronezhskie tetradi*. See also a discussion of the text in Baines, *The Later Poetry*, pp. 201–203, 205. The most apparent allusions are to the *Lay of Igor's Campaign* (the ten hawks and the ten swans of Baian's fingers strumming the strings, as opposed to Mandelstam's far less aristocratic and far more biblical bullocks); to a Rembrandt "Pieta" (via the metonym of Rembrandt, his *Night Watch;* see also *SS* 1: 364 and discussion in the text below); and to Pushkin's "Ne dai mne Bog soiti s uma" (lines 2–3 and 7–8 are an obvious polemic with Pushkin's "anticivic" poem) and his "Pamiatnik"

(line 22). The most important polemical and therefore meaningful allusion is to Pasternak's "On vstaet. Veka. Gelaty," from his "Georgian" cycle "Khudozhnik" (1936). The cycle appeared in *Znamia* 4 (1936) and elicited more than one response from Mandelstam. In this poem, Pasternak presented the poet as a folkloric warrior on a high horse riding into the "epoch," and pointedly not as a Baian (*gusliar*) or a narrator of magic tales (*balakir'*). The ostensible allusion is to the seventh stanza: "Like a thunderstorm, uniting on the road life and chance, death and passion, you shall pass through minds and lands, to fall into eternity as a legend." Mandelstam's poem is, obviously, a kenotic response to Pasternak's high-minded attempt to inscribe himself into Soviet modernity.

67. NM 1, pp. 216–220 ("Oda").

68. "Mandelstam's 'Ode to Stalin,'" *Slavic Review* 34, no. 4 (1975): 683–691.

69. Jangfeldt, "Mandel'štam's 'Ode to Stalin.'" K. Taranovsky discussed both the *Slavic Review* and Jangfeldt's texts in light of two authentic versions made available to him in "Dve publikatsii 'Stalinskoi ody' O. E. Mandel'shtama," *Scando-Slavica* 23 (1977): 87–88. The publication of the "Ode" in *SS* 4 follows the text established by Taranovsky.

70. NM 1, pp. 216–220. See also Baines, *The Later Poetry*, pp. 174–198, which closely follows the account of Nadezhda Mandelstam, although in more detail.

71. For the list of poems constituting *The Second Voronezh Notebook*, see Baines, *The Later Poetry*, pp. 242–243. The same list with only minor variations may be found in O. Mandelstam, *Voronezhskie tetradi*, pp. 35–80.

72. NM 1, pp. 212ff.

73. *SS* 4, pp. 143–145.

74. Most of Mandelstam's letters of this period end with an urgent plea for an answer by telegraph—a good indication of the sense of isolation Mandelstam was experiencing.

75. Mandelstam, *SS* 2, pp. 280ff.

76. Pasternak's growing visibility and importance during the congress, culminating in Nikolai Bukharin's high praise, prompted Lilia Brik's letter on behalf of the dead Maiakovskii, which in its turn culminated in Stalin's formulation (suggested by Lilia Brik): "Maiakovskii was and remains the best and most talented poet of our Soviet epoch" (E. J. Brown, *Mayakovsky: A Poet in the Revolution* [Princeton, 1973], p. 370). See also G. de Mallac, *Boris Pasternak, His Life and Art* (Norman, Okla., 1981), pp. 142ff.

77. For the accounts of the incident, see NM 1, pp. 25–27, 145–149, 152–157, 214. See also Iu. Krotkov, "Pasternak," *Grani* 64 (1967): 62; and O. Ivinskaia, *V plenu vremeni* (Paris, 1978), pp. 75–82. Two more recent summaries can be found in "Zamechaniia" and in L. Fleishman, *Pasternak v tridtsatye gody* (Jerusalem, 1983), pp. 163–178 ("Arest Mandel'shtama").

78. For Mandelstam, the term *master* had a negative connotation, as it designated older poets no longer needed by the new Soviet state except for their expertise as versifiers. This was what Mandelstam had in mind when in

the "apartment" poem he refused to "master" (see Vl. Vasilenko's review of Mandelstam's *Stikhotvoreniia* [1928] in *Izvestiia*, July 6, 1928). See also the debates on Acmeism in *Literaturnyi Leningrad* in 1933–34. In this respect, Mikhail Bulgakov's designation of his novel's protagonist as "master" represents an attempt to restore the term's traditional honorable connotation.

79. NM 1, p. 220.

80. B. Bettelheim, "Remarks on the Psychological Appeal of Totalitarianism," in *Surviving, and Other Essays* (New York, 1979), pp. 319ff.

81. Cf. Mikhail Bakhtin's understanding of language, or words, as a locus of clashing *attitudes* of speakers (elaborated in *Problemy poetiki Dostoevskogo* [Moscow, 1963], esp. "Slovo u Dostoevskogo"; "Slovo v romane," in *Estetika slovesnogo tvorchestva* [Moscow, 1979]; and in the final chapter of Voloshinov's *Marksizm i filosofiia iazyka* [Leningrad, 1929], on "nesobstvenno-priamaia rech'"). In a sense, the poetics of Acmeism, particularly in Mandelstam, model this particular aspect of language insofar as they conjoin conflicting usages of poetic expressions. Even where the focus of the work falls on a "mythic" elaboration of a rhetorical item, the same operation of "clash" obtains. Cf. Akhmatova's recollection that Mandelstam's advice was "to clash words with diametrically opposing meanings" ("Mandel'shtam," in Akhmatova, *Sochineniia*, vol. 2). However, this orientation toward "the word of the other," foregrounded in Acmeist poetics (Ronen, "Leksicheskii povtor"), is common to any ideological text and, as such, represents a certain ideological position. It is itself a myth (as R. Barthes defines the term) linked to other myths comprising the contemporary ideological universe. Cf. R. Timenchik, "Tetkst v tekste u akmeistov," in *Tekst v tekste, Trudy po znakovym sistemam*, vol. 14 (Tartu, 1981), p. 73.

82. Akhmatova, *Sochineniia*, vol. 2, pp. 147–154.

83. "Nąshedshii podkovu" (*SS* 1: 140) bore the subtitle "Pindaricheskii otryvok" (Pindaric fragment), which places this most "irregular" of Mandelstam's poems in the Pindaric tradition, not via Russian classical poetry but by bypassing it. On this poem, see Broyde, *Osip Mandel'štam and His Age*, pp. 169–199.

84. Letter of January 21, 1937 (*SS* 2, pp. 280ff.).

85. Compare Mandelstam's words from *Journey to Armenia*, "the oceanic news of Maiakovskii's death," with the "oceanic" metaphor here and in the "Conversation about Dante," where he likens the composition of blood to that of the ocean, salt, and the sun: "krov' soliarna, solonna."

86. G. Kozintsev, "Tynianov i kino," and S. Eizenshtein, "Neposlannoe pis'mo Tynianovu," in *Vospominaniia o Iurii Tynianove*, ed. V. A. Kaverin (Moscow, 1983), pp. 262–271 and 272–277, respectively.

87. "Novoe chuvstvo prirody i istorii, *chuvstvo tainstvennoi blizosti mira i prisutstviia beskonechnogo v konechnom sostavliaet sushchnost' vsiakoi podlinnoi romantiki*" (A. Blok, "O romantizme" [1919]). In Blok, this state signified the "proximity to the World Soul." See A. Blok, *SS* 5, p. 363.

88. Frank J. Miller, "The Image of Stalin in Soviet Russian Folklore," *The Russian Review* 39, no. 1 (1980): 60ff.

89. I. Stalin, *Sochineniia*, vol. 4 (Moscow, 1949), pp. 46–61. The speech containing these famous six vows was made the day before Lenin's entombment, on January 26, 1924: "We vow to thee, Comrade Lenin, that we will with honor fulfill this thy testament [*My klianemsia, tovarishch Lenin, chto my s chest'iu vypolnim etot tvoi zavet*]." And so forth, six times. The words *klianemsia* and *zavet*, needless to say, belong to the scriptural vocabulary, the first to the Old Testament, the second to both the New and the Old Testaments (*Novyi i Vetkhii Zavet*). They emphasize the sacred nature of the leadership transition, sanctify its legitimacy, and correspond to the self-image that Stalin would later so assiduously cultivate. As the "Ode" demonstrates, Mandelstam knew well how to "read" Stalin's speeches. Compare Stalin's vows to Genesis 26:3: "For unto thee and thy seed I will give all these countries, and I will perform the oath [*kliatvu*] which I swear [*klialsia*] unto Abraham thy father." See also Stalin's June 1931 speech on the six conditions for industrialization.

90. Viach. Ivanov, "Pindar, Pif. 1," *Zhurnal ministerstva narodnogo prosveshcheniia*, nos. 7–8 (1899), *Otdel klassicheskoi filologii*, pp. 50–51.

91. *Izvestiia*, October 2, 1936.

92. *Apollodorus* 1, 2: 2. There may be another, metonymic or contiguous, association of Stalin with the myth of Prometheus, which is focused on the Caucasus, the place of Stalin's birth and of Prometheus's punishment.

93. On the Stalin cycle, see C. Brown, "Into the Heart of Darkness"; and Baines, *The Later Poetry*, pp. 174–198. On the function of cycles in Mandelstam's poetics, see NM 1, pp. 198–212; and the work of Taranovsky and Ronen.

94. *SS* 1: 330–331.

95. Cf. O. Ronen, "Mandel'štam's Kaščej," in *Studies Presented to Professor Roman Jakobson by His Students* (Cambridge, Mass., 1968), pp. 252–264; and Baines, *The Later Poetry*, pp. 170–173. The poem is "Ottogo vse neudachi," *SS* 1: 337.

96. C. Brown, "Into the Heart of Darkness," pp. 598–600. "Vooruzhennyi zren'em uzkikh os," *SS* 1: 367.

97. NM 1, pp. 216–220; and Baines, *The Later Poetry*, pp. 174–198. Nadezhda Mandelstam, for example, insists that the words of the "wasps" poem "I neither draw, nor sing" are in direct opposition to the persona of the poet in the "Ode," where he indeed draws. This observation, although backed by the authority of, perhaps, the sharpest reader of Mandelstam's poetry, has the flaws of any literal interpretation. In the "wasps," Mandelstam neither "draws nor sings," but in the poem written the same day, February 8, 1937, he "sings while the soul is moist and the throat dry" (*SS* 1: 365). The same may be said about another poem (one among many) where a similar reversal takes place: "Do not compare, a living man cannot be compared" (*SS* 1: 352). But in February, seventeen days later, the poet breaks his own vow: "Like the martyr of chiaroscuro Rembrandt, / I have gone deep into the mute time, / But the sharpness of my burning rib / Is guarded neither by those guards / Nor by this warrior who is asleep under the thunderstorm" (*SS* 1: 364). Here the poet compares himself not only to his brother artist but also to the subject of the artist's painting: either the Crucifixion or Christ's Resurrection from the tomb

(viz., the "burning rib," the "sleeping warrior," the "guards"). Cf. C. Brown, "Into the Heart of Darkness," p. 385. On this subject, cf. also K. Taranovsky, *Essays on Mandel'štam*, pp. 113ff.

98. For the text of Pasternak's "Stalin" poem and its versions, see his *Stikhi 1936–1956*, in *Works*, vol. 3: *Stikhi dlia detei. Stikhi 1912–1957, ne sobrannye v knigi avtora. Stat'i i vystupleniia* (Ann Arbor, 1961), pp. 138–139, 256. See also "Zamechaniia."

99. See especially Pasternak's 1913 poem "Bliznetsy" (Twins). It begins, appropriately for Mandelstam, with the motif of solitary confinement: "Hearts and companions, we freeze, we—[freeze] like twins in cells of solitary confinement" (B. Pasternak, *Stikhotvoreniia i poemy*, p. 495). The collection is permeated with astral thematism—another aspect that Mandelstam, who would soon be composing his "stellar" cycle (including "Verse on the Unknown Soldier"), must have found appealing.

100. Mandelstam, *SS* 4, p. 140. If I am reading this letter correctly, the "Ode" represented another instance in the dialogue between the two poets in the 1930s. After all, the "wolf" cycle was prompted by, among other things, Pasternak's "Krasavitsa moia, vsia stat'," and certain lines in Pasternak's "Vse naklonen'ia i zalogi" read like an admonition to Mandelstam put together from bits and pieces of Mandelstam's own poetry (the "Ariosto" cycle, *SS* 1: 267–270). The admonition may actually have affected Mandelstam, since its echoes are audible in "Esli b menia nashi vragi vziali" (*SS* 1: 372).

101. "Klialsia Gospod' i ne raskaetsia . . ."(Ps. 109: 4); "Ne narushu zaveta Moego . . . Odnazhdy Ia poklialsia sviatostiiu Moeiu: solgu li Davidu?" (Ps. 88: 35–36).

102. *SS* 1: 367.

103. H. Bergson, *Creative Evolution* (New York, 1944), pp. 153, 188–194.

104. NM 1, p. 218; Baines, *The Later Poetry*, p. 175.

105. *SS* 1: 86–87. For an analysis of this poem, see C. Brown, *Mandelstam* (Cambridge, 1973), pp. 237–245; and G. Freidin, "Time, Identity, and Myth in Osip Mandelstam" (Ph.D. diss., University of California, Berkeley, 1979), pp. 164–168.

106. Cf. Derzhavin's ode "Bog."

107. St. Augustin's *Confessions* and those of Rousseau.

108. K. Clark, "Utopian Anthropology as a Context for Stalinist Literature," in *Stalinism: Essays in Historical Interpretation*, ed. Robert C. Tucker (New York, 1977). Cf. I. Nusinov, *Vekovye Obrazy* (Moscow, 1937).

109. The appropriation of Prometheus to Christianity is by no means an uncommon theme in modern European literature. "If the identification of Prometheus with Christ," wrote one scholar, "was the result of a mistake which was as much historical as ideological, then, it has to be recognized, rarely has a mistake been more productive" (R. Trousson, *Le thème de Prométhée dans la littérature européenne*, vol. 2 [Geneva, 1964], p. 479).

110. Apart from the "prayer of the cup" at Gethsemane, compare line 10 of stanza 5 with Matt. 27: 34: "Dali Emu pit' uksusa, smeshannogo *s zhelch'iu* i, otvedav, ne khotel pit'."

111. Reported by N. Khardzhiev (see NM 1, p. 268).
112. "Gde sviazannyi i prigvozhdennyi ston," *SS* 1: 356.
113. See Sir James Frazer, *The New Golden Bough* (New York, 1959), p. 35 ("The Roots of Magic").
114. "Khrani menia, moi talisman." See Ronen, "Osip Mandel'štam."
115. Frazer, *The New Golden Bough,* p. 35.
116. To cite A. A. Potebnia (*Malorusskaia narodnaia pesnia* (Voronezh, 1877], p. 21), the "fundamental formula of a spell [*zagovor*] . . . constitutes a verbal representation in which a given or contrived phenomenon is compared to one that is desired, with the purpose of fulfilling the latter."
117. R. Barthes, *Mythologies* (New York, 1972), esp. pp. 117–121. Significantly for the history of myth in contemporary culture, Mandelstam praises myth in "Pushkin i Skriabin" in virtually the same words Barthes uses (p. 118) to damn it: "It is this constant game of hide-and-seek between the meaning and the form which defines myth." Compare this with Mandelstam's idea of a poet "playing hide-and-seek with God." On the problem of this sort of concealment, see J. Derrida, "La pharmacie de Platon," in *La dissémination* (Paris, 1972), where we find the following definition of a text: "Un texte n'est un texte que s'il cache au premier regard, au premier venu, la loi de sa composition et la regle de son jeu" (p. 71).
118. "Prodigal Son" is the title of a chapter in NM 2.
119. Contrary to the sense conveyed in NM 1, Mandelstam's friend B. S. Kuzin recalled that Aleksei Nikolaevich Tolstoi was a magnanimous actor in the arbitration between Mandelstam and Sargidzhan, who allegedly used force against the poet's wife (Kuzin, "Ob. O. E. Mandel'shtame," p. 122): "A. Tolstoi, it was plain to see, did not try to add to the yapping of the dogs from the Writers' Union that had been loosed on Mandelstam. He did not even respond to the symbolic slap he received from O.E. in any way that might have worsened the clouds gathered over him."
120. "The Procurator's cheek twitched, and he said: 'Bring me the accused'" (M. Bulgakov, *Belaia gvardiia. Teatral'nyi roman. Master i Margarita* [Moscow, 1973], p. 438). Dostoevskii, *Polnoe sobranie sochinenii,* vol. 11, p. 28.
121. NM 1, p. 220.
122. NM 2, p. 103.

BIBLIOGRAPHY

Adamovich, Georgii. *Odinochestvo i svoboda*. New York, 1955.
Adrianov, S. "'Roza i krest' A. Bloka." *Vestnik Evropy* 11 (1913).
———. "Tret'ia Rossiia." *Novaia Rossiia* (later on *Rossiia*) 1 (March 1922).
Afanas'ev, A. N. *Poeticheskie vozzreniia slavian na prirodu: Opyt sravnitel'nogo izucheniia slavianskikh predanii i verovanii v sviazi s mificheskimi skazaniiami drugikh narodov*. Parts 1–3. Moscow, 1865–69.
Akhmatova, Anna. *Sochineniia*. 3 vols. Edited by G. P. Struve and B. A. Filippov. Vols. 1 and 2. Washington, D.C.: Inter-Language Literary Associates, 1965 and 1968. Vol. 3. Paris: YMCA Press, 1983.
———. *Stikhotvoreniia i poemy*. Edited, compiled, and annotated by Viktor Zhirmunskii, with an Introduction by A. A. Surkov. Leningrad, 1976.
———. *Vecher*. St. Petersburg, 1912.
Aksakov, S. T. "Istoriia moego znakomstva s Gogolem." In *Gogol' v vospominaniiakh sovremennikov*. Edited by S. Mashinskii. Moscow, 1952.
Al'manakh muz. Petrograd, 1916.
A-mi. "Zametka liubitelia stikhov." *Zavety* 1 (1912).
Annenskii, I. *Knigi otrazhenii*. Edited, compiled, and annotated by N. T. Ashimbaeva, I. I. Podol'skaia, and A. V. Fedorov. Moscow, 1979.
———. *Stikhotvoreniia i tragedii*. Edited, annotated and with an Introduction by A. Fedorov. Leningrad, 1959.
———. *Teatr Evripida. Polnyi stikhotvornyi perevod I. F. Annenskogo*. St. Petersburg, 1908.
Annenskii, V. I. [V. Krivich]. "Innokentii Annenskii po semeinym vospominaniiam i rukopisnym materialam." *Literaturnaia mysl'. Al'manakh* 3. Leningrad, 1925.
Arbour, R. *Henri Bergson et les lettres françaises*. Paris, 1955.
Arseniev, Nicholas. *Holy Moscow*. London, 1940.
Arvatov, B. "Kontrrevoliutsiia formy." *Lef* 1 (1923).
Asmus, V. "Estetika Bergsona." *Na literaturnom postu* 2 (1929).
Aucouturier, M. "The Legend of the Poet and the Image of the Actor in the Short Stories of Pasternak." *Studies in Short Fiction* 3 (1966).

———. "The Metonymous Hero, or the Beginnings of Pasternak the Novelist." *Books Abroad* (now *World Literature Today*) 44 (Spring 1977).
———. "Smena vekh i russkaia literatura 20-kh godov." In *Odna ili dve russkikh literatury? Mezhdunarodnyi simpozium, sozvannyi fakultetom slovestnosti Zhenevskogo Universiteta i Shveitsarskoi Akademiei Slavistiki, Zheneva, 13-14-15 aprelia 1978.* Lausanne, 1981.
Averbakh, L. *Na putiakh kul'turnoi revoliutsii.* Moscow, 1929.
Averbakh, L., S. Firin, and M. Gorky, eds. *Belomor: An Account of the Construction of the New Canal Between the White Sea and the Baltic Sea.* Written by L. Averbakh, B. Agapov, S. Alimov et al. Translated, edited, and with a special Introduction by Amabel Williams-Ellis. New York, 1935.
Averintsev, S. "Morfologiia kul'tury Osval'da Shpenglera." *Voprosy literatury* 1 (1968).
Azadovskii, K. "Put' Aleksandra Dobroliubova." In *Uchenye zapiski Tartuskogo gosudarstvennogo universiteta,* no. 459. *Tvorchestvo Aleksandra Bloka i russkaia kul'tura XX veka: Blokovskii sbornik III.* Tartu, 1979.
Baevskii, V., and A. Koshelev. "Poetika Bloka: Anagrammy." In *Uchenye zapiski Tartuskogo gosudarstvennogo universiteta,* no. 459. *Tvorchestvo Aleksandra Bloka i russkaia kul'tura XX veka: Blokovskii sbornik III.* Tartu, 1979.
Baines, Jennifer. *Mandelstam: The Later Poetry.* Cambridge, London, and New York, 1976.
Bakhrakh, A. "'Dopolnitel'nyi' Mandel'shtam." *Russkaia mysl'* (New York), April 19, 1981.
———. "Pis'ma Mariny Tsvetaevoi." *Mosty* (Munich) 5 (1960).
Bakhtin, Mikhail. "Iz lektsii po istorii russkoi literatury: Viacheslav Ivanov." In *Estetika slovsnogo tvorchestva.* Moscow, 1979.
———. *Problemy poetiki Dostoevskogo.* Moscow, 1963.
———. "Slovo v romane." In *Estetika slovesnogo tvorchestva.* Moscow, 1979.
———. *Voprosy literatury i estetiki: Issledovaniia raznykh let.* Moscow, 1975.
Bal'mont, Konstatin. *Poeziia kak volshebstvo.* Moscow, 1916.
———. *Sonety solntsa, meda i luny.* 2d ed. (1st ed. Moscow, 1917). Berlin, 1921.
———. *Stikhotvoreniia.* Edited, compiled, annotated, and with an Introduction by Vl. Orlov. Leningrad, 1969.
Baron, Salo W. *The Russian Jews Under Tsars and Soviets.* New York and London, 1975.
Barthes, R. *Mythologies.* Selected and translated by Annette Lavers. New York, 1972.
———. *S/Z. An Essay.* Translated by Richard Miller, with a Preface by Richard Howard. New York, 1974.
Bazarov, V. "Bogoiskateli i bogostroiteli." *Vershiny* (1909).
Bel'kind, E. "A. Blok i Viacheslav Ivanov." In *Blokovskii sbornik II. Trudy Vtoroi nauchnoi konferentsii, posviashchennoi izucheniiu zhizni i tvorchestva A. A. Bloka.* Tartu, 1977.

Bibliography

Belyi, Andrei. "Dnevnik pisatelia. Pochemu ia ne mogu kul'turno rabotat'." *Zapiski mechtatelei* 2–3 (1921).
———. "Dnevnik pisatelia." *Rossiia* 2/11 (1924).
———. *Glassolaliia: Poema o zvuke*. Moscow, 1917. (Title page: *Glassololiia*.) Edited and with an Introduction by Dmitrij Tschizewskij. Munich, 1976. (Reprint of the 1922 edition.)
———. *Kubok metelei*. Moscow, 1908.
———. *Lug zelenyi*. Moscow, 1910.
———. *Masterstvo Gogolia*. Moscow, 1934.
———. *Nachalo veka*. Moscow and Leningrad, 1933.
———. *Simvolizm*. Moscow, 1910.
———. "Venok ili venets." *Apollon* 11 (1910).
———. "Zhezl Aarona." In *Skify* 1 (1917).
Bem, A. "O Mandel'shtam, 'O prirode slova.'" *Volia Rossii* (Prague) 6–7 (1923).
Bendix R. *Max Weber: An Intellectual Portrait*. New York, 1960.
———. "Max Weber's Sociology Today." *International Social Science Journal* 17 (1965).
Berberova, N. *Kursiv moi: Avtobiografiia*. Munich, 1972.
Berdiaev, N. "K psikhologii revoliutsii." *Russkaia mysl'* 29, no. 3 (1908).
Berenshtam, Vl. "Voina i poety: Pis'mo iz Petrograda." *Russkie vedomosti*, January 1, 1915.
Bergson, Henri. *Creative Evolution*. Translated by Arthur Mitchell. New York, 1944.
———. *L'energie spirituelle; essais et conferences*. 160th ed. Paris, 1976.
———. *Essai sur les données immediates de la conscience*. 22d ed. Paris, 1924.
Berkovskii, N. "O proze Mandel'shtama." In *Tekushchaia literatura*. Moscow, 1930.
———. "O proze Mandel'shtama." *Zvezda* 5 (1925).
Berlin, Sir Isaiah. *Personal Impressions*. Edited by Henry Hardy, with an introduction by Noel Annan. New York, 1981.
Bernshtein, S. "Golos Bloka" (1921). Prepared for publication by A. Ivich and G. Superfin. *Blokovskii sbornik II. Trudy Vtoroi nauchnoi konferentsii, posviashchennoi izucheniiu zhizni i tvorchestva A. A. Bloka*. Tartu, 1977.
Beskin, O. "O. Mandel'shtam. 'O poezii'" (review). *Pechat' i revoliutsiia* 6 (1929).
Bettelheim, Bruno. *Surviving, and Other Essays*. New York, 1979.
Blok, Aleksandr. *Sobranie sochinenii*. 8 vols. Edited by V. N. Orlov, A. A. Surkov, and K. I. Chukovskii. Moscow and Leningrad, 1960–64.
Bloom, Harold. *The Anxiety of Influence: A Theory of Poetry*. New York, 1973.
Bobrov, Sergei. "O. Mandel'shtam. 'Tristia'" (review). *Pechat' i revoliutsiia* 4 (1923).
Bondarenko, P. *Protiv mekhanicheskogo materializma i men'shevistvuiushchego idealizma v biologii*. Moscow and Leningrad, 1931.

Bibliography

Borland, H. *Soviet Literary Theory and Practice During the First Five-Year Plan: 1928–1932*. New York, 1950.
Borozdin, A. *Ocherki po istorii russkoi literatury: Russkaia narodnaia slovesnost' i drevniaia pis'mennost'*. N.p., 1913.
Brik, L. "Maiakovskii i chuzhie stikhi. Iz vospominanii." *Znamia* 3 (1940).
Brik, Osip. "Zvukovye povtory." In *Poetika: Sborniki po teorii poeticheskogo iazyka*. Petrograd, 1919.
Briusov, V. "'Al'manakh Tsekha poetov,' kn. 2 (Pg., 1921) and 'SOPO. Pervyi sbornik stikhov' (M. 4-yi god 1-go veka [1921])" (review). *Pechat' i Revoliutsiia* 3 (1921).
———. "God russkoi poezii." *Russkaia mysl'* 5 (1914).
———. "Literaturnaia zhizn' Frantsii: Nauchnaia poeziia." *Russkaia mysl'* 6 (1909).
———. "O 'rechi rabskoi' v zashchitu poezii." *Apollon* 9 (1910).
———. "Segodniashnii den' russkoi poezii." *Russkaia mysl'* 7 (1912).
———. *Sobranie sochinenii*. 7 vols. Moscow, 1975–77.
———. "Sredi stikhov" (review of Osip Mandelstam's *Vtoraia kniga*). *Pechat' i revoliutsiia* 6 (1923).
———. "Vchera, segodnia i zavtra russkoi poezii." *Pechat' i revoliutsiia* 7 (1922).
Brown, Clarence. "Into the Heart of Darkness." *Slavic Review* 26, no. 4 (1967).
———. *Mandelstam*. Cambridge, 1973.
———. *The Prose of Osip Mandelstam: The Noise of Time. Theodosia. The Egyptian Stamp*. Translated, with a critical essay, by Clarence Brown. 2d ed., with corrections (1st ed., 1964). Princeton, 1967.
Brown, Edward J. *Mayakovsky: A Poet in the Revolution*. Princeton, 1973.
———. *The Proletarian Episode in Russian Literature: 1928–1932*. New York, 1953.
———. "Roman Osipovich Jakobson 1896–1982: The Unity of His Thought on Verbal Art." *The Russian Review* 42, no. 1 (1983).
———, ed. *Major Soviet Writers: Essays in Criticism*. Oxford, London and New York, 1973.
Brown, Peter. "The Saint as Exemplar in Late Antiquity." *Representations* 1, no. 2 (1983).
———. *Society and the Holy in Late Antiquity*. Berkeley and Los Angeles, 1982.
Broyde, Steven. *Osip Mandel'štam and His Age: A Commentary on the Themes of War and Revolution in the Poetry, 1913–1923*. Cambridge, Mass., 1975.
Bukhshtab, B. "The Poetry of Osip Mandelstam." *Russian Literature Triquarterly* 1 (1971).
Bulgakov, Mikhail. *Belaia gvardiia. Teatral'nyi roman. Master i Margarita*. Moscow, 1973.
Bulgakov, S. "Geroizm i podvizhnichestvo." In *Vekhi: Sbornik statei o russkoi intelligentsii*. 3d ed. Edited by M. O. Gershenzon. Moscow, 1909.

Bibliography

Burke, Kenneth. *The Philosophy of Literary Form: Studies in Symbolic Action*. 3d ed. Berkeley and Los Angeles, 1973.
Buslaev, F. I. "Dogadki i mechtaniia o pervobytnom cheloveke." In *Sochineniia*, vol. 1. St. Petersburg, 1908.
Buzeskul, V. *Antichnost' i sovremennost': Sovremennye temy v antichnoi Gretsii*. 2d ed. St. Petersburg, 1914.
Carré, Meyrick H. *Realists and Nominalists*. Oxford, 1946.
Challis, N., and H. W. Dewey. "The Blessed Fools of Old Russia." *Jahrbuch für Geschichte Osteuropas* 22 (1974).
Chernov, V. "Etika i politika." *Zavety* 3 (1912).
Chudakova, M. *Poetika Mikhaila Zoshchenko*. Moscow, 1979.
Chukovskaia, L. *Pamiata Anny Akhmatovoi*. Paris, 1976.
Chukovskii, K. "Anna Akhmatova: Mnogoobrazie likov." In *Pamiat': Istoricheskii sbornik*, vol. 2, edited by N. Gorbanevskaia. Paris, 1979.
Chukovskii, N. "Vstrechi s Mandel'shtamom." *Moskva* 8 (1964).
Chuzhak, N., ed. *Literatura fakta. Pervyi sbornik materialov rabotnikov LEF'a*. Moscow, 1929.
Clark, Katerina. "Utopian Anthropology as a Context for Stalinist Literature." In *Stalinism: Essays in Historical Interpretation*, edited by Robert C. Tucker. New York, 1977.
Cohen, Stephen F. *Bukharin and the Bolshevik Revolution: A Political Biography, 1888–1938*. New York, 1973.
Cohn, R. G. *Towards the Poems of Mallarmé*. Berkeley and Los Angeles, 1965.
Dal', Vl. *Tolkovyi slovar' zhivogo velikorusskago iazyka*. 3d ed., corrected and expanded. 4 vols. Edited by I. A. Boduen-de-Kurtene. St. Petersburg and Moscow, 1903–9.
Dal'nii, G. *See* G. G. Superfin.
Danchenko, V. *Dante Alig'eri: Bibliograficheskii ukazatel' russkikh perevodov i kriticheskoi literatury na russkom iazyke 1762–1972*. Moscow, 1973.
Dante Alighieri. *La Divina Commedia*. Edited and annotated by C. H. Grandgent, revised by Charles S. Singleton. Cambridge, Mass., 1972.
———. *The Divine Comedy of Dante Alighieri*. 3 vols. Translated and with commentary by John D. Sinclair. New York, 1939.
———. *Novaia zhizn'. Bozhestvennaia komediia*. Translated by A. Efros and M. Lozinskii, with commentary by E. Solonovich, S. Averintsev, A. Mikhailov, and M. Lozinskii. Moscow, 1967.
Derrida, Jacques. *Of Grammatology*. Translated by Gayatri Chakravorty Spivak. Baltimore, 1976.
———. "La pharmacie de Platon," In *La dissemination*. Paris, 1972.
Detienne, Marcel. *The Garden of Adonis*. Translated by Janet Lloyd, with an Introduction by J.-P. Vernant. Sussex, England, 1977.
Dinershtein, E. "A. K. Voronskii: Iz perepiski s sovetskimi pisateliami (Vstupitel'naia stat'ia)." In *Literaturnoe nasledstvo*, vol. 93. *Iz istorii sovetskoi literatury 1920–1930-kh godov: Novye materialy i issledovaniia*. Moscow, 1983.

Dix, Dom Gregory. *The Shape of the Liturgy*. 2d ed. London, 1945.
Dodds, E. R. *The Greeks and the Irrational*. Berkeley and Los Angeles, 1951.
Dolgopolov, Leonid. *Na rubezhe vekov: O russkoi literature kontsa XIX–nachala XX*. Leningrad, 1977.
———. *Poema Aleksandra Bloka "Dvenadtsat'."* Leningrad, 1979.
Dostoevskii, F. M. *Polnoe sobranie sochinenii*. 30 vols. Leningrad, 1972–.
Driver, S. "Acmeism." *Slavic and East European Journal* 2 (1968).
Druzin, V. "E. Bagritskii, *Iugo-Zapad*" (review). *Zvezda* 6 (1928).
Dunlop, John B. *Starets Amvrosy: Model for Dostoevsky's Starets Zossima*. Belmont, Mass., 1972.
Durkheim, E. *Elementary Forms of the Religious Life*. Translated by Joseph Ward Swain. New York, 1915.
"Dva pis'ma N. Ia. Mandel'shtam." In *Pamiat': Istoricheskii sbornik*, vol. 1. Moscow, 1976; New York, 1978.
Edmonds, J., ed. *Lyra Graeca*, vol. 1. London, 1928.
Efros, A. "Vestnik y poroga: Dukh klassiki." In *Liricheskii krug: Stranitsy poezii i kritiki*, vol. 1. Moscow, 1922.
Eikhenbaum, Boris. *Anna Akhmatova: Opyt analiza*. St. Petersburg, 1923.
———. "O shatobriane, o chervontsakh i russkoi literature." *Zhizn' iskusstva* 1 (1924).
———. "Sud'ba Bloka." In *Ob Aleksandre Bloke*. Petrograd, 1921.
Eliot, T. S. *The Three Voices of Poetry*. New York, 1954.
Elliott, R. C. *The Power of Satire: Magic, Ritual, Art*. Princeton, 1960.
Ellis [L. L. Kobylinskii]. "O zadachakh i tseliakh sluzheniia kul'ture." *Trudy i dni* 4–5 (1912).
———. *Russkie simvolisty*. Moscow, 1910.
Empson, William. *Seven Types of Ambiguity*. New York, 1947.
Eng-Liedmeier, Jeanne van der. "Mandel'štam's poem 'V Peterburge my sojdemsja snova.'" *Russian Literature* 7/8 (1974).
Erberg, K. "O vozdushnykh mostakh kritiki." *Apollon* 2 (1909).
Erenburg, Ilia. *Liudi, gody, zhizn': Kniga pervaia i vtoraia*. Moscow, 1961.
———. *Portrety sovremennykh poetov*. Moscow, 1923.
Erlich, V. *Russian Formalism: History—Doctrine*. 3d ed. New Haven and London, 1981.
Etkind, E., ed. and comp. *Frantsuzskie stikhi v perevode russkikh poetov XIX–XX vv*. Moscow, 1969.
Fanger, D. *The Creation of Nikolai Gogol'*. Cambridge, Mass., 1979.
Faresov, A. I. *Protiv techeniia: N. S. Leskov. Ego zhizn', sochineniia, polemika i vospominaniia o nem*. St. Petersburg, 1904.
Fedotov, G. P. *The Russian Religious Mind*. Cambridge, Mass., 1946.
Filosofov, D. "Druz'ia ili vragi." *Russkaia mysl'* 8 (1909).
———. "'Sborniki po teorii poeticheskogo iazyka. Vypusk I' (Petrograd, 1916)" (review). *Rech'*, September 26, 1916.
Flammarion, C. *Popular Astronomy*. Authorized translation by J. E. Gore. 1907.

Bibliography

Fleishman, L. "Epizod s Bezymenskim v *Puteshestvii v Armeniiu*." *Slavica Hierosolymitana* 3 (1978).
———. "Neizvestnaia stat'ia Osipa Mandel'shtama." *Wiener Slawistischer Almanach* 10 (1982).
———. "O gibeli Maiakovskogo kak literaturnom fakte." *Slavica Hierosolymitana* 4 (1979).
———. *Pasternak v dvadtsatye gody*. Munich, n.d. [1981].
———. *Pasternak v tridtsatye gody*. Jerusalem, 1983.
Florenskii, Pavel. *Stolp i utverzhdenie istiny: Opyt pravoslavnoi feoditsei v dvenadtsati pis'makh*. Moscow, 1914.
Florovskii, Georgii. *Puti russkogo bogosloviia*. 2d ed. Edited by I. Meiendorf. Paris, 1981.
Forsh, O. *Sumashedshii korabl'*. Moscow, 1931.
Frazer, Sir James. *The New Golden Bough*. Edited and abridged by Theodore H. Gaster. New York, 1959.
Freidin, G. "Time, Identity, and Myth in Osip Mandelstam." Ph.D. diss., University of California, Berkeley, 1979.
———. "The Whisper of History and the Noise of Time in the Writings of Osip Mandelstam." *The Russian Review* 37, no. 4 (1978).
Freud, S. *The Interpretation of Dreams*. Translated and edited by James Strachey. New York, 1965.
———. *The Standard Edition of the Complete Psychological Works of Sigmund Freud*. 24 vols. London, 1953–74.
Fridliand, V. "Krugovorot professora istorii" (review of B. Iu. Vipper, *Krugovorot istorii*). *Pechat' i revoliutsiia* 6 (1923).
Friedberg, Maurice. *Russian Classics in Soviet Jackets*. New York and London, 1962.
Fussell, Paul. *Great War in Modern Memory*. Oxford, 1975.
Gal'skii, V. [Vadim Shershenevich]. "O. Mandel'shtam. Kamen'. Stikhi" (review). *Novaia zhizn': Literaturno-obshchestvennyi al'manakh*. Vol. 4 (Moscow, 1916).
Galakhov, Vas. *See* V. V. Gippius.
Gardner, E. G. *Dante and the Mystics*. New York, 1968.
Geertz, Clifford. *The Interpretation of Cultures: Selected Essays*. New York, 1973.
———. *Local Knowledge: Further Essays in Interpretive Anthropology*. New York, 1983.
Gershenzon, M. O. *Petr Chaadaev: Zhizn' i myshlen'e*. St. Petersburg, 1908.
———, ed. *Vekhi: Sbornik statei o russkoi intelligentsii*. 3d ed. Moscow, 1909.
Gershenzon, M. O., and Viach. Ivanov. *Perepiska iz dvukh uglov*. Berlin, 1922.
Gertsen, Aleksandr [A. Herzen]. *O razvitii revoliutsionnykh idei v Rossii*. Vol. 3 of *Sochineniia*. Moscow, 1956.
———. *Sochineniia*. 9 vols. Moscow, 1955–58.
Gifford, Henry. "Mandelstam and Pasternak: The Antipodes." In *Russian and*

Slavic Literature, edited by R. Freeborn, R. R. Milner-Gulland, and C. A. Ward. Cambridge, Mass., 1976.
———. *Pasternak: A Critical Study.* Cambridge, 1977.
Ginzburg, Lidiia. "Iz starykh zapisei." In *O starom i novom.* Leningrad, 1982.
———. *O lirike.* 2d ed. Leningrad, 1974.
———. *O starom i novom.* Leningrad, 1982.
———. "Poetika Osipa Mandel'shtama" (1966). In *O lirike.* Leningrad, 1974. Also in *O starom i novom.* Leningrad, 1982.
———. "Tynianov-uchenyi." In *Vospominaniia o Iurii Tynianove,* edited by V. A. Kaverin. Moscow, 1983.
Gippius, V. V. *Lik chelovecheskii.* St. Petersburg and Berlin, 1922.
———. *Puskhin i khristianstvo.* Petrograd, 1915.
———. [Vas. Galakhov]. "Tsekh poetov." *Zhizn'* (Odessa) 5 (1918).
Girard, R. *Violence and the Sacred.* Translated by Patrick Gregory. Baltimore and London, 1977.
Gleason, A. *European and Muscovite; Ivan Kireevsky and the Origins of Slavophilism.* Cambridge, Mass., 1972.
Glebov, Igor' [B. V. Asaf'ev]. *Skriabin. Opyt kharakteristiki.* Berlin, 1923.
Gofman, Viktor. "Iazyk simvolistov." In *Literaturnoe nasledstvo,* vols. 27–29. Moscow, 1937.
Gogol', Nikolai. *Polnoe sobranie sochinenii.* 14 vols. Edited by N. F. Bel'chikov and B. V. Tomashevskii. Moscow, 1940–52.
Gollerbakh, E. "Peterburgskaia Kamena." *Novaia Rossiia. Obshchestvenno-literaturnyi i nauchnyi ezhemesiachnyi zhurnal* (Petrograd) 1 (1922).
———. "Staroe i novoe." *Novaia russkaia kniga* (Berlin) 7 (1922).
Goodman, Felicitas D. *Speaking in Tongues: A Cross-Cultural Study of Glossolalia.* Chicago, 1972.
———. *Trance, Healing, and Hallucination.* New York, 1974.
Gorbachev, G. *Ocherki sovremennoi russkoi literatury.* 2d ed., enlarged. Leningrad, 1925.
———. *Sovremennaia russkaia literatura.* 2d ed., revised and enlarged. Leningrad, 1925.
Gornfel'd, Arkadii G. *Knigi i liudi: Literaturnye besedy I.* St. Petersburg, 1908.
———. "Khudozhestvennoe slovo i nauchnaia tsifra." *Literaturnaia mysl'. Al'manakh,* vol. 1. Petrograd, 1922.
———. Letter to the Editor. *Krasnaia gazeta* (Leningrad), November 28, 1928.
Gorodetskii, Sergei. "Muzyka i arkhitektura v poezii." *Rech'* 17 (30) (June 1913).
———. "Nekotorye techeniia v sovremennoi russkoi poezii." *Apollon* 1 (1913).
———. "Poeziia kak iskusstvo." *Lukomor'e* 18 (April 30, 1916).
———. "Stikhi o voine v 'Apollone.'" *Rech',* November 3, 1914.
———. *Stikhotvoreniia i poemy.* Leningrad, 1974.
———, ed. *Styk: Pervyi sbornik stikhov Moskovskogo Tsekha poetov.* With In-

troductions by A. V. Lunacharskii and S. M. Gorodetskii. Moscow, 1925.

Gorodetzky, Nadejda. *The Humiliated Christ in Modern Russian Thought*. London and New York, 1938.

Graham, Stephen. *The Way of Martha and the Way of Mary*. New York, 1916.

Greenberg, Louis. *The Jews in Russia: The Struggle for Emancipation*. With an Introduction by Alfred Levin. New York, 1976.

Greenblatt, Stephen. *Renaissance Self-Fashioning*. Chicago, 1980.

Griakalova, N. Iu. "Fol'klornye traditsii v poezii Anny Akhmatovoi." *Russkaia literatura* 25, no. 1 (1982).

Griftsov, B. "V. V. Gippius, 'Pushkin i khristianstvo'" (review). *Russkaia mysl'* 37, no. 1 (1916).

Grigor'ev, A. and I. Petrova. "Mandel'shtam na poroge tridtsatykh godov." *Russian Literature* V-2 (1977).

Gromov, P. *Blok. Ego predshestvenniki i sovremenniki*. Moscow and Leningrad, 1966.

Gruzdev, I. "Sovremennaia russkaia poeziia." *Kniga i revoliutsiia* 3 (1923).

Gumilev, Nikolai. "Nasledie simvolizma i akmeizm." *Apollon* 1 (1913).

―――. *Neizdannye stikhi i pis'ma*. Edited and annotated by G. P. Struve. Paris, 1980.

―――. *Sobranie sochinenii*. 4 vols. Edited by B. A. Filippov and G. P. Struve. Washington, D.C., 1962–68.

Hackel, Sergei. *The Poet and the Revolution: Alexander Blok's "The Twelve."* Oxford, 1975.

Haimson, L. H. *The Russian Marxists and the Origins of Bolshevism*. Cambridge, Mass., 1955.

Harris, Jane Gary. "Autobiographical Theory and the Problem of Aesthetic Coherence in Mandelstam's *The Noise of Time*." *Essays in Poetics* 9, no. 2 (1984).

―――. Introduction to Osip Mandelstam, *The Complete Critical Prose and Letters*. Ann Arbor, 1979.

Hastings, James, ed. *Encyclopaedia of Religion and Ethics*. 12 vols. New York, n.d.

Henry, Hélène. "Étude de fonctionnement d'un poème de Mandel'stam." *Action poétique* 63 (1975).

Henry, Peter. "Imagery of *Podvig* and *Podvizhnichestvo* in the Works of Garshin and the Early Gor'kii." *Slavonic and East European Review* 61, no. 1 (1983).

Heracleitos. *Geraklit Efesskii, Fragmenty*. Translated by Vladimir Nilebder. Moscow, 1910.

Herzen, A. *See* A. Gertsen.

Holland, Norman N. *5 Readers Reading*. New Haven, 1975.

Hope, A. D. "The Blind Swallow: Some Parleyings with Mandelstam." In *The Pack of Autolycus*. Canberra and Norwalk, Conn., 1978.

Hughes, H. Stuart. *Oswald Spengler: A Critical Estimate*. New York and London, 1952.

Hughes, Robert P. "Nothung, the Cassia Flower, and a 'Spirit of Music' in the Poetry of Aleksandr Blok." *California Slavic Studies* 6 (1971).

Hulme, T. E. *Speculations: Essays on Humanism and the Philosophy of Art.* 2d ed. Edited by Herbert Read, with a Frontispiece and Foreword by Jacob Epstein. London and New York, 1936.

Iakubinskii, L. P. "Skoplenie odinakovykh plavnykh v prakticheskom i poeticheskom iazykakh." In *Poetika: Sborniki po teorii poeticheskogo iazyka.* Petrograd, 1919.

Iser, Wolfgang. *The Act of Reading: A Theory of Aesthetic Response.* Baltimore and London, 1978.

Ivanov, Georgii. "Osip Mandel'shtam" (review of O. E. Mandelstam, *Sobranie sochinenii,* 1955). *Novyi zhurnal* 43 (1955).

———. *Peterburgskie zimy.* New York, 1952.

———. "Voennye stikhi." *Apollon* 4–5 (1915).

Ivanov, Viach. *Cor ardens.* 2 vols. Moscow, 1911–12.

———. "Dostoevskii i roman-tragediia." *Russkaia mysl'* 32, no. 6 (1911).

———. "Ellinskaia religiia stradaiushchego boga." *Novyi put'* 1–3, 5, 8–9 (1904).

———. "Orfei." *Trudy i dni* 1 (1912).

———. *Po zvezdam.* St. Petersburg, 1909.

———. *Prozrachnost'. Vtoraia kniga liriki.* Moscow, 1904.

———. "Religiia Dionisa: Ee proiskhozhdenie i vliianie." *Voprosy zhizni* 6, 7 (July 1905).

———. *Rodnoe i vselenskoe.* Moscow, 1917.

———. *Sobranie sochinenii.* 3 vols. Edited and with an Introduction by O. Decharte. Brussels, 1971–79.

———. *Stikhotvoreniia i poemy.* Edited, compiled, and annotated by R. E. Pomirchii, with an Introduction by S. S. Averintsev. Leningrad, 1976.

Ivanov-Razumnik, R. V. [Ivanov, Razumnik Vasilievich]. "Gertsen o nashikh dniakh." In *A. I. Gertsen: 1870–1920.* Petrograd, 1920.

———. *Istoriia russkoi obshchestvennoi mysli.* 2 vols. St. Petersburg, 1907.

Ivanova, E. V. "Valerii Briusov i Aleksandr Dobroliubov." *Izvestiia Akademii nauk SSSR. Seriia literatury i iazyka* 40, no. 3 (1981).

Ivinskaia, Ol'ga. *V plenu vremeni: Gody s Borisom Pasternakom.* Paris, 1978 (title page: Moscow, 1982).

Izenberg, Charles. "Associative Chains in *Egipetskaia marka.*" *Russian Literature* V-3 (1977).

Izgoev, A. S. "Na perevale. Zhizn' i publitsistika." *Russkaia mysl'* 33, no. 27 (1912).

Jakobson, Roman O. "Co je poesie." *Volné směry* 30 (1933–34).

———. "Linguistics and Poetics." In *Style in Language,* edited by T. Sebeok. Cambridge, Mass., 1960.

———. "The Metaphoric and Metonymic Poles." In R. O. Jakobson and Maurice Halle, *The Fundamentals of Language.* The Hague and Paris, 1956.

Bibliography

———. *Noveishaia russkaia poeziia (Nabrosok pervyi). Victor Khlebnikov.* Prague, 1921.
———. "O pokolenii, rasstrativshem svoikh poetov." In *Smert' Vladimira Maiakovskogo.* Berlin, 1931. English translation by Edward J. Brown: "On a Generation That Squandered Its Poets." In *Major Soviet Writers: Essays in Criticism,* edited by E. J. Brown. Oxford, 1973.
———. "Poetry of grammar and grammar of poetry." *Lingua* 21 (1968).
———. "Randbemerkungen zur Prosa des Dichters Pasternak." *Slavische Rundschau* 7 (1935).
Jangfeldt, Bengt. *Majakovskij and Futurism: 1917–1921.* Stockholm Studies in Russian Literature, no. 5. Stockholm, 1976.
———. "Osip Mandel'štam's 'Ode to Stalin.'" *Scando-Slavica* 22 (1976).
Joravsky, David. *The Lysenko Affair.* Cambridge, Mass., 1970.
———. *Soviet Marxism and Natural Science, 1917–1932.* New York, 1961.
Kagarov, E. *Kul't fetishei, zhivotnykh i rastenii v drevnei Gretsii.* St. Petersburg, 1913.
Karlinsky, Simon. *Marina Cvetaeva: Her Life and Art.* Berkeley and Los Angeles, 1966.
———. *Marina Tsvetaeva.* Berkeley and Los Angeles, 1985.
———. *The Sexual Labyrinth of Nikolai Gogol.* Cambridge, Mass., 1976.
Karpovich, Mikhail. "Moe znakomstvo s Mandel'shtamom." *Novyi zhurnal* 49 (1957).
Katanian, V. *Maiakovskii: Literaturnaia khronika.* 4th ed., expanded. Moscow, 1961.
Kaverin, V. A., ed. *Vospominaniia o Iurii Tynianove.* Moscow, 1983.
Kenez, Peter. *Civil War in South Russia, 1919–1920: The Defeat of the Whites.* Berkeley and Los Angeles, 1977.
Khardzhiev, Nikolai I. "Vosstanovlennyi Mandel'shtam." *Russian Literature* 7/8 (1974).
Khardzhiev, Nikolai I., and Vl. Vl. Trenin. *Poeticheskaia kul'tura Maiakovskogo.* Moscow, 1969.
Khlebnikov, Velemir. *Sobranie sochinenii.* 5 vols. Revised reprint of *Sobranie proizvedenii* (Moscow, 1928–33). With an Introduction and additions by Vladimir Markov. Munich, 1968.
———. *Sobranie proizvedenii.* 5 vols. Edited by N. Stepanov. Leningrad, 1928–33.
Khlebnikov, Velemir, and Aleksei Kruchenykh, *Dokhlaia luna.* Moscow, 1913.
Khodasevich, Vl. *Literaturnye stat'i i vospominaniia.* New York, 1954.
———. "Literaturnyi subbotnik—o novykh stikhakh." *Utro Rossii* 30 (January 30, 1916).
———. *Nekropol'.* Brussels, 1939.
———. "O Mandel'shtame." *Dni* 65 (1922).
Kholodovich, A. A. "O 'Kurse obshchei lingvistiki' F. de Sossiura." Foreword to Ferdinand de Saussure, *Trudy po iazykoznaniiu,* translated and edited by A. A. Kholodovich. Moscow, 1977.

"Kirik Levin, 'A. I. Gertsen: Lichnost' i ideologiia'" (review). *Pechat' i revoliutsiia* 6 (1922).

Kliuchevskii, V. O. *Kurs russkoi istorii*. 2d ed., revised. 5 vols. Moscow, 1937. (Reprint of the 1922 edition.)

Kniazhin, V. [Ivoilov], ed. *Pis'ma A. Bloka*. Moscow, 1925.

Knox, R. A. *Enthusiasm: A Chapter in the History of Religion with a Special Reference to the XVII and XVIII Centuries*. Oxford, 1950.

Kondakov, N. P. *Ikonografiia Bogomateri*. 2 vols. Petrograd, 1915.

Konovalov, D. G. *Religioznyi ekstaz v russkom misticheskom sektantstve: Issledovanie*. Part I, vyp. 1: *Fizicheskie iavleniia v kartine sektantskogo ekstaza*. Sergiev Posad, 1908.

Kotrelev, N. V., and R. D. Timenchik, comps., "Blok v neizdannoi perepiske i dnevnikakh sovremennikov (1898–1921)." In *Literaturnoe nasledstvo*, vol. 92, bk. 3. Moscow, 1982.

Kozmin, B., ed. *Pisateli sovremennoi epokhi. Biobibliograficheskii slovar' russkikh pisatelei XX veka*. Vol. 1. Moscow, 1928.

Kranikhfel'dt, Vl. "Literaturnye otkliki." *Sovremennyi mir* 8 (1909).

Krivich, V. *See* V. I. Annenskii.

Krotkov, Iurii. "Pasternak." *Grani* 64 (1967).

Kruchenykh, A. *See* Khlebnikov, Velemir, and A. Kruchenykh.

Kuzin, B. S. "Ob O. E. Mandel'shtame." *Vestnik russkogo studencheskogo khristianskogo dvizheniia* 140, nos. 3–4 (1983).

Kuzmin, Mikhail A. "Parnasskie zarosli." In *Zavtra: Literaturno-kriticheskii sbornik*, vol. 1. Edited by E. Zamiatin, Mikhail Kuzmin, and Mikhail Lozinskii. Berlin, 1923.

———. "Radlova. 'Soty'" (review). *Zhizn' iskusstva* 16 (1918).

———. *Sobranie stikhov*. 3 vols. Edited, with introductions and commentary, by John E. Malmstad and Vladimir Markov. Munich, 1977–78.

———. *Uslovnosti: Stat'i ob iskusstve*. Petrograd, 1923.

Kuzmina-Karavaeva, E. I. *See* E. Skobtsova.

Lacan, Jacques. *The Language of the Self: The Function of Language in Psychoanalysis*. Translated, with notes and commentary, by Anthony Wilden. New York, 1968.

———. "La relation d'objet et les structures freudiennes." *Bulletin de Psychologie* 10 (1957).

———. "La signification du phallus: Die Bedeutung des Phallus." In J. Lacan, *Ecrits*. Paris, 1966.

Larin, B. "O 'Kiparisovom lartse.'" *Literaturnaia mysl': Al'manakh*, vol. 2. Petrograd, 1923.

Leikina-Svirskaia, V. R. *Russkaia intelligentsiia v 1900–1917 gg*. Moscow, 1981.

Lelevich, G. "Gippokratovo litso." *Krasnaia nov'* 1 (1925).

Lerner, N. "Osip Mandel'shtam. 'Shum vremeni'" (review). *Byloe* 6 (1925).

Letter to the Editor. *Dni* 5 (November 3, 1922).

Lévi-Strauss, Claude. *Structural Anthropology*. Translated by Claire Jacobson and Brooke Grundfest Schoepf. New York, 1963.

Levin, Iu. I. "O sootnoshenii mezhdu semantikoi poeticheskogo teksta i

Bibliography

vnetekstovoi real'nost'iu (Zametki o poetike Mandel'shtama)." *Russian Literature* 10/11 (1975).

———. "Zametki o krymsko-ellinskikh stikhakh O. Mandel'shtama." *Russian Literature* 10/11 (1975).

Levin, Iu. I., D. M. Segal, R. D. Timenchik, V. N. Toporov, and T. V. Tsiv'ian. "Russkaia semanticheskaia poetika kak potentsial'naia kul'turnaia paradigma." *Russian Literature* 7/8 (1974).

Levin, Kirik. *A. I. Gertsen: Lichnost' i ideologiia.* 2d ed. Petrograd, 1922.

Levinton, G. "'Na kamennykh otrogakh Pierii' Osipa Mandel'shtama: Materialy k analizu." *Russian Literature* V-2 and V-3 (1977).

———. "Zametki o fol'klorizme Bloka." In *Mif, fol'klor, literatura.* Edited by V. G. Bazanov et al. Leningrad, 1978.

Levinton, G., and R. D. Timenchik. "Kniga K. F. Taranovskogo o poezii O. E. Mandel'shtama." *Russian Literature* VI-2 (1978).

Lewin, Moshe. "The Social Background of Stalinism." In *Stalinism: Essays in Historical Interpretation,* edited by Robert C. Tucker. New York, 1977.

Lezhnev, A. "Literaturnye zametki." *Pechat' i revoliutsiia* 4 (1925).

———. "Uzel." *Krasnaia nov'* 8 (1926).

Lezhnev, A., and D. Gorbov. *Literatura revoliutsionnogo desiatiletiia.* Kharkov, 1929.

Lezhnev, Isai. "Velikii sintez." *Novaia Rossiia* 1 (1922).

Lipkin, S. "Ugl', pylaiushchii ognem." *Vnutrennie protivorechiia* 7 (1984).

Literaturnoe nasledstvo. Vol. 92: *Aleksandr Blok: Novye materialy i issledovaniia.* 3 bks. Moscow, 1980–83.

———. Vol. 93: *Iz istorii sovetskoi literatury 1920–1930-kh godov: Novye materialy i issledovaniia.* Moscow, 1983.

Livshits, Benedikt. *Polutoroglazyi strelets.* New York, 1978. (Reprint of the 1933 Moscow edition.)

Lomunov, K. N., ed. *Literaturnye vzgliady i tvorchestvo slavianofilov: 1830–1850 gg.* Moscow, 1978.

Losskii, N. O. *Intuitivnaia filosofiia Bergsona.* 3d ed. Petrograd, 1922.

Lossky, Victor. "Les startsy d'Optino." *Contacts* 33 (1961).

Lotman, Iu. M. "O sootnoshenii zvukovykh i smyslovykh zhestov v poeticheskom tekste." In *Semiotika teksta. Trudy po znakovym sistemam,* vol. 11. Tartu, 1979.

Lotman, Iu. M., and B. A. Uspenskii. "Rol' dual'nykh modelei v dinamike russkoi kul'tury (do kontsa XVIII veka)." In *Trudy po russkoi i slavianskoi filologii* 28 (*Uchenye zapiski Tartuskogo gosudarstvennogo universiteta* 414). Tartu, 1977.

Lozinskii, M. *Gornyi kliuch.* 2d ed. (1st ed., 1916). Petrograd, 1922.

Lunacharskii, A. V. "Taneev i Skriabin." *Novyi mir* 6 (1925).

Lunts, Lev. "Tsekh poetov." *Knizhnyi ugol* 8 (1922).

Lur'e, Artur. "Detskii rai." *Vozdushnye puti.* New York, 1963.

L'vov-Rogachevskii, V. *A History of Russian Jewish Literature.* Translated by Arthur Levin, with an Introduction, "Russian Literature and the Jews," by B. Gorev. Ann Arbor, 1979.

———. *Russko-evreiskaia literatura*. Moscow, 1922.
McClelland, James C. *Autocrats and Academics: Education, Culture, and Society in Tsarist Russia*. Chicago, 1979.
McKenzie, John L. *Dictionary of the Bible*. London, 1965.
McLean, Hugh. "A Linguist Among Poets." *International Journal of Linguistics and Poetics* 3 (1983).
———. *Nikolay Leskov: The Man and His Art*. Cambridge, Mass., 1977.
———. "Smert' Vladimira Maiakovskogo" (review). *Slavic Review* 36, no. 1 (1977).
Maguire, Robert A. *Red Virgin Soil: Soviet Literature in the 1920s*. Princeton, 1968.
Maiakovskii, Vladimir. *Polnoe sobranie sochinenii*. 13 vols. Moscow, 1955–61.
Makovskii, Sergei. *Na Parnase serebrianogo veka*. Munich, 1962.
Maksimov, Dmitrii. *Poeziia i proza Aleksandra Bloka*. Leningrad, 1981.
———. *Valerii Briusov*. Leningrad, 1969.
Malia, Martin. *Alexander Herzen and the Birth of Russian Socialism, 1812–1855*. Cambridge, Mass., 1961.
Mallac, Guy de. *Boris Pasternak, His Life and Art*. With a Foreword by Rimbydas Silbajoris. Norman, Okla., 1981.
Mallarmé, Stéphane. *Les noces d'Hèrodiade. Mystère*. With an Introduction by Gardner Davis. Paris, 1959.
Malmstad, John E. "Mikhail Kuzmin: A Chronicle of His Life and Times." In M. A. Kuzmin, *Sobranie stikhov*, edited, with introductions and commentary, by John E. Malmstad and Vladimir Markov. Vol. 3: *Nesobrannoe i neopublikovannoe. Prilozheniia. Primechaniia. Stat'i o Kuzmine*. Munich, 1977.
———. "A Note on Mandel'štam's 'V Peterburge my sojdemsja snova.'" *Russian Literature* V-II (1977).
Malraux, André. *The Voices of Silence*. Translated by Stuart Gilbert. Princeton, 1978.
Malyshev, V. I. "Bibliografiia sochinenii protopopa Avvakuma i literatury o nem 1917–1953 gg." *Trudy Otdela drevne-russkoi literatury Instituta russkoi literatury Akademii nauk SSSR* (Pushkinskogo doma) 10 (1954).
Mandel'shtam, Nadezhda Ia. "Motsart i Sal'eri." *Vestnik russkogo studencheskogo khristianskogo dvizheniia (Le Messager)* 103 (1972).
———. *Vospominaniia*. New York, 1970.
———. *Vtoraia kniga*. Paris, 1972.
Mandel'shtam, Osip E. *The Complete Critical Prose and Letters*. Edited, annotated, and with an Introduction by Jane Gary Harris. Translated by Jane Gary Harris and Constance Link. Ann Arbor, 1979.
———. *Egipetskaia marka*. N.p., 1928.
———. *Journey to Armenia*. Translated by Sydney Monas, with an Introduction by Henry Gifford. San Francisco, 1979.
———. *Kamen'*. St. Petersburg, 1913.
———. *Kamen'*. Petrograd, 1915.
———. *Kamen'. Pervaia kniga stikhov*. Moscow, 1923.

Bibliography

———. Letter to the Editor (reply to Gornfel'd). *Vecherniaia gazeta* (Moscow) December 10, 1928.

———. *O poezii*. Moscow, 1928.

———. *The Prose of Osip Mandelstam* (*The Noise of Time. Theodosia. The Egyptian Stamp*). Translated, with a Critical Essay by Clarence Brown. 2d ed., with corrections (1st ed., 1964). Princeton, 1967.

———. "Pshenitsa chelovecheskaia." *Nakanune* (Berlin), June 7, 1922. Reprinted in L. Fleishman, "Neizvestnaia stat'ia Osipa Mandel'shtama." *Wiener Slawistischer Almanach* 10 (1982).

———. *Razgovor o Dante*. Edited and annotated by A. A. Morozov, with an Afterword by L. E. Pinskii. Moscow, 1967.

———. *Selected Essays*. Translated and with an Introduction by Sydney Monas. Austin, 1977.

———. *Shum vremeni*. Leningrad, 1925.

———. *Sobranie sochinenii*. 3 vols. and supplement. Edited by G. P. Struve and B. A. Filippov. Vol. 1, 2d ed. (n.p., 1967). Vol. 2, 2d ed. (n.p., 1971). Vol. 3 (n.p., 1969). Supplement (vol. 4), edited by Nikita Struve et al. (Paris, 1981).

———. *Stikhotvoreniia*. Moscow, 1928.

———. *Stikhotvoreniia*. Edited, compiled, and annotated by N. I. Khardzhiev, with an Introduction by A. L. Dymshits. Leningrad, 1973.

———. *Tristia*. Berlin, 1921 (1922).

———. *Voronezhskie tetradi*. Edited, annotated, and with an Afterword by V. Shveitser. Ann Arbor, 1980.

———. *Vtoraia kniga*. Moscow, 1923.

"Mandelstam's 'Ode to Stalin.'" *Slavic Review* 34, no. 4 (1975).

Mandrykina, L. A. "Iz rukopisnogo naslediia Akhmatovoi." *Neva* 6 (1979).

Markov, Vladimir. *The Longer Poems of Velemir Khlebnikov*. Berkeley and Los Angeles, 1962.

———. "Mysli o russkom futurizme." *Novyi zhurnal* 38 (1954).

———. "Poeziia Mikhaila Kuzmina." In M. A. Kuzmin, *Sobranie stikhov*, edited, with introductions and commentary, by John E. Malmstad and Vladimir Markov. Vol. 3: *Nesobrannoe i neopublikovannoe. Prilozheniia. Primechaniia. Stat'i o Kuzmine*. Munich, 1977.

———. *Russian Futurism: A History*. Berkeley and Los Angeles, 1968.

———, ed. and comp. *Manifesty i programmy russkikh futuristov*. Vol. 27 of *Slavische Propyläen*. Munich, 1967.

———, ed. and comp. *Russian Imagism: 1919–1924. Anthologie*. Vol. 15.2 of *Bausteine zur Geschichte der Literatur bei den Slawen*. Giessen, 1980.

Martinez, L. "Le noir et le blanc. A propos de trois poèmes de Mandelstam." *Cahiers de linguistique d'orientalisme et de slavistique* 3–4 (1974).

Maslov, D. "Pechat' pri Vrangele." In *Antanta i Vrangel': Sbornik statei*. Moscow and Petrograd, 1923.

Matveev, Pavel. "L. N. Tolstoi i N. N. Strakhov v Optinoi pustyni." *Istoricheskii vestnik* 4 (1907).

Mauss, Marcel. *A General Theory of Magic*. Translated by Robert Brain. London, 1972.
———. *The Gift: Forms and Functions of Exchange in Archaic Societies* [Essai sur le don, forme archaïque de l'échange, 1925]. Translated by Ian Cunnison, with an Introduction by E. E. Evans-Pritchard. New York, 1967.
Medvedev, Zh. *The Rise and Fall of T. D. Lysenko*. Translated by I. Michael Lerner. New York, 1969.
Meeks, Wayne A. *The First Urban Christians: The Social World of Apostle Paul*. New Haven, 1983.
Men'shutin, A., and A. Siniavksii. *Poeziia pervykh let revoliutsii: 1917–1920*. Moscow, 1964.
Merezhkovskii, D. S. *Petr i Aleksei*. In *Khristos i Antikhrist*, vol. 3. St. Petersburg, 1907.
———. *Vechnye sputniki*. St. Petersburg, 1896.
Mikhail, Bishop (Old Believers). "Afonskaia smuta (ob Imiabozhtsakh)." *Rech'*, June 4 (May 22), 1913.
Miller, Frank J. "The Image of Stalin in Soviet Russian Folklore." *The Russian Review* 39, no. 1 (1980).
Mindlin, E. *Neobyknovennye sobesedniki*. Moscow, 1968.
Minskii, N. M. [Vilenkin]. "Blok i Dante." *Sovremennye zapiski* (Paris) 7 (October 5, 1921).
———. *Na obshchestvennye temy*. St. Petersburg, 1909.
———. "Narod i intelligentsiia." *Russkaia mysl'* 9 (1909).
———. *Pri svete sovesti: Mysli i mechty o tseli zhizni*. 2d ed. St. Petersburg, 1897.
———. *Religiia budushchego: Filosofskie razgovory*. St. Petersburg, 1905.
Mints, Z. G. "A. Blok i V. Ivanov." In *Edinstvo i izmenchivost' istoriko-literaturnogo protsessa. Ucheny zapiski Tartuskogo gosudarstvennogo universiteta*, no. 604. *Trudy po russkoi i slavianskoi filologii. Literaturovedenie*. Tartu, 1983.
Mirskii, D. S. [Prince D. Sviatopolk-Mirskii]. *A History of Russian Literature*. Edited and abridged by Francis J. Whitfield. New York, 1973.
———. "O. Mandel'shtam, 'Shum vremeni'" (review). *Sovremennye zapiski* 25 (1925).
———. "O. Mandel'shtam, 'Shum vremeni'" (review). *Blagonamerennyi* (Brussels) 1 (1926).
———. "Osip Mandel'shtam, 'Vtoraia kniga'" (review). *Blagonamerennyi* 2 (1926).
———. "Valerii Iakovlevich Briusov." *Sovremennye zapiski* 25 (1924).
Miturich, Pavel. Unpublished memoirs on Khlebnikov's death.
Mochulskii, Konstantin. *Vladimir Solov'ev: Zhizn' i uchenie*. Paris, 1936.
Morozov, Aleksandr A. "Mandel'shtam v zapisiakh dnevnika S. P. Kablukova." *Vestnik russkogo studencheskogo khristianskogo dvizheniia (Le Messager)* 129, no. 3 (1979).

Bibliography

———. "Pis'ma O. E. Mandel'shtama V. I. Ivanovu." In *Gosudarstvennaia publichnaia biblioteka SSSR imeni V. I. Lenina. Zapiski Otdela rukopisei.* Vol. 34. Moscow, 1975.
Mother Maria. *See* E. Skobtsova.
Muratov, P. P. "Khudozhestvennoe obozrenie (Starina i sovremennost'. Eklektizm i arkhaizm. 'Apollon')." *Russkaia mysl'* 31, no. 1 (1910).
———. "Stil' epokhi." *Russkaia mysl'* 31, no. 1 (1910).
Musatov, V. V. "Nekrasov v poeticheskom soznanii Mandel'shtama." *N. A. Nekrasov i russkaia literatura vtoroi poloviny XIX–nachala XX vekov. Mezhvuzovskii sbornik nauchnykh trudov,* no. 64. Kostromskoi gosudarstvennyi pedagogicheskii institut. Yaroslavl, 1982.
Nedobrovo, N. V. "Obshchestvo revnitelei khudozhestvennogo slova v Peterburge." *Trudy i dni* 2 (1912).
Nekrasov, N. A. *Sobranie sochinenii.* Edited by K. I. Chukovskii. Moscow, 1965–67.
Nevedomskaia, V. "Vospominaniia o Gumileve." *Novyi zhurnal* 38 (1954).
Nietzsche, Friedrich. *On the Genealogy of Morals.* Translated and with an Introduction by Walter Kaufman and R. J. Hollingdale. New York, 1969.
Nikitin, N. "Kamni." In *Zavtra: Literaturno-kriticheskii sbornik,* vol. 1. Edited by E. Zamiatin, Mikhail Kuzmin, and Mikhail Lozinskii. Berlin, 1923.
Nikol'skii, K. T. *Posobie k izucheniiu ustava bogosluzheniia Pravoslavnoi Tserkvi.* 6th ed., expanded and revised. St. Petersburg, 1900.
Nilsson, Nils Ake. "Life as Ecstasy and Sacrifice: Two Poems by Pasternak." *Scando-Slavica* 5 (1959).
———. "Mandel'shtam's Poem 'Voz'mi na radost'.'" *Russian Literature* 7/8 (1974).
———. "Ship Metaphors in Mandel'štam's Poetry." In *To Honor Roman Jakobson.* Vol. 2. The Hague, 1967.
Novitskii, P. "Iz istorii krymskoi pechati v 1919–1920 gg." *Pechat' i revoliutsiia* 1 (1921).
Nusinov, I. *Vekovye obrazy.* Moscow, 1937.
O Vladimire Solov'eve. Sbornik Pervyi. Moscow, 1911.
Ob Aleksandre Bloke. Petrograd, 1921.
Obolenskii, V. "Krym pri Vrangele." *Na chuzhoi storone* (Berlin and Prague) 9 (1925).
Odna ili dve russkikh literatury? Mezhdunarodnyi simpozium, sozvannyi fakultetom slovestnosti Zhenevskogo Universiteta i Shveitsarskoi Akademiei Slavistiki, Zheneva, 13–14–15 aprelia 1978. Lausanne, 1981.
Odoevtseva, Irina. *Na beregakh Nevy.* Washington, D.C., 1967.
Oksenov, Innokentii. "O. Mandel'shtam. Kamen'. Stikhi. 'Giperborei,' P. 1916" (review). *Novyi zhurnal dlia vsekh* 2–3 (1916).
———, ed. *Sovremennaia russkaia kritika.* Leningrad, 1925.
Olesha, Iu. *Zavist'.* Moscow, 1927.
Ol'khovyi, B. "O poputnichestve i poputchikakh," Parts 1 and 2. *Pechat' i revoliutsiia* 5 and 6 (1929).

"Osip Mandel'shtam, 'Kamen'" (review). *Letopis'* 5 (1916).
"Osip Mandel'shtam, 'Kamen',' i Grigorii Aronson, 'Lirika'" (review). *Vestnik znaniia* 5–6 (1916).
The Oxford Dictionary of the Christian Church. 2d ed. S.v. "Grace." London, 1977.
Palei, Abram. "Vospominaniia ob A. G. Gornfel'de." *Al'manakh bibliofila.* Vol. 5. Moscow, 1978.
Pamiat': Istoricheskii sbornik 1–4. Moscow, 1976–79; Paris and New York, 1978–81.
Panofsky, D., and E. Panofsky. *Pandora's Box: The Changing Aspects of a Mythical Symbol.* 2d ed., revised. New York, 1965.
Parnakh, Valentin. "The Russian World of Literature." *The Mennorah Journal* 12, no. 3 (1926).
———. *Samum.* Paris, 1919.
Parnok, Sofiia (Andrei Polianin). "O. Mandel'shtam. 'Kamen'.' Stikhi. 'Giperborei.' Petrograd. 1916" (review). *Severnye zapiski* 4 (1916)
———. *Sobranie stikhotvorenii.* Edited, compiled, annotated and with an Introduction by S. Poliakova. Ann Arbor, 1979.
Pasternak, Boris. *Stikhotvoreniia i poemy.* Edited, compiled, and annotated by L. A. Ozerov, with an Introduction by A. D. Siniavskii. Moscow and Leningrad, 1965.
———. *Works.* 4 vols. Ann Arbor, 1959–61.
Pasternak, E. B., and E. V. Pasternak. "Boris Pasternak: Iz perepiski s pisateliami." In *Literaturnoe nasledstvo.* Vol. 93: *Iz istorii sovetskoi literatury 1920–1930-kh godov.* Moscow, 1983.
Pater, Walter. "A Study of Dionysus: The Spiritual Form of Fire and Dew." In *Greek Studies. A Series of Essays.* New York, 1899.
Pavlovich, Nadezhda. "Optina Pustyn': Pochemu tuda ezdili velikie pisateli." In *Prometei* 12 (1980).
———. "Vospominaniia ob Aleksandre Bloke." In *Blokovskii sbornik. Trudy nauchnoi konferentsii, posviashchennoi izucheniiu zhizni i tvorchestva A. A. Bloka.* Tartu, 1964.
Pertsev, V. "V. Buzeskul, 'Antichnost'' i sovremnennost'"" (review). *Golos minuvshego* 5 (1913).
Pertsov, P. *Literaturnye vospominaniia.* Moscow and Leningrad, 1933.
Petrov, V. P. "Zagovory." In *Iz istorii russkoi sovetskoi fol'kloristiki,* edited by A. A. Gorelov. Leningrad, 1981.
Piast, Vladimir [Vl. Pestovskii]. "Dva slova o chtenii Blokom stikhov." In *Ob Aleksandre Bloke.* Petrograd, 1921.
———. "Osip Mandel'shtam, 'Kamen'"" (review). *Den',* January 21, 1916.
———. *Vstrechi.* Moscow, 1929.
Pil'niak, Boris [B. Vogau]. *Golyi god.* Petrograd, Moscow, and Berlin, 1921.
Platonov, S. F. *Ocherki po istorii smuty v Moskovskom gosudarstve.* 3d ed. St. Petersburg, 1910.
———. *Sokrashchennyi kurs russkoi istorii dlia srednei shkoly.* 8th ed. St. Petersburg, 1914.

Bibliography

Poetika: Sborniki po teorii poeticheskogo iazyka. Petrograd, 1919.
"Poeziia vne grupp." *Rech'*, December 9, 1913.
Poggioli, Renato. *The Poets of Russia: 1890–1930.* Cambridge, Mass., 1960.
Pokrovskii, N. V. *Siiskii ikonopisnyi podlinnik.* Vyp. 1. St. Petersburg, 1895.
Poliakova, Sofiia. *Zakatnye ony dni: Tsvetaeva i Parnok.* Ann Arbor, 1983.
Polianina, Serafima. "Ol'ga Vaksel'." *Chast' rechi* (New York) 1 (1980).
Polnyi pravoslavnyi bogoslovskii slovar'. St. Petersburg, 1913.
Polonskii, Viacheslav. *Ocherki literaturnogo dvizheniia revoliutsionnoi epokhi.* Moscow, 1929.
———. *Ocherki sovremennoi literatury.* Moscow, 1930.
Potebnia, A. A. *Estetika i poetika.* Moscow, 1976.
———. *Malorusskaia narodnaia pesnia.* Voronezh, 1877.
———. *Mysl' i iazyk.* 4th ed. Introduction by V. I. Khartsiev. Vol. 1 of *Polnoe sobranie sochinenii.* Odessa, 1922.
Poznanskii, N. *Zagovory: Opyt issledovaniia proiskhozhdeniia i razvitiia zagovornykh formul. Zapiski istoriko-filologicheskogo fakul'teta Petrogradskogo Universiteta,* vol. 136. Petrograd, 1917.
Preobrazhenskii, P. F. "Al. Gertsen i K. Leont'ev: Sravnitel'naia morfologiia tvorchestva." *Pechat' i revoliutsiia* 2/5 (1922).
Przybylski, R. "Arcadia Osipa Mandelsztama." *Slavia Orientalis* 13, no. 3 (1964).
Punin, Nikolai. "O. Mandel'shtam 'Tristia'" (review). *Zhizn' iskusstva* 41 (October 17, 1922).
Pushkin, A. S. *Polnoe sobranie sochinenii.* 6 vols. Edited by M. A. Tsiavlovskii. Leningrad, 1936–38.
Raeff, Marc. *The Origins of the Russian Intelligentsia: The Eighteenth-Century Nobility.* New York, 1966.
Rancour-Laferrière, Daniel. "Potebnja, Šklovkij, and the Familiarity/Strangeness Paradox." *Russian Literature* IV-1 (1976).
Raudar, M. N. "Obrazy severa i severnoi kul'tury v tvorchestve Anny Akhmatovoi." In *Skandinavskii sbornik,* vol. 24. Tallin, 1981.
Read, Christopher. *Religion, Revolution, and the Russian Intelligentsia, 1902–1912 (The Vekhi Debate and Its Intellectual Background).* London, 1979.
Reformatskaia, N. V., ed. *Maiakovskii v vospominaniiakh sovremennikov.* Moscow, 1963.
Reisner, L. *Avtobiograficheskii roman.* In *Literaturnoe nasledstvo.* Vol. 93: *Iz istorii sovetskoi literatury 1920–1930-kh godov.* Moscow, 1983.
Remizov, A. "Po povodu knigi L. Shestova 'Apofeoz bespochvennosti.'" *Russkaia mysl'* 7 (July 1905).
Riasanovsky, Nicholas. *A Parting of Ways: Government and the Educated Public in Russia, 1801–1855.* Oxford, 1976.
———. *Russia and the West in the Teachings of the Slavophiles.* Cambridge, Mass., 1952.
Rohde, Erwin. *Psyche: The Cult of Souls and Belief in Immortality Among the Greeks.* Translated from the 8th edition by W. B. Hillis. N.p., 1925.
Ronen, Omry. *An Approach to Mandel'štam.* Jerusalem, 1983.

Bibliography

———. "A Beam upon the Axe: Some Antecedents to Osip Mandel'štam's 'Umyvalsja nočiu na dvore.'" *Slavica Hierosolymitana* 1 (1977).

———. "Četvertoe soslovie: Vierte Stand or Fourth Estate? (A Rejoinder)." *Slavica Hierosolymitana* 5–6 (1981).

———. "The Dry River and the Black Ice: Anamnesis and Amnesia in Mandel'štam's poem 'Ia slovo pozabyl, čto ia xotel skazat'.'" In *Slavica Hierosolymitana* 1 (1977).

———. "An Introduction to Mandel'štam's *Slate Ode* and *1 January 1924:* Similarity and Complementarity." *Slavica Hierosolymitana* 4 (1979).

———. "K siuzhetu 'Stikhov o neizvestnom soldate' Mandel'shtama." *Slavica Hierosolymitana* 4 (1979).

———. "Leksicheskii povtor, podtekst i smysl v poetike Osipa Mandel'štama." In *Slavic Poetics: Essays in Honor of Kiril Taranovsky*, edited by Roman Jakobson, C. H. van Schoneveld, and Dean S. Worth. The Hague, 1973.

———. "Mandel'shtam, Osip Emilyevich." In *Encyclopaedia Judaica: Year Book 1973*. Jerusalem, 1973.

———. "Mandel'štam's Kaščej." In *Studies Presented to Professor Roman Jakobson by His Students*. Cambridge, Mass., 1968.

———. "Osip Mandel'štam: An Ode and an Elegy." Ph.D. diss., Harvard University, 1976.

Rowland, Mary F., and Paul Rowland. *Pasternak's Doctor Zhivago*. Carbondale, 1967.

Rozanov, I. "Obzor khudozhestvennoi literatury za dva goda." In *Literaturnye otkliki. Stat'i*. Moscow, 1923.

———. *Putevoditel' po sovremennoi russkoi literature*. 2d ed. Moscow, 1929 (Reprinted: Leipzig, 1973).

Rozanov, Vasilii. *Apokalipsis nashego vremeni*. Sergiev Posad, 1917–18.

———. *Temnyi lik: Metafizika khristianstva*. Würzburg, 1975. (Reprint of the 1911 St. Petersburg edition.)

Rozental', S. "Teni starogo Peterburga." *Pravda*, August 30, 1933.

Rozhdestvenskii, Vs. *Stranitsy zhizni; iz literaturnykh vospominanii*. Leningrad, 1962.

Rubinshtein, M. M. "Filosofiia i obshchestvennaia zhizn' v Rossii: Nabrosok." *Russkaia mysl'* 30, no. 3 (1909).

Ruderman, M. "O. Mandel'shtam, 'Stikhotvoreniia'" (review). *Novyi mir* 8 (1928).

———. "Poet i chitatel'." *Literaturnaia gazeta*. September 17, 1932.

Russkaia proza XVIII veka. Edited and annotated by G. P. Makogonenko and A. V. Zapadov, with an Introduction by G. P. Makogonenko. Moscow and Leningrad, 1950.

Sabaneev, L. *Skriabin*. Moscow, 1916.

Saianov, V. "K voprosu os sud'bakh akmeizma." *Na literaturnom postu* 17–18 (1927).

Said, Edward. *Beginnings: Intention and Method*. New York, 1975.

Saussure, Ferdinand de. *Kurs obshchei lingvistiki*. Translated by A. M.

Sukhotin. Revised according to the 3d French edition and with an Introduction by A. A. Kholodovich. Moscow, 1977.
Savinkov, B. *Vospominaniia terrorista*. 2d ed. Kharkov, 1926.
Scherrer, Jutta. *Die St. Petersburger Religiös-Philosophischen Vereinigungen: Die Entwicklung des religiösen Selbstverständnisses ihrer Intelligencija-Mitglieder (1901–1917)*. Vol. 19 in *Forschungen zur osteuropäischen Geschichte*. Berlin, 1973.
Schlegel, A. W. *Comparaison entre "Phèdre" de Racine et celle d'Euripide*. Oxford, 1962. (Reprint of the 1807 Paris edition.)
Schlott, Wolfgang. *Zur Funktion antiker Göttermythen in der Lyrik Osip Mandel'štams*. Europäische Hochschulschriften, series 16, vol. 18 in Slawische Sprachen und Literaturen. Frankfurt am Main and Bern, 1981.
Segal, D. M. "Mikrosemantika odnogo stikhotvoreniia." In *Slavic Poetics: Essays in Honor of Kiril Taranovsky*, edited by Roman Jakobson, C. H. van Schoneveld, and Dean S. Worth. The Hague, 1973.
———. "O nekotorykh aspektakh smyslovoi struktury 'Grifel'noi ody' O. E. Mandel'shtama." *Russian Literature* 2 (1972).
———. "Pamiat' zreniia i pamiat' smysla (Opyt semanticheskoi poetiki. Predvaritel'nye zametki)." *Russian Literature* 7/8 (1974).
Selivanovskii, A. "Razgovor o poezii." *Literaturnaia gazeta*, September 17, 1932.
Seward, Barbara. *The Symbolic Rose*. New York, 1960.
Shapir, Nikolai. "Filosofsko-kul'turnye ocherki." *Severnye zapiski* 9 (September 1913).
———. "Uchitel'stvo literatury." *Russkaia mysl'* 34, no. 4 (1913).
Shestov, Lev [L. Shvartsman]. *Apofeoz bespochvennosti*. 2d ed. Moscow, 1905.
Shils, Edward. *Center and Periphery: Essays in Macrosociology*. Chicago, 1975.
Shklovskii, Viktor. "Babel': Kriticheskii romans." *Lef* 2 (1924).
———. *Gamburgskii schet*. Leningrad, 1928.
———. "Iskusstvo kak priem." In *Poetika: Sborniki po teorii poeticheskogo iazyka*. Petrograd, 1919.
———. "O poezii i zaumnom iazyke" (1916). In *Poetika: Sborniki po teorii poeticheskogo iazyka*. Petrograd, 1919.
———. *O teorii prozy*. Moscow and Leningrad, 1925.
———. "Potebnia" (1916). In *Poetika: Sborniki po teorii poeticheskogo iazyka*. Petrograd, 1919.
———. *Razvertyvanie siuzheta*. Petrograd, 1921.
———. *Sentimental'noe puteshestvie*. Berlin, 1923.
———. *Zhili-byli*. In *Sobranie sochinenii*, vol. 1: *Rasskazy i povesti*. Moscow, 1973.
Shletser, Boris [B. Schloezer]. *A. Skriabin*. Vol. 1: *Lichnost'. Misteriia*. Berlin, 1923.
Shtakenshneider, E. A. *Dnevnik i zapiski*. Edited by I. N. Rozanov. Moscow and Leningrad, 1934.
Shtif, N. I. *Pogromy na Ukraine: Period Dobrovol'cheskoi armii*. Berlin, 1922.
Skobtsova, E. [Mother Maria; E. I. Kuzmina-Karavaeva]. "Vstrechi s

Blokom (K piatnadtsatiletiiu so dnia smerti)." *Sovremennye zapiski* (Paris) 63 (1937).

Skvortsov, N. A. *Arkheologiia i topografiia Moskvy. Kurs lektsii chitannykh v Imperatorskom Moskovskom Arkheologicheskom institute imeni Nikolaia II-go v 1912–13 godu.* Moscow, 1913.

Sluchevskii, K. K. *Stikhotvoreniia i poemy.* Leningrad, 1962.

Smolitsch, I. *Russisches Mönchtum: Entstehung, Entwicklung und Wesen, 988–1917.* Würzburg, 1953.

Solov'ev, Vl. *Sobranie sochinenii.* 9 vols. Edited by S. M. Solov'ev and E. M. Radlov. St. Petersburg, 1911.

———. *Stikhotvoreniia i shutochnye p'esy.* With an Introduction and annotations by Z. G. Mints. Leningrad, 1974.

Spengler, Oswald. *The Decline of the West.* 2 vols. Translated by Charles F. Atkinson. New York, 1928.

Stalin, Iosif. *Sochineniia.* 13 vols. Moscow, 1949–52.

Stanevich, Vera. "O Sal'erizme." *Trudy i dni* 7 (1914).

Starr, Frederick. *Red and Hot.* New York, 1983.

Steiner, P. "Poem as Manifesto: Mandel'štam's 'Notre Dame.'" *Russian Literature* V-3 (July 1977).

Steklov, Iu. M. *N. G. Chernyshevskii, ego zhizn' i deiatel'nost'.* 2d ed., revised and expanded. 2 vols. Moscow, 1928.

Stepanov, N. "O. Mandel'shtam, 'Stikhotvoreniia' (1928)" (review). *Zvezda* 6 (1928).

———. "B. Pasternak, Dve knigi" (review). *Zvezda* 11 (1927).

Stepun, F. *Byvsjee i nesbyvsheesia.* 2 vols. New York, 1956.

Stilman, L. "The All-Seeing Eye in Gogol." In *Gogol from the Twentieth Century: Eleven Essays,* edited by Robert A. Maguire. Princeton, 1974.

Struve, G. P. "Ital'ianskie obrazy v poezii Osipa Mandel'shtama." In *Studi in onore di Ettore Lo Gatto e Giovanni Maver,* edited by G. Sansoni. Rome, 1962.

———. *Russian Literature Under Lenin and Stalin: 1917–1953.* Norman, Okla., 1971.

———. *Neizdannyi Gumilev.* Paris, 1982.

Struve, Nikita. *Ossip Mandelstam.* Paris, 1982.

Struve, P. B. "Religiia i sotsializm." *Russkaia mysl'* 8 (1909).

Superfin, G. G. [G. Dal'nii]. "Po povodu trekhtomnogo sobraniia O. Mandel'shtama." *Vestnik russkogo studencheskogo khristianskogo dvizheniia* 97 (1970).

Superfin, G. G., and Timenchik, R. D. "Pis'ma A. Akhmatovoi k V. Ia. Briusovu." In *Gosudarstvennaia publichnaia biblioteka SSSR imeni V. I. Lenina.* Vol. 32: *Zapiski otdela rukopisei.* Moscow, 1972.

Syromiatnikov, S. N. "Liubov' u Vladimira Solov'eva." *Novoe vremia* (May 9, 1910).

Tager, Elena. "O Mandel'shtame." *Novyi zhurnal* 186 (1965).

Taranovsky, Kiril. "Dve publikatsii 'Stalinskoi ody' O. E. Mandel'shtama." *Scando-Slavica* 23 (1976).

———. *Essays on Mandel'štam*. Cambridge, Mass., 1976.
———. "K publikatsii 'Ody Stalinu.'" *Scando-Slavica* 23 (1976).
———. "Tri zametki o poezii Mandel'shtama." *International Journal of Slavic Linguistics and Poetics* 12 (1969).
Terras, Victor. "Classical Motives in the Poetry of Osip Mandelstam." *Slavic and East European Journal* 3 (1966).
Thomas, Keith. *Religion and the Decline of Magic*. New York, 1971.
Thompson, d'Arsy W. *A Glossary of Greek Birds*. Hildesheim and Olms, 1966.
Timenchik, R. D. "Po povodu *Antologii peterburgskoi poezii epokhi akmeizma*." *Russian Literature* V-4 (1977).
———. "Tekst v tekste u akmeistov." In *Tekst v tekste. Trudy po znakovym sistemam*, vol. 14. Tartu, 1981.
———. "Zametki ob akmeizme." *Russian Literature* 7/8 (1974).
———. "Zametki ob akmeizme II." *Russian Literature* V-3 (1977).
———. "Zametki ob akmeizme III." *Russian Literature* IX-II (1981).
Timenchik, R. D., V. N. Toporov, and T. V. Tsiv'ian. "Akhmatova i Kuzmin." *Russian Literature* VI-3 (1978).
Todd, W. M. III. "*Eugene Onegin*: 'Life's Novel.'" In *Literature and Society in Imperial Russia: 1800–1914*, edited and with an Introduction by W. M. Todd III. Stanford, 1978.
———. *Fiction and Society in the Age of Pushkin: Ideology, Institutions, and Narrative*. Cambridge, Mass., 1986.
———. "Pushkin, Aleksandr Sergeevich." In *The Handbook of Russian Literature*, edited by Victor Terras. New Haven, 1985.
Toddes, E. A. "Mandel'shtam i Tiutchev." *International Journal of Slavic Linguistics and Poetics* 17 (1974).
Tomashevskii, B. "Literatura i biografiia." *Kniga i revoliutsiia* 4 (1923).
———. *Teoriia literatury. Poetika*. Moscow and Leningrad, 1925. (6th ed., Moscow, 1931.)
Trotskii, Lev. *Literatura i revoliutsiia*. 2d ed. Moscow, 1924.
———. *Literature and Revolution*. Translated by Rose Strunsky. Ann Arbor, 1971.
Trousson, Raymond. *Le thème de Prométhée dans la littérature européenne*. 2 vols. Geneva, 1964.
Tschizewskij, Dmitrij. Introduction to *Anfänge des russischen Futurismus*, edited by D. Tschizewskij. Wiesbaden, 1963.
Tsvetaeva, Marina. "Istoriia odnogo posviashcheniia." *Oxford Slavonic Papers* 9 (1964).
———. *Izbrannye proizvedeniia*. Compiled, edited, and annotated by A. Efron and A. Saakiants, with an Introduction by V. Orlov. Moscow and Leningrad, 1965.
———. *Proza*. New York, 1953.
———. *Stikhotvoreniia i poemy*. 5 vols. Compiled and edited by Alexander Sumerkin. New York, 1980–
Tucker, Robert C. "Stalinism as Revolution from Above." In *Stalinism: Es-*

says in Historical Interpretation, edited by Robert C. Tucker. New York, 1977.
Tynianov, Iurii. *Arkhaisty i novatory.* Leningrad, 1929.
———. "Blok i Geine." In *Ob Aleksandre Bloke.* Petrograd, 1921.
———. *Poetika. Istoriia literatury. Kino.* Edited by E. A. Toddes, A. P. Chudakov, and M. O. Chudakova. Moscow, 1977.
———. *Problema stikhotvornogo iazyka.* Moscow, 1965. (1st ed., 1924.)
Ushakov, D. N., ed. *Tolkovyi slovar' russkogo iazyka.* 4 vols. Moscow, 1935–40.
Ustrialov, N. *Skazaniia sovremennikov o Dmitrii Samozvantse.* 3d ed. 2 parts. St. Petersburg, 1859.
Utechin, S. V. *Russian Political Thought: A Concise History.* New York and London, 1963.
Vagin, E. "Osip Mandel'shtam—khristianin v XX veke." *Novoe russkoe slovo,* December 10, 1978.
Vaginov, K. *Garpagoniada.* Ann Arbor, 1983.
———. *Kozlinaia pesn'.* Leningrad, 1928.
Vainshtein, E. V. *Deistvuiushchee zakonodatelstvo o evreiakh: po svodu zakonov s raziasneniiami.* Kiev, 1911.
Vaksel', Ol'ga. "O Mandel'shtame. Iz dnevnika." *Chast' rechi* (New York) 1 (1980).
Valentinov, N. [N. Vol'skii]. *Encounters with Lenin.* Translated by Paul Rosta and Brian Pearce, with a Foreword by L. Shapiro. London, 1968.
Vasilenko, Vl. "O. Mandel'shtam, 'Stikhotvoreniia'" (review). *Izvestiia,* July 6, 1928.
Veselovskii, A. N. *Istoricheskaia poetika.* Edited, annotated, and with an Introduction by Viktor Zhirmunskii. Moscow, 1940.
Ves' Peterburg na 1909 g. Adresnaia i spravochnaia kniga g. S.-Peterburga. St. Petersburg, 1909.
Vetlugin, G. N. *Polnaia spravochnaia kniga o pravakh evreev: s raziasneniiami, opredeleniiami i resheniiami Pravitelstvuiushchago Senata.* St. Petersburg, 1913.
Vinogradov, V. "O simvolakh Anny Akhmatovoi." In *Literaturnaia mysl': Al'manakh,* vol. 1. Petrograd, 1922.
Vipper, B. Iu. *Krugovorot istorii.* Moscow and Berlin, 1923.
Vladislavlev, I. *Russkie pisateli.* 4th ed. Moscow, 1924.
Voloshin, Maksimilian. "Liki tvorchestva." *Apollon* 2 (1909).
———. *Stikhotvoreniia.* Edited by L. A. Evstigneeva. Leningrad, 1977.
———. "Vospominaniia (April 1932)." Edited by Susan Smernoff Lazinger. *Slavica Hierosolymitana* 5–6 (1981).
Voloshinov, V. N. *Marksizm i filosofiia iazyka: Osnovnye problemy sotsiologicheskogo metoda v nauke o iazyke.* Leningrad, 1929.
Voronskii, A. *Na styke.* Moscow, 1923.
Vossler, Karl. *Mediaeval Culture: An Introduction to Dante and His Times.* 2 vols. Translated by William Cranston Lawton. New York, 1929.

Bibliography

Vygodskii, D. "Poeziia i poetika: Iz itogov 1916 g." *Letopis'* 1 (1917).
Vytorpskii, Erast. *Istoricheskoe opisanie Kozel'skoi Optinoi pustyni, vnov' sostavlennoe.* Troitse-Sergievskaia Lavra, 1902.
Weber, Max. *From Max Weber: Essays in Sociology.* Edited by H. H. Gerth and C. Wright Mills. New York, 1958.
———. *Max Weber on Charisma and Institution Building.* Edited and with an Introduction by S. N. Eisenstadt. Chicago, 1968.
Weidle, Vl. "O poslednikh stikhakh O. Mandel'shtama." *Vozdushnye puti* 2 (1961).
Welsh, Andrew. *Roots of Lyric: Primitive Poetry and Modern Poetics.* Princeton, 1978.
West, Daphne M. *Mandelstam: The Egyptian Stamp.* Birmingham Slavonic Monographs, no. 10 (1980).
West, James. *Russian Symbolism: A Study of Vyacheslav Ivanov and the Russian Symbolist Aesthetic.* London, 1970.
Wilson, Edmond. "Legend and Symbol in Doctor Zhivago," *The Bit Between My Teeth: A Literary Chronicle of 1950–1965.* New York, 1965.
Windelbandt, Wilhelm. *A History of Philosophy.* 2 vols. Translated by James H. Tufts. New York, 1958. (Revision of 1901 edition.)
———. *Istoriia novoi filosofii v ee sviazi s obshchei kul'turoi i otdel'nymi naukami.* 2 vols. Translated from the 2d German edition. St. Petersburg, 1904–5.
Yates, Frances A. *Giordano Bruno and the Hermetic Tradition.* London, 1964.
"'Zakat Evropy' Shpenglera." *Novaia Rossiia* (Petrograd) 1 (1922).
"Zamechaniia o peresechenii biografii Osipa Mandel'shtama i Borisa Pasternaka." In *Pamiat': Istoricheskii sbornik* 4. Moscow, 1979; Paris, 1981.
Zamiatin, Evgenii. *Litsa.* With an Introduction by M. Koriakov and an Afterword by V. Bondarenko. New York, 1967.
———. *A Soviet Heretic: Essays by Yevgeny Zamyatin.* Edited and translated by Mira Ginzburg. Chicago, 1970.
Zaslavskii, D. I. "Skromnyi plagiat ili razviaznaia khaltura." *Literaturnaia gazeta* 3 (1929).
Zelinskii, F. F. *See* T. Zielinski.
Zernov, Nicholas. *Eastern Christiandom: A Study of the Origins and Development of the Eastern Orthodox Church.* New York, 1961.
Zhirmunskii, Viktor M. "Preodolevshie simvolizm" (1916). In *Voprosy teorii literatury.* Leningrad, 1928.
———. "Po Vostochnoi Galitsii s sanitarnym otriadom." *Russkaia mysl'* 37, no. 2 (1916).
———. *Voprosy teorii literatury.* Leningrad, 1928.
Zhukov, P. D. "Levyi front isskusstv." *Kniga i revoliutsiia* 3/27 (1923).
Zhukovskii, Vas. *Sobranie sochinenii.* 4 vols. Moscow and Leningrad, 1959–60.
Zielinski, Tadeusz. [F. F. Zelinskii]. "Ideia vozmezdiia v antichnoi tragedii i zhizni." *Russkaia mysl'* 33, no. 11 (1912).
———. *Iz zhizni idei.* 3 vols. Vol. 2: *Drevnii mir i my,* 2d ed. St. Petersburg, 1905. Vol. 3: *Soperniki khristianstva.* St. Petersburg, 1907.

———. "Kharakter antichnoi religii v sravnenii s khristianstvom." *Russkaia mysl'* 29, no. 2 (1908).
———. "Tragediia pravdy." *Russkaia mysl'* 34, no. 11 (1911).
———. "'Venetsianskii kupets' i 'Kol'tso Nibelunga.'" *Russkaia mysl'* 32, no. 1 (1911).
Zinger, N. "Osip Mandel'shtam. 'Egipetskaia marka'" (review). *Izvestiia*, September 27, 1928.
Zorgenfrei, V. A. "A. A. Blok." *Zapiski mechtatelei* 6 (1922).
Zorkaia, N. M. *Na rubezhe stoletii. U istokov massovogo iskusstva v Rossii 1900–1910 godov*. Moscow, 1976.
Zoshchenko, Mikhail. *Izbrannoe*. 2 vols. Leningrad, 1978.

INDEX

"Academy of Verse," 29
Acmeism, 29, 40, 60, 109, 296n23; principles of, xi, 45, 58, 155. *See also individual poets*
Aeschylus, 261, 268
"Aestheticism," 43
Agnosticism, 27
Akakii Akakievich, 216, 219. *See also* Coat allegory
Akhmatova, Anna, 2, 20, 46, 60, 255; *Anno Domini*, 2; *Chetki*, 81; critics on, 188, 270, 271; on Mandelstam, 146, 147, 250
Aleksei (tsarevich; son of Peter the Great), 108, 111, 115
Allegories, 184–85
Ambiguity, 105, 108, 111, 204–5
Amnesia, 78
Anamnesis, 78, 120, 168, 178, 193, 194, 210; poetics of, 161, 162, 250
Andersen, Hans Christian, 36, 201; "Snow Queen," 36–37
Androgyne, 44, 53
Annenskii, Innokentii, 28, 37, 183, 185, 188, 295n16; *Thamyris the Cythara Player*, 56–58, 100; works on Hippolytus myth by, 61–62, 63–64, 67–68, 75
Antichrist, 116
Antigone, 77, 78, 204, 206, 207, 209, 248
Anti-Semitism, 22, 53, 292n51
"Anxiety of influence," 44, 176
Aphrodite, 61, 76, 77, 96
Apocalypse, 156
Apogamy, 337n51

Apollonian-Dionysian dichotomy, 57, 87, 91
Apollon journal, 19, 29, 30, 36, 48, 61
Arbenina, Ol'ga, 126, 128–29
Architecture as metaphor, 40, 45
Asmus, V., 332n15
Assassination plots, 23
Atheism, 27
Attraction and repulsion, 53–54
Authority of authorship, 16–17, 268
Autobiography of Mandelstam (The Noise of Time). *See* Mandelstam, Osip: Prose
Averbakh, L., 273, 274
Avvakum (archpriest), 109–10, 111, 220, 271
Axis imagery, 264, 267–68
Azef, E., 103

Baines, J., 370n103, 373n13, 374n19, 375n24, 377n44, 378nn58, 66, 381n93
Bal'mont, Konstantin, 23, 35, 201, 294n5
Baron, Salo W., 287n95
Barthes, Roland, 37, 158; *Mythologies*, x
Baudelaire, Charles, 107, 360n12
Beethoven, Ludwig van, 81; Ninth Symphony, 87, 210
Belinskii, Vissarion, 17
Belyi, Andrei, 15, 28, 78, 196, 279n19, 288n115, 290n128, 294n10, 298n37, 334n33, 340n79, 343n15, 345n28, 347n43, 348n49, 349n57; "Magic of Words," 173; *St. Petersburg*, 103; *Symbolism*, 157

411

Bergson, Henri, 156, 170, 173, 267, 332*n*15, 342*n*8, 352*n*78, 355*n*112, 356*n*125, 358*n*139, 372*n*9
Bernshtein, S. N., 13, 283*n*61
Bettelheim, Bruno, 255
Blok, Aleksandr, x, xi, 10, 23, 28, 169; cult of, 12, 13; "Dances of Death, The," 151; mystical revelation in, 43, 44, 45; on Mandelstam, 6, 15, 152–53; "On the Contemporary State of Russian Symbolism," 18, 28–29; personal thematics in, 47, 48; *Puppet Theater*, 10, 40; "Steps of the Commendatore," 159–60, 181; themes in, 18, 19, 193, 262; "Twelve, The," 53, 168
Blood imagery, 10, 337*n*54
Bloody Sunday (1905), 95
Borisov, V., 324*n*53
Briusov, Valerii, 23, 28, 29, 35, 61, 87; on Mandelstam, 152; "Poetu," 38
Brotherhood, 195
Brown, Clarence, 21, 30, 89, 95, 195, 250, 251, 264, 277*n*3, 281*n*36, 293*n*2, 308*n*46, 316*n*118, 319*n*11, 320*n*23, 324*n*55, 329*n*109, 331*n*11, 369*n*88, 378*n*58, 382*n*97
Brown, E. J., 284*n*63, 285*n*67, 364*n*42, 379*n*76
Brown, P., 277*n*2, 279*n*19, 285*n*75
Broyde, S., 359*n*8
Buddhist motif, 156, 230, 264, 343*n*11, 375*n*20
Bukharin, Nikolai, 32, 224, 254, 273
Bulgakov, Mikhail, 250, 271
Burke, Kenneth, 341*n*1
Burliuk, D., 359*n*12
Burning metaphor, 24, 70, 95
Byron, George Gordon, 9

Catharsis, 14, 59, 98
Catholicism, 81
Catullus, 211
Censorship, 18, 169
Center and periphery, 4, 7, 9, 12–14, 31, 128
Chapaev (film), 246
Charisma of poets, xi, 4, 31, 60, 111; of Russian literature, 204; charismatic authority, 3–4, 11–12, 278*n*7; "charis-matic institution," x. *See also* Mandelstam, Osip
Chastity, 64–65, 77
Chekhov, Anton, 18
Chernyshevskii, Nikolai, 18, 184; *What Is to Be Done*, 17
Chiliastic interpretations, 77, 108, 116, 155
Chorus, 95–96, 97, 98
Christ: *imitatio Christi*, 60, 71–72, 75–76, 78, 79–80, 185; in Mandelstam's poetry, 50–54. *See also* Eucharistic theme; Kenotic interpretation; Martyrdom
Christianity, 27, 54, 76; revelation of, in Russia, 75–79
"Christianity of the Spirit," 69
Chthonic mythology, 154, 155, 156, 185, 203, 208
Chudakov, A. P., 339*n*75, 351*n*65
Chudakova, M. O., 339*n*79, 351*n*65
Chukovskii, K. I., 253
Coat allegory, 218–21, 234, 235
Cohen, S. F., 292*n*152, 355*n*109, 374*n*18
Cohn, R. G., 335*n*42
Color imagery, 78, 96, 97, 136–37, 139
Confessional mode, 47, 48–52, 91
Conflicting worlds, theme of, 51–52
Coster, Charles de, 31, 273; *Légende de Uylenspiegel*, 216–17
Critics on Mandelstam, 7, 152, 187–89, 190, 194, 210, 211
Crown and wreath imagery, 146, 150, 152
Cult, 15–16, 158; of poet, 13, 69, 182, 204, 268; of sensuality, 208; of supreme leader, 32, 240, 268. *See also individual poets*
Cyclicity, 156, 157

Dal, Vladimir, 171–72
Dante Alighieri, 40, 86, 201; Beatrice in, 133, 144; Leah in, 132–33; Matilda in, 133, 144; *Veltro*, 236–37
Daronositsa, 121, 329*n*106
"Dead word," 157, 158
Death: death-in-love, 213; as *imitatio Christi*, 72–73, 80, 96, 97, 310*n*68; of old world, 191, 192–93; of poet, 185, 190, 198, 203; and resurrection, 15, 155, 198, 200

Index

Decembrists, 17, 152
Den' (newspaper), 56
Derrida, Jacques, 37
Derzhavin, Gavriil, 8, 119
Dice game imagery, 112, 113
Dionysus, 27, 57, 58, 87, 91, 204
Dis manibusque sacrum, 99–100. *See also* Gift imagery
"Distance" in poetry, 65, 67
Dmitrii (tsarevich and saint), 102, 108, 110, 111, 112, 326n73
Dostoevsky, F. M., 17, 18, 94, 227; *Brothers Karamazov*, 16; *Idiot, The*, 248; *Possessed, The*, 116; "Pushkin speech," 141
Dreams, 2, 3, 5, 15, 278n6
"Dreyfus Affair." *See* Mandelstam–Gornfel'd Affair
Durkheim, Emile, x; *Elementary Forms of the Religious Life*, 11

Education, public, 18
Ego-Futurism, 343n16
Eikhenbaum, Boris, 7, 12, 13, 188, 291n145, 306n22, 308n49, 335n38, 358–59n5, 366n64
Einstein, Albert, 227
Eliot, T. S., 98
Empson, William, 67
Encyclopaedia Judaica Yearbook, 131
Engine and machine imagery, 191, 193
Epiphanic state, 82
Equestrian and racing imagery, 8, 216, 242–44, 247
Eros, 37, 53, 57, 208; in "Heart" poem, 42, 43, 44, 45; in Phaedra poems, 94, 99
Esenin, Sergei, 10
"Eternal recurrence," 59, 77, 80
Eucharistic theme, 113, 167, 168, 185, 201, 247; *eucharistia*, 119–20; martyrdom and, 120–23
Euripides, 63, 74, 78, 88, 91, 98, 111
Exegetic symbolism, 132
Exter, Alexandra, 125
Eyes imagery, 165–66, 167, 168

False Dmitrii, 102, 114–15
Fatal flaw, 63–64
Federation of Soviet Writers, 222

Fedorov, N., 146
Filippov, Boris, 20
Filofei (monk), 114
Fin de siècle, 157, 168
Finnish-Methodist church, 30
First Five-Year Plan, 223, 224
Flame imagery, 70, 95
Fleishman, L., 280n29, 317n6, 318n10, 353n96, 362n30, 367n72, 375n20, 379n77
Flesh imagery, 39–40, 41, 42
Florenskii, Pavel, 196
Folkloric elements, xi, 95, 101, 111, 114
Formalism, 8, 60, 174, 175
Forsh, Ol'ga, 178
"Fourth estate," 220, 229, 231
Frazer, Sir James, 2, 72, 140, 155, 201
Freiburg school, 173
Freud, Sigmund, 2, 12, 121, 137, 282n55, 307n43
Frye, Northrop, 141
Futurism, 7, 28, 29, 63, 109, 157–58, 174, 176, 297n28, 300n49, 304n8, 314n108, 321n26, 339n75, 343n15, 345n30, 350n57, 355n104, 358n5, 364n49

Gasparov, B., 336n49, 371n112
Gautier, Théophile, 133, 335n38
Geertz, Clifford, 11, 279n11, 282n51, 283n60
Gender polarity, 137
Genesis, Book of, 2–3
Gershuni, Gersh, 24
Gethsemane, symbolism of, 270–71
Gift imagery, xi, 3, 4, 100–101, 102, 103, 239; charisma of poet and, 120–23, 128; in "Take for the sake of joy," 197–201; Mandelstam's other gift poems, 105–7; *Manibus sacrum* motif, 119; reciprocity, 238; time and gift-giving, 118, 119–20. *See also* Prestation
Ginzburg, L., 14, 280n31, 282n42, 284n64, 303n3, 317n1, 324n55, 326n74, 327n76, 333n24, 338n61, 356n117, 359n8, 360n17
Gippius, V. V. (Bestuzhev), 25–26, 78; *Pushkin and Christianity*, 69–70, 96
Gippius, Zinaida, 28

413

Index

Gogol, Nikolai, 7, 16, 60, 216, 219, 235; "A Few Words about Pushkin," 16; "Vii," 165, 167–68

Gollerbakh, E., 187, 346n37

Gorky, Maxim, 273

Gornfel'd, Arkadii, 31, 217, 221, 222, 229, 273, 292n151, 337n54. *See also* Mandelstam–Gornfel'd Affair

Greeks, ancient, 63, 69; Christianity and, 72–73, 76–77. *See also* Hellenic spirit in Russia

Greenberg, Louis, 287n95

Grigor'ev, Apollon, 86

Gruzdev, I., 321n26

Gulag, 20

Gumilev, Nikolai, 10, 29, 38, 40, 60, 193, 281n41; on the Word, 64, 182, 200, 201, 283n56; "The Word," 175

Hades, 100

Hegelian dialectics, 42

Heine, Heinrich, 210

Helen of Troy, 138, 139, 141, 143–44

Hellenic spirit in Russia, 81, 87, 94, 110, 115, 137, 196, 203; "Hellenistic" understanding of language, 174–75; Kremlin-Acropolis, 171, 172

Helleno-Christian ideal, 78–79, 81

Hephaestus, 244

Heraclitus, 112

Herzen, Alexander, 22, 108, 111, 171; *My Past and Thoughts,* 110

Hesiod, 157, 191

Hippolytus myth, 61, 63, 75, 77, 91, 96, 97, 216; Christian interpretation of, 67–68; Mandelstam as Hippolytus, 78, 79, 206, 209, 247, 249

Holy men, 16–17, 18

Homologies, 182, 199, 243

Honey, as symbol, 197–200

Horace, 119

Host, 64–65, 121, 194. *See also* Eucharistic theme

Hubris, 58

Hughes, Robert P., 295n10, 317n2

Humility, 77

Iakutian Soviets, Congress of, 263

Icons, 323n48; Icon of Our Lady, 111, 113

Imagery, 147–48, 150–51. *See also* Gift imagery; Stars imagery; *and other individual motifs*

Imagism, 161, 176

Imitatio Christi. *See* Christ; Death; Kenotic interpretation; Phaedra myth

Immortality, 203

Incest myth, 55, 57, 58, 60, 208; development of in Mandelstam's poetry, 75–76, 124, 130; and Mandelstam's Jewish heritage, 131–35; as metaphor for poet and land, 65, 67, 74, 75, 77; in "Return" poem, 136–41; in terms of Christian martyrdom, 77–78, 89, 94, 96, 99

Ineffable, conception of, 37

Intelligentsia, 17, 171, 226, 227, 229, 271

Intensity, attribute of, 11–12, 17, 282n55. *See also* Charisma of Poets

Ionov, I. I., 223

Isaiah, 269

Iser, W., 326n71

Ivanov, Georgii, 36

Ivanov, Viacheslav, 23, 59, 78, 91, 94, 108, 141; *Across the Stars,* 42–43; friendship with Mandelstam, 25, 26–27; influence of, 28, 29, 61, 155, 158, 159, 185; on Dionysus, 203–4; on "hermitage" poets, 27–28; "Skriabin's View of Art," 69, 70–71, 72; "Testaments of Symbolism," 29

Ivan the Terrible, 108

Ivanov-Razumnik, R. V., 326n70, 351n71

Izvestiia, 223

Jakobson, Roman, 10, 140, 199; *Noveishaia russkaia poeziia,* 172; "On a Generation That Squandered Its Poets," 8

Jangfeldt, Bengt, 252

Jews in Russia, 9, 21–22, 48, 103, 125, 126; Messiah and, 78. *See also* Mandelstam, Osip

John, Gospel of, 175

John the Baptist, 67

Joseph and his coat of many colors, 6, 136, 138, 150; coat allegory, 216, 220, 246; as metaphor, 217, 242, 268; story of, 1, 2–3, 4–5

Judeo-Roman *v.* Greek and universal, 77–78

Juvenal, 91

Index

Kablukov, Sergei Pavlovich, 30
Kafka, Franz: "Penal Colony," 123
Kaliaev, Ivan, 23
Karlinsky, S., 316n118, 324n55, 328n93, 348n48
Karpovich, Mikhail, 24–25
Kartashev, A. V., 78
Kautsky, K., *The Erfurt Program,* 22
Kenotic interpretation, 96, 97, 114, 117, 122, 220, 310n68; kenotic *imitatio Christi,* 115, 123, 134, 194, 227, 268, 270; kenotic martyrdom, 116; kenotic resignation, 235
Kerenskii, A. F., 142
Khardzhiev, Nikolai, 7, 12, 13–14, 317n8, 348n49, 372n7
Khlebnikov, Velemir, 8, 81, 160–61, 176, 177, 281n32, 283n56, 306n28, 314n103, 335n38, 339n72, 349n55, 354n102, 360n12, 368n81
Khodasevich, Vladislav, 38, 45, 178, 239
Kiev, 125–26
Kinship, 137–38, 141–42, 146
Kolos, Iakub, 263–64
Komissarzhevskaia, Vera, 59
Konovalov, D. G., 346n33
Krasnaia gazeta, 217
Kruchenykh, A., 360n12
Krug press, 86
Kuzin, B. S., 232, 372n9
Kuzmin, Mikhail, 28, 35, 85, 86, 156–57, 293n4

Lacan, Jacques, 37
Land and Factory publishing house, 273, 274
Leah, 128, 129, 130, 132–34, 141, 143
Left Front of Arts, 188
Lelevich, G., 189, 191, 192
Lenin, Vladimir, 17, 228, 262
Leningrad State Publishing House, 217
Leont'ev, Konstantin, 16
Lermontov, Mikhail, 8, 191, 193, 255; *Masquerade,* 235; "Molitra," 38
Leskov, Nikolai, 16
Letters from Mandelstam, 7, 25–26, 27, 131, 183, 252, 253, 260, 261
Levin, Iu., 305n14, 319n14, 342n7, 361n24
Levin, K., 318n10

Levinton, G., 299n44, 303n81, 327n77, 328n96, 329n104, 345n26, 364n44
Lévi-Strauss, Claude, 337nn52, 55, 56
Lewin, M., 292n152, 355n109
Light imagery, 98–99, 143, 322n38
Literature in Russia, 12–13, 17–19, 31, 204; politics and, 169–76
Literaturnaia gazeta, 230
Livshits, Benedikt, 274
Logos, 7, 157, 168, 180
Losskii, N., 332n15, 342n8
Lot's daughters, 130, 137, 139
Love, 77, 146, 198, 200
Lozinskii, L., 311n76, 314n106
Lozinskii, Mikhail, 122, 201, 311n76, 314n106
Lunacharskii, A., 319n14

McLean, H., 281n34, 285n77, 364n42
Magic, 33, 44, 55, 98, 113, 127, 136, 148, 154, 162, 173, 347n43, 379n66; magic tokens, 234; sympathetic magic, 194, 196, 198, 199, 340n75; verbal magic, xi, 55, 158, 181–83, 194, 195, 284n65, 294n5, 333n27, 336n47, 352n82, 364n44, 365n53, 383n116
Maguire, R., 273
Maiakovskii, Vladimir, 10, 109, 165; "Backbone Flute, The," 93–94, 205–6; *Mystery-Bouffe,* 220, 229; in public recitals, 7, 14; "Sergeiu Eseninu," 166; *Vladimir Maiakovskii: A Tragedy,* 58
Malia, M., 326n70
Mallarmé, Stéphane, 133, 188; "Don du poème," 135, 201, 207
Malmstad, J., 293n4, 355n114, 357n128
Mandelstam, Emile (father), 2
Mandelstam, Flora (mother), 2
Mandelstam, Nadezhda (wife), xiii, 11, 125, 126; on husband's works, 123, 215, 224, 270, 271; on "Return" poem, 127–28, 130–31, 135; on Stalin ode, 250, 251–52, 254–55, 264; on translation scandal, 31–32, 291n143
Mandelstam, Osip: in Armenia, 217, 237; baptism of, 29, 30; "biographical" principle in poems of, 84–85; as charismatic poet, 11–12; Christian mimesis in, 71–73; in Crimea, 118, 119, 124–25, 126, 142, 143, 147; as cult figure,

Mandelstam, Osip (*continued*)
12, 13–15, 16; dream and prophecy in "Return," 135–41; during World War I, 81–83; etymological mythologizing of, 164–65, 167–68; historical influences in work, 107–9, 112, 114–15; as Jew, 1, 9, 47, 48, 103, 130, 131, 132, 134, 135; as Jew and Christian, 76–77, 78; language of, 140–41, 146, 338n62; later alternative viewpoints of, 231, 236, 237–38; mythologies brought together, 242–43; name, significance of, 1–2; in public recital, 6–8; self-presentation of, ix, x, 57, 97–99, 122–23, 124, 134, 204, 207; Stalin ode, 261–63, 264, 266–67; translation scandal, 216, 217, 221, 222, 229, 273–74; as translator, 211, 223–24; travels and higher education of, 24–49, 32, 33, 154–55; Voronezh poems, 245, 246, 247, 250, 252; youth and early education of, 21–23. *See also* Mandelstam-Gornfel'd Affair

—Poems: "Arbenina" cycle, 197; "Avtoportret" (Self-Portrait), 79–80, 238; "Batiushkov," 120; "Bessonnitsa. Gomer. Tugie parusa" (Insomnia. Homer. Taut sails), 75–76, 128; "Den' stoial o pitai golovakh . . ." (It was a five-headed day), 246; "Dovol'no kuksit'sia! Bumagi v stol zasunem" (Enough of frowning . . .), 243; "Drozhzhi mira dorogie" (The dear leaven of the world), 247–48; "Dykhanie" (Breathing), 34–37, 41, 302n76; "Emu kavkazskie krichali gory" (The mountains of the Caucasus . . .), 132; "Eta noch' nepopravima" (This night cannot be undone), 96–97; "Grifel'naia oda" (Slate Ode), xii, 8, 41, 86, 113, 167, 176; "Ia budu metat'sia po taboru ulitsy temno" (I shall dash about the gypsy band of a dark street), 86; "Ia nenavizhu svet" (I hate the light), 57; "Ia ne uvizhu znamenitoi Fedry" (I shall not see the famous Phaedra), 89–91; "Ia s dymiashchei luchinoi vshozhu" (Holding a smoldering chip), 232; "Ia skazhu tebe s poslednei priamotoi" (I shall tell you as directly as I can), 144–45; "Ia slovo pozabyl, chto ia khotel skazat" (I have forgotten the word), 201–4, 206; "Ia v khorovod tenei, toptavshikh nezhnyi lug" (Into the round dance of shadows), 212–13; "I Shubert na vode, i Motsart v ptich'em game" (And Schubert . . .), 15; "Iz omuta zlogo i viazkogo" (Out of the evil and miry pool), 48–49, 51–52, 301n65; "K nemetskoi rechi" (To the German Tongue), 232, 271; "Kak etikh pokryval i etogo ubora" (O the splendor of these veils . . .), 92–93; "Kak oblakom serdtse odeto" (The heart is clothed as though in a cloud), 37–39, 42, 44–45, 61–62, 302n76; "Kholodnaia vesna. Golodnyi Staryi Krym" (It's a cold winter. The Old Crimea starves), 238; "Kogda b ia ugol' vzial dlia vysshei pokhvaly" (Ode to Stalin), 256–60; "Kontsert na vokzale" (Concert at the Railroad Station), 189–92, 194; "Kvartira tikha, kak bumbaga" (The flat is still like a sheet of paper), 239–41; "Lamarck," 224–28; "Liubliu pod svodami sedyia tishiny" (Under the bridal veil . . .), 209–10; "My zhivem, pod soboiu ne chuia strany" (We live, sensing no country . . .), 242; "Na kamennykh otrogakh Pierii" (On the rocky slopes of Piaeria), 297n35; "Na rozval' niakh, ulozhennykh solomoi" (In a peasant sledge lined with straw), 107–12; "Nashedshii podkovu" (He Who Found a Horseshoe), 8, 42, 112–13, 215–16; "Net, nikogda nichei ia ne byl sovremennik" (No, never have I been anybody's contemporary), 9–10, 163–65, 281n40; "Neumolimye slova . . . Okamenela Iudeia" (The implacable words), 50–51, 52–53, 301n68; "Ne veria voskresen'ia chudu" (Not believing in the miracle of the Resurrection), 296n27; "Noch' na dvore. Barskaia lzha!" (It's night outside), 236–37; "O etot vozdukh, smutoi p'ianyi (O this air, drunk with trouble), 106; "Notre Dame," 294n9; "1 January 1924," xii, 15, 206, 207, 211, 217, 220; "Ot syroi prostyni govoriashchaia" (Talking out of a damp sheet), 246; "Polnoch' v Moskve" (It's midnight in Moscow), 218, 229–30, 244; "Rakovina" (Seashell), 297n31, 302n73; "Segodnia mozhno sniat' dekal'komani" (Today one can make decals), 244; "Sestry—tiazhest' i nezhnost'—odinakovy vashi primety" (Sisters—heaviness and tenderness . . .), 145–46, 197, 298n36; "S mirom dershavnym ia byl lish' rebiacheski sviazan" (With the Imperial world . . .), 232; "Solominka" (The Straw), 133–34, 267, 301n66; "Sredi sviashchennikov levitom molodym" (A young Levite among priests), 78–79; "Stansy" (I do not wish among the hothouse youth), 245; "Ubity med'iu vechernei" (Killed by the brass of the evening), 302n74; "V belom raiiu lezhit bogatyr" (In a white paradise, a hero reposes), 81–82; "Vek" (The Age), 10, 112, 165–66, 192; "Venitseiskoi zhizni mrachnoi i besplodnoi" (Venetian Life), 148–52; "Vernis' v smesitel'noe lono" (Return to the incestuous womb), 124–26, 127; "V khrustal'nom omute kakaia krutizna" (How precipitous is this crystal pool!), 302n72; "Vlez besenok v mokroi sherstke" (The little demon, his fur wet . . .), 249–50; "V ogromnom omute prozrachno i temno" (The enormous pool is transparent and dark), 49–50, 51, 301n65, 302n72; "Vooruzhennyi zren'em uzkikh os" (Armed with the eyesight of slender wasps), 267; "Vot daronositsa kak solntse zolotoe" (Here is the Gift), 121–22; "Voz'mi na radost' iz moikh ladonei" (Take for the sake of joy . . .), 197–201; "V Peterburge my soidemsia snova" (We shall gather again in Petersburg), 179–84, 296n27; "V Petropole prozrachnom my umrem" (In Petropolis, translucent . . .), 155–56; "V tot vecher ne gudel strel'chatyi les organa" (That evening, the Gothic forest of the organ was silent), 296n27; "Vy pomnite, kak beguny" (Do you remember how the race runners), 243–44; "Za gremuchuiu doblest' griadushchikh vekov" (For the sake of the thundering glory), 233–34, 236; "Zasnula chern' . . ." (The Palace Square), 33, 292n153; "Za to, chto ia ruki tvoi ne sumel uderzhat'" (Because I knew not how to hold on to your hands . . .), 129–30; "Zolotistogo meda struia . . ." (Golden, a stream of honey . . .), 143–44; "Zverinets. Oda miru" (Bestiary. A Dythyramb to Peace), 83, 87; "Zvuk, ostorozhnyi i glukhoi" (The sound, cautious and hollow), 296n27. *See also* Christ; Gift imagery; Incest myth; *and other individual images and themes*

—Prose, 32; "Badger's Hole, The," 159, 160; "Bloody Mysterium of January 9," 95–96; *Conversation About Dante*, 238; *Egyptian Stamp, The*, 8, 30, 31–32, 213–15, 216, 220, 228; "Few Words Concerning Civic Poetry, A," 81; *Fourth Prose, The*, 217, 220, 221, 228, 229, 374n16; "François Villon," 174; "Fur Coat," 219–20; "Humanism and the Present," 172, 195–96, 209; *Journey to Armenia*, 237; *Noise of Time, The* (autobiography), 20, 21, 23–24, 30, 191, 206, 211, 220; "On the Addressee," 214; "On the Interlocutor," 65; "On the Nature of the Word," 175, 177–78, 191; "Petr Chaadaev," 65–66, 122, 142; "Pushkin and Skriabin," 68–71, 73, 83, 91, 156, 198; "Streams of Slapdash," 223–24, 241; "Word and Culture," 160, 161–62, 173–74, 175, 177–78

Mandelstam–Gornfel'd Affair, 32, 273–74
Mark, Saint, 133
Marriage. *See* Mystical marriage
Martyrdom, 42, 72; of poet, 68, 110, 123
Marx, Karl, 54
Mary and Martha, 132–33, 144, 334n35
Mauss, Marcel, 118, 122, 199; *The Gift*, xi, 119
Melpomene, 91
Memory, 120, 204, 244
Men'shutin, A., 368n74
Merezhkovskii, D. S., 19, 69, 71, 72, 203; *Christ and the Antichrist*, 115–17

Messianism, 68, 82, 114, 123
Metapoetry, 141
Meter in Mandelstam's poetry, 35, 90, 95, 197, 260, 262
Metonymy, 95, 96, 141, 144, 199, 242
Michelangelo: "Creation of Adam," 175–76
Mint, symbolism of, 199–200
Mirsky, D. S., 115
Miturich, Pavel, 8
Mnemosyne, 79, 80
Modernism, 28, 195
Mommsen, Theodor, 25
Morozov, A., 286n92, 288n110, 314n106, 319n16
Moscow subway, 224, 227
Moskovskii komsomolets, 220, 228
Müller, Max, 176
Music as metaphor, 40, 148, 191, 193
Myth and myth-making, 27, 33, 154–55, 158
Mystical Anarchists, 23
Mystical marriage, 43, 45, 47–48, 53, 208; between poet and land, 67, 68; in Phaedra poems, 94–99; in "Return" poem, 136–37
Mysticism, 42, 43

Nabokov, Vladimir, 21
Nadson, Semen, 23
Naming of children, 1–2, 267
Narbut, V., 60, 223, 273
Nationalism. *See* Populism
"Negative parallelism," 113–14
Nekrasov, N. A.: "About the Weather," 239
Neologisms, 157, 160, 161
New Economic Policy (NEP), 31, 32, 87, 172, 210, 211, 219, 220, 235
Nietzsche, Friedrich, 2, 54, 76, 77, 108, 155, 156, 184, 185, 201; *Birth of Tragedy out of the Spirit of Music,* 193, 288n116, 289n118, 297n28, 303n79, 305n14, 309n53, 311n72, 312n86, 319n14
Nikitin, N., 360n12
Noah and the flood, 151
Nominalism, 172–73, 175
Novyi mir, 231

Odysseus, 143
Oedipus, 77, 78, 111, 136, 201, 207, 248; Mandelstam as, 206, 207, 209
Ogarev, Nikolai, 110
Old Believers, 24
Olesha, Iu.: *Envy,* 215
On Guard journal, 189
Ontogenetic-phylogenetic recapitulation, 80, 123, 134
Optina Hermitage, 16
Orpheus, 72, 74–75, 180, 182–83
Orphic mysteries, 63, 76, 183, 201, 203
Origins, importance of, 40–41
Ovid, 211, 255
Oxymorons, 4, 147–48, 150, 152

Pandora myth, 100
Paperno, I., 285n79
Parnakh, Valentin, 214
Parnok, Sophia, 214
Parny, Evariste, 211
Paronomastic wordplay, 41, 52, 152, 162, 180, 199, 221, 263, 267
Parthenogenesis, 207
Pascal, Blaise, 51
Passion of Christ, 72, 96, 97. *See also* Christ
Pasternak, Boris, 8, 215, 217–18, 239, 254, 275, 364n44, 379n66; "Garden of Gethsemene," 85; "Hamlet," 166–67; "Ia ponial: vse zhivo," 264–66; as Jew, 21, 286n93; "Krasavitsa moia, vsia stat'," 234–35; *My Sister-Life,* 110; other poems, 218, 230, 231; *Safe Conduct,* 81
Pater, Walter, 133
Paternalistic symbolism, 266, 267, 268, 270
Paul the Apostle, 72, 185
Peasant Commune, 87, 195
Peasants, 234, 236
Penelope, 143–44
People's Commissariat of Culture, 126, 331n11
Persephone myth, 100, 156, 199, 200
Personal thematics in poetry, 47
Petersburg, 101, 151; as New Jerusalem, 78
Peter the Great, 101, 108
Petrine metaphor, 230, 231, 375n20

418

Petrograd House of Arts, 178
Petrograd Union of Poets, 152
Petrov, V., 284 n65
Phaedra myth, 67, 78; *imitatio Christi* in Phaedra poems, 88, 96, 97, 99; "Phaedra-Russia," 74–75, 77, 206, 241
Phylogenetic-ontogenetic recapitulation, 80, 123, 134
Plato, 160, 175, 201
Poet, x–xi, 211; ambiguity and, 102–3, 136; bond of, with audience and reader, 13, 14–15, 59, 60; loneliness of, 45; necessity of conflict to, 58–59; otherness of, 48, 50, 54; poetic principles, 154–62; Russian attitudes toward, 8–10, 14; task of, xi, 177–78, 196; as tragic hero, 58–59. *See also* Christ; Cult; Martyrdom; Mystical marriage
Poetic exchange. *See* Gift imagery
Poet's Club, 152
Poets' Guild, 29, 81, 155
Pogroms, 126
Poliakova, S., 316 n118
Political metaphors, 168
Pool imagery, 50, 52–53, 54, 134, 142
Popova, Elekonida, 246
Populism, 42, 43, 155, 176
Potebnia, Alexander, 162, 168, 170, 173, 176
Pound, Ezra, 195
Poznanskii, N., 336 n47
Pravda, 175, 178
Presses, nongovernment, 170
Prestation, 122, 134, 198, 234, 238
Prolepsis, 84, 112
Prometheus motif, 100, 261, 263, 268, 269
Propaganda, 169
Prophecy, 42
Providence, 77
Psalms, 267
Psychoanalysis, 98, 158
Punin, Nikolai, 188, 270, 271
Puns, 39, 167–68, 203, 204, 213, 244, 249
Pushkin, Aleksander, 16, 17, 61, 69, 80, 86, 119, 255; *Boris Godunov,* 90; cult of, 69–70, 147, 182; *Feast During the Plague,* 144, 151; *Gabriliad,* 211; influence of, 146–47; "Krivtsovu," 181, 182;

Little Tragedies, 90; "Poet and the Crowd, The," 42; "Prophet, The," 211; "Tale About Tsar Saltan," 172. *See also* Mandelstam, Osip: Prose

Rachel, 132, 133, 134, 138, 141, 144
Racine, Jean Baptiste, 88, 90–91, 93, 95; *Phèdre,* 62–63, 83, 98
Rancour-Laferrière, D., 346 n37
Recitals, public: of poetry, 7, 25, 59, 81, 152
Redemption theme, 68, 73, 75, 77
Reed, Meyne, 223, 274
Reed imagery, 51, 52, 53, 134
Religious intolerance, 30
Religious-Philosophical Assembly, 29, 68, 308 n47
Religious syncretism, 42, 71, 72
Repatterning, 245, 246
Repetition, 148, 181
Resurrection theme, 15, 155, 185
Return, theme of, 142, 143
Revelation, 77, 78
Romantic idealism, 43
Romanticism, European, 17
Rome, 62, 63, 76–77, 114
Ronen, Omry, xii, 122, 131–32, 134, 135, 164, 284 n65, 296 n23, 301 n64, 317 n3, 327 n74, 329 n109, 335 n40, 340 n76, 341 n83, 349 n55, 353 n94, 357 n127, 359 n8, 362 n33, 363 n34, 365 n54, 368 n80, 373 n10, 374 n19, 383 n114; *Approach to Mandelstam, An,* xii
Roscelinus, 173
Rose, as symbol, 147
Rozanov, I. N., 163, 291 n145, 347 n42
Rozanov, Vasilii, 72, 289 n116, 309 n52, 311 n74; *Apocalypse of Our Time,* 156
Russia. *See* Christianity; Hellenic spirit in Russia; Jews in Russia; Literature in Russia; Messianism; Poet
Russianness, gift of, 104, 105
Russian Orthodox Church, 30, 110, 120–21, 148, 155, 200
Russkaia mysl' (journal), 29, 61

Sacrament, 99, 164–65, 185, 197
Sacred, concept of, 10, 11, 12–13, 27–28
Sacrifice, 59–60, 72; human sacrifice, 112, 113

Said, E., 297n28, 314n104
Salvation, theme of, 60
Sappho, 41
Saturn, 150, 151
Saussure, Ferdinand de, 25, 170, 172, 283n61
Saussurian structuralism, 13
Savinkov, Boris (Ropshin), 23
Schiller, J. C. F. von: "Ode to Joy," 87, 210
Schism (17th century), 101, 108
Schlegel, A. W., 67, 80; *Comparaison entre le Phèdre de Racine et celle d'Euripide,* 63
Schlott, W., 315n114, 322n38, 324n53
Schopenhauer, Arthur, 156
Sechenov, 37
Segal, D., 297n32, 319n14, 327n77, 338n67, 342n7, 361n24, 371n114
Self-mockery, genre of, 215
Self-presentation, 30, 33. *See also* Mandelstam, Osip
Seneca, 91
Sergei, Grand Duke, 23
Shakhty trial, 223–24
Shamanistic quality in poetry, xi, 7, 14, 181, 182, 199, 284n65
Shershenevich, Vadim, 167, 300n57, 346n34
Shestov, Lev, 183, 185, 289nn116, 118
Shils, Edward, x, 11, 17, 128
Shklovskii, Viktor, 8, 161, 162, 175, 178, 194, 237, 284n65, 289n116, 345n31, 346n37, 349n54, 351n69, 353n93, 361n25; *Resurrection of the World, The,* 122
Silenus, 58, 304n5
Sinani, Boris, 21–22, 24, 327n76
Siniavskii, A., 368n74
Skriabin, Alexsandr, 70–71, 91; *Mysterium,* 96; "Poem of Fire, The," 24. *See also* Mandelstam, Osip: Prose
Slavic Review, 252
Socialism, 171
Socialist-Revolutionary Party, 22, 23, 24
Sodom, 138, 139
Sologub, Fedor, 35
Solov'ev, Vladimir, 53, 69, 80, 185
Sophocles, 77, 78, 111, 136
Spengler, Oswald, 156, 319n14, 342n8, 343n14

Stalin, Joseph, 230, 254, 263; background for ode to, 250–55; in other works by Mandelstam, 237, 241–42, 245–46; poetic iconography and poet's persona, 268–71
Stalinist era, 13, 229
Stalin revolution, 14, 20, 32, 227, 228, 229
Starchestvo, institution of, 16
Starets. *See* Holy men
Stars imagery, 57, 102–3, 166, 167, 193
Stein, Gertrude, 148
Stone imagery, 41, 42, 95
Struve, Gleb, 20
Struve, N., 303n80, 326n69, 339n73, 352n85, 355n112
Sturm und Drang, 44, 155
Suicide, 10
Sun imagery, 74, 75, 142, 143, 180, 198, 310n76; in Phaedra poems, 96–99; in "Return" poem, 137, 138–39
Superfin, G., 306n23
Surikov, Vasilii (painter): *Boiarynia Morozova,* 109–10
"Susanna and the Elders," 150, 152
Swallow imagery, 208, 216, 332n23
Symbolist movement, 28, 29, 40, 54, 108–19, 174–75; revolt against, 6, 57, 58, 60–61, 64
Synecdoche, 110, 141, 144, 146, 182, 247
Syntax in Mandelstam's poetry, 35

Taranovsky, Kiril, 51, 131, 134, 135, 311n76, 312n77, 320n23, 322n37, 329n109, 333n33, 335n42, 359n8, 366n62, 367n67, 372n8, 379n69, 382n97
Tenishev School, 21, 22
Terras, V., 365n54
Terrorism, 23–25
Theosophy, 70, 71, 76
Theurgy, 61, 77–78, 158, 173; *theurgos,* 27
"Third Testament," 69, 71, 72, 115
Thomas the Apostle, 168
Tikhonov, Nikolai, 275
Time, 119, 146, 194, 204
Timenchik, R., 286n90, 287n107, 293n34, 303n81, 306n23, 314n105, 319n14, 342n7, 354n98, 361n24, 363n42, 380n81

Time of Troubles, 101, 105
Tintoretto: "Susanna and the Elders," 150, 152
Tiutchev, Fedor, 51, 90, 191, 193
Todd, W., 283*n*60, 286*n*83, 301*n*59
Toddes, E., 302*n*70, 339*n*75, 359*n*8
Tolstoy, Lev, 17, 18; *War and Peace,* 82; "What Is Art," 11
Toporov, V., 319*n*14, 342*n*7, 361*n*24
"Tower" salon, 25, 28
Trenin, Vl., 348*n*49
Trotsky, Leon, 194, 261; *Art and Revolution,* 175
Tsiv'ian, T., 319*n*14, 342*n*7, 361*n*24
Tsvetaeva, Marina, 8–9, 10, 83, 119, 316*n*118; "Dmitrii! Marina! V mire," 101–2; "Iz ruk moikh-nerukotvornyi grad," 103–4; "Mimo nochnykh bashen," 105
Tsygal'skii, Colonel, 126
Turgenev, Ivan, 18
Twins and doubling, image of, 11, 145, 147, 264, 266, 268
Tynianov, Iurii, 260, 261, 281*n*34, 282*n*47, 291*n*145, 295*n*16, 306*n*22, 344*n*21, 353*n*95, 357*n*129, 359*n*20, 361*n*25, 367*n*74; "Space Between, The," 210, 211

Underworld, descent into, 227. *See also* Orphic mysteries; Persephone myth

Vaginov, Konstantin, 237; *Goat Song,* 215
Vainshtein, E., 287*n*95
Venice, 150–51
"Verbal magic." *See* Magic
Verlaine, Paul: "Art poétique," 199–200, 201, 218, 364*n*44
Veselovskii, A. N., 99, 113, 141, 176, 182, 195; *Historical Poetics,* 159–60; "Psychological Parallelism and Its Forms from the Perspective of Poetic Style," 158–59
Vetlugin, G., 287*n*95
Vico, Giambattista, 88, 108, 156, 305*n*14, 319*n*14
Villon, François, 44, 45, 99
Vipper, B., 319*n*14
Virgil, 112, 157, 201
Voloshin, Maksimilian, 201
Vol'pe, Tsezar', 237
Voronezh Theater, 252
Voronskii, A. K., 86, 273
Vygotskii, D., 46

Waller, Fats: "Honeysuckle Rose," 148
War Communism, 229, 235
Wasp imagery, 267
Weber, Max, x, 3, 4, 11–12, 60, 181, 211
Wilamowitz-Moellendorff, U. von, 67, 80
Wilde, Oscar: *Salome,* 67
William of Ockham, 173
Wing imagery, 172
Wolf imagery, 233, 236–37
Wrangel, P. N., 126, 142, 147, 228
Writers' commune, 178
Writers' Union, 252

Zabolotskii, Nikolai, 237
Zaslavskii, D. I., 274
Zenkevich, Mikhail, 60
Zeus, 100, 268, 270
Zhirmunskii, Viktor, 46–47, 187–88
Zhukovskii, Vasilii, 80
Zielinski, Tadeusz, 141, 155
Zoshchenko, Mikhail, 31; *Mishel' Siniagin,* 215, 217, 218–19; "Pleasantries of Culture," 235
Zvezda, 237

Designer:	Sandy Drooker
Compositor:	G&S Typesetters, Inc.
Text:	10/12 Bembo
Display:	Bembo

www.ingramcontent.com/pod-product-compliance
Lightning Source LLC
Chambersburg PA
CBHW030125240426
43672CB00005B/21